Lori Hollander-Strong

D0982878

READING
ACQUISITION

READING ACQUISITION

Edited by

PHILIP B. GOUGH
University of Texas at Austin
LINNEA C. EHRI
City University of New York Graduate School
REBECCA TREIMAN
Wayne State University

LEA LAWRENCE ERLBAUM ASSOCIATES, PUBLISHERS
1992   Hillsdale, New Jersey   Hove and London

Lawrence Erlbaum Associates, Inc., Publishers
365 Broadway
Hillsdale, New Jersey 07642

Library of Congress Cataloging-in-Publication Data
Reading acquisition / edited by Philip B. Gough, Linnea C. Ehri,
Rebecca Treiman.
    p. cm.
Essays developed from a conference attended by the authors in 1986
at the Cognitive Science Center, University of Texas at Austin.
Includes bibliographical references and indexes.
ISBN 0-8058-0113-8
1. Reading—Congresses. 2 Language acquisition—Congresses.
I. Gough, Philip B. II. Ehri, Linnea C. III. Treiman, Rebecca.
IV. University of Texas at Austin. Center for Cognitive Science.
372.4—dc20   91-42029
                                                       CIP

Printed in the United States of America
10 9 8 7 6 5 4 3 2 1

Contents

Preface   **ix**

1. **Studies in the Acquisition Procedure for Reading:
   Rationale, Hypotheses, and Data**   **1**
   Brian Byrne

2. **Reading, Spelling, and the Orthographic Cipher**   **35**
   Philip B. Gough, Connie Juel, and Priscilla L. Griffith

3. **Rhyme, Analogy, and Children's Reading**   **49**
   Usha Goswami and Peter Bryant

4. **The Role of Intrasyllabic Units in Learning to Read and Spell**   **65**
   Rebecca Treiman

5. **Reconceptualizing the Development of Sight Word Reading
   and Its Relationship to Recoding**   **107**
   Linnea C. Ehri

6. **The Representation Problem in Reading Acquisition**   **145**
   Charles A. Perfetti

7. **Cognitive and Linguistic Factors in Learning to Read**   **175**
   William E. Tunmer and Wesley A. Hoover

8. **Reading Stories to Preliterate Children: A Proposed
    Connection to Reading**   215
    Jana M. Mason

9. **Dyslexia in a Computational Model of Word Recognition
    in Reading**   243
    Mark Seidenberg

10. **Identifying the Causes of Reading Disability**   275
    *Donald Shankweiler, Stephen Crain, Susan Brady,
    and Paul Macaruso*

11. **Speculations on the Causes and Consequences of Individual
    Differences in Early Reading Acquisition**   307
    Keith E. Stanovich

12. **Whole Language Versus Code Emphasis: Underlying
    Assumptions and Their Implications for Reading Instruction**   343
    I. Y. Liberman and A. M. Liberman

Author Index   367

Subject Index   379

Contributors

Susan Brady, Haskins Laboratory, New Haven, Connecticut

Peter Bryant, University of Oxford, England

Brian Byrne, The University of New England, Australia

Stephen Crain, Haskins Laboratory, New Haven, Connecticut

Linnea C. Ehri, Graduate School, City University of New York

Usha Goswami, University of Cambridge, England

Philip B. Gough, University of Texas at Austin

Priscilla L. Griffith, University of South Florida, Tampa

Wesley A. Hoover, Southwest Educational Development Laboratory, Austin, Texas

Connie Juel, University of Virginia, Charlottesville

A. M. Liberman, Haskins Laboratories, New Haven, Connecticut

I. Y. Liberman, Haskins Laboratories, New Haven, Connecticut

Paul Macaruso, Massachusetts General Hospital, Boston

Jana M. Mason, University of Illinois, Urbana-Champaign

Charles A. Perfetti, University of Pittsburgh, Pennsylvania

Mark Seidenberg, University of Southern California, Los Angeles

Donald Shankweiler, Haskins Laboratories, New Haven, and University of Connecticut, Storrs

Keith E. Stanovich, Ontario Institute for Studies in Education, Toronto, Canada

Rebecca Treiman, Wayne State University, Michigan

William E. Tunmer, Massey University, New Zealand

Preface

Reading Acquisition emerged several years after its contributors participated in a conference on beginning reading organized by Phil Gough. The conference was funded by the Sloan Foundation and was held in March 1986 at the Cognitive Science Center, University of Texas at Austin. Chapters were drafted and circulated before the conference, presented at the conference, and then completed afterward. Various events disrupting the life of the first editor delayed publication of the book until two additional editors offered their assistance. At this point, all of the chapters were revised and updated, and some new chapters were added. We would like to thank Sarah Weatherston and Jennifer Gross for their help in the editorial process.

The conference was a 3-day affair. Its purpose was to bring together psychologists doing basic research in reading and making interesting discoveries about the processes involved in learning to read. Those who attended and made presentations were Peter Bryant, Brian Byrne, Linnea Ehri, Usha Goswami, Phil Gough, Wes Hoover, Connie Juel, Ingvar Lundberg, Jana Mason, Chuck Perfetti, Don Shankweiler, Mark Seidenberg, Keith Stanovich, and Bill Tunmer. Becky Treiman was there in spirit and in print, but her corporeal form remained at home with her 1-month-old baby. Isabelle Liberman also was invited but could not attend.

The chapters in *Reading Acquisition* address various processes and problems in learning to read. These include the manner in which acquisition gets underway, the contribution of story listening experiences, the process of learning to read words, and the way readers represent information about written words in memory. In addition, the chapters consider how phonological awareness, onsetrime awareness, and syntactic awareness contribute to reading acquisition, how learning to spell is involved, and how reading ability can be explained as a combination of decoding skill and listening comprehension skill. Finally, the contributors address the causes of reading difficulties and suggest how to study these causes.

Byrne begins by focusing on novice learners who have little understanding of how reading works. He proposes that they adopt a default acquisition procedure to read words. This involves building nonanalytic associations between some aspect of each printed word and the corresponding spoken word. Even though novices may learn to read "families" of words such as *fat* and *bat* in this way, this learning does not, on its own, force them to shift to analytic alphabetic reading. Learners' logographic approach changes only when they gain access to a mental representation of speech at the level of phonemes and when they learn how letters symbolize phonemes.

Gough, Griffith, and Juel further discuss the distinction between logographic and alphabetic word reading. They propose that children learn to read their first few words by selecting some attribute of each word that distinguishes it from the other words that they know. Although learning by selective association is easy at first, it becomes more difficult as children encounter more words and must figure out new words on their own. To be successful readers, Gough, Griffith, and Juel claim that children must learn the alphabetic cipher. Gough and his colleagues argue that the same is true for spelling. Reading and spelling are fundamentally similar because knowledge of the cipher is at the heart of both skills.

Goswami and Bryant discuss the connection between phonological awareness and reading. It is often assumed that phonemic awareness is the only type of phonological awareness that is important in learning to read and spell. It is further assumed that children who are aware of phonemes become good readers because they can learn the relationships between individual phonemes and individual graphemes. Goswami and Bryant argue, in contrast, that there are other phonological paths to literacy. Preschool children are sensitive to rhyme and to alliteration, and they use this knowledge in learning to read. For example, children who know how to read *beak* may successfully read the new word *peak* by applying their awareness of rhyme.

Treiman extends this consideration of phonological units other than phonemes. Her theme is that spoken words contain units that are intermediate in size between syllables and phonemes and that these units play a role in learning to read and spell. Treiman reviews the evidence that English syllables consist of onset and rime units. She argues that children are more aware of onsets and rimes than they are of single phonemes. As a result, children often deal with printed words in terms of units that correspond to onsets (e.g., initial *bl*, initial *s*) and units that correspond to rimes (e.g., *-ight, -eck*). Intrasyllabic units also play a role in learning to spell. Treiman suggests that children's awareness of onset and rime units should be put to use in the teaching of reading and spelling.

Ehri focuses on the role of phonological knowledge in learning to read words by sight. She rejects the conventional idea that mature readers learn to read sight words by rote memorizing visual forms linked to meanings in memory. She proposes instead that sight words are learned as spellings linked systematically to pronunciations. Her proposal explains why phonological recoding skill is central for learning to read words by sight. Ehri traces the development of sight word reading from a time when prereaders use strictly visual cues to a time when readers analyze spellings as symbols for the phonemic structure of words.

Perfetti extends the discussion of the way that specific words are learned with a proposal that is highly compatible with Ehri's view. He describes a theory of word reading that specifies the form of lexical representations in memory and proposes two principles of development, redundancy and specificity. In this theory, phonemic knowledge is central to the quality of the spellings that are stored in memory. With development, representations become more complete and more specific.

Tunmer and Hoover expand the scope of reading ability to include comprehension and metalinguistic awareness as well as word reading processes. They present evidence for what they call the simple view of reading—that reading ability can be explained as a combination of decoding skill and listening comprehension skill. Tunmer and Hoover discuss how these skills develop. Phonological awareness is critical for developing decoding skill. Syntactic awareness is critical for developing comprehension skill. Also, syntactic awareness may help children acquire phonological recoding skill. At first, beginners learn to combine their knowledge of the constraints of sentence contexts with incomplete graphophonemic information to identify unfamiliar words in text. Successful identification improves their ability to read these specific words and also improves their knowledge of grapheme–phoneme correspondences. As the latter knowledge grows, beginners become more proficient at phonological recoding. Tunmer and Hoover also argue that decentration is critical for reading development.

Mason pursues the development of reading comprehension skill by discussing the impact of parents' and teachers' reading of storybooks on young children's listening comprehension and subsequent reading development. She suggests that reading to children helps them build a repertoire of concepts about written language structure and helps them develop strategies for remembering and comprehending text.

Seidenberg returns our attention to the processes involved in word reading as he considers how skilled and unskilled readers recognize words. He rejects the conventional idea that readers read words by accessing a single representation in lexical memory. Instead, he proposes a connectionist view of word reading. He discusses how his model behaves when simulated on a computer and applies this model to describe various causes of dyslexia.

Shankweiler, Crain, Brady, and Macaruso discuss how the cause or causes of reading disability can best be identified. Should one compare groups of children who are the same age but who differ in reading ability, or should one compare groups of children who are the same in reading level but who differ in age? Recently, some researchers have advocated the use of reading level-match designs. Shankweiler and his colleagues defend the use of age-match designs under certain conditions. The evidence that they review suggests that poor readers' problems stem from a deficit in the processing of phonological information.

From his review of the vast literature on the causes of reading problems, Stanovich concurs that deficiencies in phonological processing are the primary proximal cause of early reading failure. In addition, Stanovich argues, some poor readers have trouble forming accurate orthographic representations of printed words. Stanovich also discusses the cognitive consequences of early reading problems. These, he argues, are profound and general.

Liberman and Liberman examine positive and negative features of two contrasting approaches to the teaching of reading, the whole language approach and the code emphasis approach. The main problem with a whole language approach is its assumption that learning to read is as effortless as learning to speak. A code emphasis approach correctly recognizes that speech and reading follow very different developmental paths.

Several of the chapters use phonetic symbols. These are: /i/ as in b*ee*t, /e/ as in b*ai*t, /u/ as in b*oo*t, /o/ as in b*oa*t, /ɪ/ as in b*i*t, /ɛ/ as in b*e*t, /æ/ as in b*a*t, /a/ as in h*o*t, /ʌ/ as in b*u*t, /ay/ as in b*i*te, /ɔ/ as in b*ou*ght, /oy/ as in b*oy,* /ə/ as in sof*a,* /ŋ/ as in si*ng,*/č/ as in *ch*ip, /š/ as in *sh*ip, and /ǰ/ as in *J*ill.

Linnea C. Ehri
Rebecca Treiman

READING
ACQUISITION

1 Studies in the Acquisition Procedure for Reading: Rationale, Hypotheses, and Data

Brian Byrne
The University of New England

Imagine a child who is taught to read just two things, the words *fat* and *bat*. The child knows none of the names or sounds of the letters of the alphabet and can read no other words. Will this child deduce that the letter *f* corresponds to the phoneme /f/ and that the letter *b* corresponds to the phoneme /b/? The main experiments reported in this chapter address this kind of question. What precedes that report is a justification for doing the experiments, two hypotheses, and some preliminary experimental data. I am concerned with what I call the *default acquisition procedure* for reading.

RATIONALE

Investigations of reading acquisition by experimental psychologists are of two types. One is primarily correlational, and it seeks to characterize the children who find reading difficult. The second approach focuses on the learning task itself, usually on the successive stages through which the child goes on the way to reading mastery. The correlational approach has a long history, whereas the detailed study of the acquisition process is more recent. I present a brief critical review of correlational studies, out of which emerges an appeal for continued close attention to the learning process, along with some methodological assumptions that I think are worth making.

Correlational studies generally compare groups of good readers and poor readers on some laboratory task or psychometric measure thought likely to be critically involved in the mastery of reading and in which some children may reasonably be considered to be deficient. The early emphasis was on the integrity

1

of the "visual word center." Damage to or weakness in this center was viewed as undermining sight–sound associations for words (see Benton, 1980). Orton (1925) advanced the view that reading failure resulted from lack of full hemispheric specialization, producing confusing competition from the nondominant hemisphere's reversed images. The emphasis on visual processes continued with the development of training techniques to inculcate appropriate visuospatial discriminations and eye movements (Frostig & Maslow, 1973). At the same time other avenues were being explored, particularly the notions of a generalized problem of cross modal integration (Birch & Belmont, 1964) and of difficulties in sequential perception (Bakker, 1971). More recently, attention has shifted to the language faculty, with reports of deficiencies in almost all linguistic functions (see Stanovich, 1986a). Vellutino (1979) provided researchers with an exhaustive review of the hundreds of experiments motivated by these quite plausible ideas, and others have kept the review process up to date (e.g., Perfetti, 1985; Stanovich, 1986b).

A consensus viewpoint is emerging. First, none of the *nonlinguistic* deficiencies that has been explored accounts for very much in the way of reading group differences once the research is scrutinized closely for proper subject selection, task design, experimental control, and so forth. Second, the best designed studies are the ones that implicate language or language-related functions in reading disabilities. Hence, it is sensible to assume that the causes of dyslexia are to be found somewhere in the language module. The range of possibilities is still quite large, however, because problems in syntactic, lexical, and morphological development, in speech perception and memory coding, and in "metalinguistic" (especially phonemic) awareness have all been identified in poor readers (Liberman & Shankweiler, 1985; Stanovich, 1986a).

The factors mentioned so far as causes of reading disability have either been confined to one modality or concerned with intermodal integration. Hypotheses also exist about *general* processes as the culprits in reading disability. Modality-free deficiencies could be expected to affect a good deal more than just reading. The global construct of intelligence is an obvious candidate in this category. Interestingly, in many studies of poor-reader groups the mean IQ is in the low average range (Stanovich, 1986a). Other suggestions for modality-free deficiencies include generating a response on the basis of partial information (Wolford & Fowler, 1984) and learning an irregular rule system (Morrison, 1984).

Finally, difficulties in visual perception as underlying reading disability may not be a dead issue. Work by Lovegrove and his colleagues (see Lovegrove, Martin, & Slaghuis, 1986, for a summary) has provided interesting data that are rather awkward for the dominant language-module set of hypotheses—they report abnormalities in transient visual processes in a high proportion of "specifically reading disabled" children.

It should be obvious from this short review that one of the problems of the field is an embarrassment of riches. There are more than enough correlates of reading skill that could serve, and have been advanced, as explanations of reading problems. This is true even if attention is restricted to the language domain, which many analysts suggest should be the case. In a recent review on the topic, based largely on their own careful and extensive research, Liberman and Shankweiler (1985) identified

> three problems of the poor reader—difficulty in becoming aware of sublexical structure for the purpose of developing word-recognition strategies, unreliable access to the phonological representations in the internal lexicon for naming objects and for performing metalinguistic tasks involving phonological properties of words, and finally, the deficient use of phonetic properties as a basis for the short-term working memory operations that underlie the processing of connected language in any form. (p. 15)

Liberman and Shankweiler outlined how each one could undermine some part of the reading process and learning to read, and they noted the need to determine how these abilities are related.

One thing that could be said about this rather long list of possible causes of reading problems is that it is needed, because reading is multifaceted and because there are many kinds of problems. This is a standard line of reasoning. In my view, however, it is premature. There is considerable uncertainty surrounding the typology of reading difficulties. Apparently different aspects of reading may in fact be related; "low level" problems may be at the root of "high level" ones, like comprehension difficulties (Perfetti & Lesgold, 1979). I cannot explore all of these issues here, but my point is that, given the uncertainty about a typology of reading difficulties and given that fewer explanatory constructs than reading problems may be needed, there may well be too much explanatory power for the job at hand. A way is needed to constrain the power. Economy of explanation characterizes the scientific endeavor and should be invoked in this branch of science.

It is possible that the explanatory power available could be constrained if it were required that each of the many hypothetical causes of reading problems fits a well-worked-out account of the acquisition procedure. In cases where the deficiency could not be made to fit, there would be prima facie evidence that it was either indirectly related to reading skills through joint variation with some third factor, itself a product of low levels of reading skill, or it was based on faulty experimentation. If the acquisition procedure remains only vaguely formulated, one can hold too readily that some deficiency "obviously" explains mastery problems. For instance, while analysis of learning to read took no account of different orthographic systems and their conceptual demands, it was easy enough to believe that a general deficiency in crossmodal integration would disrupt the process (Birch & Belmont, 1964). But when it became clear to psychologists that alphabetic systems might make very special demands on the learner—that is, when the analysis of the acquisition procedure had advanced—it became sensible to enquire whether the generality of the supposedly deficient process could be sustained in the face of facts about various orthographies. The claim that there were very few reading problems in Japan (Makita, 1968) sat uncomfortably with the crossmodal integration hypothesis. The *coup de grâce* was delivered by Rozin, Poritsky, and Sotsky (1971) when they showed that children with histories of reading problems in English could rapidly learn to read some words in Chinese, which also requires sight–sound integration. It suddenly looked as if the problem was not one of matching phoneme and grapheme but of being conscious of the phoneme's existence in the first place. If the speculation about a special difficulty in being aware of phonemic segmentation (Gleitman & Rozin, 1977) had been in place earlier, the sensory integration hypothesis might have been subjected to more critical examination right from the start.

The overabundance of possible causes is not the only reason to be cautious about the state of the art of dyslexia research that is based on the correlational method. Another reason is that some of the phenomena may turn out to be epiphenomena, or of uncertain reliability, and thus go the way of earlier, plausible "causes" of reading problems. There exist already a few chinks in the armor. For instance, one of the central pieces of data in support of impoverished verbal short-term memory in poor readers—lack of a phonetic confusion effect (Shankweiler, Liberman, Mark, Fowler, & Fischer, 1979)—has not always been easy to replicate (Byrne & Ledez, 1983; Hall, Ewing, Tinzmann, & Wilson, 1981; Morais, Cluytens, Alegria, & Content, 1986). And, lest it be thought that I cannot turn a critical eye on my own research, I mention that Simpson and Byrne (1987) demonstrated that earlier data, in which adult poor readers were shown to be less able (or willing) to code words phonetically in a memory task (Byrne & Ledez, 1983), may have been an artifact of inadequate matching of the subjects with their controls. As well, Winbury (1985) reported a frank failure to replicate data from Byrne and Shea (1979), who showed that poor readers make very few recognition errors on the basis of phonetic properties of speech. According to Winbury, the problem may reside in low reliability of the task in question, which is continuous recognition of a long list of spoken words.

This is clearly not a systematic critique of currently held views about possible causes of reading difficulties nor is it meant to be. It simply expresses some of my uneasiness about the state of knowledge that is based on correlational studies. Cherished beliefs in the field of reading have been undermined before. That the data are not always perfectly secure invites caution about the level of understanding of the issues and should, I think, encourage the converging approach of formulating and testing a theory of acquisition per se. At the least, this enterprise should produce some order in a field in which almost every aspect of psychological variation has been linked to reading progress. One should then be able to locate the points in the acquisition process at which the surviving solid individual differences exert their influences.

THE ACQUISITION PROCEDURE FOR READING

The acquisition process generally has been thought of as a sequence of stages. The model proposed by Frith (1985) is representative of these schemes. Others have suggested different pathways to reading mastery (e.g., Marsh, Friedman, Welch, & Desberg, 1981), but most incorporate something like Frith's stages (see Stuart & Coltheart, 1988). I will not review the proposals in detail here because my data only speak to what is happening during the child's very earliest contacts with orthography. But two aspects of the discussion surrounding the stage approach do merit attention—whether there is an inevitable sequence of stages that all successful readers pass through, and what drives the change from one stage to another.

Frith (1985) used the terms *logographic, alphabetic,* and *orthographic* to describe the stages of reading acquisition. Logographic reading occurs when the child uses some graphic cue(s) to read words without accompanying insights into the mapping of graphemes onto phonemes. Gough and Hillinger (1980) analyzed logographic reading as paired-associate, a point to which I return. Long words like *MacDonalds* are within the capabilities of logographic readers, though there is no understanding that *M* represents /m/. In the second, alphabetic, stage the child has discovered simple grapheme–phoneme relations and uses them in reading. The final stage, the orthographic, is reached when the child uses letter groups to identify words, ideally by correspondence to morphemic units, and when the route from print to the lexicon is not necessarily via phonology. For a full and critical discussion of Frith's model, see Ehri (1991).

Although not contesting the existence of stages of the sort Frith suggested, Stuart and Coltheart (1988) disputed the proposed sequencing. In particular, they argued that a child might launch directly into the alphabetic stage. This can occur if the child understands the phonemic organization of the speech stream and the way these segments are represented by letters at the time the child begins to read words. Stuart and Coltheart's evidence included the fact that phonological knowledge and letter–sound knowledge, measured prior to school, combined to predict reading age after a mere nine months of schooling.

In my formulation of the acquisition procedure, I incorporate Stuart and Coltheart's (1988) point while trying to preserve an interesting implication of models like Frith's (1985)—that there is just a single route to skilled reading. I do this by proposing the notion of the *default option*—the acquisition procedure that applies unless the child has access to certain initial representations of phonological structure ("phonemic awareness"). In brief, I argue that the relationship between phonemic awareness and progress in reading acquisition is as follows: Phonemic awareness is essential for progress to the alphabetic stage. If the child's usable knowledge about speech structure does not include the phonemic principle, he or she will read logographically at first (the default option). Breaking free of the logographic stage depends on achieving phonemic awareness.

This simplifying assumption of just one acquisition procedure is representative of a common way to proceed in science. It is usual to make a testable assertion with minimal components, to confront it with the data, and to retreat from it into complexity only when it is shown to be insufficient for explanatory purposes. I am pessimistic that we will ever gain a firm understanding of early reading and reading failure if it really is the case that there are many acquisition procedures. We already have several identifiably different instructional methods and, by hypothesis, variation in several critical mental capacities. If we add several initial learning strategies to the mix, the degrees of freedom are enormous.

What provokes the child to move from logographic to alphabetic reading? Two answers traditionally have been suggested. One is that confrontation with print itself, with its implicit information about grapheme–phoneme relations, is sufficient. The child deduces, unaided, that *f* represents /f/ by learning to read families of words like *fish, frog, fall,* and so on. This hypothesis lies behind the Bloomfield and Barnhart (1961) "linguistic" method, which uses large word families without direct instruction in phonemic structure. The alternate position is that the child needs independent information about the segmental nature of the speech stream and the way this is represented by the letters of the alphabet. Traditional "phonics" instruction makes this assumption. I present evidence in favor of this latter position.

HYPOTHESES

From the previous considerations I advance two hypotheses. First, I hypothesize that the default acquisition procedure for reading is to build nonanalytic associations between the spoken word and an aspect of the print sequence. That is, logographic reading is the first stage. This stage can be circumvented if the child has access to a mental representation of speech at the level of the phoneme and knows how letters symbolize phonemes. My second hypothesis is that for the logographic (nonanalytic) reader merely learning to read words that are arranged to reveal grapheme–phoneme relations will not force a shift to alphabetic reading. Independently provided information about phonemic structure is required for this shift to occur.

DATA I: ADULT ACQUISITION
OF AN ARTIFICIAL ORTHOGRAPHY

I begin the empirical section of this chapter with an in-principle demonstration of nonanalytic learning of an orthography by literate adults. I also demonstrate that nonanalytic acquisition is very persistent and that providing independent information about the speech structures that the orthography represents leads to analytic acquisition. The present account is brief—for a full description, see Byrne (1984) and Byrne and Carroll (1989).

The orthography that I taught my adult subjects in Experiment 1 of Byrne (1984) is exemplified in Fig. 1.1a. Its elements represent subphonemic features. The ones of particular interest are the symbols for voicing, < for voiced sounds, ∩ for unvoiced. The phonemes /z/ and /b/ are both voiced. Their unvoiced counterparts are /s/ and /p/. The input to the subjects was the four symbol–sound pairs in a paired-associated paradigm, and the subjects were trained until they could reliably say a phoneme when its symbol was presented. The question of interest was whether, after training, the subjects had discovered the mapping of orthographic elements onto the phonetic elements. Discovery was tested by presenting the participants with one of the partially new symbols of Fig. 1.1b.

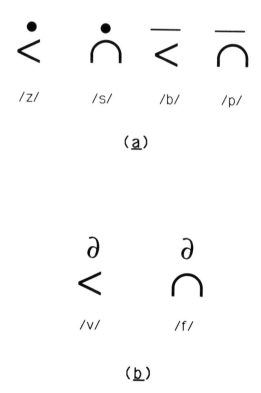

FIG. 1.1.   (a) Symbols and corresponding phonemes used in training phase of adult feature-based orthography experiments; (b) examples of stimuli used in transfer phase.

The subjects were told the symbol said either /f/ or /v/ and asked to choose. Someone who realized what the voicing symbols stood for should be able to solve the transfer task correctly even though the transfer symbol was partially new. There were eight test items of this sort.

What transpired was that even though the subjects could rapidly "read" the four symbols at the end of the training session, their performance on the transfer phase was exactly chance (later results restored my reputation as an honest experimenter). Thus, the acquisition procedure was nonanalytic in the sense that no evidence of insight into the most basic speech–symbol isomorphism emerged even though the system in itself was acquired. I can anticipate part of my later argument by likening my subjects to children who can read *cat* without any knowledge of what the individual letters represent, or indeed that they could represent anything individually at all.

In Experiments 2 and 3 of Byrne (1984) I demonstrated that the nonanalytic acquisition just described was not due to the fact that only four symbol–sound pairs needed to be learned. First, using the stimuli of Fig. 1.1a, new subjects learned that the symbols represented the syllables *fan, fit, pan,* and *pit.* Thus, the components of the stimuli that stood for ± voice in Experiment 1 now stood for two values of syllable rime, *an* and *it.* Literate adults certainly have access to the syllabic components of onset and rime—that is, in contrast to the case for phonetic features, syllabic structure is transparent. Transfer was tested by presenting a partially new symbol, like one of those in Fig. 1.1b, and requiring a forced choice between, for instance, *man* and *mit.* On this occasion, transfer was successful. Thus the problem in Experiment 1 was most likely due to the level of symbol–sound mapping represented by the orthography rather than the number of associations required. Further, analytic acquisition only occurs when the subject has available a suitably fine-grained representation of the critical speech structures. To continue the analogy with the situation facing the child learner, discovery of the way that letters represent phonemes will be possible if the learner has access to a suitable representation of the phonemic structure of speech. If the child does not have this access, acquisition of print–speech associations will remain logographic.

In Experiment 3, I returned to the use of phonemes and made the burden of acquisition heavier by increasing the number of items to be learned to eight. Even though many subjects found the acquisition stage burdensome, and hence should have found it useful to discover a systematic relationship between symbol and sound, on the average there was no successful generalization to the partially new symbols, confirming the picture emerging from the first two experiments.

The transfer procedure that I used in these three experiments was a demanding test of whether subjects had extracted information about the basic mapping embodied in the orthography. Certainly in later experiments, to be described shortly, those subjects who successfully generalized also gave insightful verbal reports of the mapping, using phrases like "this (+ voice symbol) is used for dark sounds." It is now well established that in concept learning situations and categorization experiments there can exist evidence of acquisition of the governing principles well below the level at which subjects can give any account of what they are learning, and even in the presence of explicit denials that there is anything to learn at all (Brooks, 1977, 1978; Reber, 1969). Thus, it may be that different techniques, requiring less in the way of effortful problem solving, would in fact expose evidence of subjects having acquired the principle of the orthography. Carroll and I tested this possibility (Byrne & Carroll, 1989).

We used a "savings" paradigm, which permits an assessment of how learning a second item list is affected by acquisition of a previous list of related items. Twenty-four subjects were first taught four symbol–sound pairs, such as those in Fig. 1.1a. After reaching criterion of three errorless passes through the four-item list, subjects were required to learn four new items comprising, as in the first learning stage, two pairs of phonemes minimally distinguished by voicing. The upper parts of the orthographic symbols were new; the lower parts were the signs that stood for voiced or unvoiced. For half of the subjects, however, voicing symbols were reversed in Stage 2, so that < now represented the unvoiced member of the pair and ∩ the voiced. For the other subjects the system was kept consistent throughout the entire experiment. Our reasoning was that if there were some implicit learning of the orthographic principle by which voicing was represented then subjects in the reverse condition should be disrupted during the second training stage, relative to the control subjects.

There was no evident at all of negative (or positive) savings. The mean errors made in reaching the criterion in the second stage were 4.2 for the reversal group and 4.4 for the savings controls. During Stage 1 the respective means were 4.8 and 3.4, a nonsignificant difference, $t(22) = .73$. It seems clear that the learning done by these subjects with this writing system is genuinely nonanalytic.

Furthermore, nonanalytic reading proved remarkably persistent. In another experiment in Byrne and Carroll (1989), one group of subjects learned the systematic orthography of Fig. 1.1a, applied to eight phonemes, and another learned an unsystematic system—the same visual symbols and phonemes, but linked so that voicing and place were not consistently represented by the component symbols. Both groups were then given 300 trials, each consisting of one pass through the eight-item list. Thus, each subject had a total of 2,400 exposures to examples of the orthography. We measured reaction time (RT) to respond with the phoneme when the symbol was shown. There turned out to be no RT advantage for the systematic group after the 4 hours' training that the experiment took. This finding stands in marked contrast to one of Brooks' (1977). He found a clear RT advantage for subjects taught a systematic but novel *alphabetic* orthography compared to subjects taught a nonsystematic version of the same phoneme–(novel)-grapheme pairs. So it appears that our subjects did not figure out the symbol–feature mapping. Had they done so, they would presumably have shown the RT advantage of Brooks' subjects (who of course already knew of the existence of phonemic segments by dint of being skilled readers).

Again to anticipate later argument, these data showing the persistence of nonanalytic learning have a parallel with a finding of Seymour and Elder's (1986). They followed a group of children taught by "whole-word" methods throughout the first year of schooling. At the end of the year, most of the children could not read words they had not been taught—they had not figured out the basic grapheme–phoneme mappings despite exposure to words that embodied those mappings for a long period of time.

I now return to the experiments of Byrne (1984). The final three experiments concerned the effects of explicit prior instruction in articulatory phonetics upon acquisition and transfer of the orthography on the basis of phonetic features. The story, briefly, is that if subjects were told about voicing and place prior to being exposed to the writing system they succeeded in the transfer phase provided that the examples used in the prior instruction were the phonemes used during ac-quisition of the orthography. The more specific the phonetics lesson the better the generalization, to the extent that all eight subjects in the final experiment, in which the orthography–speech links were explicitly pointed out, gave perfect or close to perfect transfer performances (mean, 94%). The comparison worth drawing this time is with the apparent success of reading programs that direct the learner's attention explicitly to the existence of phonemes, the sound segments represented by an alphabet (e.g., Bradley & Bryant, 1983; Byrne & Fielding-Barnsley, 1989; Williams, 1980).

DATA II: PAIRED-ASSOCIATE LEARNING
OF THE FIRST WORDS

I now turn to the first of a series of experiments using preliterate children as subjects. In this first set, I examine in more detail the claim of Gough and his colleagues (Gough & Hillinger, 1980; Gough, Juel, & Griffith, this volume) that the logographic phase is an instance of paired-associate (PA) learning. The claim is important because, if it is correct, then the process of early word learning will be illuminated by the considerable amount that is known about PA learning. The work was done in conjunction with Jennifer Shumack.

Experiment 1

The primary experimental evidence that Gough and Hillinger (1980) quoted in favor of their PA view were studies that showed that beginning readers are faster to learn lists of dissimilar than similar words (e.g., Otto & Pizzilo, 1970–1971). This observation fits an analysis of PA learning that holds that learners seek an attribute of the stimulus to serve as a connection to the response. The more the stimulus list shares attributes, the more errors in response selection will occur. But by itself the evidence advanced is ambiguous because the typical lists used in word-learning experiments have both high interstimulus similarity and high interresponse similarity. The poorer performance in learning to read a list containing RAT, RAN, and RAG than a group like CUT, FIN, and WEB[1] might stem from the response similarity and not the stimulus confusability. If this turned out to be true, the case for viewing early learning as essentially PA is weakened because it is known from laboratory studies that response similarity is not nearly as detrimental to the acquisition of associations as is stimulus overlap (Underwood, 1953). In the first experiment, the two sources of confusability are unconfounded.

Method

We selected 8 preschool children who could not read any of the words used in the study and who did not know the names or sounds of any of the constituent letters. There were 4 of each sex, with an average age of 54 months. On each of four consecutive school days, the children were individually taught a separate word list, counterbalanced in a Latin square so that each list was learned equally often in the four order positions. The lists, created by crossing the variable auditory similarity with visual similarity, are presented in Table 1.1 and were comprised of words judged by the preschool staff to be in the children's vocabularies.

Each word was printed in lower case letters on a card. For the first two passes through a list the experimenter showed the child a card, told him or her what it "said" and asked the child to repeat it. After Trial 2 the child was asked to pronounce each word as it was shown. If the subject failed to produce a response or gave an incorrect one the experimenter gave the correct word and again asked for repetition of it. The list was presented this way eight times, in a prearranged order each time, making the maximum score on each list 24.

Results and Discussion

In Table 1.2 are the mean correct responses for each list. As expected, the visually and auditorily less similar list was learned best. The two visually similar lists were acquired most poorly, and equally so. The list that rhymed but was visually distinct (TWO, BOO, YOU) was intermediate. A one-way analysis of variance yielded a significant F-value of 6.40 ($p < .01$). By Fisher's least significant difference (LSD) test, with p set at .05, all differences except that between RAT, RAN, RAG and SEE, SET, SEW were significant.

The data confirm what other research has found, that similar lists are learned more slowly than less similar ones. Moreover, they indicate that the problem lies primarily in visual not acoustic similarity. This is because SEE, SET, SEW was

---

[1]Throughout the text, upper case letters are used to represent print sequences taught to subjects. In the actual experiments, lower case print of the kind currently found in beginning reading texts was used.

TABLE 1.1
Word Lists Used in Experiment 1

| | | Auditorily | |
		More Similar	Less Similar
Visually	More Similar	RAT RAN RAG	SEE SET SEW
	Less Similar	TWO BOO YOU	CUT FIN WEB

as difficult to learn as RAT, RAN, RAG, and both were harder than TWO, BOO, YOU. There was some difficulty attributable to sound similarity, however (TWO, BOO, YOU vs. CUT, FIN, WEB), a fact that indicates that these preliterate children were sensitive enough to rhyme for it to be a source of confusion in the acquisition of print/speech pairs. Overall the data are consistent with the contention that the course of early reading acquisition fits the paired-associate paradigm, because the pattern of results is what would be predicted from what is known about the effects of variations in stimulus and in response overlap: most problems are created by stimulus similarity; the fewest occur when both stimuli and responses are quite distinct; response similarity produces only minor interference.

Experiment 2

In the first experiment meaningful words were used. There is the possibility that the results were the product of some unknown and possibly idiosyncratic seman-

TABLE 1.2
Mean Correct Responses for Each List Type, Experiment 1 (Maximum 24)

| | | Auditorily | |
		More Similar	Less Similar
Visually	More Similar	12.1	12.0
	Less Similar	15.8	19.9

tic factors, word familiarity, and so on. Thus in the next study lists of nonwords were used. We also took the opportunity to make the phonological structure of the items uniform; they were all consonant-vowel (CV) syllables. In Experiment 1 they varied between CV and consonant-vowel-consonant (CVC) and were not always identical within lists (SEE, SET, SEW). But although experimental nicety was the motivation behind the study, it is being reported here because of an interesting result that was itself the consequence of a design fault.

Method, Results, and Discussion

The syllable lists are presented in Table 1.3. As in the earlier study, preschoolers ($n = 9$) were each taught all four lists, a separate one on each of four consecutive days of attendance. The maximum score was again 24, and the results are shown in Table 1.4.

What transpired at first puzzled us. The previous result of low acquisition rates of *both* visually more similar lists, this time VOY, VOW, VOO and TAY, QAY, VAY, did not occur. Instead, TAY, QAY, VAY was learned as quickly as JIE, ZHY, FUY and REE, ZAR, DOW, and better than VOY, VOW, VOO, $F(3, 24) = 9.85$, $p < .01$, with the only significant contrast being between VOY, VOW, VOO and the rest. Recall earlier we had found that RAT, RAN, RAG and SEE, SET, SEW were both poorly learned. But we believe we have an explanation of this discrepancy between the experiments—scanning strategy. Notice that we rather carelessly permitted the two visually similar lists to vary in the locus of similarity—with one (VOY, VOW, VOO) it is in the left-most two letters, with the other (TAY, QAY, VAY) it is in the right-most two. In contrast, the real word lists of the earlier experiment were uniform in this respect. One might think, as we did, that for preliterate children this is not an important factor prior to the development of a left–right order of processing. But it turns out that our pre-

TABLE 1.3
Nonsense Syllable Lists Used in Experiment 2

| | | Auditorily | |
		More Similar	Less Similar
	More Similar	TAY QAY VAY	VOY VOW VOO
Visually			
	Less Similar	JIE ZHY FUY	REE ZAR DOW

TABLE 1.4
Mean Correct Responses for Each List Type, Experiment 2 (Maximum 24)

| | | Auditorily | |
		More Similar	Less Similar
Visually	More Similar	14.7	8.1
	Less Similar	15.9	15.2

schoolers had in fact received a good deal of information about the left-initial organization of English orthography, even though they could not in fact read any of our words or letters. It was common practice in the school for the teachers to print each child's name on any work they were doing (pasting, painting, etc.), often while the child watched, and to draw attention to the fact that unless one started on the left-hand side of the paper one would run out of room. Thus the children could be thought of as possessing an empty left–right scanning strategy. Hence in this experiment problems arise when it is the left letter that is common to all three words (VOY, VOW, VOO) because that is where the children's attention is initially focused.

This brings me to the point I want to make. It is that the list TAY, QAY, VAY was acquired no less readily than TIE, ZHY, FUY and REE, ZAR, DOW, despite being internally more similar than these other lists. It appears that in this experiment the children did not take advantage of the greater distinctiveness of the words in the latter two triads, which in turn indicates that the aspect of print that was the object of association was limited to a single letter. This belies the claim that global distinctiveness is what young readers learn about. I am not saying that the cue will always be a letter—in this experiment for two of the lists a single letter was all that differentiated the words, and so it is not surprising that that is what was used as a basis of discrimination. But what I suggest is that the child will attach the speech unit to a single *feature* of the word and not take advantage of redundant information in the print form. This will make it more difficult for the acquisition of a sight vocabulary, of course, because many words share single features (e.g., letters, length, particular subletter strokes, etc.), whereas all words except homographs are differentiated at some level of patterning.

In sum, these two experiments provide data that are consistent with the proposition that reading in the logographic stage is an instance of paired-associate learning. Stimulus similarity is more detrimental to acquisition than response similarity, consistent with Underwood's (1953) observations. Furthermore, the second experiment showed that subjects are *selective*. They select an element of the stimulus to serve as one side of the association. This phenomenon fits the analysis of PA learning provided by Greeno, James, DaPolito, and Polson (1978). The learner seeks out a single attribute of a stimulus, sufficient to distinguish it from the others being acquired. As well, if our analysis of the influence of preschool practices on word scanning strategy is correct, it seems that attribute selection is not random in the case of these children learning these words. They select the left-most letter.

However, acknowledging that early printed-word knowledge is PA in character does not necessarily exhaust our understanding of what is learned. Consider the (plausible) case of a child who has learned to read a small group of words and has selected the initial letters as the distinctive stimulus attributes. It is conceivable that this learning experience is all that is needed to provoke useful insights into phonemic structure: If printed words can be subject to analysis (attribute selection), why not spoken words? If there is a usable construct, "left-most visual component," why not a useful construct, "initial sound"? The typical learning experiment, with latency and error rates as data, is in principle incapable of exploring the associations more deeply. What is needed is a technique that can do exactly that—lay bare what is acquired under the influence of PA learning. In the next section I report a series of experiments aimed at this kind of exploration, exploiting the transfer paradigm used in the artificial orthography experiments of Byrne (1984) that were reported earlier.

DATA III: DOES ACQUISITION OF WORD FAMILIES PROVOKE DISCOVERY OF THE ALPHABETIC PRINCIPLE?

The standard way to assess what a child has discovered after learning a list of printed words is to request the child to read new words composed of the letters used in the training list. Typically, very young children cannot transfer to new words, leading to the conclusion that alphabetic reading has not been established (Carnine, 1977; see Ehri, 1991, for a review). But there is always a problem in interpreting failure in psychological experiments, particularly failure by the child subject. The problem is that there may be some critical knowledge in place that is masked by the experimental procedures (see Hamburger & Crain, 1984, for an example in the field of syntactic development). Thus a child may deduce that *f* represents /f/, *i* represents /I/, and *n* represents /n/ after learning a group of words containing those three letters and yet be unable to read the new word *fin* because he or she has not learned to assemble pronunciation from print for unseen items. In other words, an understanding of the alphabetic principle may be established but not the ability to harness this knowledge to read new words. Haddock (1976) presented evidence that this in fact can occur in reading, and

Brown, Kane, and Long (1989) analyzed the general problem of transfer of knowledge by young children and its suppression by task factors.

In the experiments reported in this section, done in conjunction with Ruth Fielding-Barnsley, we relieved the children of the need to read new words. Instead, our test of the presence of the alphabetic principle was modeled on the adult studies reported earlier. The children were taught to read a word family like FAT and BAT and then tested for transfer with a new word like FUN. They were told that it said either "fun" or "bun" and were asked to choose. We reasoned that providing the responses would lighten the child's computational load and hence be more likely to reveal a grasp of the alphabetic principle if it existed. The procedure is described in detail in Experiment 3 and subsequently more briefly.

Experiment 3

Method

Subjects.   The participants were 7 boys and 4 girls attending the University of Connecticut preschool, or the Uralla preschool in Australia, average age 53 months (range 47–57). None of the children could read any of the words used in the experiment nor give names or render pronunciations for the critical letters involved, F and B. Screening was conducted using a large card on which were printed all 26 letters. These were interspersed with line drawings of common objects to ensure that children with no letter knowledge could still experience some success in the task. In this initial study we decided to use as a criterion of exclusion the ability to read the critical letters F and B. Only 2 children of the 13 screened could do so. Most children knew the names or sounds for only a very few letters, generally the initial letters of their names. Some knew none at all.

Materials.   The words FAT, BAT, FIG, BIG, FELL, BELL, FUN, BUN, FIN, and BIN were each printed on a white 12.5 cm × 7 cm card, in lower case letters in the "sticks and circles" style common in initial reading.

Procedure.   Following screening, the training phase proceeded as follows: The experimenter drew a sketch of a bat on a piece of paper and asked the child what it was (each knew). The child was then presented with the card with BAT on it and was told that the word said "bat." The card was placed below the picture. Next a picture of a very fat boy was drawn, and the child told that this was "fat." The word FAT was shown and placed beneath the drawing. The words "bat" and "fat" were repeated several times by the experimenter and by the child while the experimenter pointed to the word–picture pairs. Following this, the cards were placed in front of the child, one closer to the subject than the other, and the child was asked, "which one says 'fat,' put it with its picture; which one says 'bat,' put it with its picture." Corrective feedback was provided, and the procedure was repeated until the subject succeeded in placing the cards correctly five consecutive times. After this, the pictures were removed and the cards presented to the child one at a time in a random order, with the child being asked to read each one. The criterion in this learning phase was also five consecutive successes with the pair of words. If the child had difficulties reaching the criterion, the picture matching procedure was reintroduced.

In the test phase the experimenter first drew a sketch of a (hamburger) bun and told the child what it was ("a bun"). Then some party balloons were drawn and the child told they were "fun." Immediately following, the printed word FUN was shown. The child was told it said "bun" or "fun," and asked to say which. No feedback was provided. The test sequence comprised eight such forced choices, each time using a pair of pictures and one word. The other items were the words BIG (drawing of a very tall house) and FIG (a fig), BELL (a bell) and FELL (a stick man on his back), and BIN (a garbage can) and FIN (shark with a prominent fin). On the first pass through the words FUN, BIG, FELL, and BIN were tested, then, using the same picture pairs, the words BUN, FIG, BELL, and FIN. Each child was checked on memory for the trained pair FAT and BAT halfway through the test procedure and retrained to criterion (this time three successful readings of the words) if necessary.

Pilot testing had revealed the need to provide the subjects with pictorial versions of the forced-choice items to guarantee that they would in fact respond with one of the two words. In the pilot work without the drawings, for example, one child offered the response "fat" when asked whether FUN said "fun" or "bun" (an observation that anticipates the major result of this study).

Results and Discussion

All but two of the subjects reached criterion on FAT and BAT with about 10 minutes of training. The two children required two learning sessions. Two children needed reminding of the correct responses to FAT and BAT in the middle of the test stage, on the basis of their failure to produce three error-free readings of the pair immediately upon retesting. All children always volunteered one of the items (e.g., "big" or "fig") in the forced-choice transfer phase.

Mean correct response level during the forced-choice test was 4.2, 53% ($s =$ 1.1), statistically indistinguishable from the guessing level of 4.0. It appears, therefore, that the training procedure did not produce usable knowledge of the pertinent letter–phoneme relations. The results are consistent with the proposition that initial reading acquisition is nonanalytic. Although each child must have been using the F–B discrimination as the basis of word learning, they apparently could not use what they had learned in a partially new situation. They had not, it seems, deduced that F represents /f/ and B, /b/.

The results are, of course, consistent with many other hypotheses as well. One is that the child really is an analytic learner but the knowledge did not (or could not) support correct performance during the generalization test. This could arise if the child simply did not perceive a connection between the training and test phases, or if the knowledge gained was suppressed by the forced-choice task. This is tantamount to saying that the testing technique masked the acquired analytic understanding, that it is in fact insensitive to letter–sound knowledge. This possibility is the subject of Experiment 4.

Experiment 4

The aim of this simple experiment was to see if children who did have extensive letter–sound knowledge but no (relevant) word reading skill could successfully solve the forced-choice task used in the generalization phase. If they could, it would undermine the claim that failure in Experiment 2 was due to the insensitivity of the testing technique.

Method

We needed subjects who had prior knowledge of the phonemes represented by F and B but who could not read any of the 10 words (FAT and BAT, plus the eight test items, FUN, etc.). A kindergarten teacher in a local public school was asked to nominate suitable children, and testing confirmed that the seven who were nominated knew what sounds F and B represented. None could read FAT and BAT. Mean age was 63 months.

The subjects were simply presented with the forced-choice task, that is, without prior training in reading FAT and BAT. These two words were added to the pool of test items, yielding ten in all.

Results and Discussion

Even though none of these kindergarteners was capable of reading any of the test words, each one achieved maximum scores (10) on the choice test. This is clear evidence that letter–sound knowledge will support correct performance on the transfer measure and supports the belief that the technique has a reasonable degree of sensitivity.

Two differences between Experiments 3 and 4 need noting. One is that the subjects in the latter experiment were older. The second is that these subjects could be assumed to have overlearned the letter–sound relations, presumably prior to coming to school or in the first few months of kindergarten. Either or both of these factors might explain the different outcomes. However, in the following experiments it will become clear that neither one alone nor their combination can fully account for the results.

Experiment 5

Even if it was the case that learning to read FAT and BAT in Experiment 3 was accomplished nonanalytically, it is not clear if the failure of analysis was due specifically to difficulty children have deducing letter–phoneme relations for themselves. After all, there were only two associations to be learned, and this number may not force analytic learning. In Experiment 5, this question was confronted in a fashion analogous to Experiment 2 in Byrne (1984) in which components of syllables rather than components of phonemes were the critical elements of speech structure (see the previous discussion). The units of language that were the objects of association with the orthography for Experiment 5 were words, specifically LITTLE BOY and BIG BOY. Children can apprehend the existence of words before they can access the concept of phoneme (Fox & Routh, 1975; Liberman & Shankweiler, 1985). The analogy with Experiment 2 in the adult series breaks down beyond this point because the orthographic symbols were not the same as in the basic experiment (FAT and BAT). For preliterates they could have been, logically, but we sacrificed scientific precision for ethics (that is, we decided against teaching that FAT said "little boy" and BAT said "big boy").

This study is also relevant in part to the possibility raised initially that the learning was in fact analytic but did not influence transfer performance. If acquisition–transfer dissociation occurs then it could be expected to also be in operation whatever the units of acquisition are.

Method

There were 12 subjects, 6 boys and 6 girls. In this study mean age was 52 months (range 47–57). All were attending the University of Connecticut preschool or the Uralla preschool in Australia, and all were screened in the same manner as in Experiment 3. The material consisted of the following phrases printed on cards, one phrase per card: LITTLE BOY, BIG BOY, LITTLE TRUCK, BIG TRUCK, LITTLE FISH, BIG FISH, LITTLE FOOT, BIG FOOT, LITTLE CAT, BIG CAT. Training consisted of associating the phrases LITTLE BOY and BIG BOY with sketches of a small and large boy, done by the experimenter, followed by verbal responses to the words alone. The criteria of acquisition employed in Experiment 3 were used. The generalization test also consisted of eight items; on each occasion the child was required to respond with one of the appropriate phrases when shown a printed phrase (e.g., LITTLE FISH) and a picture pair drawn by the experimenter (a big and little fish). This forced-choice technique was again successful in always eliciting one of the appropriate responses.

Results and Discussion

The course of acquisition was quite similar to that in the first experiment except that no child needed two training sessions to reach criterion. Again, there were two children who required some degree of retraining on the learned pair of phrases halfway through the test session.

Mean generalization score was 5.5 or 69% ($s = 1.9$), significantly higher than chance, $t(11) = 2.69$, $p < .05$. Individual scores revealed that some children performed knowledgably during transfer (three scored the maximum of 8) and some were clearly guessing (there were six scores between 2 and 5). The other three children each scored 6 correct. On the whole, therefore, there was generalizable knowledge of print–speech pairings gained during the training phase. It seems safe to conclude that the failure of generalization that occurred in the first experiment was not due to children being broadly nonanalytic nor to a general dissociation between acquisition and transfer stages in this experimental arrangement. When the elements of speech that the orthographic items represent are themselves readily available to reflection, as words are, then analytic learning seems possible as indicated by successful transfer. But not all children transfer, as the individual scores show, and a major research question is which ones do and why.

Experiment 6

Critical readers will note a likely confounding between Experiments 3 and 5. The items that were targets for deductive acquisition are both linguistically and orthographically more salient in Experiment 5—the words *little* and *big* versus the phonemes /f/ and /b/. Thus the differential success of generalization performance could be due to visual or to linguistic differences. In Experiment 6 this was tested by adopting a uniform "orthography" constructed from simple geometric forms, which represented "fat" and "bat" for one subject group, and "little boy" and "big boy" for another.

Method

The "writing" used for acquisition consisted of two distinct initial segments, a red triangle and a blue circle, each followed by the same green square (see Fig. 1.2). For one group of 12 preschoolers, screened in the normal manner (mean age was 50 months), these pairs of symbols were trained as representing "fat" and "bat." The children were told that this was the writing of the Voltrons (stars of a current television show about aliens). The other group ($n = 12$, mean age also 50 months) was treated identically except that the symbols stood for "little boy" and "big boy." Generalization was assessed by pairing one of the left-most symbols (e.g., the red triangle) with a new form (see also Fig. 1.2), analogous to FUN and LITTLE FISH, and presenting the usual forced choice, "fun" or "bun" (etc.) for Group 1, and "little fish" or "big fish" (etc.) for Group 2.

Results and Discussion

First, it was noted that acquisition was very rapid. In Group 1 (*fat, bat*), all but three children reached the criteria without error. In contrast, in Experiment 3

| | EXPERIMENT 6 | | EXPERIMENT 7 | EXPERIMENT 8 | EXPERIMENT 9ᵃ |
	Group 1	Group 2			
ACQUISITION					
Δ □	fat	little boy	clean chair	sat	hug
O □	bat	big boy	dirty chair	mat	hot
TRANSFER					
Δ ✚	fun	little cat	clean dog	sum	jug
O ✚	bun	big cat	dirty dog	mum	jot
Δ ◇	fig	little fish	clean face	sad	dug
O ◇	big	big fish	dirty face	mad	dot
Δ ✳	fell	little truck	clean plate	sow	tug
O ✳	bell	big truck	dirty plate	mow	tot
Δ ☆	fin	little foot	clean car	set	rug
O ☆	bin	big foot	dirty car	met	rot

FIG. 1.2. The "Voltron" writing system; (a) in Experiment 9 the Voltron symbols were inverted to maintain left-right correspondence between orthographic and speech sequences. (Under Acquisition are the words associated with the symbols in Experiments 6–9. Under Transfer, only the correct responses for each item in the forced-choice task are presented. In actual testing, both relevant words or phrases (e.g., *fun* and *bun* or *big cat* and *little cat*) were provided to the subject in conjunction with a single Voltron sequence. See text for further explanation.)

no child did so even though they were of the same age. In Group 2 there were eight children who made no errors during acquisition. These facts suggest the likely salience of simple geometric forms over conventional English letters.

The generalization performance for Group 1 was 3.6 (45%) and for Group 2 was 4.5 (56%—not significantly above the chance value of 50%). There is thus a prima facie case that the comparative results of Experiments 3 and 5, which used conventional spelling and in which the words-in-phrases condition (Experiment 5) produced significant generalization, may have depended on the visual distinctiveness of LITTLE BOY, BIG BOY compared to FAT, BAT. However, we noted that two of the Group 2 children scored 8 out of 8, and one 7 out of 8 (the probability of 7 out of 8 by chance is approximately .03). In contrast, not one child in Group 1 (*fat, bat*) did so well. Thus we were tempted to believe that some children gained usable knowledge of print–speech relations at the word level (as in Experiment 1), which *none* did when phonemes-in-words were the targets. Hence, a partial replication of Experiment 6 was conducted.

Experiment 7

There are reasons to believe that the adjective *little* may form a particularly tight bond with a following noun, tantamount perhaps to a compound noun. Richards (1977) reported some experimental data to this effect and commented in support on the fact that languages sometimes have diminutive forms, like *-lein* or *-chen* in German (*Mannlein, Herzchen*), *-li* in Swiss (*Fuessli*), and *-let* in English (*ringlet, droplet*). Thus it seemed possible that "little boy" may act as something of a unit, as is postulated for "fat" and "bat," and hence produce unreliable transfer because successful performance demands that the distinctive components ("little" and "big") be separated from their accompanying common elements ("boy"). The case for *big* having similar properties is not as strong, but it is interesting to note at least that bigness sometimes assumes the status of a prefix, as in *supertanker* and *superstar* (English), and *Riesenhunger* and *Riesenslalom* (German). Hence in the replication we used the same Voltron orthography but changed the adjective–noun pairs.

Method

This study used the acquisition pairs *clean chair* and *dirty chair*, associated with the symbols that represented "fat" and "bat," and "little boy" and "big boy" in the previous experiment (Fig. 1.2). Preschool children ($n = 12$, mean age 54 months), screened for relevant word and letter knowledge, were again used. The procedure was identical to that in Experiment 6. Transfer items are shown in Fig. 1.2.

Results and Discussion

Mean transfer performance was 4.83, 60%, ($s = 0.94$), yielding a t value of 3.07 ($p < .02$). Thus, there is again some evidence of usable knowledge of the most basic print–speech mapping when the speech items are words, which stands in contrast to what happens when the isomorphism occurs at the phoneme level. The level of performance was hardly overwhelming, however: No child scored 7 or 8 out of 8, though there were three scores of 6. The role of transfer failures of this global sort in learning to read invites investigation.

Experiment 8

In this experiment and the next one, the generality of the child's inability to learn letter–sound relations from word families was tested. First we changed the initial phonemes from /f/ and /b/ to /s/ and /m/. The selection was not simply random. It resulted from our observation that when preschoolers did know the sounds or names of letters, or both, *s* was by far the most commonly known, with *m* a clear though distant second for sound. The relevant data are in Table 1.5.

TABLE 1.5
Proportions of Preschool Children (*n* = 77) Knowing the Names and Sounds of Individual Letters

Letter	Name	Sound	Letter	Name	Sound
A	.23	.07	N	.16	.01
B	.18	.09	O	.53	.05
C	.32	.09	P	.20	.10
D	.07	.00	Q	.01	.00
E	.19	.03	R	.22	.05
F	.23	.07	S	.49	.33
G	.10	.05	T	.07	.05
H	.14	.01	U	.18	.01
I	.31	.01	V	.19	.02
J	.23	.05	W	.40	.00
K	.29	.03	X	.41	.00
L	.10	.01	Y	.16	.00
M	.37	.19	Z	.27	.05

Method

Training ("sat" and "mat") and transfer items are presented in Fig. 1.2. Appropriate pictures were drawn for each of the words, and the procedure throughout was the same as in the basic FAT–BAT experiment. There were 13 subjects, and mean age was 55 months.

Results and Discussion

Mean generalization score was 3.8 (47%). Thus even using phonemes that may have special salience does not appear to make it easier for children to extract letter–sound correspondence from suitably arranged word families.

Experiment 9

So far, the discriminable portions of the print and speech sequences have been the first; *f* and *b*, for example. These correspond to the syllable onset (just one phoneme in these cases). But there is evidence that rime (e.g., the /æt/ in /fæt/) is a readily detectable unit of speech for children. Lenel and Cantor (1981) demonstrated that preliterate youngsters are sensitive to rhyme (i.e., rime identity in two or more words) at a time when other research has shown them to be relatively insensitive to onset identity (e.g., Treiman & Breaux, 1982). Thus, we decided to see if preschoolers could deduce the relationships holding between rime and orthographic units in a suitably arranged word pair.

Method

The words "hug" and "hot" were selected as acquisition items. In contrast to previous pairs, they share a common beginning but have different endings (rimes). The Voltron symbols were reversed to maintain the left-to-right correspondence between orthography and speech—that is, the common element (green square) was left-most, followed by red triangle (*hug*) or blue circle (*hot*). The transfer items are also shown in Fig. 1.2. There were 12 subjects (average age 63 months) selected in the standard way from a local kindergarten.

Results and Discussion

As usual, the result of interest is performance in the transfer task: The mean was 3.6 (45%). The picture of the unbiased acquisition procedure as nonanalytic was thus confirmed in this case even when the relatively salient component, rime, was the speech object of interest.

Experiment 10

In all of the studies conducted to this point, there have been just two acquisition items. This is the minimum required by logic to allow for deduction of the basic correspondences (F → /f/, etc.). Furthermore, the training has been to modest criteria—five successive errorless trials of word–picture matching and the same number of "reading" trials. Although this has proven sufficient for some children to acquire transferable knowledge of print–word relationships (Experiments 5, 6, and 7), extraction of print–phoneme correspondences may require more stringent training conditions. It is possible that the hypothesis of nonanalytic acquisition has been protected so far by making it too easy for children to attach the whole speech sequence (e.g., "fat") to a single component of the orthography. If the hypothesized learning process disappears as soon as it is no longer possible to associate words (spoken) with single orthographic components, it would lose most of its interest. After all, in real classrooms children learn to read large numbers of words, sometimes arranged in overlapping families. In Experiment 10, the essential structure of the acquisition task was changed by increasing the number of items to 4.

Method

The learning set consisted of *fat, bat, fin*, and *bin*. Voltron orthography was again used, with "fat" and "bat" represented in the same way as in Experiment 6, and "fin" and "bin" having the same initial symbols as "fat" and "bat" (red triangle and blue circle, respectively), and a common final symbol (black star). Therefore, no single symbol uniquely represented one word—the red triangle, for example, was part of the graphic sequence for both "fat" and "fin." So learners were forced to conditionalize their responses on some property of the orthographic *pattern*. Under these circumstances, analytic acquisition would appear to be an efficient learning strategy.

Acquisition proceeded in stages. In Stage 1 (the first day), *fat* and *bat* were taught to the normal criteria. Then *fin* and *bin* were taught to the same level. In

Stage 2 (second and subsequent days), the child was presented with the four words in randomized orders and required first to match each up to its appropriate picture. This was continued, with feedback, until the criterion of five successive errorless passes through the four-word list was achieved. Then the subject was asked just to read the words, to the same criterion. If necessary, extra days were used for this second training stage.

Fourteen children (mean age of 53 months) were recruited from local pre-schools.

Results and Discussion

Of the 14 subjects, 4 could not learn the full list before being judged to be unsettled by continuing failure (after a total of 4 days training). They were terminated from the experiment. However, 5 children went through the entire acquisition regime without any errors. The remainder made a number of errors, mostly in Stage 2, the four-item list. The errors were systematic in the sense that erroneous responses were in most cases (90%) a word that shared either onset (e.g., "fin" for "fat," 50%) or rime (e.g., "fin" for "bin," 40%) with the target. Only 10% were of the "fat"–"bin" sort.

Two types of transfer items were used, the normal *fun–bun* group, and words that tested for analytic acquisition of the links between orthographic symbol and rime, namely, *pin, pat, skin, skat, flin* (as in the nursery rhyme character), *flat, spin,* and *spat.* Suitable line drawings were prepared for each of these items.

Mean correct performance on the onset transfer test (*fun, bun,* etc.) was 50%, and for rime (*pin, pat,* etc.) was 55% (not significantly higher than chance). The extra demands of learning a longer word list without a singular mapping of symbol onto speech item did not drive the children to deduce the basic relationships between orthography and speech segment captured by the orthography. Nonanalytic acquisition appears relatively persistent.

Experiment 11

The final experiment to be reported in this section was conceived in an attempt to ease the preliterate child into analytic acquisition of symbol–phoneme links by means of successful performance in the transfer stage at a more transparent linguistic level, the word. This was the kind of thinking behind Rozin and Gleitman's (1977) syllabic teaching device. In the current study, a jump was made from successful performance on the *little boy–big boy* task to *fat* and *bat,* with no intermediate syllabic stage. That is, this study represents the minimal easing-in situation, a justifiable starting place.

Method

The basic design was to test a group of children on the *little boy–big boy* task (as in Experiment 6), and then to take the successful subjects through the *fat–bat* condition. To this end, 13 children were selected from a local kindergarten class (mean age was 63 months). They were screened in the usual way for letter knowledge, which was minimal and included none of the critical letters. The subjects were older than their counterparts in Experiment 6 (Group 2), a deliberate move to try to ensure a higher level of performance at transfer. Successful transfer on *little fish* and so on was defined as 7 or 8 correct out of 8. Of the 13 children, 10 reached this criterion, 3 scoring 7 and the rest 8. These 10 children were then taught "fat" and "bat" as responses to a new set of Voltron symbols. For half of the children one symbol set was used for *little boy, big boy* and the other set for *fat, bat,* with the symbol–speech item arrangement reversed for the other half. This was to ensure that any performance differences were not due to some uncontrolled difference in visual distinctiveness between the patterns.

Results and Discussion

Mean transfer performance on *fun* and so on was 3.6 (45%). The highest score was 5 out of 8. Being successful in transfer at the word level is of no assistance when it comes to the phoneme level. The failure of these particular children to deduce symbol–sound relationships cannot be due to a generalized failure in this kind of task. There really is something inaccessible about the phoneme.

The results of the nine experiments reported in this section show that preliterate children are unable to extract regularities linking sublexical components of print and speech after learning, to a low criterion, the minimal number of words that would permit rule extraction, when the measure of rule deduction is transfer to partially new items. The learning that did take place fits the definition of logographic, and it is analogous to the nonanalytic acquisition that characterized the adult performance reported in the DATA I section. In addition, the data from the first two child experiments (DATA II), error rates in learning to read more and less similar word lists, support the idea that nonanalytic, logographic reading is an instance of paired-associated learning. It appears, therefore, that confrontation with an orthography that represents low-level properties of language— phoneme and phonetic feature in the case of the child and adult experiments respectively—does not provoke insight into fundamental speech–orthography isomorphism. To return to the debate about reading instruction, teaching children to read word families is, by itself, no guarantee that the children will work out grapheme–phoneme correspondences for themselves. The links between print and speech may retain the status of paired-associates.

Of course, more substantial exposure to word groups, typical of real classrooms, might well be a sufficient stimulus for the learner to move to alphabetic reading. But I know of no strict test of the hypothesis that whole-word learning is sufficient to generate alphabetic insight. This is because it is impossible to isolate children from all information about phonological organization and letter symbolization (see Byrne, 1987, for a discussion of this point). The nearest one can come in naturalistic research is to capitalize on different teaching techniques, with more or less emphasis on direct instruction in phonemic structure, letter–sound relations, and decoding. Perhaps the best known study of this sort is Barr's (1974–1975). She found that children taught by "phonics" methods were using a decoding strategy by the end of a year's instruction, as indicated by the kinds of errors they made. The whole-word method, however, left all but two children using a sight–word strategy by the end of the year. In addition, the Seymour and Elder (1986) data, though not based on a comparative study, indicated poor decoding skills in children taught by nonphonics methods for a year.

Research with children later in their schooling does show that whole-word trained readers do in fact develop phonological-based reading strategies as indicated, for example, by the appearance of nonword errors (Thompson, 1986). In an unpublished study by Britton (1988), third-grade children who had had whole-word instruction for their entire school careers were capable of decoding nonwords. (Interestingly, their performance was much poorer than that of a comparison group from a phonics orientation, though the two groups were no different in reading irregularly spelled words, which presumably depend more on word-specific associations.) But the problem with interpreting those data is the one mentioned earlier—the impossibility of knowing what information about phonology and graphemics the children had been given both inside and outside the classroom.

DATA IV: CONDITIONS NECESSARY FOR ACQUISITION OF THE ALPHABETIC PRINCIPLE

The final set of experiments that I report concern the conditions that promote an understanding of the alphabetic principle as operationalized by the transfer paradigm of the preceding section. The hypothesis under test is that providing information about the relevant structures of speech, the phonemes, and how they are represented by letters will enable the child who can read a word family to compute the phonemic value of the critical letter in a previously untaught word. The description is brief—for a full account see Byrne and Fielding-Barnsley (1989).

The hypothesis is justified by several related sets of observations: The first is the general correlation between phonemic awareness and reading ability (see Bryant & Bradley, 1985, for a review). Second, measures of phonemic awareness taken *prior to* reading instruction predict later reading skill (e.g., Bryant, Bradley, MacLean, & Crossland, 1989). Third, phonemic awareness training has been found to improve subsequent reading skill (e.g., Bradley & Bryant, 1983;

Williams, 1980). However, other observations indicate that the relationship between phonemic awareness and reading ability is of a special sort. In particular, phonemic awareness is necessary but not sufficient for alphabetic reading—there are children who have reasonable levels of phonemic awareness but who are poor at those reading tests that tap decoding skill like nonword reading (Gough & Juel, 1987; Tunmer, Herriman, & Nesdale, 1988). The data to be reported show that letter–sound knowledge is needed in addition to phonemic awareness to ensure an understanding of the alphabetic principle.

The basic structure of the experiments was to provide preliterate children with increasing amounts of information about phonemic organization and how letters represent sounds in the hope that the children would gain insight into the alphabetic principle. We began with 12 children screened in the usual way to ensure minimal or nonexistent knowledge of the alphabet. They were first subjected to a new training routine that aimed to alert them to the separability of the initial sounds in all of the training and transfer items of the SAT, MAT set. The child was required to break each word up ("s . . . at," "m . . . at," "s . . . ow," "m . . . ow," and so on). The experimenter exemplified the segmentation and provided feedback on performance. We discovered that only 8 of the 12 children could segment the words successfully under our instructional regime. All 12 children were then taught to read SAT and MAT and subsequently tested in the transfer task ("does SOW say 'sow' or 'mow'?," etc.) to see if those who had learned to segment could now perform well at transfer. Our reasoning was that awareness of the separate status of /s/ and /m/ might result in the deduction that these sounds are represented by separate visual symbols.

It turned out, however, that none of the successful segmenters performed to the criterion of 7 out of the 8 transfer items correct. Nor did any of the other four children. It seems that awareness of segmental structure of the words being learned does not guarantee emergence of insight into the alphabetic principle.

We then trained a second aspect of phonemic awareness, phoneme identity. Because a child can segment "sat" and "sow," it does not follow that he or she is aware of the identity of the two initial sounds. But even if a child under our training regime came to understand that S represents the first sound in "sat" by a process of deduction during acquisition of the words SAT and MAT, failure at transfer would be expected unless identity of the initial sounds in the training and related transfer words ("sat" and "sow", for example) was also known. Our segment identity training procedure involved the children telling us which word out of a pair, for example "sow" or "mow", started with the same sound as "sat". We worked through all of the pairs of transfer words, each time comparing them with one or another of the two training words "sat" and "mat". The children were given feedback on their performance on each trial. As with the first component of phonemic awareness, segmentation, we discovered that only some of the children succeeded—5 out of the 12, including 4 who had learned the segmentation procedure.

We then retrained the basic reading items, SAT and MAT, and reran the transfer task. But for a second time we were faced with continued failure at transfer, even among the four children who had passed both phoneme awareness procedures. Therefore, knowing the relevant segmental structure of words and the identity of the relevant sounds in pairs of words did not provide sufficient information for our young subjects to acquire working knowledge of the alphabetic principle.

Finally, we directly taught all 12 children the critical symbol—phoneme relations—that S says /s/ and M says /m/. All learned very quickly. Then we tested with the transfer procedure for a third time. Now we obtained a very interesting result. All four of the children who succeeded in both phonemic awareness tasks—phoneme segmentation and phoneme identity—performed perfectly at transfer. In addition, each of the two children who passed one of the phonemic tasks but not the other also performed well at transfer. Thus, 6 of the 12 children succeeded at transfer, and all 6 had passed on at least one of the aspects of phonemic awareness. But none of the remaining six subjects, all of those in fact who had failed both aspects of phonemic training, performed to criterion at transfer despite having readily acquired the symbol–sound associations in the final training session. Phonemic awareness by itself is not sufficient to produce alphabetic insight, but when it is supplemented by relevant letter-sound knowledge understanding of the alphabetic principle can be demonstrated. Learning the sounds that the letters represent is not sufficient either. That needs to be supplemented by appropriate insights into segment separability and identity. Phonemic awareness and letter–phoneme knowledge act in a complementary fashion to generate an understanding of alphabetic orthography as children learn to read their first words.

In subsequent studies (Experiments 1 and 2 of Byrne & Fielding-Barnsley, 1990) we considerably increased the amount of phonological training in an attempt to separately assess the efficacy of teaching phoneme identity and word segmentation. We found that children who profited from extensive instruction in phoneme identity alone showed a grasp of the alphabetic principle, as evidenced by successful transfer after learning to read a two-word family. Training in how to segment words ("m . . . at," etc.), was not so clearly related to learning the alphabetic principle. The correlation between segmentation score and subsequent transfer performance was a nonsignificant .20, whereas it was .49 ($p < .05$) for identity and transfer. Furthermore, what beneficial effect segmentation training had may have been mediated by knowledge of phoneme identity—all children taught segmentation who passed at transfer also demonstrated a grasp of identity, whereas successful segmenters who did not understand identity failed at transfer. These and other data have led us to suggest that activities that alert children to the existence of shared sounds in words may be particularly helpful as a basis for reading acquisition, as also suggested by Bradley and Bryant (1983).

One further aspect of the data is worth noting—the relative robustness of the alphabetic principle once it is understood. In the experiments just described, children were trained in phonemic awareness (identity or segmentation) for the sounds /s/ and /m/, trained to read SAT and MAT, and tested for transfer in the usual way. In the final stage, they were taught two new words, FIN and BIN, taught the sounds for F and B, and tested for transfer ("does FUN say 'fun' or 'bun'," etc.). There was *no* phonemic awareness instruction for /f/ and /b/. Despite this, the majority of children who passed transfer for S and M also passed F and B. This was the first time in a long series of studies that the alphabetic principle was in evidence in children not given phonemic awareness training in the critical sounds. The data encourage the view that once the principle is grasped, it spreads to other sounds and letters that occur in the developing reading vocabulary. We also believe that the data make it proper to use the term "insight" to describe the stage of the acquisition process we are examining in these training studies. An insight typically transcends the particular context in which it was initially gained. A general principle has been discovered.

SUMMARY AND CONCLUSIONS

I have argued that we need a way to constrain hypotheses about reading development and reading difficulties in view of the fact that a great number of variables have been identified as correlating with progress in reading. I suggested that one way to achieve some constraint is to postulate a reading acquisition procedure with as few parameters as possible. Stage models, like Frith's (1985), are attractive in that they (often implicitly) assume that all apprentices take the same steps on the way to reading mastery. Some recent data from Stuart and Coltheart (1988) cast doubt on the uniformity assumption, but a way to partially preserve it is through the notion of a default acquisition procedure. I suggested that, in the absence of accessible knowledge of phonemic structure in the child, the natural strategy the learning reader will adopt is to build associations between the words in language and an aspect of the print sequences that represent them. The associations, which can be thought of in the framework of paired-associate learning, are not realized at the level of letter–phoneme links, even when the words the child can read could potentially reveal those links. Information about the segmentation of speech into phonemic units is needed.

I first argued by analogy from studies of adults acquiring a feature-based orthography that showed that learners can read an orthography without knowing its basic isomorphism with speech and that this can persist for a long time. The data from preliterate children I have presented are consistent with the hypotheses. First, error rates from children's attempts to learn to read word lists had the hallmarks of paired-associate learning: Stimulus similarity disrupted learning, and there was evidence that attributes of the stimuli were selected as bases for the associations. In subsequent studies, using a transfer paradigm, children learned to read word families like FAT and BAT. The learning was structured to potentially reveal symbol–phoneme associations, but the children failed in fact to deduce these associations for themselves. The sensitivity of the transfer test used to assess exactly what had been acquired was confirmed (Experiment 4), and in several other experiments (e.g., Experiments 5 and 11) results indicated that the failure at the phoneme level was not due to a generalized inability to transfer symbol–speech associations to partially new situations. Finally, the training studies show that the grip of the default acquisition procedure can be broken by the provision of information about phonemic structure and how the phonemes are represented by graphemes.

As I see it, the chief merit of this kind of argument is that it treats a certain common kind of reading difficulty, characterized by failure to develop analytic links between print and speech (Boder, 1973), simply as an extension of the default acquisition procedure. It also directs attention toward the instructional process in explaining both success and failure in learning to read, something that Calfee (1983) urged on researchers some time ago.

I want to close with references to some case studies of adult disabled readers (Johnston, 1985). In the three cases presented, the origins of the disabilities seem to be in the early conception that reading is largely remembering. As one interviewee put it: "I had learned symbols . . . and 1 and 2 and 3, which were symbols . . . so I wanted that for five-letter words. . . . I had this idea that . . . I was going to know just by looking at it. . . . But there's no way you could possibly take all the words in the dictionary and just learn them by sight . . . " (Johnston, 1985, p. 157). It seems too that the three men were in a sense trapped by their early success in reading by remembering. One, at least, "got great marks" for standing up in class and "reading" via memorization of stories. At a certain point, anxiety about being exposed began to drive coping strategies that were counterproductive to genuine reading development. Functional fixation of the default acquisition procedure was established.

Johnston (1985) referred to these men's "misconceptions" about the nature of reading, but I would recast them as natural assumptions. This aside, if the picture painted by these case studies is accurate, then the burning research question becomes why some individuals cannot or do not break out of the initial strategy. It seems likely to me that in pursuing this matter we will be considering mainly the intersection of the default acquisition procedure and the instructional setting.

ACKNOWLEDGMENTS

This research was funded by the Australian Research Council and the University of New England. I thank the children who formed the bulk of the subjects for this research, their parents, and the following principals and directors for their kind cooperation: Marie Backhouse (Armidale City Public School); Bronwen Bell

(Hobbit House); Gloria Cook (Armidale Community Preschool); Annabelle Daunt-Watney and Louise Pearce (St. Peter's Preschool); Sue-Ellen Dean (Galloway Street Preschool); Charlotte Madison (University of Connecticut Preschool); John Reid (Newling Public School); Dianne Tegart (Uralla Preschool); and John Turnbull (Ben Venue Public School).

REFERENCES

Bakker, D. J. (1971). *Temporal order in disturbed reading: Developmental and neuropsychological aspects in normal and reading-retarded children.* Rotterdam: Rotterdam University Press.

Barr, R. C. (1974–1975). The effect of instruction on pupil reading strategies. *Reading Research Quarterly, 10,* 555–582.

Benton, A. L. (1980). Dyslexia: Evolution of a concept. *Bulletin of the Orton Society, 30,* 10–26.

Birch, H., & Belmont, L. (1964). Auditory–visual integration in normal and retarded readers. *American Journal of Orthopsychiatry, 34,* 852–861.

Bloomfield, L., & Barnhart, C. L. (1961). *Let's read: A linguistic approach.* Detroit: Wayne State University Press.

Boder, E. (1973). Developmental dyslexia: A diagnostic approach based on three atypical reading–spelling patterns. *Developmental Medicine and Child Neurology, 15,* 663–687.

Bradley, L., & Bryant, P. E. (1983). Categorizing sounds and learning to read—a causal connection. *Nature, 301,* 419–421.

Britton, D. (1988). *The persistence of early reading instruction effects on reading strategies.* Unpublished master's thesis, University of New England, Armidale, N.S.W., Australia.

Brooks, L. R. (1977). Visual pattern in fluent word identification. In A. S. Reber & D. L. Scarborough (Eds.), *Toward a psychology of reading: The proceedings of the CUNY conferences* (pp. 143–181). Hillsdale, NJ: Lawrence Erlbaum Associates.

Brooks, L. R. (1978). Nonanalytic concept formation and memory for instances. In E. Rosch & B. B. Lloyd (Eds.), *Cognition and categorization* (pp. 169–211). Hillsdale, NJ: Lawrence Erlbaum Associates.

Brown, A. L., Kane, M. J., & Long, C. (1989). Analogical transfer in young children: Analogies as tools for communication and exposition. *Applied Cognitive Psychology, 3,* 275–293.

Bryant, P. E., & Bradley, L. (1985). *Children's reading problems.* Oxford, England: Blackwell.

Bryant, P. E., Bradley, L., Maclean, M., & Crossland, J. (1989). Nursery rhymes, phonological skills and reading. *Journal of Child Language, 16,* 407–428.

Byrne, B. (1984). On teaching articulatory phonetics via an orthography. *Memory & Cognition, 12,* 181–189.

Byrne, B. (1987). Is the interactive view premature? *Cahiers de Psychologie Cognitive, 7,* 444–450.

Byrne, B., & Carroll, M. (1989). Learning artificial orthographies: Further evidence of a non-analytic acquisition procedure. *Memory & Cognition, 17,* 311–317.

Byrne, B., & Fielding-Barnsley, R. (1989). Phonemic awareness and letter knowledge in the child's acquisition of the alphabetic principle. *Journal of Educational Psychology, 81,* 313–321.

Byrne, B., & Fielding-Barnsley, R. (1990). Acquiring the alphabetic principle: A case for teaching recognition of phoneme identity. *Journal of Educational Psychology, 82,* 805–812.

Byrne, B., & Ledez, J. (1983). Phonological awareness in reading-disabled adults. *Australian Journal of Psychology, 35,* 185–197.

Byrne, B., & Shea, P. (1979). Semantic and phonetic memory codes in beginning readers. *Memory & Cognition, 7,* 333–338.

Calfee, R. (1983). Review of "Dyslexia: Theory and Research." *Applied Psycholinguistics, 4,* 69–79.

Carnine, D. W. (1977). Phonics versus look-say: Transfer to new words. *Reading Teacher, 30,* 636–640.

Ehri, L. C. (1991). Development of the ability to read words. In R. Barr, M. Kamil, P. B. Mosenthal, & P. D. Pearson (Eds.), *Handbook of reading research* (Vol. 2, pp. 383–417). New York: Longman.

Fox, B., & Routh, D. K. (1975). Analyzing spoken language into words, syllables, and phonemes: A developmental study. *Journal of Psycholinguistic Research, 4,* 331–342.

Frith, U. (1985). Beneath the surface of developmental dyslexia. In K. E. Patterson, J. C. Marshall, & M. Coltheart (Eds.), *Surface dyslexia:* Neuropsychological and cognitive studies of phonological reading (pp. 301–330). Hillsdale, NJ: Lawrence Erlbaum Associates.

Frostig, M., & Maslow, P. (1973). *Learning problems in the classroom: Prevention and remediation.* New York: Grune & Stratton.

Gleitman, L. R., & Rozin, P. (1977). The structure and acquisition of reading I: Relations between orthographies and the structure of language. In A. S. Reber & D. L. Scarborough (Eds.), *Toward a psychology of reading: The proceedings of the CUNY conferences* (pp. 1–53). Hillsdale, NJ: Lawrence Erlbaum Associates.

Gough, P. B., & Hillinger, M. L. (1980). Learning to read: An unnatural act. *Bulletin of the Orton Society, 30,* 179–196.

Gough, P. B., & Juel, C. (1987). *Is there reading without phonological awareness?* Paper presented at the Annual Meeting of the American Educational Research Association, Washington, DC.

Greeno, J. G., James, C. T., DaPolito, F., & Polson, P. G. (1978). *Associative learning: A cognitive analysis.* Englewood Cliffs, NJ: Prentice-Hall.

Haddock, M. (1976). Effects of an auditory–visual method of blending instruction on the ability of prereaders to decode synthetic words. *Journal of Educational Psychology, 68,* 825–831.

Hall, J. W., Ewing, A., Tinzmann, M. B., & Wilson, K. P. (1981). Phonetic coding in dyslexics and normal readers. *Bulletin of the Psychonomic Society, 11,* 520–527.

Hamburger, H., & Crain, S. (1984). Acquisition of cognitive compiling. *Cognition, 17,* 85–136.

Johnston, P. H. (1985). Understanding reading disability. *Harvard Educational Review, 55,* 153–177.

Lenel, J. C., & Cantor, J. H. (1981). Rhyme recognition and phonemic perception in young children. *Journal of Psycholinguistic Research, 10,* 57–68.

Liberman, I. Y., & Shankweiler, D. (1985). Phonology and the problems of learning to read and write. *Remedial and Special Education, 6,* 8–17.

Lovegrove, W., Martin, F., & Slaghuis, W. (1986). A theoretical and experimental case for a visual deficit in specific reading disability. *Cognitive Neuropsychology, 3,* 225–267.

Makita, K. (1968). The rarity of reading disability in Japanese children. *American Journal of Orthopsychiatry, 38,* 599–614.

Marsh, G., Friedman, M., Welch, V., & Desberg, P. (1981). A cognitive-developmental theory of reading acquisition. In G. E. MacKinnon & T. G. Waller (Eds.), *Reading research: Advances in theory and practice, Vol. 3* (pp. 199–221). San Diego, CA: Academic Press.

Morais, J., Cluytens, M., Alegria, J., & Content, A. (1986). Speech-mediated retention in dyslexics. *Perceptual and Motor Skills, 62,* 119–126.

Morrison, F. (1984). Reading disability: A problem in rule learning and word decoding. *Developmental Review, 4,* 36–47.

Orton, S. T. (1925). "Word-blindness" in school children. *Archives of Neurology and Psychiatry, 14,* 581–615.

Otto, W., & Pizzilo, C. (1970–1971). Effect of intralist similarity on kindergarten pupils' rate of word acquisition and transfer. *Journal of Reading Behavior, 3,* 14–19.

Perfetti, C. A. (1985). *Reading ability.* New York: Oxford University Press.

Perfetti, C. A., & Lesgold, A. (1979). Coding and comprehension in skilled reading and implications for reading instruction. In L. B. Resnick & P. Weaver (Eds.), *Theory and practice of early reading, Vol. 1* (pp. 57–84). Hillsdale, NJ: Lawrence Erlbaum Associates.

Reber, A. S. (1969). Transfer of syntactic structure in synthetic languages. *Journal of Experimental Psychology, 81,* 115–119.

Richards, M. M. (1977). Ordering preferences for congruent and incongruent English adjectives in attributive and predicative contexts. *Journal of Verbal Learning and Verbal Behavior, 16,* 489–503.

Rozin, P., & Gleitman, L. R. (1977). The structure and acquisition of reading II. The reading process and the acquisition of the alphabetic principle. In A. S. Reber & D. L. Scarborough (Eds.), *Toward a psychology of reading: The proceedings of the CUNY conferences* (pp. 55–141). Hillsdale, NJ: Lawrence Erlbaum Associates.

Rozin, P., Poritsky, S., & Sotsky, R. (1971). American children with reading problems can easily learn to read English represented by Chinese characters. *Science, 71,* 1264–1267.

Seymour, P. H. K., & Elder, L. (1986). Beginning reading without phonology. *Cognitive Neuropsychology, 3,* 1–36.

Shankweiler, D., Liberman, I. Y., Mark, L. S., Fowler, C., & Fischer, F. W. (1979). The speech code and learning to read. *Journal of Experimental Psychology: Human Learning and Memory, 5,* 531–545.

Simpson, L., & Byrne, B. (1987). Phonemic awareness in reading-disabled adults: A follow-up and extension. *Australian Journal of Psychology, 39,* 1–10.

Stanovich, K. E. (1986a). Cognitive processes and reading problems in learning-disabled children: Evaluating the assumption of specificity. In J. Torgesen & B. Wong (Eds.), *Psychological and educational perspectives on learning disabilities* (pp. 87–131). San Diego, CA: Academic Press.

Stanovich, K. E. (1986b). Matthew effects in reading: Some consequences of individual differences in the acquisition of literacy. *Reading Research Quarterly, 21,* 360–407.

Stuart, M., & Coltheart, M. (1988). Does reading develop in a sequence of stages? *Cognition, 30,* 139–181.

Thompson, G. B. (1986). When nonsense is better than sense: Nonlexical errors to word reading tests. *British Journal of Educational Psychology, 56,* 216–219.

Treiman, R., & Breaux, A. M. (1982). Common phoneme and overall similarity relations among spoken syllables: Their use by children and adults. *Journal of Psycholinguistic Research, 11,* 569–598.

Tunmer, W. E., Herriman, M. L., & Nesdale, A. R. (1988). Metalinguistic abilities and beginning reading. *Reading Research Quarterly, 23,* 134–158.

Underwood, B. J. (1953). Studies of distributed practice: X. The influence of intralist similarity on learning and retention of serial adjective lists. *Journal of Experimental Psychology, 45,* 253–259.

Vellutino, F. R. (1979). *Dyslexia: Theory and research.* Cambridge, MA: MIT Press.

Williams, J. P. (1980). Teaching decoding with an emphasis on phoneme analysis and phoneme blending. *Journal of Educational Psychology, 72,* 1–15.

Winbury, N. E. (1985). A developmental investigation of the use of phonetic and semantic codes in good and poor readers (Doctoral dissertation, University of Connecticut, 1984). *Dissertation Abstracts International, 45,* 1079A–1080A.

Wolford, G., & Fowler, C. A. (1984). Differential use of partial information by good and poor readers. *Developmental Review, 4,* 16–35.

2

Reading, Spelling, and the Orthographic Cipher

Philip B. Gough
Connie Juel*
Priscilla L. Griffith
University of Texas at Austin

When does reading begin? There may have been a time when we thought that it began with reading instruction, but students of emergent literacy (Sulzby & Teale, 1991) have persuaded us that many children know a great deal about reading before they enter school. They know something about the uses and functions of print, they know something about the form of their orthography and its books, and they know something about the nature of the forms of discourse.

Still, although their literacy may be emerging, no sensible person would call them literate. Conventional literacy begins when they begin to recognize specific words. The acquisition of literacy is primarily the acquisition of word recognition skill.

This is not to equate literacy with word recognition; there is much more to reading than recognizing words. After recognizing the word *letter*, readers must decide whether it means a character or a missive; they must disambiguate it. After deciding on the meaning of each word in the sentence *Juan showed her baby pictures*, readers must decide whether *baby* or *pictures* is the direct object; they must parse the sentence. After understanding each sentence in a discourse, readers must assemble them into a larger framework; they must build a discourse structure. And after understanding the discourse, readers must integrate it with what they already know; they must assimilate the text.

But readers must also do these things when they listen. These are linguistic skills, not just of reading, but of comprehension in general. So we equate literacy not with word recognition, but rather with the product of that skill and comprehension (Gough & Tunmer, 1986; Hoover & Gough, 1990; Tunmer & Hoover, this volume). Reading (R) equals the product of decoding (D) and comprehension (C), or $R = D \times C$.

---

*Connie Juel is presently at the University of Virginia, Charlottesville.

If our view is correct, then the reader is simply one who can recognize words and comprehend them. But preliterate children can already comprehend. They have internalized the phonology and syntax of their native language, they have acquired a vocabulary of thousands of words, and they can understand stories and follow instructions. What they cannot do is read stories or follow instructions in print. What they must learn, then, is word recognition. Our concern then is with the way that children learn to recognize words.

THE FIRST WORDS

At some point, whether in the home, a shopping mall, or at school, children must learn to recognize their first words. How is this done?

The idea that beginning readers read in a different way than skilled readers is widely accepted. Unlike skilled readers, beginning readers are supposed to see words "globally" or as "wholes," to view them as if they were Chinese characters, or to recognize words as they might recognize a tree or a face.

As we see it, there is something correct in such claims, but there is also something wrong. What is correct is the suggestion that children do not look at the word the way skilled readers do, registering each (or at least most of) its component letters. What is wrong is the claim that this is because children are seeing the word globally, or as a whole, or registering the word as a gestalt.

Our belief is that children begin to recognize words by means of what we call *selective association* (see also Byrne, this volume). That is, children learn to recognize their first words by selecting some cue, some attribute or feature, that distinguishes each word from others they have noticed. A child then might select some part of a word, like a particular letter (e.g., the *d* in *dog*) or pair of letters (e.g., the matching *ee*'s in *feet*), or a particular property of the word as a whole (e.g., its length or its font).

We emphasize that we do not hold that children will always select the same property or even the same kind of property across different words. In some instances, a child may select a cue because it bears a physiognomic resemblance to the word's meaning. Thus we would guess that a child might notice the *oo*'s in *moon,* or the humps in *camel,* or the tail on *donkey.* In other instances, the child might select a cue because it is associated with a word's sound, like the *b* in *bee,* or the *j* in *jail* (see Ehri & Wilce, 1985). In still others, the child might notice that this word is long, or that one short (Lipscomb & Gough, 1990).

There may be tendencies to choose one or another class of cues in or even across individual children. But we believe that the cue selected will ultimately depend more on the similarities and differences among the set of words the child is trying to distinguish than anything else. The child will select any cue that will work.

In a first test of this notion, Gough (unpublished) asked 32 four- and five-year-olds to learn to read four words presented on flash cards. Half the children learned a set of similar words (*bag, bat, rag,* and *rat*), and the other half learned a set of dissimilar words (*box, leg, sun,* and *rat*). For each child, one of the four flashcards was sullied by a thumbprint in the corner. Using the standard method of paired-associate learning with anticipation and correction, the child was trained to a criterion of two successive correct trials on all four words.

Although the dissimilar list was mastered faster than the similar list, the thumbprinted word was mastered first (and equally fast) in each list. But when the child was then shown (without comment) a clean card bearing the word that had been accompanied by the thumbprint, less than half of the children could identify that word. In contrast, when each child was then shown a card bearing only the thumbprint, nearly all of them could identify the word that had accompanied it. Finally, when the children were shown a card bearing the thumbprint and another word, nearly all of them identified the word as the one that had accompanied the thumbprint in training.

To us, the important aspect of these results is not that the children had learned which word went with the thumbprint, but that they had learned the thumbprint to the exclusion of the word. This result clearly demonstrates that the child's learning of these words was selective. But to show that the child will select a conspicuous extraneous cue obviously falls short of showing that the child will be equally selective when (as in the case of an ordinary word on a clean flashcard) no one cue is equally salient. Our next experiment was aimed at this point.

We asked a different set of preschoolers to learn 4 four-letter words (*lamb, duck, fish,* and *pony*) by means of flashcards, again to a criterion of two successive correct responses to all four words. Then we asked the children whether they could recognize the words when we hid parts of them, and we showed them (on separate trials and in random order) the first and last half of each word. We reasoned that, although we could not anticipate which cue the child would select to learn each word (it might well be different for each child, and for each word), if that cue was to be found in the first half of the word it would not be found in the second, and vice versa. Thus we predicted that if we cross-classified the children's responses in a 2 × 2 table (right vs. wrong on the first half of the word by right vs. wrong on the second half), we would see a negative contingency.

This is just what we observed. We found that children were twice as likely to recognize the second half of a word when they could *not* recognize the first. They were half again as likely to recognize the first half when they failed on the second as when they succeeded on the latter half. Thus most children learned to recognize a cue in one half of the word but not the other; they selected one cue.

Taken together, we believe that these results strongly support the idea that children learn to recognize their first words through selective association.

THE FAILURE OF SELECTIVE ASSOCIATION

Children could continue to learn in this way, but they face two serious problems. Although it is easy to find partial cues that distinguish a handful of words, this task becomes increasingly difficult as additional words must be added. In the end, many words can be identified on the basis of no partial cue, for every one of their proper subsets of ordered letters is shared with some other word; the only thing that distinguishes such a word is its full spelling. The result then is that learning by selective association begins easily but gets progressively harder.

The second problem is that selective association provides no way of recognizing a novel word. The importance of this problem cannot be overemphasized. It is obvious in the abstract that every word we can read must have been novel to us exactly once. But because we adults seldom encounter such words in text, it is easy to forget that children's experience is very different: Beginning readers encounter novel words on almost every page they read.

To read ordinary text, children must be able to identify unfamiliar words. It is widely supposed that context will provide the children with the help they need. There certainly are times when context will permit one to infer the identity or at least the meaning of an unknown word. But we think such cases are rare, because in real text most words are unpredictable (Gough, 1983; Gough, Alford, & Holley-Wilcox, 1981). Moreover, as Alford (1980) pointed out, the extent to which context points to a particular word is, in ordinary text, positively correlated with the frequency of the word (and negatively correlated with its length). Words that are predictable tend to be short and common, whereas words that are unpredictable tend to be long and uncommon. Thus context will fail children exactly where they most need help.

What children need is a way to recognize novel words on the basis of their form. We should remember that the vast majority of these words are already known to children in their phonological form, for in the early grades almost all of the words that readers encounter are already part of the child's vocabulary. So if there was a way to convert the printed form into a phonological form, children could readily recognize them.

Fortunately, an alphabetic language like English affords a mechanism that works for many of its words. An alphabetic orthography is based on a system of rules that map letter strings onto phonological forms; the letters of printed words represent the phonemes of spoken ones. If children could internalize this system, they would have a way of transforming the novel into the familiar, and they could decode the message.

THE CIPHER

It is common to think of writing as a code and reading as decoding. However, we would note that cryptologists use the term *code* in two senses. One is generic; it characterizes any kind of secret writing system. In this sense, an alphabetic orthography like English is indeed a code. But within the class of codes, cryptologists (e.g., Kahn, 1967) distinguish two kinds, codes and ciphers. Codes are arbitrary, like using *007* to represent *James Bond*. Ciphers in contrast are systematic, like using *kbnft cpoe* to encode the same message. It should be clear that in this narrower sense English orthography is a cipher rather than a code.

The orthographic cipher of English (in short, the cipher) is very complex. A simple cipher would map each letter onto a single phoneme and each phoneme onto a single letter. But English has only 26 letters to map onto more than three dozen phonemes, so it could not be simple; either a letter must represent more than one phoneme, or some phonemes must be represented by more than one letter. Moreover, English orthography was woven by history (Scragg, 1974), and like most such fabrics the basic pattern has been stitched and darned, and altered and augmented many times.

Consider only the mappings of initial letters onto initial phonemes. For only a minority of the letters (*b, d, f, l, n, r, v, z*) is it possible to identify the phoneme it represents. For the other 19, at least one additional letter must be identified before the identity of the word's first phoneme can be determined; in some cases, at least four more letters are required (compare *chord* and *chore*). The vast majority of the letter–sound correspondences of the English cipher are context dependent.

Our basic premise is that to become a skilled reader the child must master this cipher. The child must give up trying to learn to read each word by memorizing a unique cue for that word. Instead, the child must master the system by which printed words are mapped onto spoken ones; the child must internalize the cipher. We also hold that the child can only do this through cryptanalysis.

In making this assertion, we are trying to make three points. First, we argue that learning is distinct from teaching, that whatever or however they might be taught, what will determine how children read is what they internalize. Second, we argue that if they are to read with any degree of skill, they must internalize the cipher. That is, we argue that there is only one way to read well and that is with the aid of the cipher. Thus however children are taught, whether by phonics, whole language, or some eclectic method, they must master the cipher, or they will read poorly if at all. Third, we argue that even when the attempt is made to teach the cipher directly, as in synthetic phonics, the rules that children are taught are not the rules that they must internalize.

As we have pointed out elsewhere (Gough & Hillinger, 1980), the rules of phonics are explicit, few in number, and slow. In contrast, the rules of the cipher are implicit, very numerous, and very fast. Our assumption is that the two are distinct. Indeed, we are intrigued by the suggestion that what the child has internalized are not rules at all but might instead be a system of analogy (Goswami, 1986) or even a connectionist system (Seidenberg & McClelland, 1989; Seidenberg, this volume). Whatever the form of the cipher, whether it consists of rules, analogies, or connections, we contend that it does *not* consist of the rules taught consciously in phonics.

We assume then that the process of reading acquisition is aptly and accurately described as a process of cryptanalysis, of codebreaking, or better, of cipherbreaking. We have argued (Gough & Hillinger, 1980) that for children to be successful four conditions must be met. First, children must have cryptanalytic intent. Second, they must be aware of the letters in the written word. Third, they must be aware of the phonemes in the spoken word. Fourth, they must be given written words paired with spoken words. Given all four things, children will internalize the cipher and become what we will call a *cipher reader*. Lacking any one of them, they must continue to read by selective association; they must remain *code* or *cue* readers.

Three of the prerequisites are easily provided (or at least encouraged) by instruction, if not by the child's natural environment. But little in the child's environment promotes phonemic awareness. How phonemic awareness is acquired seems to us an important mystery. But however it is acquired, it seems clear to us, as to many others, that phonemic awareness is the key to reading acquisition. We believe, however, that its role in this process is not direct. Instead, we believe that it is important because it is necessary for the acquisition of the cipher.

CUE VERSUS CIPHER

When children begin to internalize the cipher their way of reading changes. Where they had been associating spoken words with partial cues, now they will perceive the letters of each word and apply the cipher to those letters. Instead of associating whole (i.e., unanalyzed) spoken words with selected parts of printed ones, children who master the cipher will now systematically map visual form onto phonological form, converting a string of letters into a string of phonemes. Where they had been code or cue readers they will now become cipher readers.

This hypothetical change in the child's way of reading has a number of testable consequences. A first and trivial prediction is that acquisition of the cipher will make the child a better reader. It will increase the child's accuracy and speed in word recognition (if only because the cue reader will have no cue for the recognition of most words). Many studies (e.g., Baron, 1979; Gough, Juel, & Roper/Schneider, 1983) have reported substantial correlations between the child's ability to read pseudowords and his or her ability to read real words; indeed, Curtis (1980) found the ability to read pseudowords to be the single best predictor of reading ability she examined. Moreover, this correlation remains significant when the effects of intelligence (Stanovich, Cunningham, & Feeman, 1984; Stanovich, this volume) and even reading progress (i.e., how far the child has gone in his basal reading series; Souther, 1986) are partialed out.

Although acquisition of the cipher will generally increase the child's ability to recognize words, it should not do so uniformly across words. We have no reason to expect that the cipher will facilitate the recognition of familiar words; where the code reader has a well-practiced cue (e.g., for the recognition of his or her own name), the cipher is not needed. Indeed, what we expect is that the influence of knowledge of the cipher will vary inversely with word familiarity; the less familiar a word, the more important the cipher will be.

This reasoning turned on its head led us to predict that, if we were to measure the effect of word familiarity on the individual child's word recognition accuracy, the slope of that function should decrease with the child's knowledge of the cipher (i.e., with the child's ability to read pseudowords). Using a computer program that, given the child's current place in the basal reader series, tallied how often each of the words had occurred prior to that date, Gough et al. (1983) found that the slope of the regression of error on word frequency for the individual child correlated positively (and significantly) with that child's score on the pseudoword test.

The acquisition of the cipher not only has consequences for the probability that the child will make a reading error, but it also influences the nature of that error. When the cipher reader makes an error, we construe it as a misapplication of the cipher: a failure to register a letter, a failure to apply a particular rule, or even an erroneous application of a rule. The resulting string of phonemes will conform to the phonological rules of English. It may form a word, but it is at least as likely that it will not, that it will instead constitute a nonsensical string, a pseudoword. Thus we expect that a substantial proportion of the cipher reader's errors will be nonwords. In contrast, if true code readers produce an error at all (they may well just fall silent, or ask about the word, or say "I don't know that one"), the error must be a real word. Thus we predicted that the proportion of oral reading errors that are real words would go down as knowledge of the cipher increased. We (Gough et al., 1983) found that score on a test of pseudoword reading correlates significantly with the proportion of oral reading errors that are nonwords.

Although many of the cipher reader's errors will be nonwords, the cipher reader will also make word errors. These will be of two sorts: those that arise, randomly as it were, from misapplication of the cipher (e.g., misreading *slice* as *slick*); and those that arise from an overreliance on context (e.g., misreading Little Miss Muffet's *tuffet* as *chair*). Cue readers could be expected to make even more of the latter type of word errors (cf. Stanovich, 1980). But we expect them to make an additional sort of word error. The cue reader can be thought of as a child with a bag of spoken words that he or she is trying to associate with printed ones. When cue readers encounter an unfamiliar word and notice in it a cue associated with one of the words in the reader's repertoire, they will produce that word erroneously. But if cue readers identify no familiar cue, they may simply reach into their bag of words and offer one of those words as a wild (if educated) guess. In either event, what distinguishes such an error from errors resulting from overreliance on context (or cipher misapplication) is that it must be drawn from the child's previous reading history. Therefore, we predicted that among word errors the proportion of words that could be found in the basal readers that the child had read would be greater for cue readers than for cipher readers, and that is what we found (Gough et al., 1983).

The cipher reader's word recognition thus differs quantitatively and qualitatively from that of the code reader. We also have evidence that the acquisition of the cipher leads to significant changes in the child's spelling.

THE CIPHER AND SPELLING

Prior to the cipher the child can only spell from memory. But the acquisition of the cipher gives the child the ability to generate spellings, to create them when they have not been seen before, or even to recreate them when they have.

There has been much interest in recent years in the phenomenon of "invented spelling" (Read, 1986), that is, in spellings created by children for words they have not seen before. What such studies seem to have shown is that the child's first spellings are phonemic, resulting from application of sound–spelling rules to the sounds of words. What seems to be overlooked in this account is that, in order to apply the sound–spelling rules, children must be aware of the sounds to which those rules apply. If children lack phonemic awareness, such rules are utterly useless to them.

In our theory the spelling of cue readers could not resemble "invented spelling," for they lack the knowledge of the cipher that yields such spellings. The spelling of the code reader must differ from the spelling of the cipher reader in at least four ways. First, as in the case of word recognition, we must make the trivial prediction that spelling ability will increase with the acquisition of the cipher, not for every word (for the code reader can surely spell some words from memory) but because it will at least enable the child to generate spellings for novel words and because it may (and we suspect does) relieve the burden on memory for familiar words. In support of this, Juel, Griffith, and Gough (1986) reported that score on the Bryant test of decoding correlates significantly with score on the spelling subtest of the Wide Range Achievement Test.

Not only should the acquisition of the cipher lead to increases in correct spelling, it should also lead to changes in the quality of the child's spelling errors. For one thing, the child's errors should obviously become more "phonetic," and so they should increasingly resemble the target word. In fact, we have found that cipher readers make ten times as many phonetic spelling errors as code readers, and that the Bryant test is significantly correlated with the proportion of target letters to be found in the child's spelling errors (Gough et al., 1983; Juel, Griffith, & Gough, 1985).

The more interesting implication is associated with the absence of the cipher. Consider how the cue reader (i.e., the child without knowledge of the cipher) must spell. Clearly, the child may be able to retrieve a spelling from memory. (From the very beginning, most children correctly spell their names.) Failing this, the code reader is faced with a hopeless task. The child who knows that *camel* is the one with the humps might record the *m*, but the rest of the spelling will be nothing but luck. That is, if the code reader puts down any letters in addition to *m*, it is only a matter of chance if they happen to be letters that were also in the target word, and most such letters would be random intrusions. This leads then to the prediction that the proportion of letter intrusions (i.e., letters that are not found in the target word) in the child's spelling errors will correlate negatively with knowledge of the cipher as measured by pseudoword reading. Such a finding was reported by Juel et al. (1985).

More striking evidence of the absence of the cipher is provided by two other kinds of spelling errors. One is the substitution of an entire word, which we suppose could happen either because of a memory retrieval error or because the child has no idea what to write and decides to put down something he or she *can* remember; such an error should not be produced by a child who is trying to relate print to phonological form. The other is the intrusion of nonalphabetic material like digits and other symbols, which reflects a failure to grasp the basic alphabetic principle. Such errors are rare but they do occur, and we have observed them only in pure code readers (i.e., children who can read no pseudowords at all).

The acquisition of the cipher has profound consequences for the child's reading and spelling. In our view the cipher is the *sine qua non* of literacy, but we recognize that there is more to it than this. The cipher is necessary, but it is not sufficient for either word recognition or spelling. The child must learn more than the cipher.

BEYOND THE CIPHER

Consider word recognition. The cipher will enable the reader to correctly decode many words, like *gum, hot,* and *pink,* but it will miscode many exception words, like *pint, shoe,* and *tongue.* Equally problematic is the fact that any number of letter sequences are polyphonic in the cipher (compare *ea* in *meat, steak, head, theater, theatrical,* and *pineapple*). To correctly apply the cipher in these cases requires word-specific, lexical information.

The same problems arise in spelling. The cipher supports the spelling of many words, like *hand, arm,* and *leg,* but it provides little help with irregulars like *Mrs., colonel,* and *yacht.* Moreover, most English phonological sequences are polygraphic (i.e., they can be spelled in more than one way), and word-specific information must be used to select the correct spelling. So spelling, too, requires a good deal of word-specific information.

Observations like these have led Baron (1979) and Treiman (1984) to propose that reading and spelling might be based on two distinct mechanisms, one rule based (to us, the cipher) and the other word specific. To test this notion, they asked children to read three lists, one of regular words (List R), one of exception words (List E), and one of pseudowords (List N). They reasoned that the pseudowords could be read only with the cipher and the exception words only with the word-specific mechanism, whereas the regular words might be read with either. They predicted that, on the basis of their common factors, the correlations between R and N (based on the rule mechanism) and between R and E (based on the word-specific mechanism) would be higher than the correlation between E and N (which share no mechanism). In several studies they have found this to be the case.

In these studies, however, Baron and Treiman have repeatedly found high positive correlations between the pseudoword and exception lists. This suggested to us (Gough & Walsh, 1991) that, rather than relying on separate mechanisms, the recognition of pseudowords and exception words might instead be based on the same foundation. To further examine this relationship, Gough and Walsh, like Baron and Treiman, asked first and second graders to read a list of exception words (e.g., *shoe* and *tongue*) and a list of pseudowords. However, their pseudowords were homophones (*shoo* and *tung*) of the exception words. If exception words and pseudowords are read by separate mechanisms, we should see that there are some children ("Chinese" readers) who could read more exception words than their homophonic counterparts. Gough and Walsh found no such children; every child could read at least as many pseudohomophones as exception words and most could read more.

What this suggests is that word-specific knowledge, rather than being deployed in a separate mechanism, is instead gathered within the same mechanism with the cipher. Metaphorically, it is assembled "on top of" the cipher. Consistent with the notion, Gough and Walsh found that children who have the cipher (i.e., cipher readers) learn to read and spell new exception words faster and more accurately than children who do not.

There is more to literacy than the cipher, but we hold that reading and spelling are both built on the cipher. In neither case is the cipher sufficient. Knowledge of the cipher alone cannot determine the pronunciation of any word that contains any polyphonic letter or letter sequence (and these abound) or the pronunciation of exception words. Nor can knowledge of the cipher alone yield the correct spelling of exception words or any polygraphic phonological form. Thus specific lexical knowledge must be added to the cipher to achieve both skilled reading and spelling. We hold, however, that the cipher is the foundation for both skills.

DO CHILDREN READ AND SPELL DIFFERENTLY?

A serious challenge to this view has been put forward by Bradley and Bryant. These investigators have argued that, in an early stage of normal reading (and one that may persist in retarded reading), reading and spelling are "surprisingly separate" (Bradley & Bryant, 1979, p. 512), that they "are managed in very different ways" (Bradley & Bryant, 1985, p. 176), and that children "use different strategies for these two skills" (Bradley, 1986, p. 2).

Bryant and Bradley did not come to these conclusions by examining the interdependence of reading and spelling across children, for that correlation is nearly perfect. For example, as part of her dissertation research, Griffith (1987) asked a number of first and third graders to read and spell (on separate occasions) the same set of words. She found a correlation of .83 between the reading and spelling of the first graders and .84 for the third graders. Given that the reliabilities (as measured by Cronbach's alpha) of both tests were approximately .90, the correlations could scarcely have been higher.

Rather than looking at the correlation between reading and spelling across individuals, Bradley and Bryant took the novel approach of looking at this correlation within individual children. In several studies, they asked young readers to read and spell the same set of words and then cross-classified the words according to whether each word was read and spelled correctly or incorrectly. As most of us would expect, they found that although children can usually read and spell (or fail to read and spell) the same words, there are words that they can read but not spell. But they also observed a surprising result: Beginning readers can sometimes spell words that they cannot read.

At first sight this is counterintuitive, for it evokes an image of the children writing down words that they then cannot recognize. But this, of course, is not what Bryant and Bradley observed. Rather, what they found is that when children are asked to read a set of words on one occasion and spell them on another, they sometimes misread words that they spell correctly *some other time*.

It occurred to us that the inconsistencies observed by Bradley and Bryant might have reflected not an independence between reading and spelling but rather an inconsistency *within* early reading and spelling. Bryant and Bradley (1979) rejected this interpretation because they found that when they asked their subjects to reread and respell those words that they had spelled correctly but misread, the children spelled and misread them again.

However, we remained curious about the consistency of early reading and spelling and its possible connection with the Bradley–Bryant phenomenon. To satisfy this curiosity, we asked 20 beginning readers in an Oxford elementary school to read and spell the same 28 words twice, in four separate sessions spread over a week. Twenty of these words were regular consonant-vowel-consonant words like *bus, leg,* and *mat,* the kind of word that Bradley and Bryant found to yield the anomalous inconsistency. (In fact, most of the words were taken from their papers.)

When we then tallied the words in a fourfold contingency table (Table 2.1) we saw almost exactly the pattern reported by Bradley and Bryant. Our 20 readers read and spelled most of the words correctly and neither read nor spelled still others. All told, their reading and spelling was consistent on almost three-

TABLE 2.1
Probability of Reading and Spelling the Same Words

SPELLING		READING WRONG	READING RIGHT
	RIGHT	.10	.60
	WRONG	.12	.18

quarters of the words. Almost 20% were read correctly but misspelled, and 1 word in 10 was misread but spelled correctly.

However, when we tallied the first and second readings (and spellings) in exactly the same way (Table 2.2), we did not see what Bradley and Bryant did. That is, we did not see that the words misread but spelled correctly on the first trial were again misread but spelled correctly on the second. Instead, we saw virtually the same inconsistency within reading and spelling as we (and they) had observed between them.

Our results suggest that children exhibit the same inconsistency in successive readings (or spellings) as they do between reading and spelling. If the fact of such inconsistency in the latter case is to be taken as evidence that children read and spell using different mechanisms, then by parity of argument we should conclude that children read (and spell) differently on different occasions. We resist both conclusions. A more parsimonious explanation of the facts is that beginning readers read and spell in the same way on different occasions; they simply do so inconsistently.

TABLE 2.2
Probability of Reading and Spelling the Same Words Twice

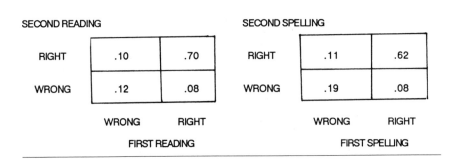

SECOND READING		FIRST READING WRONG	FIRST READING RIGHT
	RIGHT	.10	.70
	WRONG	.12	.08

SECOND SPELLING		FIRST SPELLING WRONG	FIRST SPELLING RIGHT
	RIGHT	.11	.62
	WRONG	.19	.08

We agree with Bradley and Bryant that this inconsistency merits attention, and we are inclined to agree with at least some aspects of their interpretation of it. For example, Bryant and Bradley (1979) found that when the correctly spelled but previously misread words were subsequently presented in a list of nonsense syllables, many were now read correctly. They concluded that this was due to an increase in phonological processing, or what we would call an increased reliance on the cipher; this seems quite reasonable to us.

We must also agree with them that spelling cannot be simply the mirror image of reading. For one thing, the ambiguities of spelling (e.g., whether /ǰ/ should be recorded as *j, g, dg,* or something else) do not coincide with the ambiguities of reading (e.g., whether *ea* is to be mapped onto /e/, or /i/, or /ɛ/, or a diphthong); polygraphy is not the same as polyphony. For another thing, spelling may well require an explicit use of phonology that reading does not, as the results of Kimura and Bryant (1983) would appear to show.

However, we think it is wrong to conclude that children "read by eye and spell by ear," for we believe that to do this is to be blinded (by the sight of a minor inconsistency, obtained with only a particular sort of words for a very short time, and even then inconsistently) to the overwhelming consistency of reading and spelling both across readers and across words. We continue to believe that consistency exists because reading and spelling have a common basis, and that is the cipher. We conclude then that reading and spelling are built on the same foundation, and that is the cipher.

REFERENCES

Alford, J. A., Jr. (1980). *Lexical and contextual effects on reading time.* Unpublished doctoral dissertation, University of Texas at Austin.

Baron, J. (1979). Orthographic and word-specific mechanisms in children's reading of words. *Child Development, 50,* 60–72.

Bradley, L. (1986). *Poor spellers, poor readers: Understanding the problem.* Occasional paper 2. University of Reading, Reading and Language Information Centre, School of Education.

Bradley, L., & Bryant, P. E. (1979). The independence of reading and spelling in backward and normal readers. *Developmental Medicine and Child Neurology, 21,* 504–514.

Bradley, L., & Bryant, P. E. (1985). *Rhyme and reason in reading and spelling.* Ann Arbor: University of Michigan Press.

Bryant, P. E., & Bradley, L. (1979). Why children sometimes write words which they cannot read. In U. Frith (Ed.), *Cognitive processes in spelling* (pp. 355–370). Orlando, FL: Academic Press.

Curtis, M. E. (1980). Development of components of reading skill. *Journal of Educational Psychology, 72,* 656–669.

Ehri, L. C., & Wilce, L. S. (1985). Movement into reading: Is the first stage of printed word learning visual or phonetic? *Reading Research Quarterly, 20,* 163–179.

Goswami, U. (1986). Children's use of analogy in learning to read: A developmental study. *Journal of Experimental Child Psychology, 42,* 73–83.

Gough, P. B. (1983). Context, form, and interaction. In K. Rayner (Ed.), *Eye movements in reading: Perceptual and language processes* (pp. 203–211). Orlando, FL: Academic Press.

Gough, P. B., Alford, J. A., Jr., & Holley-Wilcox, P. (1981). Words and contexts. In O. J. L. Tzeng & H. Singer (Eds.), *Perception of print* (pp. 85–102). Hillsdale, NJ: Lawrence Erlbaum Associates.

Gough, P. B., & Hillinger, M. L. (1980). Learning to read: An unnatural act. *Bulletin of the Orton Society, 30,* 179–196.

Gough, P. B., Juel, C., & Roper/Schneider, D. (1983). A two-stage model of initial reading acquisition. In J. A. Niles & L. A. Harris (Eds.), *Searches for meaning in reading/language processing and instruction* (pp. 207–211). Rochester, NY: National Reading Conference.

Gough, P. B., & Tunmer, W. E. (1986). Decoding, reading, and reading disability. *Remedial and Special Education, 7,* 6–10.

Gough, P. B., & Walsh, M. A. (1991). Chinese, Phoenicians, and the orthographic cipher of English. In S. A. Brady & D. P. Shankweiler (Eds.), *Phonological processes in literacy: A tribute to Isabelle Y. Liberman* (pp. 199–209). Hillsdale, NJ: Lawrence Erlbaum Associates.

Griffith, P. L. (1987). *The role of phonological and lexical information in word recognition and spelling.* Unpublished doctoral dissertation, University of Texas at Austin.

Hoover, W. A., & Gough, P. B. (1990). The simple view of reading. *Reading and Writing, 2,* 127–160.

Juel, C., Griffith, P. L., & Gough, P. B. (1985). Reading and spelling strategies of first-grade children. In J. A. Niles & R. Lalik (Eds.), *Issues in literacy: A research perspective* (pp. 306–309). Rochester, NY: National Reading Conference.

Juel, C., Griffith, P. L., & Gough, P. B. (1986). Acquisition of literacy: A longitudinal study of children in first and second grade. *Journal of Educational Psychology, 78,* 243–255.

Kahn, D. (1967). *The codebreakers.* New York: Macmillan.

Kimura, Y., & Bryant, P. E. (1983). Reading and writing in English and Japanese. *British Journal of Developmental Psychology, 1,* 129–144.

Lipscomb, L., & Gough, P. B. (1990). Word length and first word recognition. In J. Zutell & S. McCormick (Eds.), *Thirty-ninth Yearbook of the National Reading Conference.* Chicago: National Reading Conference. Pp. 217–222.

Read, C. (1986). *Children's creative spelling.* London: Routledge & Kegan Paul.

Scragg, D. G. (1974). *A history of English spelling.* Manchester, England: Manchester University Press.

Seidenberg, M. S., & McClelland, J. L. (1989). A distributed, developmental model of word recognition and naming. *Psychological Review, 96,* 523–568.

Souther, A. (1986). *A two-stage model of early reading acquisition.* Unpublished doctoral dissertation, University of Texas at Austin.

Stanovich, K. E. (1980). Toward an interactive-compensatory model of individual differences in the development of reading fluency. *Reading Research Quarterly, 16,* 32–71.

Stanovich, K. E., Cunningham, A. E., & Feeman, D. J. (1984). Intelligence, cognitive skills, and early reading progress. *Reading Research Quarterly, 19,* 278–303.

Sulzby, E., & Teale, W. (1991). Emergent literacy. In R. Barr, M. L. Kamil, P. B. Mosenthal, & P. D. Pearson (Eds.), *Handbook of reading research* (Vol. 2, pp. 727–757). New York: Longman.

Treiman, R. (1984). Individual differences among children in reading and spelling styles. *Journal of Experimental Child Psychology, 37,* 463–477.

3 Rhyme, Analogy, and Children's Reading

Usha Goswami
University of Cambridge

Peter Bryant
University of Oxford

There can be little doubt that phonological awareness plays an important role in reading. The results of a large number of studies amply demonstrate a strong (and consistent) relationship between children's ability to disentangle and to assemble the sounds in words and their progress in learning to read (Bradley & Bryant, 1983; Lundberg, Olofsson, & Wall, 1980; Stanovich, Cunningham, & Cramer, 1984). There is also evidence that successful training in phonological awareness helps children learn to read, particularly when that training is combined with experience with alphabetic letters and written words (Bradley & Bryant, 1983; Fox & Routh, 1984; Goldstein, 1976; Olofsson & Lundberg, 1985; Williams, 1980). Put together, these two sets of data are convincing evidence that phonological awareness is a powerful causal determinant of the speed and efficiency of learning to read.

ONE OR MORE THAN ONE KIND OF PHONOLOGICAL AWARENESS?

The enterprise of establishing the importance of phonological awareness has been a strikingly successful one. It has immediate educational implications, and it will also undoubtedly play a great part in theories about learning to read. However, it is only a first step. We must now think about the nature of the pathway between phonological awareness and reading. The two are connected, and the connection is almost certainly a causal one, but what form does the connection take? How exactly does a child's skill in handling sounds affect the way he or she comes to grips with written language?

This question has not been discussed a great deal, and one of the reasons for this relative silence is probably that the answer seems so obvious. After all, alphabetic letters represent sounds in words, and an essential part of learning to read and to spell must be to conquer these letter–sound relationships. To do that children must be able to break a word up into its constituent sounds (segmenting) and also to put sounds together to build up a word (blending). If they can segment and blend, and if they know which letter represents which sound, then they should be able to read and spell a whole host of words like *cat* and *Wales*.

The argument is virtually indisputable. It is almost impossible not to believe that the three-stage pathway (phonological awareness–letter sound rela-tionships–reading and spelling *cat*) is an essential part of learning to read. However, there are good reasons also for wondering whether it is the only link between phonological awareness and learning to read, and the main point of our chapter is to argue for the existence of another significant link between these two skills.

There are two reasons why the letter–sound pathway might not be the only connection. One is that it would not account for all that much. In English simple letter–sound relationships do not work or only work very approximately with a large number of written words. It is an irregular orthography, and many words simply cannot be spelled phonologically. Of course one can add rules, such as that a final *e* is silent and has the effect of lengthening the vowel of the preceding syllable, but even so there will be a tremendous number of exceptions. The system will deal with *cat* and *Wales* but not with *yacht* and *Gloucester*. One way to deal with such irregularity is to postulate a completely different type of pathway, and that is what many psychologists have done. Dual route models— one route phonological, the other visual—are popular today, and one of the main features of these models is to send words that cannot be deciphered on a pho-nological basis down the visual pathway. Something of the sort may indeed happen, but we argue that it is also possible to stay with the phonological route and still explain how many words that elude letter–sound rules are read.

Our second reason for wondering whether there are other phonological paths to literacy is the distinct possibility that there are several different types of phonological awareness, each with a different effect on reading. There is a tendency to talk about phonological awareness as one homogeneous whole, but that seems improbable to us. The skill is tested in so many different ways, and the tests have such vastly different levels of difficulty, that it is difficult to believe that they all test exactly the same thing. One can demonstrate that children as young as 4 years are aware of rhyme and alliteration without too much difficulty (e.g., Bradley & Bryant, 1983; Kirtley, Bryant, Maclean, & Bradley, 1989; Maclean, Bryant, & Bradley, 1987), but other tests are much harder. The Liber-man, Shankweiler, Fischer, and Carter (1974) phoneme tapping test seems to be possible only for 6-year-olds and above. The Bruce (1964) and Rosner and Simon (1971) subtraction task (*sand* to *sad*) is even more difficult. Bruce only found consistent success in children as old as 8 years—some time, it should be noted, after they had learned to read.

Of course it is possible that these and other tests of phonological awareness all measure exactly the same skill or set of skills and that the only reason for these striking differences in difficulty is the differing, extraneous cognitive demands made by the various tasks over and above their phonological component. But another possibility is that there is a set of different phonological skills that affect reading in different ways.

This alternative might seem farfetched at first, but that is only because phonological awareness is generally held to be synonymous with segmenting and blending sounds when, in fact, it need not be restricted to only those two things. One has only to think of the forms of phonological awareness that are probably the first to arrive and certainly the easiest to demonstrate in young children. Rhyme, and to a certain extent alliteration, play an obvious part in young children's lives, and so it is not at all surprising that, as we have already noted, several studies have shown that children as young as 4 are on the whole capable of saying whether words rhyme or not and also whether they begin with the same sound or not. But rhyming is a very different activity than segmenting and blending.

Sets of rhyming words are in effect categories. If a child realises that *mat, hat, bat,* and *cat* rhyme, he or she is dealing with a category of words that have a common sound. The evidence on rhyming and alliteration suggests very strongly that preschool children have formed many such categories.

These categories are potentially important as far as reading goes, because when a child has to learn about spelling patterns he or she will encounter another kind of category, orthographic categories, that consist of words that share a common spelling pattern. These words will often have a sound in common too and thus will map onto the rhyming categories that the child has already formed. It seems to us to be extremely likely that experience with the first kind of category (rhyme and alliteration) will play a significant role in helping the child to form the second kind of category (orthographic). This is our hypothesis.

It is interesting to note that orthographic categories of this sort often transcend simple letter–sound relationships. Words like *cat* and *hat* can be deciphered by using simple letter–sound relationships, whereas words like *light* and *fight* cannot. Hence categorizing on the basis of orthography could be an advantage to a child trying to come to grips with the irregularities of spelling–sound correspondences in English.

To make a convincing case for our hypothesis we need three kinds of evidence. First, we need to show that there is a relationship between the preschool child's sensitivity to rhyme and alliteration and eventual progress in learning to read and to spell, and we also need evidence that the relationship is a causal one. Second, we have to show that children are aware of and use orthographic categories at an early stage in learning to read. This issue is a controversial one, and we should note at this stage that if it is true that children can form orthographic categories, then they should be able to use these to read new words by analogy.[1] Third, our hypothesis is that there is a direct connection between rhyming categories and orthographic categories. So we would predict a strong relationship between children's skill at rhyming and children's ability to make analogies between the spelling patterns in words in reading. We now consider each of these three questions in turn.

RHYME AND READING

To establish a causal relationship between a child's preschool skills at rhyme and alliteration and his or her later success in reading, one has to show two things. One is that there is a relationship between these two skills, and the other is that training the former skill improves the latter. There is evidence to support both propositions, and it can be described quite briefly here because it has been summarized a number of times in other places (Bryant & Bradley, 1985; Bryant & Goswami, 1987).

Correlations and Longitudinal Predictions

Three longitudinal studies have shown a striking relationship between children's early rhyming skills and their later progress in reading. The first was by Lundberg et al. (1980). They originally saw 143 children in kindergarten and then tested their reading and spelling in their first and second years at school. They gave children a number of tests of phonological awareness, which included tests of segmentation, blending, and phoneme reversal, and also a test of rhyme production. Using path analyses, the authors found that the two most powerful predictors of reading in Grade 1 were the task that involved segmenting phonemes and one that involved reversing their order. At this stage there was a positive relationship, though of a smaller order, between the rhyme production scores and reading. In the second year, reading scores were best predicted by the children's previous success at reversing phonemes and at rhyme production. So the relationship between rhyme and reading was relatively durable.

The strength and persistence of this relationship were confirmed in a large-scale longitudinal study by Bradley and Bryant (1983, 1985). They tested the ability of 400 4- and 5-year-old children to detect rhyme and alliteration. The tests were oddity tasks: In each trial the child heard 3 or 4 words, all but one of which rhymed (or started with the same sound), and had to judge which was the odd one out.

---

[1]In work on reading, people have often referred to this kind of inference as an "analogy" (Glushko, 1979). To read a nonsense word like *jation* from a real word like *nation* has been described as reasoning by analogy.

Then over the following 3- to 4-years measures were taken of the children's progress in reading and spelling and also in learning about mathematics. The main question was whether there would be a relationship between the early measures of sensitivity to rhyme and alliteration and the children's reading later on, and also whether this relationship would be specific to reading and spelling. That was the reason for putting in a mathematics test. If the hypothesis is right then rhyme should be related specifically to reading and not at all to mathematics.

This was what happened. The rhyme and alliteration scores were consistently and strongly related to reading and spelling but not to mathematical achievement. The relationship with reading and spelling was significant in a series of fixed order multiple regressions in which the dependent variables were the final reading or spelling or mathematics scores. The steps in these multiple regressions were the children's age, their vocabulary level at the beginning of the project, their W.I.S.C. scores, their memory for the words in the rhyme or alliteration test, and finally performance in the rhyme and alliteration test. Thus these multiple regressions measured the relationship between the initial rhyme or alliteration performance and reading after the influence of verbal abilities, intelligence, and memory had been partialed out (Bradley & Bryant, 1985). Rhyme and alliteration accounted for a significant amount of the additional variance in the final reading and spelling tests but not in the tests of mathematical achievement. Again, measures of the children's ability to categorize words by their common sounds were strongly related to reading, and again the relationship lasted for some time.

The third empirical demonstration that rhyme predicts reading was slightly more complex. Ellis and Large (1987) examined the relationship between a number of metalinguistic tasks, including the Bradley/Bryant rhyme tests, and the reading and spelling development of 40 children over a three-year period. The children were first seen at age 5 and then at yearly intervals until age 8. The metalinguistic tasks were given at each yearly follow up. At age 8, three groups of five children were selected, who were respectively of high IQ but poor reading (Group A), of high IQ and good reading (Group B), and of low IQ and poor reading (Group C). Ellis and Large then compared the patterns of development for these three groups by comparing their performance on the different metalinguistic tasks over the 3 years of the study.

The most important measure in discriminating between Groups A and B turned out to be Bradley and Bryant's rhyme subtest. Group B children were significantly better at this test than Group A children, in spite of the fact that Group A children were matched with those in Group B in intelligence. The second most important discriminator was a test of rhyme production. Thus differences in rhyming ability seemed to be the most important distinguishing factor between good and poor readers who were matched for IQ. This result suggests that rhyming ability is an important determinant of later reading development.

With Groups A and C (both groups equally poor at reading, but with different

IQ levels) the relationship with rhyme was again extremely important. This time the tests associated with IQ discriminated between the two groups, and the tests associated with reading development did not. The tests that turned out to be most strongly related to reading were rhyme production and Bradley and Bryant's rhyme test. So again, rhyming skill was shown to play a key role in the later development of reading. Finally, the comparison between Groups B and C (good reading, high IQ, and poor reading, low IQ) again showed performance on Bradley and Bryant's rhyme test to be the most important discriminator.

These three studies seem to show a powerful connection between rhyme and reading. Is there any contrary evidence? The only research that we know of that does not show a particularly strong relationship between rhyming and reading is not longitudinal. This is work by Stanovich et al. (1984), who gave 49 6-year-old children 10 phonological awareness tasks as well as a test of reading. Two of these phonological tasks involved rhyme. In one the children had to supply a rhyme and in the other to choose rhymes. The other tasks all involved detecting single consonants. Most of the correlations among the 10 tasks were strong, but the correlations between rhyme and the other tasks, though positive, were relatively low. Furthermore, the correlations between the two rhyme tests and the children's performance in a reading test were not significant. However, as the authors noted, there was a ceiling effect in the rhyme scores, and this may well have been the reason for the lack of a connection. It is possible that the important rhyme scores are those taken before children go to school and thus before that ceiling is hit.

Intervention

To show that a preschool measure predicts how well children learn to read is not enough to establish a cause of reading. The two skills might be related because they are both determined by some unknown third factor. Longitudinal predictions cannot escape the threat of the tertium quid. To avoid that one needs a training experiment.

Studies in which children are trained in phonological awareness in the hope that it will improve their reading and spelling have not, for a number of reasons, been completely convincing (Bryant & Goswami, 1987). Attempts to train rhyme are unfortunately no exception. We know of only one intervention study that involves rhyme. This was part of the large-scale project run by Bradley and Bryant (1983). Some time after it started they took 64 6-year-old children and split them into four matched groups. One was trained over a period of 2 years in rhyme and alliteration. A second was trained for 2 years in rhyme and alliteration and in the second year also learned how the sounds that rhymed could be expressed in alphabetic letters. A third (control) group was taught to categorize the same words semantically for 2 years, and the final group formed an unseen control. A year later (when the children were eight years old) they were given standardized tests of reading, spelling, and mathematics.

The two groups trained in sound categorization (rhyme and alliteration) were better in the reading and spelling tests than the control groups, though the effect was only significant for the group given experience with alphabetic letters. The training effects were specific: There were no effects on mathematics.

The most important comparison was between the group trained just in sound categorization and the group trained in semantic categorization. A difference between these two groups would be strong evidence for a causal link between phonological awareness and reading. In fact the first group was ahead by 3 to 4 months on all the standardized tests of reading and spelling. However, because of the lack of significance, we cannot conclude that there was a definite effect.

There were significant differences between the group trained in sounds and letters and the two control groups. Although this result has some practical significance, it does not take us any further forward with the question about the effects of experience with rhyme. The study included no controls for the extra experience that the successful group had with alphabetic letters.

It is difficult to reach a definite conclusion about cause and effect from this study. To produce a 3- to 4-months' improvement in standardized reading and spelling tests is something of an achievement, and the result certainly suggests a causal relationship, but the fact that this effect was not significant gets in the way of a confident conclusion that the causal connection must exist.

One possible reason for the failure to reach significance is that, as in the Stanovich et al. (1984) study, the children were too old. After all, the hypothesis is about the effects of what happens to the child *before* he or she goes to school, and so a more direct test would be an intervention study in which children are taught about rhyme and alliteration years before they begin to learn to read and write. Nevertheless, there are distinct signs from the study just described that training in rhyme can speed a child's progress in reading even when that training is quite late in the day. When one considers the longitudinal studies and the intervention studies together one finds a great deal of evidence to support the hypothesis of a strong and specific causal link between rhyming skills and reading, and one finds no convincing evidence against this notion.

ANALOGIES AND READING

An obvious fact about English orthography is that words that share the same sounds often contain the same spelling patterns. This is especially true of words that rhyme: These usually have the same vowels and terminal consonants. So the spelling pattern of the rime of the syllable is frequently identical. This means that in principle a child might be able to read new words by making analogies to the spelling patterns of known words. The child could work out the sound of an unfamiliar written word (e.g., *peak*) by making an analogy from a known word with the same spelling pattern (e.g., *beak*). Such analogies would also enable children to work out how to read new *irregular* words that can be put into rhyming categories. Words like *light* and *fight* have an irregular spelling pattern, but this spelling pattern is consistent across a large number of rhyming words (e.g., *night, might, right, tight* . . .) although not all (e.g., *bite*). This means that the use of analogies that are based on rhyme will help children to read *both* regular and irregular words.

Analogies between the spelling patterns in words need not be limited to orthographic categories that are based on rhyme. Many words sound similar at the beginning (e.g., *beak, bean, bead, beat*), a relationship partly captured by alliteration. Children who can use analogies to read new words should in principle make these analogies between the beginnings of words as well as between the ends of words, so that knowing a word like *beak* should help in reading a new word like *bean* or *bead*. However, as orthographic categories based on the spelling patterns at the beginnings of words do not map naturally onto phonological categories that the child already has, as is the case with common spelling patterns at the ends of words and rhyming categories, children may use analogies between the beginnings of words much less frequently in reading.

How good is the evidence that children use analogies to read new words? Surprisingly, although some models of skilled reading in adults recognize the potential importance of analogies in reading (Glushko 1979, 1981; Kay & Marcel 1981), children's ability to make analogies between the spelling patterns in words has received little attention. In the studies that have been done, analogy is seen either as a sophisticated strategy only used in the final stages of reading development (Marsh, Desberg, & Cooper, 1977; Marsh, Friedman, Desberg, & Saterdahl, 1981; Marsh, Friedman, Welch, & Desberg, 1980), or as a strategy available to kindergarteners (Baron, 1977).

Marsh and his coworkers claimed that analogy is used only in the final stage of reading development after the stages of rote learning (learning each word as an holistic pattern), substitution (guessing on the basis of some of the letters in the word and context), and grapheme–phoneme conversion (letter-by-letter decoding on the basis of grapheme–phoneme correspondences). They claimed that "there are qualitative differences between the strategies used by beginners and skilled readers" (Marsh et al., 1980, p. 351). However, the possible link between rhyming and analogy suggests that analogies may be used much earlier in reading development. Furthermore, given that analogy can also be an inappropriate strategy to use on occasion (for example, *beak* is not a good analogy for reading *break*), it seems quite likely that analogy would be important in the early stages of learning to read before a child becomes aware of the many inconsistencies in spelling–sound relations in English.

Marsh and his coworkers carried out a number of studies in support of their claim that there is a strong developmental increase in the use of analogy as reading improves. These studies all used essentially the same method. Children of differing ages were given nonsense words to read either in isolation (Marsh et al., 1977, 1981) or in text (Marsh et al., 1980). The nonsense words could either be read by analogy to real words or on the basis of letter–sound correspondences. The nonsense words were always chosen so that the use of analogy would lead to a pronunciation that differed from one that was based on spelling–sound rules. An example would be *puscle*, which can be pronounced either by analogy to *muscle* or by grapheme–phoneme correspondences (*puskle*). This enabled the comparison of these two different reading strategies at different ages.

The prediction that Marsh and his coworkers were making was that older children should rely more on analogies than on grapheme–phoneme correspondences, whereas young children should rely more on grapheme–phoneme correspondences than on analogies. This was the result that they consistently found. However, their conclusion depended on the assumption that children at all the reading levels tested knew the written words on which the analogy had to be based. If 7-year-old children do not know words like *muscle*, then nothing can be concluded about their ability to use analogies in reading by testing them with nonsense words like *puscle*. Yet Marsh and his colleagues did not ensure that the real word analogues necessary for reading the nonsense words were known to the younger children in any of their studies, even though the words that they used (*muscle, piety*) were quite difficult. The developmental increase that they consistently found (e.g., 14% analogies at age 7, 34% analogies at age 10, and 38% analogies at college level; Marsh et al., 1980) could thus have been an artifact arising from the younger children knowing or remembering fewer analogous base words.

Thus, the evidence that analogy is a sophisticated strategy used only by children in the final stages of reading development is not at all convincing. Seven-year-olds and even younger children may be perfectly capable of using analogies in reading if they know the words on which analogies are meant to be based. This is the claim made by Baron (1977), who suggested that analogy is a strategy used naturally even by kindergarteners.

Baron taught kindergarteners words and sounds such as *b, at, bat, ed, red*, and then tested transfer to reading new words such as *bed* and *rat* (which can be read by analogy to the taught words), and *bad* and *bet* (which Baron argued can only be read by combining some of the letter–sound correspondences learned in the training words). Children's performance on words such as *bed* and *rat* was about 90% correct, compared to 15% for *bad* and *bet*. From this, Baron argued that analogy strategies are more natural in the beginning stages of reading than correspondence strategies.

However, this conclusion can be challenged for two reasons. One is that half of the "correspondence" test words could be read by analogy as well, as they contained consonant–vowel units that could be extracted from the *beginnings* of the training words: An analogy could in principle be made between the segment *ba-* in *bat* and *bad*. If analogy strategies are more natural in the beginning stages of reading, children should also use analogy to help them here. The second reason is that the children were trained on the rimes in the analogous words (the

-ed and *-at* segments) but not in the correspondence words (e.g., *-ad* and *-et*). This alone could explain the superior performance on the analogous words. Thus it cannot necessarily be concluded from this experiment that kindergarteners are capable of using analogy to read new words.

Therefore, these studies do not provide good evidence that children are able to use analogies in reading, and it is also unclear whether analogy is a strategy restricted to older readers or whether it is available at all reading levels. In an attempt to examine these questions, Goswami (1986) carried out an experiment to establish whether children can make analogies between the spelling patterns in words in reading and whether such analogies are available to children right from the beginning stages of learning to read.

The experiment was introduced as a game about working out words. Children aged from 5 to 8 years were asked to read words and nonsense words that were either analogous or nonanalogous to "clue" words that they were given, such as *beak*. The clue word was present throughout each session so that the basis for making analogies to some of the test words was available to all the children. No hint of how the clue word should be used was given by the experimenter, who simply said, "This is your clue word. This word says '(beak)'. What does this say?" when presenting the other (test) words. Examples of the test words used for the clue word *beak* would be *bean* and *peak* (analogous) or *bask* and *lake* (nonanalogous). If children can make analogies between the spelling patterns in words in reading, they should read more analogous than nonanalogous words correctly when a clue word like *beak* is present but should not read more analogous than nonanalogous words correctly when a clue word is not provided.

Fifty-three children were tested, and they were divided into three different reading levels. These reading level groups were based on performance on the Schonell Graded Word Reading Test (Schonell & Goodacre, 1971). The youngest group (Group 1—mean age 5;4) did not score on the test and were not yet reading. Group 2 (mean age 6;10) had a mean reading age of 6;10 on the Schonell test, and Group 3 (mean age 7;1) had a mean reading age of 7;4.

Goswami (1986) found that children at all three reading levels could make analogies between the ends of words, and that the children in Groups 2 and 3 could also make analogies between the beginnings of words. At all three reading levels the children read significantly more analogous words correctly when analogies could be made between the ends of the clue and test words than they did when analogies could be made between the beginnings of the clue and test words. Also, they read more words correctly when analogies could be made from the clue words than when no basis for analogy was provided. It is surprising and exciting that even the nonreading group made some analogies between the rimes (the end portions of words: *at* is the rime in *cat*). (This result has since been replicated by Goswami, 1988.) The children in the two reading groups made significantly more analogies between rimes than between the spelling patterns at the beginnings of words.

There were no differences in the number of analogies made between the clue words and the spelling patterns at the ends of the real words and at the ends of the nonsense words, although more analogies were made between the clue words and the spelling patterns at the beginnings of the real words than the nonsense words. Finally, and most strikingly, there were no differences in the number of analogies made by Groups 2 and 3, which means that analogies are used in reading irrespective of reading level.

We can conclude that even very young children make analogies when they are trying to read new words. Some analogies between the spelling patterns in words are actually made by children who are not yet formally reading. The significantly stronger effect found at all reading levels for analogies between the ends of words compared to analogies between the beginnings of words supports the hypothesis that the use of analogies in reading is closely related to rhyming.

SPECIFIC CONNECTIONS
BETWEEN RHYME AND ANALOGY

Our final prediction is of a specific relation between children's rhyming ability and their use of analogies to read new words. Words that rhyme are often spelled in the same way. Children who group together words that rhyme are creating phonological categories of words that sound similar at the ends. These phonological categories are often identical to orthographic categories of words that share the same spelling patterns at the ends (rimes). The expectation that words that have common spelling patterns will share common sounds underlies the use of analogies in reading. Because an analogy strategy seems to be available to children from the very beginning of learning to read, the extent to which children use analogies could depend on their rhyming skill. Thus children who are skilled at recognizing rhymes may be more likely to make analogies between the spelling patterns in words than children who are less skilled at recognizing rhymes.

To show that there is a specific connection, one would have to establish that analogy is related to rhyming more than it is to other phonological skills. This prediction was tested by including two different measures of phonological skills in the study just described. These were the Bradley and Bryant oddity tests for rhyme and alliteration (Bryant & Bradley, 1985) and a test of phonological segmentation devised by Content, Morais, Alegria, and Bertelson (1982). The latter test took the form of a game in which two puppets spoke a secret language. One puppet (operated by the experimenter) said a word and the other (operated by the child) repeated it without either the initial (*bean-ean*) or the final (*bean-bea*) phoneme.[2] It was the child's task to decide what the second puppet's word, the one without the relevant phoneme, would sound like.

---

[2]Obviously, the stimuli used in the original experiment, which was conducted in French, were not words like *bean*. The example given is taken from Goswami's (1986) experiment, in which the children were given all the analogous words used in her study in the phoneme deletion task.

TABLE 3.1
Three-Step Multiple Regressions Relating Rhyming and Phoneme Deletion to Analogy

	Beta	% Variance	F	p
Dependent Variable: Analogy B				
Step 1: BPVS (Same for all)	0.44	19.5	8.00	0.006
Step 2: B & B Beginning	0.19	3.6	1.50	0.23
B & B Middle	0.37	13.1	6.20	0.02
B & B End	0.36	12.6	5.95	0.02
Phoneme Deletion				
Initial	0.31	9.1	4.06	0.052
Final	0.34	7.7	3.36	0.08
Step 3: BPVS x Phonological Meas.				
BPVS x B & B Beginning	0.79	0.54	0.22	0.64
BPVS x B & B Middle	0.35	0.13	0.06	0.81
BPVS x B & B End	0.76	0.72	0.33	0.57
BPVS x Initial	0.85	0.92	0.41	0.53
BPVS x Final	5.24	0.13	6.44	0.02
Dependent Variable: Analogy E				
Step 1: BPVS (Same for all)	0.55	30.1	14.18	0.001
Step 2: B & B Beginning	0.28	7.8	4.01	0.05
B & B Middle	0.40	14.8	8.56	0.006
B & B End	0.54	28.4	21.90	0.000
Phoneme Deletion				
Initial	0.36	12.4	6.92	0.01
Final	0.42	11.9	6.56	0.02
Step 3: BPVS x Phonological Meas.				
BPVS x B & B: Mimimum tolerance level reached.				
BPVS x B & B Middle	1.49	2.4	1.42	0.24
BPVS x B & B End	0.07	0.0	0.00	0.95
BPVS x Initial	1.89	4.5	2.65	0.11
BPVS x Final: Minimum tolerance level reached.				

The reason for including the second task was to test the prediction that a child's ability to use analogies would have a weaker connection with this kind of segmentation than with rhyme. To examine our prediction, a number of fixed order multiple regressions was run in which the dependent variable was always a measure of the use of analogy. In half of the regressions this measure was of the percentage of analogies made between the beginnings of the clue and test words

TABLE 3.2
Three-Step Multiple Regressions Relating Rhyming to Analogy E

	Beta	% Variance	F	p
Dependent Variable: Analogy E				
Step 1: BPVS (Same for all)	0.55	30.1	14.18	0.001
Step 2: Initial Phoneme Deletion (Same for all)	0.36	12.4	6.92	0.01
Step 3: B & B Beginning	0.27	7.3	4.54	0.04
B & B Middle	0.32	8.9	5.67	0.02
B & B End	0.48	20.2	16.83	0.000
Step 1: BPVS (Same for all)	0.55	30.1	14.18	0.001
Step 2: Final Phoneme Deletion (Same for all)	0.42	11.9	6.56	0.02
Step 3: B & B Beginning	0.15	1.8	0.96	0.33
B & B Middle	0.29	5.9	3.56	0.07
B & B End	0.53	16.5	12.36	0.001

(Analogy B), and in the other half this measure was of the percentage of analogies made between the ends of the clue and test words (Analogy E).

There were three steps in each multiple regression, which always came in the same order. The first was a measure of the children's vocabulary (British Picture Vocabulary Scales; Dunn, Dunn, & Whetton, 1982; a British version of the PPVT). The second was one of the two phonological measures, and the third was the interaction between the first two variables.

These results are summarized in Table 3.1, which shows that for Analogy B the only variables to account for a significant amount of additional variance in these regressions were scores on the Bradley and Bryant tests of rhyme. The Morais et al. measures of segmentation fell short of significance and so did the Bryant and Bradley alliteration measure. For Analogy E, the relationship with rhyme was even stronger, but here the relationship with phoneme deletion also became significant. A series of further multiple regressions were thus run for Analogy E, stepping out both verbal skills and phoneme deletion before considering the link with rhyming. The results of these regressions are shown in Table 3.2. It is clear that the only consistently significant relationship was between the rhyming subtest and analogies between the ends of words. These significant results with rhyme provide convincing evidence for our hypothesis of a specific connection between rhyming and analogy.

We think that these last results demonstrate that analogy is the essential link in the chain that starts with a child's preschool experiences with rhyme and ends with skilled reading and writing. Our idea is that the rhyming categories that a child builds up in his or her early years form the basis for the orthographic categories that in turn are the basis for the use of analogy, and which thus play a central role in learning to read (Goswami & Bryant, 1990).

CONCLUSION

We have discussed the evidence that relates to our three predictions. On the whole this evidence is positive. There is a clear connection between rhyming skills and learning to read, and it looks as though this relationship is a causal one. It also seems that analogies pervade early reading and are used as soon as children start learning to read. Furthermore, there seems to be a strong link between the two skills: Children who are better at rhyming make more analogies.

One important question raised by these results is the origin of these skills. We obviously need to know about the effects of the child's environment on rhyming, because this is clearly an activity that might vary a great deal between families and perhaps between cultures. This in turn could well affect the child's progress in reading. Another urgent need is to look at poor readers. It seems very likely that an inefficient use of analogy contributes to reading backwardness. Because poor readers are so bad at rhyming, they must find analogies extremely difficult, and in fact a consequent failure in the use of analogies could be the pathway between difficulties in rhyming and difficulties in reading.

REFERENCES

Baron, J. (1977). Mechanisms for pronouncing printed words: Use and acquisition. In D. LaBerge & S. J. Samuels (Eds.), *Basic processes in reading: Perception and comprehension* (pp. 175–216). Hillsdale, NJ: Lawrence Erlbaum Associates.

Bradley, L., & Bryant, P. E. (1983). Categorizing sounds and learning to read—a causal connection. *Nature, 301,* 419–421.

Bradley, L., & Bryant, P. E. (1985). *Rhyme and reason in reading and spelling.* Ann Arbor: University of Michigan Press.

Bruce, D. J. (1964). The analysis of word sounds by young children. *British Journal of Educational Psychology, 34,* 158–170.

Bryant, P. E., & Bradley, L. (1985). *Children's reading problems.* Oxford, England: Blackwell.

Bryant, P. E., & Goswami, U. (1987). Phonological awareness and learning to read. In J. Beech & A. Colley (Eds.), *Cognitive approaches to reading* (pp. 213–243). New York: Wiley.

Content, A., Morais, J., Alegria, J., & Bertelson, P. (1982). Accelerating the development of phonetic segmentation skills in kindergarteners. *Cahiers de Psychologie Cognitive, 2,* 259–269.

Dunn, L. M., Dunn, L. M., & Whetton, C. (1982). *British picture vocabulary scale.* Berks., England: NFER-Nelson.

Ellis, N., & Large, B. (1987). The development of reading: As you seek so shall you find. *British Journal of Psychology, 78,* 1–28.

Fox, B., & Routh, D. K. (1984). Phonemic analysis and synthesis as word attack skills: Revisited. *Journal of Educational Psychology, 76,* 1059–1064.

Glushko, R. J. (1979). The organization and activation of orthographic knowledge in reading aloud. *Journal of Experimental Psychology: Human Perception and Performance, 5,* 674–91.

Glushko, R. J. (1981). Principles for pronouncing print: The psychology of phonography. In A. M. Lesgold and C. A. Perfetti (Eds.), *Interactive processes in reading* (pp. 61–84). Hillsdale, NJ: Lawrence Erlbaum Associates.

Goldstein, D. M. (1976). Cognitive–linguistic functioning and learning to read in preschoolers. *Journal of Educational Psychology, 68,* 680–688.

Goswami, U. (1986). Children's use of analogy in learning to read: A developmental study. *Journal of Experimental Child Psychology, 42,* 73–83.

Goswami, U. (1988). Orthographic analogies and reading development. *Quarterly Journal of Experimental Psychology, 40A,* 239–268.

Goswami, U., & Bryant, P. E. (1990). *Phonological skills and learning to read.* Hillsdale, NJ: Lawrence Erlbaum Associates.

Kay, J., & Marcel, A. (1981). One process, not two, in reading aloud: Lexical analogies do the work of non-lexical rules. *Quarterly Journal of Psychology, 33,* 397–413.

Kirtley, C., Bryant, P. E., Maclean, M., & Bradley, L. (1989). Rhyme, rime and the onset of reading. *Journal of Experimental Child Psychology, 48,* 224–245.

Liberman, I. Y., Shankweiler, D., Fischer, F. W., & Carter, B. (1974). Explicit syllable and phoneme segmentation in the young child. *Journal of Experimental Child Psychology, 18,* 201–12.

Lundberg, I., Olofsson, A., & Wall, S. (1980). Reading and spelling skills in the first school years predicted from phonemic awareness skills in kindergarten. *Scandinavian Journal of Psychology, 21,* 159–173.

MacLean, M., Bryant, P., & Bradley, L. (1987). Rhymes, nursery rhymes and reading in early childhood. *Merrill-Palmer Quarterly, 33,* 255–282.

Marsh, G., Desberg, P., & Cooper, J. (1977). Developmental strategies in reading. *Journal of Reading Behavior, 9,* 391–394.

Marsh, G., Friedman, M. P., Desberg, P., & Saterdahl, K. (1981). Comparison of reading and spelling strategies in normal and reading disabled children. In M. P. Friedman, J. P. Das, & N. O'Connor (Eds.), *Intelligence and learning* (pp. 363–367). New York: Plenum Press.

Marsh, G., Friedman, M. P., Welch, V., & Desberg, P. (1980). A cognitive–developmental approach to reading acquisition. In G. E. MacKinnon & T. G. Waller (Eds.), *Reading research: Advances in theory and practice* (Vol. 3, pp. 199–221). San Diego, CA: Academic Press.

Olofsson, A., & Lundberg, I. (1985). Evaluation of long term effects of phonemic awareness training in kindergarten: Illustrations of some methodological problems in evaluation research. *Scandinavian Journal of Psychology, 26,* 21–34.

Rosner, J., & Simon, D. P. (1971). The Auditory Analysis Test: An initial report. *Journal of Learning Disabilities, 4,* 384–392.

Schonell, F., & Goodacre, E. (1971). *The psychology and teaching of reading* (5th ed.). Edinburgh, Scotland: Oliver & Boyd.

Stanovich, K. E., Cunningham, A. E., & Cramer, B. (1984). Assessing phonological awareness in kindergarten children: Issues of task comparability. *Journal of Experimental Child Psychology, 38,* 175–190.

Williams, J. (1980). Teaching decoding with an emphasis on phoneme analysis and phoneme blending. *Journal of Educational Psychology, 72,* 1–15.

4 The Role of Intrasyllabic Units in Learning to Read and Spell

Rebecca Treiman
Wayne State University

Many investigators have proposed that children's knowledge of spoken language plays an important role in their acquisition of printed language (e.g., Gough & Hillinger, 1980; Liberman, 1983). Therefore, studies of the structure of spoken language provide an important foundation for studies of the way that children learn to read and write. In this chapter, I focus on one particular aspect of spoken language structure—phonological units that are intermediate in size between syllables and phonemes. I ask what role these units might play in learning to read and spell. The first section of the chapter reviews the linguistic status of intrasyllabic units. I then discuss the role of these units in the development of phonological awareness in children. Next, I consider the effects of intrasyllabic units on the way that children learn to read and spell. The chapter concludes with a discussion of how children's awareness of intrasyllabic units might be put to use in the teaching of reading and spelling.

THE STRUCTURE OF THE ENGLISH SYLLABLE

Until recently, there was little discussion of the syllable within the field of linguistics. Some linguists mentioned the syllable only to ignore it; others asserted that the syllable played no role in phonological organization. In recent years, linguists have begun to pay more attention to syllables and their structure. There are several competing views about the structure of the syllable. One position (e.g., Hooper, 1972) is that the syllable is a linear string of phonemes. In this view, there are no levels of structure intermediate between the syllable and the phoneme. This idea is depicted in the top panel of Fig. 4.1 by reference to the

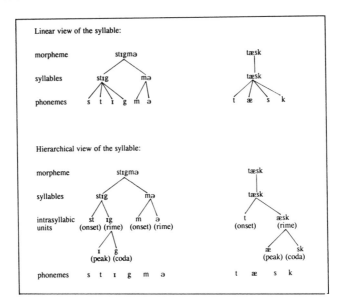

FIG. 4.1. Linear and hierarchical views of the syllable.

English words *stigma* (/stɪ'gmə/) and *task* (/tæsk/).[1] Another and more popular view (e.g., Clements & Keyser, 1983; Davis, 1989; Fudge, 1969, 1987, 1989; Hockett, 1967/1973; Selkirk, 1982; Vergnaud & Halle, 1979) is that the phonemes in a syllable are organized into groups or units. There exists a hierarchy of phonological units, with some units being intermediate in size between the syllable and the phoneme.

The bottom panel of Fig. 4.1 depicts the most widely accepted hierarchical view of the English syllable (Fudge, 1969, 1987, 1989; Hockett, 1967/73; Selkirk, 1982; Vergnaud & Halle, 1979). In this view, the syllable has two major subunits, the *onset* and the *rime*. The onset, or initial consonant portion of the syllable, may be a single phoneme (e.g., the /t/ in /tæsk/), or it may be a two-phoneme cluster (e.g., the /st/ in /stɪg/) or three-phoneme cluster (e.g., the /spr/ in /spre/). Syllables do not necessarily have an onset (e.g., /æsk/). The second major unit of the syllable, the rime, consists of the vowel and any following consonants. Thus, /spre/ has the rime /e/, /stɪg/ has the rime /ɪg/, and /tæsk/ has the rime /æsk/. The rime itself must contain a *peak* or vowel nucleus. Some linguists claim that a liquid (/l/, /r/) or a nasal (/m/, /n/, /ŋ/) that follows the vowel can be part of the peak (Fudge, 1969; Selkirk, 1982; Vergnaud & Halle, 1979). For example, the /l/ in /mɪlk/ and the /n/ in /mɪnt/ are thought to belong

---

[1]The symbol ' indicates a stressed vowel (stress is only indicated for words of more than one syllable).

to the peak. The rime may also contain a consonantal *coda*. Thus, the coda of /tæsk/ is /sk/ and the coda of /čɪnts/ is /ts/. The peak and the coda are in turn composed of phonemes. Linguistic evidence for this hierarchical view of the English syllable is reviewed by Selkirk (1982).

A fair amount of behavioral evidence supports the hierarchical view of the syllable in the bottom panel of Fig. 4.1 over the linear view. (See Treiman, 1988, for a detailed discussion.) In general, the evidence suggests that certain groups of phonemes tend to behave as units, whereas other groups of phonemes are less likely to do so.

In one investigation of syllable structure (Treiman, 1986, Experiment 1), college students heard pairs of consonant–vowel–consonant–consonant (CVCC) words on each trial. They were asked to blend the two words into one new word by taking part of the first word followed by part of the second one. For example, as Table 1 shows, /pækt/ (*packed*) and /nʌts/ (*nuts*) can combine to yield /pʌts/ (*putts*), /pæts/ (*pats*), or /pæks/ (*packs*). The first response, /pʌts/, is called a C/VCC response. It divides each stimulus between the initial consonant and the

TABLE 4.1
Results of Blending Studies with College Students

Stimulus type	Sample Stimuli	Possible Responses			Proportion of Responses of each Type			
CVCC words (Treiman, 1986, Exp. 1)	pækt + nʌts	C/VCC pʌts	CV/CC pæts	CVC/C pæks	C/VCC .91	CV/CC .05	CVC/C .01	other .04
CCVC words (Treiman, 1986, Exp. 2)	frel + slæt	C/CVC flæt	CC/VC fræt	CCV/C fret	C/CVC .23	CC/VC .62	CCV/C .03	other .12
CCCV syllables (Treiman, 1986, Exp. 6)	spli + skrɔ	CC/CV sprɔ	CCC/V splɔ		CC/CV .21	CCC/V .62	other .17	
VCC syllables, postvocalic liquids (Treiman, 1984, Exp. 3)	arz + ɪld	V/CC ald	VC/C ard		V/CC .21	VC/C .49	other .30	
VCC syllables, postvocalic nasals (Treiman, 1984, Exp. 3)	ʌns + æmd	V/CC ʌmd	VC/C ʌnd		V/CC .43	VC/C .38	other .19	
VCC syllables, postvocalic obstruents (Treiman, 1984, Exp. 3)	ipt + uks	V/CC iks	VC/C ips		V/CC .58	VC/C .20	other .22	

remainder of the syllable, that is, at the boundary between the onset and the rime. The onset of *packed*, /p/, is combined with the rime of *nuts*, /ʌts/, to yield /pʌts/. The response /pæts/ is a CV/CC division, breaking the stimuli within the rime. The CVC/C response is /pæks/. This response also divides the syllables within the rime. If people group the phonemes in the syllables into onset and rime units, C/VCC blends should predominate. In fact, as the first row of Table 4.1 shows, over 90% of all responses were C/VCC blends.

Does the preference for C/VCC blends shown in the experiment just described reflect an onset/rime division of the syllable, or do people combine the first phoneme of the first stimulus with the second, third, and fourth phonemes of the second stimulus regardless of the linguistic structure of the stimuli? If the findings reflect linguistic structure, different results should be obtained for CCVC and CCCV stimuli. To address this issue, I carried out a second experiment (Treiman, 1986, Experiment 2). This time, the stimuli were CCVC words like /frel/ (*frail*) and /slæt/ (*slat*). As Table 4.1 shows, people most often combined the first two phonemes of the first word with the third and fourth phonemes of the second word. For example, the most common response to /frel/ plus /slæt/ was /fræt/. People tended to join the onset of the first word with the rime of the second word. They did not usually join the first phoneme of the first word with the second, third, and fourth phonemes of the second word.

To determine whether three-consonant onsets tend to behave as units, as two-consonant onsets do, I devised an experiment with CCCV stimuli as shown in Table 4.1 (Treiman, 1986, Experiment 6). In this experiment, unlike the two just described, most of the stimuli and responses were nonsense words. For the stimuli /spli/ and /skrɔ/, the CC/CV blend is /sprɔ/ and the CCC/V blend is /splɔ/. (A C/CCV blend is precluded, because this blend would not yield a new syllable.) Over 60% of the time, people produced CCC/V blends. They joined the first three consonants, or onset, of the first stimulus with the last phoneme, or rime, of the second stimulus. The results of the three experiments just described cannot be explained by supposing that people tend to combine phonemes in certain serial positions of the stimulus syllables. Rather, with the single-syllable words and nonwords used in these experiments, college students prefer an onset/rime division.

Additional evidence that speakers of English treat syllables in terms of onset and rime units comes from spontaneous errors in the production of speech (e.g., MacKay, 1972; Shattuck-Hufnagel, 1983; Stemberger, 1983). In speech errors, people are more likely to treat a vowel and a following consonant as a unit than an initial consonant and a vowel as a unit. In the error *Let Hucky drink → Luck Hucky drink* (from Stemberger, 1983), both the /ʌ/ and /k/ of *Hucky* are anticipated. These two phonemes behave as a unit, replacing the /ɛ/ and /t/ of *let*. Such an error is more probable than one like *Hut Hucky drink*, in which /h/ and /ʌ/ behave as a unit.

Most of the evidence for onset and rime units comes from studies with single-syllable words. This has led some linguists (e.g., Davis, 1989) to argue that words are actually divided into a word-initial onset and another unit that consists of the rest of the word. With a one-syllable word like /tæsk/, this "remainder" unit, /æsk/, looks like a rime. With a two-syllable word like /stɪ'gmə/, however, the remainder unit, /ɪ'gmə/, is not the same as a rime. Although Davis' arguments have been rebutted on theoretical grounds (Fudge, 1989), more research is needed to study the units within multisyllabic words. I suspect, along with Fudge (1989), that word-initial onsets have a special status but that each syllable of a multisyllabic word consists of an onset and a rime.

Theoretically, the distinction between rimes and remainders of words is important. In terms of implications for phonological awareness, reading, and spelling, the distinction is probably less important. Most of the words that beginning readers encounter contain a single syllable. For example, 90% of the preprimer and primer words in the listing of Harris and Jacobson (1972) are monosyllabic. With one-syllable words, the rime and the remainder of the word are identical.

Rime units such as the /æsk/ of /tæsk/ and the /ɪlk/ of /mɪlk/ are not simple strings of phonemes. Rimes, like syllables, contain subunits. To study the nature of these subunits, I used a blending task like that described earlier (Treiman, 1984, Experiment 3). This time the stimuli were VCC syllables. As Table 4.1 shows, one group of people received stimuli with liquid phonemes (/r/ and /l/) after the vowel. For example, /arz/ and /ɪld/ can combine to yield /ald/ (a V/CC blend) or /ard/ (a VC/C blend). People made over twice as many VC/C blends as V/CC blends with these stimuli. Another group of people received VCCs with postvocalic nasals (/m/, /n/, and /ŋ/). For example, /ʌns/ and /æmd/ can yield the V/CC blend /ʌmd/ or the VC/C blend /ʌnd/. Subjects in the nasal group made roughly equal numbers of V/CC and VC/C blends. A third group of people had stimuli with obstruents (which include stops and fricatives) after the vowel. The stimuli /ipt/ and /uks/, for example, can join to form the V/CC /iks/ or the VC/C /ips/. Here, V/CC blends outnumbered VC/C blends by a ratio of almost three to one. These results suggest that liquids are closely linked to the preceding vowel. Liquids perhaps are part of the syllable's peak. Obstruents are less closely bound to the vowel. They may be part of the coda rather than part of the peak. Nasals seem to have a status intermediate between that of liquids and obstruents.

The observed difference between liquids and nasals does not support the view of some linguists (Fudge, 1969; Selkirk, 1982; Vergnaud & Halle, 1979) that nasals can be part of the peak in the same way that liquids can. In this case, there seems to be a discrepancy between the behavioral evidence and certain linguistic theories. The linguistic theories suggest a two-way distinction—liquids and nasals versus other consonants. The word game results suggest a three-way distinction—liquids versus nasals versus obstruents. Despite this apparent discrepancy, it is clear that adults are sensitive to the linguistic structure of the rime. They treat it differently depending on the type of phoneme that follows the vowel. The rime, like the syllable, has an internal structure.

To summarize, there appear to be linguistic units intermediate in size between the syllable and the phoneme. The two primary units of the syllable are the onset and the rime. Vowel-liquid sequences within rimes seem to be particularly cohesive, whereas vowel-obstruent sequences are less cohesive.

SYLLABLE STRUCTURE AND THE
DEVELOPMENT OF PHONOLOGICAL AWARENESS

Many researchers have investigated children's awareness of the phonological units of spoken language. These studies are motivated by the idea that language awareness plays an important role in learning to read and write (e.g., Gough & Hillinger, 1980; Liberman, 1983; Rozin & Gleitman, 1977; Tunmer & Bowey, 1984). For alphabetic writing systems, awareness of phonemes is thought to be especially critical. For example, if children are not aware that the spoken syllables /blæst/ and /bʌg/ begin with the same sound, they will not fully understand why the printed versions of these words begin with the same letter.

Most of the early research on phonological awareness was based on the implicit assumption that syllables are linear strings of phonemes, that there are no units intermediate in size between syllables and phonemes. Consequently, researchers examined children's awareness of syllables and phonemes. They did not consider children's awareness of intrasyllabic units. Several studies (Fox & Routh, 1975; Hardy, Stennett, & Smythe, 1973; Leong & Haines, 1978; Liberman, Shankweiler, Fischer, & Carter, 1974; Treiman & Baron, 1981) have compared syllabic awareness and phonemic awareness. Children were found to achieve an awareness of syllables earlier than they achieve an awareness of phonemes. For example, in the study of Liberman et al. (1974), about half of the preschool and kindergarten children could learn to tap once for each syllable in a spoken word (e.g., one tap for *but*, two taps for *butter*, three taps for *butterfly*). Few preschoolers and kindergarteners could master the analogous task with phonemes (e.g., one tap for *oo*, two for *boo*, three for *boot*). Not until first grade did a majority of the children succeed on the phoneme counting task.

The idea that syllables have an internal structure suggests that these early studies may have overlooked some important steps in the development of phonological awareness. In particular, there may be a point at which children are fairly good at analyzing spoken syllables into onsets and rimes but have trouble analyzing onsets and rimes into their component phonemes. For some words, of course, an analysis into onsets and rimes is the same as a phonemic analysis. As an example, /bo/ contains the onset /b/ and the rime /o/. The onset and the rime of this syllable are single phonemes. For the many English syllables that are more complex than CVs, however, an analysis into onsets and rimes is less detailed than an analysis into phonemes. For example, a child who could not go beyond an onset/rime division of the syllable would be aware that /blo/ begins with /bl/ and ends with /o/. However, this child could not analyze /bl/ as a /b/ phoneme followed by an /l/ phoneme. A child who was restricted to the level of onsets and rimes would also lack awareness that the /ep/ of /grep/ consists of /e/ followed by /p/.

There may also be a point in the development of phonological awareness when children can analyze rimes into peaks and codas but cannot analyze peaks and codas into their constituent phonemes. For example, some children may be able to divide /ɪlk/ into the peak /ɪl/ and the coda /k/. However, they may think of /ɪl/ as a single unit. Similarly, some children may be aware that /æsk/ consists of /æ/ and /sk/ but unaware that /sk can be analyzed into /s/ and /k/.

Recent findings support the idea that the awareness of intrasyllabic units is easier than and developmentally prior to the awareness of phonemes. In reviewing this research, I first consider the evidence that the ability to divide syllables into onset and rime units develops at a young age. Next, I discuss the evidence that children have difficulty dividing initial consonant clusters into their component phonemes at a time when they can separate single initial consonants from the remainder of the syllable. I then ask whether rimes are difficult to divide into phonemes.

Awareness of Onsets and Rimes

Many young children can divide spoken syllables at the onset/rime boundary in a variety of phonological awareness tasks. Rhyme production tasks and alliteration production tasks are one way to assess children's ability to analyze syllables into onsets and rimes. A child who can give /bot/ or /sot/ as a rhyme for /got/ must be aware, at some level, that all three syllables contain the rime /ot/. Likewise, a child who offers /tɛn/ as starting with the same sound as /tæp/ is presumably aware that these words share an onset. Maclean, Bryant, and Bradley (1987), who worked with children averaging 3 years, 8 months in age, reported that 42% of the children produced at least one correct response in a rhyme production task and that 35% produced at least one correct response in an alliteration production task. Calfee, Chapman, and Venezky (1972) used a rhyme production task with kindergarteners (mean age 5 years, 9 months) and found that 53% of the children generated at least one rhyme. Stanovich, Cunningham, and Cramer (1984) and Yopp (1988) also reported that kindergarteners performed well in rhyme production tasks. Thus, some young children are able to produce rhyme and alliteration.

Forced-choice tasks provide another way to assess children's awareness of onsets and rimes. A child who responds correctly to such questions as, "Which word rhymes with *bed—sled* or *ring*?" is presumably aware that *bed* and *sled* share the /ɛd/ unit. Knafle (1973, 1974) and Stanovich et al. (1984) found that kindergarteners did relatively well on forced-choice rhyme and alliteration tests, and Lenel and Cantor (1981) found above-chance performance on a forced-choice rhyme task among four-year-olds. However, the 3-year-olds tested by Maclean et al. (1987) showed little success in a forced-choice rhyming task.

Children's ability to deal with onset and rime units can also be assessed by word pair comparison tasks. In one study, Treiman and Zukowski (1991) introduced children to a puppet who liked pairs of words that contained some of the same sounds. In the onset/rime condition of the study, the puppet liked pairs such as *plank* and *plea,* which share a CC onset. The puppet also liked pairs such as *spit* and *wit,* which share a VC rime. Pairs such as *twist* and *brain* or *rail* and *snap* were not pleasing to the puppet. Children heard each pair of words and judged whether the puppet liked it. The experimenter praised correct responses and corrected wrong ones. Using this procedure, 56% of the preschoolers (mean age 5 years, 1 month) and 74% of the kindergarteners (mean age 5 years, 9 months) reached criterion in the onset/rime task. These findings agree with other results in showing that some children can divide syllables at the boundary between the onset and the rime before they learn to read.

Kindergarteners' relatively good performance in the onset/rime comparison task of Treiman and Zukowski (1991) contrasts with their poor performance in the apparently similar tasks of Calfee et al. (1972). In an initial sounds task, Calfee et al. asked children whether two words started with the same sound. In a rhyming task, Calfee et al. asked children whether two words sounded the same at the end. Kindergarteners performed at chance levels in both tasks, even though some of the same children succeeded in the rhyme production task. The procedure of Treiman and Zukowski (1991), with its use of a puppet and its provision of feedback by the experimenter, may have allowed children to show their abilities to a greater extent than the procedure of Calfee et al. (1972).

Oddity tasks provide another way to assess children's ability to analyze syllables into onset and rime units. A child who can say that *cap* is the odd word out in the set *cap, doll, dog* must be aware that *doll* and *dog* share the onset /d/, whereas *cap* does not have this onset. A child who can say that *rail* is the odd word in *top, rail, hop* must know that the rime of *rail* is not the same as the rime of *top* and *hop.* Five-year-olds score above chance on both these tasks, suggesting that they have some ability to divide syllables at the onset/rime boundary (Bowey & Francis, 1991; Kirtley, Bryant, Maclean, & Bradley, 1989). Even some 3-year-olds can perform the tasks when pictures are used (Maclean et al., 1987).

Finally, certain phoneme deletion tasks, such as the deletion of /f/ from *feel* to produce *eel,* can be carried out at the level of onsets and rimes. Although deletion tasks are among the hardest phonological awareness tasks (e.g., Yopp, 1988), some kindergarteners can learn to delete sounds in words if the sounds are onsets (Calfee et al., 1972; Dow, 1987; Stanovich et al., 1984).

To summarize, phonological awareness tasks that can be solved by dividing the syllable into an onset and a rime are easier than other kinds of phonological awareness tasks. Many children can perform onset/rime tasks before they begin to read.

Awareness of Phonemes Within Cluster Onsets

Syllable onsets may be single consonants or consonant clusters. Although many young children can deal with cluster onsets as units, they have difficulty dividing them into their component phonemes. This difficulty surfaces in a variety of tasks. One of the first studies to document children's problems with cluster onsets was that of Barton, Miller, and Macken (1980, Experiment 1). Children between four and five years of age were taught to give the "first sound" of words like *mouse*. For these words, the onset is a single phoneme. The children could perform this task with only a small amount of training. The children were then asked to give the "first sound" of words like *swing* and *train*. Some children (about a third of those tested) consistently produced the first consonant of the cluster. Others (about 20%–40% of those tested, depending on the cluster) consistently produced the entire cluster. For example, these children said that *swing* began with /sw/ rather than /s/. The remaining children gave a combination of single-consonant and cluster responses.

A study by Treiman (1985a, Experiment 2) used a phoneme recognition task to assess children's ability to analyze word-initial consonant clusters into phonemes. Twelve children with an average age of 5 years, 5 months were asked whether spoken syllables like /spa/, /sap/, /sa/, and /nik/ began with /s/. If children can analyze two-phoneme onsets into their component phonemes, they should response "yes" to the first three syllables and "no" to the last. If children can analyze /spa/ into /sp/ and /a/ but have difficulty dividing /sp/ into /s/ and /p/, erroneous "no" responses to /spa/ would be expected. The task was presented with the help of a puppet who was said to like all "words" that began with the target sound. After a series of practice trials, children heard a tape-recorded list of test syllables and were asked whether the puppet liked each one. Children more often failed to recognize the initial consonant in syllables like /spa/ (28% error rate) than in syllables like /sap/ (14% error rate) and /sa/ (12% error rate). The children did fairly well at rejecting the syllables that began with other phonemes (13% erroneous "yes" responses). Apparently, 5-year-olds have some difficulty recognizing an initial phoneme within a cluster onset.

The results just presented show that children have more trouble recognizing the first consonant of a cluster than a syllable-initial single consonant, even though both phonemes are in the first position of the stimulus. In an unpublished study, I compared 5-year-olds' ability to recognize the second consonant of a cluster with their ability to recognize a syllable-initial single consonant. Again, the phonemes had the same position in the stimulus, both being the second phoneme of a three-phoneme stimulus. For example, I compared children's ability to recognize /m/ in the one-syllable stimulus /smi/ and the two-syllable stimulus /əmi'/. In /smi/, /m/ is the first consonant of the stressed second syllable according to most linguistic theories of syllabification and according to behavioral data (Treiman & Danis, 1988).

The experiment included four conditions, one with each of the targets /m/, /n/, /l/, and /r/. Each condition had four practice stimuli and twelve test stimuli. Half of the stimuli contained the target phoneme and half did not. In the /m/ condition, for example, /smi/ and /əmi'/ contained the target, whereas /sko/ and /əko'/ did not. Sixteen children, ranging in age from 4 years, 11 months to 5 years, 8 months (mean age 5 years, 3 months) participated. Following the procedure used in the experiment just described, potential subjects who scored randomly in the experiment or who scored perfectly in the first session were replaced with other subjects. If children perform at floor or ceiling, the role of linguistic factors on performance cannot be assessed. Four potential subjects were replaced for the first reason and one was replaced for the second reason. The procedure was similar to that of the earlier experiment. Children were told that a puppet liked all "words" that contained the target sound. They listened to a series of syllables and judged whether the puppet liked each one. Four different puppets were used, one for each target. Children worked with two targets in the first session of the experiment and the remaining two targets in the second session.

If children have more difficulty recognizing the second consonant of a cluster than a syllable-initial single consonant, they should more often miss the target in a stimulus like /smi/ than in a stimulus like /əmi'/. This prediction was supported. Children missed the target 50.5% of the time (chance level performance) on the syllables like /smi/. They missed the target 39.1% of the time for the /əmi'/ stimuli. Although this rate is still quite high, it is significantly lower than the error rate on the /smi/ stimuli (across subjects, $t[15] = 1.88$, $p < .05$, one tailed; across stimuli, $t[11] = 2.99$, $p < .01$, one tailed). For negative stimuli, the error rates were 32.3% for CCV stimuli and 30.2% for VCV' stimuli.

Overall, the error rates in the /smi/, /əmi'/ experiment were higher than those in the /spa/, /sap/, /sa/ experiment. Children may have more trouble recognizing a phoneme in the middle of a stimulus than a phoneme at the beginning of a stimulus. However, the most important result of the two experiments is that, when position in the stimulus is held constant, a consonant that is part of an onset cluster is harder to detect than a consonant that is itself the onset. Five-year-olds have a certain amount of difficulty analyzing two-consonant onsets into their constituents and recognizing the individual phonemes within them. By age 7, these difficulties have largely disappeared for normal readers and spellers (Bruck & Treiman, 1990).

Difficulties with word-initial clusters also surface in phoneme substitution tasks. In one study (Treiman, 1985a, Experiment 1), children were taught a word game in which they had to substitute two fixed phonemes for two of the original phonemes in a three-phoneme syllable. Because phoneme substitution tasks are among the hardest phonemic awareness tasks (Golinkoff, 1978), 8-year-olds served as subjects. In the CCV condition, each child attempted to learn two games using the same CCV syllables as stimuli. About 2 weeks elapsed between the learning of the two games. In Game A, the child replaced the first and second phonemes of each stimulus—the onset—with two fixed phonemes. As Table 4.2 shows, /gwe/ became /sle/ and /fru/ became /slu/. In Game B, the child replaced the second and third phonemes of each stimulus. Thus, /gwe/ became /gli/ and /fru/ became /fli/. In the CCV condition, Game A should be easier than Game B because it treats the onset as a unit. Game B, which requires the child to divide the stimuli within the onset and to replace part of the onset and the rime, should be harder. As Table 4.2 shows, Game A was in fact easier than Game B according to all four measures of performance—number of correct responses, position of first correct response, longest run of consecutive correct responses, and number of different correct responses.

Taken alone, the results of the CCV condition would be consistent with another hypothesis—that children can more easily replace the first two phonemes of a three-phoneme syllable than the last two phonemes. However, the results of the CVC condition, to be described later, do not support this hypoth-

TABLE 4.2
Sample Stimuli and Results for Phoneme Substitution Experiment with Children

| | CCV Condition | | CVC Condition | |
	Game A	Game B	Game A	Game B
Sample stimuli and responses	gwe sle fru slu	gwe gli fru fli	fɛg lʌg ju̯t lʌt	fɛg tʌl ju̯t jʌl
Number of correct responses (maximum = 18)	8.42	5.13	7.21	9.00
Position of first correct trial	8.17	11.92	9.50	9.00
Length of longest run of correct responses	6.67	4.29	6.21	7.88
Number of different correct responses (maximum = 6)	4.00	2.71	3.75	3.88

From Treiman, 1985a, Experiment 1.

esis. It appears that children are better able to treat the onset as a unit, replacing the entire onset, than to subdivide it.

Difficulties in analyzing word-initial clusters into phonemes also appear in phoneme deletion tasks. In the study of Bruck and Treiman (1990), 7-year-old children in the first and second grades had an error rate of less than 8% when required to delete the entire onset of a spoken syllable (e.g., /prov/ → /ov/). The error rate jumped above 60% when children were asked to delete just the first consonant of a cluster onset (e.g., /floy/ → /loy/). Even third graders showed an error rate of 50% in this task. Thus, onset clusters cause substantial difficulty in the deletion task. Morais, Cluytens, and Alegria (1984) and Miller and Limber (1985) have reported similar results.

To summarize, children have trouble analyzing syllable-initial consonant clusters into phonemes in a variety of phonological awareness tasks. It is not possible to pinpoint an exact age at which children become able to segment cluster onsets because their performance varies with the demands of the task. For example, it is much easier for children to judge that /floy/ starts with /f/ than to delete the /f/ and produce the remaining syllable (Bruck & Treiman, 1990).

Awareness of Phonemes Within Rimes

Just as young children have difficulty appreciating the internal structure of the syllable onset, so they have difficulty appreciating the internal structure of the rime. For example, picking the odd word in the triad *mop, lead, whip* requires one to analyze the words' rimes into phonemes and to realize that *op* and *ip* share a phoneme (the final consonant) that *ead* does not share. Picking the odd word in the triad *cap, can, cot* also requires one to analyze the rimes into phonemes and to focus on the vowel. Five-year-olds perform more poorly on these kinds of oddity problems than on problems that can be solved with an onset/rime division of the syllable (Bowey & Francis, 1991; Kirtley et al., 1989; Stanovich et al., 1984).

The phoneme substitution task of Treiman (1985a, Experiment 1) also tested children's ability to divide rimes into phonemes. In the CVC condition of this study, each child tried to learn two games using the same CVC stimuli. In Game A, the child replaced the first and second phonemes of each stimulus with two fixed phonemes. In Game B, the child replaced the second and third phonemes of each stimulus with two fixed phonemes. Examples appear in Table 4.2. In the CVC condition, I predicted that Game B would be easier than Game A. This is because Game B replaces the rime as a whole, whereas Game A requires the child to divide the syllable within the rime and to replace the onset and part of the rime. The results, shown in Table 4.2, revealed a significant superiority for Game B over Game A for two of the four dependent variables—number of correct responses and length of longest run of correct responses. The other two measures showed nonsignificant differences but in the expected direction. In the overall analysis of the phoneme substitution data, no main effect of game type (A or B) or condition (CCV or CVC) was found. Rather, Game A tended to be easier than Game B in the CCV condition and Game B tended to be easier than Game A in the CVC condition. The interaction between game type and condition, which was significant for all four dependent variables, shows that the syllabic structure of the stimuli affects children's performance.

Summary and Implications for the Teaching of Phonological Awareness

Many prereaders can divide spoken syllables into onset and rime units. When the onsets and rimes coincide with phonemes, the analysis into onsets and rimes might appear, at first glance, to be a phonemic analysis. When the onsets and rimes are larger than single phonemes, however, it becomes clear that the children have not managed to fully analyze the syllables into phonemes.

Findings from illiterate adults support the idea that larger units such as syllables and rimes are more accessible than phonemes (see Bertelson & de Gelder, 1989, for a review). Adults who do not know an alphabetic writing system can often make judgments about rhyme. They perform fairly well too on syllabic analysis tasks. However, these adults are very poor at analyzing spoken words into phonemes. Thus, although phonemes may play a tacit role in speech production and speech perception, they are not as available to conscious awareness as larger units of speech. Special experiences, such as those involved in learning to read and write an alphabet, may be required for the emergence of phonemic awareness (see Gattuso, Smith, & Treiman, 1991).

Previous classifications of phonological awareness tasks (e.g., Golinkoff, 1978) have suggested that two factors determine how difficult the task will be—the cognitive requirements of the task and the linguistic level that the task taps. For example, recognition tasks, which require one to judge whether a unit is present or absent, are easier than substitution tasks. Tasks that tap the linguistic level of the syllable are easier than tasks that tap the linguistic level of the phoneme. The results reviewed here suggest that the dimension of linguistic level be expanded to include not only syllables and phonemes but also intrasyllabic units. Cognitive demands being equal, tasks that can be solved on the basis of an onset/rime division are easier for both children and adults than tasks that require a full analysis into phonemes.

Because phonological awareness plays an important role in learning to read and write, it has been suggested that phonological awareness skills be taught prior to or during initial reading and spelling instruction. Several programs (Rosner, 1974; Rozin & Gleitman, 1977; Williams, 1980) begin with the analysis of words into syllables and proceed to the analysis of syllables into phonemes.

In an early stage of Rosner's program, for example, children omit a designated syllable in a two-syllable word like *cowboy*. Only later do they learn to omit a phoneme from a one-syllable word. The researchers just cited found that even disadvantaged children have relatively little difficulty learning syllabic analysis. For example, the inner-city 4-year-olds in Rosner's study could learn to delete one syllable from a two-syllable word. However, the next step—the analysis of syllables into phonemes—was difficult. Even after a full school year of training, Rosner's 4-year-olds did not reach the level of phonemic analysis.

The difficulty in progressing from syllabic analysis to phonemic analysis in these programs may arise in part because an intermediate step is missing. This step is the analysis of syllables into intrasyllabic units. The research that I have reviewed suggests the value of developing and testing programs that include this intermediate step. In such a program, children would first be taught to divide spoken words into syllables. They would then learn to divide syllables into onsets and rimes. Only after children have mastered this step would the analysis of onsets and rimes into smaller units be introduced. Early on, then, a word like /spɛl/ would be divided into /sp/ and /ɛl/. Not until later would children be required to analyze /sp/ into /s/ and /p/ and /ɛl/ into /ɛ/ and /l/.

Linguistic phenomena such as the greater cohesiveness of vowel-liquid sequences than vowel-obstruent sequences should be considered in the design of phonological awareness training programs. For example, children could learn to analyze the vowel-obstruent sequence /ɛt/ into /ɛ/ plus /t/ before they learn to analyze the vowel-liquid sequence /ɛl/ into /ɛ/ plus /l/. With a rime like /ɪlk/, children could analyze it into /ɪl/ and /k/ before they break it down completely into phonemes. The rime /ɪsk/, in contrast, would be analyzed into /ɪ/ and /sk/, because /s/ and /k/ form a unit. As these examples show, phonological awareness training programs can be based on what we know about syllable structure. Research is required to determine whether such programs are more successful than those that are designed without this component.

Although theories of syllable structure were not explicitly considered in designing the phonological awareness training programs referred to previously, certain aspects of the programs *are* consistent with these theories. For example, Rosner (1974) taught children to substitute one single initial consonant for another before requiring them to substitute one phoneme of a cluster for another. More explicit and comprehensive consideration of syllable structure may lead to improved phonological awareness training programs.

Because phonological awareness plays an important role in the acquisition of reading and writing, our ideas about phonological awareness and its development will influence our theories of reading and spelling. Behind traditional views of reading and spelling is the notion that there are two levels of phonological awareness—awareness of syllables and awareness of phonemes. The idea that there is an intermediate level to consider—the awareness of intrasyllabic units— calls for a fresh look at children's reading and spelling skills.

SYLLABLE STRUCTURE
AND CHILDREN'S READING

One important skill that children must master in learning to read is decoding. Given an unfamiliar printed word, children must be able to figure out which spoken word it symbolizes. That is, they must be able to map from print to speech. Previous discussions of this mapping process (e.g., Coltheart, 1978) have emphasized two levels at which it may take place. The first level involves mappings from single graphemes to single phonemes. For example, readers may know that the printed letter *b* corresponds to the phoneme /b/. Although rules of this kind often involve single letters, they may also involve groups of letters such as *sh* and *ck* that correspond to single phonemes. A letter group such as *bl*, which corresponds to a sequence of two phonemes, is not a unit in this view. In addition to grapheme–phoneme mappings, readers are thought to use memorized links between whole printed words and whole spoken words. These are called word-specific associations. Because most preprimer and primer words contain a single syllable, the earliest word-specific associations often link printed syllables to spoken syllables. The distinction between grapheme–phoneme rules and word-specific associations lies at the core of dual process models of reading.

Standard dual process models imply that children can read a printed word like *blast* in one of two ways. They can use the grapheme–phoneme correspondences $b \rightarrow$ /b/, $l \rightarrow$ /l/, $a \rightarrow$ /æ/, $s \rightarrow$ /s/, and $t \rightarrow$ /t/, or they can remember that the letter string *blast* corresponds to the spoken syllable /blæst/. The idea that children use correspondences either at the level of phonemes or at the level of syllables is based on the notion that the syllable is a linear string of phonemes, that there are no phonological units intermediate between the syllable and the phoneme. If syllables and phonemes are the only phonological units that are available to children, then children must either treat the printed syllable as a whole or parse it into units that correspond to phonemes. Children who cannot use grapheme–phoneme rules have no choice but to learn words as "sight words."

The existence of phonological units intermediate in size between syllables and phonemes raises the possibility of correspondences between print and speech that are based on these intermediate units. If intrasyllabic units exist, children have other options than grapheme–phoneme rules and whole-word memorization. One such option, as Goswami and Bryant (this volume) also argue, is the use of orthographic units that correspond to onsets and rimes. For example, children may parse the printed word *blast* into two parts, *bl* and *ast*. Children may pronounce the word using links between the letter group *bl* and the onset /bl/ and the letter group *ast* and the rime /æst/. In this view, children do not derive the correspondence between *bl* and /bl/ from knowledge of the correspondences between *b* and /b/ and *l* and /l/. Instead, children store the correspondence between *bl* and /bl/ separately, as a memorized unit. Children use this correspondence whenever they encounter *bl* at the beginning of a word. Likewise, children may use a link between *ast* and /æst/ rather than separate rules linking *a* and /æ/, *s* and /s/, and *t* and /t/. If the units of printed words are related to the units of spoken words, children should use units like *ast,* which correspond to rimes, to a greater degree than units like *bla,* which do not correspond to a single constituent of the spoken syllable.

Many previous studies of children's reading have found evidence for units like *ast,* although they have not offered a theoretical justification for focusing on units like *ast* over units like *bla.* For example, Baron (1979, Experiment 1) asked poor fourth-grade readers to pronounce nonsense words that shared their vowel(s) and final consonant(s) with real words. Given a nonsense word like *reen,* the children pronounced it as /rɪn/ about as often as they pronounced it as /rin/. If children used only rules at the level of single phonemes, /rin/ pronunciations should have predominated. This is because *r* is tyically pronounced a /r/, *ee* is typically pronounced as /i/, and *n* is typically pronounced as /n/. Children's many /rɪn/ pronunciations suggest that they parsed *reen* into *r* and *een.* They sometimes read *een* as /ɪn/ because they knew that *een* is pronounced in this way in the common real word *been.*

With real words, too, many researchers have implicitly assumed that children use vowel-final consonant units. For example, Backman, Bruck, Hébert, and Seidenberg (1984) compared children's ability to pronounce words like *paid* and words like *hope.* The former words are considered regular but inconsistent in that the unit *aid,* although pronounced in the typical way (/ed/) in *paid,* is pronounced otherwise (/ɛd/) in *said.* Words like *hope* are considered regular in that the unit *ope* always corresponds to /op/. Second and third graders made significantly more errors on regular inconsistent words like *paid* than on regular words like *hope.* About one-third of their errors on a word like *paid* were pronunciations that rhymed with *said.* Apparently, children sometimes use a rule that links the multiletter unit *aid* to the sequence of phonemes /ɛd/. Children do not just use grapheme units like *ai* and *d,* which correspond to single phonemes.

Researchers such as those just cited may have studied units like initial *p* and final *aid* because these units, intuitively, seem most natural. However, these researchers do not discuss why readers might favor some multiletter units over others. For example, why do children parse *reen* into *r* and *een*? Is a division into *ree* plus *n* equally likely? Should a word like *sail,* which shares the initial *sai* unit with *said,* be classified as a regular inconsistent word, just as *paid* is classified as regular and inconsistent? Without a basis for deciding among possible multiletter units, theories of reading are not sufficiently constrained.

Linguistic theories of syllable structure can help constrain our theories of reading by suggesting which types of multiletter units are most likely to be used. For example, because the letter groups *bl* and *ast* correspond to the onset and rime units of the spoken syllable /blæst/, people may employ the units *bl* and *ast* when reading *blast*. Readers may be less likely to use *bla* than *ast* because *bla* does not correspond to a natural constituent of the syllable, whereas *ast* does.

My hypothesis, then, is that correspondences between print and speech are not restricted to the level of whole words or the level of single phonemes. In addition to word-specific associations and grapheme–phoneme correspondences, readers also use mappings that involve intrasyllabic units. This hypothesis is attractive to those who stress the close relationship between printed language and spoken language.

What is the evidence that readers use multiletter units in printed words that correspond to intrasyllabic units in spoken words? Results like those of Baron (1979) and Backman et al. (1984), which were discussed previously, suggest that children divide printed words into one letter group that corresponds to the onset and another letter group that corresponds to the rime. However, these researchers did not systematically compare vowel-final consonant units with initial consonant-vowel units.

Fortunately, a number of studies have compared readers' use of different multiletter units within words. Studies with adults will be mentioned only briefly, because the units that adult readers use may not be the same as the units that children use. Findings of Santa, Santa, and Smith (1977) suggested that, with words like *blast*, both *bla* and *ast* function as units. However, more recent results (Bowey, 1990; Glushko, 1981; Taraban & McClelland, 1987; Treiman & Chafetz, 1987; Treiman, Goswami, & Bruck, 1990; Treiman & Zukowski, 1988) show that college students rely more on units like *ast*, which correspond to the rimes of spoken syllables, than units like *bla*, which do not correspond to a single constituent of the syllable. For example, Treiman and Zukowski (1988) asked people to pronounce nonwords like *saip* and *vaid*. The first nonword, *saip*, shares the *sai* of *said*. The second nonword, *vaid*, shares the *aid* of *said*. *Said* is one of a very few English words in which *ai* is pronounced as /ɛ/. Although /ɛ/ pronunciations of *ai* were not very frequent, these pronunciations were more common in nonwords like *vaid* than in nonwords like *saip*. This finding suggests that people have a link between the letter group *aid* and the rime /ɛd/. Although some researchers have found that readers use initial consonant-vowel units to some extent (Johnson & Venezky, 1976; Kay, 1985; Taraban & McClelland, 1987), these units do not seem to be as important as vowel-final consonant units. For adults, then, the units of printed words bear a close relationship to the units of spoken words.

On theoretical grounds, one can argue that children must use units like *ast* even more than adults do. This argument is based on the finding that many children, at the time they begin to read, are aware of onset and rime units. However, they have difficulty analyzing complex onsets and rimes into their component phonemes. Children who can segment /blæst/ into /bl/ and /æst/, but who are not aware that /bl/ is composed of /b/ plus /l/ and that /æst/ is composed of /æ/, /s/, and /t/, may be unable to learn the grapheme–phoneme mappings $b \rightarrow$ /b/, $l \rightarrow$ /l/, $a \rightarrow$ /æ/, $s \rightarrow$ /s/, and $t \rightarrow$ /t/. However, these children may be able to learn the correspondences between bl and /bl/ and ast and /æst/. Thus, beginning readers may rely heavily on onset and rime units. Adults may have less need for larger units, because they can fully analyze spoken words into phonemes.

Of course, a theoretical argument that children read words in terms of onset and rime units is less convincing than an empirical demonstration. Empirical evidence does exist to support the view that children use multiletter units that correspond to onsets and rimes to a greater degree than other types of multiletter units.

In an early study relevant to the issue of multiletter units, Santa (1976–1977) worked with second graders, fifth graders, and adults. Subjects first practiced naming words and pictures. During this practice phase, the words were printed with normal spacing between the letters. The practice phase was omitted for the adults. In the test phase, pairs of words and pictures were presented simultaneously. Subjects had to judge as quickly as possible whether the picture illustrated the word. The words were presented in one of five forms. They could be intact, as in the practice phase (*blast, check*), or they could have two spaces after the first letter (*b last, c heck*), second letter (*bl ast, ch eck*), third letter (*bla st, che ck*), or fourth letter (*blas t, chec k*). The fifth graders and adults responded equally quickly in all conditions. For these subjects, the task may be insensitive due to ceiling effects. When the second graders' data were examined alone, a significant effect of spacing was found. The second graders responded faster when the words were divided after the second letter than when the words were divided at other points. In fact, the second graders responded as quickly to words divided after the second letter—a form to which they had presumably not been exposed before the experiment—as to the intact words with which they had practiced. Santa did not present the data for "different" judgments, nor did she break down the results by the type of stimulus. It would be valuable to know whether the superiority for divisions after the second letter was the same for words like *check,* in which the first two consonants correspond to a single phoneme and so are a unit (a grapheme) in the traditional sense, and for words like *blast,* in which the first two consonants correspond to two phonemes. Despite these limitations, Santa's results are consistent with the idea that children use vowel-final consonant units in reading. These units seem to be more natural than initial consonant-vowel units. Just as the vowel of a spoken syllable is more closely linked to the consonant(s) that come(s) after it than to the consonant(s) that come(s) before, the vowel of a printed word seems to form a better unit with the following letter(s) than with the preceding one(s).

Research by Goswami (1986, 1988; Goswami & Bryant, this volume) has made a similar point. In one representative study, Goswami (1986) showed children a real-word "clue" and asked them to try to use this clue to read *related items* and *control items*. In the real-word condition, the related items and control items were real words. For instance, the clue word might be *beak*. Half of the related words shared the vowel and final consonant of the clue word. For example, the related work *peak* occurred with the clue word *beak*. The other half of the related words shared the initial consonant and vowel with the clue word. For example, the related word *bean* also occurred with the clue word *beak*. Control words, or those for which the clue was not expected to be helpful, included *lake* and *rain*. Beginning readers about 7 years old benefited from the presence of the clue word. They read more related items when a clue word was present than when no clue word was given. Importantly, this benefit was greater for words that shared the vowel and final consonant with the clue word than for words that shared the initial consonant and vowel with the clue word. Thus, *beak* was more helpful in deciphering *peak* than in deciphering *bean*. Goswami's experiment also included a nonsense word condition, in which the clue word *beak* was paired with nonwords like *beal* (initial CV shared), *neak* (final VC shared), and *pake* (control item). The results in the nonsense-word condition were similar to those in the real-word condition.

A group of 5-year-olds who could not yet read any words on a standardized reading test also participated in Goswami's (1986) experiment. Not surprisingly, these children did not do very well at decoding the related items even when a clue word was provided. However, the children succeeded more often on related items that shared a vowel-final consonant unit with the clue word (7.4% correct responses) than on related items that shared an initial consonant–vowel unit with the clue word (0.9% correct responses). Similar results were reported by Goswami (1988).

Goswami's finding that children typically benefit more from clue words that share their end letters with a CVC target (e.g., *beak–peak*) than clue words that share their beginning letters with a CVC target (e.g., *beak–bean*) has been interpreted in terms of the linguistic structure of speech. However, it is possible that the results have nothing to do with linguistic structure. Children may find it easier to make analogies that are based on the ends of words than analogies that are based on the beginnings of words. To address this question, Goswami (in press) compared children's ability to use clue words like *trim* as a basis for reading unknown words like *trot* with their ability to use clue words like *wink* as a basis for reading unknown words like *tank*. If analogies that are based on the ends of words are easier than analogies that are based on the beginnings of words, children should perform better on *wink–tank* than on *trim–trot*. If analogies that are based on onsets and rimes are more natural than analogies that are based on other units, children should perform better on *trim–trot* (which share an onset) than on *wink–tank* (which share part of a rime). The results generally supported the linguistic structure hypothesis.

Findings of Wise, Olson, and Treiman (1990) further suggested that segmenting printed words into onset and rime units helps children learn to pronounce the words, at least over the short term. In these studies, first graders were pretested for their ability to pronounce words like *pond* and *clap* presented on a computer screen. Then, during a training phase, children touched each word with a special pen. The orthographic segments were highlighted and a speech synthesizer simultaneously pronounced the segments. We compared two types of segmentation. In the onset/rime condition, the segments for *pond* were *p* and *ond* and the segments for *clap* were *cl* and *ap*. For example, the letter *p* was highlighted while the speech synthesizer pronounced /pə/; then the letters *ond* were highlighted and /and/ was pronounced. In the postvowel condition, the segments for *pond* were *po* and *nd* and the segments for *clap* were *cla* and *p*. After the onset/rime or postvowel training, children were retested on their ability to pronounce the words. A short-term posttest immediately followed each block of training; a long-term posttest was given at the end of the half-hour session. On the short-term posttest, children showed more improvement on words for which onset/rime segmentation training had been given than on words for which postvowel segmentation training had been given. A similar trend was seen on the long-term posttest, but the results were weaker than those for the short-term posttest.

Recent findings of Treiman et al. (1990) further supported the idea that children use onset and rime units in addition to grapheme and phoneme units when they decode nonwords. We asked first graders, good and poor third-grade readers, and adults to pronounce nonsense words like *tain, goach, goan,* and *taich*. The first two nonwords share their vowel-final consonant unit with a number of real words, including *rain, main,* and *coach*. The second two nonwords share their vowel-final consonant unit with few or no real words. If people use their knowledge of vowel-final consonant units to help them pronounce the nonwords, they should therefore do better on *tain* and *goach* than on *goan* and *taich*. In contrast, if people use only grapheme–phoneme correspondences to pronounce the nonwords, they should do equally well on *goan* and *taich* as on *tain* and *goach*. This is because the two types of nonwords contain the very same graphemes. All groups of subjects performed better on the nonwords with the more common vowel-final consonant units than on the nonwords with the less common vowel-final consonant units. This result supports the idea that vowel-final consonant units play a role in the pronunciation process. Indeed, the more real words that shared a nonword's vowel-final consonant unit, the fewer errors people made on the nonword. The number of real words that contained the nonword's initial consonant-vowel unit had no significant effect, suggesting that initial consonant-vowel units are less important than vowel-final consonant units. Children's performance was influenced by their knowledge of the grapheme-phoneme correspondences in the nonword as well as by the frequency of the nonword's vowel-final consonant unit. This result suggests that children use grapheme–phoneme correspondences in addition to vowel-final consonant units.

Indirect evidence for a role of onset and rime units in word pronunciation comes from findings that children's ability to pronounce a letter depends on the position of the letter within the word or syllable. According to the results of many studies with monosyllabic real and nonsense words (Fowler, Liberman, & Shankweiler, 1977; Seidenberg, Bruck, Fornarolo, & Backman, 1986; Shankweiler & Liberman, 1972; Treiman & Baron, 1981; Venezky, 1976), children misread consonants in final position more often than consonants in initial position. For example, children more often pronounce *n* correctly when it begins a syllable, as in *nud,* than when it ends a syllable, as in *dun.* If children relied only on grapheme–phoneme correspondences to pronounce the syllables, their success on *nud* would lead us to suppose that they knew the correspondence between the letter *n* and the phoneme /n/. That children sometimes misread *n* when it occurs in final position suggests that they use correspondences at the level of onsets and rimes. When decoding *nud,* children may use correspondences between initial *n* and the onset /n/ and between final *ud* and the rime /ʌd/. When decoding *dun,* children use correspondences between initial *d* and /d/ and between *un* and /ʌn/. Because children parse *nud* into *n* and *ud* and *dun* into *d* and *un,* the knowledge that initial *n* is pronounced as /n/ does not allow them to deduce that the final *n* in *un* is pronounced as /n/. To make such an inference—to acquire a link between *n* and /n/ that is valid for both initial and final *n*s— children may need to analyze rimes into their component phonemes. As I have shown, this is difficult for some children.

Consonants are especially hard to pronounce when they occur in initial clusters. In one experiment (Treiman, 1985a, Experiment 4), I asked first and second graders to pronounce nonsense words like *smoo, soom, kree,* and *keer.* The first graders in particular had more trouble on the nonwords with initial consonant clusters than on the nonwords without clusters. Using a strict criterion, according to which all of the phonemes had to be pronounced correctly for the response to be counted as correct, the first graders made an average of 74% errors on nonwords like *smoo* and 61% errors on nonwords like *soom.* Using a lenient criterion, according to which the pronunciation of the vowel was disregarded, the children made 60% errors on cluster items and 36% errors on noncluster items. If children use only grapheme–phoneme correspondences to decode the nonwords, they should perform equivalently on the two types of nonwords. Children who have a general rule that links the letter *m* to the phoneme /m/ should be able to apply this rule to the *m* of *smoo* and the *m* of *soom.* That children who can decode *soom* cannot always decode *smoo* suggests that the children use not only correspondences at the level of single phonemes but also correspondences at the level of onsets and rimes. Although children know the correspondence between single initial *s* and the onset /s/ and single initial *m* and the onset /m/, this knowledge does not necessarily allow them to deduce that initial *sm* corresponds to the complex onset /sm/. To make such an inference, children must be able to analyze /sm/ into /s/ and /m/—something that is difficult for many young children.

In sum, the data do not support the idea that children have only two options in reading words—memorized associations between whole words or syllables and their pronunciations on the one hand, and grapheme–phoneme correspondences on the other hand. Although units at these levels *do* play a role in the pronunciation process, children also use units that are intermediate in size between syllables and phonemes. Many possible intermediate-sized units exist, including initial consonant-vowel units like *bla* and vowel-final consonant units like *ast*. Although children may use initial consonant-vowel units to some extent (e.g., Zinna, Liberman, & Shankweiler, 1986), vowel-final consonant units are more important.

Why do children prefer orthographic units like *bl* and *ast* over orthographic units like *bla* and *st?* One hypothesis is that children favor *bl* and *ast* because these groups of letters correspond to the natural phonological constituents of the syllable. Many young children, even before they begin to read, are aware that the spoken syllable /blæst/ contains the onset /bl/ and the rime /æst/. When confronted with the printed word *blast,* children use orthographic units that symbolize the phonological units, namely *bl* and *ast*.

There is, however, an alternative explanation of why readers use units like *bl* and *ast*. People may prefer these units because they have relatively consistent pronunciations. In English, many vowels have more than one pronunciation. (Some consonants do too, but irregularity is more widespread for vowels.) For example, *ea* can be pronounced as /i/ (as in *beat*), /e/ (as in *steak*), or /ɛ/ (as in *head*). Descriptions of English orthography that emphasize correspondences between graphemes and phonemes, like Venezky's (1970), must acknowledge the several pronunciations of *ea* as a case of irregularity. However, when one considers the following consonant the irregularity becomes less blatant. For words that end in *eam* and *each,* for example, *ea* is always pronounced as /i/ in the large collection of words studied by Venezky. In *ead,* the /ɛ/ pronunciation is more likely. Although consideration of the following consonant often increases the degree to which one can predict the pronunciation of a vowel, consideration of the preceding consonant usually does not. For example, *a* has a stable pronunciation when followed by *ng* (*bang, sang, hang*) but has many different pronunciations when preceded by *c* (*cat, call, car;* Wylie & Durrell, 1970).

Although there has not yet been a systematic study of which multiletter units have the most consistent pronunciations, the observations just described suggest that the pronunciations of vowel-final consonant units are more stable than the pronunciations of initial consonant-vowel units. If descriptions of English orthography included correspondences involving larger units in addition to correspondences involving graphemes and phonemes, the pronunciations of words would be more predictable than usually thought. Thus, readers may parse printed words into an initial consonant unit and a vowel-final consonant unit because these units have relatively consistent pronunciations, not because these units correspond to the onsets and rimes of spoken syllables. However, this argument does not explain why Goswami's (1986, 1988) nonreaders benefited from shared

VCs but not shared CVs. These children, who could not read any words on a standardized reading test, had probably not yet learned that vowel-final consonant units are more reliable guides to pronunciation than initial consonant-vowel units. I suspect that the English writing system evolved in such a way that the final consonant influences the pronunciation of the vowel because spoken syllables are composed of an onset and a rime. The onset and rime units in the spoken language may help to explain *both* the nature of the writing system and the fact that people—even children with little previous reading experience—prefer vowel-final consonant units.

Standard dual process theories of reading maintain that readers pronounce novel strings of letters without reference to specific words that they know. They do so by means of rules that link print and speech at the level of phonemes. These theories do not include a role for units that are intermediate in size between single phonemes and whole words. The evidence that readers use orthographic units like *bl* and *ast* does not sit well with standard dual route theories. This, along with other limitations of the theories, has led to the postulation of new types of theories.

One new theory retains a central idea of dual process theory—that readers have a system of abstract rules by which they generate pronunciations for novel letter strings. In the modified view, however, the rules are not restricted to the level of phonemes and the level of whole words. Readers also use rules that are based on intermediate-sized units. I refer to models of this kind as *modified dual process models*. One model of this type is that of Patterson and Morton (1985).

Another view is that nonwords (and words) are pronounced by activating and synthesizing the pronunciations of similar known words. The processes used to pronounce novel letter strings are not sharply different in this view from the processes used to pronounce familiar words. For example, an unfamiliar letter string like *vaid* activates a set of familiar words that perhaps includes *paid, said,* and *vain*. The pronunciations of the activated words are in some way combined to yield a pronunciation for *vaid*. I refer to models of this type as *analogy models*. Glushko's (1979) model falls into this category. Seidenberg and Mc-Clelland (1989; see Seidenberg, this volume) recently implemented a related model.

There has been much debate between proponents of standard or modified dual process models and proponents of analogy models (see Humphreys & Evett, 1985). Although modified dual process models and analogy models superficially appear quite different, the issue of orthographic units is important in both types of models. According to modified dual process models, people read novel words by using correspondences between groups of letters and groups of phonemes. Do all possible multiletter units participate in such correspondences, or are some units more important than others? According to analogy models, people read novel words by activating known words that share letters with the novel stimulus. Are words that share certain groups of letters more highly activated than words that share other groups of letters? Until the modified dual process model and the analogy model are fleshed out by specifying which kinds of orthographic units are used, the models are incomplete and cannot be truly compared.

The research that I have reviewed suggests that multiletter units that correspond to onset and rimes are more important than other multiletter units. These results could be interpreted within modified dual process models by postulating that readers use rules that are based on units like *aid* rather than, or to a greater extent than, rules that are based on units like *vai*. Indeed, Patterson and Morton's (1985) model makes exactly this claim. The results could also be interpreted within analogy models by postulating that a nonword like *vaid* strongly activates words like *said* and *paid* but weakly activates, or does not activate at all, words like *vain*. Such a claim was made by Glushko (1979). Once assumptions about orthographic units are built into the models, modified dual process models and analogy models may turn out to be not all that different.

Seidenberg and McClelland's (1989) version of the analogy model, unlike Glushko's (1979), does not grant a special status to units like *aid*. According to Seidenberg and McClelland, any preference for units like *aid* over units like *vai* arises because the former units usually have more consistent pronunciations than the latter. As I have discussed, this view has difficulty explaining Goswami's (1986, 1988) finding that even young children prefer vowel-final consonant units to initial consonant-vowel units. This view also has difficulty explaining Treiman and Zukowski's (1988) finding that the *ai* of *vaid* is more likely to be pronounced as /ɛ/ than the *ai* of *saip*. Besides *said,* there are no other English words in which *sai* is pronounced as /sɛ/ or *aid* is pronounced as /ɛd/. Seidenberg and McClelland's model would seem to predict that words that share their initial letters with *said* would be as likely to elicit /ɛ/ pronunciations of *ai* as words that share their final letters with *said*. I tentatively conclude that vowel-final consonant units must be granted a special status in models of word recognition and pronunciation.

SYLLABLE STRUCTURE
AND CHILDREN'S SPELLING

In the case of spelling, as in the case of reading, researchers have assumed that two different processes are available to children (e.g., Ellis, 1982). First, children can use associations between single phonemes and single graphemes. They can spell /blo/ as *blow* on the basis of links from /b/ to *b*, /l/ to *l*, and /o/ to *ow*. Second, children can use associations between whole spoken words and whole printed words. They can memorize that /blo/ is spelled as *blow*. Dual process models of spelling have been criticized (e.g., Campbell, 1983) as have dual process models of reading. One problem with standard dual process models of spelling is that they do not include links from groups of phonemes to groups of graphemes. Theories of syllable structure can suggest which groups of phonemes are likely to play a role in spelling. Spellers may associate groups of phonemes that constitute natural units of the syllable with groups of graphemes.

Intrasyllabic units may be especially important for children learning to spell because of children's difficulty in analyzing intrasyllabic units into phonemes. Because a full analysis of spoken words into phonemes is beyond the capability of many young children, children may have trouble learning links from single phonemes to single graphemes. Consider a child who can divide /blo/ into /bl/ and /o/ but who has difficulty analyzing /bl/ into /b/ followed by /l/. This child may be able to spell single word-initial /b/ with *b* and single word-initial /l/ with *l,* but may be unable to deduce that the word-initial /bl/ cluster is spelled with *b* followed by *l.* Or, consider a child who is unable to analyze /ɛl/ into /ɛ/ plus /l/. This child may fail to spell /ɛl/ with an appropriate vowel letter followed by *l* or *ll.* Rather, the child may spell the unit /ɛl/ with the single letter *l,* as suggested by the letter's name.

As I pointed out earlier, the onset/rime division of the spoken English syllable seems to be reflected in the writing system. Vowel plus final consonant (or cluster) units appear to have more stable spellings than initial consonant (or cluster) plus vowel units. For example, /ay/ can be spelled in several ways, including *i* followed by final *e* (as in *file*), *y* (*my*), and *igh* (*fight*). Consideration of the consonant that follows /ay/ narrows the range of possible spellings. For example, /ay/ is often spelled with *igh* when followed by /t/ (*fight, sight, night*) or when at the end of a syllable (*sigh, nigh*). It is rarely spelled with *igh* when followed by a consonant other than /t/. In contrast, the consonant that precedes a vowel does not usually help to specify the vowel's spelling. These observations have not yet been subjected to a detailed test, but if they are correct one could suggest that the writing system itself reflects the onset/rime division of the syllable.

Several studies have implicitly assumed that children use onset and rime units in spelling without giving a theoretical rationale for this assumption. For example, Waters, Bruck, and Seidenberg (1985) found that good third-grade spellers had more success on words whose final VCs are spelled in the same way in all other rhyming words than on words whose final VCs are spelled in different ways in rhyming words. Thus, words like *dish* were easier to spell than words like *beef,* presumably because /š/ is always spelled as *ish,* whereas /if/ can be spelled as *eef, ief,* or *eaf.* These investigators did not consider whether the consistency of spelling of the initial CV has a similar effect. For example, /bɪ/ may be spelled in several ways, including *bi* as in *big, bee* as in *been,* and *bui* as in *build.* Does this variability make it difficult for children to spell words that begin with /bɪ/? According to the present hypothesis, variability in the spelling of initial CVs should be less harmful than variability in the spelling of rimes.

A study by Treiman and Zukowski (1988) is the only one, to my knowledge, to directly compare spellers' use of final vowel–consonant units and initial consonant-vowel units. This study was carried out with college students. We examined how often people spelled a phoneme like /ɛ/ as *ai*, as in the unusual real word *said*. People were asked to spell three types of nonwords—those like /vɛd/, in which /ɛ/ is followed by /d/, as it is in /sɛd/, those like /sɛp/, in which /ɛ/ is preceded by /s/, and those like /vɛp/, in which /ɛ/ is neither preceded by /s/ nor followed by /d/. Overall, *ai* spellings of /ɛ/ were quite infrequent. However, people produced more such spellings for nonwords like /vɛd/ than nonwords like /sɛp/ and /vɛp/. This result suggests that adults use rime units like /ɛd/ to a greater degree than onset plus vowel units like /sɛ/ in spelling.

Although a study like that of Treiman and Zukowski (1988) has not yet been done with children, recent evidence is consistent with the idea that children use intrasyllabic units in spelling. This evidence comes from two different sources. The first is children's spelling of onset clusters. The second is children's spelling of vowel-consonant units in rimes that match the names of letters. I discuss the two phenomena in turn.

Spelling of Onset Clusters

If children can analyze a spoken word like /blo/ into /bl/ and /o/ but have difficulty analyzing /bl/ into /b/ and /l/, they may err in spelling the /bl/ onset. Although they can spell single initial /b/ with *b* and single initial /l/ with *l*, they may be unable to deduce that /bl/ is spelled with *b* followed by *l*. Findings of several studies are consistent with this claim.

One sign that children have trouble spelling cluster onsets comes from a study of classroom writings produced by 43 first-grade children (Treiman, 1985b, 1991). These children were all taught by the same first-grade teacher; they were members of her class during two successive school years. The teacher used a *language-experience* approach to the teaching of reading and writing. Every morning the children spent about half an hour writing. They wrote on large sheets of unlined paper, accompanying their stories with pictures. They dictated what they had written to the teacher or the teacher's aide. The adult wrote what the children dictated on the child's paper, but did not point out or correct the child's spelling errors. The children were exposed to conventional spelling in this way and through their reading materials, but correct spelling was not stressed during the writing period. Children felt free to invent a spelling when they did not know the conventional spelling of a word. All the children whose spellings were studied were White, middle class, native speakers of English. None of the children were considered to have an articulation problem.

The collection of spellings from throughout the school year (which included both correctly spelled words and incorrectly spelled words) contained 425 instances of word-initial clusters. Of these, 390 contained two phonemes (e.g., /bl/) and 35 had three phonemes (e.g., /spr/). In many cases children spelled the clusters correctly, as in the first example of Table 4.3. Correct spellings occurred

TABLE 4.3
Examples of First Graders' Spelling of Words with Cluster Onsets

Child's Spelling	Standard Spelling
blo	blow
chrap	trap
skrach	scratch
bow	blow
sube	stubby
sret	street
set	street
aslep	asleep
hasak	haystack

in 259 of the 425 cases, or 66%. These correct spellings could arise for several reasons. Children may have memorized the conventional spelling of the whole word or of the cluster. Or, children may have analyzed the cluster into phonemes and spelled each phoneme with the correct letter. In 44 cases or 10% of the total, children represented all of the phonemes in the cluster but spelled one of them in an unconventional way. For example, the second error in Table 4.3 uses *ch* rather than *t* for the /t/ in /træp/. This error makes sense given the similarity in sound between /t/ before /r/ and /č/ (Barton et al., 1980; Read, 1975; Treiman, 1985c).

Almost all of the remaining spellings—114 of 425 or 27%—stemmed from failure to represent one or more phonemes of the cluster.[2] For two-phoneme initial clusters, children omitted the second phoneme of the cluster much more often than the first phoneme. There were 93 cases in which only the second phoneme of the cluster was omitted, 1 case in which only the first phoneme was omitted, and 1 case in which both phonemes were omitted. For three-phoneme initial clusters, the second phoneme alone was omitted 5 times, the third phoneme alone was omitted 10 times, and both the second and third phonemes were omitted 4 times. The first phoneme of a three-phoneme initial cluster was never omitted. Thus, children's most common type of error in spelling an initial cluster was failure to represent a phoneme. The omitted phoneme tended to be the second phoneme in the case of two-phoneme clusters and the second or third phoneme in the case of three-phoneme clusters.

Misspellings of word-initial consonant clusters also occur under the more controlled conditions of experiments (Bruck & Treiman, 1990; Marcel, 1980; Miller & Limber, 1985; Treiman, 1991). These errors are found for both real

---

[2]The remaining 8 spellings of word-initial clusters had a vowel between the consonants of a two-phoneme cluster. In 6 cases the vowel letter represented a vowel phoneme that occurred elsewhere in the word (e.g., *form* for *from*); in 2 cases an extra vowel was inserted (e.g., *pilad* for *played*).

words and nonsense words and for a wide variety of initial clusters. For example, kindergarteners and first graders who know that *p* represents /p/ and that *r* represents /r/, who can spell /poy/ with initial *p* and /roy/ with initial *r*, and who correctly pronounce /pr/, do not always spell /proy/ with initial *p* followed by *r* (Treiman, 1991). They sometimes leave out the *r*. First graders sometimes spell /ste/ (*stay*) and /se/ (*say*) alike, writing *say* for both. Although some children change their spellings when shown that they have written the two words alike, others claim that even though the two words sound different they are spelled in the same way (Treiman, 1991).

Before concluding that spelling errors like *say* for *stay* reflect the unitary nature of the syllable onset, some alternative explanations for these errors must be ruled out. Perhaps children sometimes omit the second (and third) phonemes of clusters because these are often the second (and third) phonemes of words. Phonemes that occur later in a word may be more susceptible to omission than phonemes that occur earlier in a word. If so, children should be as likely to omit the /l/ of *along* as the /l/ of *blow*, because /l/ is the second phoneme in both words. Children should be as likely to omit the /r/ of *garage* as the /r/ of *street*, because /r/ is the third phoneme in both words. The data do not support these predictions. In the spellings of the first graders from the language-experience classroom, the omission rates for consonants like the /l/ of *blow* and the /r/ of *street* (i.e., the second and third consonants of cluster onsets) far exceeded the omission rates for consonants like the /l/ of *along* and the /r/ of *garage* (i.e., consonants that are considered by linguists to be syllable-initial but not word initial; Treiman, 1985b). In an experiment with children reading and spelling at the second-grade level, children were more likely to omit the /m/ of /smi/ than the /m/ of /əmi'/ (Bruck & Treiman, 1990). Thus, whether a consonant is a single-phoneme onset (as in /əmi'/) or part of an onset cluster (as in /smi/) is an important determinant of omission rate when position in the stimulus is held constant.

Perhaps children sometimes fail to spell the second and third consonants of onset clusters because these consonants are often the liquids /r/ and /l/. Liquids may be more susceptible to omission than are the obstruents (e.g., /p/, /f/) that occur in the first positions of onset clusters. However, obstruents can occur in the second positions of onsets when the first consonant is /s/. I found a relatively high omission rate for the obstruents /p/, /t/, and /k/ when they occurred in the second positions of onset clusters (Treiman, 1985b). For example, children were much more likely to omit the /p/ of /sp/ than the /p/ of /pr/ or /pl/. The effects of linguistic structure far outweigh any effects of consonant type.

Further support for the linguistic structure hypothesis comes from the finding that omissions of the second consonants of cluster onsets do not just occur at the beginnings of words. Consider the word /pətro'l/ (*patrol*). According to most linguists, the syllables in this word are /pə/ and /trol/. The /tr/ cluster forms the onset of the second syllable. Psycholinguistic evidence from adults (Treiman &

Danis, 1988) supports this claim. Because /tr/ forms a syllable onset in /pətro'l/, children should sometimes misspell this word as *patol* or *pachol,* just as they sometimes misspell /trol/ as *tol* or *chol.* Errors like *parol* for *patrol* should be relatively uncommon, just as errors like *rol* for *troll* are. A recent study with first graders (Treiman, 1991) found that errors like *patol* and *pachol* do outnumber errors like *parol.* Apparently, omissions of the second consonant of an onset characterize onset clusters in general. They are not restricted to onset clusters at the beginnings of words.

To summarize, first graders who can spell syllable-initial /b/ with *b* and syllable-initial /l/ with *l* do not always spell syllable-initial /bl/ with *b* followed by *l.* They sometimes omit the *l,* spelling /bl/ with just *b.* These errors seem to arise because the children lack awareness that /bl/ consists of /b/ followed by/l/. Children consider /bl/ to be a unit rather than a sequence of two separate phonemes. They may use the letter *b* to stand for the entire unit because they consider /bl/ to be more similar to /b/ than to /l/, as adults appear to do (Stemberger & Treiman, 1986).

Use of Letter–Name Knowledge in Spelling of Rimes

I have argued that some first graders misspell onset clusters because they fail to appreciate the internal structure of these clusters. The spelling errors reflect children's difficulty analyzing intrasyllabic units of speech—onsets in this case—into their component phonemes. If this argument is correct, children's difficulties in analyzing other types of intrasyllabic units into phonemes should also affect their spelling. Earlier, I reviewed evidence that vowels and following consonants, or rimes, tend to behave as units. Findings with adults suggest that vowels and following liquids are particularly cohesive, perhaps because they make up the syllable's peak. Vowels and nasals show an intermediate degree of cohesiveness; vowels and following obstruents show even less cohesion. Are these aspects of syllable structure also reflected in children's spelling?

To address this question, I returned to the spellings produced by the first graders in the language-experience classroom. I asked how the children spelled words containing VC(C) sequences that match the name of a letter. For example, one child misspelled /farm/ (*farm*) as *frm.* Apparently, this child used *f* to stand for the phoneme /f/ and *m* to stand for the phoneme /m/. Rather than using a vowel letter to represent /a/ and a consonant letter to represent /r/, the child spelled the /ar/ sequence with the single letter *r.* This child seemed to use her knowledge that *r* is named /ar/ in spelling the word /farm/. Another child spelled *helped* as *hlpt,* employing *l* to stand for the entire /ɛl/ sequence. This error makes sense given that the name of the letter *l* is /ɛl/. Similar errors have been observed by Ehri (1984) and others.

Some investigators (e.g., Gentry, 1982; Henderson, 1980) have suggested that children pass through a stage in learning to spell during which they use a letter–name strategy whenever possible. During this stage, children spell all sequences of phonemes that make up the name of a letter with that letter. In contrast, I predict that letter–name spellings are more common for some letters than for others. Letter–name spellings should be most frequent when the phonemes in the letter's name are most cohesive. Thus, letter–name spellings should be especially common for *r* and *l*. As I have discussed, the vowel-liquid sequences that make up these letters' names are difficult to analyze into phonemes. Letter–name spellings should be less frequent for *m* and *n*, whose names contain a vowel phoneme followed by a nasal phoneme. Letter–name spellings should be even less frequent for *f, h, s,* and *x*. The names of these letters contain an obstruent consonant after the vowel. Vowel-obstruent sequences seem to be less cohesive than other vowel-consonant sequences.

With my first-grade sample, the results suggested, though not conclusively, that letter–name spellings are more frequent for some letters than for others. With /ar/ (*r*) and /ɛl/ (*l*), the first graders failed to include a vowel in their spelling in 26 of 156 cases, yielding a rate of 16.7% vowel omissions. Examples include the aforementioned *hlpt* for *helped* and *frm* for *farm*. With *m* and *n,* the vowel was omitted 33 of 316 times, for a rate of 10.4% vowel omissions. Examples are *hm* for *him* and *n* for *in*. Children only attempted 11 words that contained sequences corresponding to the letter names *f, h, s,* and *x*. In none of the 11 cases did they omit the vowel. Although the rate of vowel omissions appears to be highest for liquids, intermediate for nasals, and lowest for obstruents, the difference among these three categories only reached the .06 level of significance in a chi-square test. This was largely due to the small number of cases in the postvocalic obstruent category. As these results show, it can be difficult to draw firm conclusions about children's spelling only on the basis of naturalistic data. In this case, as in certain other cases, children do not choose to spell a large number of words of the kind one wishes to study.

In an attempt to overcome this limitation, I carried out an experiment with 22 first-grade children (mean age 6 years, 8 months) whose teacher did not employ a language-experience approach to the teaching of reading and writing. The children were all native speakers of English. They were tested during October and early November. The experiment began with a pretest. Children were shown the consonant letters *r, l, m, n, f,* and *s* and the vowel letters *a, e,* and *i*. Colored magnetic letters were used, and children were asked to give the name of each letter. The children knew all the letter names. The experimenter then explained that the child would be asked to spell some "words." She said that most were not real words but the child should try to spell them as best as he or she could. The child repeated each item before spelling it and the experimenter corrected any erroneous repetitions. For each item, the experimenter placed the first letter of the spelling on the magnetic board. The child was asked to finish the word using the letters *r, l, m, n, f, s, a, e,* and *i*. These letters were arranged haphazardly by the side of the board.

TABLE 4.4
Proportion of Errors in Three Categories in First Graders' Spellings Ending with Vowel-Liquid,
Vowel-Nasal, and Vowel-Obstruent Letter-Name Sequences

Type of Letter–Name Sequence	Examples	Proportion of Errors in Various Categories		
		Letter-Name Errors[a]	Vowel Errors[b]	Other Errors
Vowel-liquid	yar, vɛl	.45	.45	.11
Vowel-nasal	bɛm, vɛn	.07	.79	.15
Vowel-obstruent	pɛs, bɛf	.04	.92	.04

[a]CC misspellings in which both consonants are spelled correctly but the vowel is omitted.
[b]CVC misspellings in which both consonants are spelled correctly but the vowel is spelled incorrectly.

The test contained 24 items. There were three CVC syllables that ended with each of the letter–name sequences /ar/, /ɛl/, /ɛm/, /ɛn/, /ɛf/, and /ɛs/. Examples are shown in Table 4.4. The experimenter did not tell the child whether his or her spellings of these items were correct. There were also six filler items. These were syllables such as /fæn/ and /lɪf/ whose rimes did not correspond to the name of any letter. The experimenter helped the child to spell the fillers, thereby demonstrating that three-letter spellings consisting of a consonant, a vowel, and another consonant were correct for some items. The order of the 24 items was randomly chosen for each child.

On average, children produced correct spellings 44% of the time for the syllables with vowel-liquid letter–name sequences, 54% of the time for the vowel-nasal items, and 63% of the time for the vowel-obstruent items. Analyses of variance across subjects, $F(2, 42) = 3.62$, $p < .05$, and across stimuli, $F(2, 15) = 3.95$, $p < .05$, showed that the differences among the three types of syllables were reliable. Post hoc tests (Tukey's) were carried out for both the analysis by subjects and the analysis by items. Correct spellings were significantly more common for vowel-obstruent letter–name syllables like /bɛf/ and /pɛs/ than for vowel-liquid letter–name syllables like /yar/ and /vɛl/ ($p < .05$). This was true even though, judging from the Harris and Jacobson (1972) lists, words containing vowel-liquid letter–name sequences are more frequent than words containing vowel-obstruent letter–name sequences at the preprimer, primer, and first-grade levels. On the basis of their exposure to real words like *car* and *help,* children should have done best on nonwords like /yar/ and /vɛl/, not worst.

How do children misspell syllables like /yar/ and /vɛl/? Do they make many errors like *yr* and *vl*—errors that suggest the use of letter–name knowledge? To address this question I divided children's misspellings into three categories. The first type of error is *letter-name errors,* or spellings in which both consonants are spelled correctly but the vowel is omitted. As Table 4.4 shows, close to half of the children's errors on syllables with vowel-liquid letter–name sequences were of this type. Less than 10% of the errors on the other letter–name stimuli fell into this category. This difference was statistically significant across subjects, $F(2, 16) = 8.69$, $p < .005$; only those 9 children who made at least one error on all three types of stimuli were included in this and subsequent analyses across subjects; across stimuli, $F(2, 15) = 13.19$, $p < .001$. Post hoc tests showed that children made a higher proportion of letter–name errors on stimuli with vowel-liquid letter–name sequences than on stimuli with vowel-nasal or vowel-obstruent letter–name sequences, which were indistinguishable. Thus, letter–name misspellings are more common for r and l than for $m, n, f,$ and s.

Another type of error is a *vowel error*. Here, both consonants are spelled correctly. The vowel is also represented but with the wrong letter. Examples of vowel errors are *yer* for /yar/ and *baf* for /bɛf/. Vowel errors do not reveal an attempt to use a letter to spell all of the phonemes in its name. The proportion of such errors varied as a function of stimulus type; across subjects, $F(2, 16) = 12.26$; across stimuli, $F(2, 15) = 26.77$; $p < .001$ for both. As Table 4.4 shows, vowel errors were more common for stimuli with vowel-obstruent and vowel-nasal letter–name sequences than for stimuli with vowel-liquid letter–name sequences ($p < .05$).

Finally, *other errors* did not fit into either of the categories just described. They included spellings like *vai* for /vɛl/ and *ymn* for /yɛm/. The proportion of such errors did not vary for the three types of stimuli; across subjects, $F(2, 16) = 1.73$; $p = .21$; across stimuli, $F(2, 15) = 1.71$, $p = .22$.

These results suggest that letter–name spellings are not equally common for all letters, as has sometimes been implied (e.g., Gentry, 1982; Henderson, 1980). Rather, letter–name spellings vary in frequency with the phonological properties of the letters' names. These spellings are most common when the phonemes in a letter's name are highly cohesive, for example /a/ and /r/. Letter–name spelling errors are less common when the phonemes in a letter's name have a lower degree of cohesion, for example /ɛ/ and /s/.

According to the idea that syllables contain an onset and a rime, sequences like /ɛ/ and /s/ do form a unit, albeit a weaker one than /a/ and /r/. This is because a vowel and a following obstruent both belong to the syllable's rime. However, first graders seem to have little difficulty analyzing the vowel-obstruent unit into phonemes and spelling each phoneme with a separate letter. It may be that younger children would show a higher rate of letter–name errors with s and f. Although further research is needed, it appears that children's letter–name spellings can shed light on their grouping of phonemes within the syllable. Sequences like /ar/ are tightly bound and are difficult to analyze into individual phonemes. Consequently, children sometimes spell these sequences with a single letter.

Conclusions About Spelling

A phoneme's role in the syllable structure is important for spelling, just as it is for reading. Thus, children more often fail to spell the /l/ of /blo/ than the /l/ of /əlo'n/. They are more likely to omit the /ɛ/ of /vɛl/ than the /ɛ/ of /vɛs/. These results do not support the idea that children use only correspondences at the level of single phonemes to spell words. If so, omissions should not vary with the phoneme's role in the syllable structure. The results suggest that children use links between speech and print at the level of intrasyllabic units. Because of their difficulty in analyzing an onset like /bl/ into /b/ followed by /l/, children learn or invent a spelling for the entire /bl/ cluster. Because of their difficulty in analyzing the peak /ɛl/ into /ɛ/ plus /l/, children treat /ɛl/ as a unit for purposes of spelling.

At the earliest stages of learning to spell, it is possible that some children do not possess links between speech and print at the level of single phonemes. To such children, the knowledge that syllable-initial /t/ is spelled as *t,* syllable-final /æt/ is spelled as *at,* and syllable-final /ʌst/ is spelled as *ust* may be separate and unconnected facts. Only later may these children learn that /t/, wherever it occurs in the syllable, is generally spelled as *t.* Other children may use both correspondences at the level of single phonemes and correspondences at the level of larger units from the beginning. In either case, larger units play an important role in the spelling process.

Standard dual process models of spelling, which neglect correspondences between groups of phonemes and groups of graphemes, must therefore be rejected. In their place, one could propose a rule-based model that includes rules linking groups of phonemes to groups of graphemes as well as rules at the levels of syllables and phonemes. One could also propose an analogy model in which novel words are spelled by activating and synthesizing the spellings of known words (e.g., Campbell, 1983). Within each of these theoretical frameworks, it is important to determine which groups of phonemes are systematically linked to spellings. Theories of syllable structure can suggest some likely candidates.

IMPLICATIONS OF SYLLABLE STRUCTURE
FOR READING AND SPELLING INSTRUCTION

A number of investigators (e.g., Gough & Hillinger, 1980; Liberman, 1983) have suggested that children must be able to explicitly analyze spoken words into phonemes in order to master an alphabetic writing system. In this view, children who are equipped with phonemic analysis skills can learn links from graphemes to phonemes and vice versa. Without these skills, children have no recourse but to read and spell words (or syllables) as wholes. Support for the relationship between phonemic analysis ability and alphabetic knowledge comes from studies showing that phonemic analysis correlates with and predicts reading and spelling success (e.g., Lundberg, Olofsson, & Wall, 1980; Stanovich et al., 1984; Treiman & Baron, 1981). In addition, phonological awareness training helps children learn correspondences between printed and spoken words (e.g., Ball & Blachman, 1988; Bradley & Bryant, 1983; Byrne, this volume; Fox & Routh, 1984; Lundberg, Frost, & Peterson, 1988; Treiman & Baron, 1983).

If the goal of initial reading and spelling instruction is to teach correspondences at the level of single phonemes, and if these correspondences cannot be learned until children are able to analyze spoken syllables into phonemes, training in phonemic analysis should precede instruction in spelling–sound relationships. Reading and spelling instruction should begin when pupils can analyze syllables into phonemes and should focus on correspondences between graphemes and phonemes. Williams' (1980) program exemplifies this approach. After learning to analyze spoken words into syllables, children proceed to the analysis of syllables into phonemes. When children are able to segment spoken syllables like /bæt/ into phonemes, letters are introduced. The child learns the pronunciations of a small number of letters, including *b, a,* and *t.* Next, the child learns to decode words and nonwords like *bat* and *ab* that are made up of these letters as well as to spell syllables like /bæt/ and /æb/. Later, additional letters and more complex words are introduced.

An advantage of the approach just described is that it teaches children tools that they can use to read and spell large numbers of unfamiliar words. However, a disadvantage may lie in the assumption that the *only* such tools are rules that link graphemes and phonemes. Even if we grant that children must *eventually* learn correspondences between print and speech at the level of phonemes, instruction need not begin at the phoneme level. As I have argued, children's difficulty in analyzing syllables into phonemes makes it hard for them to learn and use grapheme–phoneme correspondences. The basic notion that print represents speech might be more easily understood, especially by children with poor phonological skills, if it were introduced by reference to a larger, more accessible unit of sound.

Rozin and Gleitman (1977) proposed to teach children that spoken words and printed words are related by starting at the level of syllables rather than at the level of phonemes. In their view, children can begin to learn about the relationships between print and speech *before* they are able to divide spoken words into phonemes. Once pupils in Rozin and Gleitman's program are able to segment familiar multisyllabic words into syllables, they are shown that spoken syllables can be represented visually. For example, /sænd/ is represented by a picture of sand; /wɪč/ is represented by a picture of a witch. These two pictures are combined to symbolize the spoken word /sændwɪč/. This phase of Rozin and Gleitman's program is intended to teach children that printed symbols stand for sounds and that these symbols can be put together to represent words and sentences. Rozin and Gleitman maintain that children grasp these concepts more easily when they are introduced at the level of the syllable than when they are introduced at the level of the phoneme. Only when children have achieved success at the syllable level does instruction in grapheme–phoneme relationships begin.

Rozin and Gleitman's use of higher-level units—in their case, syllables—to introduce the concept that print represents speech seems to be helpful. In their study, pupils from low-achieving populations learned this concept relatively easily, achieving fair success with the syllabary system. However, the concept did not readily transfer to the level of phonemes as Rozin and Gleitman had hoped. Although the idea of beginning with a level higher than the phoneme may be good, the syllable may not be the ideal choice for English. Because English has so many different syllables, children who memorize symbols for only a small number of syllables can decode only a limited number of words. The children will be unable to pronounce or spell new multisyllabic words that are composed of unfamiliar syllables. More seriously, the children will be unable to decode unfamiliar single-syllable words, which make up many of the words that beginning readers encounter (Harris & Jacobson, 1972). Thus, children who have difficulty going beyond the syllable level, as many of Rozin and Gleitman's pupils had, are poorly equipped to deal with the English writing system. These children will be better off than those who rely solely on whole-word memorization, in that they will be able to read and spell *some* words that have not been taught, but they will be unable to handle a wide variety of new words.

Rozin and Gleitman (1977), by concentrating on relationships between print and sound at the level of syllables, may have chosen a level that is too high. Their program may give children the idea that print and speech are related but may not give them the tools to read and spell large numbers of unfamiliar words. Williams (1980), by beginning at the level of single phonemes, may be using a level that is too low for at least some children. Although her program teaches skills that can be used to read and spell many new words, correspondences at the phoneme level are difficult for some children to grasp. If the syllable level is too high and the phoneme level is too low to serve as a good introduction to the English writing system, what level might be appropriate? The level of onsets and rimes, I suggest, may be a suitable candidate.

The idea that reading and spelling instruction could begin at the level of onsets and rimes is based on three assumptions. First, children have less difficulty analyzing spoken syllables into onsets and rimes than into phonemes. Second, the English writing itself embodies an onset/rime division of the syllable. Vowel plus final consonant (or cluster) units have relatively stable spellings. Third, beginning readers and spellers naturally link print and speech at the level of onsets and rimes. They often prefer correspondences at this level to correspondences at the phoneme level.

An onset/rime approach to reading and spelling would begin by teaching children to analyze spoken words into syllables. Next, pupils learn to analyze syllables into onsets and rimes. At this point, correspondences between print and speech at the level of onsets and rimes are introduced. It would be possible, perhaps beneficial, to teach a small number of words as sight words before this point. However, this preliminary instruction would not be designed to convey the idea that parts of printed words correspond to parts of spoken words in a predictable way. In an onset/rime approach to spelling, children analyze the spoken word /bɛl/ into /b/ and /ɛl/. They are taught that initial /b/ is spelled with b and that final /ɛl/ is spelled with ell. Likewise, they analyze the spoken word /šay/ into /š/ and /ay/, learning that initial /š/ is spelled with sh and that final /ay/ is spelled with (as one possibility) y. Children analyze /blæst/ into /bl/ and /æst/ and learn to spell the sequence /bl/ with the letters bl and the sequence /æst/ with the letters ast. A similar approach is used for reading. Children divide a printed word like blast into bl and ast and read it by means of correspondences between bl and /bl/ and ast and /æst/.

In some ways, the program just proposed is similar to traditional approaches that focus on correspondences at the level of phonemes. For example, children in phonics programs are taught that initial /b/ corresponds to b, that initial /š/ corresponds to sh, and that final /ay/ can correspond to y. In other ways, however, this program differs significantly from standard phonics approaches. Children memorize that /bl/ corresponds to bl in the same way that they memorize that /š/ corresponds to sh. Even though they may already know the correspondences between /b/ and b and /l/ and l, children are not expected to derive for themselves the correspondence between /bl/ and bl. As discussed earlier, young children have difficulty making such inferences; they sometimes misspell /bl/ with just the letter b. In the present view, children should be explicitly taught that /bl/ corresponds to bl. Likewise, children are taught that /ɛl/ corresponds to ell in the same way that they are traditionally taught that /oy/ corresponds to oy. Just as children in traditional phonics programs are not expected to deduce that oy is pronounced as /oy/ based on knowledge about the sounds of o and y (even though such a deduction is theoretically possible, given that /oy/ is a diphthong), children at this stage of the onset/rime program are not expected to deduce that ell is pronounced as /ɛl/.

Once children have achieved a certain degree of success at the level of onsets and rimes, correspondences between print and speech at the level of phonemes are introduced. Children are first trained to segment onsets and rimes of spoken syllables into phonemes. As I discussed earlier, theories of syllable structure can provide a basis for such training. Then children begin to learn correspondences between phonemes and graphemes. Children already know, for example, that the unit /sm/ is spelled as sm and that the unit /ɪm/ is spelled as im. Their attention is now drawn to the fact that the letter groups sm and im both contain the letter m. Because children have been taught to analyze /sm/ into /s/ plus /m/ and /ɪm/ into /ɪ/ plus /m/, they can notice that both groups of phonemes contain an /m/.

In this way, children begin to understand that the phoneme /m/ is generally represented with the letter *m*. As another example, once children are aware that the /æt/ rime of /bæt/ and /sæt/ consists of /æ/ followed by /t/, they can realize that syllable-final /t/ is represented with *t*, just as syllable-initial /t/ is. Thus, children in an onset-rime program are taught correspondences between phonemes and graphemes, but these correspondences are introduced only after correspondences at the level of onsets and rimes.

The proposed program shares an advantage with Williams' (1980) program in that it gives children tools that can be used to read and spell a relatively large number of unfamiliar words. If children at the onset/rime stage of the program know that /b/ is spelled as *b*, that /š/ is spelled as *sh*, and that /ɛl/ is spelled as *ell*, they can in principle spell the word /šɛl/ even if this word has not previously been taught. As another example, children who can read *men* and *bat* can deduce the pronunciations of *mat* and *Ben*. Because the inferences are based on onsets and rimes, they should be easier than inferences that are based on phonemes.

The proposed approach shares an advantage with Rozin and Gleitman's (1977) program as well. The concept that printed words symbolize spoken words is introduced by reference to a level that is more accessible than the level of phonemes. However, by focusing on correspondences at the level of onsets and rimes rather than the level of syllables, the proposed program may avoid one disadvantage of Rozin and Gleitman's approach—that children who know correspondences between a limited number of syllables and their pronunciations can read and spell relatively few new words. Children who know correspondences between a limited number of onsets and rimes and their pronunciations can, if the onsets and rimes are carefully selected, read and spell a fair number of new one-syllable words (see Wylie & Durrell, 1970). Even if children have difficulty progressing from the level of onsets and rimes to the level of phonemes, they can experience some success with unfamiliar words.

An onset/rime approach to reading and spelling instruction is not a completely novel idea. It is consistent with the common practice of teaching words in "word families." The families typically consist of words like *bat, cat,* and *hat*—words that share a rime rather than an initial CV. Theories of syllable structure provide a theoretical rationale for this practice. A program of reading and spelling instruction that is more fully and explicitly founded on what we know about syllable structure may well prove to be beneficial. Certainly, the idea is attractive enough to merit further study.

CONCLUSIONS

Many investigators have assumed that because the English writing system *can* be described, used, and learned at the level of phonemes, it *must* be described, used, and learned at this level. I have argued that these assumptions are not necessarily correct. Units larger than the phoneme and smaller than the syllable must also be considered. Descriptions of the English writing system have typically focused on correspondences between graphemes and phonemes. I have suggested that, by supplementing rules at this level with rules at higher levels, the number of apparent exceptions to the rules is reduced. The English writing system may be more predictable than usually thought when the level of onsets and rimes is taken into account. On the basis of traditional descriptions of the English writing system, it has been proposed that fluent readers parse printed words into graphemes. They use correspondences between graphemes and phonemes to generate pronunciations for the words. Similarly, spellers use links from phonemes to graphemes. I have argued that, in addition to correspondences at the level of phonemes and graphemes, readers and spellers also use correspondences that are based on higher-level units such as onsets and rimes. Finally, although children must eventually learn rules at the level of phonemes, such rules are not easy or natural in the early stages of learning to read and write. Children may more readily learn links between groups of letters and groups of phonemes. Reading and spelling instruction that begins with larger units may be more successful than instruction that begins at the phoneme level.

ACKNOWLEDGMENTS

Preparation of this chapter was supported by a Research Career Development Award from NICHD (HD20276). Thanks to Andrea Zukowski and Jennifer Gross for a careful reading of the manuscript.

REFERENCES

Backman, J., Bruck, M., Hébert, M., & Seidenberg, M. S. (1984). Acquisition and use of spelling–sound correspondences in reading. *Journal of Experimental Child Psychology, 38,* 114–133.

Ball, E. W., & Blachman, B. A. (1988). Phoneme segmentation training: Effect on reading readiness. *Annals of Dyslexia, 38,* 208–225.

Baron, J. (1979). Orthographic and word-specific mechanisms in children's reading of words. *Child Development, 50,* 60–72.

Barton, D., Miller, R., & Macken, M. A. (1980). Do children treat clusters as one unit or two? *Papers and Reports on Child Language Development, 18,* 93–137.

Bertelson, P., & de Gelder, B. (1989). Learning about reading from illiterates. In A. M. Galaburda (Ed.), *From reading to neurons* (pp. 1–23). Cambridge, MA: MIT Press.

Bowey, J. A. (1990). Orthographic onsets and rimes as functional units of reading. *Memory and Cognition, 18,* 419–427.

Bowey, J. A., & Francis, J. (1991). Phonological analysis as a function of age and exposure to reading instruction. *Applied Psycholinguistics, 12,* 91–121.

Bradley, L., & Bryant, P. E. (1983). Categorizing sounds and learning to read—a causal connection. *Nature, 301,* 419–421.

Bruck, M., & Treiman, R. (1990). Phonological awareness and spelling in normal children and dyslexics: The case of initial consonant clusters. *Journal of Experimental Child Psychology, 50*, 156–178.

Calfee, R. C., Chapman, R. S., & Venezky, R. L. (1972). How a child needs to think to learn to read. In L. W. Gregg (Ed.), *Cognition in learning and memory* (pp. 139–182). New York: Wiley.

Campbell, R. (1983). Writing nonwords to dictation. *Brain and Language, 19*, 153–178.

Clements, G. N., & Keyser, S. J. (1983). *CV phonology: A generative theory of the syllable.* Cambridge, MA: MIT Press.

Coltheart, M. (1978). Lexical access in simple reading tasks. In G. Underwood (Ed.), *Strategies of information processing* (pp. 151–216). Orlando, FL: Academic Press.

Davis, S. (1989). On a non-argument for the Rhyme. *Journal of Linguistics, 25*, 211–217.

Dow, M. L. (1987). *The psychological reality of sub-syllabic units.* Unpublished doctoral dissertation, Department of Linguistics, University of Alberta.

Ehri, L. C. (1984). How orthography alters spoken language competencies in children learning to read and spell. In J. Downing & R. Valtin (Eds.), *Language awareness and learning to read* (pp. 119–147). New York: Springer-Verlag.

Ellis, A. W. (1982). Spelling and writing (and reading and speaking). In A. W. Ellis (Ed.), *Normality and pathology in cognitive functions* (pp. 113–146). Orlando, FL: Academic Press.

Fowler, C. A., Liberman, I. Y., & Shankweiler, D. (1977). On interpreting the error pattern in beginning reading. *Language and Speech, 20*, 162–173.

Fox, B., & Routh, D. K. (1975). Analyzing spoken language into words, syllables, and phonemes: A developmental study. *Journal of Psycholinguistic Research, 4*, 331–342.

Fox, B., & Routh, D. K. (1984). Phonemic analysis and synthesis as word attack skills: Revisited. *Journal of Educational Psychology, 76*, 1059–1064.

Fudge, E. C. (1969). Syllables. *Journal of Linguistics, 5*, 253–286.

Fudge, E. (1987). Branching structure within the syllable. *Journal of Linguistics, 23*, 359–377.

Fudge, E. (1989). Syllable structure: A reply to Davis. *Journal of Linguistics, 25*, 219–220.

Gattuso, B., Smith, L. B., & Treiman, R. (1991). Classifying by dimensions and reading: A comparison of the auditory and visual modalities. *Journal of Experimental Child Psychology, 51*, 139–169.

Gentry, J. R. (1982). An analysis of developmental spelling in GNYS AT WRK. *The Reading Teacher, 36*, 192–200.

Glushko, R. (1979). The organization and synthesis of orthographic knowledge in reading aloud. *Journal of Experimental Psychology: Human Perception and Performance, 5*, 674–691.

Glushko, R. J. (1981). Principles for pronouncing print: The psychology of phonography. In A. M. Lesgold & C. A. Perfetti (Eds.), *Interactive processes in reading* (pp. 61–84). Hillsdale, NJ: Lawrence Erlbaum Associates.

Golinkoff, R. M. (1978). Phonemic awareness skills and reading achievement. In P. Murray & J. Pikulski (Eds.), *The acquisition of reading* (pp. 23–41). Baltimore, MD: University Park Press.

Goswami, U. (1986). Children's use of analogy in learning to read: A developmental study. *Journal of Experimental Child Psychology, 42*, 73–83.

Goswami, U. (1988). Orthographic analogies and reading development. *Quarterly Journal of Experimental Psychology, 40A*, 239–268.

Goswami, U. (in press). Learning about spelling sequences: The role of onsets and rimes in analogies in reading. *Child Development.*

Gough, P. B., & Hillinger, M. L. (1980). Learning to read: An unnatural act. *Bulletin of the Orton Society, 30*, 179–196.

Hardy, M., Stennett, R. G., & Smythe, P. C. (1973). Auditory segmentation and auditory blending in relation to beginning reading. *Alberta Journal of Educational Research, 19*, 144–158.

Harris, A. J., & Jacobson, M. D. (1972). *Basic elementary reading vocabulary.* London: Macmillan.

Henderson, E. H. (1980). Developmental concepts of word. In E. H. Henderson & J. W. Beers (Eds.), *Developmental and cognitive aspects of learning to spell: A reflection of word knowledge* (pp. 1–14). Newark, DE: International Reading Association.

Hockett, C. F. (1973). Where the tongue slips, there slip I. In V. Fromkin (Ed.), *Speech errors as linguistic evidence* (pp. 910–936). The Hague: Mouton. (Original work published 1967)

Hooper, J. B. (1972). The syllable in phonological theory. *Language, 48*, 525–540.

Humphreys, G. W., & Evett, L. J. (1985). Are there independent lexical and non-lexical routes in word processing? An evaluation of the dual-route model of reading. *Behavioral and Brain Sciences, 8*, 689–740.

Johnson, D. D., & Venezky, R. L. (1976). Models for predicting how adults pronounce vowel digraph spellings in unfamiliar words. *Visible Language, 10*, 257–268.

Kay, J. (1985). Mechanisms of oral reading: A critical appraisal of cognitive models. In A. W. Ellis (Ed.), *Progress in the psychology of language* (Vol. 2, pp. 73–105). London: Lawrence Erlbaum Associates.

Kirtley, C., Bryant, P., Maclean, M., & Bradley, L. (1989). Rhyme, rime, and the onset of reading. *Journal of Experimental Child Psychology, 48*, 224–245.

Knafle, J. D. (1973). Auditory perception of rhyming in kindergarten children. *Journal of Speech and Hearing Research, 16*, 482–487.

Knafle, J. D. (1974). Children's discrimination of rhyme. *Journal of Speech and Hearing Research, 17*, 367–372.

Lenel, J., & Cantor, J. (1981). Rhyme recognition and phonemic perception in young children. *Journal of Psycholinguistic Research, 10*, 57–67.

Leong, C. K., & Haines, C. F. (1978). Beginning readers' analysis of words and sentences. *Journal of Reading Behavior, 10*, 393–407.

Liberman, I. Y. (1983). A language-oriented view of reading and its disabilities. In H. Myklebust (Ed.), *Progress in learning disabilities* (Vol. 2, pp. 81–101). New York: Grune & Stratton.

Liberman, I. Y., Shankweiler, D., Fischer, F. W., & Carter, B. (1974). Explicit syllable and phoneme segmentation in the young child. *Journal of Experimental Child Psychology, 18*, 201–212.

Lundberg, I., Frost, J., & Petersen, O. -P. (1988). Effects of an extensive program for stimulating phonological awareness in preschool children. *Reading Research Quarterly, 23*, 263–284.

Lundberg, I., Olofsson, A., & Wall, S. (1980). Reading and spelling skills in the first school years predicted from phonemic awareness skills in kindergarten. *Scandinavian Journal of Psychology, 21*, 159–173.

MacKay, D. G. (1972). The structure of words and syllables: Evidence from errors in speech. *Cognitive Psychology, 3*, 210–227.

Maclean, M., Bryant, P., & Bradley, L. (1987). Rhymes, nursery rhymes, and reading in early childhood. *Merrill-Palmer Quarterly, 33*, 255–281.

Marcel, T. (1980). Phonological awareness and phonological representation: Investigation of a specific spelling problem. In U. Frith (Ed.), *Cognitive processes in spelling* (pp. 373–403). San Diego, CA: Academic Press.

Miller, P., & Limber, J. (1985, October). *The acquisition of consonant clusters: A paradigm problem.* Paper presented at the Boston University Conference on Language Development, Boston, MA.

Morais, J., Cluytens, M., & Alegria, J. (1984). Segmentation abilities of dyslexics and normal readers. *Perceptual and Motor Skills, 58*, 221–222.

Patterson, K. E., & Morton, J. C. (1985). From orthography to phonology: An attempt at an old interpretation. In K. E. Patterson, J. C. Marshall, & M. Coltheart (Eds.), *Surface dyslexia: Neuropsychological and cognitive studies of phonological reading* (pp. 335–359). Hillsdale, NJ: Lawrence Erlbaum Associates.

Read, C. (1975). *Children's categorization of speech sounds in English* (NCTE Research Report No. 17). Urbana, IL: National Council of Teachers of English.

Rosner, J. (1974). Auditory analysis training with prereaders. *The Reading Teacher, 27,* 379–384.

Rozin, P., & Gleitman, L. R. (1977). The structure and acquisition of reading II: The reading process and the acquisition of the alphabetic principle. In A. S. Reber & D. L. Scarborough (Eds.), *Toward a psychology of reading: The proceedings of the CUNY conferences* (pp. 55–141). Hillsdale, NJ: Lawrence Erlbaum Associates.

Santa, C. M. (1976–1977). Spelling patterns and the development of flexible word recognition strategies. *Reading Research Quarterly, 12,* 125–144.

Santa, J. L., Santa, C. M., & Smith, E. E. (1977). Units of word recognition: Evidence for the use of multiple units. *Perception and Psychophysics, 22,* 585–591.

Seidenberg, M. S., Bruck, M., Fornarolo, G., & Backman, J. (1986). Word recognition skills of poor and disabled readers: Do they necessarily differ? *Applied Psycholinguistics, 6,* 161–180.

Seidenberg, M. S., & McClelland, J. L. (1989). A distributed, developmental model of word recognition and naming. *Psychological Review, 96,* 523–568.

Selkirk, E. O. (1982). The syllable. In H. Van der Hulst & N. Smith (Eds.), *The structure of phonological representations, Part II* (pp. 337–383). Dordrecht, Holland: Foris.

Shankweiler, D., & Liberman, I. Y. (1972). Misreading: A search for causes. In J. F. Kavanagh & I. G. Mattingly (Eds.), *Language by ear and by eye: The relationships between speech and reading* (pp. 293–317). Cambridge, MA: MIT Press.

Shattuck-Hufnagel, S. (1983). Sublexical units and suprasegmental structure in speech production planning. In P. F. MacNeilage (Ed.), *The production of speech* (pp. 109–136). New York: Springer-Verlag.

Stanovich, K. E., Cunningham, A. E., & Cramer, B. (1984). Assessing phonological awareness in kindergarten children: Issues of task comparability. *Journal of Experimental Child Psychology, 38,* 175–190.

Stemberger, J. P. (1983). *Speech errors and theoretical phonology.* Bloomington: Indiana University Linguistics Club.

Stemberger, J. P., & Treiman, R. (1986). The internal structure of word-initial consonant clusters. *Journal of Memory and Language, 25,* 163–180.

Taraban, R., & McClelland, J. L. (1987). Conspiracy effects in word pronunciation. *Journal of Memory and Language, 26,* 608–631.

Treiman, R. (1984). On the status of final consonant clusters in English syllables. *Journal of Verbal Learning and Verbal Behavior, 23,* 343–356.

Treiman, R. (1985a). Onsets and rimes as units of spoken syllables: Evidence from children. *Journal of Experimental Child Psychology, 39,* 161–181.

Treiman, R. (1985b). Phonemic analysis, spelling, and reading. In T. Carr (Ed.), *New directions for child development: The development of reading skills* (Vol. 27, pp. 5–18). San Francisco: Jossey-Bass.

Treiman, R. (1985c). Phonemic awareness and spelling: Children's judgments do not always agree with adults'. *Journal of Experimental Child Psychology, 39,* 182–201.

Treiman, R. (1986). The division between onsets and rimes in English syllables. *Journal of Memory and Language, 25,* 476–491.

Treiman, R. (1988). The internal structure of the syllable. In G. Carlson & M. Tanenhaus (Eds.), *Linguistic structure in language processing* (pp. 27–52). Dordrecht, The Netherlands: Kluwer.

Treiman, R. (1991). Children's spelling errors on syllable-initial consonant clusters. *Journal of Educational Psychology.*

Treiman, R., & Baron, J. (1981). Segmental analysis ability: Development and relation to reading ability. In G. E. MacKinnon & T. G. Waller (Eds.), *Reading research: Advances in theory and practice* (Vol. 3, pp. 159–198). San Diego, CA: Academic Press.

Treiman, R., & Baron, J. (1983). Phonemic-analysis training helps children benefit from spelling-sound rules. *Memory and Cognition, 11,* 382–389.

Treiman, R., & Chafetz, J. (1987). Are there onset- and rime-like units in written words? In M. Coltheart (Ed.), *Attention and performance XII: The psychology of reading* (pp. 281–298). Hillsdale, NJ: Lawrence Erlbaum Associates.

Treiman, R., & Danis, C. (1988). Syllabification of intervocalic consonants. *Journal of Memory and Language, 27,* 87–104.

Treiman, R., Goswami, U., & Bruck, M. (1990). Not all nonwords are alike: Implications for reading development and theory. *Memory and Cognition, 18,* 559–567.

Treiman, R., & Zukowski, A. (1988). Units in reading and spelling. *Journal of Memory and Language, 27,* 466–477.

Treiman, R., & Zukowski, A. (1991). Levels of phonological awareness. In S. A. Brady & D. P. Shankweiler (Eds.), *Phonological processes in literacy: A tribute to Isabelle Y. Liberman* (pp. 67–83). Hillsdale, NJ: Lawrence Erlbaum Associates.

Tunmer, W. E., & Bowey, J. A. (1984). Metalinguistic awareness and reading acquisition. In W. E. Tunmer, C. Pratt, & M. L. Herriman (Eds.), *Metalinguistic awareness in children* (pp. 144–168). Berlin: Springer-Verlag.

Venezky, R. L. (1970). *The structure of English orthography.* The Hague: Mouton.

Venezky, R. L. (1976). *Theoretical and experimental base for teaching reading.* The Hague: Mouton.

Vergnaud, J. -R., & Halle, M. (1979). *Metrical phonology.* Unpublished manuscript.

Waters, G. S., Bruck, M., & Seidenberg, M. S. (1985). Do children use similar processes to read and spell words? *Journal of Experimental Child Psychology, 39,* 511–530.

Williams, J. P. (1980). Teaching decoding with an emphasis on phoneme analysis and phoneme blending. *Journal of Educational Psychology, 72,* 1–15.

Wise, B. W., Olson, R. K., & Treiman, R. (1990). Subsyllabic units in computerized reading instruction: Onset-rime versus postvowel segmentation. *Journal of Experimental Child Psychology, 49,* 1–19.

Wylie, R. E., & Durrell, D. D. (1970). Teaching vowels through phonograms. *Elementary English, 47,* 787–791.

Yopp, H. K. (1988). The validity and reliability of phonemic awareness tests. *Reading Research Quarterly, 23,* 159–177.

Zinna, D. R., Liberman, I. Y., & Shankweiler, D. (1986). Children's sensitivity to factors influencing vowel reading. *Reading Research Quarterly, 21,* 465–480.

Reconceptualizing the Development of Sight Word Reading and Its Relationship to Recoding

Linnea C. Ehri
City University of New York Graduate School

OVERVIEW

Many researchers and teachers have adopted a dual route view to explain how readers read words out of context. This view holds that words are read in one of two ways, either by phonological recoding or by sight. Phonological recoding[1] involves translating letters into sounds by application of letter–sound rules and then recognizing the identities of words from their pronunciations. Sight word reading involves reading words by establishing direct connections between the visual forms of words seen in print and their meanings in memory as a result of much practice reading the words. According to dual route theory, the connections formed are arbitrary rather than systematic, they are learned by rote, and they do not involve letter–sound relations.

This view of sight word reading has several weaknesses. Most importantly, the evidence collected to support it is essentially negative evidence against phonological recoding as an explanation. Few studies have been conducted with spellings that are totally arbitrary and that lack letter–sound relations to show that visual-semantic connections and not visual-phonological connections form the basis of sight word reading. Furthermore, this view does not explain why it is necessary for beginners to have phonological awareness and phonological recod-

---

[1]In this chapter, the term *recoding* rather than decoding is used to refer to the process of transforming spellings into pronunciations by application of letter–sound rules. Recoding is preferred to decoding because it has this more specific meaning. The term *decoding* is ambiguous and may be used either as a synonym for recoding or as a reference to the general process of reading printed words either by recoding or by sight.

ing skill in order to learn to read words, yet this necessity has been demonstrated by research.

In this chapter I propose an alternative conception of sight word reading that involves establishing systematic visual-phonological connections between the spellings of words and their pronunciations in memory. Readers use their knowledge about letter–sound relations to form these connections. This process differs from phonological recoding in that word-specific connections rather than translation rules are used to read words. As a result, the words are accessed directly in memory from their printed forms rather than indirectly from pronunciations, and information about the spellings of specific words is retained in memory and amalgamated with information about pronunciations and meanings. It is this amalgam that is accessed directly when sight words are seen. My conception of sight word reading differs from the sight word route of dual route theory in that the kind of connection enabling readers to find specific words in memory is a systematic connection between spellings and pronunciations rather than an arbitrary connection between spellings and meanings. Evidence is drawn from several studies to support these claims.

I then consider how sight word reading develops according to my perspective. Three successively emerging phases are proposed, each distinguished by the kind of word-specific connection that is established between visual forms and word identities in memory. During the logographic or visual cue reading phase, readers know little about the letter–sound system so they read words by rote memorizing connections between visual cues and meanings of words. During the phonetic cue reading phase, readers use their rudimentary knowledge of letter names or sounds to form partial connections between spellings and pronunciations. During the cipher reading phase, readers use their phonemic segmentation and phonological recoding skill to form complete connections that secure the entire spelling of the word in memory as a visual symbol for phonemic units in its pronunciation.

SIGHT WORD READING ACCORDING
TO DUAL ROUTE THEORY

What are some common views about sight word reading? Just about everyone agrees that readers recognize sight words as single holistic units without segmenting and attending to letters one at a time and without sounding out and blending letters sequentially. One sign that readers are reading words by sight is that they read the words immediately without hesitation.

Authorities differ in their views about the kinds of words that are read by sight (Hood, 1977). To some people, sight words are the entire set of words that a reader has learned to access in memory. Others restrict the term to irregularly spelled words that cannot be read accurately through phonological recoding, for example, *island* and *sword*. Still others restrict sight words to high frequency words that comprise a reader's core vocabulary, for example, function words and words on the Dolch (1939) list. Because high frequency words are practiced so often, they are thought to be read as wholes instantly by accessing memory.

Authorities also differ in their view about the factors that determine whether readers employ sight word access or phonological recoding to read words. At the outset of learning to read, whether beginners use one or the other approach is thought by some to depend on how the beginners are taught to read (Barr, 1972, 1974–1975; Beck, 1981) and whether they practice reading words that conform to the phonics rules they are taught (Juel & Roper/Schneider, 1985). In a phonics instructional program the goal is to teach children to read words by phonological recoding. This is best accomplished by having children read words that are regularly spelled and that contain letter–sound relations that the children have been taught (e.g., *at, sat, bat, mat, fat, rat;* Richek, 1977–1978). In a whole-word, meaning emphasis program the goal is to teach children to recognize word meanings by sight. This is accomplished by teaching children to read visually distinctive words (e.g., *boy, children, farm, house, rabbit, wagon;* Richek, 1977–1978) and by having them read and reread these words in meaningful contexts.

According to other authorities, whether beginning readers read words by sight or by phonological recoding depends not only on how they were taught to read but also on their skills and strategies, their stage of development, and their prior experience reading the words in question (Ehri, 1978, 1987; Gough & Hillinger, 1980; Marsh, Friedman, Welch, & Desberg, 1981). Children start out using sight word memory and then add recoding to their repertoires when this skill is acquired. They use sight word memory for words they have read before several times, and they use recoding for words they have never read and words seen infrequently. Phonics-trained readers may acquire superior recoding skill, especially at first, but those children in a whole-word program who make progress in learning to read also acquire recoding skill. Even though they are not taught phonics rules, whole-word trained readers are thought to induce letter–sound relations implicitly as they practice reading and thereby learn how to recode (Gough & Hillinger, 1980). Also, concurrent instruction in spelling may help whole-word trained readers improve their recoding skill (Ehri & Wilce, 1987a; Uhrey, 1989).

One issue that has divided researchers is whether and how the sight word reading of more mature readers who have learned to recode differs from the sight word reading of immature beginning readers who cannot recode. Another issue is what happens when words that are recoded several times become sight words. Does the prior recoding influence the sight word reading process, or are the two ways of reading words established independently?

Information processing theorists have described the mental processes used to read words by sight memory and by recoding. According to one popular view, dual route theory, readers can read words using one of two routes into their mental lexicons (i.e., dictionary of words stored in memory). The first is a visual route that leads directly into the lexicon to the word's meaning. The second is a phonological route that leads indirectly into the lexicon; readers first apply letter–sound translation rules to derive the word's pronunciation and then find a word matching this pronunciation in the lexicon (Baron, 1977, 1979; Barron, 1981, 1986; Bryant & Bradley, 1980; Coltheart, Davelaar, Jonasson, & Besner, 1977; Frith, 1979; Treiman & Baron, 1983). These two routes are considered to operate independently when words are read, with the visual route being faster than the phonological route. A difference in speed occurs because, in recoding words, readers must process all of the letters in their proper order to derive the word's pronunciation and then use the pronunciation to access meaning, whereas in sight word reading readers can simply process the visual cues to access meaning.

According to dual route theory, words are read visually by retrieving associations between the visual form of the word and its meaning. These associations are already stored in memory from previous readings of the word. The visual-spatial cues in these associations may be some of the letters or the sequence of letters recognized as a legal or frequent orthographic pattern. The cues may involve boundary letters plus configuration or length information, or they may even be nonalphabetic. However, no sounds or recoding rules are involved in the associations. Thus, the associations are arbitrary and must be learned by rote. Visual-meaning associations are formed in memory through repetition and practice. Learning them takes substantial time, like learning Chinese characters, because the visual cues in the associations are word-specific and unsystematic. Phonological information about words recognized by sight is said to be activated *postlexically*. That is, pronunciations of the words are not retrieved from memory until after their meanings are identified.

The other route in dual route theory is phonological. Printed words are converted into pronunciations through the application of letter–sound rules or other kinds of recoding rules. The pronunciations are then used to enter the lexicon and retrieve meanings. As readers improve at phonological recoding, they automatically apply letter–sound rules to many different spelling patterns. They execute this process fairly rapidly although never as rapidly as visual word reading.

This difference in speed is evidenced by the common finding that readers are slower at reading words they have never seen before than words that are familiar (Ehri & Wilce, 1983; Perfetti & Hogaboam, 1975). According to dual route theory, although a word may be phonologically recoded several times, this route never becomes part of the reader's memory for that specific word. Rather each time the word is read, the reader repeats the same routine of applying letter–sound rules, deriving a pronunciation, and using the pronunciation to find the word in lexical memory.

Many studies have been conducted to determine which route readers use to read words. Generally, phonological recoding is not used to read words that the reader has read several times before (Gough, 1984). This is true even among children as young as first grade (Barron & Baron, 1977). Phonological recoding is used mainly to read unfamiliar words, low frequency words, difficult words, and nonsense words that have not received sufficient exposure to enter memory. Once words become familiar in print they are read by sight.

FLAWS AND SOURCES OF CONFUSION IN THE DUAL ROUTE VIEW

Until recently the dual route view of word reading has dominated the thinking of many researchers. Most previous criticisms of dual route theory have concerned the phonological route. However, its view of sight word reading is equally inadequate as an explanation not only of how words are read by sight but also of how beginners learn to read words by sight. I review some of the weaknesses of this theory and then propose an alternative view that is more in accord with the evidence. (For more extensive critical discussions of the theory, see Barron, 1986; Glushko, 1979, 1981; Henderson, 1982; Humphreys & Evett, 1985.)

Dual route theorists propose a very specific definition of sight word reading that makes certain claims about how words are stored in memory. However, results of their studies do not provide direct evidence for these claims. The evidence is mainly negative indicating that words are not read by phonological recoding. For example, Barron and Baron (1977) had subjects decide whether pairs of pictures and words were similar in meaning. Subjects had to repeat the word *double* while performing the task. If readers are phonologically recoding the words to access their meanings, then repeating *double* should interfere because it uses the same speech processes as recoding does. Results failed to reveal any effects of interference. From this finding of no difference it was concluded that readers use the visual-semantic route of dual route theory to read words, not the phonological route. However this is not the only sight word theory that fits the data. There are other possibilities, one of which is described in the next section.

A conceptual weakness of dual route theory is its view of how sight words are learned. According to dual route theory, rote memory underlies the learning of sight words, particularly irregularly spelled words but also regularly spelled words. It is reasoned that because words like *island* and *sword* contain unpronounced letters, they cannot be recoded successfully by means of letter–sound translation rules and therefore must be memorized. Although memory is clearly involved, I question whether the memory process is a rote process. Rote memory is used to learn relationships that are arbitrary and unsystematic. However, few English word spellings are totally arbitrary in the sense that they contain no letters that conform to English letter–sound spelling conventions. Most spellings that are considered irregular are only partially so. For example, *island* and *sword* each contain only one irregular letter. All the other letters correspond to sounds in the words' pronunciations. In using memory processes to read these words, readers are more apt to take advantage of any available systematic relations than to ignore them and rote memorize the entire form.

In fact, studies comparing the reading of irregularly spelled words, regularly spelled words, and nonsense words suggest that irregular spellings are processed similarly to regular spellings and also similarly to nonsense spellings that must be recoded rather than read by sight. Treiman and Baron (1983) found very high positive correlations between readers' skill in reading regularly and irregularly spelled words, $r = .73$, and in reading irregularly spelled words and nonsense words, $r = .67$. If readers ignore systematic relations when learning to read irregular spellings as sight words, then one would not expect such high correlations. Also, Lovett (1987) found no difference in normal readers' speed to read regularly spelled and irregularly spelled words that were known by sight to these children (i.e., the words were high frequency), indicating that the two words types were processed similarly.

In sum, dual route theory's claim that rote memory is used in learning to read words by sight appears illogical. Irregular spellings as well as regular spellings of words contain letter–sound relations that readers recognize as systematic. It is highly unlikely that these relations are ignored in favor of rote memory. An explanation is presented shortly describing how readers use these systematic relations in learning to read both irregular and regular spellings by sight.

Another shortcoming of dual route theory is that it cannot adequately accommodate the evidence regarding the course of development of word reading skill. Various studies indicate that phonological recoding is necessary to learn how to read. English is an alphabetic system. Beginners need to learn how the system works in order to succeed in learning to read (Biemiller, 1970; Chall, 1983; Gleitman & Rozin, 1977; Gough & Hillinger, 1980; Gough & Tunmer, 1986; Liberman, Shankweiler, Liberman, Fowler, & Fischer, 1977; Perfetti, 1985; Rozin & Gleitman, 1977). However, other evidence indicates that once readers become familiar with the printed forms of words, they stop recoding them and read them by sight (Gough, 1984; Stanovich, 1986). As children gain reading experience, fewer and fewer words are read by recoding and more and more are read by sight. This begins to happen as early as first grade (Barron & Baron, 1977). Because dual route theory conceptualizes sight word reading as a separate, visually based route that neither involves nor requires phonological recoding, the theory cannot explain why beginning readers need to learn how to phonologically recode words to learn to read. Why not just have them practice reading words by sight from the outset?

Jorm and Share (1983) have offered one explanation for the value of phonological recoding. They suggest that being able to recode enables beginners to read unfamiliar words successfully on their own, thereby providing themselves with many "positive learning trials" in which to set up visual-semantic routes for the words in memory. However, this contribution does not make phonological recoding a necessity for learning to read, only a facilitator. It allows the possibility that children who lack recoding skill can still learn to read words effectively although they may progress more slowly and may depend on external aids, either a literate tutor to identify unfamiliar words or informative context to enable them to guess the unfamiliar words. However, evidence shows that children who cannot phonologically recode do not become good readers (Gough & Tunmer, 1986). Dyslexics are typically deficient in phonological recoding skill (Firth, 1972; Vellutino, 1979) and also in spelling skill that requires phonological knowledge (Ehri, 1986). Phonological awareness along with letter knowledge are the strongest predictors of beginning reading achievement ($r = .58$ to $.68$), stronger even than intelligence ($r = .39$ to $.41$; Share, Jorm, Maclean, & Matthews, 1984; Stanovich, this volume). This evidence suggests that phonological recoding skill is not a mere facilitator but rather is a prerequisite for becoming a successful reader. Dual route theory cannot explain how this could be.

AN ALTERNATIVE CONCEPTION OF SIGHT WORD LEARNING

It is puzzling that researchers have accepted the idea of a direct, independent, phonologically devoid, visual route into the lexicon given that the evidence bears primarily on the phonological recoding side of the theory. Even those who would like to believe that readers use phonological recoding to read words (Gough, 1972) have accepted dual route theory's description of visual processing (Gough, 1984).

It is possible to devise an alternative explanation of sight word reading that does not eliminate phonological processes but rather only omits phonological recoding, which evidence has shown to not be involved (Barron & Baron, 1977; Gough, 1984). Suppose that a reader encounters an unfamiliar word in a story and phonologically recodes it. The word recurs several times. At some point the reader's memory for that specific word should take over and eliminate the need for phonological recoding. What processes are being used at this point to read the word from memory?

According to dual route theory, a nonphonological visual-semantic route is being used. However, given that letter–sound relations were used initially to read the word, why should they drop out of processing when memory takes over? Why should arbitrary, nonphonological, visual-semantic connections form the newly established route into memory? Being arbitrary, the visual cues are much harder to associate with particular words in memory in order to know how to read them. In contrast, letter–sound cues are not arbitrary. They connect the visual form of the word directly to its pronunciation in memory, because readers know how to interpret letters as symbols for sounds.

An alternative conceptualization to the visual-semantic route of dual route theory is a visual route that is paved with phonological information leading into lexical memory.[2] Because letter–sounds were used initially to recode the word, it makes good sense that they would be retained and would participate in the reading-by-memory operation. Setting up a visual-phonological route into memory involves forming specific connections between visual cues seen in the word and its pronunciation stored in memory. The visual cues consist of a sequence of letters. The connections linking the letters to the pronunciation are formed out of readers' knowledge of letter–sound correspondences and other orthographic regularities linking print to speech. When readers see a word they have never seen before they phonologically recode the word. This begins the process of setting up a visual-phonological route for that word leading from its spelling directly to its pronunciation in memory. Once such routes are set up, readers can look at spellings and immediately retrieve their specific pronunciations without resorting to translation rules and recoding.

To clarify the distinction between this visual-phonological route for reading sight words and the visual-semantic route depicted in dual route theory, a diagram has been created that portrays the visual cues in the printed word and how they are connected to parts of the word in memory. *The matter of connections is a crucial one, for this is what determines how easy it is for readers to retrieve words in memory from the visual forms that they see.* Connections are formed and set up in memory from prior experiences reading words. In Fig. 5.1, connections are portrayed by solid and dotted lines; the solid lines represent connections that are formed out of *systematic* prior knowledge that makes the connections predictable, and the dotted lines represent connections that are *arbitrary* and rote memorized. The lines connect various types of visual units—individual letters, letter clusters, and whole spellings—to various kinds of units in lexical memory—individual phonemes, onset consonants, rime stems, whole pronunciations of words, and also meanings of words. Each unit is depicted by a line that encircles the unit.

Readers who have full knowledge of how the orthographic system symbolizes units in speech form many systematic connections linking visual spelling units seen in print to pronunciations stored in memory. These connections depicted in Fig. 5.1 form the visual-phonological route. As a result of prior recoding experiences with the word, individual letters are connected to individual phonemes within the word. Knowledge of letter–sound correspondences is used to form these connections. Also, individual letters are connected to the whole pronunciation because each letter–phoneme connection occupies a position within the

---

[2]I express gratitude to my colleague Professor Carl Spring at the University of California, Davis, for discussing this theory with me.

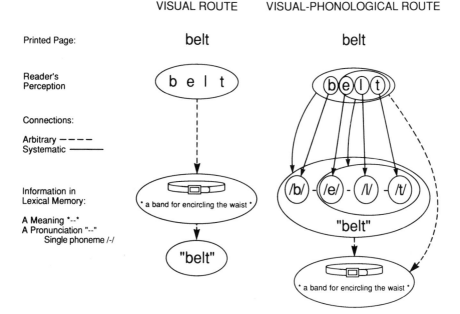

FIG. 5.1. Diagram contrasting the connections that are established in reading words by the visual-semantic route of dual route theory and by the visual-phonological route of the theory described here.

pronunciation, making it an intrinsic part of the whole. Moreover, the whole spelling is connected to the whole pronunciation in that the sequence of letters corresponds to the sequence of blended phonemes in the pronunciation. Other connections may be formed out of letter sequences within the spelling as well, for example, the rime stem *-elt* connected to the rime unit *-elt* in the pronunciation (see Goswami & Bryant, this volume; Treiman, this volume). The knowledge used to form this connection may come from other known words having this same spelling pattern and pronunciation, for example, *melt, felt, pelt,* and *welt* (Goswami, 1986).

The critical connections that enable readers to find specific words in lexical memory by means of this visual-phonological route are connections linking spellings to pronunciations rather than to meanings. However, connections between spellings and meanings are easily formed in the process of establishing visual-phonological routes. These connections are depicted in Fig. 5.1. Readers already know connections between pronunciations and meanings from speech. When spellings are connected to pronunciations, the connections extend to meanings as well, perhaps automatically. In addition, readers form direct connections between spellings and meanings when they interpret the words they read. This comes about as follows. The visual-phonological connections that readers have formed for a word make that spelling a visual symbol for its pronunciation. This means in effect that readers "see" the pronunciation when they look at the spelling, and this event creates direct links between the spelling and its meaning. Thus, readers access not only pronunciations but also meanings directly when they learn to read words by means of a visual-phonological route.

Whereas connections between spellings and pronunciations are systematic, connections between spellings and meanings are arbitrary. There is no inherent link between a spelling and its referent. As Fig. 5.1 shows, the connections forming the visual-semantic route of dual route theory are arbitrary. No prior knowledge is available for use in linking spelllings directly to their meanings. Some authors have suggested that readers may use their knowledge of orthographic regularities to form visual routes (Barron, 1986; Juel, 1983). However, even though a spelling may be recognized as containing some type of orthographic regularity—a letter combination that the reader recognizes as being orthographically legal or as occurring frequently in other words—this regularity does not make the connection between the spelling and meaning systematic unless the letters symbolize a known morphographic unit, such as a root word (e.g., *sign* in *signature*) or affix (e.g., past tense *-ed*). However, most spellings lack this type of regularity. It is true that orthographic regularity makes the spelling more structured and perhaps easier to remember. However, ease of stimulus learning by itself is not what is critical to sight word reading. Rather what is critical is the quality of the access route, that is, the kind and number of connections between the spelling and the word in lexical memory.

Comparison of the two routes in Fig. 5.1 clearly reveals the major strength of the visual-phonological route and the major weakness of the visual-semantic route for explaining how readers read sight words. The quality and number of connections differ dramatically. The visual-phonological route consists of many systematic connections, whereas the visual-semantic route consists of one or at most a few arbitrary connections. This makes the visual-phonological route much more stable and well established in memory and subject to much less forgetting.

Another strength of the visual-phonological route is its ability to handle the access problem, that is, to explain how readers can look at a spelling and instantly find that particular word in lexical memory while ignoring thousands of other words. Readers need an access route that is highly selective and that clearly targets one word and bypasses all others. Visual-phonological access routes do this easily. Visual-semantic routes do not. In English, spellings systematically symbolize pronunciations of words not meanings. Letters in spellings symbolize a sufficient number of phonemes to distinguish words from even their closest phonological neighbors. Thus, access routes built out of spellings that are linked to phonemes are fully capable of handling the access problem. In contrast, it is hard to imagine how access routes built out of spelling–meaning connections could accomplish the same feat.

In sum, sight word reading is a stable, reliable process, particularly in readers who possess phonological recoding skill. Consider the huge number of words that mature readers are able to recognize by sight. Consider their ability to look at a spelling and access that particular word in memory instantly while bypassing thousands of other words. Consider that words are read by sight after only a few exposures to the word, and that readers remain able to read words by sight even when the words are read infrequently. An adequate explanation for readers' capabilities with words requires a theory that specifies how many systematic connections are established linking specific printed words to their pronunciations and meanings in lexical memory and how these connections are easily remembered. The visual-phonological route in Fig. 5.1 is a much better candidate for this theory than the visual-semantic route of dual route theory.

WHICH SIGHT WORD ROUTE INTO MEMORY
DOES THE EVIDENCE SUPPORT?

Let us consider evidence bearing on the question of whether a visual-semantic route or a visual-phonological route better explains how readers process English word spellings when they read them by sight. Most of the studies conducted by dual route theorists are not very informative on this question because the words used to examine visual processing are not devoid of phonological information. For example, irregular spellings have commonly been used, yet as noted previously many of the letters in irregular spellings correspond to sounds in pronunciations. Because phonological processing has not been eliminated from the picture, these studies do not tell us about the use of a visual-semantic route to read words.

A few studies have examined people's ability to read words whose spellings bear no relationship to sound (e.g., *xdn* to symbolize *chair*) and have compared performance on these words to performance on words that exhibit systematic letter–sound correspondences. Brooks (1977) reported several experiments that he and Baron conducted using artificial orthography. In one study, adults were given 400 trials of practice to learn to read two types of spellings, one containing letter–sound correspondences and one having letters related arbitrarily to words. If dual route theory is correct that all sight words are read by a nonphonological visual route, then one would expect readers to learn to read both types of words with equal skill following lots of practice when the words acquire sight status. However, results showed something else. These results are reproduced in Fig. 5.2. During the first 200 trials, words having systematic letter–sound relations (labeled *orthographic*) were read more slowly than arbitrarily spelled words (labeled *paired associate*), whereas during the second 200 trials, systematic words were read more rapidly than arbitrary words. In another similar study Spring (1978) found that, during several overlearning trials when both types of

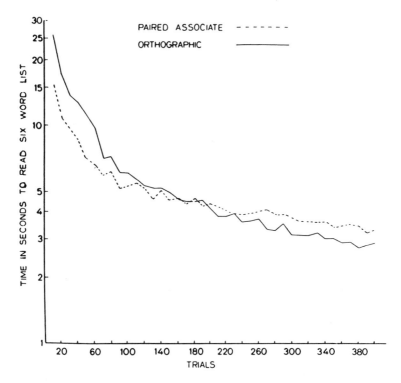

FIG. 5.2. Time taken in seconds (log scale) to read each of two sets of six words over 400 trials of practice. The paired associate set consisted of arbitrary spellings. The orthographic set consisted of systematic phonological spellings. *Note.* From "Visual Pattern in Fluent Word Identification" by L. Brooks, in *Toward a Psychology of Reading* (p. 153) by A. S. Reber and D. L. Scarborough, 1977, Hillsdale, NJ: Lawrence Erlbaum Associates. Copyright 1977 by Lawrence Erlbaum Associates, Inc. Reprinted by permission.

words presumably had achieved sight word status, the phonologically spelled words were read faster than the arbitrarily spelled words.

It appears that systematically spelled words are read faster than arbitrarily spelled words when both become sight words. This suggests that the two types of sight words are not processed similarly. Our explanation of the difference is that the connections linking spellings to lexical memory are more numerous and of higher quality for phonologically spelled words than for arbitrarily spelled words. This facilitates memory access in the former case. Also, word reading speed is greater because the phonological spellings are linked directly to pronunciations, whereas the arbitrary spellings are linked only indirectly to pronunciations through meanings.

Wilce and I also performed a study comparing readers' ability to learn to read systematic and arbitrary spellings of words (Ehri & Wilce, 1985). Results agreed with the aforementioned studies in showing that the two kinds of spellings are learned differently. Specifically, we taught kindergarteners to read two kinds of words by sight—systematic spellings in which letters corresponded to some sounds in words (e.g., *msk* for *mask*, *jrf* for *giraffe*) and arbitrary spellings exhibiting no letter–sound relations (e.g., *uhe* for *mask*, *wbc* for *giraffe*). Children were given several trials to learn to read six words of each type, each set taught on a different day. We found that word learning was not the same for the two types of words. Whether kindergarteners learned to read systematic or arbitrary spellings more easily depended on their word reading skill. Nonreaders learned to read arbitrary spellings more readily than systematic phonetic spellings. In contrast, beginning readers learned systematic spellings more readily than arbitrary spellings. It was not the case that readers read systematic phonetic spellings better because they could phonologically recode the words; the words had to be read from memory because they lacked letters for all the sounds.

These results indicate that different processes are used to read systematic and arbitrary spellings by sight and that the particular processes used depend on the readers' word reading skill. The reason nonreaders did not learn systematic phonetic spellings as easily as arbitrary spellings in this study is that they lacked the letter–sound knowledge needed to form visual-phonological connections in memory. This was verified on pretests showing that the nonreaders knew only a few letter–sound relations. The reason beginning readers learned systematic spellings better than arbitrary spellings is that they possessed and used their letter–sound knowledge to form systematic connections in memory. On pretests these readers knew all of the letter names and most letter–sounds.

In this same study we examined what information subjects remembered about letters in the systematic and arbitrary spellings they had learned to read. Of interest here are performances of 12 of the best readers who learned to read all six words in both sets perfectly (i.e., two perfect trials in a row), indicating that they had stored connections for both types of spellings in memory. We reasoned that if readers had formed letter–sound connections in learning to read systematic spellings but not arbitrary spellings, then they should remember more of the letters in the systematic spellings. However, if they learned to read both word types in the same way using an arbitrary visual route, then no difference in letter memory should be apparent.

Results of a spelling recall test given after the reading trials supported the first hypothesis. The mean number of initial and final letters recalled correctly in systematic spellings was 10.8, or 90.3% correct, whereas the mean recalled in arbitrary spellings was 5.0, or 41.7% correct. The high recall of letters in systematic phonetic spellings was not solely a result of subjects' ability to guess these letters from their letter–sound knowledge nor of their familiarity with conventional spellings of the words: Forty-two percent of the sounds could be spelled in more than one way (e.g., *j-g, k-c, s-z*), and 75% of the correct initial and final letters were not conventional (e.g., *kom* for *comb*).

These results are consistent with the idea that, in learning to read sight words, readers remember letter information in systematic phonetic spellings differently from the way they remember letter information in arbitrary spellings. When readers learn phonetic spellings as sight words, they form connections between letters and sounds. In contrast, when readers learn nonphonetic spellings as sight words, they pay less attention to letter identities.

In sum, results of our study and the studies by Brooks (1977) and Spring (1978) indicate that whether words are spelled systematically or arbitrarily makes a big difference in how readers learn to read the words by sight. Whereas dual route theory is incapable of explaining this difference, the present theory does fit the data.

DISTINCTION BETWEEN READING WORDS
BY VISUAL-PHONOLOGICAL CONNECTIONS
AND BY PHONOLOGICAL RECODING

I have distinguished between reading sight words by means of the strictly visual route of dual route theory and reading sight words by means of a visual-phonological route. Let me also clarify how the visual-phonological route differs from phonological recoding. The main difference involves the unit that is used to locate a specific word in the lexicon: a blend of phonemes versus a sequence of letters. According to dual route theory, phonological recoding involves applying letter–sound rules to transform a spelling into a blend of phonemes that is used to enter lexical memory and locate the real word with that pronunciation. The word is not recognized until this phonological match is achieved. In contrast, when words are read by a visual-phonological sight route the spelling itself is used to enter lexical memory and locate the word's pronunciation. No intermediate translation step is required. Connections are established between letters in the word's spellings and phonemes in its pronunciation, making direct access to that specific word possible. Recoding rules may be used to set up this sight route. However, once the word has been recoded several times, the rules and the translation and phonological matching routines drop out to be supplanted by specific connections linking the spelling directly to its pronunciation in memory.

Letters in spellings are processed as symbols for phonemes in the pronunciations of specific words in the course of forming visual-phonological connections. As a result, spellings become amalgamated to pronunciations and are retained in memory as orthographic "images" of the words, that is, visual letter-analyzed representations (Ehri, 1980, 1984, 1987). These representations also become amalgamated to meanings in memory. It is this amalgam that is accessed directly when sight words are read and recognized by means of visual-phonological connections.

According to this view, readers should be able to read familiar spellings that have become sight words faster than they can read unfamiliar spellings that must be recoded, even when the two types of spellings are phonologically identical. For example, once the word *seed* is set up in memory this way, readers should be able to read it faster than they can read *ceed* or *sead* or *cead,* which they have never seen. This is because the former word is read by accessing word-specific visual-phonological connections in memory, whereas the latter words are read by applying general phonological recoding routines.

Reitsma (1983) conducted a study providing supportive evidence. In his study, second-grade Dutch readers were familiarized with the pronunciations of 20 pseudowords. Then they practiced reading 10 of the words. Then their ability to read these 10 words plus 10 alternative unseen spellings of the same words (homophonic spellings) plus 10 control words was tested. Children read the practiced spellings faster than the homophonic and control spellings, indicating that they learned to recognize the specific patterns of letters in the words they read. In another experiment, Reitsma (1983) showed that the difference was not due to subjects' hearing the words that were read more times. Reitsma (1983) found that only a few exposures to the spellings of words were necessary to make a difference—as few as four exposures in one experiment. My explanation of why children read practiced spellings faster than alternative unpracticed forms is that visual-phonological connections were established between the practiced spellings and their pronunciations in memory, enabling readers to access pronunciations directly from the spellings rather than indirectly through recoding rules.

Wilce and I performed a study comparing beginning readers' speed to read familiar real words (e.g., *cat, book, see, stop, jump, red*), nonsense words (e.g., *nel, jad, mig, fup*), and to name single digits (Ehri & Wilce, 1983). The subjects were skilled and less skilled readers in first, second, and fourth grades. We reasoned that if readers process familiar real words by sight rather than by recoding, they ought to read familiar words faster than nonsense words. If they process familiar words as single units, then they ought to read the words as fast as they can name digits. Being able to read words as units is thought to become possible when spellings are fully connected (amalgamated) to pronunciations in memory (Ehri, 1978, 1980).

Both skilled and less skilled readers at all grade levels read familiar words much faster than nonsense words, indicating that they were not recoding the words but rather were reading them by sight. All of the skilled readers but only the oldest less skilled readers (fourth graders) were able to read the words as fast as name the digits, indicating that only some of the readers had formed complete connections between spellings and pronunciations.

In a second experiment we gave skilled and less skilled readers several practice trials to read real and nonsense words. This practice enabled skilled readers to read the nonsense words as fast as the real words and digits, indicating that the nonsense words had become completely connected sight words. However, even 18 practice trials did not allow poor readers to read nonsense words as fast as real words and real words as fast as digits.

Our explanation for the difference between skilled and less skilled readers is that only the skilled readers possessed adequate recoding skill to form complete connections between spellings and pronunciations in memory. The connections formed by poor readers in learning to read the words by sight were partial and failed to specify the entire word's pronunciation, because poor readers lacked sufficient knowledge of grapheme–phoneme correspondences to form a complete set of connections. In reading words, therefore, they took longer to retrieve the pronunciations from memory. Poor readers' weak recoding skill was evidenced by errors and longer latencies in the nonsense word recoding task.

These results provide support for the distinction between recoding and sight word reading and for the contribution that recoding makes to sight word reading. Moreover, they indicate that readers may differ in their skill at forming visual-phonological connections to read words by sight.

If phonological recoding and visual-phonological sight word reading are different ways to read words, and if the process of recoding words establishes visual-phonological connections for those words in memory, then we would expect readers in a spelling recall task to remember specific letters in words that they previously recoded rather than to produce alternative phonologically plausible spellings. However, if words are simply recoded over and over and never established as sight words in memory, then readers should not be biased to spell words using the same letters that they saw when they recoded the words.

I sought evidence for this prediction in a study with second graders who practiced reading 8 pseudowords spelled in one of two ways (Ehri, 1980). For example, half of the subjects read *bistion* and half read *bischun* pronounced identically. Then they wrote out the words from memory. If subjects were simply recoding the words, they should not remember whether they saw *-tion* or *-chun*. However, if letter–sound connections are retained in memory from reading words, then spellings should reflect this. I found evidence for specific letter memory in subjects' misspellings. Every subject who saw *bistion* and misspelled it included *-st-* but never *-ch-* in their misspelling. Conversely, every subject who saw *bischun* and misspelled it included *-ch-* but never *-st-*. In other words, subjects recalled letters that they had seen rather than other phonologically equivalent letters.

Our studies combine with Reitsma's (1983) experiments to provide evidence for the distinction between reading words by phonological recoding and reading words by accessing a visual-phonological sight route in memory. Results support the idea that when words are phonologically recoded several times, word-specific connections linking spellings to pronunciations are established in memory. Once established, readers use these connections rather than phonological recoding to read the words and also to spell them.

Results of the previously described study by Brooks (1977), using artificial orthography, can be interpreted in terms of the distinction between reading words by phonological recoding and reading words by setting up word-specific letter–

sound connections in memory. Recall that in this study subjects practiced reading six phonologically spelled (labeled *orthographic*) and six arbitrarily spelled (labeled *paired associate*) words for 400 trials. (See Fig. 5.2). During the first 200 trials phonological words were read more slowly than arbitrary words. During the last 200 trials the reverse occurred. The distinction between reading words by phonological recoding and by visual-phonological sight may explain the difference in word reading performance between the early and late phases of practice. During the early phase systematically spelled words were read slower than arbitrarily spelled words, because readers were phonologically recoding the systematic words, whereas they were reading the arbitrary words by sight using a visual-semantic route. Other research (Gough, 1984) shows that phonological recoding is a slower process than sight word reading, particularly when readers are unfamiliar with the letter–sound relations. During the later phase of practice, systematically spelled words were read faster than arbitrarily spelled words because readers began processing the systematic spellings differently once the letter–sound system became familiar. They shifted from recoding to sight word reading and began establishing visual-phonological connections that linked spellings to their specific pronunciations in memory. As the number of connections increased for each word and became more effective in distinguishing one word from another, and as systematic spellings became linked directly to pronunciations in memory, processing speed continued to increase beyond that involved in reading words by sight using a visual-semantic route.

DEVELOPMENT OF SIGHT WORD READING

How does my reconceptualization of sight word reading fit with evidence on the course of development of sight word reading skill? In my previous research I have proposed a theory of printed word learning and conducted several studies to obtain evidence bearing on the theory. (See Ehri, 1978, 1980, 1984, 1987, for reviews.) My earlier descriptions differ slightly from the connectionist view developed previously but are essentially the same idea. The connectionist formulation focuses on the nature of the access route into memory and the kinds of connections that are formed linking spellings to pronunciations, whereas my earlier theory focused on the nature of the spelling representation that is established in memory when these connections are formed.

In languages such as English in which words are spelled alphabetically to symbolize phonemes, sight word reading can be analyzed as developing in several phases. I describe these phases briefly here and then provide details later. Each phase is defined by the kind of connections that are formed between visual cues seen in print and information about a specific word stored in memory. During the first phase when children begin recognizing words in their environment but have little knowledge about letters, they form connections that are arbitrary. Salient visual cues seen in or around a word are linked to the meaning and pronunciation of the word in memory but the link is not phonological. These connections are learned by rote. The visual route described by dual route theory depicts this phase. I have called this *visual cue reading* and also *logographic reading* (taken from Frith's, 1985, theory) in my previous work to indicate that the connections are strictly visual and nonphonetic (Ehri, 1991; Ehri & Wilce, 1985).

During the second phase when children learn about letter names or sounds, they use their knowledge to form systematic visual-phonological connections between letters seen in words and sounds detected in their pronunciations. However, the connections are incomplete. Only some of the letters seen in spellings are linked to sounds, usually initial or initial and final letters. I have called this the rudimentary alphabetic phase or *phonetic cue reading* (Ehri, 1991; Ehri & Wilce, 1985, 1987a, 1987b).

During the third phase, students continue to use the alphabetic principle to read words by sight but in a more mature way. When readers acquire phonemic segmentation skill and phonological recoding skill, they use this knowledge to form complete visual-phonological connections in learning to read sight words. Individual letters are linked to individual phonemes. Also the sequence of letters is connected to the blend of phonemes. I adopt Gough and Hillinger's (1980) term to denote this type of sight word reading, calling it *cipher sight word reading* to indicate that spellings are fully analyzed as visual symbols for phonemic constituents in pronunciations. Let me review in more detail the characteristics of each phase and evidence regarding its development.

Logographic Phase of Sight Word Learning: Visual Cue Reading

During the first logographic phase, readers read words by selecting and forming connections out of visual cues that are arbitrarily related to the word's meaning and that bear no relationship to the word's pronunciation. The visual cues selected might be part of the spelling or adjacent to the spelling. Examples of such visual cues are a circle at the end (e.g., *hero*), or two tall posts in the middle of the spelling (e.g., *yellow*), or a thumbprint next to the word (Gough & Hillinger, 1980), or a logo behind a word as in *McDonald's* printed on golden arches. Children who have learned to identify letter shapes may select letters as cues. However, letters are selected because they are visually salient or distinctive, not because they have anything to do with sounds in the word.

Occasionally a visual cue that is semantically related to the word's meaning might be found, such as the tail on the end of *dog* or the humps in the middle of *camel*. Such connections involving visual cues that are built out of prior knowledge and that systematically link the spelling to its meaning may be effective in enabling a child to remember how to read those words, although other words having the same cues (e.g., *leg* and *timer*) may be mistaken as the same words. Unfortunately for the perpetuation of this phase, it is hard to find meaning-bearing cues in most spellings.

Because most connections formed between spellings and meanings are arbitrary, they are easily forgotten unless practiced frequently. Because the visual cues forming the connections are not unique to individual words, children mistake visually similar words for one another. Because the visual cues are connected to meanings rather than to pronunciations, readers may produce synonyms rather than one specific word when they read spellings. Thus word reading during this phase is not very accurate or reliable.

Several studies have revealed that when logographic readers are able to read signs in their environment, such as *McDonald's, Pepsi,* or *STOP,* they do it by remembering visual cues accompanying the signs. They pay little attention to letters in the signs (Dewitz & Stammer, 1980; Goodman & Altwerger, 1981; Harste, Burke, & Woodward, 1982; Hiebert, 1978; Masonheimer, Drum, & Ehri, 1984). In the study by Masonheimer et al. (1984), children between the ages of 3 and 5 years were selected for their expertise at reading environmental signs. When they were shown the same signs without any environmental cues, most of the experts were no longer able to read the signs. When letters were altered and presented with their logos in the signs (e.g., *Pepsi* changed to *Xepsi*), most children did not even notice the changes. The children who were unable to read signs out of context and who failed to detect letter alternations could read few if any words in isolation and knew names of only 62% of the letters. According to the present theory these children were logographic readers. They were reading the signs by accessing connections that they had formed between salient visual cues in or near the words and the words' meanings. Their knowledge of letter names and sounds was not sufficiently developed to allow them to form the visual-phonetic connections that characterize the next phase of development.

In the Masonheimer et al. (1984) study, 6 out of the 102 sign reading experts deviated from this pattern of performance. They could read the signs without environmental cues present, they recognized immediately that the letter-altered signs were incorrectly printed, and they attempted to recode the unfamiliar spellings (e.g., *Xepsi*). These children were more advanced in their word reading development as well. They had mastered letter names and could read several words in isolation. According to my theory, these children were reading words in the signs differently from the logographic readers. They were accessing visual-phonetic connections rather than visual-meaning connections.

In other environmental print studies (Goodman & Altwerger, 1981; Harste et al., 1982), researchers have observed that logographic readers produce variable rather than exact wordings when they read signs and labels. For example, they might read *Crest* as "brush teeth" or "toothpaste" and *Dynamints* as "fresh-a-mints." I interpret this use of synonymous terms rather than exact pronunciations to read words as evidence that logographic readers form connections between visual cues and the meanings of printed words rather than between visual cues and pronunciations. This contrasts with later phases of sight word reading where the involvement of letter–sound connections restricts the word accessed in memory to a single pronunciation.

Unless the sight words learned during the logographic phase are practiced frequently, they are easily forgotten because the connections linking spellings to meanings in memory are arbitrary. Supporting this view, Mason (1980) found that logographic-phase readers could learn to read 3 or 4 printed words on a 10-item list but they could not read these words 15 minutes later. Also, when children were shown the words with the case of some of the letters altered from upper to lower case or lower to upper case, they could no longer read the words. In contrast, more advanced readers were still able to read the words despite case changes. This finding supports the idea that logographic readers do not perceive letters as members of conceptual categories with invariant shapes and specific identities (i.e., names) when they learn to read words by sight (Adams, 1990). Rather they only notice visual properties of letters such as straight, curved, or crossed lines. One reason for this is that they have not learned the shapes and names or sounds of many letters. Gough, Juel, and Roper/Schneider (1983) found that logographic readers sometimes included numbers when they spelled words, indicating that they did not distinguish letters as a special kind of symbol.

Rudimentary Alphabetic Phase of Sight Word Learning: Phonetic Cue Reading

The shift to the next phase occurs when readers learn the shapes and names or sounds of most alphabet letters and when they acquire low-level phonemic awareness that enables them to focus on beginning and ending sounds in words and in letter names (Tunmer, Herriman, & Nesdale, 1988; Tunmer & Hoover, this volume). During this second phase, learners begin using their letter knowledge to form visual-phonetic connections between letters seen in spellings and sounds detected in pronunciations of words they are learning to read. For example, in learning to read *ball,* they recognize that *b* connects with /b/ and that *ll* connects with /l/ in the pronunciation of the word. These two connections are stored in memory, enabling children to access the word's pronunciation the next time they see its spelling.

Even if beginners know only letter names, not letter sounds, they can use phonetic information in the name to create a connection. For example, in learning to read *jail,* readers who recognize that the first and final letters say their own names when the word is spoken are able to form connections linking these two letters to the pronunciation in lexical memory. The next time they see the spelling they access the pronunciation in memory using these connections.

Of course, the reader must possess sufficient phonetic segmentation skill to detect the presence of separate sounds in the pronunciations of words and also in letter names (e.g., detecting /b/ in *bee*). Detecting first and final sounds in pronunciations is easier than detecting embedded sounds, particularly sounds in consonant blends, for example, the /l/ in *black* (Treiman, 1985a). Special training may be required for beginners to detect sounds in blends (Ehri & Wilce, 1987b).

At the beginning of this phase readers may use only one or two letters to form connections, usually the first or last letters in spellings. Such connections allow readers to remember how to read these words but also cause them to misread other words having the same visual-phonetic cues, for example, *jail* and *jewel*. As readers gain experience reading various words in this way, as they learn more letter–sound relations, and as their phonemic segmentation skill improves, they can use more of the letters in spellings to form access routes connecting spellings with pronunciations in memory.

This second phase contrasts with the first phase in several ways. Whereas connections in the first phase are arbitrary, connections in this phase are systematic. They are built out of what the child knows about letter names or letter–sound relations. Whereas only one connection may be formed during the logographic phase, several connections may be formed during Phase 2 if readers use more than one letter. These differences make word reading more reliable during Phase 2 than during Phase 1 because the words are easier to remember how to read. However, as in Phase 1, reliability is less than perfect because the letter cues used to read specific words also appear in other words. Another difference between the two phases is that in Phase 1 the primary connection is between a spelling and its meaning, whereas in Phase 2 the primary connection is between a spelling and its pronunciation. This too makes word reading in Phase 2 more reliable because letters are connected to one specific word rather than to a meaning that may include synonymous words.

In a study mentioned earlier (Ehri & Wilce, 1985) we obtained evidence for the difference between Phase 1 visual cue reading and Phase 2 phonetic cue reading, and we determined when readers shift from Phase 1 to Phase 2 in learning to read words out of context. In this study we compared readers in their ability to learn to read two types of spellings—arbitrary spellings having distinctive visual cues that we thought Phase 1 readers would find useful for learning to read words, and systematic spellings having visual-phonetic cues that we thought Phase 2 readers would find useful for learning to read words. The arbitrary spellings contained no letters corresponding to sounds in pronunciations. However, they were more distinctive visually than the other set of spellings in that all of the letters were different across words, and the size and ascending or descending positions of the letters were varied (e.g., *uHE* to spell *mask*). The systematic spellings were simplified phonetic spellings containing letters that corresponded to some of the sounds in words (e.g., *MSK* to spell *mask*). Some letters recurred across words and letters were uniform in size, making phonetic spellings less distinctive visually than the other set.

The subjects in our study were kindergarteners who were grouped according to their word reading skill. The least mature readers were those who could read few if any preprimer words in isolation and who knew only some letters and only a few letter–sound relations. We called these *prereaders*. The next group could read a few preprimer words (from 1 to 11) and knew most letter names and sounds. We called these *novice* readers. The most mature group could read from 11 to 36 preprimer words and knew most letter names and sounds. We called these *veteran* beginning readers.

We asked whether children in each of the groups would learn to read visual spellings or phonetic spellings more easily. We reasoned that logographic readers should form visual-semantic connections more easily than visual-phonetic connections and hence should learn to read the arbitrary spellings more easily than the systematic spellings. In contrast, alphabetic readers should form visual-phonetic connections more easily than visual-semantic connections and hence should learn the systematic spellings more easily. Because the prereaders knew few letter names or sounds, we expected them to perform like logographic readers. Novices and veterans knew most letter names and sounds, so we expected them to perform like alphabetic readers.

As predicted, prereaders learned arbitrary, visually distinctive spellings more easily than systematic phonetic spellings whereas novices and veterans learned the systematic spellings more easily than the arbitrary spellings. The results are depicted in Fig. 5.3. This evidence is consistent with our view that logographic readers learn sight words by forming connections out of arbitrary, visually distinctive cues, whereas alphabetic readers form connections out of letter–sound cues.

In the word learning task involving systematic phonetic spellings, it was not the case that Phase 2 readers were reading the words by recoding them. Novice readers exhibited little recoding skill on the preprimer word reading task. Furthermore, most of the simplified spellings were not recodable (e.g., *LFT* for *elephant, PNSL* for *pencil*). Rather spellings had to be stored in memory. This suggests that the novice and veteran readers were reading the phonetic spellings by sight. That they learned to read phonetic spellings better than visual spellings indicates that they were learning to read the sight words by forming connections between letters and sounds.

Results of this study indicate that the shift from Phase 1 to Phase 2 happens early. The ability to learn sight words by forming visual-phonetic connections was evident in the group of novice readers who had just moved into reading as indicated by the fact that they could read only a few preprimer words out of context. The only group that did not learn phonetic spellings more easily than visual spellings was the group of prereaders who knew few letter sounds and

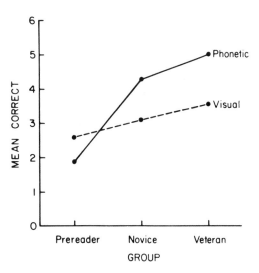

FIG. 5.3.   Mean number of systematic phonetic and arbitrary visual spellings identified correctly in the word-learning task as a function of beginning reader group. *Note.* From "Movement into Reading: Is the First Stage of Printed Word Learning Visual or Phonetic?" by L. C. Ehri and L. S. Wilce, 1985, *Reading Research Quarterly, 20,* p. 169. Copyright 1985 by the International Reading Association. Reprinted by permission.

could not read words out of context. These findings suggest that as soon as children learn their letters and become able to read even a few words in isolation, they have moved from the logographic to the alphabetic phase of sight word reading.

In another study, we obtained further evidence clarifying how Phase 2 readers process words using visual-phonetic connections and what knowledge is required to do this more effectively (Ehri & Wilce, 1987b). In this study, we created through training two groups of readers who differed in their ability to process connections between letters in spellings and sounds in pronunciations of words. We selected kindergarten novice readers who could name 9 out of 10 target letters but could read only a few preprimer words and no target words. Half of the children were given instruction and practice in how to produce phonetic spellings of words (mostly nonsense) constructed out of consonants, consonant blends and long vowels (e.g., *ĒK, TĀN, SNŌL, TĪNS,* pronounced "eak," "tain," "snoal," "tines"). The other half of the sample practiced spelling single, isolated consonant and vowel sounds, the same 10 sounds that appeared in the nonsense words. These treatments yielded two groups of readers that were alike in their knowledge of letter–sound relations but that differed in their ability to segment pronunciations of words into sounds and to connect letters to these sounds to spell words.

Following training, both groups were given seven trials to learn to read the phonetic spellings of 12 real words that all began with *S* and that were constructed out of the same letter sounds used in training (e.g., *SĒL, SŌP, SLĪS, SĀLS,* pronounced "seal," "soap," "slice," "sails"). We compared various aspects of the two groups' performances to determine whether spelling-trained subjects were better at forming visual-phonetic connections than control subjects.

The spelling-trained group learned to read more words than the control group. Mean performances across trials are presented in Fig. 5.4. However neither group mastered the list. On the seventh and final trial, the spelling-trained group read a mean of 46% of the words, and the control group read a mean of 28% of the words. The list proved difficult because the words were similarly spelled and also because subjects lacked the ability to recode the words. Their recoding deficit was apparent on a word reading pretest; blending was not taught during spelling training; and only a minority of their correct readings of target words were preceded by observable sounding out and blending behaviors. Most recoding attempts resulted in failure. That subjects learned to read some words despite a lack of recoding skill is interpreted to indicate that they were learning to read the words by sight, that is, by forming connections to create access routes into lexical memory.

In examining the course of sight word learning, we found that subjects did not read words consistently across trials. They would read a word correctly but then subsequently forget it or misread it as another word. Both groups continued to read correctly only 30%–31% of the words they read correctly at least once. Children were inconsistent because they failed to process enough letter cues to fully determine word identities. As a result, they either forgot the words or

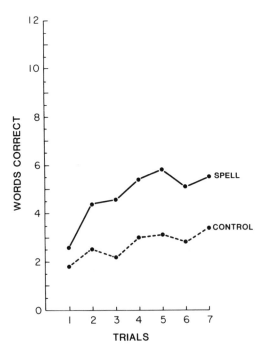

FIG. 5.4. Mean number of words read correctly across trials in the word learning task for subjects given spelling training and for control subjects given sound–letter training. *Note.* From "Does Learning to Spell Help Beginners Learn to Read Words?" by L. C. Ehri and L. S. Wilce, 1987, *Reading Research Quarterly, 22,* p. 55. Copyright 1987 by the International Reading Association. Reprinted by permission.

confused them with other words having the same letter cues. This supports the idea that subjects were using partial cues in words to form connections into memory.

Analysis of subjects' errors revealed that the kind of connections they were forming were partial connections between some of the letters in spellings and some of the sounds in pronunciations. We examined whether subjects' misreadings of words were influenced by letters they saw in the words. Spelling-trained subjects pronounced significantly more letters in their misreadings than control subjects, $M = 66\%$ versus 49%. This difference indicates that spelling-trained readers processed more phonetic cues in words than control subjects. Many of the misreadings were other words on the list. The proportion of letters pronounced in these misreadings was greater for spelling-trained than for control subjects, $M = 64\%$ versus 49%. This value was above chance for trained subjects but not for control subjects, indicating that trained subjects were processing phonetic cues when they misread words rather than randomly guessing words.

We obtained further evidence that subjects were forming partial letter–sound connections by analyzing the relative difficulty of learning different words in the list of 12 words. One trained subject told us that it was easy to read the word *sop* (*soap*). All she needed to see was the *p*. Indeed, this was the only word ending in *p*, and it shared the fewest letters with other words on the list. It turned out that children correctly read *sop* more often than any other word. In contrast, the two words read least often, *sals* (*sails*) and *slis* (*slice*), shared the highest proportion of letters (52%) with other words on the list. Correlational analyses verified that words sharing more letters with other words were read less accurately than words sharing fewer letters. Correlations were high for both groups, but the value was substantially higher for spelling-trained subjects than for control subjects, $r = -.91$ versus $-.60$. Thus partial letter–sound cues influenced word reading performance with the impact much greater among spelling-trained than control subjects.

Another characteristic besides letter overlap that distinguished the words in this list was their meaningfulness. For example, *soap* and *snake* are more meaningful to young children than *sight, soles,* or *sake* (i.e., for the sake of). We obtained meaningfulness rankings for these words from adults and then correlated these values with the numbers of subjects reading each word correctly at least twice. The correlation was significantly different from zero for control subjects, $r = .59$ ($p < .05$), but not for spelling-trained subjects, $r = .32$ ($p > .05$). Apparently, control subjects depended on lexical access routes that involved connections between spellings and meanings, whereas spelling-trained subjects did not.

Thus, control subjects' word learning was influenced by both word meaningfulness and letter–sound cues, whereas trained subjects' word learning was influenced only by letter–sound cues. These findings suggest that as readers improve at Phase 2 reading, that is, as they learn to form more connections between letters and sounds to access lexical memory, letter–sound connections take over as the primary basis for distinguishing among words to read them and connections between spellings and meanings become less important. This is not to say that more advanced Phase 2 readers stop processing word meanings but only that they cease to depend on print-meaning connections as access routes to read sight words. This is not surprising, because spelling-meaning connections are not as reliable as spelling-pronunciation connections for retrieving specific words designated by the spellings in lexical memory.

After the word learning task subjects were given two spelling tests and a phoneme segmentation task. Performances on these posttests confirmed that the spelling-trained group was better at forming visual-phonetic connections. Spelling-trained subjects were superior in spelling nonsense words, were better able to match up correct spellings to pronunciations on a multiple choice spelling recognition test, and outperformed controls in dividing nonsense words into their constituent phonemes. Spelling-trained subjects' ability to handle consonant blends in all of these tasks far exceeded that of controls.

Spelling-trained subjects' superior performances on these tasks support our explanation of why spelling training improves sight word reading. It enables readers to form superior access routes that are comprised of multiple connections between letters seen in spellings and sounds in pronunciations that are stored in memory. The ability to form such connections requires more than simple letter–sound knowledge. Both groups knew constituent letter sounds equally well. In addition, phonetic segmentation skill is needed so that readers can detect constituent sounds in the pronunciations of words in order to connect letters in spellings to those sounds.

In a longitudinal study, Share et al. (1984) found that the two best predictors of beginning reading achievement during the first two years of instruction were letter-name knowledge and phonemic segmentation skill. As we have explained, both of these skills play central roles in our theory of how sight word reading gets underway and grows during Phase 2.

Mature Alphabetic Phase of Sight Word Learning: Cipher Reading

Cipher sight word reading refers to the process of reading sight words by setting up connections in memory between the entire sequence of letters in spellings and phonemic constituents in the word's pronunciation. Not only are individual letters or digraphs linked to phonemes but also the sequence of letters is connected to the blend of phonemes such that part–part as well as part–whole relations are established leading from print into memory. These connections are diagrammed in Fig. 5.1.

The connections are considered to be phonemic rather than phonetic because cipher readers recognize the size and the abstract nature of the "sounds" they are connecting to letters (e.g., *b* symbolizes /b/ rather than /bi/ or /bə/ in *beaver*), they conceptualize the pronunciation as a sequence of phoneme-size units, and they analyze the "sounds" according to conventional phonemic categories rather than according to phonetic criteria. Cipher readers possess phonological recoding skill and they use this to analyze spellings fully as visual symbols for phonemic constituents of pronunciations. Silent letters are distinguished and marked as exceptions (Ehri & Wilce, 1982) or they are recognized as parts of mor-phophonemic spelling units, for example, final -*e* marking a preceding vowel as tense (long; Venezky, 1970). Letters in a spelling are connected to the word's pronunciation in a way that fully determines the pronunciation and consequently the meaning and that excludes words with similar pronunciations. Thus sight word reading at this phase becomes an exceedingly reliable process.

It is highly adaptive for readers to learn to process phonemic rather than phonetic connections because English orthography symbolizes the phonemic structure of language more closely than the phonetic structure. A phonetic tran-scription depicts all the distinctions that make one sound different from another, whereas a phonemic transcription represents only those distinctions that make a difference to meaning. One example involves aspiration. A phonetic transcrip-tion of the labial sound /p/ in *pit* and *spit* includes the fact that the former sound is aspirated whereas the latter is not. (One can detect the difference in aspiration by holding one's hand in front of one's mouth and feeling the difference in the amount of air ejected when /p/ in the two words is articulated.) In contrast, a phonemic transcription ignores this difference. The orthography agrees with the phonemic transcription in classifying the sounds as both *p*.

Another example involves voicing. A phonetic transcription of /t/ in *stick* includes the fact that voicing onset of the vowel makes this sound more similar to /d/ in *Dick* than to /t/ in *tick*. Perceptually, the two sounds /st-/ and /d/ are more similar also. Researchers showed this in a study in which they excised /s/ from tape recordings of words like *stick,* played the excised word to listeners, and found that the word was heard as *Dick* rather than *tick* (Reeds & Wang, 1961). In contrast, phonemic and orthographic transcriptions ignore this phonetic fact and classify the sound as /t/. Treiman (1985b) observed novice beginning readers to analyze sounds such as /t/ in *stick* phonetically rather than phonemically and to spell /t/ in *stick* as *d*. More experienced readers never made this mistake.

In my view, cipher readers do not make errors that are phonetically valid but phonemically wrong because they have learned how the phonemic system works. Some of this knowledge has come from their experiences with speech but also some of it has come from learning how the spelling system symbolizes speech phonemically. During the course of learning to read and spell, readers' concep-tualizations about phonemes in speech have been shaped by orthography as they have reconciled their insights about the sounds in words with the way the words are spelled (Ehri, 1984; Ehri & Wilce, 1980, 1986; Ehri, Wilce, & Taylor, 1987). In the previous example, cipher readers never would think of or spell the

/t/ in *stick* as *d* because they have learned from the spelling system that such blends are /st/, never /sd/. This sort of knowledge about the phonemic structure of words and how spellings symbolize this phonemic structure distinguishes Phase 3 cipher readers from Phase 2 phonetic cue readers.

Phase 3 readers are thought to differ from Phase 2 readers in several respects. As explained previously, the connections formed by Phase 2 readers are partial and phonetic, whereas the connections of Phase 3 readers are formed out of the complete array of letters connected to the phonemic structure of the word. This is made possible by the acquisition of phonemic segmentation and recoding skills. Because Phase 3 readers know how to analyze pronunciations into a sequence of phonemes, and because they know which letters typically symbolize these phonemes, they can analyze the phonemic function of all the letters in a word's spelling and store these connections in memory to use in recognizing the printed word. In contrast, the sounds used by Phase 2 readers may be as small as phonemes or as large as syllables. Because Phase 2 readers have processed only some of the letters in spellings, they mistake other words having the same letters for these words. Phase 3 readers make few if any confusions in reading similarly spelled words because they have processed all of the letters in these spellings.

We conducted a study to compare the word reading performances of Phase 2 and Phase 3 readers (Ehri & Wilce, 1987a). This difference in reading ability was created experimentally. Beginning readers who knew letters and could read a few words but could not recode were selected. To create a group of Phase 3 cipher readers, we trained half of the subjects to recode words (mostly nonsense) comprised of consonants, short vowels, and consonant blends (e.g., *sab, sist, stum*). To create a group of Phase 2 phonetic cue readers, we gave the other subjects isolated letter–sound practice. After training both groups were given several posttests to assess their ability to learn to read words and to spell words.

The word reading posttest consisted of 15 similarly spelled words comprised of CVCs and consonant blends (e.g., *bend, blond, dot, lamp, lap*). Subjects were given up to 7 trials to learn the words. Several differences between the two groups were apparent. Cipher readers learned to read most if not all of the words, whereas phonetic cue readers learned to read only a few words. On the final trial, the mean proportion of words read correctly was 93% for cipher readers but only 32% for phonetic cue readers. Cipher readers had an easier time learning to read the set of similarly spelled words for two reasons. In contrast to phonetic cue readers they were better able to recode the words, and their superior recoding skill enabled them to form more complete connections linking spellings to pronunciations in memory to read the words by sight.

Whereas the cipher readers showed consistent gains on successive word reading trials, the phonetic cue readers did not. Often cue readers would read words correctly on one trial and then fail to read them correctly on later trials. Whereas cipher readers continued to read correctly 72% of the words they read correctly once, cue readers read only 35% of the words consistently. This was because cue readers either forgot the connections or confused them with connections established for other words, which was very likely because many words shared some of the same letters.

Both groups of subjects pronounced over half of the letters they saw in the words, indicating that cue as well as cipher readers were processing letter–sound connections to learn the words. Cipher readers pronounced significantly more letters in their misreadings than cue readers, suggesting that they were more adept at using letter–sound relations. Analysis of intralist intrusion errors confirmed that cue readers were mixing up words on the basis of partial letter cues, primarily initial letters. Cue readers produced some semantic intrusion errors that often preserved first letters, for example, saying *light* or *lantern* for *lamp*. No cipher reader produced any misreadings of this sort. It may be that when readers begin attending primarily to letter–sound cues in reading words, semantically related words are suppressed because readers realize that sounds in the words do not match up well enough with spellings.

Subjects' memory for the spellings of words they had learned to read was examined to obtain additional evidence about connections stored in memory. Not suprisingly, cipher readers remembered significantly more correct spellings and more correct letters of various types than phonetic cue readers. Vowels were recalled better (78% vs. 49%) as were consonant blends (70% vs. 12%). There was one exception: Phonetic cue readers recalled almost as many initial and final consonants in the words as cipher readers and the difference was not significant statistically ($M = 79\%$ vs. 90%, $p > .05$). Cue readers' recall of initial and final consonants may have been good because these letters formed the connections that they had used in learning to read the words. The spellings of one cue reader provided extra support for this hypothesis. This child spelled 97% of the first and final letters correctly but few middle letters correctly. In addition, when she wrote these words she capitalized the initial and final letters as they had appeared in the words she had seen, but she wrote most of the medial letters in lower case, even though these too had been seen in capital letters. Apparently, this cue reader attended to and remembered connections between boundary letters and sounds during the word reading task but ignored medial letter–sound relations.

Although subjects who were trained to recode nonsense words outperformed control subjects in learning to read real words, one might wonder whether our laboratory-trained subjects were truly Phase 3 cipher readers rather than simply more advanced Phase 2 phonetic cue readers. That they learned to read most of the similarly spelled words indicates that they were processing letter–sound connections in words fairly completely. All but one reader attained a perfect score on at least one trial. However, there was some inconsistency in their word reading across trials, and they remembered how to spell only 37% of the words they practiced reading. Readers who attain the cipher phase of reading in the real world might be expected to know the spelling system better than this.

Although the third phase of word reading has been portrayed as discrete and qualitatively different from the second phase, the *transition period* between phases is probably quantitative and continuous. Attaining the idealized state of a cipher reader as I have described it very likely involves a gradual process of acquiring the various skills and sources of knowledge that enable the reader to function fully in this manner. That movement from Phase 2 to Phase 3 is gradual should not be surprising because the development of sight word reading involves acquiring and integrating a complex set of skills rather than a single simple capability. Complex skills do not emerge all at once. In our study, we attempted to train novice kindergarten readers to function like Phase 3 readers. Although our trained subjects performed like cipher readers in some respects, it is probably more accurate to regard them as transitional in their skills.

Evidence in the foregoing training study does not allow us to distinguish whether cipher readers read the similarly spelled words by sight or by phonological recoding. However, other studies provide clearer evidence that when readers recode words repeatedly, they establish visual-phonological connections between spellings and pronunciations in memory. In the study by Reitsma (1983) described earlier, children read familiar spellings of words faster than phonologically equivalent alternative spellings that they had not read before. In our study (Ehri & Wilce, 1983), skilled readers read familiar words much faster than they read nonsense words, in fact, as fast as they named single digits. A likely explanation is that visual-phonemic connections were formed in memory enabling readers to read the familiar words by sight.

We have performed several studies indicating that when cipher readers learn to read specific words, the spellings of the words influence their conception of phonemes in the words when there is ambiguity. This is interpreted to reflect the process of using the cipher to establish complete connections between letters in spellings and phonemes in pronunciations of words when they are learned as sight words (Ehri, 1984). Examples of words having phonemes that are ambiguous are "pi*t*ch versus rich," "ba*d*ge versus page," "can *y*ou versus menu." A phoneme corresponding to the italicized letter can be found in the pronunciations of pair members yet the phoneme is symbolized in only one of the spellings, making its presence in the pronunciation ambiguous.

In one study we taught fourth-grade normal readers, presumably cipher sight word readers, to read unfamiliar words that contained ambiguous phonemes (Ehri & Wilce, 1980). Half of the spellings included letters corresponding to the phonemes and half did not. To determine whether subjects acquired the idea that some of the words contained these extra phonemes, we gave them an oral phonemic segmentation task (no spellings present) in which they used tokens to mark the sequence of phonemes as they pronounced them in each word. Children detected extra phonemes in words having extra letters in their spellings but not in words lacking these extra letters. Two other studies using different words and tasks yielded similar results (Ehri & Wilce, 1986; Ehri et al., 1987).

Our interpretation of these findings is that when cipher readers learn to read words they form complete connections between letters in spellings and phonemes in pronunciations and retain the spellings in memory as orthographic "images" amalgamated to pronunciations and symbolizing their phonemes. The presence of an extra letter prompts the detection of an ambiguous phoneme, a connection is formed, and the extra letter symbolizing its phoneme is retained in the orthographic image. Orthographic images sit in memory and influence readers' conception of the phonemic structure of words. When readers are asked about phonemes in words, they consult spelling-pronunciation amalgams. Additional evidence supporting this view is considered elsewhere (Ehri, 1984).

Cipher reading is intended to portray that point in development when readers become able to process letters as phonemic symbols in learning to read words by sight. However, I have not specified what kinds of words readers should be able to handle. English words vary in number of letter, number of syllables, and letter–sound regularity. Readers may be able to use the cipher in learning to read short, regularly spelled, monosyllabic words by sight, but they may regress to phonetic cues in processing multisyllabic words or even to logographic cues in processing words with spellings that defy their letter–sound knowledge. In addition, there are many English spellings whose regularity is not primarily phonemic but rather morphophonemic or morphographic (Becker, Dixon, & Anderson-Inman, 1980; Venezky, 1970). Learning to read these words by sight may require knowing higher order spelling regularities and how these letter patterns are connected systematically to subunits in pronunciations or in meanings. More research is needed on how readers learn to read various kinds of words by sight and whether the concept of cipher sight word reading is useful in explaining how readers learn to read longer and more complex words.

CONCLUDING COMMENTS

In this chapter I have attempted to present theory and evidence indicating how sight words are established in memory. The kinds of words that are learned by sight are not limited to high frequency words and irregularly spelled words. Rather they include all words that have been read often enough to initiate the formation of connections into memory. The kinds of readers that read words by sight are not limited to those who have been taught in sight word instructional programs. Rather they include all readers who have practiced specific words often enough to read them by accessing memory. I have tried to show that sight word learning is not a rote memory process but rather involves remembering systematic connections between spellings and pronunciations of words. I have suggested that it is the establishment of systematic connections that enable readers to recognize sight words so rapidly and to remember how to read infrequently seen words.

One of the hallmarks of skilled reading is the ability to read words accurately and rapidly out of context (Perfetti, 1985; Stanovich, 1980). This context-free word reading is not carried out by a process of phonological recoding (Gough, 1984). This conclusion has proved troublesome to researchers such as Gough and Tunmer (1986) who would like to regard all word reading as involving recoding skill. The present view of sight word reading provides a solution by showing how phonological recoding is central. I suggest that context-free word reading skill depends centrally on recoding knowledge because it is this knowledge that allows readers to establish the network of connections leading from a word's spelling to its pronunciation in memory when the word is established as a sight word. One of the weaknesses of dual route theory's view of sight word reading is that it does not explain why beginners must possess phonological recoding skill in order to become skilled sight word readers. In contrast, my view of sight word reading makes letter–sound knowledge a necessity. This knowledge is needed to form a complete network of visual-phonological connections in lexical memory.

My view of sight word reading and its emergence in beginning readers carries implications for reading instruction. Before students can begin to read independently they need to be taught letter shapes, names, and sounds plus rudimentary phonetic segmentation skill. These skills might be fostered by the use of pictorial mnemonics to teach letter–sound associations (Ehri, Deffner, & Wilce, 1984) and by inventive spelling practice to teach phonetic segmentation (Ehri & Wilce, 1978b). Words that students are taught to read at the outset should contain at least some letter–sound relations that students recognize so that the words can be learned by sight using phonetic cues to form connections into memory. The same words should be read repeatedly to allow connections to form. Students can begin reading words before they have learned all the major letter–sound relations and how to recode. However, to move from use of phonetic cues to use of the cipher in their sight word reading, most students will probably require instruction and practice in how to recode. Few will be able to induce the system on their own.

Neither a phonics program nor a whole-word instructional program is completely suitable for facilitating the development of sight word reading as I have conceptualized it. Phonics programs prepare students for independent word reading by teaching them letters and letter–sound relations at the outset. Also, phonics programs teach learners recoding skill that is important for attaining Phase 3. However, by having students practice reading many different words sharing a small set of letter–sound correspondences rather than practice fewer words repeatedly, phonics programs may not help students develop strong sight vocabularies. Moreover, phonics programs may require students to begin recoding word patterns before students have gained much experience as phonetic cue readers. It may be that phonetic cue reading is important preparation for cipher reading. This possibility awaits further study.

Whole word instructional programs provide more practice on individual words. However, one weakness is that beginners may be pushed into sight word reading before they have the requisite letter knowledge and phonemic segmentation skill to function as phonetic cue readers. Also the words that beginners are required to read by sight in whole word programs have spellings that may be quite uninterpretable in terms of readers' letter–sound knowledge, thus precluding their use of phonetic cues in learning to read the words.

The present theory of sight word reading explains why poor readers are not very skilled at reading words. Not only are they unable to phonologically recode words very accurately or rapidly, but also their poor recoding skill precludes their learning to read words by sight using the cipher. In developing sight word reading skill they never get far enough beyond Phase 2 to become proficient at Phase 3. The connections formed between letters in spellings and sounds in pronunciations are partial and incomplete, not only because poor readers lack knowledge of some letter–sound relations, particularly vowels (Shankweiler & Liberman, 1972), but also because they are poor at segmenting pronunciations into constituent phonemes (Liberman et al., 1977). Although they do learn to read words by sight, they are slower and less accurate than skilled readers because the partial connections do not attach spellings securely to their pronunciations in memory (Ehri, 1989). Research is needed to explore further these deficits in poorer readers' sight word reading skill.

ACKNOWLEDGMENTS

Preparation of this chapter was supported in part by a grant from the National Institute of Child Health and Human Development (HD 23719).

REFERENCES

Adams, M. J. (1990). *Beginning to read: Thinking and learning about print*. Cambridge, MA: MIT Press.

Baron, J. (1977). Mechanisms for pronouncing printed words: Use and acquisition. In D. Laberge & S. J. Samuels (Eds.), *Basic processes in reading: Perception and comprehension* (pp. 175–216). Hillsdale, NJ: Lawrence Erlbaum Associates.

Baron, J. (1979). Orthographic and word specific mechanisms in children's reading of words. *Child Development, 50*, 587–594.

Barr, R. C. (1972). The influence of instructional conditions on word recognition errors. *Reading Research Quarterly, 7*, 509–529.

Barr, R. C. (1974–1975). The effect of instruction on pupil reading strategies. *Reading Research Quarterly, 10*, 555–582.

Barron, R. W. (1981). Development of visual word recognition: A review. In G. E. Mackinnon & T. G. Waller (Eds.), *Reading research: Advances in theory and practice* (Vol. 3, pp. 119–158). San Diego, CA: Academic Press.

Barron, R. W. (1986). Word recognition in early reading: A review of the direct and indirect access hypotheses. *Cognition, 24*, 93–119.

Barron, R. W., & Baron, J. (1977). How children get meaning from printed words. *Child Development, 48,* 587–594.

Beck, I. L. (1981). Reading problems and instructional practices. In G. E. Mackinnon & T. G. Waller (Eds.), *Reading research: Advances in theory and practice* (Vol. 2, pp. 55–95). San Diego, CA: Academic Press.

Becker, W. C., Dixon, R., & Anderson-Inman, L. (1980). *Morphographic and root word analysis of 26,000 high frequency words.* Eugene: University of Oregon College of Education.

Biemiller, A. (1970). The development of the use of graphic and contextual information as children learn to read. *Reading Research Quarterly, 6,* 75–96.

Brooks, L. R. (1977). Visual pattern in fluent word identification. In A. S. Reber & D. L. Scarborough (Eds.), *Toward a psychology of reading: The proceedings of the CUNY conferences* (pp. 143–181). Hillsdale, NJ: Lawrence Erlbaum Associates.

Bryant, P. E., & Bradley, L. (1980). Why children sometimes write words which they do not read. In U. Frith (Ed.), *Cognitive processes in spelling* (pp. 355–370). San Diego, CA: Academic Press.

Chall, J. S. (1983). *Stages of reading development.* New York: McGraw-Hill.

Coltheart, M., Davelaar, E., Jonasson, J. T., & Besner, D. (1977). Access to the internal lexicon. In S. Dornic (Ed.), *Attention and performance VI* (pp. 535–555). Hillsdale, NJ: Lawrence Erlbaum Associates.

Dewitz, P., & Stammer, J. (1980). *The development of linguistic awareness in young children from label reading to word recognition.* Paper presented at the National Reading Conference, San Diego, CA.

Dolch, E. W. (1939). *A manual for remedial reading.* Champaign, IL: Garrard Press.

Ehri, L. C. (1978). Beginning reading from a psycholinguistic perspective: Amalgamation of word identities. In F. B. Murray (Ed.), *Development of the reading process,* IRA Monograph No. 3 (pp. 1–33). Newark, DE: International Reading Association.

Ehri, L. C. (1980). The development of orthographic images. In U. Frith (Ed.), *Cognitive processes in spelling* (pp. 311–338). San Diego, CA: Academic Press.

Ehri, L. C. (1984). How orthography alters spoken language competencies in children learning to read and spell. In J. Downing & R. Valtin (Eds.), *Language awareness and learning to read* (pp. 119–147). New York: Springer-Verlag.

Ehri, L. C. (1986). Sources of difficulty in learning to spell and read. In M. L. Wolraich & D. Routh (Eds.), *Advances in developmental and behavioral pediatrics* (pp. 121–195). Greenwich, CT: JAI Press.

Ehri, L. C. (1987). Learning to read and spell words. *Journal of Reading Behavior, 19,* 5–31.

Ehri, L. C. (1989). The development of spelling knowledge and its role in reading acquisition and reading disability. *Journal of Learning Disabilities, 22,* 356-365.

Ehri, L. C. (1991). Development of the ability to read words. In R. Barr, M. L. Kamil, P. B. Mosenthal, & P. D. Pearson (Eds.), *Handbook of reading research* (Vol. 2, pp. 383–417). New York: Longman.

Ehri, L. C., Deffner, N. D., & Wilce, L. S. (1984). Pictorial mnemonics for phonics. *Journal of Educational Psychology, 76,* 880–893.

Ehri, L. C., & Wilce, L. S. (1980). The influence of orthography on readers' conceptualization of the phonemic structure of words. *Applied Psycholinguistics, 1,* 371–385.

Ehri, L. C., & Wilce, L. S. (1982). The salience of silent letters in children's memory for word spellings. *Memory and Cognition, 10,* 155–166.

Ehri, L. C., & Wilce, L. S. (1983). Development of word identification speed in skilled and less skilled beginning readers. *Journal of Educational Psychology, 75,* 3–18.

Ehri, L. C., & Wilce, L. S. (1985). Movement into reading: Is the first stage of printed word learning visual or phonetic? *Reading Research Quarterly, 20,* 163–179.

Ehri, L. C., & Wilce, L. S. (1986). The influence of spellings on speech: Are alveolar flaps /d/ or

/t/? In D. Yaden & S. Templeton (Eds.), *Metalinguistic awareness and beginning literacy* (pp. 101–114). Exeter, NH: Heinemann.

Ehri, L. C., & Wilce, L. S. (1987a). Cipher versus cue reading: An experiment in decoding acquisition. *Journal of Educational Psychology, 79,* 3–13.

Ehri, L. C., & Wilce, L. S. (1987b). Does learning to spell help beginners learn to read words? *Reading Research Quarterly, 18,* 47–65.

Ehri, L. C., Wilce, L. S., & Taylor, B. B. (1987). Children's categorization of short vowels in words and the influence of spellings. *Merrill-Palmer Quarterly, 33,* 393–421.

Firth, I. (1972). *Components of reading disability.* Unpublished doctoral dissertation, University of New South Wales.

Frith, U. (1979). Reading by eye and writing by ear. In P. A. Kolers, M. Wrolstad, & H. Bouma (Eds.), *Processing of visible language* (Vol. 1, pp. 379–390). New York: Plenum Press.

Frith, U. (1985). Beneath the surface of developmental dyslexia. In K. E. Patterson, J. C. Marshall, & M. Coltheart (Eds.), *Surface dyslexia: Neuropsychological and cognitive studies of phonological reading.* (pp. 301–330). London: Erlbaum.

Gleitman, L. R., & Rozin, P. (1977). The structure and acquisition of reading I. Relations between orthographies and the structure of language. In A. S. Reber & D. L. Scarborough (Eds.), *Toward a psychology of reading: The proceedings of the CUNY conferences* (pp. 1–53). Hillsdale, NJ: Lawrence Erlbaum Associates.

Glushko, R. J. (1979). The organization and activation of orthographic knowledge in reading aloud. *Journal of Experimental Psychology: Human Perception and Performance, 5,* 674–691.

Glushko, R. J. (1981). Principles for pronouncing print: The psychology of phonography. In A. M. Lesgold & C. A. Perfetti (Eds.), *Interactive processes in reading* (pp. 61–84). Hillsdale, NJ: Lawrence Erlbaum Associates.

Goodman, Y. M., & Altwerger, B. (1981). *Print awareness in preschool children: A working paper. A study of the development of literacy in preschool children.* Occasional Paper No. 4, Program in Language and Literacy, University of Arizona.

Goswami, U. (1986). Children's use of analogy in learning to read: A developmental study. *Journal of Experimental Child Psychology, 42,* 73–83.

Gough, P. B. (1972). One second of reading. In J. F. Kavanagh & I. G. Mattingly (Eds.), *Language by eye and by ear: The relationships between speech and reading* (pp. 331–358). Cambridge, MA: MIT Press.

Gough, P. B. (1984). Word recognition. In P. D. Pearson (Ed.), *Handbook of reading research* (pp. 225–253). New York: Longman.

Gough, P. B., & Hillinger, M. L. (1980). Learning to read: An unnatural act. *Bulletin of the Orton Society, 30,* 180–196.

Gough, P. B., Juel, C., & Roper-Schneider, D. (1983). Code and cipher: A two-stage conception of initial reading acquisition. In J. A. Niles & L. A. Harris (Eds.), *Searches for meaning in reading/language processing and instruction. Thirty-second yearbook of the National Reading Conference* (pp. 207–211). Rochester, NY: National Reading Conference.

Gough, P. B., & Tunmer, W. E. (1986). Decoding, reading, and reading disability. *Remedial and Special Education, 7,* 6–10.

Harste, J. C., Burke, C. L., & Woodward, V. A. (1982). Children's language and world: Initial encounters with print. In J. Langer & M. Smith-Burke (Eds.), *Bridging the gap: Reader meets author* (pp. 105–131). Newark, DE: International Reading Association.

Henderson, L. (1982). *Orthography and word recognition in reading.* San Diego, CA: Academic Press.

Hiebert, E. (1978). Preschool children's understanding of written language. *Child Development, 49,* 1231–1234.

Hood, J. (1977). Sight words are not going out of style. *The Reading Teacher, 30,* 379–382.

Humphreys, G. W., & Evett, L. J. (1985). Are there independent lexical and nonlexical routes in word processing? An evaluation of the dual-route theory of reading. *The Behavioral and Brain Sciences, 8,* 689–705.

Jorm, A. F., & Share, D. L. (1983). Phonological recoding and reading acquisition. *Applied Psycholinguistics, 4,* 103–147.

Juel, C. (1983). The development and use of mediated word identification. *Reading Research Quarterly, 18,* 306–327.

Juel, C., & Roper/Schneider, D. (1985). The influence of basal readers on first grade reading. *Reading Research Quarterly, 20,* 134–152.

Liberman, I. Y., Shankweiler, D., Liberman, A. M., Fowler, C., & Fischer, F. W. (1977). Phonetic segmentation and recoding in the beginning reader. In A. S. Reber & D. L. Scarborough (Eds.), *Toward a psychology of reading: The proceedings of the CUNY conferences* (pp. 207–225). Hillsdale, NJ: Lawrence Erlbaum Associates.

Lovett, M. W. (1987). A developmental approach to reading disability: Accuracy and speed criteria of normal and deficient reading skill. *Child Development, 58,* 234–260.

Marsh, G., Friedman, M., Welch, V., & Desberg, P. (1981). A cognitive-developmental theory of reading acquisition. In G. E. Mackinnon & T. G. Waller (Eds.), *Reading research: Advances in theory and practice* (Vol. 3, pp. 199–221). San Diego, CA: Academic Press.

Mason, J. (1980). When *do* children begin to read: An exploration of four-year-old children's letter and word reading competencies. *Reading Research Quarterly, 15,* 203–227.

Masonheimer, P. E., Drum, P. A., & Ehri, L. C. (1984). Does environmental print identification lead children into word reading? *Journal of Reading Behavior, 16,* 257–271.

Perfetti, C. A. (1985). *Reading ability.* New York: Oxford University Press.

Perfetti, C. A., & Hogaboam, T. (1975). Relationship between single word decoding and reading comprehension skill. *Journal of Educational Psychology, 67,* 461–469.

Reeds, J. A., & Wang, W. S. -Y. (1961). The perception of stops after *s. Phonetics, 6,* 78–81.

Reitsma, P. (1983). Printed word learning in beginning readers. *Journal of Experimental Child Psychology, 36,* 321–339.

Richek, M. A. (1977–1978). Readiness skills that predict initial word learning using two different methods of instruction. *Reading Research Quarterly, 13,* 200–222.

Rozin, P., & Gleitman, L. R. (1977). The structure and acquisition of reading II: The reading process and the acquisition of the alphabetic principle. In A. S. Reber & D. L. Scarborough (Eds.), *Toward a psychology of reading: The proceedings of the CUNY conferences* (pp. 55–141). Hillsdale, NJ: Lawrence Erlbaum Associates.

Shankweiler, D., & Liberman, I. Y. (1972). Misreading: A search for causes. In J. F. Kavanagh & I. G. Mattingly (Eds.), *Language by eye and by ear: The relationships between speech and reading* (pp. 293–317). Cambridge, MA: MIT Press.

Share, D. L., Jorm, A. F., Maclean, R., & Matthews, R. (1984). Sources of individual differences in reading acquisition. *Journal of Educational Psychology, 76,* 466–477.

Spring, C. (1978). Automaticity of word recognition under phonics and whole word instruction. *Journal of Educational Psychology, 70,* 445–450.

Stanovich, K. E. (1980). Toward an interactive compensatory model of individual differences in the development of reading fluency. *Reading Research Quarterly, 16,* 32–71.

Stanovich, K. E. (1986). Matthew effects in reading: Some consequences of individual differences in the acquisition of literacy. *Reading Research Quarterly, 21,* 360–406.

Treiman, R. (1985a). Phonemic analysis, spelling, and reading. In T. Carr (Ed.), *New directions for child development: The development of reading skills* (Vol. 27, pp. 5–18). San Francisco: Jossey-Bass.

Treiman, R. (1985b). Spelling of stop consonants after /s/ by children and adults. *Applied Psycholinguistics, 6,* 261–282.

Treiman, R., & Baron, J. (1983). Individual differences in spelling: The Phoenician-Chinese distinction. *Topics in Learning and Learning Disabilities, 3,* 33–40.

Tunmer, W. E., Herriman, M. L., & Nesdale, A. R. (1988). Metalinguistic abilities and beginning reading. *Reading Research Quarterly, 23,* 134–158.

Uhrey, J. (1989). *The effect of spelling instruction on the acquisition of beginning reading strategies.* Unpublished doctoral dissertation, Teachers College, Columbia University, New York.

Vellutino, F. R. (1979). *Dyslexia: Theory and research.* Cambridge, MA: MIT Press.

Venezky, R. L. (1970). *The structure of English orthography.* The Hague: Mouton.

6 The Representation Problem in Reading Acquisition

Charles A. Perfetti
University of Pittsburgh

In 1976 a series of three conferences on the "Theory and Practice of Early Reading" was held at the University of Pittsburgh's Learning Research and Development Center. The published proceedings required three volumes for its 45 contributions (Resnick & Weaver, 1979). The conference focused on *early* reading rather than skilled reading because more was known about early reading. As Resnick and Weaver (1979) observed in their introduction to the published proceedings, "It is in recognition of the differential state of scientific knowledge about decoding and comprehension that we choose to limit the focus of these volumes to early reading" (p. 5).

I have been skeptical about this assumption that decoding is well understood and comprehension is not. (Of course after a long period of research on comprehension any disparity should be greatly reduced.) The principles controlling printed word recognition remain the subject of scientific contention, and the alphabetic and phonological knowledge sources that underlie the acquisition of these processes are only now beginning to be fully appreciated. Moreover, the contrast between decoding and comprehension is not necessarily the only important one for beginning reading. What is critical is the difference between the processes of the learner and those of the skilled performer. The most important question for reading acquisition is how a child moves from the initial learning state to more advanced stages of reading skill.

Seen from this perspective, the areas of knowledge and ignorance in the scientific study of reading are not, respectively, decoding and comprehension but rather skilled reading and the processes of becoming a skilled reader. What we know a lot about is *skilled* word recognition and *skilled* comprehension. What we still know much less about are the processes of word recognition (and comprehension) that serve a child as he or she learns how to read. Even less is known about the processes by which the learning reader acquires higher levels of word recognition skill, moving from "novice" to "expert."

The central theoretical questions for beginning reading in this view are these: How does the child mentally represent printed words at each point of reading development? How does the child access these representations during encounters with print? How do word representation and word access change with experience and instruction? That is, how does learning occur? It is my impression that answers to these questions are not very well developed, although there are a number of promising beginnings. There is no doubt that we know a lot about beginning reading in some ways; there are lots of data. However, these data do not allow much specifically to be said about *representation, access,* and *change of representation.* In what follows I hope to make clear why these are the central questions and what it might mean to begin to answer them.

THE REPRESENTATION QUESTION

The general form of the representation question is: How are words represented in the mind? It may be possible to have a theory of reading acquisition without addressing the representation of words, as Gibson and Levin (1975) appear to have done by focusing on the acquisition of distinctive visual features as the essential process of learning to read. But behind any process of pattern recognition is the form of knowledge that allows recognition. This is the representation question. Reading cannot be addressed without at least an implicit assumption regarding this question. The access question is how a printed word comes to cause a reader's mental representation of a word to be activated and accessed by a printed stimulus. Although the representation question and the access question are intertwined, in empirical terms almost hopelessly so, they can be conceptualized and described separately for some purposes.

Although several debates remain active, years of research have provided important empirical generalizations about access to printed words. Prominent among the important facts is that word recognition is holistic in appearance and nonholistic in reality.

The appearance of holistic word perception goes back at least to Cattell's (1886) studies of word perception and the word superiority effect. The idea that words are perceived as "wholes" has been influential. Advocates of meaning-emphasis instruction pointed to evidence that words are read as a whole and to Gestalt psychologists' demonstrations of holistic perceptual processes (Williams, 1979). Cues of word shape and word length, along with partial information from letters, would constitute holistic perception.

It is now fairly clear that, whatever the appeal of the whole word hypothesis at the phenomenal level, word identification is mediated by letter perception. The individual constituent letters of the word are the units of its identification. Cues of word shape and word length appear to be of some significance, but they carry a very small share of the identification burden compared with letters.

Exactly how word recognition processes use the information of constituent letters is the central theoretical question in word identification. There are a number of models concerning word identification that provided a central role to constituent letters. Some models are strongly interactive (Rumelhart & Mc-Clelland, 1981), and others are more weakly interactive (Morton, 1969) or somewhat more bottom up (Gough, 1972; Massaro, 1975). The model of Forster (1979), which emphasizes a functionally isolated autonomous lexicon, is a particularly interesting contrast to the more fully interactive models of Rumelhart and McClelland. Although the bottom-up model of Forster is incompatible in its details with a fully interactive model, there is an interesting common ground in a hybrid model. I refer to this hybrid as the *Restricted-Interactive model* of word recognition.

THE RESTRICTED-INTERACTIVE MODEL

There are both autonomous and interactive components in the identification of words. Each of these becomes important for the development of reading. However the general preference for interactive models among reading researchers has partially masked the important autonomous aspects of word recognition. These autonomous aspects of word recognition are reflected in constraints on how context contributes to skilled reading. The Restricted-Interactive model reflects these constraints while allowing interactive processes.

A restricted-interactive model incorporates the fully interactive connections among representations of words, letters, and phonemes (Rumelhart & Mc-Clelland, 1981). It can allow a threshold mechanism that is raised or lowered by local semantic influences (Morton, 1969). The representation of letters and words in a hierarchical system having both top-down and bottom-up activation proves to be a powerful system as Rumelhart and McClelland have shown. Most important is the fairly natural way this system captures intraword context effects. The word superiority effect, the superior perception of a letter when it is in a word, and a range of related phenomena are elegantly explained by the principles of bidirectional activation (letters to words and vice versa). It demonstrates that phenomenologically compelling holistic word perception is mediated by perception of constituent letters while retaining in some sense the idea that not all the constituent letters need to be "seen." Some letters get a relatively high proportion of their activation from perceptual features and others get a relatively high proportion of their activation from the word.

The power of fully interactive models may be enhanced further by their connectionist successors, which assume that a words' representation is distributed over a matrix of connections rather than occupying a specific higher level node (McClelland, 1986; Seidenberg & McClelland, 1989; Seidenberg, this volume). These parallel distributed processing models offer a very powerful inductive machinery for learning to recognize complex patterns.

Although it can be argued that these interactive models are too powerful (i.e., they contain too many free parameters or too few *a priori* constraints), I want to assume that the principles they embody are the correct ones for word reading. Indeed, because I want to argue for constraints on interactions, assuming the correctness of the interactive framework makes things more interesting.

Now for the constraints. There are three of them that converge on a general principle: *The semantic output of word recognition is only weakly constrained by context.* (1) The early stages of word activation include a general <u>nonselective</u> set of semantic and syntactic attributes. Prior context does not preselect the semantic value of a word but rather influences which meaning will be carried over to the next stage of the reading process (i.e., comprehension). (2) The mechanism for these contextual influences is constrained. It relies on activation that spreads through a lexical network. It does not readily admit influence from outside the links of this network. For example, general knowledge or the theme of a discourse does not influence the early stages of lexical access. (3) In normal skilled reading, lexical access is so rapid that contextual influences are minimal. Thus the constraints of (1) and (2) that context does not preselect word meaning and that it does not include import of general knowledge are applicable to rapidly executing processes. Slowly executing processes are more permissive of broader influences.

There is a fair body of research that supports these constraints on lexical access. That word meaning is not preselected by context is consistent with the research of Swinney (1979), Tanenhaus, Lieman, and Seidenberg (1979), and Seidenberg, Tanenhaus, Lieman, and Bienkowski (1982). Although this conclusion appears to be challenged in experiments by Glucksberg, Kneuz, and Rho (1986), there are enough questions about methodological issues in this research (Seidenberg et al., 1982) to allow us to retain this constraint against prior selection of meaning by context.

As for the scope-of-influence constraint, there are two components. First, that lexical access is not influenced by imported knowledge has been shown by Seidenberg et al. (1982) and by Kintsch and Mross (1985) in priming experiments. Kintsch and Mross (1985) for example found no priming effects in a lexical decision task when words used as primes were thematically related through the discourse to the target word but were not lexically related to it. For example, replicating Swinney (1979), Kintsch and Mross (1985) found that in a text about a man running to catch a plane, the reading of the word *fly* primed both its contextually appropriate associate, *plane,* and its inappropriate associate, *insect,* but not an unassociated word that could have been activated by the theme of the discourse, *gate.* The second constraint of this type is that the spread of activation may be restricted to one link in a lexical network. DeGroot (1983) found that priming did not occur between words that were linked only through an intermediate word (e.g., *bull—[cow]—milk*). Although such effects extend to two-word links in other experiments, the conclusion remains that the spread of activation is limited.

Finally, because the evidence concerning constraints on lexical access comes from experiments that depart in some ways from actual reading, the question of their applicability to normal reading can be raised. Mitchell and Green (1978) argued that reading was too rapid for context effects. Indeed, word identification occurs too rapidly in skilled reading for context to have much advance effect on meaning selection. This is consistent with evidence from crossmodal priming experiments. However, it is perfectly possible for identification thresholds to be momentarily affected by local contexts, and it is inevitable that eventual meaning selection be completely determined by context. There remains doubt only about the locus (on the activation level of words before they are seen?) and the source (only from immediately preceding words?) of context effects. If the source is truly limited to preceding lexical associations then context would have a very limited effect, because only highly redundant word sequences could provide context facilitation.

Even if these limits on context are as severe as they appear, this does not trivialize the role of context in actual reading. It simply would make clear that context does its work postlexically. Meanwhile, the eye-movement evidence of Ehrlich and Rayner (1981) should be kept in mind. They found that both the duration and the probability of a fixation were influenced by a word's predictability. Effects on durations can be considered postlexical, but effects on probabilities of fixations require a different level of explanation. (Although note that one cannot easily argue that a word's threshold has been modified by context when it has not even been fixated.) Word skipping effects may represent responses to *regions* of text redundancy rather than to context effects on specific words. In any case, there seems to be every reason to assume that context effects operate at the lexical level in ordinary reading.

Thus I am arguing for two characteristics of word reading that are superficially contradictory. One is that word recognition is interactive, permissive of multiple sources of information that are mutually activated without constraints. The other is that word recognition is autonomous, not widely permissive of influences beyond highly constrained sources perhaps internal to the lexicon. There is nothing incompatible about these claims. The Restricted-Interactive model combines the interactive principles of McClelland and Rumelhart (1981) and the autonomous principles of Forster (1979). The lexicon is an isolable language subsystem. Some operations within this subsystem, such as word recognition, are not easily penetrated by information *outside* it. But the information *within* it can operate interactively. Interactive and autonomous processes coexist. It is just a matter of where the constraints are.

Phonemic and Orthographic Information

The Restricted-Interactive Model as described so far is silent on two questions that are critical for learning to read: What about speech codes, and what about orthographic rules? The interactive model of Rumelhart and McClelland (1981) allows a phonemic level but does not use it. It does not allow orthographic rules or even multiletter units. Connections are between position-coded individual letters and words. (But see Seidenberg & McClelland, 1989, for a connectionist model that uses multiletter units and a phonemic level.) It is a general characteristic of connectionist models that they do not represent rules. Rules are considered emergent properties of systems of connections that show rule-like behavior. A reader may behave in accordance with an orthographic rule or a rule mapping orthography to pronunciation, for example, pronouncing *mane* with a long vowel, but this rule is not used in accessing the word or even in producing it.

I embrace the idea of an emergent rule in this sense: The processing mechanism is ignorant of the rule's existence. The rule is knowable by a somewhat more reflective cognitive component. Skilled word recognition, like any process that executes rapidly, is based on direct contact with input not on reference to rules. Of course the concept of rules has had a different tradition in psychology and especially in psycholinguistics. This tradition holds that rules represent implicit knowledge and must have psychological reality to account for rule-like performance. Such psychological reality is almost axiomatic in explaining syntactic and phonological abilities. However for processes such as skilled word recognition that are primarily perceptual and require virtually no integration of information over time, rules have a different status. They essentially reflect probabilistic co-occurrence relations acquired through print experience. A reasonable claim for orthographic rules in short is that they constitute an important kind of information that skilled readers have but use only indirectly as they get instantiated in particular lexical representations.

For phonemic information my claim is similar but different in important ways. I believe that in skilled reading lexical access involves phonemic information obligatorily. Neither "direct access" nor "speech recoding" quite captures this idea of obligatory speech activation. It is not that letters are recoded into phonemes and then phoneme strings are used to access a word, and it is not that a string of letters directly accesses the word. Rather phonemic information is activated *during* lexical access as an intrinsic part of the process. This activation of speech codes occurs almost always because speech codes are part of the lexical representation. However, because letters and letter strings are also associated with phonemes, the opportunity for phonemic activation is doubled: activation of phonemes by letters and activation of phonemic word shapes by words. An interactive model extends naturally to allow such activation.

By this account, whether speech codes are "prelexical" or "postlexical" depends on the definition of access and how rapidly it occurs. (For one kind of evidence that prelexical speech processes occur, see Perfetti & Bell, 1991, and Perfetti, Bell, & Delaney, 1988; for another, see Van Orden, 1987.) When words are unfamiliar or when readers are unskilled, a rather high level of phonemic activation may build up before semantic codes are sufficiently activated. Whether this semantic activation ought to be equated with "lexical access" is a different question. But in real reading, as opposed to lexical decision tasks, it is hard to imagine what "lexical access" can refer to except a point at which the reader is prepared to name the word or to make some judgment about its meaning. (The reader certainly does not decide whether it is a word.)

Whether the name of a word is available before its meaning attributes is a meaningless question in general. The answer surely depends on a more precise characterization of meaning. When reading a sentence such as *John brought his dog with him*, there are several meaning features that might be aroused as part of the access of *dog—animal, four-legged animal, domestic four-legged animal, family pet*, and so on. Why should all these potential meaning features be aroused before the name *dog* is aroused? Or after? Some may precede, some may follow, but the name *dog* is inevitably and quickly aroused in some form.

To complicate things realistically, suppose the preceding text has referred to John's dog *Sam*. Will the reader recognize the referential identity of *dog* and *Sam* before the name *dog* is aroused? The answer is not clear, but it is surely an unprincipled answer, that is, one that depends on particular circumstances. The point is that when contextually relevant meanings, or references, are considered along with static lexically based semantic features, these questions of "recoding" and "direct access" get very cumbersome. Automatic phonemic activation as part of access at least handles matters in a straightforward way. The name code is always quickly accessed. Some meaning features may precede this name activation but certainly not all of them and, under some circumstances, probably not many of them. (For more on why this is a good way to think about speech processes in reading, see Perfetti & McCutchen, 1982, or Perfetti, 1985, Chapter 4.)

An important implication of this model is that there are no qualitative differences in the representation of words. In particular, the distinction between "regular" and "irregular" words has no bearing on representation. Expert representations comprise specific words and their constituent letters, whether they have more or less predictable pronunciations. The empirical basis for a regularity effect, in which words with fully predictable pronunciations based on grapheme–phoneme correspondences are supposed to be accessed more quickly than words with less predictable pronunciations, has been undermined by experiments by Seidenberg et al. (1982). Regular words have an advantage only at low frequencies. For words that have been encountered with high frequency the links between word representation and letters are strong enough that there is little time for build up of activation between letters and phonemes. However for a low-frequency word this activation is helpful for a regular word and less so for an irregular word.

A final issue is whether expert representations serve both production and perception, that is, both spelling and reading. My assumption is that they do. A specific word representation contains information about its constituent letters. It is this representation that is consulted for both spelling and reading. The access routes are different in the two cases, but the representation is the same. Indeed, *the quality of the lexical representation is reflected in idealized spelling performance.* (I say "idealized" because actual spelling reflects information processing constraints of sequencing, memory, and pattern verification, all of which can go awry.) This means that even for skilled readers many words, those that cannot be spelled, are imperfectly represented.

Summary

The characterization of an expert representation system is an important part of a theory of acquisition. In the case of reading acquisition, the critical representation system is a visually accessible lexicon. There are a number of models of adult word recognition that are consistent with most of the facts of word recognition. The model I propose is not another model of word recognition but rather a set of principles that embodies a class of models that I refer to as the Restricted-Interactive Model. The principles are that in skilled reading there are *restrictions* on the use of nonlexical knowledge in word identification. General knowledge and expectations have little or no influence on the initial access of a word. At the same time the identification processes are *interactive* in the use of intralexical information. That is, links between letters and words, letters and phonemes, and phonemes and words permit reciprocal activation. It is likely also that multiletter units and multiphoneme units are established as part of the lexical component. Phonemic activation always occurs as a part of lexical access. A single representation serves both reading and spelling, and the quality of the representation is indexed by idealized spelling performance.

THE ACQUISITION QUESTION

The acquisition question is: How does a child come to have a representation system something like this Restricted-Interactive system (or any other candidate for an expert system)? Answering this question proves to be rather difficult, partly because the question has not been asked in this way. Researchers have asked whether phonics or whole word teaching is better, whether letter names should or should not be taught, and whether various skills are prerequisites for learning how to read. Such questions are very important, but the research on them seems to have had little contact with theoretical issues and hence has had limited impact on fundamental theoretical issues.

In recent years however some important theoretically guided research has begun to shed light on fundamental issues. The acquisition question has been addressed by Ehri in her theory of word amalgamation (1978, 1980, 1984), by Gough and Hillinger (1980) in their two-stage theory of acquisition, by Liberman and Shankweiler (1979; Shankweiler, Liberman, Mark, Fowler, & Fischer, 1979) in their arguments for the centrality of speech codes in acquisition, and by Bryant and Bradley (1980) in their claim that reading and spelling draw on different representations, to name just a few examples. (See also the theoretically motivated papers by Byrne, 1991, Stanovich, 1991, and Gough & Juel, 1991.) Each of these lines of research has contributed to our understanding of acquisition. Furthermore, there have been some bold attempts, less successful perhaps, to answer the acquisition question by characterizing stages of development (Chall, 1967; Ehri & Wilce, 1983; Marsh, Desberg, & Cooper, 1976).

A descriptive theory of acquisition and eventually some explanatory theory of acquisition are exactly what is needed, although the attempts so far must be judged as preliminary. The fact is that there is as yet an inadequate database for anything beyond the most general theory of acquisition. Given the vast amount of research on early reading, this probably seems an extravagant claim. We lack theoretically motivated detailed studies of children in various stages of progress in learning to read that will tell us about lexical representation. Again, there are some exceptions to this generalization, and recent research by Ehri (Ehri, 1991; Ehri & Wilce, 1985) provides a good example of how children in different stages of prereading and early reading might exhibit different word representation strategies.

Nevertheless, the general state of affairs means that a theory of representation acquisition has some general constraints but few particular ones. In what follows I describe what I think an acquisition theory might look like, in general terms, noting also at least some empirical support for the theory. Because the phrase *representation acquisition* is a bit awkward, I refer simply to *acquisition*. However, the issue is representations—what are they like? How does a reader acquire them? How do they change with increasing skill?

There are two general components of the acquisition of lexical expertise to be addressed. First is the general course of acquiring a *functioning* lexical representation system. Second is the course of acquiring an *autonomous* lexical representation system. The first entails attention to a number of important issues. What is the role of phonological awareness in acquisition of a functioning lexicon? Of orthographic knowledge? Of rules, both of grapheme–phoneme correspondences and of orthography? Do production and perception use the same representation?

ACQUIRING FUNCTIONAL LEXICAL
REPRESENTATIONS

Although I assume that reading is essentially a linguistic process and that linguistic processes are implicitly rule governed, I suggest that rules have a minor role in the acquisition of lexical representations. *The major essential development in learning to read is the acquisition of individual word representations.*

To simplify the argument, assume that three arbitrary levels of reading skill can be identified. Level 1 corresponds to an average midyear first-grade student; Level 2 perhaps corresponds to a second- or third-grade student; and Level 3 corresponds to a fifth-grade student. (The grade levels are quite arbitrary.) Here are the fundamental changes in the lexicon to be seen with increasing skill level: (a) the number of lexical entries increases; and (b) the quality of lexical representations improves. I consider each of these in turn.

Increasing the Number of Entries

The number of words that can be read increases with experience. There are three possible ways to account for this increase. First, with age children learn more words through both printed and aural exposure. Increased size of the lexicon merely reflects the acquisition of new words, that is, vocabulary growth. Second, the number of entries increases generatively, that is, because the child learns decoding rules that are based on grapheme–phoneme correspondences and orthographic regularities that extend his or her aural lexicon to his or her printed lexicon. Third, the number of entries increases because the child has increasing exposure to specific words. The words the child sees are the words he or she acquires.

Each of these explanations is incomplete at best. The first is actually empirically false, because some of the words that get added to the printed lexicon were originally available through spoken language. Some words that are fairly common in the child's language are added to the print lexicon fairly late; *ache* is probably an example of this. Still, it is obvious that a significant portion of new entries into the printed lexicon are new entries into the general lexicon. The proportion of new entries (relative to other sources of lexical growth) probably increases with reading experience.

The second and third explanations are not easily dismissed, but they are incomplete. The second, that new entries reflect increased scope of decoding rules, fails to explain the acquisition of so-called "irregular" words that show less frequent grapheme–phoneme correspondences. Clearly such words are acquired throughout the period of learning to read. The third seems to restrict acquisition to specific word learning and does not generalize to words not specifically learned. It is possible that a reader does not have a high quality representation of a printed word without having experienced it visually, but the decoding system allows the reading of previously encountered words already represented through spoken language.

Because the decoding model and specific word learning model have complementary problems, a sensible model for acquiring new words might seem to be a dual-mechanism model, with one mechanism that is based on decoding rules gradually acquired and expanded and made context sensitive and the other that is based on specific pattern learning. The dual-mechanism learning model is thus parallel to dual route lexical access models that postulate both a "recoding" route and a "direct" route to the lexicon (Baron, 1977). (See Stanovich & West, 1989, for evidence that children acquire both generalized, phonologically based and experience based, word-specific representations.)

By this dual route account the difference between Level 1 and Level 2, for example, is this: Level 1 has some decoding principles and some specific words; the Level 2 reader has a larger lexicon (a) because of learning more specific words, and (b) because of increasing the power of decoding rules. But this, if it means anything, must mean that the influence of (b) is on words yet to be encountered in print. That is, decoding rules generatively increase the potential of the lexicon. At Level 2 some new words might have been added to the lexicon through decoding and by Level 3 still more words have been added. A word, once acquired, may be represented strictly as a specific unit.

The point is that the number of lexical entries may increase both because of decoding and specific word learning; however the effect of the decoding mechanisms is on the number of specific words acquired. They have no other significance, at least for the acquisition of a lexicon. If they are to have further significance, it will have to be in allowing an alternative access route to specific words.

It is important to notice what is at issue here. Decoding rules of some sort are important in providing a backup process in reading never-encountered words. (Context has this value also.) But as a word becomes represented in the lexicon, decoding becomes only indirectly important. That is, it has provided the links between letters and phonemes that can be activated to assist recognition. However with increasing word familiarity, these links lose their ability to be of much assistance.

Figure 6.1 illustrates the suggestion I am making about acquisition. The general course of acquisition is one of increasing the number of entries. Both regular and irregular words increase. There is some increase also in the power and scope of decoding rules, which become increasingly context sensitive. (If someone prefers to call these analogies rather than decoding rules I have no quarrel with that; however I doubt that we can agree on the ultimate decidability of rule-governed versus analogic nature of processes in general.)

Thus there are two interdependent acquisitions across observation levels. The number of actual lexical entries increases and the potential number of entries increases. These two acquisitions are mutually facilitative. The more powerful

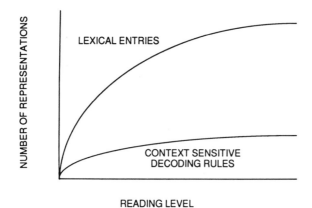

FIG. 6.1. Two growth trajectories that describe increases in the reader's lexicon. See text for explanation.

the context-sensitive decoding rules (or analogic capabilities), the more entries the learner can acquire. And the more entries , the more powerful the decoding rules. Lexical learning (as opposed to lexical access) is highly interactive.

Finally, although these two acquisitions are interactive, their trajectories are probably different. The acquisition trajectory for specific words continues throughout the reading life of the individual, probably as an exponential function. The acquisition trajectory for rules is a lower one, perhaps asymptoting fairly early for practical purposes.[1] It appears that I am suggesting that acquisition of the lexicon is essentially a matter of what is often called "sight" vocabulary. Indeed this interpretation is not too far off, although this may seem out of character for a linguistically based view of reading. The notion of sight vocabulary is a bit imprecise, however, in terms of what the child comes to know; it implies, for example, holistic patterns. The present account emphasizes the acquisition of specific (but abstract) letter patterns, reinforced by sublexical links with phonemes. There is no possibility in this account for holistic patterns playing a major role in recognition. This observation leads directly to the next major acquisition, the change in the quality of lexical representations.

Increasing the Quality of Representations

Increasing skill not only brings about more entries but also produces changes in the representations. There is always a question in development as to whether

---

[1]Actually a distinction between rule-governed and analogic might suggest two possible trajectories. Analogical processes should be constant, and hence potential analogic lexical entries should increase with the number of actual lexical entries and would have a longer trajectory than that for a rule-based process.

developmental changes are fundamental, reflecting restructuring of knowledge, or incremental, reflecting assimilation of new knowledge by existing structures. I am not sure whether such a question is decidable even in principle. I am more certain that I am in no position to decide it in the specific case of lexical acquisition. However, I can suggest that the idea of representation quality can be usefully applied to learning to read.

There are two principles that characterize the development of lexical representation quality: precision and redundancy. These principles are developed as follows.

Precision. The precision principle is that fully specified representations are superior to partially specified ones. Representations that become more fully specified can be said to be more precise. The advantage of a fully specified representation is that it is *determinant* with respect to the input features that will trigger it. In the case of word reading this means that a given letter string will be sufficient to activate a specific word and to quickly bring about the recognition of that word rather than some other word. It also means that there can be less reliance on context. In short, only in a system with fully specified representations can the input features, the constituent letters in this case, easily control recognition.

In contrast to precise representations are variable representations. The variable representations include free variables in the positions where the precise, fully specified representations include specific letters (or "constants"). (One might also think of precise representations as having bound variables rather than free variables.)

To illustrate what this means for word reading, Fig. 6.2 shows three levels of precision for the words *iron, tongue,* and *ukulele,* which are three irregular words from a commonly used sight vocabulary list. The three levels correspond arbitrarily to the same hypothetical first-, third-, and fifth-grade readers as before. The reader at Level 1 has imprecise representations for all three words. For *iron,* the identity of the second vowel is a free variable rather than a constant. For *tongue,* not only is the identity of the vowel letter unknown but the number of letters following the *n* is also unknown. (However, the reader knows something follows the *n.*) Over the levels, the representations for all words increase in precision. *Ukulele,* by this example, undergoes a reversal in which a precise but incorrect letter is represented at Level 2 and replaced by a variable at Level 3.

There are several nonarbitrary choices in the representation changes depicted in Fig. 6.2. One is that early representations for English words are likely to include initial letters, a well-established fact of beginning reading (Marchbanks & Levin, 1965; Williams, Blumberg, & Williams, 1970). A representation with variables is more likely to have these variables in medial and final portions of the word. A second assumption is that vowels are more likely to be variables than are consonants. Evidence for this assumption is indirect and is based on findings that

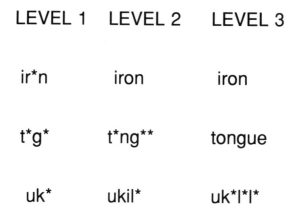

LEVEL 1   LEVEL 2   LEVEL 3

ir*n   iron   iron

t*g*   t*ng**   tongue

uk*   ukil*   uk*l*l*

FIG. 6.2. Change in representation precision over three hypothetical skill levels in the acquisition of reading for the words *iron, tongue,* and *ukulele.* Asterisks denote free variables in the representation. For example, at Level 1 the reader's representation for *tongue* does not include precise knowledge concerning the second letter nor concerning how many letters follow the *n.*

reading errors are especially frequent for words with complex vowels (Liberman, Shankweiler, Orlando, Harris, & Berti, 1971) and on the fact that vowel letters enter into more variable phonemic mappings than do consonants.

An important principle is that phonemic values play a large role in determining which letters get represented. It is the phonemic variability of vowels that makes them more likely for variable representations. However, phonemic principles also make predictions concerning the representation of consonants. For example, nasal consonants that precede stop consonants are more likely to be unrepresented or to be represented by assimilating a preceding vowel, for example, *tongue* may be missing the *n* or the *o* or more generally represent the nasal vowel nucleus as a variable, as shown for Level 1 (Fig. 6.2). As examples of phonemic influences, consonant clusters, for example, *string* and medial syllables of multisyllabic words (see *ukulele,* Fig. 6.2), may be prone to variable representation.

There is a question here of how to understand the concept of variable representation. The essence of the concept is the instability and changeability of the representation. It is applied to a representation that is in a state of change. It does not necessarily imply a representation that includes incorrect letters. However, cases in which a learner seems to have an incorrect representation probably should be thought of as variable except for those rare conditions in which a reader, for some reason, has a deeply held faith in an incorrect spelling. Such an incorrect representation will be very difficult to establish as a string of constants because actual inputs will never contain those specific letters. "Variable" does not imply only momentarily incorrect spellings. It entails also incomplete representations. Thus the precision principle is that lexical representations evolve toward completeness and specification.

Redundancy.   The second principle of qualitative changes in representation is the redundancy principle. Just as representations become more fully specified, they also increase in their inclusion of redundant information sources. The main source of redundancy is between letters and phonemes and, more generally, between orthographic strings and phonemic strings.

Consider the immature representation. It is not only imprecise in its orthography, but it is also more dependent on it. Phonemic information is less reliable because the learner is gradually acquiring the mapping system. In fact, one can think of the phonemic information connected to grapheme strings as having the same kind of variability illustrated previously for the orthography. There are two major changes in quality that have the same effect. First, the representation of phonemes changes. How it changes is a complex affair perhaps dependent on method of instruction. Figure 6.3 illustrates just one possibility across three hypothetical levels of skill not necessarily identical to the levels of Fig. 6.2. (To emphasize this possibility, the three levels are illustrated as Levels 0, 1, and 3.) At Level 0 the representation reflects the reader's knowledge that the letter *i* is associated with the phoneme /ay/, its name. That means there is imperfect phonemic help in accessing the word. Still there is some, and the /ay/ might assist restricting the search space for recognition to *i*-initial words. This level may correspond to the stage of phonetic-cue reading identified by Ehri and Wilce (1985). At Level 1 things are different because the reader has experienced quite a bit of print and, in some cases, perhaps some direct "phonics" instruction. Either from direct learning or from indirect induction the representation now includes multiple phonemic values for each letter in *iron*. Some are the names of the letters, but in general there is the array of phonemes contained in the language associated to letters in a many-to-one and many-to-many fashion. This representation provides some phonemic assistance to lexical access, but it is limited. The limitations arise from the fact that phoneme–grapheme mappings are weak and not yet context-sensitive. The letter *r*, for example, causes activation of a diffuse set of phonemic representations: /ar/, /r/, and perhaps /ru/, /ro/, and other representations that include inappropriate vowel environments. Thus there is a diffuse activation at the phonemic level with the result being a relatively low net activation of the word.

By Level 3 there has been a reversal in phoneme proliferation with fewer phonemes now represented. Phoneme representation has become context sensitive. A finer picture of this representation would be to show intermediate orthographic units. That is, letter strings intermediate between individual letters and words could have a separate representation. (This is not reflected in Fig. 6.3 to avoid clutter and because the effect of an intermediate level is readily repre-

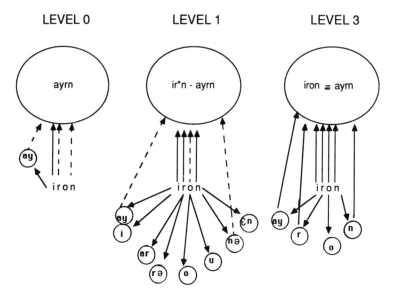

FIG. 6.3. Development of redundant phonemic information over three hypothetical levels of reading acquisition. The levels are not necessarily identical to those of Fig. 6.2. The large circles are word representations containing spellings and pronunciations (a pronunciation only at Level 0), and the small circles are phonemes and phoneme sequences that are associated with specific letters. Thus each level represents the word *iron,* but the form of the representation begins as a phonemic object at Level 0, includes variable orthographic information at Level 1, and at Level 3 includes a fully specified orthographic representation "bonded" to the phonemic representation. (An analogy to chemical bonding is intended.) Meanwhile, the representation of phonemes changes in two directions, beginning impoverished at Level 0, proliferating at Level 1, and by Level 3 reducing to mainly those that are sensitive to the orthographic context imposed by the word *iron.* The solid arrows indicate strong activation patterns and the dashed arrows weak ones.

sented by a more restricted connection at the single letter level.) In effect, the representation now includes knowledge that *ir* at the beginning of a word is strongly mapped to /ayr/ and that final *n* is always /n/. Notice that this first mapping will later be modified to accommodate new acquisitions (e.g., *irritate*). To illustrate that the representation system is still developing, the letter *o* activates the phoneme /o/, one of its context-free phonemes. But the overall effect is that there are now word-specific phoneme values to assist word access. The second development is the bonding of orthographic with phonemic representations. At Level 0 there is no orthographic representation at all, so this could be thought of as a very early encounter with a word known to the child through spoken language. At Level 1 the representation includes an underspecified orthographic representation, in the spirit of Fig. 6.2. Because of its variable representation, it is only weakly bonded to the word *iron* (/ayrn/). By Level 3 the reader has had enough experience with *iron* or with related printed words that the orthographic representation consists solely of constants and is strongly bonded to the word *iron* (/ayrn/), as represented in Fig. 6.3 by the double bond.[2] These two developments, the strengthening of context-dependent grapheme–phoneme connections and the bonding of orthographic and phonemic representations, are not independent. Indeed they are virtually the same thing described at two levels. This is the development of redundancy. At the constituent level phonemes are redundant with respect to the letters. At the word level the pronunciation is redundant with the spelling. Across levels the letters are redundant with the spelling and the phonemes are redundant with the pronunciation. Notice that any *one* kind of representation can be eliminated and lexical access can still occur in principle. The string of letters *i-r-o-n* is sufficient to trigger a bonded representation (*iron*-/ayrn/) and so is a string of phonemes. The redundancy advantage is that redundancy overdetermines lexical access. The redundancy advantage is important in reading both for bootstrapping the identification of unfamiliar words and for the rapid automatic recognition of familiar words.

In summary I take the acquisition of a functioning lexical representation system to involve increases in the number of orthographically addressable lexical entries and increases in the quality of the lexical representations. In short, the child comes to know more words and to know more about these words. The increase in quantity comes primarily through the acquisition of specific words. The increase in quality is a matter of gains in precision and redundancy of lexical representations. Fully specified orthographic and phonemic representations replace variable and unreliable ones. In the next section I take up the question of bringing this functional lexicon to a level of autonomy.

ACQUIRING AN AUTONOMOUS LEXICON

The functional lexicon represents words so that they can be visually accessed. Beyond this the representation system of the skilled reader acquires the property of autonomy. In terms of the Restricted-Interactive Model the lexicon acquires some restrictions on its access. The lexicon changes from a wide-open public tavern in which anything goes to a private club in which access is restricted to elite members with proper orthographic credentials.

This private club metaphor goes awry if it implies a lexicon of *less* flexibility.

---

[2]This bonding idea, I now recognize, is approximately the same concept as Ehri's (1978, 1980) "amalgamation" of information sources. Ehri especially emphasized the combining of visual orthographic information with phonetic information in the child's acquisition of word recognition.

Surely the advancement of reading skill leads to more access not less. The restrictions, thus, are not on absolute access but on access privilege: First access rights go to correctly specified grapheme strings then only to the other sources of information.

The main characteristic of an autonomous lexicon is its impenetrability. By definition, knowledge and expectations cannot penetrate an autonomous lexicon. This characteristic does not apply to the functional lexicon of the beginning reader for whom knowledge and expectations, and context in general, contribute heavily to the activity of identifying words. This interactive access process also is characteristic of older readers of low skill (Perfetti & Roth, 1981; Stanovich, 1980). The question is how does the lexicon acquire impenetrability? And, fundamentally, what exactly is it that is impenetrable?

Before considering these questions it is useful to clarify why an impenetrable lexicon is of value to the reader. Superficial analysis indeed leads to the opposite conclusion, namely that it is a fully interactive lexicon that is valuable. Such a lexicon allows information from all sources to penetrate lexical representations and makes the job of recognition easier. However this is a misleading analysis. The reader is served by expectations, knowledge, and beliefs in forming interpretations not in recognizing words. If expectations, knowledge, and beliefs actually penetrated the lexical representations, the identification of a word could become a hit-or-miss affair. Only if the graphic input has privileged status in access can accurate word identification take place. Merely postponing the influence of expectations, knowledge, and beliefs a few precious milliseconds, so that it is the output of the identification process that is influenced, will make a more efficient system. It is characteristic of the young reader and the low-ability older reader to be rather context dependent in word identification (Perfetti & Roth, 1981; Stanovich, 1980). The general principle is that a slow identification process will enable penetration of expectations to occur, and readers of low skill have slow identification processes. Moreover, even skilled readers will show contextual influences when their basic identification processes are retarded by altering the identifiability of the words (Perfetti & Roth, 1981).

The acquisition of a context-free autonomous lexicon thus must be part of learning to read. However it has not been clear what such an acquisition entails except experience with words. I propose that the critical events for the acquisition of autonomy are the acquisition of *fully specified and redundant* lexical representations. Autonomy follows naturally from the acquisition of such representations. As lexical entries become fully specified they also become "encapsulated." Because the graphic representation has no "holes" in it, it can be triggered by graphic input in a totally deterministic way. It is the encapsulated, self-contained character of a representation that makes it a specialized data structure responsive only to appropriate input features. (This claim of course is in the spirit of Fodor's, 1983, modularity thesis. See also Perfetti, 1990, and Stanovich, 1990, for applications of modularity to reading.)

Identifying representation quality as the critical element for autonomy appears to ignore practice. Although it may be necessary, how can a fully specified and redundant representation be sufficient for autonomy? Practice is indeed important. However, practice has already taken place on route to establishing the fully specified and redundant representation. As continued access to this representation occurs there should be some consequences. The speed of access should increase, for example. Speed of access, however, is a by-product of highly skilled automated recognition not its defining characteristic. Thus the question reduces to how much practice is required for autonomy? Certainly practice extended over years of reading helps maintain the autonomy of access and continues to add new entries to the autonomy subsection of the lexicon. However, it is possible that the practice that is sufficient to establish the high quality (fully specified and redundant) representation is sufficient to make it autonomous. Thus my suggestion is that the reading lexicon contains two sublexicons: a developing functional lexicon with representations under specified, and an autonomous lexicon with representations fully specified and redundant. A given word moves from the developing functional lexicon to the autonomous lexicon just when it becomes fully specified and redundant. This is essentially a word-by-word process.

This again raises the question of how to decide what the quality of a given word representation is. The key measure, I suggest, is spelling, and the concepts of variability and facility have to be applied. The idealized situation is a spelling test in which all possible performance constraints are reduced: Paper and pencil are available; the words are short; and the subject has the opportunity to verify his or her spelling. Variability and facility enter in the following way. It is not sufficient for the child to spell the word correctly one time. The child must spell it correctly repeatedly over different testing situations. And it is not sufficient for the spelling to be uncertain or effortful. Perhaps speed of correct spelling can be taken as an index of facility along with distractibility—how easily a subject can be influenced to change his or her mind about the correct spelling given two or three plausible alternatives. The details of defining an individual reader's representation quality is a tricky matter. On the other hand the principle seems clear enough. Reliable, confident, and facile spelling is an index of high quality representation. By hypothesis it is also an index of an autonomous representation.

My proposal then is that the reader's lexicon can acquire impenetrability as a result of the quality of its representation, which in turn is the result of knowledge (orthographic and phonemic) and practice (at lexical access). One question is whether there is anything in this claim that is not included in the concept of *automaticity?* The difference between automaticity and acquired impenetrability is a matter of entailments. Automaticity entails either processes that occur without allocation of resources or processes that are not easily inhibited. Thus research on the development of automaticity relies either on dual task methods to demonstrate automaticity as processing low in resource demands or Stroop-inspired interference methods to demonstrate automaticity as processing that resists inhibition. The literature on reading includes mainly research of the latter kind, in which pictures of objects with words printed on them are presented to children (Guttentag & Haith, 1978; Rayner & Posnansky, 1978; Schadler & Thissen, 1981; Stanovich & West, 1981). With familiar words, there is an interference effect when children are asked to name pictures and ignore words. This interference has been found by the end of first grade (Guttentag & Haith, 1978; Schadler & Thissen, 1981; Stanovich, Cunningham, & West, 1981). However, if the automaticity question is cast in terms of resource allocation rather than processing without intention, automaticity is largely acquired between first and second grade but continues to develop through adulthood (Horn & Manis, 1987).

The entailments of acquired impenetrability are slightly different. Impenetrability leaves open the question of whether resources are required by the impenetrable process. It assumes that the impenetrable process cannot be penetrated or inhibited. A younger reader might have impenetrable processes that nevertheless require resources. However, it is generally the case that the potential for resource savings is a function of the representation quality just as impenetrability is. Where representation quality is low, the reader may direct more resources to lexical access. Where representation quality is high, resource demands are reduced because access is overdetermined by input features. However, the supposition that word reading can in general be completely attention free might not be correct. Even the simplest letter comparison processes seem to demand attention (Posner & Boies, 1971). It is best to think of resource costs as a matter of degree and not as an all-or-none distinction between attention-free and attention demanding. Speed of processing is commonly used as an index of automatized responding. In the present account speed of access is a result of representation quality and an intrinsic characteristic of impenetrability. Only rapidly executed processes can be computationally autonomous. Slower processes reflect higher-level contributions to some process that is intrinsically altered by being slowed down. For example, when a novel word is read it is processed outside the autonomous lexicon, which fails to serve up a representation to the lexical processor. The problem solving component, after some time, gains access to what the lexical processor has, which is a novel string of letters and some decoding rules.[3]

Phonological Knowledge

Phonological knowledge is clearly critical in skilled reading. The heart of lexical access is the activation of a phonologically referenced name code. Although this

---

[3]This description of a "lexical processor" and a "problem solving component" reflects the structure of language processing outlined by Forster (1979).

assumption does not appear to be universally shared, it should be without contention. Thus I want to focus not on the importance of phonological information,
which I merely assume, but on the role of explicit phonemic knowledge, which I
think cannot be so easily assumed.

The issue simply put is whether explicit reflective phonemic knowledge is
necessary to learn to read an alphabetic orthography. By my account the answer
is "yes and no." A distinction between *computational* and *reflective* knowledge
is important here. Computational knowledge is simply connections between
phonemes (or letter names) and letters that allow pronunciations of grapheme
strings to be partly or wholly computed. Reflective knowledge is an awareness of
the basic nature of these connections, that is, they depend on the fact that words
comprise meaningless speech segments. Some computational phonemic knowledge is necessary to gain a functional lexical representation system of any size,
and explicit reflective knowledge, or "awareness," is a sign of a more powerful
learning mechanism than implicit knowledge. However, explicit reflective
phonemic knowledge is not necessary to begin the acquisition of a functional
representation system. All that is necessary is the ability to represent some of the
graphemes of a word and to use these to compute the word's phonological
representation. Because the essence of a grapheme string is its orthography not
its pronunciation, it is possible in principle to acquire some word representations
in ignorance of connections between letters and phonemes. Thus it is possible
that initial progress in acquisition could be based only on visual information
(Gough & Hillinger, 1980). However, this is not what really happens or at least
not for very long. Children do acquire phonemic mappings to letters and this
serves the acquisition of word representations. Indeed, Ehri and Wilce (1985)
have shown that children just starting to read are disposed to take advantage of
grapheme–phoneme connections even when their knowledge of phoneme values
is little more than letter names. But taking advantage of these connections is to
use essentially computational knowledge rather than reflective knowledge.

Thus the very early computational use of phonemic information characterizes
learning how to read. Furthermore, we know that providing children with
phonemic instruction can improve their reading. Bradley and Bryant's (1983)
study showed that training backward readers in an orthographic-phonemic task
improved their reading performance. Treiman and Baron (1981) also reported
effective training that was based on segmentation knowledge. (See also
Lundberg, Frost, & Peterson, 1988). Such studies demonstrate a causal connection between phonemic knowledge and reading skill and strengthen the conclusion from many correlational studies that show beginning reading success is
predicted by prereading measures of phonological knowledge (e.g., Lundberg,
Olofsson, & Wall, 1980; Mann & Liberman, 1984; Stanovich, Cunningham, &
Cramer, 1984; see Wagner & Torgesen, 1987, and Tunmer, 1991, for reviews; for
recent research on these issues see the collection of papers in Rieben & Perfetti,
1991 and in Brady & Shankweiler 1991.)

Nevertheless, explicit reflective phonemic knowledge is not a prerequisite to reading. Perfetti, Beck, Bell, and Hughes (1987) found that first-grade children showed progress in simple word and pseudoword reading *before* they showed progress in a task of *explicit* phonemic awareness. (The task was phoneme deletion in which the child produces, for example, cat without the /k/ or without the /t/.) Because progress on a simple computation-type synthetic phonemic task ("blending" phonemes into words and syllables) preceded progress in word reading, we concluded that the relationship between explicit phonemic knowledge and reading is reciprocal in a sense. Some rudimentary phonemic knowledge—not reflective analytic knowledge—is causally necessary for progress in word reading. However a deeper reflective kind of phonemic knowledge, the kind most researchers have in mind when they refer to "phonemic awareness," has a more complex reciprocal relationship. Such awareness comes through experience with alphabetic stimuli. The typical child does not have such knowledge, or at least not in a very useful form, that is based only on his or her spoken language experience.[4] Indeed, it is hard to imagine exactly where it would come from. The child begins to treat words as having separable constituents when he or she notices that printed words have such constituents in the form of letters. When the child also notices that these alphabetic symbols have speech sounds, the child is in a good position to develop phonemic awareness. With this development comes the potential for further gains in reading. Indeed Perfetti et al. (1987) found that gains in awareness, although initially preceded by gains in reading, were then followed by further gains in reading. In short, the pattern of time-lag correlations supports a reciprocal relationship between explicit and analytic phonemic knowledge and learning to read.

Downgrading phonological awareness from causal status to reciprocal status does not diminish its importance for reading. Indeed, it allows it to be seen as a central component of reading instead of as a prerequisite. The problem with prerequisites is that there is an implication that they must be met before progress is made. If phonemic awareness and learning to read are reciprocal, phonemic awareness is no longer a prerequisite that has to be met (and cannot be met by most children) but an achievement of learning that then facilitates further learning. The glue for the redundant lexical representation and, perhaps more important, the basis for a fully specified lexical representation comes from phonemic knowledge along with alphabetic knowledge.

Nevertheless, there is the evidence of the training studies to consider. On the one hand is a clear indication that children make significant progress in word reading prior to exhibiting explicit analytic phonemic knowledge (Perfetti et al., 1987). On the other hand, there are training studies that demonstrate gains in word reading following gains in phonemic knowledge produced by training

---

[4]Actually I would stress the accessibility of the knowledge as the problem. Very young children show speech play that indicates experimentation with the meaningless sounds of language even before their speech is very well developed.

(e.g., Bradley & Bryant, 1983; Treiman & Baron, 1981). However, this is only an apparent contradiction not a real one. If we see the relationship between two competencies as prerequisite or if the overall knowledge structure is hierarchical then there is a contradiction. Phonemic knowledge and reading must have an orderly sequence. By one account, this sequence is first phonemic knowledge and then word reading. By the alternative account, the by-product account (because phonemic knowledge comes as a by-product of learning to read), the sequence is reversed: Word reading comes before phonemic knowledge.

Suppose instead that the relationship is not hierarchical but interactive. There is abstract knowledge concerning words, namely that words are systematically decomposable into meaningless segments. The segments constitute a finite generative vocabulary for words, and there are both printed segments (letters) and spoken segments (phonemes). Knowledge about the two kinds of segments can develop in tandem and probably does in many cases. Which develops more quickly may depend on the linguistic environment of the child. Either because demonstrating phonemic knowledge is difficult or because the knowledge in fact is fully inaccessible (i.e., implicit), many children will not show it until they begin to read. Some will read poorly and continue not to have access to phonemic knowledge. If they are now trained on phonemic knowledge, it might improve their reading, as the training studies suggest. If so, it does so by affecting their computational phonemic knowledge, that is, their abilities to make connections between letters, which they have already learned about, *and* phonemes, about which they have only dim inaccessible knowledge. Phonemic awareness training does not merely give them access to phonemic knowledge, but it also makes the structure of words clearer: Spoken words contain phonemes; written words contain letters; and letters and phonemes correspond. This does not mean however that phoneme knowledge is a prerequisite to reading. Instead, the child who makes normal progress in reading acquires access to his or her knowledge that letters comprise words at the same time that he or she is acquiring access to the knowledge that phonemes comprise words. From our study, we conclude the beginning reader acquires some of the print knowledge slightly in advance of *some* phonemic knowledge. A finer grained study might show something slightly different, but it probably would not show that all levels of phonemic awareness had to come first. A sensitivity to rhymes comes very early and is predictive of beginning reading (Maclean, Bryant, & Bradley, 1987), but it is not the level of phonemic analysis that we think develops alongside of reading. (See also Alegria & Morais, 1991.)

Spelling and Reading

Because my account assigns a large role to orthographically specified representations, the issue of spelling is raised. The precision principle is essentially identified with correct spellings. I assume that spelling and reading are processes that share the same lexical representation.

There are, however, apparent cases of children spelling words that they cannot read (Bryant & Bradley, 1980; but see Gough, Juel, & Griffith, this volume). Moreover, there are studies that appear to have shown that some children spell phonetically while reading nonphonetically (Frith, 1980; Jorm & Share, 1983). On the other hand, Waters, Bruck, and Seidenberg (1985) found that third-grade children, regardless of reading skill, tried to use spelling–sound correspondences in both reading and spelling.

In a study of college-age dyslexics we (Bell and Perfetti, unpublished manuscript) have been able to find only a few instances of accurate spelling of words by subjects who failed to read them. Fifteen low-ability readers were given 56 words varying in frequency and regularity to read and spell on separate occasions. (Half the words were read first and half were spelled first.) We found only 6 cases out of 640 opportunities in which a subject misread a word he or she spelled correctly, and each case was produced by a different individual reading a different word. The reading errors were generally easily understood as misreadings rather than access failures (e.g., *conscience* for *conscious* and *corpse* for *corps*). Phonemic strategies were in evidence for reading even though in other tasks these subjects showed themselves poor in lexical representations including phonology. I suggest that lexical representations of experienced readers, even readers of low ability, include phonemic and orthographic information no matter how imperfectly. For adults phonemic information plays a role in everyone's spelling.

Whether this is true for children who are learning to read remains a controversy among those who study children's spelling. There are claims that nonphonemic spelling strategies distinguish a subclass of developmental dyslexics, Boder's (1973) dyseidetics. I find the claim that there are individuals, whether normal or developmentally dyslexic, who use only a visual strategy for spelling unconvincing at best and incoherent at worst. There is a large visual component to spelling because a spelling is a spatial array of letters. Furthermore, because English spelling has a one-to-many mapping for any given phoneme or even any syllable, a grapheme–phoneme spelling rule is in principle inadequate. Correct spelling must be guided by knowledge of letter sequences.

However, the phonemic information in the word must force a phonemic component to spelling. A child who correctly spells *a-c-h-e* is not merely demonstrating a "visual" strategy that reflects how the word appears, but the child is also demonstrating phonemic knowledge that tells him or her, in some sense, the word might be spelled *a-k-e* but is not, which amounts to saying that the child learns that /k/ is sometimes spelled with a *ch* as well as a *k*.

If this assumption is correct, and it seems inevitably so to me, why have some researchers identified visual spellers and phonemic spellers as if there were two basic ways to spell that one could somehow choose, rather than two components to spelling that everyone used to a greater or lesser degree depending on the circumstances? I think one problem is that researchers have often failed to take note of this fact: If someone is not good at something, he or she has many options for how to display their weakness. Children with impoverished word representations are not good at spelling or reading.

Dyslexics in particular have this problem. When given a spelling task they have a problem because they do not know how to spell. They will try to find a representation for a word but there will not be much there. What do they do? They try to satisfy the demands of the examiner by producing a string of letters. The examiner then studies the incorrect spelling and decides that it has high or low phonemic overlap with the target or that it has high or low "visual" (orthographic) overlap with the target. There are several serious problems with this approach. First, the orthographic and phonemic information does not come in neatly separated packages. A string of letters is all you get, but these letters also have specific phonemic values in specific contexts. This is true for the letters in all but the most irregular words. Thus, the misspelling game itself is intrinsically probabilistic and statistical, and this is seldom taken into satisfactory account. A second related problem is that the reliability of the child's spelling errors is hardly ever assessed. But such assessment is important, because if the child misspells *ache* one time as *ake* and one time as *acke,* what does that mean for his or her classification as a phonemic or visual speller? Probably it reflects the child's variable coping strategy for dealing with his or her lack of knowledge. The child suspects that he or she does not have this knowledge because when he or she accesses /ek/ on the basis of its sound the child finds an impoverished representation. The child does have other knowledge however. He or she knows that some words have faithful, predictable mappings of letters and sounds and others do not. So the child tries different things and possibly gets a premature classification as a visual speller or a phonemic speller that is based on momentary manifestations of highly variable strategies. As for normal readers, I think the same argument applies in general. It is important not to overestimate a child's devotion to an alleged basic processing strategy when it might be a momentary state of an extremely variable response to inadequate knowledge.

Whatever the correct understanding of individual differences, how children spell and read remains important for an account of reading acquisition along the lines I am proposing. Bryant and Bradley's (1980) suggestion is that reading develops along visual routes and that spelling develops along phonemic routes. Their report that children could spell but not read *bun, mat, leg*, and *pat*, all regular words, is consistent with this hypothesis. However it is especially interesting that this phenomenon was readily altered by task demands. When the children read a pseudoword list that included the nonread words they were able to read them. Thus it is not a question of basic ability but either a strategy or a momentary state in response to ignorance. Bryant and Bradley prefer the strategy explanation, which is that the orthographic route is the preferred reading strategy.

My account for this phenomenon is that the child who *reliably* fails to read words that he or she can spell correctly has no lexical representation for the word or else has one that he or she is unwilling to trust. By contrast, the spelling task encourages the child to consult directly his or her phonemic knowledge and to generate correspondences. With increasing knowledge, more and more words are represented directly even if imperfectly. There is a convergence of spelling and reading, and the phenomenon observed by Bradley and Bryant disappears even for poor adult readers, as I have suggested.

Thus, on this account there is a single representation that serves both reading and spelling. It does so throughout the course of development. Because spellings can be generated without lexical access, occasional discrepancies can be observed before the number of lexical entries has grown large enough.

CONCLUSION

I have argued that the central theoretical question for a theory of reading acquisition is the development of lexical representations. My goal here has been to outline what I see as the general form of such a theory.

First, the representation system of the skilled reader requires a class of models that I call the Restricted-Interactive Model. It restricts the influence of imported knowledge on lexical access while permitting the interaction of information from within the lexicon. The acquisition of a functional representation system entails an increase in the number of lexical entries and an increase in the quality of lexical entries. Quality is a matter of upgrading representations so that they are more fully specified and redundant. Access to this lexicon becomes increasingly word specific as the quality of specific word representations increases. The acquisition of an autonomous lexicon builds on this same functional lexicon by changing the status of specific words to fully specified and redundant. This means that parts of the lexicon can become autonomous very early in reading.

Two important issues are indirectly handled by this account. In the case of phonemic knowledge, implicit computational phonemic knowledge is central to the quality of lexical representations. In the case of reflective explicit phonemic knowledge, it develops with alphabetic lexical representations and not as precursors to them. Spelling and reading use the same lexical representation. In fact, spelling is a good test of the quality of representation.

Finally there is an important question not addressed. I have described the acquisition of representations as if it were a gradual process of incrementing knowledge. It could very well be a process in which a wider-scope restructuring of the lexicon occurs at various points in response to linguistic and orthographic insights. Either possibility is consistent with our present knowledge.

ACKNOWLEDGMENTS

This chapter is based on a manuscript of the same title written in 1986, which received some distribution. In updating the manuscript for publication in this volume, I have added only a few more recent literature citations. The theory presented in the chapter, however, is unchanged from its 1986 form. Preparation of the chapter was supported in part by the Learning Research and Development Center.

REFERENCES

Alegria, J., & Morais, J. (1991). Segmental analysis and reading acquisition. In L. Rieben & C. A. Perfetti, (Eds.), *Learning to read: Basic research and its implications* (pp. 135–148). Hillsdale, NJ: Lawrence Erlbaum Associates.

Baron, J. (1977). Mechanisms for pronouncing printed words: Use and acquisition. In D. LaBerge & S. J. Samuels (Eds.), *Basic processes in reading: Perception and comprehension* (pp. 75–216). Hillsdale, NJ: Lawrence Erlbaum Associates.

Bell, L., & Perfetti, C. A. (1990). *Reading ability, "reading disability," and garden variety low reading skill: Some adult comparisons.* Unpublished manuscript.

Boder, E. (1973). Developmental dyslexia: A diagnostic approach based on three atypical reading–spelling patterns. *Developmental Medicine and Child Neurology, 15,* 663–687.

Bradley, L., & Bryant, P. E. (1983). Categorizing sounds and learning to read—a causal connection. *Nature, 301,* 419–421.

Brady, S., & Shankweiler, D. (Eds.). (1991). *Phonological processes in literacy: A tribute to Isabelle Y. Liberman.* Hillsdale, NJ: Lawrence Erlbaum Associates.

Bryant, P. E., & Bradley, L. (1980). Why children sometimes write words which they do not read. In U. Frith (Ed.), *Cognitive processes in spelling* (pp. 355–370). San Diego, CA: Academic Press.

Byrne, B. (1991). Experimental analysis of the child's discovery of the alphabetic principle. In L. Rieben & C. A. Perfetti, (Eds.), *Learning to read: Basic research and its implications* (pp. 75–84). Hillsdale, NJ: Lawrence Erlbaum Associates.

Cattell, J. M. (1886). The time it takes to see and name objects. *Mind, 11,* 63–65.

Chall, J. (1967). *Learning to read: The great debate.* New York: McGraw-Hill.

DeGroot, A. M. B. (1983). The range of automatic spreading activation in word priming. *Journal of Verbal Learning and Verbal Behavior, 22,* 417–436.

Ehri, L. C. (1978). Beginning reading from a psycholinguistic perspective: Amalgamation of word identities. In F. B. Murray (Ed.), *The development of the reading process.* (International Reading Association Monograph No. 3, pp. 1–33). Newark, DE: International Reading Association.

Ehri, L. C. (1980). The development of orthographic images. In U. Frith (Ed.), *Cognitive processes in spelling* (pp. 311–338). San Diego, CA: Academic Press.

Ehri, L. C. (1984). How orthography alters spoken language competencies in children learning to read and spell. In J. Downing & R. Valtin (Eds.), *Language awareness and learning to read* (pp. 119–147). New York: Springer-Verlag.

Ehri, L. C. (1991). Learning to read and spell words. In L. Rieben & C. A. Perfetti (Eds.), *Learning to read: Basic research and its implications.* (pp. 57–73). Hillsdale, NJ: Lawrence Erlbaum Associates.

Ehri, L. C., & Wilce, L. (1983). Development of word identification speed in skilled and less skilled beginning readers. *Journal of Educational Psychology, 75,* 3–18.

Ehri, L. C., & Wilce, L. S. (1985). Movement into reading: Is the first stage of printed word learning visual or phonetic? *Reading Research Quarterly, 20,* 163–179.

Ehrlich, S. F., & Rayner, K. (1981). Contextual effects on word perception and eye movements during reading. *Journal of Verbal Learning and Verbal Behavior, 20,* 641–655.

Fodor, J. D. (1983). *Parsing constraints and the freedom of expression.* Montgomery, VT: Bradford Press.

Forster, K. I. (1979). Levels of processing and the structure of the language processor. In W. E. Cooper and E. C. T. Walker (Eds.), *Sentence processing: Psycholinguistic studies presented to Merrill Garrett* (pp. 27–85). Hillsdale, NJ: Lawrence Erlbaum Associates.

Frith, U. (1980). Unexpected spelling problems. In U. Frith (Ed.), *Cognitive processes in spelling* (pp. 495–516). San Diego, CA: Academic Press.

Gibson, E. J., & Levin, H. (1975). *The psychology of reading.* Cambridge, MA: MIT Press.

Glucksberg, S., Kneuz, R. J., & Rho, S. (1986). Context can constrain lexical access: Implications for models of language comprehension. *Journal of Experimental Psychology: Learning, Memory, and Cognition, 12,* 323–335.

Gough, P. B. (1972). One second of reading. In J. F. Kavanaugh & I. G. Mattingly (Eds.), *Language by ear and eye: The relationships between speech and reading* (pp. 331–358). Cambridge, MA: MIT Press.

Gough, P. B., & Hillinger, M. L. (1980). Learning to read: An unnatural act. *Bulletin of the Orton Society, 20,* 179–196.

Gough, P. B., & Juel, C. (1991). The first stages of word recognition. In L. Rieben & C. A. Perfetti (Eds.), *Learning to read: Basic research and its implications* (pp. 47–56). Hillsdale, NJ: Lawrence Erlbaum Associates.

Guttentag, R. E., & Haith, M. (1978). Automatic processing as a function of age and reading ability. *Child Development, 49,* 707–716.

Horn, C. C., & Manis, F. R. (1987). Development of automatic and speeded processing of word meaning. *Journal of Experimental Child Psychology, 44,* 92–108.

Jorm, A. F., & Share, D. L. (1983). Phonological recoding and reading acquisition. *Applied Psycholinguistics, 4,* 103–147.

Kintsch, W., & Mross, F. (1985). Context effects in word identification. *Journal of Memory and Language, 24,* 336–349.

Liberman, I. Y., & Shankweiler, D. (1979). Speech, the alphabet, and teaching to read. In L. B. Resnick & P. A. Weaver (Eds.), *Theory and practice of early reading, Vol. 2* (pp. 109–132). Hillsdale, NJ: Lawrence Erlbaum Associates.

Liberman, I. Y., Shankweiler, D., Orlando, C., Harris, K. S., & Berti, F. B. (1971). Letter confusion and reversals of sequence in the beginning reader: Implications for Orton's theory of developmental dyslexia. *Cortex, 7,* 127–142.

Lundberg, I., Frost, J., & Petersen, O. -P. (1988). Effects of an extensive program for stimulating phonological awareness in preschool children. *Reading Research Quarterly, 23,* 264–284.

Lundberg, I., Olofsson, A., & Wall, S. (1980). Reading and spelling skills in the first school years predicted from phonemic awareness skills in kindergarten. *Scandinavian Journal of Psychology, 21,* 159–173.

Maclean, M., Bryant, P., & Bradley, L. (1987). Rhymes, nursery rhymes, and reading in early childhood. *Merrill-Palmer Quarterly, 33,* 255–281.

Mann, V. A., & Liberman, I. Y. (1984). Phonological awareness and verbal short-term memory. *Journal of Learning Disabilities, 17,* 592–599.

Marchbanks, G., & Levin, H. (1965). Cues by which children recognize words. *Journal of Educational Psychology, 56,* 57–61.

Marsh, G., Desberg, P., & Cooper, J. (1976, March). *Constructive memory and reading comprehension.* Paper presented at Psychonomic Society Meeting, St. Louis, MO.

Massaro, D. W. (1975). *Understanding language: An information-processing analysis of speech perception, reading, and psycholinguistics.* San Diego, CA: Academic Press.

McClelland, J. L. (1986). The programmable model of reading: Psychological and biological models. In D. E. Rumelhart & J. L. McClelland, (Eds.), *Parallel distributed processing: Explorations in the microstructure of cognition, Vol. 2* (pp. 170–215). Cambridge, MA: MIT Press.

McClelland, J. L., & Rumelhart, D. E. (1981). An interactive activation model of context effects in letter perception: 1. An account of basic findings. *Psychological Review, 88,* 357–407.

Mitchell, D. C., & Green, D. W. (1978). The effects of context and content on immediate processing in reading. *Quarterly Journal of Experimental Psychology, 30,* 609–636.

Morton, J. (1969). Interaction of information in word recognition. *Psychological Review, 76,* 165–178.

Perfetti, C. A. (1985). *Reading ability* New York: Oxford University Press.

Perfetti, C. A. (1990). The cooperative language processors: Semantic influences in an autonomous syntax. In D. A. Balota, G. B. Flores d'Arcais, & K. Rayner (Eds.), *Comprehension processes in reading* (pp. 205–230). Hillsdale, NJ: Lawrence Erlbaum Associates.

Perfetti, C. A., Beck, I. L., Bell, L., & Hughes, C. (1987). Phonemic knowledge and learning to read are reciprocal: A longitudinal study of first grade children. *Merrill-Palmer Quarterly, 33,* 283–319.

Perfetti, C. A., & Bell, L. (1991). Speech activation during the first 40 msec. of word identification: Evidence from backward masking and masked priming, *Journal of Memory and Language, 30.*

Perfetti, C. A., Bell, L., & Delaney, S. (1988). Automatic phonetic activation in silent word reading: Evidence from backward masking. *Journal of Memory and Language, 27,* 59–70.

Perfetti, C. A., & McCutchen, D. (1982). Speech processes in reading. In N. Lass (Ed.), *Speech and language: Advances in basic research and practice* (Vol. 7, pp. 237–269). San Diego, CA: Academic Press.

Perfetti, C. A., & Roth, S. F. (1981). Some of the interactive processes in reading and their role in reading skill. In A. M. Lesgold & C. A. Perfetti (Eds.), *Interactive processes in reading* (pp. 269–297). Hillsdale, NJ: Lawrence Erlbaum Associates.

Posner, M. I., & Boies, S. J. (1971). Components of attention. *Psychology Review, 78,* 391–408.

Rayner, K., & Posnansky, C. (1978). Stages of processing in word identification. *Journal of Experimental Psychology: General, 107,* 64–80.

Resnick, L. B., & Weaver, P. A. (Eds.). (1979). *Theory and practice of early reading, Vol. 1.* Hillsdale, NJ: Lawrence Erlbaum Associates.

Rieben, L., & Perfetti, C. A. (Eds.). (1991). *Learning to read: Basic research and its implications.*

Rumelhart, D. E., & McClelland, J. L. (1981). Interactive processing through spreading activation. In A. M. Lesgold & C. A. Perfetti (Eds.), *Interactive processes in reading* (pp. 37–60). Hillsdale, NJ: Lawrence Erlbaum Associates.

Schadler, M., & Thissen, D. M. (1981). The development of automatic word recognition and reading skill. *Memory and Cognition, 9,* 132–141.

Seidenberg, M. S., & McClelland, J. L. (1989). A distributed, developmental model of visual word recognition and naming. *Psychological Review, 96,* 523–568.

Seidenberg, M. S., Tanenhaus, M. K., Lieman, J. M., & Bienkowski, M. (1982). Automatic access of the meanings of ambiguous words in context: Some limitations of knowledge-based processing. *Cognitive Psychology, 14,* 489–537.

Shankweiler, D., Liberman, I. Y., Mark, L. S., Fowler, C. A., & Fischer, F. W. (1979). The speech code and learning to read. *Journal of Experimental Psychology: Human Learning and Memory, 5,* 531–545.

Stanovich, K. E. (1980). Toward an interactive-compensatory model of individual differences in the development of reading fluency. *Reading Research Quarterly, 16,* 32–71.

Stanovich, K. E. (1990). Concepts in developmental theories of reading skill: Cognitive resources, automaticity, and modularity. *Developmental Review, 10,* 72–100.

Stanovich, K. E. (1991). Changing models of reading and reading acquisition. In L. Rieben & C. A. Perfetti (Eds.), *Learning to read: Basic research and its implications* (pp. 19–31). Hillsdale, NJ: Lawrence Erlbaum Associates.

Stanovich, K. E., Cunningham, A. E., & Cramer, B. (1984). Assessing phonological awareness in kindergarten children: Issues of task comparability. *Journal of Experimental Child Psychology, 38,* 175–190.

Stanovich, K. E., Cunningham, A. E., & West, R. F. (1981). A longitudinal study of the development of automatic recognition skills in first graders. *Journal of Reading Behavior, 13,* 57–74.

Stanovich, K. E., & West, R. F. (1981). The effect of sentence context on on-going word recognition: Tests of a two-process theory. *Journal of Experimental Psychology: Human Perception and Performance, 7,* 658–672.

Stanovich, K. E., & West, R. F. (1989). Exposure to print and orthographic processing. *Reading Research Quarterly, 24,* 402–433.

Swinney, D. A. (1979). Lexical access during sentence comprehension: Reconsideration of context effects. *Journal of Verbal Learning and Verbal Behavior, 18,* 645–659.

Tanenhaus, M. K., Lieman, J. M., & Seidenberg, M. S. (1979). Evidence for multiple stages in the processing of ambiguous words in syntactic contexts. *Journal of Verbal Learning and Verbal Behavior, 18,* 427–440.

Treiman, R., & Baron, J. (1981). Segmental analysis ability: Development and relation to reading ability. In G. E. MacKinnon & T. G. Waller (Eds.), *Reading research: Advances in theory and practice* (Vol. 3 pp. 159–188). San Diego, CA: Academic Press.

Tunmer, W. E. (1991). Phonological awareness and literacy acquisition. In L. Rieben & C. A. Perfetti, (Eds.), *Learning to read: Basic research and its implications* (pp. 105–119). Hillsdale, NJ: Lawrence Erlbaum Associates.

Van Orden, G. C. (1987). A ROWS is a ROSE: Spelling, sound and reading. *Memory and Cognition, 15,* 181–198.

Wagner, R. K., & Torgesen, J. K. (1987). The nature of phonological processing and its causal role in the acquisition of reading skills. *Psychological Bulletin, 101,* 192–212.

Waters, G. S., Bruck, M., & Seidenberg, M. (1985). Do children use similar processes to read and spell words? *Journal of Experimental Child Psychology, 39,* 511–530.

Williams, J. P. (1979). Reading instruction today. *American Psychologist, 34,* 917–922.

Williams, J. P., Blumberg, E. L., & Williams, D. V. (1970). Cues used in visual word recognition. *Journal of Educational Psychology, 61,* 310–315.

7 Cognitive and Linguistic Factors in Learning to Read

William E. Tunmer
Massey University

Wesley A. Hoover
Southwest Educational Development Laboratory

The purpose of this chapter is to discuss how children learn to read and what processes are centrally involved. The chapter is divided into five sections. The first draws attention to the importance of distinguishing between the process of learning to read, the process of skilled reading, and the process of reading instruction. The second describes a model of the proximal causes of individual differences in reading comprehension performance. The third provides a conceptual framework that specifies the relationships between the learning tasks, learning strategies, and cognitive prerequisites of beginning literacy development. The fourth summarizes research on the relationship between metalinguistic abilities and learning to read. And the fifth section presents a cognitive–developmental model of metalinguistic development and reading acquisition.

PROCESS AND INSTRUCTION

A major source of confusion in reading research stems from the failure to keep separate the following three questions regarding the role of any hypothesized component skill or mental operation.

1. What is the role of the skill in learning to read?
2. What is the role of the skill in fluent reading?
3. What emphasis should be placed on teaching the skill in reading instruction?

Although these three questions are clearly interrelated, it is important to recognize that they are conceptually distinct. For example, consider the possible role of language prediction skill in reading (i.e., the ability to use prior sentence context in recognizing words). If the simplifying assumption is made that language prediction skill does or does not play an important role in each of the three aspects of reading (i.e., reading acquisition, skilled reading, and reading instruction), a total of 8 possible patterns of relationships between language prediction skill and these three logically distinct aspects of reading can be distinguished (see Table 7.1).

Patterns 1 and 5 represent the extreme views. Pattern 1 says that language prediction skill plays an important role in both learning to read and skilled reading and should be included as an essential component of reading instruction. This view is consistent with the claims of Goodman (1967) and Smith (1971), who argued that fluent reading is primarily an activity of using the syntactic and semantic redundancies of language to generate hypotheses, or guesses, about the text yet to be encountered. Efficient readers are thought to pay little attention to the bulk of the words of text because the flow of language follows a predictable pattern. Instead, they use the fewest cues possible to make a prediction and test their guess against their developing meaning. As Smith (1979) described it, skilled reading is only "incidentally visual" and "depends on using the eyes as little as possible" (p. 9). Goodman (1967) characterized reading as a rapid series of guesses, a "psycholinguistic guessing game."

The major conclusion derived from these claims was that unlike fluent readers poor and beginning readers are less able to make use of contextual redundancy in ongoing sentence processing. Smith (1971) maintained that "the more difficulty the reader has with reading, the more he relies on the visual information," and that "the cause of the difficulty is inability to make full use of syntactic and semantic redundancy, of nonvisual sources of information" (p. 221). Reading instruction should therefore place little emphasis on using visual information to

TABLE 7.1
Patterns of Relationships Between Language Prediction Skill and Aspects of Reading

Patterns	Reading Acquisition	Skilled Reading	Reading Instruction
1	+	+	+
2	+	+	0
3	+	0	+
4	+	0	0
5	0	0	0
6	0	0	+
7	0	+	0
8	0	+	+

identify individual words and should place more emphasis on using context to guess words.

The problem with these conclusions, however, is that even if the claim regarding the role of language prediction skill in fluent reading is true (see the following text for evidence that it is not), it does not *necessarily* follow that prediction skill also plays a central role in learning to read. Conversely, even if it is true that language prediction skill is important in acquiring reading ability (see the following text for evidence that it might be), it does not necessarily follow that this skill is important in fluent reading. The processes involved in skilled reading must be distinguished from the processes involved in *becoming* a skilled reader.

Pattern 5 in Table 7.1 represents the opposite view to Goodman and Smith. Supporters of this view claim that the ability to use sentence context to facilitate word recognition is not important in either learning to read or in skilled reading. Stanovich (1986), for example, argues that "compared to other prerequisite skills—such as phonological awareness—the variability in the ability to use context to facilitate word recognition is so relatively low that it may not be a major determinant of individual differences in reading acquisition" (p. 369). According to this view, then, teaching beginning readers to use context as a word recognition strategy would be of little or no benefit. Instruction should focus instead on teaching word-level skills.

Although many investigators and practitioners align themselves with one of these extreme positions, several other less extreme views are possible. For example, Pattern 2 represents the possibility that language prediction skill is essential for both learning to read and skilled reading but need not be taught. Perhaps the ability to use language prediction skill in recognizing words in an unconscious, automatic skill that comes about "naturally" as a consequence of having acquired (tacit) knowledge of the grammatical rules of spoken language.

Patterns 3 and 4 represent the possibilities that language prediction skill plays an essential role in reading acquisition but not in skilled reading and may or may not need to be taught. For example, as we argue later, the ability to *combine* knowledge of the constraints of sentence context with incomplete graphophonemic information may help children identify unfamiliar words and thus increase both their word-specific knowledge and their knowledge of grapheme–phoneme correspondences. Increased knowledge of the latter would help beginning readers become even more proficient in identifying unfamiliar words.

Pattern 6 says that language prediction skill plays no role in either reading acquisition or skilled reading but is an important component of reading instruction. Although this possibility seems unlikely, it is nevertheless conceivable. For example, instruction in using context to predict missing words in cloze tasks may facilitate the development of children's general linguistic ability. Because linguistic ability is a key factor in reading comprehension performance (see following text), training in language prediction skill may be useful.

Patterns 7 and 8 represent the possibilities that language prediction skill is essential in skilled reading but not in reading acquisition and may or may not need to be taught. It is possible that beginning readers first need to achieve a fairly high level of context-free word recognition skill before they can use context to facilitate word recognition in ongoing sentence processing. In support of this suggestion are the results of a longitudinal study by Stanovich, Cunningham, and Feeman (1984b) on the effects of context on word recognition in beginning reading. In the autumn and spring of the school year, first-grade children were asked to read coherent story paragraphs and random word lists. The dependent variable for these two conditions was the mean number of words read correctly per second. Stanovich et al. (1984b) found that although skilled readers displayed more contextual facilitation in reading coherent paragraphs than less skilled readers in the autumn, the less skilled readers received as much contextual facilitation as did the skilled readers when at a comparable level of context-free decoding later in the year.

There are probably many more patterns of possible relationships than those shown in Table 7.1, especially because it is highly unlikely that language prediction skill is related to each of the three aspects of reading in a binary fashion. The analysis may be further complicated by the possibility of different types of contextual effects on word recognition. Gough (1984) described two: "One is like sophisticated guessing, based on slowly forming, perhaps conscious, expectancies," whereas the other results from "an automatic, fast, 'cost-free' spreading activation mechanism" (p. 245). The contextual facilitation effects observed in the study by Stanovich et al. (1984b) appear to be of the automatic type that occurs in ongoing sentence processing. At the end of their study Stanovich et al. (1984b) acknowledged a distinction between the (automatic) use of context to aid ongoing word recognition and the use of context to facilitate the comprehension and memory of text. However there may be a third type of contextual facilitation, namely, the slow, deliberate use of sentence context to facilitate the acquisition of knowledge of grapheme–phoneme correspondence rules (see following text).

The important point, however, is that the questions of the role of a particular skill in reading acquisition, skilled reading, and reading instruction are conceptually distinct questions, each of which must be investigated empirically (see also Gough & Tunmer, 1986). Treating these questions separately also draws attention to different theoretical possibilities. For example, viewing reading acquisition as a process that takes place over time allows for the following:

1. Learning to read may involve qualitatively different (but perhaps overlapping) stages in which different component skills are the focus of each stage.
2. The acquisition of component skills (and related subskills) may depend on certain cognitive or linguistic abilities that may affect the rate at which children progress through the stages.

3. The acquisition of each component skill may be facilitated by particular methods of instruction, from which it follows that different methods may be appropriate at different stages in the reading acquisition process.

For any given child the best method or combination of methods would depend on the stage of reading development reached by the child and the child's level of competence in the cognitive/linguistic abilities required to master the component skills of that stage.

A MODEL OF THE PROXIMAL CAUSES
OF READING PERFORMANCE DIFFERENCES

A model of the proximal causes of reading performance differences, sometimes referred to as the *simple view* (Gough & Tunmer, 1986; Hoover & Gough, 1990; Juel, 1988; Juel, Griffith, & Gough, 1986), proposes that $R = D \times C$, where R is reading comprehension, D is decoding (i.e., word recognition), and C is listening comprehension. That reading comprehension is *some* function of decoding and listening comprehension is well established. Using multiple regression, a number of investigators have shown that decoding and listening comprehension make independent contributions to reading comprehension (e.g., Curtis, 1980).

However, the simple view makes the stronger prediction that the effect of either skill on reading ability depends on the reader's level of competence in the other skill. For example, if decoding ability is high but listening comprehension is low, the child will be a very poor reader (i.e., if $D = 1.0$, where 1.0 is perfection, and $C = 0$, then $R = 0$). Conversely, if listening comprehension is high but decoding ability is very low, the child will again be a poor reader (i.e., if $C = 1.0$ and $D = 0$, then $R = 0$). Thus each skill is assumed to be necessary, but not sufficient, for success in reading.

Let us consider arguments and evidence in support of the two component skills postulated in the model.

Listening Comprehension

Reading is now generally viewed as a derived skill that builds on spoken language; the reading process is thought to be grafted onto the listening process. Accordingly, reading has been defined as the translation from print to a form of code from which the reader can already derive meaning (Venezky, 1976). This suggests that in order to learn to comprehend text, preliterate children must discover how to map the printed text onto their existing language, which requires the ability to deal explicitly with the structural features of spoken language. Two general kinds of language problems may therefore affect reading acquisition: a deficiency in the development of oral language knowledge per se, and an inability to bring knowledge of oral language to conscious awareness.

With regard to the former, Gough (1975) argued that "knowledge of the language being read is at the heart of the reading process, and without that knowledge reading could simply not take place" (p. 15). Deficiencies in different aspects of language structure and functioning (e.g., speech perception, morphophonemic rule knowledge, lexical knowledge, syntactic knowledge, and discourse knowledge) should result therefore in different kinds of reading difficulties. For example, children who are unable to discriminate between different types of phonemes, perhaps because of a high frequency hearing loss, should encounter difficulty in analyzing speech and relating it to print. That is, they should have difficulty in learning to decode words.

There are two sources of evidence in support of this claim. First, children who suffer impairments in one or more of the various levels of language functioning are much more likely to encounter reading problems than children with normal oral language skills (Mann, 1986). Second, research on non-native speakers indicates that reading achievement (in English) is a function of English oral language proficiency.

With respect to the latter, Matluck and Tunmer (1979) examined the relation of English oral language proficiency to reading achievement among non-native speaking children attending primary schools in which the language of instruction was English. A monotonically increasing, parabolic function provided the best fit of the data, indicating that children must attain a threshold level of competence in the language being read before they can progress in reading (see Fig. 7.1). It was only when the non-native speaking children scored at fairly high levels on the language proficiency test that they demonstrated much success on standardized tests of reading achievement.

Although a second-degree polynomial regression equation accounted for approximately 33% of the variance in reading achievement, this value for R^2 probably underestimated the strength of the relation of oral language proficiency

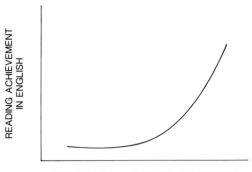

FIG. 7.1. Relation of English oral language proficiency to reading achievement in English.

to reading achievement for two reasons. First, the scores obtained from the language proficiency test were negatively skewed, which probably reflected the nature of the test. Consistent with current views of language development, the test focused on syntactic development rather than vocabulary development. The latter would have resulted in a more normal distribution of scores. Second, variability in reading achievement was found to increase at higher levels of oral language proficiency. Scatterplots of the data revealed that there were many children who performed well on the language test but poorly on the reading test, which is exactly what one would expect if language ability is necessary but not sufficient for learning to read.

Decoding and Phonological Recoding Ability

Goodman (1967) and Smith (1971, 1979) have argued that poor and beginning readers are less able to use prior sentence context to identify words as they read text. Research conducted during the past fifteen years has not supported this claim. Several studies have shown that the effect of context on speed of ongoing word recognition during reading *decreases* with increasing age, grade level, reading ability, word familiarity, and stimulus quality (see Stanovich, 1984, 1986, for reviews). On the basis of these findings, Stanovich (1980) concluded that less skilled readers compensate for difficulties in word recognition by relying more on sentence context to facilitate ongoing word recognition. In contrast, better readers are sufficiently fast and accurate at recognizing words in text to make reliance on contextual information unnecessary.

In opposition to the views of Goodman (1967) and Smith (1971) is Perfetti's (1985, 1986) verbal efficiency theory. This theory maintains that children will encounter difficulty in reading if they fail to develop skill in recognizing individual words quickly and accurately. A central claim of verbal efficiency theory is that inefficient lexical access disrupts the temporary representation of text in working memory. As words are recognized their phonological representations are stored in working memory until sufficient information has accumulated to permit assembly of the lexical entries into larger units of relational meaning called *propositions*. Because proposition encoding takes place within the limits of working memory, lexical access that is inefficient and capacity draining will disrupt the temporary representation of text in working memory, and comprehension will suffer as a result.

Evidence in support of these claims comes from studies reporting strong correlations between speed and accuracy of context-free word recognition and reading comprehension, especially among children in the lower grades (see Perfetti, 1985). Results of a longitudinal study by Lesgold, Resnick, and Hammond (1985) support the claim that word recognition efficiency in first grade is causally related to reading comprehension.

In his review of the effects of context on word recognition, Stanovich (1986) made the interesting point that the theories of reading development proposed by Goodman (1967), Smith (1971), and Perfetti (1985) were aimed at solving the same problem, namely, the working memory bottleneck in the information processing system. Goodman (1967) and Smith (1971) claimed that the skilled reader overcomes working memory limitations through minimal sampling of text and heavy use of context to predict words. In contrast, Perfetti (1985) and others have argued that the fluent reader takes in a large amount of visual information but processes it very quickly and efficiently.

The simple view of reading further proposes that an essential aspect of the development of word recognition skill is phonological recoding ability, which is the ability to translate letters and letter patterns into phonological forms. Beginning readers must eventually realize that there are systematic correspondences between elements of written and spoken language to advance beyond an initial stage of reading in which words are recognized by selective association (i.e., the pairing of a partial stimulus cue to a response, Gough & Hillinger, 1980; Hoover & Gough, 1990). Children who continue to read words as if they were Chinese logographs will be limited to reading the particular words they have learned as arbitrary patterns. Phonological recoding skill is thought to facilitate the reading acquisition process by acting as a self-teaching mechanism that, when combined with the use of sentence context cues, enables beginning readers to identify unfamiliar words (including irregular words) and to gain the practice required for developing speed and automaticity in recognizing familiar words in text (Gough & Hillinger, 1980; Jorm & Share, 1983). This in turn frees up cognitive resources for allocation to higher order cognitive functions, such as gaining meaning from text and determining the meanings of unknown words.

In support of these claims is the observation that most of the words that the beginning reader encounters in print are novel (Gough & Hillinger, 1980). Basal reading series typically employ upwards of 1500 words, each of which must be encountered a first time. Moreover, when a new word does appear in print it does not suddenly begin appearing with great frequency. Approximately 35% to 40% of the words used in basals appear only once (Jorm & Share, 1983). Thus beginning readers are continually encountering words that they have not seen before and may not set eyes on again for some time. When confronted with an unfamiliar word, children who lack phonological recoding skill will encounter difficulty in discovering the phonological representation and hence the meaning corresponding to the word.

The way that beginning readers take advantage of the correspondences between graphemes and phonemes in learning to recognize words may vary. They may use correspondences between single graphemes or digraphs (e.g., *sh, th, oa*) and single phonemes, or correspondences between groups of graphemes and groups of phonemes, or analogies, or all three (Goswami & Bryant, this volume; Treiman & Baron, 1981; Treiman, this volume). The correspondences may also draw upon morphophonemic rules that speakers of English know implicitly, such as that regular noun plural inflection is realized as /s/ when it follows a voiceless stop consonant, as in *cats,* and as /z/ when it follows a voiced phoneme, as in *dogs.*

There is now considerable convergent evidence indicating that knowledge of grapheme–phoneme correspondences is intimately related to the acquisition of basic reading skills (Backman, Bruck, Hébert, & Seidenberg, 1984; Hoover & Gough, 1990; Jorm, Share, Maclean, & Matthews, 1984; Juel, 1988; Juel et al., 1986; Manis & Morrison, 1985; Perfetti & Hogaboam, 1975; Snowling, 1980, 1981; Stanovich, Cunningham, & Feeman, 1984a; Thompson, 1986; Tunmer, 1989b; Tunmer, Herriman, & Nesdale, 1988; Tunmer & Nesdale, 1985). Direct evidence that phonological recoding skill is related to reading achievement comes from research showing that accuracy (e.g., Tunmer & Nesdale, 1985) and speed (e.g., Perfetti & Hogaboam, 1975) of naming pseudowords (e.g., *toin, sark*) are two of the tasks that most clearly differentiate good from poor comprehenders of text. Differences in performance on tasks involving pseudowords occur even when younger, normal readers are matched with older, poor readers on reading ability (Manis & Morrison, 1985; Snowling, 1980). It would be impossible to pronounce pseudowords without knowledge of the grapheme–phoneme correspondence rules because pseudowords have not been seen before and therefore could not have been learned by sight.

Detailed cross-sectional studies of the role of phonological recoding skill in learning to read also have been reported. Backman et al. (1984) examined the acquisition and use of phonological recoding skills in children from Grades 2 through 4. The children were asked to read words and nonwords containing regular and homographic spelling patterns. Homographic spelling patterns are letter sequences that have different pronunciations in different words (e.g., *o-w-n* as in *clown* and *blown*). Analyses of latencies, pronunciations, and errors revealed that younger and poorer readers were slower and less accurate in recognizing words and nonwords and performed especially poorly on words containing homographic spelling patterns. When presented with exception words and exception-regular inconsistent nonwords (e.g., *naid,* which was derived from *said* and *raid*), these readers were less likely to regularize the words, indicating that they possessed weaker knowledge of regular spelling–sound correspondences than good readers.

Consistent with this suggestion are the results of a series of studies by Manis and Morrison (1985). The studies showed that poor readers encountered greater difficulty than reading-age controls in employing more complex, conditional grapheme–phoneme correspondence rules. Conditional rules were defined as those whose application depended on either the position of the unit in the word or on the presence of a "marker" letter (e.g., *cane*). Unconditional correspondences were those in which the pronunciation of the unit did not depend on its graphemic environment or on its position in the word (e.g., *blow*).

In one study, normal Grade 2 readers and normal and poor readers in Grades 3 through 6 were asked to pronounce 50 pseudowords that varied in rule conditionality (i.e., unconditional vs. conditional). The normal Grade 2 readers were matched in reading ability (both reading comprehension and word recognition) with the Grade 6 poor readers. As anticipated, the pseudoword pronunciation accuracy of the normal readers was superior to that of the poor readers at all grade levels. More importantly, the scores of the Grade 6 poor readers were significantly lower than those of the Grade 2 normal readers of matched reading ability. Closer analysis revealed that this difference was limited to the conditional words.

Further evidence that phonological recoding ability is essential for acquiring basic reading skills comes from a longitudinal study of beginning reading by Jorm et al. (1984). They formed two groups of first-grade readers who were matched on sight word vocabulary, verbal intelligence, gender, and school but differed in phonological recoding skill. They found that the difference in phonological recoding ability gave rise to steadily increasing differences in future reading achievement that favored the group that initially had higher levels of phonological recoding skill. Juel (1988) also found that phonological recoding ability in first grade was strongly related to later reading achievement.

More recently, Gough and Walsh (1991) obtained results indicating that phonological recoding ability is essential for acquiring word-specific knowledge. They found the standard positive correlation between pseudoword naming and exception word naming ($r = .66$), but on closer examination of their data they discovered that this relationship was of a particular nature. A scatterplot revealed that there were many children who performed reasonably well on the pseudoword naming test but recognized few exception words. However, there were no children who performed poorly on the pseudoword naming test and well on the exception word naming test. These results suggest that phonological recoding ability (as measured by pseudoword naming) is necessary but not sufficient for the development of word-specific knowledge. Consistent with this interpretation, Gough and Walsh also found that beginning readers with higher levels of phonological recoding skill required fewer trials to learn unfamiliar exception words than did children with lower levels of phonological recoding ability.

Gough and Walsh concluded from these results that "word-specific information does not reside in a mechanism separate and apart from the cipher, but instead is accumulated on top of the cipher, and cannot be otherwise acquired" (p. 15). This view is in contrast to the dual-route model of word recognition, which proposes that there are two kinds of proficient readers: those who rely primarily on word-specific mechanisms for word recognition and those who rely primarily on phonological mediation in identifying words (see Barron, 1986, for further discussion).

Barron (1986) described an alternative model to the dual-route model, which he called the *single process lexical model*. This model is based largely on the work of Ehri (1984, 1986, 1987, 1989). According to this model, sublexical analyses involving the application of grapheme–phoneme correspondences result in positive learning trials (i.e., correct word identifications), which in turn lead to the amalgamation of orthographic and phonological representations in semantic memory. These amalgamated representations are thought to provide the basis for rapid and efficient access to the lexicon (see Ehri, this volume, for further discussion).

Predictions of the Simple View

The simple view predicts that the inclusion of the product of phonological recoding and listening comprehension in the regression equation for reading comprehension will account for a significantly greater amount of variance than the linear combination of the two variables alone (i.e., $aD + bC + c[D \times C]$ will correlate better with R than $aD + bC$). In support of this prediction are results from a longitudinal study by Hoover and Gough (1990). At each grade from 1 through 4, the product of listening comprehension and phonological recoding accounted for an additional significant proportion of variance in reading comprehension (see Table 7.2).

The results further revealed developmental changes in the relative contribu-

TABLE 7.2
Summary of Regression Analyes in Support of Simple View

Variable	Multiple R	Increase in R^2
Grade 1 (n = 210)		
Linear	.849	.721**
Product	.856	.011*
Grade 2 (n = 206)		
Linear	.853	.728**
Product	.865	.020**
Grade 3 (n = 86)		
Linear	.884	.782**
Product	.921	.067**
Grade 4 (n = 55)		
Linear	.922	.851**
Product.	.948	.048**

Note. Linear = Linear combination of phonological recoding and listening comprehension; Product = Product of phonological recoding and listening comprehension.
*$p < .005$.
**$p < .001$.

tions of recoding and listening comprehension to the variance in reading comprehension, with recoding accounting for more of the variance in the lower grades. This finding is related to another prediction of the model, which is that beginning readers should be able to read as well as they can listen provided that inadequate recoding skills are not holding them back. That is, when listening comprehension is represented on the horizontal axis and reading comprehension on the vertical axis, the model predicts that at increasing levels of recoding skill there should be positive slope values of increasing magnitudes between listening and reading comprehension. In addition, the intercept values for the slopes should all be zero because reading comprehension should be zero if listening comprehension is zero irrespective of the level of recoding skill. These predictions were confirmed by Hoover and Gough (1990).

A third prediction of the model is that within the population of poor readers recoding and listening comprehension should be negatively correlated. If reading comprehension is the product of phonological recoding and listening comprehension, then to achieve a low score on reading comprehension a child who performs at a high level on recoding must achieve a low score on listening comprehension and vice versa. (Poor reading comprehension also occurs when both recoding and listening comprehension skills are weak.) Thus, for increasing sample reductions on the basis of successively removing from the sample students of higher levels of reading comprehension skill, correlations between recoding and listening comprehension should go from positive to negative. This prediction was also confirmed by Hoover and Gough (1990).

The simple view also provides an account of the different forms of reading difficulty (see Gough & Tunmer, 1986). It predicts that reading problems can result from an inability to decode, an inability to comprehend, or both (see Fig. 7.2). Children who can understand a text when it is read aloud but cannot decode it even after instruction are referred to as *dyslexics*. These children fall in the lower right-hand quadrant of Fig. 7.2. Children who can decode print but who

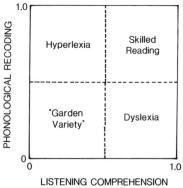

FIG. 7.2. Classification of different forms of reading difficulty according to the simple view.

have problems with listening comprehension in their native language are called *hyperlexics*. These children fall in the upper left-hand quadrant of Fig. 7.2. The remaining category of reading difficulty is composed of children who can neither decode nor comprehend and is represented by the lower left-hand quadrant. This situation tends to be the more typical one, as dyslexics and hyperlexics are relatively rare.

A CONCEPTUAL FRAMEWORK OF BEGINNING LITERACY DEVELOPMENT

The results shown in Table 7.2 indicate that the linear combination of phonological recoding and listening comprehension plus the product of these two variables accounts for almost 90% of the variance in reading comprehension performance by fourth grade. If phonological recoding and listening comprehension are indeed the proximal causes of individual differences in reading comprehension performance, what causes deficiencies in these two variables? There are of course many possibilities: intellectual impairment, gross neurological disorders, sensory deficits, attentional problems, emotional and social difficulties, poor motivation, inadequate early language environment, poor school attendance, inadequate or inappropriate school instruction, and so on. Here we focus on children who are within the normal range of intellectual and oral language abilities and who have no apparent problems in the areas just mentioned.

To account for individual differences in decoding and listening comprehension, a good place to start is the task of learning to read. Figure 7.3 provides a

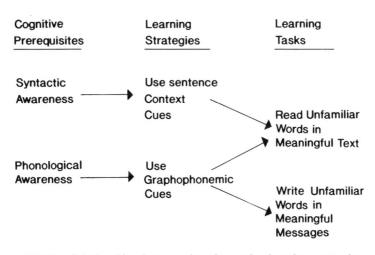

FIG. 7.3. Relationships between learning tasks, learning strategies and cognitive prerequisites of beginning literacy development.

general framework that specifies the relationships between the learning tasks, learning strategies, and cognitive prerequisites of beginning literacy development. In the "integrated" approach to teaching literacy skills that is currently used in most schools, beginning students are faced with two major learning tasks. As shown in the column on the right side of Fig. 7.3, they must learn to read unfamiliar words in meaningful, natural language texts, and they must learn to write unfamiliar words in meaningful messages, especially those relating to their personal experiences. As indicated in the middle column of Fig. 7.3, to read unfamiliar words children are normally taught two general learning strategies: to use sentence context cues and to use graphophonemic cues. In learning to write unfamiliar words, children are taught to use correspondences between phonemes and graphemes to produce conventional and preconventional spellings of words.

The question to ask at this point is what cognitive prerequisite skills are necessary to acquire the strategies of using sentence context cues and graphophonemic cues? As shown on the left side of Fig. 7.3, we hypothesize that the development of these general learning strategies depends crucially on two types of metalinguistic abilities, where *metalinguistic ability* (or awareness) is defined as the ability to reflect on and manipulate the structural features of spoken language (Tunmer & Herriman, 1984). To use sentence context cues requires the ability to reflect on the internal syntactic/semantic structure of sentences (called *syntactic awareness*), and to discover correspondences between graphemes and phonemes requires the ability to decompose spoken words into their constituent phonemic elements (called *phonological awareness*).

In the remaining sections of this chapter we examine the theoretical arguments and empirical evidence in support of the claim that phonological and syntactic awareness are essential for acquiring basic reading skills. Pragmatic, or discourse, awareness (see following text) is also hypothesized to play an important role in reading but at a later stage of reading development. Because phonological, syntactic, and pragmatic awareness are types of metalinguistic ability, the discussion begins with a brief description of the development of metalinguistic skills.

METALINGUISTIC DEVELOPMENT
AND LEARNING TO READ

It was suggested earlier that two general kinds of language problems may affect reading acquisition: a deficiency in knowledge of spoken language and an inability to bring knowledge of spoken language to conscious awareness. For most beginning readers who are native speakers, knowledge of the spoken language is sufficiently well advanced that it does not contribute to difficulties in learning to read. However, the central claim of this section is that intuitive oral language knowledge is insufficient to acquire the skills necessary for fluent reading. To learn to read children must also be able to bring their knowledge of the spoken language to bear upon the written language, which requires the metalinguistic ability to reflect on the structural features of spoken language.

Metalinguistic ability is a distinct kind of linguistic functioning that develops separately from and later than basic speaking and listening skills. The ability to perform metalinguistic operations does not come free with the acquisition of language. In support of this claim are the results of studies showing that many 5- and 6-year-old children who appear to possess normal language comprehension and speaking abilities are nevertheless unable to perform simple metalinguistic operations such as segmenting familiar spoken words into their constituent phonemes or correcting word order violations in simple sentence structures (see Tunmer, Pratt, & Herriman, 1984, for reviews of research on the development of metalinguistic abilities in children).

Research further suggests that metalinguistic development is related to a more general change in information processing capability that occurs during middle childhood, which is the development of metacognitive control over the information processing system. The results of several studies suggest that during middle childhood children become increasingly aware of how they can control their intellectual processes in a wide range of situations and tasks, including those requiring metalinguistic skills (see Flavell, 1981, 1985, for reviews).

This linkage of metalinguistic development to metacognitive development helps explain why the ability to treat language as an object of thought is not an automatic consequence of language acquisition. Unlike normal language operations, which involve automatic processing, metalinguistic operations require control processing. When comprehending or producing an utterance, older language users normally are unaware of the individual phonemes and words comprising the utterance and the grouping relationships among the utterance's constituent words unless they deliberately reflect on the structural features of the utterance. Because the gradual increase in children's control of their cognitive processes does not appear until about age 4 or 5 for most children, and even later for some, metalinguistic abilities would not be expected to develop concomitantly with the acquisition of language. Rather, the generally accepted view is that when children are acquiring their first language they consciously attempt to understand the purpose of individual speech acts by interpreting the situation as a whole, whereas they *unconsciously* attend to relationships between structural features of the utterances and features of the situations in which they occur (see Tunmer & Herriman, 1984, for further discussion).

The relationship between normal language processing and metalinguistic operations can be expressed in terms of a model of sentence comprehension that specifies a set of interacting processors in which the output of each becomes the input to the next (Tunmer & Herriman, 1984; Tunmer et al., 1988). The model provides the basis for a definition of metalinguistic awareness as the ability to use control processing to perform mental operations on the products of the mental mechanisms involved in sentence comprehension, where *products* refers to phonemes, words, structural representations of sentences, and sets of interrelated propositions. The model also provides the basis for classifying the various manifestations of metalinguistic awareness into four broad categories: phonological, word, syntactic, and pragmatic (or discourse) awareness. *Phonological awareness* refers to the ability to perform mental operations on the output of the speech perception mechanism. *Word awareness* refers to the ability to perform mental operations on the output of the lexical access mechanism. *Syntactic awareness* refers to the ability to perform mental operations on the output of the mechanism responsible for assigning intrasentential structural representations to groups of words. And *pragmatic awareness* refers to the ability to perform mental operations on the output of the mechanism responsible for integrating individual propositions into larger sets of propositions through the application of both pragmatic and inferential rules.

The development of each of these four general types of metalinguistic ability is described in Tunmer et al. (1984). Examples of phonological awareness include segmentation of words and pseudowords into phonemic segments, phoneme blending, phoneme deletion, phoneme substitution, and appreciation of puns. Examples of word awareness include segmentation of phrases and sentences into words, separation of words from their referents, appreciation of jokes involving lexical ambiguity, judgment of word length, recognition of synonyms and antonyms, and word substitution. Examples of syntactic awareness include detection of structural ambiguity in sentences, recognition of synonym relations, correction of word order violations, and completion of sentences with missing words. And examples of pragmatic awareness include detection of inconsistencies between sentences, recognition of message inadequacy, understanding of communication failures, and awareness of macrostructures.

Phonological Awareness and Learning to Read

Although word awareness develops during middle childhood (Ehri, 1975; Tunmer, Bowey, & Grieve, 1983) and appears to be related to beginning reading achievement (Bowey, Tunmer, & Pratt, 1984; Evans, Taylor, & Blum, 1979; McNinch, 1974), it is not treated separately from phonological awareness because phonological awareness implies word awareness. That is, the ability to reflect on phonemes requires an awareness that the sound used to represent a concept is not an inherent property of the concept (Morais, Alegria, & Content, 1987; Tunmer, 1989b). For example, to segment the spoken word *dog* into its constituent phonemic elements children must first be able to dissociate the (unsegmented) sound "dog" from the concept to which it refers. They can then analyze the sound into its phonemic elements.

Beginning readers must be able to analyze the internal structure of spoken words to discover how phonemes are related to graphemes. However, many school-age children find it extraordinarily difficult to reflect on and manipulate the phonemic segments of speech. Initially this may seem rather puzzling because even very young children are capable of discriminating between speech sounds and using phonemic contrasts to signal meaning differences. The important distinction, however, is that using a phonemic contrast to signal a meaning difference, which is done intuitively and at a subconscious level, is not the same as the *metalinguistic* act of realizing that the relevant difference is a phonemic difference. Consciously reflecting on phonemic segments is much more difficult for children because their is no simple physical basis for recognizing phonemes in speech. It is not possible to segment a speech signal such that each segment corresponds to one and only one phoneme (A. Liberman, Cooper, Shankweiler, & Studdert-Kennedy, 1967). Rather, the information necessary for identifying a particular phoneme often overlaps with that of another phoneme. Because phonemic segments do not exist in the acoustic signal per se but must be constructed from it, children must develop an awareness of an entity that is inherently abstract. They must develop the ability to invoke control processing to perform mental operations on the products of the mental mechanism responsible for converting the speech signal into a sequence of phonemes.

The research on speech perception may help explain why many children who have entered formal reading instruction fail to benefit from either letter–name knowledge or letter–sound knowledge in learning to recognize words. Because there is no one-to-one correspondence between phonemes and segments of the acoustic signal, it is not possible to pronounce in isolation the sound corresponding to most phonemes. Consequently, the strategy of simply "sounding out" a word like *drag* will result in /dərəægə/ a nonsense word comprising four syllables (I. Liberman & Shankweiler, 1985). Letter sounds and letter names are only imprecise physical analogues of the phonemes in spoken words. Whether children learn to associate the sound /də/ or the name /di/ or both with the letter *d*, they must still be able to segment the sound or name to make the connection between the letter *d* and the phoneme /d/. In short, beginning readers must be phonologically aware.

On logical grounds alone it would appear that at least some minimal level of explicit phonological awareness is necessary for children to be able to discover the systematic correspondences between graphemes and phonemes. Several studies provide support for the claim that phonological awareness is required to break the orthographic code. This research shows (a) that measures of phonological awareness obtained on students before they begin formal reading instruction predict their later reading achievement even when those showing any preschool reading ability are excluded (Bradley & Bryant, 1985; Tunmer et al., 1988) and when the influence of preschool reading ability is statistically controlled (Vellutino & Scanlon, 1987); (b) that phonological awareness influences reading comprehension indirectly through phonological recoding ability (Juel et al., 1986; Stanovich et al., 1984a; Tunmer & Nesdale, 1985); (c) that the more successful readers in strictly whole-word reading programs are the children who score higher on tests of phonological awareness (Morais et al., 1987); and (d) that training in phonological awareness during or before reading instruction produces significant experimental group advantages in reading achievement (Bradley & Bryant, 1985; Lundberg, Frost, & Petersen, 1988; Olofsson & Lundberg, 1985; Vellutino & Scanlon, 1987).

Although phonological awareness training may interact with spelling development to facilitate reading development (Ehri, 1989), exposure to print is not a necessary condition for the development of phonological awareness. The training study by Lundberg et al. (1988) demonstrated that preliterate children with very limited letter–name knowledge could be successfully trained in phonological awareness skills during their kindergarten year without the use of letters. Consistent with Stanovich's (1986) suggestion that small differences in phonemic segmentation ability at the beginning of reading instruction can be the genesis of large differences in reading achievement later in development, Lundberg et al. (1988) found that the differences in reading achievement between the experimental and control groups *increased* from first to second grade. Because phonemic segmentation ability has been shown to influence reading achievement through phonological recoding (see the previous discussion), it is likely that even greater differences would have been obtained if measures of phonological recoding had been used. This seems especially likely in view of Jorm et al.'s (1984) finding that differences in phonological recoding ability gave rise to steadily increasing differences in reading achievement even when sight word vocabulary, verbal intelligence, gender, and school attended at the end of the first year of reading instruction were held constant (see earlier discussion).

Evidence that some minimal level of explicit phonological awareness is necessary for acquiring knowledge of grapheme–phoneme correspondences comes from studies that have generated scatterplots of the relationship between phonological awareness and pseudoword decoding, which is regarded as a measure of phonological recoding ability (Juel et al., 1986; Tunmer, 1989b; Tunmer & Nesdale, 1985). The scatterplots have shown that, although many children performed well on phoneme segmentation and poorly on pseudoword decoding, no children performed poorly on phoneme segmentation and well on pseudoword decoding. Explicit phonological awareness appears to be necessary, but not sufficient, for acquiring grapheme–phoneme correspondence rules.

The likelihood that some minimal level of phonemic segmentation ability is necessary for learning to read does not preclude the possibility that some skills that are acquired or improved as a consequence of learning to read (and spell) may greatly improve performance on phonological awareness tasks (Tunmer, 1989a; Tunmer & Rohl, 1991). Some of these spinoff skills, which include the ability to maintain and operate on verbal material in working memory, to generate orthographic images, and to apply phoneme–grapheme correspondence rules, may even be necessary to perform more advanced phonological awareness tasks. This suggests that phonological awareness may be both a cause and a consequence of learning to read, which is a phenomenon referred to as *reciprocal causation*. According to this view, beginning readers must achieve some minimal level of phonemic segmentation ability in order to acquire basic reading skills that in turn enable them to acquire the spinoff skills that facilitate more difficult phonological awareness tasks.

Consider the phoneme deletion task, which has been found to be one of the most difficult phonological awareness tasks for beginning readers to perform (Yopp, 1988). When asked to say *skip* without the /kə/ sound, children must first segment /kə/ into its two component phonemes to isolate the target phoneme /k/. They must then hold /k/ in memory while they segment *skip* into its phonemic elements: /s/, /k/, /ɪ/, and /p/. The target phoneme /k/ is then recalled and compared with each phoneme of *skip* until a match is found. The phoneme that matches the target phoneme is then deleted from the sequence, leaving /s/, /ɪ/, and /p/. These remaining elements are then recombined to form the word *sip*, which the child says aloud. Clearly, this task requires more operations than a phoneme counting task, where the child simply segments the word or syllable and then represents each segment with a tap or counter. The phoneme deletion task places particularly heavy demands on working memory because in addition to the large number of operations the respondent must hold the results of one operation in memory while performing another operation.

If improved efficiency in verbal working memory is largely a consequence of learning to read (see Tunmer & Rohl, 1991 for arguments in support of this claim), and if performance in the phoneme deletion task depends greatly on verbal working memory ability, then one would expect performance in the phoneme deletion task also to be largely a consequence of reading achievement. Consistent with this prediction are the results of a longitudinal study of beginning reading by Perfetti, Beck, Bell, and Hughes (1987). Perfetti et al. obtained a pattern of partial time-lag correlations between phoneme deletion and pseudoword decoding that suggested that the development of phoneme deletion ability was largely an effect of learning to read.

Another very difficult phonological awareness task is the phoneme reversal task (e.g., "If I say *pat*, you say *tap*"). Yopp (1988) found that this task was too difficult for kindergarten children and therefore dropped it from her test battery. The processing demands of the phoneme reversal task may place such a great strain on working memory that the task can be performed successfully only if respondents are able to reduce the load on their memory by generating orthographic images of the words presented to them. Children and adults with even a moderate amount of reading ability probably respond to the phoneme reversal task by generating an orthographic image of the word, mentally reordering the word's letters, and then reading the result in their mind's eye. The assumption of a reciprocal relationship between the development of phonological awareness and learning to read would explain why beginning readers (Yopp,

1988), illiterate adults (Morais, Cary, Alegria, & Bertelson, 1979), and adults literate only in nonalphabetic orthographies (Read, Zhang, Nie, & Ding, 1986) are unable to perform well on phonological awareness tasks that draw heavily on the spinoff skills of reading, such as the phoneme reversal and phoneme deletion tasks.

In some cases the spinoff skills of learning to read may have an adverse effect on the performance of some phonological awareness tasks. Tunmer and Nesdale (1982, 1985) found that in a phoneme-counting task beginning readers were much more likely to make overshoot errors (i.e., errors in which the response given exceeds the number of phonemes in the item) on orally presented real words and pseudowords containing digraphs (letter pairs that represent single phonemes) than on similar words not containing digraphs. Similarly, Ehri and Wilce (1980) found that fourth-grade children were more likely to make overshoot errors on a word like *pitch* than on a matched control word like *rich*. Perin (1983) reported that even when adolescent readers were explicitly told not to think of the spelling of test stimuli they still tended to make overshoot errors on items containing digraphs or silent letters.

The process of internalizing the rules of the orthographic cipher and of acquiring orthographic representations of words appears to result in such a degree of overlearning that readers find it extremely difficult to ignore spellings when letters differ from phonemes. Children appear to segment on the basis of the number of letters in the word or on the number of letters and letter groupings in the word that they believe (perhaps mistakenly) represent individual phonemes in the corresponding spoken word. Consistent with this interpretation, Tunmer and Nesdale (1985) found that phonemic segmentation scores that were based on items *not* containing digraphs or silent letters correlated significantly with measures of reading achievement, whereas scores from items containing digraphs did not.

Another important aspect of phonological awareness is its relation to letter–name knowledge. Letter–name knowledge should help beginning readers discover grapheme–phoneme correspondences because the names of most letters contain the phoneme to which the letter normally refers. However, letter–name knowledge may interact with phonemic segmentation skill such that only children who can segment letter names, such as /bi/, /ɛf/, /ǰe/, and /ɛl/, will benefit from letter–name knowledge.

Consistent with the hypothesis of an interaction between letter–name knowledge and phonemic segmentation skill are the results of a longitudinal study by Share, Jorm, Maclean, and Matthews (1984). Share et al. found that of 39 individual attributes measured at school entry phoneme segmentation and letter–name knowledge were the two strongest predictors of reading achievement after two years of reading instruction ($r = .62$ and .58, respectively). However, in a stepwise regression analysis letter–name knowledge accounted for little additional variance in beginning reading achievement after the variance due to phonemic segmentation skill had been removed.

To investigate this issue further Tunmer and colleagues conducted two studies. The first was a training study in which an initial sample of 98 prereading kindergarten children was administered a letter–name test, the Peabody Picture Vocabulary Test, and a phonemic segmentation test (Tunmer & Lally, 1986). From this sample four training groups and one control group were formed. The four training groups, which were selected to be roughly equivalent in verbal intelligence, were as follows: low phonological awareness, low letter–name knowledge (LP–LL); low phonological awareness, high letter–name knowledge (LP–HL); high phonological awareness, low letter–name knowledge (HP–LL); and high phonological awareness, high letter–name knowledge (HP–HL).

The children in the four training groups received four computer-monitored training sessions in which they were taught simple grapheme–phoneme correspondences. The computer program was designed to highlight systematic correspondences by presenting children with sequences of words in which only one letter or letter group was varied at a time while all else remained constant. As expected, in a word-recognition posttest of the generalization of correspondence rules, the high phonological awareness/high letter–name knowledge group performed significantly better than any other group.

The purpose of the second study, which was part of a larger study (Tunmer et al., 1988), was to determine whether a similar pattern of results would occur in natural classroom settings. Included among the tests administered to a sample of 105 first-grade children were tests of pseudoword decoding, letter–name knowledge, and phonological awareness. In support of the hypothesis that phonological awareness and letter–name knowledge have a positive interactive effect on phonological recoding ability, a multiple regression analysis indicated that the product of phonological awareness and letter identification accounted for a significantly greater amount of variance in pseudoword decoding than the linear combination of the two alone.

Median splits of the letter identification and phonological awareness scores provided the basis for assigning each child to one of four groups as in the training study (i.e., LP–LL, LP–HL, HP–LL, and HP–HL). As expected, the high phonological awareness/high letter–name knowledge group performed better on the pseudoword decoding test than any other group. This pattern was especially marked when cutoff scores toward the ends of the two distributions were used for group assignment rather than median splits. The means for these four groups were 7.2, 10.4, 17.2, and 31.6, respectively. The children with low phonological awareness scores (i.e., those in the first two groups) performed poorly on the pseudoword decoding test regardless of their level of letter–name knowledge, which suggests that children may need some minimal level of phonological awareness before they can derive much benefit from letter–name knowledge (see also Byrne & Fielding-Barnsley, 1989).

Although there has been much research into the relationship between phonological awareness and learning to read, few studies have examined the role of phonological awareness in spelling development. Evidence that the ability to

TABLE 7.3
Performance of Three Spelling-Age Matched Groups on Three Measures

Group	n	WRAT Spelling Scores	Phonemic Segmentation Scores	Pseudoword Spelling Scores	Phonetically Plausible Spelling Errors
Grade 2					
Good	15	18.40	17.13[a]	13.73[a]	55.73[a]
Grade 3					
Average	15	18.40	15.80[a]	14.13[a]	51.47[a]
Grade 5					
Poor	15	18.40	10.93[b]	10.13[b]	39.47[b]

Note. WRAT = Wide Range Achievement Test. For each measure, means not sharing common superscript are significantly different, Newman-Keuls multiple range test, $p < .001$, .01, and .05, respectively.

access the phonological structure of spoken words is important in the very beginning stages of spelling acquisition comes from analyses of the "invented" spellings of preliterate children (Read, 1971; Treiman, this volume). The creation of such preconventional spellings as *fre* for *fairy* and *klr* for *color* requires the ability to segment both letter names and spoken words into their constituent phonemic elements. In support of this interpretation of invented spellings are the results of a study by I. Liberman, Rubin, Duques, and Carlisle (1985) that showed that the phonological accuracy of preconventional spellings in kindergarten children was related to measures of phonological awareness even when general intelligence was taken into account.

Phonological awareness also appears to be important in later stages of spelling development. Rohl and Tunmer (1988) used a spelling–age match design to test the hypothesis that deficits in phonologically related skills are linked to difficulties in acquiring basic spelling knowledge. In support of the hypothesis, Rohl and Tunmer found that when compared with poor fifth-grade spellers average third-grade and good second-grade spellers performed significantly better on a phonological awareness test, made fewer errors in spelling pseudowords, and made spelling errors that were more phonetically accurate (see Table 7.3).

Syntactic Awareness and Learning to Read

Syntactic awareness is the ability to reflect on and manipulate aspects of the internal grammatical structure of sentences. It is not until middle childhood that children develop the ability to do this. Pratt, Tunmer, and Bowey (1984) found that when the task required children to focus their attention on sentence structure, specifically, when they were asked to "unjumble" short sentences containing word-order violations, 5- and 6-year-old children performed rather poorly. When asked to correct utterances like *Tim the juice drank* and *kicked his ball Stephen,* which were spoken by a toy puppet who could not "talk properly," the 5-year-old children scored 48% and the 6-year-old children scored 76%.

A commonly used measure of syntactic awareness is the oral cloze task in which the child is asked to produce the missing words in orally presented sentences. The cloze task can be regarded as a measure of syntactic awareness because it requires the child to analyze the structure of the sentence to select the word that is most appropriate to the surrounding semantic and syntactic context. Research indicates that performance on cloze tasks correlates positively with reading comprehension scores (Bickley, Ellington, & Bickley, 1970); that training on cloze tasks transfers positively to reading comprehension (Kennedy & Weener, 1973); that of the various subtests of the Illinois Test of Psycholinguistic Abilities, the Grammatical Closure subtest (an oral cloze test) correlates most highly with early reading achievement (Newcomer & Hammil, 1975); and that of seven tests of oral-language syntactic abilities on which second-grade poor readers were significantly deficient in comparison to normal readers, the Grammatical Closure subtest was identified as the best discriminator (Vogel, 1974).

Research also indicates however that even though good readers possess better language prediction skills than poor readers, they rely *less* on context to identify words in *ongoing* sentence processing. That is, good readers' word reading speed is not improved as much by having a context for the words as poor readers' speed (see earlier discussion and Stanovich, this volume). Perfetti, Goldman, and Hogaboam (1979), for example, found that skilled readers displayed smaller context effects on a word recognition task but were better than less-skilled readers at using context to predict missing words in written and oral cloze tasks. This raises the question of why better predictive skills are associated with greater reading proficiency.

One possibility is that the poorer performance of less-skilled readers on cloze tasks is a consequence of their difficulty in learning to read. The evidence linking language prediction skill and reading ability is correlational, typically involving designs in which reading-disabled children are matched in age with normal readers. The problem with such designs is that the normal readers have received greater exposure to written language than their chronological age matches. A possible consequence of greater reading experience is the development of verbal abilities, which renders normal readers superior to less-skilled readers on tasks involving verbal materials.

A second possibility is that syntactic awareness is causally related to learning to read. There are at least two ways in which syntactic awareness may influence reading development. One way is by enabling readers to monitor their ongoing comprehension processes more effectively (Bowey, 1986). Comprehension monitoring is an executive function that skilled readers use to make sense of incoming textual information (Wagoner, 1983). It has been described as the process of keeping track of whether comprehension is proceeding smoothly and, if not, taking remedial action (Baker & Brown, 1984).

Many poor readers appear to encounter difficulty in following the content and structure of the passage they are reading. When a breakdown in comprehension occurs these children either fail to detect it, or if they do detect it they are unable to employ the "fix-up" strategies necessary to improve their understanding of text. One strategy that syntactically aware children are able to use is to check that their responses to the words of the text conform to the surrounding grammatical context. Evidence in support of this suggestion comes from Weber's (1970) study of first graders' oral reading errors. She found that good readers were much more likely than poor readers to correct word recognition errors that did not fit the syntax and meaning of sentences, which may indicate that the good readers were more aware of when they were not comprehending text.

A second strategy that syntactically aware children can employ is to make intelligent guesses about the meanings of difficult words in prose passages. Consistent with this suggestion are the results of studies showing that better readers are superior at deriving the meanings of unknown words from text even when differences in knowledge base are controlled (Sternberg, 1985).

The second way that syntactic awareness may influence reading is by helping children acquire phonological recoding skill. This may occur in three ways. First, because the acquisition of knowledge of grapheme–phoneme correspondences is a process that takes place over time, beginning readers will not be able to recode all of the unfamiliar words that they encounter. Syntactically aware children however will be able to reflect on the structural features, both semantic and syntactic, of sentences to combine knowledge of the constraints of sentential context with incomplete graphophomenic information to identify unfamiliar words, which further increases their knowledge of grapheme–phoneme correspondences. This contextual facilitation may be especially important in learning more complex rules, such as those whose application depends on either the position of the letter in the word or on the presence of a "marker" letter. As noted earlier, Manis and Morrison (1985) found that disabled readers encountered greater difficulty employing conditional rules than reading-age controls. However, there were no differences between the groups in the application of unconditional rules involving one-to-one correspondences.

Second, the ability to use context may help beginning readers discover that some spelling patterns (i.e., *homographic* spelling patterns) are associated with more than one pronunciation. The letter sequence *ough*, for example, is pronounced differently in the words *cough, rough,* and *dough*. When confronted with an unfamiliar word containing a homographic spelling pattern, beginning readers who possess such knowledge can generate alternative pronunciations until one matches a word in their listening vocabulary. Children who have yet to acquire this knowledge and are poor at using sentence-context cues to discover polyphonic letter sequences may be restricted to pronouncing *flown* like *clown* or *clear* like *bear* and receive misleading learning trials as a result.

Research indicates that homographic spelling patterns may be a major stumbling block for beginning readers. For example, Backman et al. (1984) concluded from the results of their study (described earlier) that "it is the ability to cope with homographic patterns that distinguishes skilled and unskilled readers, rather than the ability to read unambiguous spelling patterns" (p. 129). Similarly, Manis and Morrison (1985) found that the effects of rule consistency were significantly greater for disabled readers than for reading-age controls.

Third, several investigators have argued that the ability to use context may help beginning readers learn to recognize genuine exception words, such as *stomach* and *ocean* (Gough & Hillinger, 1980; Jorm & Share, 1983). Because no word is spelled completely arbitrarily, even exception words provide some accurate phonological cues to the word's identity (Gough & Hillinger, 1980). When beginning readers apply their knowledge of grapheme–phoneme correspondences to such words, the result will often be close enough to the correct phonological form that sentence-context cues can be used to arrive at a correct identification. Consistent with this suggestion are the results of a study by Adams and Huggins (1985) on the word recognition skills of good and poor readers in Grades 2 through 5. They found that the accuracy of recognizing irregular words of "intermediate familiarity" (which varied with age and ability) improved markedly with context for *every* age and ability group.

It must be emphasized, however, that it is the *combination* of language prediction skills (i.e., syntactic awareness) and emerging phonological recoding skills that provides the basis for acquiring basic reading skills. Exclusive reliance on contextual guessing to identify unfamiliar words will result in little progress. As Gough (1983) has shown, context will enable the skilled reader under ideal conditions to predict no more than one word in four. Moreover, the words that can be predicted correctly are typically frequently occurring function words (e.g., *on, the, to*) rather than less frequent but more meaningful content words. The average predictability of content words in running text is about .10, as compared to about .40 for function words. These findings suggest that for beginning readers heavy reliance on context to identify unfamiliar words will result in little progress, as the words that beginning readers can correctly predict from context will tend to be the words that they can already recognize (Gough & Hillinger, 1980). Consistent with these suggestions is research by Biemiller (1970), who found in a longitudinal study of first graders' oral reading errors that progress in reading was determined in part by how early children shifted their attention to graphic information.

The major disadvantage of relying totally on context to guess words is that not only will this strategy result in missed learning trials when the context is insufficient to make a guess, but also it will result in *misleading* learning trials when a prediction is contextually appropriate but nevertheless incorrect (Jorm & Share, 1983). Deficient and misleading data will almost certainly impede progress. Language prediction skills will be useful only if they are applied to the problem of breaking the orthographic code. Consistent with this claim, Biemiller (1970) reported that the most advanced stage of beginning reading that emerged from his analysis of first graders' oral reading errors was one in which the readers made use of *both* graphic and contextual information in learning to identify unfamiliar words.

Further evidence in support of this claim comes from a study by Evans and Carr (1985) that compared the effects of two instructional approaches (decoding oriented vs. language experience oriented) on beginning reading development. They found that the use of context to make predictions was positively correlated with reading achievement but only in the group that had received instruction in decoding skills. Evans and Carr concluded from their findings that "a focus on predictive context utilization 'worked' in the [decoding-oriented] classrooms because it was combined with print-specific skills taught through word analysis activities, but did not work in the [language experience-oriented] classrooms because the children had few resources for dealing with unfamiliar words" (p. 343–344).

Several studies using a variety of different tasks (e.g., judgment of grammaticality, correction of word-order violations, and oral cloze) have demonstrated that syntactic awareness is related to beginning reading achievement (see Ryan & Ledger, 1984, for a review). For example, Willows and Ryan (1986) found that measures of syntactic awareness were significantly related to beginning reading achievement even when general cognitive ability and vocabulary level were controlled. However, as noted earlier, the evidence linking syntactic awareness and reading ability is based primarily on studies comparing good and poor readers of similar age and intelligence. The problem with this type of design is that it yields uninterpretable results when a difference in some reading-related variable is found. The difference could be either a cause or a consequence of reading failure.

To avoid the problem of interpretation resulting from differential exposure to print, Tunmer, Nesdale, and Wright (1987) used a reading-level match design in which good, younger readers were matched with poor, older readers in reading ability and verbal intelligence. Children in second grade and fourth grade were identified as poor, average, and good readers. The second-grade good readers were carefully matched with the fourth-grade poor readers on four measures of reading ability (real word recognition, pseudoword naming, reading fluency, and reading comprehension) and verbal intelligence. The results showed that the good, younger readers scored significantly better than the poor, older readers on two measures of syntactic awareness, one an oral cloze task and the other a task in which the children were asked to "unscramble" short sentences containing word-order violations (e.g., *jumped Jack the log*). Tunmer et al. concluded from their findings that the older, poor readers were developmentally delayed in syntactic awareness and this delay might have retarded reading achievement, because both measures were strongly associated with reading achievement at each grade level. Consistent with these results, Bohannon, Warren-Leubecker, and Hepler (1984) found that sensitivity to word-order violations at the beginning of kindergarten, first grade, and second grade was strongly related to beginning reading achievement at the end of each grade even when verbal intelligence was held constant (see also Warren-Leubecker, 1987).

Although these results suggest that that syntactic awareness is causally related to learning to read, there remains the question of the nature of the relation of syntactic awareness to reading acquisition. As noted earlier, syntactic awareness may play an essential role in acquiring phonological recoding skill, intrasentential comprehension monitoring skill, or both. If syntactic awareness influences the development of phonological recoding skill, this effect should be observed in the initial stages of learning to read when the focus is on the acquisition of word-level skills. Syntactic awareness should also make an *independent* contribution to phonological recoding skill when phonological awareness is included in the analysis. It is possible that syntactic awareness is related to phonological recoding simply because syntactic awareness, like phonological awareness, is a metalinguistic ability and therefore shares in common with phonological awareness many of the same component skills (invoking control processing, performing mental operations on structural features of language, etc.). However, if syntactic awareness facilitates the development of phonological recoding skill by enabling children to use context to identify unfamiliar words, which in turn increases their knowledge of grapheme–phoneme correspondences, then syntactic awareness should make a contribution to the development of phonological recoding skill that is distinct from that made by phonological awareness.

To test this hypothesis, Tunmer and Nesdale (1986) conducted a study in which first-grade children were administered tests of verbal intelligence (estimated by the Peabody Picture Vocabulary Test), phonological awareness (measured by a phoneme segmentation task), syntactic awareness (measured by a word-order correction task), phonological recoding (measured by a pseudoword decoding task), and reading comprehension. The analysis of the results revealed that the correlation between syntactic awareness and phonological recoding was as great as that between phonological awareness and phonological recoding (both around .50). A path analysis was also conducted with verbal intelligence, phonological awareness, and syntactic awareness treated as exogenous variables, and phonological recoding and reading comprehension as endogenous variables (see Fig. 7.4). The most important findings were that phonological and syntactic awareness each made an independent contribution to phonological recoding skill and influenced reading comprehension indirectly through phonological recoding. These results suggest that phonological and syntactic awareness may be equally as important in acquiring phonological recoding skill.

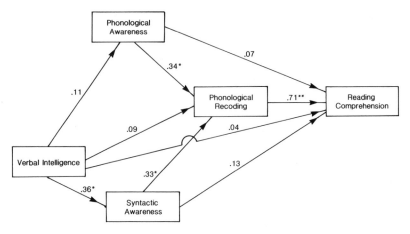

FIG. 7.4. Path diagram displaying structure of relationships between verbal intelligence, metalinguistic measures and reading achievement measures. (Standardized beta weights are shown on each path, *$p <$ .01, **$p <$ .001.)

Research by Stanovich et al. (1984a) is consistent with these findings. Stanovich et al. included as one of their measures an oral cloze task that was intended to serve as a measure of listening comprehension. For their first-grade readers, the oral cloze task (which we regard as a measure of syntactic awareness) correlated more highly with phonological recoding than did their measure of phonological awareness (.37 vs. .33) In fact, the oral cloze task correlated more highly with phonological recoding than with any of the other variables (which included general intelligence, listening comprehension, word recognition speed, and reading comprehension). Stanovich et al. (1984a) also found that in a factor analysis the oral cloze task loaded most highly with the phonological awareness factor, not with listening comprehension as they had anticipated. These findings and those of the Tunmer and Nesdale (1986) study are consistent with the claims that phonological awareness and syntactic awareness (as measured by either the cloze or correction tasks) are metalinguistic skills and that each is significantly related to the development of phonological recoding ability.

In the Tunmer and Nesdale (1986) study, verbal intelligence was significantly correlated with syntactic awareness but not with phonological awareness (see Fig. 7.4). A possible explanation of this difference is that performance on the syntactic awareness task depended in part on vocabulary knowledge, which was used as an estimate of verbal intelligence. Vocabularly knowledge includes not only knowledge about word meanings but also information about how words can be combined with other words to form grammatical sentences. For example, in "unscrambling" a word string like *jumped Jack the log,* the child needs to know the word class associated with each word, the syntactic structures into which the verb *jumped* can enter (governed by strict subcategorization rules), and the types of nouns that can serve as subjects of *jumped* (governed by selectional restriction rules, which prevent word orderings like *the log jumped Jack*).

The results obtained by Tunmer and Nesdale (1986) have been replicated and extended in subsequent studies (Tunmer, 1989b; Tunmer et al., 1988). In one study, which is described more fully in the final section, Tunmer (1989b) found that syntactic awareness in first grade was significantly related to phonological recoding and listening comprehension in second grade even when the effects of verbal intelligence, general cognitive ability, and phonological awareness were controlled. Also, scatterplots have revealed a relationship between syntactic awareness and phonological recoding (Tunmer, 1989b; Tunmer et al., 1988). Similar to the relation between phonological awareness and phonological recoding, the scatterplots revealed that although many children performed well on syntactic awareness and poorly on pseudoword decoding, no child performed poorly on syntactic awareness and well on pseudoword decoding. These findings suggest that syntactic awareness may be essential for acquiring knowledge of grapheme–phoneme correspondences.

Pragmatic Awareness and Learning to Read

Whereas syntactic awareness is concerned with intrasentential relations, pragmatic awareness is concerned with intersentential relations. Individual propositions normally do not stand in isolation but are integrated into larger sets of propositions. This occurs through the (automatic) application of pragmatic and inferential rules that combine new information with old information. Old information includes prior knowledge, knowledge of preceding text, and knowledge of situational context.

Pragmatic awareness can thus be defined as the ability to use control processing to perform mental operations on the output of these integrative processes. It is reflected in problem-solving, communication tasks in which children are required to consciously analyze, evaluate, and edit candidate messages. Flavell (1977) suggested that these tasks require a fairly late-developing "metacommunicative" ability that involves "thinking about the message (metacommunication) rather than sending it (communication)" (p. 78). Several studies have shown that young children often fail to notice when they do not understand, as in situations in which there is insufficient or ambiguous information, or in which there are inconsistencies in the information provided (see Pratt & Nesdale, 1984, for a review). Young children seem less able to engage deliberately in the inferential and constructive processing necessary to obtain information about their own comprehension, an ability that can be referred to as *intersentential comprehension monitoring*.

In a series of studies Tunmer and colleagues investigated the development of young children's ability to detect intersentence inconsistencies in passages that were presented orally. Tunmer, Nesdale, and Pratt (1983) asked 5-, 6-, and 7-year-old children to say whether each of several three-sentence "stories" told by a puppet was a good one that made sense or a silly one that did not make sense and to justify their response. The stories differed in whether they were consistent or inconsistent and in whether the principle upon which a story's consistency depended was implicitly or explicitly stated.

The task used by Tunmer et al. was designed specifically to reduce the effects of factors that may have limited children's performance in previous studies (e.g., Markman, 1979). The task involved the use of materials that were clearly based on children's experiences, the children were told explicitly that some of the passages contained inconsistencies (i.e., were "silly"), and the logically inconsistent sentences were presented contiguously. Nevertheless, the results showed developmental trends, with many of the younger children experiencing difficulty in detecting inconsistencies. The justifications provided by these children indicated that they tended to question the empirical validity of individual sentences, rather than integrate the story as a whole and examine its overall logical structure. Subsequent studies by Tunmer and colleagues confirmed that the difficulty of detecting inconsistencies was even greater when the inconsistent sentences were interspersed among other sentences or embedded in larger segments of communication, or when the children were not led to expect that some of the passages would not make sense (Nesdale, Pratt, & Tunmer, 1985; Nesdale, Tunmer, & Clover, 1985).

Research also shows that young children are poor at detecting ambiguities in messages. Patterson, O'Brien, Kister, Carter, and Kotsonis (1981) used a version of the referential communication task developed by Glucksberg and Krauss (1966). The experimenter and child were seated at opposite ends of a table separated by an opaque screen placed across the middle of the table. Each had an identical set of cards with pictures of common objects or animals on each card. The experimental task was presented in the form of a listening game in which the child was asked to indicate whether descriptions presented by the experimenter were sufficient to select one of the pictures on the card (termed the "special one"). The messages were designed to be fully informative, partially informative, or ambiguous. The main dependent variable was the number of correct judgments about whether sufficient information had been presented to identify the target referent. Patterson et al. (1981) found that school-age but not preschool children showed evidence of effective comprehension monitoring.

Although young children are relatively effective communicators when language is embedded in a familiar perceptual and social context, the results of the aforementioned studies indicate that they function poorly on tasks that require them to attend to the structural features of language free from supportive contextual and paralinguistic cues. These findings may provide an explanation of the comprehension difficulties experienced by some beginning readers, because written language, especially that which appears in school texts, tends to be much less context dependent than the language of casual conversation, which is usually highly context dependent (as is demonstrated by the difficulty one encounters when attempting to comprehend transcripts of casual conversation).

In support of these suggestions is a considerable amount of research on reading comprehension processes in good and poor readers that indicates that poor readers are less able to monitor their comprehension processes than good readers (see reviews by Baker & Brown, 1984; Garner, 1987; Wagoner, 1983). However, because these studies have concentrated on children in the middle grades, they do not provide an answer to the question of whether intersentential comprehension monitoring is important in the beginning stages of learning to read, when the focus is primarily on the acquisition of word-level skills. Unlike phonological and syntactic awareness, there seems to be little theoretical justification for supposing that pragmatic awareness facilitates the acquisition of decoding skill. West, Stanovich, Feeman, and Cunningham (1983), for example, found that varying the amount of prior context (one sentence vs. three sentences) did not produce differences in the effects of context on word recognition in second- and sixth-grade readers, which suggests that context effects arise primarily from the sentence containing the target word.

To investigate further the role of pragmatic awareness in beginning reading development, Tunmer et al. (1988) performed a path analysis to determine the structure of relationships between phonological, syntactic, and pragmatic awareness (as measured by an oral inconsistency detection task), and phonological recoding and reading comprehension in first-grade readers. As predicted, phonological and syntactic awareness influenced reading comprehension indirectly through phonological recoding, whereas pragmatic awareness failed to make an independent contribution to either phonological recoding or reading comprehension.

Although these results suggest that pragmatic awareness is not as important as phonological and syntactic awareness in the beginning stages of reading acquisition, pragmatic awareness may become more important in later stages, when the emphasis shifts more toward text-level processes. The findings from several studies indicate that the intersentential comprehension monitoring strategies of older, poor readers can be improved by training. However, such training appears to have little or no impact on reading comprehension performance as measured by standardized tests (see Paris & Oka, 1989).

A possible explanation of the failure of comprehension strategy training to transfer positively to reading achievement is that the cumulative effects of reading failure result in negative Matthew effects in *listening* comprehension, which, according to the simple view, would adversely affect reading comprehension as well (Juel, 1988). Because of their deficient decoding skills, poor readers not only receive less practice in reading but soon begin to confront materials that are too difficult for them, which further discourages them from reading (Stanovich, 1986). Poor readers are thus prevented from taking advantage of the reciprocally facilitating relationships between reading and other aspects of development such as vocabulary growth, ability to comprehend more syntactically complex sentences, and development of richer and more elaborated knowledge bases, all of which facilitate further growth in reading comprehension by enabling readers to cope with more difficult materials. Consistent with this suggestion, Juel (1988) found in a longitudinal study of beginning reading that reading achievement itself was a major factor influencing growth in listening comprehension ability among disadvantaged children with below-average school language and listening comprehension abilities at school entry.

THE COGNITIVE–DEVELOPMENTAL MODEL OF METALINGUISTIC DEVELOPMENT AND READING ACQUISITION

The cognitive–developmental model of metalinguistic development and reading acquisition proposes that phonological and syntactic awareness influence the development of phonological recoding skill, and that along with pragmatic awareness, syntactic awareness also influences the development of listening comprehension by enabling children to monitor their ongoing comprehension processes more effectively (see Fig. 7.5). Given the importance of metalinguistic skills for early progress in reading, an important question is this: Why do some children encounter difficulty in performing the metalinguistic operations necessary for acquiring basic reading skills?

Earlier we suggested that the development of metalinguistic abilities is related to a more general change in information processing capability, the development of metacognitive control over the information processing system. In contrast to

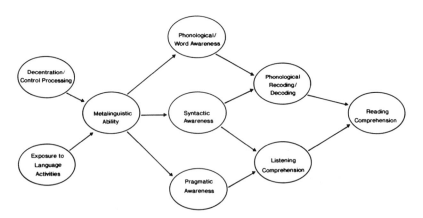

FIG. 7.5. The cognitive-developmental model of metalinguistic development and reading acquisition.

other models that focus on differences in the phonological storage and processing component of working memory (Liberman & Shankweiler, 1985; Liberman, Shankweiler, & Liberman, 1989; Shankweiler & Crain, 1986; Shankweiler, Crain, Brady, & Macaruso, this volume; Stanovich, 1988), the cognitive–developmental model ascribes greater importance to differences in the limited capacity central executive that is used to operate control processes in working memory. Metalinguistic performances such as separating a word from its referent, dissociating the meaning of a sentence from its form, and reflecting on the phonemic constituents of words require the ability to *decenter,* to shift one's attention from message content to the properties of language used to convey content. An essential feature of both metalinguistic operations and decentration is the ability to control the course of one's thoughts, that is, to invoke control processing. According to the cognitive–developmental model, then, developmental differences in control processing ability produce differences in the development of the metalinguistic abilities necessary for acquiring basic decoding and comprehension monitoring skills.

A lag in the development of control processing ability may delay early progress in reading to such an extent that it initiates what Stanovich (1986) describes as a "cascade of interacting achievement failures and motivational problems" (p. 393). Children who are developmentally delayed in control processing may therefore suffer a "double whammy." These children's level of decentration ability may be such that they cannot readily perform the low-level metalinguistic operations necessary for acquiring basic reading skills. Consequently, they will not be able to derive maximum benefit from reading instruction and will be prevented from taking advantage of the "bootstrapping" relationships between reading achievement and other aspects of development, which facilitate further growth in reading.

The claim that the development of metalinguistic ability is related to the development of decentration processes is not to suggest that metalinguistic skills emerge spontaneously in development, that is, without specific stimulation. Children must be exposed to language activities that focus their attention on the structural features of language. These activities include rhyming and sound analysis games that increase phonological sensitivity (Bryant, Bradley, Maclean, & Crossland, 1989), letter games and books that increase letter-name knowledge, games that involve the manipulation of movable letters to form preconventional spellings of words, and games and activities that involve listening to and producing "linguistic" jokes and riddles (i.e., those depending on sound similarity or structural ambiguity).

In support of the cognitive–developmental model are the results of two longitudinal studies (Tunmer, 1989b; Tunmer et al., 1988). The first (Tunmer et al., 1988) showed that decentration ability in preliterate children was more strongly correlated with overall metalinguistic ability at the beginning and end of first grade than was any other school-entry variable. The latter included measures of verbal intelligence, letter-name knowledge, and print awareness. The results further revealed that preliterate children with low levels of phonological awareness at school entry but above-average levels of decentration ability showed significantly greater improvement in phonological awareness during the school year than children with similarly low levels of phonological awareness but below-average levels of decentration ability at school entry (see Table 7.4). The mean phonological awareness score of the high-decentration ability group was above the mean of all children's phonological awareness scores at the end of the year, whereas the low-decentration ability group mean was one standard deviation below the overall mean.

A path analysis of the data from the second longitudinal study (Tunmer, 1989b) revealed that Grade 1 phonological awareness influenced Grade 2 reading comprehension indirectly through Grade 2 phonological recoding, and that Grade 1 syntactic awareness influenced Grade 2 reading achievement through *both* phonological recoding and listening comprehension (see Fig. 7.6). Neither decentration ability (as measured by concrete operations) nor verbal intelligence in Grade 1 made an independent contribution to the variability of any of the Grade 2 variables. However, decentration ability made a relatively strong independent contribution to both phonological and syntactic awareness, whereas verbal intelligence made a relatively small independent contribution to syntactic awareness only. Overall, these findings are impressive because they show that metalinguistic abilities in first grade are significantly related to listening and reading achievement in second grade, even after the effects of verbal intelligence and concrete operativity have been removed. The results further showed that decentration ability was more strongly related to metalinguistic development than was verbal intelligence, as expected.

In summary, the cognitive–developmental model proposes that during middle childhood children develop the capacity for performing metalinguistic operations when confronted with certain kinds of tasks, such as learning to read. However, as a result of a deficit or developmental delay in control processing ability, some children fail to reach the threshold level of decentration ability required to perform the low-level metalinguistic operations necessary for developing basic read-

TABLE 7.4
Mean Phonological Awareness Scores as a Function of Decentration Ability and Time of Testing

Time of Testing	Low-Decentration Ability Group Mean (n = 24)	High-Decentration Ability Group Mean (n = 16)	t(38)
Beginning of Year	4.71	4.87	.46
End of Year	11.32	16.34	3.48*

$*p < .001.$

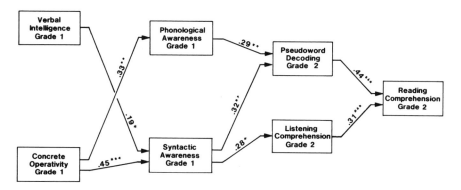

FIG. 7.6.   Path diagram displaying structure of relationships between first-grade ability measures and second-grade achievement measures. (Standardized beta weights are shown on each path, *$p < .05$, **$p < .01$, ***$p < .001$.) Reprinted from *Phonology and reading disability*, edited by Donald Shankweiler and Isabelle Y. Liberman (University of Michigan Press, 1989).

ing skills, which, in turn, would enable them to take advantage of the reciprocally facilitating relationships between reading and other cognitive skills. The cognitive–developmental model also predicts that, although some children possess the level of decentration ability necessary for acquiring metalinguistic skills, their metalinguistic development may be delayed by environmental deficits: These children may not have received sufficient exposure to the kinds of language activities that focus their attention on the structural features of spoken language. For these children, and for children with developmental delays in control processing ability, explicit training in metalinguistic skills may be required to avoid the snowballing consequences of reading failure that Stanovich (1986) described.

REFERENCES

Adams, M. J., & Huggins, A. (1985). The growth of children's sight vocabulary: A quick test with educational and theoretical implications. *Reading Research Quarterly, 20,* 262–281.

Backman, J., Bruck, M., Hébert, M., & Seidenberg, M. S. (1984). Acquisition and use of spelling-sound correspondences in reading. *Journal of Experimental Child Psychology, 38,* 114–133.

Baker, L., & Brown, A. L. (1984). Metacognitive skills and reading. In P. D. Pearson, R. Barr, M. Kamil, & P. Mosenthal (Eds.), *Handbook of reading research* (pp. 353–393). New York: Longman.

Barron, R. W. (1986). Word recognition in early reading: A review of the direct and indirect access hypothesis. *Cognition, 24,* 93–119.

Bickley, A., Ellington, B., & Bickley, R. (1970). The cloze procedure: A conspectus. *Journal of Reading Behavior, 2,* 232–249.

Biemiller, A. (1970). The development of the use of graphic and contextual information as children learn to read. *Reading Research Quarterly, 6,* 75–96.

Bohannon, J., Warren-Leubecker, A., & Hepler, N. (1984). Word awareness and early reading. *Child Development, 55,* 1541–1548.

Bowey, J. A. (1986). Syntactic awareness in relation to reading skill and ongoing reading comprehension monitoring. *Journal of Experimental Child Psychology, 41,* 282–299.

Bowey, J. A., Tunmer, W. E., & Pratt, C. (1984). Development of children's understanding of the metalinguistic term *word*. *Journal of Educational Psychology, 76,* 500–512.

Bradley, L., & Bryant, P. E. (1985). *Rhyme and reason in reading and spelling.* Ann Arbor: University of Michigan Press.

Bryant, P. E., Bradley, L., Maclean, M., & Crossland, J. (1989). Nursery rhymes, phonological skills and reading. *Journal of Child Language, 16,* 407–428.

Byrne, B., & Fielding-Barnsley, R. (1989). Phonemic awareness and letter knowledge in the child's acquisition of the alphabetic principle. *Journal of Educational Psychology, 81,* 313–321.

Curtis, M. (1980). Development of components of reading skill. *Journal of Educational Psychology, 72,* 656–669.

Ehri, L. C. (1975). Word consciousness in readers and prereaders. *Journal of Educational Psychology, 67,* 204–212.

Ehri, L. C. (1984). How orthography alters spoken language competencies in children learning to read and spell. In J. Downing & R. Valtin (Eds.), *Language awareness and learning to read* (pp. 119–147). New York: Springer-Verlag.

Ehri, L. C. (1986). Sources of difficulty in learning to spell and read. In M. L. Wolraich & D. K. Routh (Eds.), *Advances in developmental and behavioural pediatrics* (pp. 121–195). Greenwich, CT: JAI Press.

Ehri, L. C. (1987). Learning to read and spell words. *Journal of Reading Behavior, 19,* 5–31.

Ehri, L. C. (1989). The development of spelling knowledge and its role in reading acquisition and reading disability. *Journal of Learning Disabilities, 22,* 356–365.

Ehri, L. C., & Wilce, L. (1980). The influence of orthography on readers' conceptualization of the phonemic structure of words. *Applied Psycholinguistics, 1,* 371–385.

Evans, M., & Carr, T. (1985). Cognitive abilities, conditions of learning and the early development of reading skill. *Reading Research Quarterly, 20,* 327–350.

Evans, M., Taylor, N., & Blum, I. (1979). Children's written language awareness and its relation to reading acquisition. *Journal of Reading Behavior, 11,* 7–19.

Flavell, J. H. (1977). *Cognitive development.* Englewood Cliffs, NJ: Prentice-Hall.

Flavell, J. H. (1981). Cognitive monitoring. In W. Dickson (Ed.), *Children's oral communication skills* (pp. 35–60). San Diego, CA: Academic Press.

Flavell, J. H. (1985). *Cognitive development* (rev. ed.). Englewood Cliffs, NJ: Prentice-Hall.

Garner, R. (1987). *Metacognition and reading comprehension.* Norwood, NJ: Ablex.

Glucksberg, S., & Krauss, R. (1966). Referential communication in nursery school children: Method and some preliminary findings. *Journal of Experimental Child Psychology, 3,* 333–342.

Goodman, K. S. (1967). Reading: A psycholinguistic guessing game. *Journal of the Reading Specialist, 6,* 126–135.

Gough, P. B. (1975). The structure of language. In D. Duane & M. Rawson (Eds.), *Reading, perception and language* (pp. 15–37). Baltimore, MD: York Press.

Gough, P. B. (1983). Context, form and interaction. In K. Rayner (Ed.), *Eye movements in reading: Perceptual and language processes* (pp. 203–211). San Diego, CA: Academic Press.

Gough, P. B. (1984). Word recognition. In P. D. Pearson, R. Barr, M. Kamil, & P. Mosenthal (Eds.), *Handbook of reading research* (pp. 225–253). New York: Longman.

Gough, P. B., & Hillinger, M. L. (1980). Learning to read: An unnatural act. *Bulletin of the Orton Society, 30,* 179–196.

Gough, P. B., & Tunmer, W. E. (1986). Decoding, reading and reading disability. *Remedial and Special Education, 7,* 6–10.

Gough, P. B., & Walsh, M. (1991). Chinese, Phoenicians, and the orthographic cipher of English. In S. Brady & D. Shankweiler (Eds.), *Phonological processes in literacy: A tribute to Isabelle Y. Liberman.* Hillsdale, NJ: Lawrence Erlbaum Associates.

Hoover, W., & Gough, P. B. (1990). The simple view of reading. *Reading and Writing: An Interdisciplinary Journal, 2,* 127–160.

Jorm, A. F., & Share, D. L. (1983). Phonological recoding and reading acquisition. *Applied Psycholinguistics, 4,* 103–147.

Jorm, A. F., Share, D. L., Maclean, R., & Matthews, R. (1984). Phonological recoding skills and learning to read: A longitudinal study. *Applied Psycholinguistics, 5,* 201–207.

Juel, C. (1988). Learning to read and write: A longitudinal study of 54 children from first through fourth grades. *Journal of Educational Psychology, 80,* 437–447.

Juel, C., Griffith, P. L., & Gough, P. B. (1986). Acquisition of literacy: A longitudinal study of children in first and second grade. *Journal of Educational Psychology, 78,* 243–255.

Kennedy, D., & Weener, P. (1973). Visual and auditory training with the cloze procedure to improve reading and listening comprehension. *Reading Research Quarterly, 8,* 524–541.

Lesgold, A., Resnick, L. B., & Hammond, K. (1985). Learning to read: A longitudinal study of word skill development in two curricula. In G. E. Mackinnon & T. G. Waller (Eds.), *Reading research: Advances in theory and practice* (Vol.4, pp. 107–138). San Diego, CA: Academic Press.

Liberman, A. M., Cooper, F. S., Shankweiler, D., & Studdert-Kennedy, M. (1967). Perception of the speech code. *Psychological Review, 74,* 431–461.

Liberman, I. Y., Rubin, H., Duques, S., & Carlisle, J. (1985). Linguistic abilities and spelling proficiency in kindergarten and adult poor spellers. In D. B. Gray & J. F. Kavanagh (Eds.), *Biobehavioral measures of dyslexia* (pp. 163–176). Parkton, MD: New York Press.

Liberman, I. Y., & Shankweiler, D. (1985). Phonology and the problem of learning to read and write. *Remedial and Special Education, 6,* 8–17.

Liberman, I. Y., Shankweiler, D., & Liberman, A. M. (1989). The alphabetic principle and learning to read. In D. Shankweiler & I. Y. Liberman (Eds.), *Phonology and reading disability: Solving the reading puzzle* (pp. 1–33). Ann Arbor: University of Michigan Press.

Lundberg, I., Frost, J., & Petersen, O. -P. (1988). Effects of an extensive program for stimulating phonological awareness in preschool children. *Reading Research Quarterly, 23,* 263–284.

Manis, F. R., & Morrison, F. J. (1985). Reading disability: A deficit in rule learning? In L. S. Siegel & F. J. Morrison (Eds.), *Cognitive development in atypical children* (pp. 1–26). New York: Springer-Verlag.

Mann, V. (1986). Why some children encounter reading problems: The contribution of difficulties with language processing and language sophistication to early reading disability. In J. Torgesen & B. Wong (Eds.), *Psychological and educational perspectives on learning disabilities* (pp. 133–159). San Diego, CA: Academic Press.

Markman, E. (1979). Realizing that you don't understand: Elementary school children's awareness of inconsistencies. *Child Development, 47,* 742–749.

Matluck, J. H., & Tunmer, W. E. (1979, May). *Relation of oral language proficiency to reading achievement.* Paper presented at the Eighth Annual International Bilingual/Bicultural Education Conference, Seattle, WA.

McNinch, G. H. (1974). Awareness of aural and visual word boundary within a sample of first graders. *Perceptual and Motor Skills, 38,* 1127–1134.

Morais, J., Alegria, J., & Content, A. (1987). The relationship between segmental analysis and alphabetic literacy: An interactive view. *Cahiers de Psychologie Cognitive, 7,* 415–438.

Morais, J., Cary, L., Alegria, J., & Bertelson, P. (1979). Does awareness of speech as a sequence of phones arise spontaneously? *Cognition, 7,* 323–331.

Nesdale, A. R., Pratt, C., & Tunmer, W. E. (1985). Young children's detection of propositional inconsistencies in oral communications. *Australian Journal of Psychology, 37,* 289–296.

Nesdale, A. R., Tunmer, W. E., & Clover, J. (1985). Factors influencing young children's ability to detect logical inconsistencies in oral communications. *Journal of Language and Social Psychology, 4*, 39–49.

Newcomer, P., & Hammil, D. (1975). ITPA and academic achievement: A survey. *The Reading Teacher, 28*, 731–741.

Olofsson, A., & Lundberg, I. (1985). Evaluation of long term effects of phonemic awareness training in kindergarten. *Scandinavian Journal of Psychology, 26*, 21–34.

Paris, S., & Oka, E. (1989). Strategies for comprehending text and coping with reading difficulties. *Learning Disability Quarterly, 12*, 32–42.

Patterson, C. J., O'Brien, C., Kister, M. C., Carter, D. B., & Kotsonis, M. E. (1981). Development of comprehension monitoring as a function of context. *Developmental Psychology, 17*, 379–389.

Perfetti, C. A. (1985). *Reading ability.* New York: Oxford University Press.

Perfetti, C. A. (1986). Cognitive and linguistic components of reading ability. In B. R. Foorman & A. W. Siegel (Eds.), *Acquisition of reading skills: Cultural constraints and cognitive universals* (pp. 1–40). Hillsdale, NJ: Lawrence Erlbaum Associates.

Perfetti, C. A., Beck, I., Bell, L., & Hughes, C. (1987). Phonemic knowledge and learning to read are reciprocal: A longitudinal study of first grade children. *Merrill-Palmer Quarterly, 33*, 283–319.

Perfetti, C. A., Goldman, S. R., & Hogaboam, T. W. (1979). Reading skill and the identification of words in discourse context. *Memory and Cognition, 7*, 273–283.

Perfetti, C. A., & Hogaboam, T. W. (1975). The relationship between single word decoding and reading comprehension skill. *Journal of Educational Psychology, 67*, 461–469.

Perin, D. (1983). Phonemic segmentation and spelling. *British Journal of Psychology, 74*, 129–144.

Pratt, C., & Nesdale, A. R. (1984). Pragmatic awareness in children. In W. E. Tunmer, C. Pratt, & M. L. Herriman (Eds.), *Metalinguistic awareness in children: Theory, research and implications* (pp. 105–125). Berlin: Springer-Verlag.

Pratt, C., Tunmer, W. E., & Bowey, J. A. (1984). Children's capacity to correct grammatical violations in sentences. *Journal of Child Language, 11*, 129–141.

Read, C. (1971). Pre-school children's knowledge of English phonology. *Harvard Educational Review, 41*, 1–34.

Read, C., Zhang, Y., Nie, H., & Ding, B. (1986). The ability to manipulate speech sounds depends on knowing alphabetic reading: *Cognition, 24*, 31–44.

Rohl, M., & Tunmer, W. E. (1988). Phonemic segmentation skill and spelling acquisition. *Applied Psycholinguistics, 9*, 335–350.

Ryan, E., & Ledger, G. (1984). Learning to attend to sentence structure: Links between metalinguistic development and reading. In J. Downing & R. Valtin (Eds.), *Language awareness and learning to read* (pp. 149–171). New York: Springer-Verlag.

Shankweiler, D., & Crain, S. (1986). Language mechanisms and reading disorder: A modular approach. *Cognition, 24*, 139–168.

Share, D. L., Jorm, A. F., Maclean, R., & Matthews, R. (1984). Sources of individual differences in reading acquisition. *Journal of Educational Psychology, 76*, 1309–1324.

Smith, F. (1971). *Understanding reading: A psycholinguistic analysis of reading and learning to read.* New York: Holt, Rinehart & Winston.

Smith, F. (1979). *Reading without nonsense.* New York: Teachers College Press.

Snowling, M. (1980). The development of grapheme-phoneme correspondences in normal and dyslexic readers. *Journal of Experimental Child Psychology, 29*, 294–305.

Snowling, M. (1981). Phonemic deficits in developmental dyslexia. *Psychological Research, 43*, 219–234.

Stanovich, K. E. (1980). Toward an interactive compensatory model of individual differences in the development of reading fluency. *Reading Research Quarterly, 16*, 32–71.

Stanovich, K. E. (1984). The interactive-compensatory model of reading: A confluence of developmental, experimental and educational psychology. *Remedial and Special Education, 5,* 11–19.

Stanovich, K. E. (1986). Matthew effects in reading: Some consequences of individual differences in the acquisition of literacy. *Reading Research Quarterly, 21,* 360–406.

Stanovich, K. E. (1988). Explaining the difference between the dyslexic and garden-variety poor readers: The phonological-core variable-difference model. *Journal of Learning Disabilities, 21,* 590–604.

Stanovich, K. E., Cunningham, A. E., & Feeman, D. J. (1984a). Intelligence, cognitive skills and early reading progress. *Reading Research Quarterly, 19,* 278–303.

Stanovich, K. E., Cunningham, A. E., & Feeman, D. J. (1984b). Relation between early reading acquisition and word decoding with and without context: A longitudinal study of first-grade children. *Journal of Educational Psychology, 4,* 668–677.

Sternberg, R. (1985). *Beyond IQ: A triarchic theory of human intelligence.* Cambridge, England: Cambridge University Press.

Thompson, G. B. (1986). When nonsense is better than sense: Non-lexical errors to word reading tests. *British Journal of Educational Psychology, 56,* 216–219.

Treiman, R., & Baron, J. (1981). Segmental analysis ability: Development and relation to reading ability. In G. E. Mackinnon & T. G. Waller (Eds.), *Reading research: Advances in theory and practice* (Vol.3, pp. 159–198). San Diego, CA: Academic Press.

Tunmer, W. E. (1989a). Conscience phonologique et acquisition de la langue écrite. In L. Rieben & C. A. Perfetti (Eds.), *L'apprenti lecteur: Recherches empiriques et implications pedagogiques* (pp. 197–220). Paris: Delachaux Et Niestle.

Tunmer, W. E. (1989b). The role of language-related factors in reading disability. In D. Shankweiler & I. Y. Liberman (Eds.), *Phonology and reading disability: Solving the reading puzzle* (pp. 91–131). Ann Arbor: University of Michigan Press.

Tunmer, W. E., Bowey, J. A., & Grieve, R. (1983). The development of young children's awareness of the word as a unit of spoken language. *Journal of Psycholinguistic Research, 12,* 567–594.

Tunmer, W. E., & Herriman, M. L. (1984). The development of metalinguistic awareness: A conceptual overview. In W. E. Tunmer, C. Pratt, & M. L. Herriman (Eds.), *Metalinguistic awareness in children: Theory, research and implications* (pp. 12–35). New York: Springer-Verlag.

Tunmer, W. E., Herriman, M. L., & Nesdale, A. R. (1988). Metalinguistic abilities and beginning reading. *Reading Research Quarterly, 23,* 134–158.

Tunmer, W. E., & Lally, M. R. (1986, July). *The effects of letter-name knowledge and phonological awareness on computer-based instruction in decoding for prereaders.* Paper presented at annual meeting of the Australian Reading Association, Perth, Western Australia.

Tunmer, W. E., & Nesdale, A. R. (1982). The effects of digraphs and pseudowords on phonemic segmentation in young children. *Applied Psycholinguistics, 3,* 299–311.

Tunmer, W. E., & Nesdale, A. R. (1985). Phonemic segmentation skill and beginning reading. *Journal of Educational Psychology, 77,* 417–427.

Tunmer, W. E., & Nesdale, A. R. (1986). [Path analysis of the relation of phonological and syntactic awareness to reading comprehension in beginning readers]. Unpublished raw data.

Tunmer, W. E., Nesdale, A. R., & Pratt, C. (1983). The development of young children's awareness of logical inconsistencies. *Journal of Experimental Child Psychology, 36,* 97–108.

Tunmer, W. E., Nesdale, A. R., & Wright, A. D. (1987). Syntactic awareness and reading acquisition. *British Journal of Developmental Psychology, 5,* 25–34.

Tunmer, W. E., Pratt, C., & Herriman, M. L. (1984). *Metalinguistic awareness in children: Theory, research and implications.* Berlin: Springer-Verlag.

Tunmer, W. E., & Rohl, M. (1991). Phonological awareness and reading acquisition. In D. J.

Sawyer & B. J. Fox (Eds.), *Phonological awareness in reading: The evolution of current perspectives* (pp. 1–30). New York: Springer-Verlag.

Vellutino, F. R., & Scanlon, D. M. (1987). Phonological coding, phonological awareness and reading ability: Evidence from a longitudinal and experimental study. *Merrill-Palmer Quarterly, 33,* 321–363.

Venezky, R. L. (1976). *Theoretical and experimental bases for teaching reading.* The Hague, The Netherlands: Mouton.

Vogel, S. A. (1974). Syntactic abilities in normal and dyslexic children. *Journal of Learning Disabilities, 7,* 103–109.

Wagoner, S. A. (1983). Comprehension monitoring: What it is and what we know about it. *Reading Research Quarterly, 18,* 328–346.

Warren-Leubecker, A. (1987). Competence and performance factors in word order awareness and early reading. *Journal of Experimental Child Psychology, 43,* 62–80.

Weber, R. M. (1970). First graders' use of grammatical context in reading. In H. Levin & J. P. Williams (Eds.), *Basic studies in reading* (pp. 147–163). New York: Basic Books.

West, R. F., Stanovich, K. E., Feeman, D. J., & Cunningham, A. E. (1983). The effect of sentence context on word recognition in second- and sixth-grade children. *Reading Research Quarterly, 19,* 6–15.

Willows, D., & Ryan, E. (1986). The development of grammatical sensitivity and its relationship to early reading achievement. *Reading Research Quarterly, 21,* 253–266.

Yopp, H. K. (1988). The validity and reliability of phonemic awareness tests. *Reading Research Quarterly, 23,* 159–177.

8 Reading Stories to Preliterate Children: A Proposed Connection to Reading

Jana M. Mason
University of Illinois, Urbana-Champaign

In the United States, we have long assumed that reading story books to young children is important for the acquisition of literacy. At present, story book reading represents a compelling issue because large numbers of children are not good readers. In the face of demands for higher levels of literacy achievement (e.g., Stedman & Kaestle, 1987), how important is reading to children? What evidence is there from research that supports story book reading as a valuable entry step for the acquisition of literacy?

Although it is generally accepted that phonological awareness and codebreaking skills are essential for learning to read (Adams, 1990; Tunmer & Nesdale, 1985) and that these concepts are acquired in part from alphabet knowledge and analysis of words into sounds (Ehri, 1983; Mason, 1984a), it is not known whether story listening skills are also an essential aspects of learning to read. It is conceivable that reading story books to children fosters listening comprehension and then reading comprehension by clarifying written language features and functions.

Reading to children, even if important for literacy development, does not replace activities that foster phonological awareness (Cunningham, 1989). Children who grow up in families where reading to children occurs infrequently are less likely to be successful readers, but they can learn to read (Gerstein & Dimino, 1990; Heath, 1983; Wells, 1986). Moreover, some societies do not engage in the practice of reading to children. S. Sinha (personal communication) cites India as an example of a society where not even children of the educated classes are read to at home or in school.

It is reasonable to suppose that in the United States, given the nature of the English language and our letter- and word-focused beginning reading instruction

215

(Mason, Anderson, Omura, Uchida, & Imai, 1990), reading to children is a way to introduce literacy (Anderson, Hiebert, Scott, & Wilkinson, 1985). Hearing and discussing texts with literate persons could help young children establish connections between oral language and written text structures and maintain a sense of text meaningfulness (Holdaway, 1979, 1986; Sulzby, 1986a, 1986b). Such connections are valuable because "written language is often decontextualized from a physical context. That is, the meaning must be carried . . . without the oral language aids of paralinguistic cues and a shared physical context" (Purcell-Gates, 1986, p. 262). Moreover, home story book reading is usually mediated by caring adults. A protective umbrella of explanations, interpretations, and clarifications is provided at the right moments by adults who know what their children know and how to connect story information to their children's background experiences.

That children do learn about written language from being read to is evident from the fact that well-read-to children develop a "book language" way of talking (Chafe, 1982; Chomsky, 1979; Sulzby, 1985; Tannen, 1982). According to Purcell-Gates (1986), not only do these children expect books to be more syntactically integrated than oral language, but also they mimic book phrases and words in their oral language, even using nonoral word orders such as inversion of the subject and a verb.

Reading books to children provides opportunities to hear new words in meaningful contexts and leads to acquisition of a larger, more fully featured oral vocabulary (Elley, 1989). A large reading vocabulary is not needed in the first one or two years of schooling because children are learning to read texts that have controlled vocabularies. However, by the third or fourth grade, school textbook companies allow many new words to appear in their books. Children who have been read to in the earlier years will be better prepared for the expanded vocabularies in these texts. One study (Humphreys & Davey, 1983) supports this hypothesis, showing that children's listening vocabulary skills in third grade predict their reading comprehension two years later.

Reading books to children is a source for the development of listening comprehension (Peterman, 1988) as well as for learning about written textual features (Pappas, 1985). It also fosters a way of thinking that enhances reading comprehension (Olson, 1984; Wells, 1985, 1986). These figure into acquisition of effective strategies for text comprehension.

Finally, mounting research evidence suggests that reading books to children can ease the process of learning to decode the written word. Repeated readings of books are especially effective in contributing to knowledge about the print itself as children become better able to write, spell, and read words (McCormick & Mason, 1989a). Children acquire concepts about the conventions of print such as directionality of print, word boundaries, and punctuation markers (Clay, 1979, 1985). Conceivably, repeated book reading to children permits them to concentrate on words and letter–sound patterns while maintaining an understanding of the text meaning.

The first section of this chapter examines distinctions between oral and written language and suggests why written texts contain language structures that could be more difficult to acquire than oral language structures. The second section shows how story book reading activities enable children to link their listening and speaking skills to text comprehension. The third section reviews connections between story book reading and later reading achievement by describing studies that relate home literacy activities to later reading. The fourth section reviews intervention research that connects story book reading interventions to children's beginning reading achievement.

DISTINCTIONS BETWEEN ORAL AND WRITTEN LANGUAGE

Written language contains many linguistic properties that are unlike those of oral language. Although both vary in formality, written language usually contains more formal characteristics. The act of writing a text is a slow and deliberate process, and the reading of a text is usually a lonely activity. By contrast, speech is rapid and can be effortless, usually taking place in a social environment. Because the oral and written language processes are different and produce different outcomes, as Chafe (1985) discussed, some language structures that are featured in written language occur infrequently in oral language. Because written language comprehension depends in part on understanding the written syntax, it cannot be assumed then that knowledge of oral language structures is sufficient for understanding written language.

Five potential problems presented by the differences between oral and written language can be derived from Perera's (1984) framework of physical, situational, functional, form, and structural characteristics.

Physical Differences

Young children's speech is tied to the concrete world and to an immediate setting, but because written language is not so constrained, children must learn to imagine unfamiliar characters, situations, and events. They must learn to think in terms of a past and future, not merely the present. Although as readers they can review (reread) a message, this is beneficial only if they know where to look in the text, how to place and interpret events, and how to picture and remember actions they have never experienced and people whom they have never met. Complications of unfamiliar causes or effects, event sequences, problems, and intentions may make a text quite difficult to comprehend. Understanding a text is not likely to be easy, then, for children who have not been exposed to these concepts though books at home.

Ferreiro and Teberosky (1982) found that children vary in their ability to conceive of reading as voiceless and to distinguish between oral conversation and a news item or a fairy tale. Mason, McCormick, and Bhavnagri (1986) noted that children unaccustomed to having stories read to them were bothered by inadequate story book pictures. One child reconciled the problem of a story about a farm that did not include a picture of a horse by stating that the (missing) animal must have walked off the page! Other children severely criticized the unrealistic pictures of animals. Older children dealt with the problem of an unfamiliar story line or character by retelling the story in the first person, letting themselves be the protagonist. These examples suggest that children struggle with differences between oral and written language and that some construct strategies to resolve or lessen the apparent problems.

Situational Differences

Interchanges between speakers and listeners are usually face to face, whereas writers and readers are usually isolated from each other. Whereas the audience for one's oral language is usually present and well defined, the audience for a written communication is an abstract entity, which the writer might try to personalize by imagining a particular reader. Thus, speakers can make an ongoing assessment of their listeners' attention, whereas writers only hope that their readers understand their written ideas.

The listener not only hears the talk of the speaker but interprets gestures and facial expressions for added understanding, and the speaker reacts to the listener's nonverbal expressions and comments for feedback on clarity, tone, and impact. If speech referents are unclear, the listener may ask for more information under the implicit turntaking rules of conversation. Compensating tools for writers include language ties such as "this" and "that" after introducing a topic. Subtle connections such as "a . . . the," "John . . . he," "chocolate . . . this/it" are also used (Halliday & Hasan, 1976). The reader, then, needs to make backward or forward searches of the text, defer understanding, and continue reading, or even check another source to achieve an understanding of the text. Thus, to become effective reading comprehenders, young children need to learn a number of new strategies to search out meaningful text connections. Possibly, some of these strategies are initiated through adult–child interchanges about stories that adults are reading aloud.

Functional Differences

People generally use oral language for immediate communication and written language for communicating with others over time or distance. According to Halliday (1977), children's oral language functions are: instrumental (to get something), regulatory (to control), interactional (to establish social relationships), personal (to express individuality), imaginative (to express fantasy), heuristic (to explore and learn), and informative (to convey information). Children make greater functional use of oral language than written language initially because they do not know how to use written language and because their teachers usually have them perform very limited functions, such as learning to read written text and writing to fill in answers to written questions (Mason, 1984b). However, Milz (1985) found that some teachers allow first-grade children to write for a number of different purposes: to establish ownership by labeling, to build relationships through notes and interactive journals, to remind themselves and others using notes to do things, to request information or assistance, to record information, and to create their own stories. Children would have a broader understanding of written texts if they could experience differential functions for written language.

Form Differences

At the letter and sound level, the 26 letters of the alphabet are used to represent about 40 sounds in English speech. However, these sounds are complexly characterized with about 70 letters and letter combinations in English orthography (Ehri & Wilce, 1987). For example, the letter *k* almost always has the /k/ sound, but that sound may be represented by at least five letters or letter combinations: *k, c, ck, qu,* and *ch.* Each written letter is a distinct visual form, and each written word is set off with spaces and indentations, punctuation, and capitalization. In contrast, oral language has no definite boundaries between phonemes, and even word boundaries may be obscured when we speak informally, using forms such as "gonna," "dontcha," or "gimme." Thus, many children have difficulty hearing and segmenting words into phonemes as well as identifying and matching phonemes with letters. Practices of teaching letters with alphabet books and blocks and of pointing out words while reading to children should help acquaint children with form differences.

At the word level, oral and written language differences are also considerable. A young child's oral language corpus contains about 3,000 different words (Hall, Nagy, & Linn, 1984), a third-grader reads about that number of words, and an adult's reading vocabulary is larger by a factor of three or more (Nagy, personal communication). A typical first-grade reading text may contain about 300 different words, whereas the written language corpus in third through twelfth-grade textbooks contains 5 million or more words (Caroll, Davies, & Richman, 1971). It is said that somewhere between third and fourth grade a rapid expansion of the written language corpus occurs. A plausible preparation for this expansion is for adults to read to children, which would enable the children to hear and remember new words in context (Elley, 1989). With many words securely established in listening vocabularies, children should be less overwhelmed when meeting them in new written contexts.

Structural Differences

Syntactic structures differ in speech and writing. Speakers tend to be highly redundant, whereas writers strive to be concise. Speech is also less well structured, as evidenced by the high frequency of incomplete sentences, slang expressions, and meaningless vocalizations that function as place holders and allow time for thought. Writers, by contrast, may edit again and again until their pieces are well structured. In addition, although writers cannot mimic intonation, they can emulate elements of informal speech in some narrative texts with dialect, contractions, and elliptical phrases. They may also use subordinate and relative clauses, appositive and participial phrases, and passive verb constructions (Leu, 1982).

Although knowledge of oral language structures could be a sufficient base for understanding some written stories, knowledge of written language structures that is based on opportunities to hear others use more formal, book language should be more helpful. Moreover, transfer of discourse comprehension skills from listening to reading should be easier for narratives than for expository texts because narratives contain more oral language structures. Expository texts contain less familiar content and structure (Bock & Brewer, 1985).

Some research suggests that when written text is made more like speech beginning readers can process it more readily. Amsterdam (1985), who had first-grade children repeat and later recall "primerese" and "natural language" versions of fables, found significantly more meaningful consolidation with the natural language versions of the texts. Allen (1985) found that primary-grade children performed better on inferential comprehension tasks when the texts were closely linked to their oral language. However, these studies do not show whether children make improvements in their reading in general as a result of reading oral language-like texts.

If these five characteristics of language (Perera, 1984) that distinguish oral from written language are made apparent to children during story reading or in discussions about the stories, the children should be better prepared to read and understand written texts (Mason & Allen, 1986). Adults, for example, could reread favorite texts, point out physical characteristics of a text they are reading aloud, highlight situational differences, give reasons for listening to a story, talk about print and new words in texts, and rephrase unfamiliar written text structures.

STORY BOOK READING ACTIVITIES
THAT LINK ORAL AND WRITTEN LANGUAGE

Adults can mediate the written language as they read to children and listen to their retellings. The supporting systems that adults offer are subtle, but the salient features can be uncovered through analyses of transcribed adult–child talk about books. The research described next presents examples of adult–child, book-focused interchanges. The first example is from audiotaped sessions of a four-year-old child of parents with professional-level occupations retelling the same story (Lartz & Mason, 1988). The second example is from a set of videotapes of Head Start mothers who read predictable books with their children and helped them learn to recite the books. The third example is from videotaped sessions of teachers reading stories to their kindergarten classes (Mason, Peterman, Powell, & Kerr, 1989). These studies illuminate the roles that adults as well as children play in clarifying text meaning and in making written language more accessible.

Retelling a Story

The effect of retelling a story many times was traced with one kindergarten child, Jamie (Lartz & Mason, 1988). After an adult read the story *Danny and the Dinosaur* by Syd Hoff (1958) to Jamie, she handed the book to her and asked her to retell it. Then, for the next seven weeks in once-a-week sessions, Jamie's retellings were audiotaped as she leafed through the book. Lartz did not reread the book, and parents said the child did not have the book at home, although she could have seen it at her preschool or at the library. Lartz avoided asking questions so that the child's emerging strategies for constructing sensible retellings would be determined by the child. However, she answered all of Jamie's questions and kept her on the task of retelling the whole story during each session. Thus, the child's comments and questions elucidated her own attempts to distinguish oral from written language and to solve the riddle of making written language make sense.

Table 8.1 presents Jamie's retellings for one text segment. It depicts her struggles to make the text fit with the pictures, the story line, and eventually the print itself. All of the adult's comments and responses to the child are in brackets. Jamie's retellings and reading attempts are in quotes, with subquotes for the invented dialogue.

As Jamie retold the story, particularly during the first few sessions, she made heavy use of the pictures in order to connect the characters with the series of events in the story. Presumably because she had been read to frequently, Jamie did not ask about obvious oral and written language differences. Except for one mild objection to this repetitive task (asking, "Don't you have any other books?"), she did not need to be told a function for retelling the story. Over the sessions, her recollections became more like written language structures, and her vocabulary frequently mirrored words from the text. Because she had been read the story only once, most of the phrases were her own inventions. In Session 4, for example, she said, "Then a quiet voice said." In Session 6, her written story-like dialogue included, "I wish I could play with them if they were real." During the last two sessions, she began to focus on the print itself, asking for help to read

TABLE 8.1
Jamie's Retelling of One Story Segment

Text	Danny loved dinosaurs. He wished he had one. "I'm sorry they are not real," said Danny. "It would be nice to play with a dinosaur." "And I think it would be nice to play with you," said a voice. "Can you?" said Danny. "Yes," said the dinosaur.
Session 1	He found some dinosaurs. "What do you want to do? Want to go for a ride?" So they went out the door.
Session 2	He found some dinosaurs. They were big. But one of them looked at him and said, "Hi." [inaudible] "Yes," he said.
Session 3	. . .and he saw dinosaurs [long pause] Danny wished they were real. [To adult: I wish they were real, but Danny doesn't know. . .] "It would be nice to play with you," said a voice. "Where should we go?"
Session 4	. . .and he saw some dinosaurs. Danny looked at them and thought he could have one. They weren't moving. Danny said, "I'm sorry they aren't real, but if they were real, I would play with them." Then a quiet voice said, "I would like to play with you."
Session 5	. . .and he [pause] dinosaur. He wished he could play with one. [Adult points to text, saying: Look what this says.] Danny loved dinosaurs. He wished he had one. [Adult comments: You just said that good.] "I would like to play with one," said the dinosaur. "You would?" said Danny.
Session 6	And he saw some dinosaurs. He wished he could have one. He said, "I'm sorry they are not real. I wish I could play with them if they were real. "Oh, it would be nice to play with you," said a voice. "Would you?" said Danny. "Yes."
Session 7	Danny loves dinosaurs. He wished he could have some. "I think I'm s-s-aid. [To adult: Is this first or is this first? Adult: This is first—I'm s-sorry.] "sorry they are not real," said Danny. "I wished that I could have some—have one. I wanted—I want to- -[To adult: I] don't know what this is. Adult: It] "It would be nice to play with you." [Adult: with—] "with a dinosaur." "I am, and I would like to play with you," said a voice. "You would?" said Danny. "Yes I would," saud the dinosaur.
Session 8	And he saw a dinosaur. Dan liked dinosaurs. He wished he could have one— [self-corrects]—Danny loved dinosaurs. He wished he could have one. "I wish that—[self-corrects]—I am sorry they are not real," said Danny. If they were, I wish that I could have one to play with. "It would be nice to play with you," said a voice. "Would you—you would?"

and beginning to reconcile words she seemed to know were on the page with her sense of the text. She did not attempt to read every word but chose instead to mix word reading with story telling. Lartz supported the child by establishing and holding her to the task, answering all of her questions, and by responding to her comments about the text.

Most of Jamie's retellings involved a process of combining pictures and re- membered text events with written language-like elaborations. This story book activity was providing the child with opportunities to operate with written lan- guage forms and structures. When the story line made sense and seemed to fit the context, she also began to search for and use words that appeared in the text, suggesting that the story book activity also fostered word analysis and letter–sound analysis. However, this did not mean that she had learned to read words out of context. In the last session, Jamie's retelling of five sentences was evaluated. Although she had correctly said 81% of the printed words from these five sentences in her retelling, when the sentences along with the pictures were given out of the book context, she could only say 61% of the words. When the same sentences were represented without their pictures, she could identify only one word, "Danny." Thus, the child showed competency in mimicking written language structures and identifying words when she had the supporting picture and story line context. She could not read words out of context.

Parent–Child Story Book Reading Activity

To understand how parents in low-income families might help their children acquire background concepts for learning to read, text materials were set home for parents to read to their children at home. Parent–children book reading interactions were videotaped and transcribed (Kerr, Mason, & McCormick, 1991). The question was whether mothers, many of whom were themselves poor readers and who had not often read stories aloud to their children, would effectively help their children make sense of written language features and learn to recite the text. Tables 8.2 and 8.3 show two of the mother–child interactions, using the predictable book *Snowman* by McCormick and Mason (1989b). The book contained the following text and illustrations:

Page 1 text: One big snowball. [Picture of large snowball.]

Page 2 text: Two big snowballs. [Picture of one snowball on top of the other.]

Page 3 text: Eyes and nose. [Picture of snowman includes button eyes and carrot nose.]

Page 4 text: Great big smile. [Picture of snowman includes upturned mouth.]

Page 5 text: Hi Frosty. [Picture of snowman includes scarf and hat.]

The Table 8.2 transcript shows that the child paid attention to picture information rather than the print when this story was read. The mother accepted the child's preference for understanding the text through pictures, but occasionally helped her connect the picture to the print by pointing to one and then the other. She repeatedly asked the child to label pictures, and these labels were often the same as the printed words. She did not give a reason for reading but did orient the child to the test as a whole by asking what the book was about.

The Table 8.3 transcript shows a mother providing a similar focus on the meaning of the text. This mother encouraged her child to see a reason for reading the book, namely, to learn how to build a snowman. She pointed to text and

TABLE 8.2
Mother and Four-Year-Old Heather Reading the Book *Snowman*

Mother:	Right here. We'll try this one. [The mother puts the *Snowman* book, which the child received in the mail that morning, in front of Heather and agrees to read.] What is that? [Mother points to picture on cover.]
Heather:	Oh, snowman.
Mother:	So what do you think that book's about? Hmmm? Do you know? [Heather opens book.] What's that?
Heather:	Big egg man. [Heather traces the picture with her finger.]
Mother:	No that's one big snowball. [Mother points to the first word. Heather turns the page.]
Heather:	Two. [Heather points to picture.]
Mother:	Two what?
Heather:	Two snowballs.
Mother:	Two snowballs. [Heather turns page.] Ohh, what was put on there? [Mother points to picture.]
Heather:	Nose, eyes. [Heather points to each in the picture.]
Mother:	Eyes and nose. [Mother points to print as she corrects child.]
Heather:	Eyes and nose. [Heather turns the page.]
Mother:	Ohh, what else?
Heather:	A smile.
Mother:	A smile? [Mother checks that she heard the child correctly.]
Heather:	Uh-huh. [Heather turns the page and shrugs shoulders to indicate that she doesn't know what this page says.]
Mother:	What did you call him when you first opened the book, do you remember?. . . Hi, Frosty.
Heather:	Hi Frosty. [Heather closes the book.]

picture to help him focus on the pictures and to connect pictures with the print, and told him, "It says . . ." She also provided many situational cues by interpreting, rephrasing, and relating the text to the child's experiences. Although ignoring the printed words, the child did pay attention to the whole story and often commented appropriately.

Both mothers dealt with some of the oral–written language distinctions by pointing to picture and print, by asking questions about the text ideas, and by encouraging the child to expand on them. Each used nonverbal and verbal cues to

TABLE 8.3
Mother and Four-Year-Old Eric Reading the Book Entitled *Snowman*

The mother asked Eric which story he wanted to read first.

Eric:	I want to do this one about Christmas. [Eric points to the *Snowman* book.]
Mother:	Snowman?
Eric:	Snowman, yeah, 'cause it's Christmas already.
Mother:	What is that? [Mother points to picture on cover.]
Eric:	Snowman.
Mother:	I'll bet they're showin' you how to make a snowman, ain't they? [Mother opens book.] See. They made a great big snowball. [Mother points to picture.]
Eric:	No, a circle one. [Eric traces circle with finger.]
Mother:	When it ever snows, maybe we can make a snowman. [Looks enthusiastically at Eric and turns page.] Then we'll make two balls. See, they set this ball on top of this one. [Mother points to picture.]
Eric:	Turn the page.
Mother:	Turn the page? You better look so you'll know how to make a snowman. [Mother turns the page.]
Eric:	Then they made eyes. [Eric points to picture.]
Mother:	What's that? [Mother points to picture of the nose.]
Eric:	Umm, a carrot, umm, nose.
Mother:	Yes [Eric laughs] and there's his eyes!
Eric:	That's a funny nose.
Mother:	A big ole long nose ain't it? [Mother turns the page.]
Eric:	And dots for eyes. Dots for eyes.
Mother:	He's smiling. Look at him. [Mother points to picture.]
Eric:	Uh-huh. He's happy.
Mother:	It says, a great big smile. [Mother points to words as she says them.] Is that a happy snowman?
Eric:	Yes. Well, I want to color it.
Mother:	You want to color it? [Mother turns page.] They even put a hat on it—
Eric:	—You know—[Eric points to page number.]
Mother:	and a scarf—
Eric:	—number six!

(*Continued*)

TABLE 8.3
(*Continued*)

Mother:	Yeah, that's page number six. Look at them funny arms. [Mother points to arms. Eric laughs.] He's only got three fingers.
Eric:	Mommy, I want to color it.
Mother:	Ahh. [Mother closes book.]
Eric:	I want to color—[Eric reaches for his crayons.]
Mother:	No, we got another story book here to look at to see what it's about. You might want to color that. [Picks up other book she was asked to read with the child.]

help her child focus on the right information and stay on task. Each elaborated as she read the text to hold the child's attention and keep the text meaningful. Each added information to tie the text with the child's experiences. Thus, the mothers helped their children interpret picture information within the story context, they informally introduced the text itself, allowing the children to attend to pictures, and they made sure the children understood the vocabulary. In so doing, both children began learning about written language features and were able to take over some of the book reading by holding the book, turning the pages, and repeating some of the written text. Later transcripts show that these children did learn to recite the texts.

Kindergarten Teacher/Class Story Reading

Children can learn when parents read to them but it is possible for teachers to carry on valuable story reading interactions with whole-class groups? To help answer this question, six teachers agreed to be videotaped as they read three children's books to their class (Mason, Peterman, & Kerr, 1989; Mason, Peterman, Powell, & Kerr, 1989). Two of the teachers' interactions with students as they read the story *Strega Nona* by Tomie de Paola (1975) are excerpted in Table 8.4. In these transcripts, *T* refers to the teacher and *C* to one or more children. Remarks in brackets with quotation marks indicate text being read by the teacher. Teachers' actions are in the right-hand column.

Book reading lessons in these kindergartens were found to contain a three-part routine. Before reading the book, teachers pointed to the title and read it and then readied children for the text content. They also described reasons for listening. During reading, they elaborated on the text to clarify story events and asked questions about what was meant, highlighting new vocabulary terms and rephrasing text segments that they thought children would not understand. After reading, they reviewed the listening goals, usually by asking questions. A discussion of the story sequence and resolution often followed in which the text structure was reviewed. Some arranged for follow-up activities in which children wrote words

TABLE 8.4
Teachers' Story-Book Interactions with Kindergarten Children

Before reading

T: The name of this book is *Strega Nona, Strega Nona.*	Teacher emphasizes each word of the title and underlines each word with her finger.
C: Wow! That sounds different!	
T: That's a different name, isn't it? Does it sound like English?	
C: No.	
T: No, it sounds like [inaudible].	
C: [inaudible]	
C: Spanish.	
T: Could be Spanish-like when we talked about ah—Christopher Columbus.	
C: Know why I think it's Spanish? My brother knows Spanish.	
T: Does he? Matthew?	
C: It might be French.	
T: Maybe. That's another language, isn't it? Maybe it's French.	
C: Chinese.	
T: This is an old tale retold and illustrated by Tommie de Paola—I think that's how you say his name.	Points to print.
C: It's in French	
T: You think so?	
C: No, it's in –	
T: Marlon?	
C: Spanish	
C: Spanish, yeah.	
T: Well, it doesn't really tell us,	
C: It means to draw the pictures and make the words.	
T: So it looks like the same man, Tommie, drew the pictures, and he retold an old tale. What is it to retell an old tale—you think, Alex?	Points to author's name.

(Continued)

TABLE 8.4
(*Continued*)

C: It means—to read it all over.

T: To retell is to read it over again or tell it over again. So he's retelling—he is telling it over again. What is a tale? Matthew?

C: A tale is some old story that is not true—it won't never, never happen.

T: Oh, a tale is a story that will never, never happen. Do you agree, Justin?

C: Ah—Yeah.

T: A tale—you think a tale is a story—

C: That never, never happens.

T: Matthew says that never, never happens.   Points to Caldecott award on cover.
Well, maybe—that might be what is is—a tale
is a story that never, never happens. And
you notice that when he illustrated this
book he did such a good job, he got a
prize. The pictures are beautiful.

C: He got that little coin.

T: Uh-huh. That's an award that they put on
the front of a book when the pictures are
extra nice. So he won an award. By
looking at the cover, who do you think or
what do you think this book is going to be
about?
[The discussion continues.]

During the reading

T: [Begins reading text: "In a town of Calabria a   Points to picture of townspeople.
long time ago .... because Strega Nona did
have a magic touch."] Here are the people   Puts hand around mouth and whispers
in the town and some of them are saying   question.
"Do you know what Strega Nona did?"

T: Here comes the priest and the sisters of the   Points to picture at bottom of page.
convent. Now, they seem sort of
important. Does anyone know who they
are? Who are they, Alex?

C: They're people from—like churches.

T: From church, yes, the people from church.   points to pictures across top of page.
And even they went to see Strega Nona.
[Reads: "She could cure a headache with
oil, water, and a hairpin."] Right up here
these three pictures show Strega Nona
taking oil—that's what it says on that   Points to oil.
container—

TABLE 8.4
(Continued)

C: And water.

T: And some water–from there. And a hairpin from her hair. Now she has a hairpin, probably something that would hold her hair in place– And some oil–And the word oil O-I-L–	Points to picture and own hair. Picks up a bottle of cooking oil and points to label on bottle.
C: And there's water over here.	Child points to water container on table.
T: And some water-and she'd mix those all together and the person would get rid of their headache and feel a lot better. [Story reading continues.]	Puts hand on her head as though suffering from a headache.

After reading

T: Is this a real story or a pretend story?

C: False–false.

C: A fairy tale.

T: Yeah, it's an old tale. It really isn't true, is it? Is there such a thing as a witch?

C: No.

T: You don't think so?

C: A witch can [inaudible].

C: There can't be–there can't be a magic pot.
[Story discussion continues.]

---

to extend their print knowledge. The transcripts indicate that teachers do try to help children understand written language constructs. Also, follow-up evaluations of children's recall of the story indicate that the nature of the classroom discussion that their teacher had led did affect children's recall of the story.

These studies indicate that story book reading does provide oral–written language links. It can be carried out at home and in school and may have a positive effect on children's written language development. Adults can capture children's attention with written stories and help them focus on story ideas and some of the printed words. They can lay out functional goals for listening, clarify story information with elaboration and syntactic structures with rephrasing, and review the story to make the story structure understood. Thus, it appears that the compelling activity of listening to a story can lead children to a better understanding of complex written language forms and to a deeper interpretation of story ideas.

CONNECTIONS BETWEEN STORY READING
AND LATER READING ACHIEVEMENT

Although story reading to children seems to be connected to ongoing comprehension and recall, few studies have shown that it is directly related to later reading achievement. One reason is that reading to children is embedded in a package of viable emergent literacy activities. Earlier research showed that family socioeconomic status (SES) and availability of print in the home are correlated with reading achievement (Thorndike, 1976). Since then, more narrowly defined family factors (White, 1982), such as academic guidance, attitude toward education, parent aspirations for their children, conversations in the home, reading materials, and cultural activities, have been found to contribute more directly to early reading achievement and account for more variance than does SES. Iverson and Walberg (1982), in a review of 18 crossnational correlational studies of school-aged children, also found that ability and achievement are closely linked to intellectual stimulation in the home and to the sociopsychological environment, namely, academic guidance, achievement, family intellectuality, work habits, and language, rather than to broader measures of parent occupation and amount of education. Share, Jorm, Maclean, Matthew, and Waterman (1983), who analyzed the relationships among children's early reading achievement, language ability, SES, and home atmosphere, concluded

> [F]amilies of children who have higher early reading achievement at school entry tend to engage in more literary activities, prefer educational non-commercial television viewing, have higher occupational status and higher educational aspirations for their children. [A rich educational environment contributes by] providing oral language skills and to a lesser extent by providing specific reading skills. (p. 85)

Overall, then, there is only a correlational link between families who maintain a literate atmosphere for their children, which usually includes story book reading, and children who are more successful readers.

Another difficulty in connecting reading to children to reading competency is that few longitudinal studies in reading have been initiated in the preschool years, when parents read to their children. Studies by Wells and his colleagues (Moon & Wells, 1979; Wells, 1981, 1982, 1986) offer important evidence that reading to children is important that is based on data collected from parent–child conversations, parent interviews, child interviews, and assessments by teachers and researchers. The Moon and Wells study revealed high correlations, ranging from .55 to .79, that connected reading at age 7 with preschool knowledge of literacy, parent interest in literacy, and parents' quality of feedback and richness of interaction with their children. Wells (1981) found that reading at age 7 was also connected to children's language before age 4, a range of preschool activities, preschool interest and concentration on literacy, and story comprehension. Wells

(1982) indicated that listening to a story read aloud during parent conversations at age 3 was significantly associated with oral language ability and knowledge of literacy at age 5 and reading comprehension at age 7. Wells (1986) described a close association between reading achievement at age 7 and at age 10. Thus, although the reports are based on small data sets, there appears to be a link between story reading during the preschool years and later reading achievement. Other studies of this nature are needed to confirm the causal connection.

A third reason that story reading to children has not been conclusively connected to reading achievement is that beginning reading tests emphasize letter and word recognition whereas book reading to children may benefit listening skills immediately and reading comprehension skills later. One explanation for a focus on word recognition was articulated by Lesgold, Resnick, and Hammond (1985): "We can consider reading as consisting of the skills that underlie listening plus word recognition skills. The listening skills are already appearing spontaneously by the time children begin to read, so effort should center on word recognition" (p. 109). But is this a reasonable assumption? Listening skills do vary and could be affected by storybook reading. Storybook activity at home could be an unmeasured correlate of listening skills as well as a predictor of children's success at learning to read. If oral language competencies are differentiated through vocabulary and listening comprehension tests, possible differences in home literate atmosphere and book reading activity could be evaluated. Results might show that differences in later reading are closely connected to early listening skills. This possibility was considered in the next study.

In the first report of a longitudinal study for which nearly complete data were available for 100 children (Mason & Dunning, 1986), children from two schools were tested at the beginning and end of the kindergarten and first-grade years. Parents filled out a questionnaire regarding their support for literacy and their children's involvement in literacy. Questionnaire items that were significantly correlated with later reading test variables included the following: regularity of reading to children, the number of children's books in the home, the frequency of reading and writing by the children, the frequency of help in reading and writing by the parents, and the frequency of story telling at home (Table 8.5).

At the beginning of kindergarten children were tested on their abilities to define words, classify familiar concepts, and form analogies. They also tried to repeat written-language-like sentences and they chose pictured answers to questions after listening to brief stories. A factor analysis determined that these tasks loaded similarly, so the scores from these tests were standardized and summed to form a single variable, called *language understanding*. A second factor in the analysis, *language fluency*, was determined principally by children's mean length utterance when they told stories from pictures.

Children were tested at the beginning and end of kindergarten and first grade with a test developed by Mason and McCormick (1979). The test included measures of children's knowledge of letters, letter–sounds, words, and stories

TABLE 8.5

Correlations Between Parent Questionnaire Variables and Language/Reading Test Variables

Parent Questionnaire	Beginning Kindergarten				End Kindergarten		Beginning Grade 1		End Grade 1
	Language Understanding	Oral Language Ability	Decoding	Env. P Labeling	Decoding	Env. P. Labeling	Decoding	Decoding	Reading/ Listening Comprehension
Reading to child at home	.39	.13	.38	.21	.28	.37	.28	.06	.25
Number of books at home	.27	.18	.35	.19	.34	.17	.31	.26	.09
Reading and writing by child at home	.31	.21	.51	.23	.48	.47	.47	.29	.18
Help by parents to read and write	.11	.09	.16	.07	.22	.29	.23	.07	.11
Story telling at home	.17	.11	.18	.04	.17	.24	.18	.12	.25
Time spent watching TV	−.10	−.14	−.16	−.06	−.12	−.03	−.14	−.13	−.08

taken from tasks requiring children to name letters, spell common words, read common words, read pseudowords, read environmental print words, and read and comment on stories. In the kindergarten tests, most of the words and all of the pseudowords were one syllable, consonant-vowel-consonant patterns. In the first-grade tests, more difficult words and two stories were added for children to read, and the letter naming and environmental print word reading tasks were dropped. At the end of first grade, children also recalled a story they had heard, and they answered questions about it.

Factor analysis determined that two factors described reading competency at the beginning of kindergarten and again at the end of kindergarten (Times 1 and 2). One factor contained spelling, letter, and common and pseudoword recognition measures and the other contained environmental print labeling. At the beginning of first grade (Time 3), one factor described all of the subtests. Included were tasks of spelling, word recognition, story reading accuracy, and responses to questions about two simple stories. At the end of first grade (Time 4), two factors were distinguished by the factor analysis. Spelling and all word recognition tasks formed one factor, and reading, listening comprehension answers, and the recollection formed the other factor. Variables for the subsequent regression analyses were then formed by standardizing and summing the measures defined from each factor analysis. Intercorrelations among these variables are listed in Table 8.6.

Simultaneous multiple regression analyses used the variables listed in Tables 8.5 and 8.6 to predict reading achievement at each time period. The beginning of kindergarten language measures, parent questionnaire variables, and all preceding reading test variables were allowed to enter as independent variables to predict reading competency at each subsequent time. A school variable was also included because School 1 had a strong phonics emphasis, whereas School 2 involved children in more book listening and reading activities.

Decoding at each testing time was predicted primarily by the earlier reading test. However, comprehension at the end of first grade was predicted by children's entering kindergarten language understanding. A diagram of the model (Fig. 8.1) summarizes the results of the regression analyses after rerunning to omit nonsignificant variables. Five regression analyses are depicted: two at the end of kindergarten, one at the beginning of first grade, and two at the end of first grade. Arrows are directed from significantly predictor variables to predicted variables. Double-headed arrows signify correlational relationships. Beta weights or correlation coefficients are shown above the lines. All variables that entered the equations with probabilities $<.05$ are represented in the model.

Children's emerging reading knowledge and skill at the beginning of kindergarten is represented by decoding (letter and word reading, spelling, and pseudoword reading) and by environmental print labeling. These are correlated with the five subtests making up language understanding and with the set of parent questionnaire items that describe home reading and writing activity. At the

TABLE 8.6
Reading and Language Test Intercorrelations

Comprehend	Time 1 Decoding	Time 1 Labeling	Time 2 Decoding	Time 2 Labeling	Time 3 Decoding	Time 4 Decoding	Time 4 Comprehension
Time 1							
Language Understanding	.59	.41	.57	.47	.57	.35	.63
Oral Language Fluency	.22	.21	.22	.21	.23	.26	.20
Decoding	–	.41	.66	.54	.62	.35	.36
Labeling		–	.33	.59	.40	.33	.19
Time 2							
Decoding			–	.68	.89	.59	.36
Labeling				–	.70	.43	.32
Time 3							
Decoding					–	.60	.37
Time 4							
Decoding						–	.27
Comprehension							–

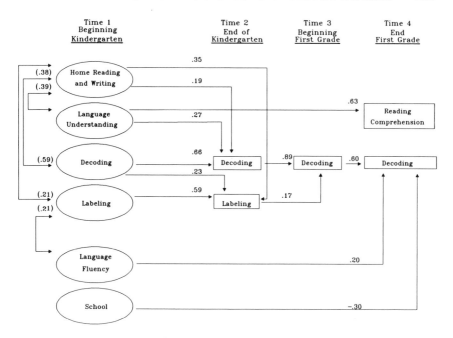

FIG. 8.1.   Model of early reading development.

end of kindergarten, decoding is predicted by the earlier decoding variable, language understanding, and home reading and writing activity. Labeling is predicted by the earlier decoding and labeling variables.

At the beginning of first grade decoding is predicted by the two earlier reading variables. Home reading and writing activity is moderately correlated at .47, but offers no additional predictive effect on the model then or at the end of first grade. Thus, children who can read and spell words in first grade are the ones who had better reading and language understanding skills in kindergarten and were more involved in literacy activities at home. These children continue with above-average performance in decoding at the end of first grade. Their decoding scores are boosted if they attended the school that emphasized phonics instruction. Inexplicably, children's entering oral language fluency also predicts decoding.

Another important finding is that at the end of first grade children's reading and listening comprehension responses are highly predicted ($r = .63$) by the entering kindergarten composite language understanding variable. This effect indicates that children's entering kindergarten ability to define and classify words and use and remember book language explains in large measure their ability to retell and answer questions about stories.

Entering kindergarten children's language understanding predicts decoding in kindergarten and predicts their comprehension at the end of first grade. Moreover, it is significantly correlated with home literacy experiences including reading to children, a range of reading and writing activities, and a number of children's books (Table 8.5). The study suggests, then, that home literacy fosters language understanding, which in turn eases the burdens of decoding and later reading comprehension. These findings appear to be at variance with the Lesgold et al. (1985) conclusions that only "word-level skills facilitate the acquisition of comprehension skills" (p. 132). Although the authors admit the possibility of "another unidentified factor that first causes word recognition and later comprehension skill" (p. 132), their data did not include language measures. Possibly, differences in children's language understanding is the unidentified other factor.

INTERVENTION RESEARCH CONNECTING STORY BOOK READING WITH READING ACHIEVEMENT

If reading stories to children could benefit early reading development, then intervention for children who are not read stories at home ought to make a difference. This final section reviews studies of book reading interventions. The studies, which involve children who might not otherwise be read to at home, help document that reading to children at home or in school has a positive effect on reading achievement.

Feitelson, Kita, and Goldstein (1986) had kindergarten teachers in Israel read to their students 3 times a week for 4 months. Matched control classrooms engaged in group games. Posttests indicated that children who were read to better understood stories, were more attentive to picture clues, were better able to infer causal relationships, and could tell more connected stories. In a second study, teachers of first-grade children either read to their students for the last 20 minutes of each weekday or continued their standard reading and writing instruction. At the end of 6 months, several posttests were administered. These included oral reading of an unfamiliar expository passage, answering comprehension questions after silently reading five short texts, and telling a story form a sequence of four pictures. Children who were read to in school produced significantly fewer word reading errors, had higher comprehension scores, and used more complex language in story telling.

Hewison and Tizard (1980) and Tizard, Schofield, and Hewison (1982) carried out a study with lower-class children in England. They found that sending books home for a year made a significant improvement in children's reading. Parents who would not otherwise read to their children were found to advance their children's reading.

McCormick and Mason (1989a) worked with children of low-income families in rural central Illinois communities. Simple-to-read predictable books were sent to half of the families and the others received pictured activity materials. Parents were asked to help their child read or use the materials. Tests of later story reading, spelling, and an ability to read words out of context revealed superior reading performance for children who had received the predictable books, and benefits were maintained into first grade. This work has been subsequently extended to children of low-income inner-city schools (Mason, Kerr, McCormick, & Sinha, 1990) and to children in small towns and fishing villages in Newfoundland (Phillips, Norris, Mason, & Kerr, 1990). First-year results indicate positive benefits accruing from shared book reading opportunities at home.

IMPLICATIONS

It appears that preschool children can learn a great deal about how to read by listening to and discussing stories with adults. The transcript examples suggest how this takes place. Children at first may be coached regarding what to listen to and look at and how the information is connected to what they know. They may be helped to understand and interpret written language structures, and they sometimes may be given hints about word forms. They may even memorize texts that are read to them repeatedly. With this support, children build a repertoire of concepts about written language structure and strategies for remembering and comprehending texts. When the text ideas are very familiar and understandable, children may turn to analysis of the print. Children can then stretch toward word recognition as they repeatedly hear and retell a story, even though they possess meager word recognition skills. If their story remembering is quite close to the actual text it is a small step to rendering a correct reading. Thus, children can learn about how to read from hearing stories read to them.

Transcript examples of story reading sessions, correlational analyses and models of reading development, and intervention research suggest that reading stories to children is linked to later reading success, although not without appropriate coaching and support from more knowledgeable adults. Through story book reading, adults acquaint children with complex information about written language forms and structures as well as strategies for reading. Adults place the activity within a meaningful context, they show children how their oral language is connected to print, and they highlight written text characteristics. They read simple stories so that children can memorize and retell stories, and they reread favorite stories, enabling children to have the meaning well in hand before working on the printed words. And, of course, they read complete stories, keeping the task whole and highly meaningful, which eases interpretation and provides opportunities for context-supported discussion.

Research is needed to examine further connections between the course of early reading development and opportunities to listen to and talk about books. The extent to which story book reading at home affects written language understanding competency and later reading and the interplay between story book reading and word recognition should be pursued. The extent to which reading to children ought to include story discussion, story rereading, story reciting, and retelling is also important. Finally, for children who are seldom read to at home, it is important to know how these techniques can be fostered in the home and integrated into kindergarten and first-grade instruction.

ACKNOWLEDGMENTS

The work upon which this chapter is based was under Contract no. 400-81-0030 and supported in part by the Office of Educational Research and Improvement Cooperative Agreement no. G0087-C1001-90 with the Reading Research and Education Center.

REFERENCES

Adams, M. J. (1990). *Beginning to read: Thinking and learning about print.* Cambridge, MA: MIT Press.

Allen, J. (1985). Inferential comprehension: The effects of text source, decoding ability, and mode. *Reading Research Quarterly, 20,* 603–615.

Amsterdam, L. (1985). *Elicited imitation: A comparison of the effects of text features.* Paper presented at the National Reading Conference, San Diego, CA.

Anderson, R. C., Hiebert, E. H., Scott, J. A., & Wilkinson, I. A. G. (1985). *Becoming a nation of readers: The report of the Commission on Reading.* Urbana-Champaign: University of Illinois, Center for the Study of Reading.

Bock, J. K., & Brewer, W. (1985). *Discourse structure and mental models* (Tech. Rep. No. 343). Urbana-Champaign: University of Illinois, Center for the Study of Reading.

Caroll, J., Davies, P., & Richman, B. (1971). *Word frequency book.* Boston: Houghton Mifflin.

Chafe, W. (1982). Integration and involvement in speaking, writing, and oral literature. In D. Tannen (Ed.), *Spoken and written language: Exploring orality and literacy, Vol. IX. Advances in discourse processes.* (pp. 35–53). Norwood, NJ: Ablex.

Chafe, W. (1985). Linguistic differences produced by differences between speaking and writing. In N. Torrance, D. Olson, & A. Hildyard (Eds.), *Literacy, language, and learning* (pp. 105–123). Cambridge, England: Cambridge University Press.

Chomsky, C. (1979). Approaching reading through invented spelling. In L. B. Resnick and P. A. Weaver (Eds.), *Theory and practice of early reading* (Vol. 2, pp. 43–65). Hillsdale, NJ: Lawrence Erlbaum Associates.

Clay, M. (1979). *Reading: The patterning of complex behavior.* Portsmouth, NH: Heinemann.

Clay, M. (1985). *Early detection of reading difficulties* (3rd ed.). Portsmouth, NH: Heinemann.

Cunningham, A. E. (1989). Phonemic awareness: The development of early reading competency. *Reading Research Quarterly, 24,* 471–472.

de Paola, T. (1975). *Stega Nona.* Englewood Cliffs, NJ: Prentice-Hall.

Ehri, L. C. (1983). A critique of five studies related to letter-name knowledge and learning to read. In L. M. Gentile, M. L. Kamil, & J. S. Blandchard (Eds.), *Reading research revisited* (pp. 143–153). Columbus, OH: Charles E. Merrill.

Ehri, L. C., & Wilce, L. (1987). Does learning to spell help beginners learn to read words? *Reading Research Quarterly, 22,* 47–65.

Elley, W. (1989). Vocabulary acquisition from listening to stories. *Reading Research Quarterly, 24,* 174–187.

Feitelson, D., Kita, B., & Goldstein, Z. (1986). Effects of reading series stories to first graders on their comprehension and use of language. *Research in the Teaching of English, 20,* 339–356.

Ferreiro, E., & Teberosky, A. (1982). *Literacy before schooling.* Portsmouth, NH: Heinemann.

Gerstein, R., & Dimino, J. (1990). Reading instruction for at-risk students: Implications of current research. *OSSC Bulletin, 35*(5).

Hall, W., Nagy, W., & Linn, R. (1984). *Spoken words: Effects of situation and social group on oral word usage and frequency.* Hillsdale, NJ: Lawrence Erlbaum Associates.

Halliday, M. A. K. (1977). *Explorations in the functions of language.* New York: Elsevier North-Holland.

Halliday, M., & Hasan, R. (1976). *Cohesion in English.* London: Longman.

Heath, S. B. (1983). *Ways with words: Language, life and work in communities and classrooms.* Cambridge, England: Cambridge University Press.

Hewison, J., & Tizard, J. (1980). Parental involvement and reading attainment. *British Journal of Educational Psychology, 50,* 209–215.

Hoff, S. (1958). *Danny and the dinosaur.* New York: Harper & Row.

Holdaway, D. (1979). *The foundations of literacy.* New York: Ashton Scholastic.

Holdaway, D. (1986). The structure of natural learning as a basis for literacy instruction. In M. Sampson (Ed.), *The pursuit of literacy: Early reading and writing* (pp. 56–72). Dubuque, IA: Kendall/Hunt.

Humphreys, L. G., & Davey, T. C. (1983). *Anticipation of gains in general information: A comparison of verbal aptitude, reading comprehension, and listening* (Tech. Rep. No. 282). Urbana-Champaign: University of Illinois, Center for the Study of Reading.

Iverson, B., & Walberg, H. (1982). Home environment and school learning: A quantitative synthesis. *Journal of Experimental Education, 50,* 144–151.

Kerr, B., Mason, J., & McCormick, C. (1991). *Literacy discourse in shared reading events.* Urbana-Champaign: University of Illinois, Center for the Study of Reading.

Lartz, M., & Mason, J. (1988). Jamie: One child's journey from oral to written language. *Early Childhood Research Quarterly, 3,* 193–208.

Lesgold, A., Resnick, L., & Hammond, K. (1985). Learning to read: A longitudinal study of word skill development in two curricula. In G. E. MacKinnon & T. G. Waller (Eds.), *Reading research: Advances in theory and practice, Vol. 4* (pp. 107–138). San Diego, CA: Academic Press.

Leu, D. (1982). Differences between oral and written discourse and the acquisition of reading proficiency. *Journal of Reading Behavior, 14,* 111–125.

Mason, J. (1984a). Early reading: A developmental perspective. In P. D. Pearson (Ed.), *Handbook of research in reading* (pp. 505–544). New York: Longman.

Mason, J. (1984b). A question about reading comprehension instruction. In G. Duffy, L. Roehler, & J. Mason (Eds.), *Comprehension instruction: Perspectives and suggestions* (pp. 39–56). New York: Longman.

Mason, J., & Allen, J. (1986). A review of emergent literacy with implications for research and practice in reading. In E. Rothkopf (Ed.), *Review of research in education* (pp. 3–48). Washington, DC: American Educational Research Association.

Mason, J., Anderson, R., Omura, A., Uchida, N., & Imai, M. (1990). Learning to read in Japan. *Journal of Curriculum Studies, 21,* 389–407.

Mason, J., & Dunning, D. (1986, April). *Toward a model relating home literacy with beginning reading.* Paper presented at the annual meeting of the American Educational Research Association, San Francisco.

Mason, J., Kerr, B., McCormick, C., & Sinha, S. (1990). Shared book reading in an early start program for at-risk children (pp. 189–198). *Thirty-ninth Yearbook. National Reading Conference:* Chicago IL.

Mason, J., & McCormick, C. (1979). *Testing the development of reading and linguistic awareness* (Tech. Rep. No. 26). Urbana-Champaign: University of Illinois, Center for the Study of Reading.

Mason, J., McCormick, C., & Bhavnagri, N. (1986). How are you going to help me learn? Lesson negotiations between a teacher and preschool children. In D. B. Yaden & S. Templeton (Eds.), *Metalinguistic awareness and beginning literacy* (pp. 159–172). Portsmouth, NH: Heinemann.

Mason, J., Peterman, C., & Kerr, B. (1989). Reading talk: How teachers read to kindergarten children. In D. Strickland & L. Morrow (Eds.), *Emerging literacy: Young children learn to read and write* (pp. 52–62). Newark, DE: International Reading Association.

Mason, J., Peterman, C., Powell, B., & Kerr, B. (1989). Reading and writing attempts by kindergarten children after book reading by teachers. In J. Mason (Ed.), *Reading and writing connections* (pp. 105–123). Needham Heights, MA: Allyn & Bacon.

McCormick, C., & Mason, J. (1989a). Fostering reading for Head Start children with little books. In J. Allen & J. Mason (Eds.), *Risk makers, risk takers, risk breakers: Reducing the risks for young learners* (pp. 154–177). Portsmouth, NH: Heinemann.

McCormick, C., & Mason, J. (1989b). *Little books.* Glenview, IL: Goodyear Press.

Milz, V. (1985). First graders' uses for writing. In A. Jaggar & M. Smith-Burke (Eds.), *Observing the language learner* (pp. 173–189). Newark, DE: International Reading Association.

Moon, C., & Wells, G. (1979). The influence of home on learning to read. *Journal of Research in Reading, 2,* 53–62.

Olson, D. (1984). "See! Jumping!" Some oral language antecedents of literacy. In H. Goelman, A. Oberg, & F. Smith (Eds.), *Awakening to literacy* (pp. 185–192). Portsmouth, NH: Heinemann.

Pappas, C. (1985). *Learning to read by reading.* Paper presented at the annual meeting of the National Reading Conference, San Diego.

Perera, K. (1984). *Children's writing and reading: Analyzing classroom language.* Oxford, England: Basil Blackwell.

Peterman, C. (1988). *The effects of story reading procedures collaboratively designed by teachers and researcher on kindergartners' literacy learning.* Unpublished doctoral dissertation, University of Illinois, Urbana-Champaign.

Phillips, L., Norris, S., Mason, J., & Kerr, B. (1990). Effect of early literacy intervention on kindergarten achievement. (pp. 199–208). *Thirty-ninth Yearbook. National Reading Conference:* Chicago IL.

Purcell-Gates, V. (1986). Three levels of understanding about written language acquired by young children prior to formal instruction. In J. Niles (Ed.), *Solving problems in literacy: Learners, teachers, and researchers* (pp. 259–265). Thirty-fifth Yearbook. National Reading Conference: Chicago IL.

Share, D. L., Jorm, A. F., Maclean, R., Matthews, R., & Waterman, B. (1983). Early reading achievement, oral language ability, and a child's home background. *Australian Psychologist, 18,* 75–87.

Stedman, L., & Kaestle, C. (1987). Literacy and reading performance in the United States, from 1880 to the present. *Reading Research Quarterly, 22,* 8–46.

Sulzby, E. (1985). Children's emergent reading of favorite storybooks: A developmental study. *Reading Research Quarterly, 20,* 458–481.

Sulzby, E. (1986a). Children's elicitation and use of metalinguistic knowledge about words during literacy interactions. In D. B. Yaden & S. Templeton (Eds.), *Metalinguistic awareness and beginning literacy* (pp. 219–234). Portsmouth, NH: Heinemann.

Sulzby, E. (1986b). Writing and reading: Signs of oral and written language organization in the young child. In W. Teale & E. Sulzby (Eds.), *Emergent literacy: Writing and reading* (pp. 50–89). Norwood, NJ: Ablex.

Tannen, D. (1982). Oral and literate strategies in spoken and written narratives. *Language, 58,* 1–21.

Thorndike, R. (1976). Reading comprehension in 15 countries. In J. Merritt (Ed.), *New horizons in reading.* Newark, DE: International Reading Association.

Tizard, J., Schofield, W., & Hewison, J. (1982). Collaboration between teachers and parents in assisting children's reading. *British Journal of Educational Psychology, 52,* 1–15.

Tunmer, W. E., & Nesdale, A. R. (1985). Phonemic segmentation skills and beginning reading. *Journal of Educational Psychology, 77,* 417–427.

Wells, G. (1981). Some antecedents of early educational attainment. *British Journal of Sociology of Education, 2,* 181–200.

Wells, G. (1982). Story reading and the development of symbolic skills. *Australian Journal of Reading, 5,* 142–152.

Wells, G. (1985). Preschool literacy-related activities and success in school. In D. Olson, N. Torrance, & A. Hildyard (Eds.), *The nature and consequences of literacy* (pp. 229–255). Cambridge, England: Cambridge University Press.

Wells, G. (1986). *The meaning makers.* Portsmouth, NH: Heinemann.

White, K. (1982). The relation between socioeconomic status and academic achievement. *Psychological Bulletin, 91,* 461–481.

9 Dyslexia in a Computational Model of Word Recognition in Reading

Mark S. Seidenberg
University of Southern California

For such a seemingly simple task, visual word recognition has been the focus of a prodigious amount of research (for reviews, see Adams, 1990; Carr & Pollatsek, 1985; Coltheart, 1987). Aside from the fact that it is the component of reading on which all other comprehension processes depend, word recognition is important because of its role in the acquisition of reading skill. Learning to recognize and pronounce words is among the first tasks confronting the beginning reader; developmental dyslexia ("reading disability") is typically associated with deficits in this domain. In addition, impairments in word recognition and naming are often observed in adult readers following brain injury; the study of these impairments has provided important clues about how reading is accomplished by the brain (see, for example, Patterson, Marshall & Coltheart, 1985). Two other reasons for interest in word recognition should also be mentioned. First, it has provided a domain in which to explore ideas about learning and the representation of knowledge that have emerged from the connectionist or "parallel distributed processing" approach (Rumelhart & McClelland, 1986). Second, it has provided a domain in which to explore important new neuroimaging techniques such as positron emission tomography (PET; Peterson, Fox, Snyder, & Raichle, 1990).

The goal of the research I have been pursuing with J. L. McClelland has been to develop a theory that provides a unified account of three aspects of word recognition: acquisition, skilled performance, and breakdown. Our strategy has been to develop a large-scale computational model that simulates detailed aspects of reading performance. We have implemented a first-generation model that brings together a broad range of behavioral phenomena within a theoretical framework that entails a novel way of thinking about the representation of lexical knowledge, its acquisition, and its use (Patterson, Seidenberg, & McClelland, 1989; Seidenberg, 1989; Seidenberg & McClelland, 1989).

Three points emerge from our experiences with the first-generation model. First, several important aspects of acquisition, skilled performance, and breakdown can all be explained in terms of a small number of central features of the computational model, principally the use of distributed representations of lexical codes, the encoding of knowledge by the weights on connections between units, and the use of a connectionist learning algorithm to set the weights. The model both simulates the results of a large number of existing studies and makes novel predictions, some of which have been tested in further studies with good results. Second, because of these features of the model, it differs from previous accounts in important ways. For example, the model does not retain the common assumption that knowledge of words is represented in terms of entries in one or more mental lexicons or the assumption that knowledge of spelling–sound correspondences is represented in terms of pronunciation rules. Because it does not respect these (and other) assumptions about lexical knowledge, the model seems somewhat counterintuitive at first; however, the force of the Seidenberg and McClelland (1989) paper is that it nonetheless accounts for detailed aspects of performance.

The third point is that although the existing model is broader in scope than any previous theory of word recognition, it is still quite limited. For example, it is restricted to monosyllabic words and therefore does not address issues that arise in connection with more complex words, such as the roles of syllabic and morphological structures in processing, and the assignment of syllabic stress. Because the model also lacks a semantic component, it does not address how readers determine the meanings of words, perhaps the central goal in word recognition. Additionally, the existing model does not employ a cascaded, stochastic mechanism for computing output; therefore, it does not simulate the time course of processing or response variability. These are important limitations which must be addressed in future work.

The significance of this research is principally that it provides an explicit account of the types of knowledge and processes involved in word recognition, a central component of reading. It also provides an explicit, computational account of the two primary tasks used in word recognition research, naming and lexical decision. The investigations of developmental and acquired forms of dyslexia represent a novel approach to understanding disordered cognition. Developmental disorders are seen as deriving from abnormalities in the initial configuration of the model or in the learning algorithm; disorders following brain injury result from damage to the normal system. This represents an advance over attempts to infer the structure of the processing system and the locus of damage from behavioral deficits. This approach also affords the possibility of establishing closer links between the behavioral disorders and their underlying biological causes.

There is already suggestive evidence linking brain abnormalities associated with dyslexia to computational properties of our model (discussed later).

Several features of the parallel distributed processing approach make it an attractive vehicle for accounts of neuropsychological disorders. Parallel distributed processing models are particularly well suited for understanding the effects of partial dysfunction. As argued by Allport (1985), standard theorizing in cognitive neuropsychology has relied on the idea that entire components are retained or abolished. But, as Allport emphasizes, ". . . such complete functional dissociations are seldom, if ever, seen . . . . What is seen every day in the clinic is reduced efficiency of performance: slower and less reliable word-finding; partial or incomplete retrieval of word meanings; increased confusability between similar items or similar constructions; and so on" (p. 36). Furthermore, although ". . . particular classes of words can be differentially affected, what appears not to occur is the permanent loss of unique, individual written or spoken word forms, leaving others in the same class intact" (p. 36).

If computational models that are based on distributed principles are "lesioned" by, for example, zeroing the output of some proportion of the processing elements, they exhibit so-called graceful degradation: There is decreased accuracy and efficiency of performance as a function of degree of damage, but there is neither a sudden catastrophic loss of ability to perform the simulated task, nor is there abolished performance on individual stimulus items. Thus, such distributed systems are compatible with many known facts about human cognitive processing, including the features of cognitive impairment noted above.

THE SEIDENBERG AND MCCLELLAND MODEL

The background for our work is provided by a large body of research by ourselves and others concerning detailed aspects of normal and impaired visual word recognition (for reviews, see Carr & Pollatsek, 1985; Coltheart, 1987; Patterson, Marshall, & Coltheart, 1985). The Seidenberg and McClelland (1989) model was an attempt to develop an integrative computational account of these phenomena. The model (illustrated in Fig. 9.1) is a lexical processing module consisting of pools of units encoding orthographic, phonological, and semantic codes. Each code is represented by patterns of activation over appropriate sets of units; each unit participates in the representation of many codes. Thus, the model uses distributed representations rather than a scheme in which units ("logogens;" Morton, 1969) correspond to individual words. Knowledge of the relations among these codes is encoded by the weights on connections between units. Lexical processing, then, involves computing the appropriate codes on the basis of written or spoken input, rather than "accessing" entries in a mental dictionary.

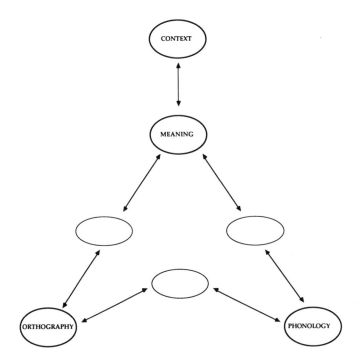

FIG. 9.1. Structure of the Seidenberg-McClelland model. Bidirectional arrows represent two independent sets of connections, one in each direction, between pools of units.

A part of this general theory has been realized as a simulation model. The model is concerned with the computation of orthographic and phonological codes in reading. Letter strings are presented as input and two types of output are produced: a pattern of activation over the phonological units, and a recreation of the input pattern over the orthographic units. These computed codes are then used in performing tasks such as naming a word aloud or making a lexical decision, according to principles set forth in the Seidenberg and McClelland (1989) paper. For example, the computed phonological code is thought to be the input to an (unimplemented) articulatory-motor module responsible for assembling the overt naming response; characteristics of the phonological code determine how rapidly the articulatory-motor response can be assembled. Similarly, lexical decisions are based on the different patterns of activation produced by words and nonwords as output.

Performance on any given word is determined by the weights, which are set during a learning phase in which the model is exposed to a large subset of the English lexicon (2897 monosyllabic words), using the backpropagation learning algorithm (Rumelhart, Hinton, & Williams, 1986). The effects of each training trial are superimposed on the weights; thus they reflect the aggregate effects of training on the entire corpus. The effect of this procedure is that the weights come to encode facts about the distribution of spelling patterns in the corpus (i.e., orthographic redundancy) and facts about the correspondences between spelling and pronunciation. These are the factors that affect subjects' performance on tasks such as lexical decision and naming.

The model's performance on different types of words and nonwords is assessed after different amounts of training and with the model configured in different ways. Performance is assessed in terms of error scores that reflect the fit between the orthographic and phonological codes computed by the model and the codes that would be produced if the model performed without error. Seidenberg and McClelland (1989) showed that the magnitudes of these error scores are systematically related to subjects' response latencies on the naming and lexical decision tasks. Much of the 1989 paper is devoted to simulations of a large number of behavioral studies from the literature, showing that the fit between error scores and latencies is quite close.

Naming

The model provides a detailed account of how written words are pronounced aloud. The weights mediating the computation from orthography to phonology encode facts about the frequency and consistency of spelling–sound correspondences in the lexicon. The model accounts for effects of lexical frequency because frequency determines how often a word is presented during the training phase; words that are presented more often have a bigger impact on the weights. For the same reason, the model performs better on words containing sublexical spelling patterns that occur in many words. In terms of computing phonological output, the model performs better on words containing spelling patterns that are associated with a single pronunciation (e.g., *-ust* in *must*, *-ike* in *like*) compared to patterns associated with more than one pronunciation (e.g., *-own* in *town*, *blown*). Thus, the model exhibits the effects of spelling–sound consistency first identified in an important paper by Glushko (1979). These outcomes are simply a consequence of how the learning algorithm operates given a significant fragment of the English lexicon to work with. Multiple exposures to consistent patterns such as *-ust* push the weights toward values that are optimal for producing the correct phonological output. Performance on inconsistent patterns such as *-own* is somewhat poorer because training on a word such as *town* has a negative effect on the weights from the point of view of *blown,* and vice versa. In such cases, given sufficient training on the words, the model produces output that is closer to the correct pronunciation than to the alternative pronunciation of the inconsistent spelling pattern; however, error scores (the discrepancy between computed and veridal phonological codes) are larger than in the case of entirely consistent words.

The model's behavior closely corresponds to that of human subjects asked to read words aloud; its performance is better on the words that subjects find easier, and worse on the words they find more difficult. There have been a large number of behavioral studies of how subjects name different types of words aloud (for reviews, see Seidenberg, 1985; Seidenberg & McClelland, 1989). Various taxonomies of word types have been proposed on the basis of different assumptions about the nature of pronunciation rules and the perceptual units relevant to pronunciation (Patterson & Coltheart, 1987). The model shows that the correct generalizations about naming performance derive from a deeper principle concerning the learning process. The accuracy of the model is such that it correctly simulates latency differences on the order of 15–25 msec.

We have also used the model to generate and test novel predictions. For example, the consistency effects observed by Glushko (1979) have replicated in only some subsequent studies (see Brown, 1987; Seidenberg, Waters, Barnes, & Tanenhaus, 1984; Taraban & McClelland, 1987). Jared, McRae, and Seidenberg (1990) described four experiments comparing sets of consistent and inconsistent words. The model correctly predicted cases where consistent words were easier than inconsistent. The magnitude of inconsistency effects was found to largely depend on the ratio of a word's "friends" (similarly spelled rhymes; e.g., *gave/save*) to its "enemies" (similarly spelled nonrhymes; e.g., *gave/have*). These are also the neighbors that have the biggest effects on the weights in the simulations. Jared and Seidenberg (1990) showed that consistency effects also occur in multisyllabic words. McRae, Jared, and Seidenberg (1990) have also used the model to simulate frequency effects in word naming, a topic that has been the focus of considerable debate (see Balota & Chumbley, 1985; Monsell, Doyle, & Haggard, 1989).

These results have important implications for theories of lexical processing and naming. The inconsistency effects, which are exhibited by people and correctly simulated by the model, are not predicted by standard "dual-route" models, in which the fundamental distinction is between regular, rule-governed words and irregular words that violate the rules ("exceptions"). This dichotomy is not rich enough to capture facts about human performance. Regular and exception words represent different points on a continuum of spelling–sound consistency. Inconsistent words such as *tint* or *leaf* represent intermediate cases; they appear to be regular, "rule-governed" items but the naming of these items is in fact affected by knowledge of exception-word neighbors such as *pint* and *deaf*. Consistency effects are somewhat smaller than suggested by Glushko's (1979) original work, but they can be detected with careful experimentation (see Jared et al., 1990), and they are theoretically important. Any number of theories can explain why a word with an irregular pronunciation might be more difficult to name than a regular word. However, the data indicate that differences among word types in terms of naming difficulty depend on the degree of consistency in the mapping between spelling and pronunciation. These differences in degree are realized in the model by the weights on connections, which reflect the aggregate effects of training on a large corpus of words.

The model thus refutes what I have termed the "central dogma" of dual-route theories (Seidenberg, 1988), namely that the naming of irregular words (such as *have*) and nonwords (such as *mave*) require separate mechanisms, table look-up and pronunciation rules, respectively. Previous theories were based on the universal intuition that no single pronunciation mechanism could produce the correct output for *gave, have,* and *mave;* however, that is what the Seidenberg and McClelland model does. It is able to do this because of the manner in which knowledge of spelling–sound correspondences is represented. There are no pronunciation rules, and there is no lexicon in which the pronunciations of irregular words are listed. Instead, knowledge of spelling–sound correspondences is encoded by the weights on connections between units encoding distributed representations. The model has sufficient resources, in the form of units and connections, to simultaneously encode both regular and irregular pronunciations of a spelling pattern (e.g., *-ave, -int*); the output that is computed changes appropriately as a function of the context in which the spelling pattern occurs (e.g., *have*/gave, *pint*/*mint*).

Note that the model behaves *as if* it contained two mechanisms. Performance on common words is largely dependent on frequency of exposure and length, not on word-internal properties such as regularity or orthographic redundancy. This type of behavior in subjects has been taken as evidence for a look-up mechanism. In effect, neighborhood effects for higher frequency words are vanishingly small. Lower frequency words are affected by word-internal structure, a characteristic previously associated with analytic processes such as parsing words into sublexical components or applying spelling–sound rules. These effects of word-internal structure reflect properties of the words in the training set. The important point is that all of these effects actually derive from the same underlying mechanism. The model cannot do table look-up because there is no table. The model cannot apply pronunciation rules because there are none. In addition, this single processing mechanism correctly predicts the broad range of consistency effects. Thus, consistency effects very strongly implicate a model of the sort we have implemented and strongly contradict the standard "rules-plus-exceptions" approach. Moreover, this same way of representing spelling–sound knowledge also explains why consistency effects interact with frequency, and it permits generalization to simple nonwords such as *mave*.

Consistency effects also provide a very important illustration of the role of computational models in psychological theorizing. Word recognition has been an important topic in the field known as "cognitive neuropsychology." Models in this area are pitched at the level of the so-called "functional architecture." Within this approach, the types of knowledge representations and processes that are relevant to a task such as naming words and nonwords aloud are posited, though never actually developed in detail; the resulting system is then invested with desirable computational processes (see Seidenberg, 1988, for discussion). For example, it has been commonly assumed that naming involves knowledge of grapheme–phoneme correspondence rules. Exactly how the rules would be represented, accessed, and applied have never been specified in detail; nonetheless, a principal theoretical claim of dual-route models is that the rules are used to produce correct phonological codes for regular, rule-governed strings. I suppose that most people in the field must have found this proposal eminently plausible, though I myself did not; I could not see how rules of the sort proposed by Venezky (1970) and others could be efficiently represented and used (Seidenberg, 1985).

Our model shows that a single computational mechanism can support the pronunciation of both "rule-governed" and "irregular" strings. The important point is that this could only be seen by actually implementing the model, that is, by being explicit enough about knowledge representations and processes to be able to see what kinds of behavior the system produced. It is interesting to imagine for a moment what would have happened if, in keeping with the "functional architecture" approach, we had merely posited a processing component—a box, if you will—without actually implementing it, arbitrarily assigning to it the capacity to generate correct output for regular words, exception words, and nonwords. Of course, no one would have taken this proposal seriously in the slightest. The important point is that all proposals pitched at the level of the functional architecture—including ones such as "apply grapheme–phoneme correspondence rules to generate the pronunciations of regular words and nonwords"—have exactly the same status as my hypothetical box: They are interesting ideas whose validity cannot be assessed unless they are more fully developed in terms of exactly what types of knowledge representations are assumed and how they are used in processing. This level of development is rarely achieved in standard functional architecture theorizing, although it is a natural byproduct of attempts to develop working simulation models.

The model contradicts one of the arguments used to challenge methods of teaching reading that emphasize the correspondences between spelling and sound (e.g., phonics). A standard argument is that English spelling–sound correspondences are highly inconsistent; therefore it would be inefficient to rely on phonological recoding in reading because the rules will fail in so many cases (see, for example, Smith, 1971). It follows from this argument that children should be taught to eschew reliance on phonological recoding and encouraged to use a direct computation from orthography to meaning, which is more efficient. This reasoning, however, depends on critical assumptions about spelling–sound knowledge that the model shows to be invalid. In particular, knowledge of spelling–sound correspondences does not have to be represented in terms of rules that necessarily fail in many cases. As in our model, this knowledge can be represented in another form, weighted connections between units, that allows efficient processing of words that are both regular and irregular from the standard point of view. The further assumption that the direct, orthography–meaning route is necessarily more efficient than an indirect, orthography–phonology–meaning route is also questionable; it cannot be established by a priori logical considerations (e.g., that a process involving two computations is necessarily less efficient than one involving one). Indeed, Van Orden, Pennington, and Stone (1990) have recently argued that phonological mediation is necessarily *more* efficient than direct access. We consider this claim again later. Here it should be noted that nothing about the correspondences between spelling and sound (or lack thereof) necessarily dictates that direct access should be dominant.

The fact that the model simulates effects of word frequency is important because it was not obvious whether a model employing distributed representations could account for phenomena related to the characteristics of individual words, such as frequency. The standard view is that frequency affects the latency to find or activate a word's entry in the mental lexicon. This requires that there be entries for individual words and a continuously updated record of each word's frequency, neither of which is incoporated in our model. The simulations suggest that both frequency and consistency effects derive from a common source, the repeated adjustment of the weights on the basis of experience. The model also clarifies questions concerning the locus of frequency effects in naming, a topic of recent controversy (Balota & Chumbley, 1985; McRae et al., 1990).

The model also provides an account of the "orthographic depth" hypothesis (Frost, Katz, & Bentin, 1987; Turvey, Feldman & Lukatela, 1984) concerning differences between orthographies in terms of the mapping between spelling and pronunciation. Essentially, there are larger effects of frequency and lexicality (word/nonword status) on naming latencies in orthographies with relatively "deep" spelling–sound correspondences (e.g., English, unvowelized Hebrew) compared to "shallow" orthographies such as Serbo-Croatian (Frost et al., 1987). We are able to simulate the effects of orthographic depth by changing the corpus used in training. For example, "shallow English" can be simulated by training the model as if English spelling–sound correspondences were entirely regular, as in Serbo-Croatian (i.e., as though HAVE and GAVE rhyme). As predicted by the orthographic depth hypothesis, frequency effects and word/nonword differences decrease in this simulation. Thus, a common architecture accounts for processing in very different orthographies; the language-specific effects due to orthographic depth reflect different degrees of consistency in the mapping between spelling and pronunciation. In the model, these are picked up by the learning algorithm and encoded by the connection strengths.

Is One Route Sufficient?

Our 1989 paper naturally emphasized the implemented model, which was principally a machine that took orthographic input and computed phonological output. It should be apparent from Fig. 9.1, however, that our general framework for lexical processing includes a second way to pronounce words. As Fig. 9.1 illustrates, a visually presented word can also be pronounced by means of a computation from orthography to meaning and then from meaning to phonology. This second route is analogous to the notion of a "lexical" pronunciation process in standard dual-route models. As we noted in 1989 (p. 558) the evidence for this second route is "compelling;" it is implicated, for example, in cases of phonological dyslexia (e.g., Derouesné & Beauvois, 1979).

The number of routes in the model has generated considerable confusion. Paap and Noel (1991), Baluch and Besner (1991), and Besner, Twilley, McCann, and Seergobin (1990) argue that our model is incorrect because it only incorporates a single pronunciation mechanism. In our 1989 paper, we emphasized the point that a single process, employing distributed representations and weighted connections between units, is sufficient to produce correct output for all types of words, not merely "rule-governed" ones. This is a novel proposal, one that is not part of standard dual-route models. That a single process could generate correct output for both HAVE and GAVE is apparent only if basic properties of parallel distributed processing systems are understood. We emphasized this aspect of the model because it refutes the central dogma mentioned previously. However, in every paper in which the model has been discussed, including Seidenberg (1988, 1989), Seidenberg and McClelland (1989), and Patterson et al. (1989), we have also discussed a second, "lexical" pronunciation mechanism that involves computations from orthography to semantics to phonology. For example, in the first paper discussing the model (Seidenberg, 1988), I wrote, "To forestall potential confusion, I should point out that in [our model] there is a second naming mechanism. . . . Thus, ours is a dual-route model. . . ." (p. 415) In fact, the model takes the "dual-route" notion to the limit: there are two ways to compute all of the codes in Fig. 9.9 (orthography, phonology, meaning). Both of the routes are discussed on pp. 558–559 of Seidenberg and McClelland (1989), where we acknowledge points of contact between our model and previous dual-route accounts, and ways in which they differ. Hence, the claim that the model is incorrect because various behavioral phenomena demand that there be two routes, whereas our model only contains one, is based on a misreading of what was said. From the fact that single route can generate correct output for both regular and exception words it does not follow that this is the only mechanism in the system.

We agree with standard dual-route models that there are two pronunciation processes; we disagree about the types of knowledge they involve and how they apply to different types of words. Insofar as the single route in the existing model is able to simulate naming latencies for monosyllabic words in some detail, it appears that the second route has little role in normal naming of these items. However, this conclusion must be qualified in three ways. First, after considerable training (250 epochs), the implemented model actually erred on a small proportion of low frequency exception words; it never learned these items.

Examples include SPOOK (the model produced a rhyme of BOOK) and WAD (which the model rhymed with HAD). The model did not have enough resources to encode the pronunciations of these words correctly. These words are ones that people might be expected to pronounce using the lexical (orthography-semantics-phonology) mechanism. Second, there may be important individual differences among even skilled readers with regard to the division of labor between the two pronunciation mechanisms. Some readers may process more of the exceptions by the lexical route; others, more of these words by the nonlexical route. These individual differences may relate to differences in amount of reading experience or differences in computational capacity (e.g., amount of neural machinery recruited for the task of reading), issues that are considered again later in the section on dyslexia. Finally, a multiplicity of ad hoc routes can be created simply by changing the instructions to the subject. For example, in recent, unpublished research, Stephen Monsell and Karalyn Patterson instructed subjects to "regularize" exception words (e.g., to read PINT as though it rhymed with MINT). Here performance involves experiment-specific strategies that might be explained by adding additional assumptions to the existing model (e.g., concerning attention, strategies for dividing words into sublexical components), rather than changing its basic assumptions. There is absolutely nothing about the model that is inconsistent with the observation that subjects can alter their strategies for performing a task.

Is Phonological Mediation Obligatory?

One of the main issues in reading research concerns the role of phonological information in the access of meaning. It has proven difficult to achieve closure on this issue despite extensive research. Our model is consistent with the idea that meaning can be activated both directly on the basis of orthographic information and indirectly by means of phonology. Again, however, it differs from other dual-route models in critical respects. Our model—and here we are referring to the Fig. 9.1 framework, not merely the part that was implemented—employs distributed representations: The spelling, pronunciation, and meaning of a word are represented by patterns of activation across simple processing units encoding each of these types of information. The presentation of a visual stimulus is assumed to initiate the computation of semantic and phonological codes in parallel (Tanenhaus, Flanigan, & Seidenberg, 1980). Over time, activation eventually spreads from phonological units to semantic units. The semantic representation of a word thus builds up over time as activation spreads from the two sources. This represents an important contrast to other dual-route accounts in which meaning is assumed to be "accessed" on the basis of one or the other of the two processing routines. In horse-race models, for example (Meyer, Schvaneveldt, & Ruddy, 1974; Paap, McDonald, Schvaneveldt, & Noel, 1987), the direct and phonologically mediated pathways operate in parallel but autonomously; the "race" between them determines which provides "access" to meaning. The Seidenberg and McClelland model incorporates the idea of two parallel computations of meaning; however, the different processes can jointly contribute to the activation of distributed semantic representations. Thus, the use of these representations affords the possibility of *partial* activation of phonology from orthography and of meaning from phonology. These outcomes are not afforded by standard dual-route models. The partial activation of these codes may be sufficient to produce phenomena such as phonological priming (e.g., Meyer et al., 1974; Shulman, Hornak, & Sanders, 1978) and the false positives in the Van Orden, Johnston, and Hale (1988) experiments.

Within this framework, the unanswered questions concern the time-course of the component computations—that is, the rate at which different types of output units are activated. Several computations—from orthography to phonology, from orthography to semantics, from phonology to meaning—are assumed to occur in parallel. In a fully implemented version of the model in Fig. 9.9, there would be connections in both directions between sets of units, creating interactive processing as in the McClelland and Rumelhart (1981) model. In connectionist models, the characteristics of these computations are determined by the weights on connections between units. Seidenberg and McClelland's simulation is quite limited, in that only the computation from orthography to phonology was implemented. Moreover, the implemented model is not a real-time system; orthographic and phonological output are computed in a single step rather than over time, and the interactive feedback loops were ignored. Hence, little can be said about detailed aspects of the time course of processing, specifically how much activation will spread from phonology to semantics for different words. This is an important issue that needs to be addressed in future simulation models. For the moment, we are assuming that the time course of processing is such that common words are recognized primarily on the basis of activation from orthography, with phonological activation contributing more to the meanings of lower frequency words. However, there may be important individual differences among readers with regard to the efficiency of the different computations. For example, skilled readers may be better at computing meanings directly from orthography, reducing the contribution of the phonological route.

Van Orden et al. (1990) have recently described a model that is offered as an alternative to dual-route accounts. They argue that skilled word recognition is exclusively phonologically mediated. This conclusion was based on both logical and empirical considerations. They note that many of the arguments for direct access depend on the assumption that knowledge of spelling–sound correspondences is represented by rules (e.g., grapheme-phoneme correspondence rules). The rules will necessarily fail to generate correct phonological codes for exception words such as *have* or *give;* hence, according to standard arguments, these words must be recognized on a direct, visual basis. Van Orden et al. correctly note that connectionist models offer an alternative way of representing spelling–

sound correspondences, namely in terms of the weights on connections between units. As our model shows, a processor employing this type of knowledge representation can generate correct phonological codes for both regular and irregular words. Van Orden et al. conclude from this that there is no logical barrier to using phonological mediation in reading all words.

The empirical evidence offered by Van Orden (1987) and Van Orden, Johnston, and Hale (1988) seems to confirm that phonological mediation is obligatory. The studies employed a semantic classification task in which subjects decide if a target word is a member of a specified category. The critical findings were a significant proportion of false positive errors when targets were homophones (e.g., *part of a horse's harness: rain*) or pseudohomophones (e.g., *article of clothing: sute*) for actual category exemplars (*rein, suit,* respectively). These effects would only occur if subjects were phonologically recoding the stimuli. Insofar as they occurred for skilled readers and did not seem to be sensitive to word frequency, Van Orden et al. concluded that phonological mediation is obligatory.

However, Jared and Seidenberg (in press) described 6 experiments using the Van Orden paradigm, suggesting that Van Orden et al. have overstated the role of phonological mediation in skilled word recognition. Specifically, the results implicate both direct and phonologically mediated recognition processes and suggest that the latter is only relevant to lower frequency words. Jared and Seidenberg (in press) showed that the false positive effects depend on several factors, including the specificity of the categories, word frequency, and the degree to which members of a homophone pair are similar in spelling (compare *rain–rein* with *wait–weight*). The critical finding, replicated in several experiments, is that false positives only occur for relatively low frequency homophones and pseudohomophones. The false positive rate for higher frequency homophones does not differ than that for nonhomophone controls. Hence, the studies provided no evidence for phonological mediation for higher frequency words. In summary, Van Orden et al. are correct in saying that arguments for direct access that are based on the properties of putative spelling–sound correspondence rules are invalid. However, it does not follow from this observation that phonological mediation is obligatory. Studies such as Jared and Seidenberg's (in press) are consistent with the older view that both direct and mediated routes contribute to the activation of meaning, with direct access predominating for skilled readers.

Lexical Decision

The model also provides a novel account of performance on the lexical decision task, which has been a principal tool in reading research. The subject's task is to decide if a letter string forms a word or not. Standard accounts of the task assume that it is performed by attempting to access an entry for the word in the mental lexicon. If lexical access is completed, the stimulus is a word; if not, it is a nonword. Initially it was assumed that "word" decisions involved accessing the meaning of the stimulus, but this was called into question by later studies showing that decision latencies are affected by other stimulus properties, such as orthographic familiarity (e.g., Balota & Chumbley, 1984).

Our account of the task differs from the standard approach in several respects. Because the model employs distributed representations, there are no entries to be accessed. The model does not incorporate the concept of lexical access that was central to previous theories, replacing it with the concept of computing several types of (distributed) output codes. Accordingly, lexical decisions cannot be performed by accessing the entry for a word in memory. Instead, we assume that decisions are based on the differing patterns of activation produced by words and nonwords. The model is blind to the lexical status of an input letter string; it processes words and nonwords in exactly the same way. However, these types of stimuli produce very different types of output. In general, the model performs better on words than on nonwords, in the sense of more accurately computing the output codes. Thus, subjects could judge whether the stimulus is a word or nonword by assessing differences in the patterns of activation produced by the two types of stimuli. Seidenberg and McClelland (1989) developed this account of lexical decision in some detail, and illustrated it by simulating several phenomena that are anomalous in terms of standard accounts of the task (e.g., frequency blocking effects, pseudohomophone effects, and changes in decision criteria as a function of properties of the stimuli in an experiment). One important aspect of this work is that it shows that lexical decisions do not necessarily require access of meaning, contrary to standard assumptions. The implemented model simulates the results of several lexical decision studies even though it is wholly lacking a semantic system. The model is compatible with the view that semantic information is relevant under some conditions, but often the decision can be based on orthography or phonology alone.

Interpreting the Error Scores

The error scores used to assess the model's performance have generated considerable confusion (Besner et al., 1990), and so it may be useful to explain them a little further. The model computes orthographic and phonological output, and there are corresponding error scores for each. The term *error score* is perhaps unfortunate, insofar as people seem to confuse the scores—which are measures of goodness of fit—with the concept of making an erroneous response on a task such as lexical decision or naming. A small error score simply means that the computed output is very close to the veridical output pattern (orthographic or phonological). "Making an error" is a different issue. The model simply computes output; we as the experimenters have to interpret its behavior, including what would count, for example, as a naming error. As an example of one plausible definition, the computed phonological output could be counted as an error if the best fit to it is provided by a code other than the correct one—if, for example, the computer output for *have* were closer to /hev/ than /hæv/.

Although calculated in the same way, the two types of error scores play very different roles in interpreting the model's behavior. Consider first the phonological error scores. The model takes a letter string as input and computes a pattern of activation over the phonological output units as output. In people, these computations are assumed to take place in real time; input units become activated and activation spreads through the network in a cascaded manner (McClelland, 1979). Thus, output representations (e.g., the phonological code used in naming words aloud) develop over time. This cascaded activation process is not implemented in the current model; output activations are computed in a single pass through the network. This simplification was entirely due to computational considerations; although the conceptual apparatus relevant to cascaded networks has been in place for some time, such systems are highly computationally intensive, slowing the simulation process by orders of magnitude. This simplification affects how we interpret the model's behavior. In people, facility in naming is assessed in terms of speed and accuracy of responding; the better a response is learned, the more rapidly and accurately it can be produced. In a cascaded model, latency would correspond to the number of processing cycles needed for output units to reach asymptotic levels of activation; accuracy would correspond to whether the computed code is correct or incorrect, given the stimulus input.

The implemented model's performance cannot be assessed in these ways, because every output is produced at the same "latency," the single pass through the network. However, this is where the phonological error scores come in. Instead of asking how long it takes the model to compute the correct output in a cascaded system, we assess how close it comes to producing the correct output on the single pass in the non-cascaded version. The error score, then, is simply a measure of the discrepancy between the computed code and the correct target code. As Cohen, Dunbar, and McClelland (1990) argued, error scores are closely related to the number of processing cycles needed for units to reach asymptotic levels of activation in a fully cascaded system. It follows that the error scores that we calculate (the sum of the squared differences between computed and target values of the units) should be correlated with measures such as naming latencies. That is what the Seidenberg and McClelland paper shows: Simulations of a large number of behavioral studies indicate that error scores are monotonically related to latencies.

The phonological error score, then, is a *statistic* that we, the modelers, calculate to assess the model's performance. There is a simple theory relating this measure to behavioral indices such as naming latency. The close fit between the error scores and behavioral data provides a substantive basis for thinking that the model is capturing some central characteristics of the naming process. The longer-term goal is to develop models that simulate the time course of processing, which will obviate the use of this statistic entirely.

Importantly, we do not assume that subjects (or, more generally, readers) calculate phonological error scores in the course of reading or pronouncing words. That is, the error scores are not assumed to have any relevance to lexical processing; they are only relevant to the narrow question of how to assess the model. This point is sometimes misunderstood (e.g., by Besner et al., 1990). Besner et al. critiqued the Seidenberg and McClelland (1989) account of lexical decision. The critique turns on the mistaken assumption that subjects actually compute phonological error scores and use them in making lexical decisions. So, for example, Besner et al. plot distributions of phonological error scores and wonder how subjects could base decisions on these distributions. Subjects cannot compute these scores because this would require having explicit specifications of the correct, target phonological codes; in our model, there is no way for subjects to access this information. Of course, we, as experimenters, can provide the correct target codes and compute the phonological error scores as one of the ways in which we assess the model's performance. This is to be distinguished, however, from the claim that *readers* compute these codes as part of the process of naming a word or making a lexical decision.

Besner et al.'s (1990) confusion apparently arose from the fact that there is a second type of error score used in assessing the model, and it is part of our theory that subjects *do* compute something very much like it in the course of performing tasks such as lexical decision. The second error score is computed with respect to the model's orthographic output. It is calculated in the same way as the phonological score, but the interpretation of this score is different. The orthographic error score reflects the difference between the computed orthographic output and the target orthographic pattern. We assume that subjects *can* derive something like this measure by comparing the initially encoded representation of the letter string and the pattern that they compute as part of the recognition process. The former can be thought of as an early, perceptual encoding of the stimulus string; the latter a computed object derived from the individual's knowledge of the lexicon. The comparison between the codes gives us an index of the familiarity of the letter string, which then plays an important role in our account of lexical decision performance. Note that, whereas deriving the phonological error score requires an *external* specification of the target pattern, deriving the orthographic error score does not because the input itself is orthographic. These distinctions between the orthographic and phonological error scores are critical to understanding and assessing the model; they are, apparently, easily misunderstood.

Does the Model Need Lexical Nodes?

The fact that the model employs distributed representations means that there are no representations for individual words. This implies that the model does not contain a lexicon, in the standard sense of that term. This aspect of the model is perhaps its most counterintuitive feature; not surprisingly, it has generated the most skepticism. The force of the Seidenberg and McClelland paper is that the model provides a better account of a broad range of word recognition phenomena than previous models. It does not do this despite the absence of lexical representations; rather it does so because of the absence of these structures. At this point it is not clear whether a model employing standard word-level representations would be able to capture this same broad range of phenomena; certainly no such model exists at this time.

It has recently been argued that our strong claim that lexical knowledge does not entail word-level representations is incorrect. Besner et al. (1990) drew this conclusion on the basis of pseudohomophone effects, which they believe implicate explicit lexical representations. In brief, the argument runs as follows. Pseudohomophones are nonwords such as *brane* that sound like words. There have been a large number of studies concerning naming and lexical decision latencies for such stimuli. Differing performance on pseudohomophones and nonpseudohomophones (*brone*) is thought to implicate lexical representations. *Brane* differs from *brone* because only the processing of *brane* is influenced by the base word *brain*. Such effects, it is argued, could only arise if the mental lexicon included an explicit representation for the word *brain*. McCann and Besner (1987) and McCann, Besner, and Davelaar (1988) reported two major findings concerning this type of stimulus. In their studies, pseudohomophones were named faster than nonpseudohomophones but yielded longer lexical decision latencies. Besner et al. (1990) believe these results are a problem for the Seidenberg and McClelland (1989) model; because the model lacks entries for individual words, there is no way for a base word such as *brain* to affect the processing of a pseudohomophone such as *brane*.

This reasoning is faulty, however, because it assumes that pseudohomophone effects could only come about by means of the direct impact of a lexical node on the processing of the derived nonword. Our model shows that the effects can arise in other ways. The model's performance on nonwords depends on how similar they are to words in the training set. (The same is true of words, of course, which is the basis of neighborhood effects.) The model does well on nonwords such as *nust*, which have many neighbors in the training corpus; it does poorly on items such as *jinje*, which do not. Pseudohomophones tend to be more wordlike than nonpseudohomophones, for obvious reasons. By design, the pseudohomophone stimuli sound like words, and the nonpseudohomophone stimuli do not. Moreover, in order to sound like words, the pseudohomophone stimuli must contain spelling patterns and sounds that occur in words; in order to not sound like words, the nonpseudohomophone stimuli must contain spelling and sound patterns that occur less often (see Seidenberg & McClelland, 1990, for discussion). In general, then, the model performs better on pseudohomophone stimuli than nonpseudohomophone stimuli—a pseudohomophone effect—even though the model lacks lexical nodes. Hence, the mere existence of pseudohomophone effects does not falsify the model, contrary to Besner et al's (1990) claims.

The issue as to whether a model of word recognition must incorporate a lexical level of representation is by no means settled. However, the emphasis on pseudohomophone effects is misplaced, in that deriving these effects does not require the introduction of lexical nodes. There are other ways to test the hypothesis that lexical representations are required; Jared et al. (1990) reported two experiments that clearly do not support this hypothesis, although further research is certainly warranted.

DEVELOPMENTAL DYSLEXIA

In the remainder of this article I discuss the model's implications concerning developmental reading disorders. Dyslexia is a controversial topic; there is little consensus concerning basic questions, such as the causes of the disorder, or even whether there is a dyslexic disorder distinct from normal variation in reading ability. This may be due in part to the nature of the reading process itself. Reading consists of a large number of perceptual and cognitive processes and involves a broad range of human skills. Given the complexity of the task and the kinds of capacities it involves, it would be very surprising if reading disability did not have multiple causes. We have to imagine a complex system with a large number of intersecting components, each of which can be damaged in differing degrees. Seen in this light, there are simply too many good reasons why the reading device could fail to function smoothly. Some of the seeming confusion in the study of dyslexia may simply reflect the fact that complex systems may break down in complex ways.

My own belief is that the understanding of reading disorders can advance beyond the categorization of subtypes typical of current research; however, progress critically depends on developing better theories of skilled reading—specifically, an explicit computational model. We are only beginning to see the development of this type of account. In its absence, researchers have attempted to infer the nature of the normal system—and the nature of reading impairments—from patterns of behavioral deficits. This approach has yielded important insights; however, its utility is limited by two factors. First, the number of components involved and the likelihood that impairments can differ in degree seem to imply a staggering variety of deficit profiles, making it difficult to derive principled generalizations.[1] Second, as we (Patterson, Seidenberg, & McClelland, 1989)

---

[1]In the neuropsychology literature, such considerations have led people to conclude that every case is unique and have motivated the use of single-case methods (e.g., Caramazza, 1984). My own view is that, although there are compelling reasons to study individual cases (and that the single-case method has a long and honorable history in areas such as psychophysics and developmental psychology), we should keep in mind that interpatient variability is one of the things we ultimately would like a theory to explain.

and others (Hinton & Shallice, 1991) have argued, it is questionable whether the loci of processing impairments can reliably be inferred from behavioral data alone. Without a theory that is explicit about how knowledge is represented and used in reading, it is hard to determine, for example, whether seemingly "visual" reading errors derive from a deficit in a part of the visual processing system or from another source; this issue is discussed further later.

Despite the limitations of the traditional methods, researchers have been able to identify a small number of plausible possible bases for the disorder. The approach we have employed has the potential to integrate these various proposals in a way that will also account for the broad variability that is seen among individuals. Moreover, the approach prepares the way for capitalizing on advances in our knowledge of the biological bases of dyslexia, so as to achieve a theory of brain-behavior relationships in reading.

Our work on dyslexia has been motivated by the following vision: Imagine that we develop a model of skilled reading. If the model is computational, then it will be explicit in terms of the types of knowledge and processes involved. If it is a connectionist model, it may say something about how the skill is acquired. With this model in hand, we could attempt to *generate* the patterns associated with dyslexic reading by modifying the architecture of the model or impairing its ability to function. We could then see how impairments to different components of the reading process affect performance. Instead of trying to *infer* which component of the process is impaired on the basis of one or another type of behavioral evidence, we could use the simulation process to *derive* and thereby *explain* the entire range of behaviors.

This is the vision; of course, nothing quite like this has been achieved as yet. The existing simulation model of normal performance is limited in scope; even within its restricted domain (the recognition and pronunciation of monosyllabic words), it is far from complete. Still, I think that something *has* been achieved thus far in terms of understanding some basic aspects of word recognition, and the power of the approach advocated here is such that we can already gain some insight about dyslexia by examining implications of the model even in its current rudimentary state. The immediate gains are that we can see how different existing proposals about the bases of dyslexia relate to each other; we can explore how they cause different types of reading problems and how they interact; and we can begin to get a handle on the interreader variability that is a problem for standard classificatory schemes. The model also suggests a new hypothesis about a cause of dyslexia, which has some biological plausibility.

Orthographic Deficits

In Fig. 9.2, I have schematically illustrated the main components of the existing model. The figure is intended to illustrate that dyslexia could derive from impairments in different components of the system and from different types of impairments within the components. Consider first the orthographic representations. In

Component of the model: **Type of dyslexia:**

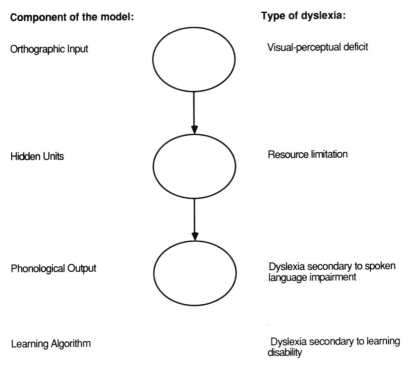

Orthographic Input   Visual-perceptual deficit

Hidden Units   Resource limitation

Phonological Output   Dyslexia secondary to spoken
                                                    language impairment

Learning Algorithm   Dyslexia secondary to learning
                                                    disability

FIG. 9.2.   Some possible causes of dyslexia and their isomorphs in
the Seidenberg-McClelland model.

the implemented model, these representations are treated as givens; the model
starts by encoding a letter string as a pattern of activation across the orthographic
units. In reality, of course, letter recognition is itself a computational process. An
impairment in this component would result in a failure to activate appropriate
orthographic representations. This could result because of anomalies in visual–
perceptual processes or because of damage to the orthographic representations
themselves. Impairments within this component would have important consequences for the system, limiting what could be learned (e.g., about the mapping
between spelling and pronunciation, or between spelling and meaning) and the
level of efficiency the system could achieve.[2]

---

[2]One other effect of an orthographic deficit is that it would interfere with the computation of
orthographic output. In the model, this occurs by means of recurrent connections from orthographic
input units to hidden units back to the orthographic units. I believe that this computed orthographic
code corresponds to the "orthographic images" discussed by Ehri (this volume; see also Seidenberg
& Tanenhaus, 1979). Poor reading would then result if, as Ehri argues, these images play an
important role in the acquisition of word recognition (and spelling) skills.

Of course, the idea that dyslexia derives from some kind of visual processing impairment is familiar to all reading researchers. It is also well known that this hypothesis fell into disfavor because a large body of research failed to consistently isolate a visual processing impairment in dyslexic children (see Adams, 1990, Stanovich, this volume, Vellutino, 1979, for discussion). Perspectives on this question may be changing once again, however, for several reasons. First, there is a growing body of psychophysical evidence implicating early visual processing impairments in at least some dyslexic children (Lovegrove, Martin, & Slaghuis, 1986). This is another case in which the understanding of behavioral deficits has greatly benefited from advances in theories of normal function (here, theories of early vision). Second, as this section of the chapter suggests, if such deficits exist, they do not exhaust the range of possible causes of dyslexia. Hence, there is no basis for a return to a single-factor theory of dyslexia, which was another failing of the visual processing hypothesis in its earlier incarnations.

Most important from my perspective, however, is that the modeling approach provides the hope of understanding exactly how a visual processing impairment of one sort or another would affect the reading process. We would like to have an account that explains how, for example, a deficit in the transient processing system (Breitmeyer, 1978) would affect particular aspects of processing. Later I describe some preliminary simulations that examine how one type of damage to the orthographic representations affects learning within the Seidenberg and McClelland (1989) model. Here the main point is that it can be taken as a prediction of the model that there should be forms of dyslexia that derive from a visual processing impairment and that the effects of this type of deficit on reading can be explored through simulation.

Resource Limitations

Referring again to Fig. 9.2, a second component of the model is the layer of hidden units. Functionally, these units come to represent higher-order correlations between the orthographic and phonological codes. The model's ability to simulate human performance depends on there being sufficient resources—units and connections—to encode these correlations. Given the size of the target corpus, the architecture of the existing model—400 input units, 200 hidden units, 460 output units—allows it to encode this knowledge in a way that results in close simulations of normal naming performance. Reducing the number of hidden units, however, leads to a decrement in performance. Seidenberg and McClelland (1989) described a replication of their main simulation with one major change: Whereas the "normal" model was configured with 200 hidden units, the "dyslexic" simulation was configured with only 100 hidden units. With fewer computational resources, the model was still able to learn; however, it performed poorly on irregular words and nonwords even after extensive training. The model was able to encode crude generalizations about the correspondences between spelling and pronunciation and performed fairly well on high-frequency, regular words such as *must* or *like*, and on simple nonwords. However, it did not have the computational resources to cope well with irregular words such as *have* or *said*. This pattern corresponds to the behavior seen in many dyslexic children (e.g., Seidenberg, Bruck, Fornarolo, & Backman, 1986).

The simulations suggest the novel hypothesis that at least some forms of developmental dyslexia may derive from a limitation in terms of the computational resources available for mastering word recognition. Such a limitation might result if for some reason too little neural machinery were allocated to the reading task in the course of development. Of course, we are not suggesting that dyslexics lack 100 reading neurons. The units in the model are not intended to be biologically realistic; they can be thought of as representing the idealized performance of large groups of neurons. Still, the computational consequence of a resource limitation, and how this limitation might be realized in the brain, should be clear.

Interestingly, there is suggestive neurophysiological evidence consistent with the resource-limitation hypothesis. Hynd and Semrud-Clikeman (1989) reported data from magnetic resonance imaging studies of dyslexic children showing smaller amounts of cortical tissue in areas thought to normally participate in reading. They speculated that, for unknown reasons, significant numbers of cells in reading-related areas are absent in these children, reducing their ability to learn and attend. These preliminary computational and neurophysiological explorations suggest that it may be useful to think of dyslexia as deriving in some cases from brain anomalies that limit the scope of what can be learned from experience.

It should also be observed that this line of inquiry, though at a very early stage of development, has the potential to deepen our understanding of reading disability in a very important way. Continuing advances in neuroimaging techniques and the use of methods such as postmortem histological analyses of neural tissue (e.g., Galaburda, Sherman, Rosen, Aboitiz, & Geshwind, 1985), insure that the amount of information about brain correlates of dyslexia and other cognitive and perceptual disorders will expand greatly in the near future. Of course, the "holy grail" for cognitive neuroscience is to have a theory that goes beyond correlations between anatomy (or physiology) and behavior to a theory that causally links the two. In the case of the Hynd and Semrud-Clikeman (1989) data, for example, we would like to know why a smaller mass of tissue in a particular area (principally the planum temporale) causes specific types of behavioral deficits. Why a reading disorder and not something else? Why would a particular type of neuropathology cause regularization errors or poor nonword generalization? I do not mean at all to suggest that we presently have anything like an answer to these questions. There are some suggestive anatomical data, some suggestive simulations, and a tentative link between them. My point is rather that these are the right sort of questions to be asking at this time and that this approach has the potential to provide some answers. One of the attractions of the connectionist approach is the possibility of identifying links between brain and behavior; in the case of dyslexia, we may be getting very, very close.

Earlier I mentioned the possibility of exploring the computational consequences of a visual processing impairment, but I did not describe the results of any simulations. We have in fact completed one such simulation, in which we damaged the input orthographic representation by ensuring that each letter string activated more orthographic units than in our original simulation. In terms of the model's orthographic representation, then, words were more similar to one another than normal. One can imagine this to be a consequence of a visual processing impairment that does not yield clear information about the identities of letters, making them more confusable with each other. We then retrained the model as before, using the list of 2897 monosyllables. The result of this simulation is easy to summarize: The model performed as in the simulation with 100 hidden units. That is, there was an overall decrement in terms of the level of performance that was achieved after training; the decrement was especially acute in the case of irregularly pronounced words. Generalization to nonwords was also poor.

This simulation confirms the obvious intuition that damaging the orthographic input representation will limit what the model can learn. However, the finding that the two damage simulations produced similar results has another interesting implication. One of the puzzles about the visual processing impairment hypothesis was that this type of deficit could not be observed in all children diagnosed as dyslexic, calling into question this theory of the disorder. In our simulations, two very different types of impairments yielded a "dyslexic" pattern of performance; only one of these corresponds to a visual processing deficit. I think that the simulations are confirming what many reading researchers have long suspected, that reading deficits—even a given *type* of reading error—may derive from more than one source. This might go some way toward explaining why only some children whose behavior fits the dyslexic profile exhibit visual processing deficits. This evidence motivates closer assessments of such children to determine whether they differentiate into the predicted subgroups.

Phonological Representation

Another important hypothesis about dyslexia is that, at least in some cases, it is secondary to impairments in the capacity to process speech. This is, of course, the hypothesis most closely associated with the late Isabelle Liberman and her colleagues at Haskins Laboratories (e.g., Liberman & Shankweiler, 1979; Liberman, Shankweiler, Fischer, & Carter, 1974; see I. Y. Liberman & A. M. Liberman, this volume). There is strong evidence that at least some dyslexics are impaired in their ability to analyze speech, as evidenced by poor performance on tasks such as phoneme identification, rhyming, and other word games (e.g.,

Jorm & Share, 1983; Shankweiler, Crain, Brady, & Macaruso, this volume; Stanovich, this volume). The Haskins theory is that learning to read, especially alphabetic orthographies, is parasitic on the ability to analyze speech into underlying components such as phonemes. In support of this theory, a large amount of evidence has accumulated suggesting that the ability to relate spoken and written language is strongly related to the achievement of reading skill (see Adams, 1990, for a review of the evidence and controversies).

Phonological deficits can be represented in our model in at least two ways. First, the phonological representations themselves could be damaged or fail to develop normally. Second, the representations could be intact but there could be an impairment in the ability to activate them. For example, there could be damaged connections along the pathways from hidden to phonological units, or the computation could be noisy or otherwise unreliable. These alternatives correspond to the distinction between impairments of representation versus access that is prominent in the neuropsychological literature (e.g., Shallice & Warrington, 1980).

We have not as yet simulated the effects of phonological impairments; clearly, however, they would limit what the model is able to learn about spelling–sound correspondences. What is more interesting, perhaps, is that the model generates a rich set of predictions about connections between reading and spoken-language deficits. Assume, for example, that for unknown reasons some children fail to develop adequate phonological representations. One way to simulate this would be to coarsen the phonological representations in the model, in a manner analogous to the simulation of orthographic deficits mentioned previously. The effect of this coarsening is to increase the confusability of phonemes. Assume further that these phonological representations play multiple roles in the lexical system. In reading, phonological codes are activated on the basis of orthographic input and used in overt pronunciation; the codes are sometimes also activated as part of the process of activating word meanings. These relationships are illustrated in Fig. 9.1. Although not illustrated in the figure, it could be further assumed that these phonological codes are activated in speech perception. Auditory word recognition can be seen as the computation of an internal phonological representation from acoustic input. Damage to phonological codes relevant to both reading and listening would therefore produce deficits in both modalities. Returning to the hypothetical example, coarsening the phonological representations would have at least two effects. First, it would limit the capacity to encode spelling–sound correspondences, causing a deficit in word naming; it would also impair access to meaning from phonology. Second, it would limit performance on auditory language comprehension tasks that require access to phonological representations—tasks such as judging whether two words rhyme or counting phonemes that Liberman and others have observed to be deficient in many dyslexics.

This speculation concerning the effects of a phonological impairment is relevant to another important question, which is whether all types of damage to the model will necessarily produce the same types of impaired performance. Our first two dyslexia simulations (coarsening the orthographic units and reducing the number of hidden units) did in fact yield very similar results with regard to generating phonological output. It is likely that damaged phonological representations will have similar effects. These types of damage should produce different effects in other domains, however. For example, whereas damage to the orthographic representations predicts corollary effects on other tasks using this knowledge (e.g., letter identification or matching tasks), the restriction on the number of hidden units does not. Similarly, although all three types of anomaly could impair the ability to pronounce words, only in the case of damaged phonological representations would one also expect impaired performance on tasks such as rhyming.

The fact that some types of performance can be impaired in several ways is important. Certain aspects of the model's performance are less robust than others and therefore more susceptible to disruption from several different sources. For example, higher frequency items are trained repeatedly and come to be very strongly encoded by the model. Performance on these items is less likely to be impaired by minor changes in the initial state of the model or in the learning algorithm. Lower frequency words, especially exception words, and nonwords are learned less well; they are harder to master because the model is exposed to them less often (in the case of nonwords, never). The performance on these items is therefore very sensitive to factors such as the number of units in one or another layer. Nonword performance is particularly fragile. Therefore, the model has to be seen as predicting that types of dyslexias deriving from several different causes will be associated with poor nonword performance. Of course, poor generalization to nonwords is a hallmark of dyslexic performance (Adams, 1990); the model suggests why this should be so.

Again, it must be acknowledged that this story is by no means complete. The phonological representations in the existing model only capture some very general characteristics of this type of knowledge, making it difficult to simulate detailed patterns of impaired performance. Moreover, it is sometimes argued that the phonological representations used in reading aloud are different from the ones employed in listening (e.g., Monsell, 1987). One would also have to explore the other types of phonological impairment, for example, ones that would be produced in the model by eliminating connections between hidden and phonological units or by increasing the noise in the computation.

Questions concerning the role of phonology in reading are central to understanding dyslexia. There are a number of theories as to why a phonological deficit would interfere with the acquisition of reading skill. Our type of modeling provides a way to explicate what is meant by phonological deficits and to investigate their causal effects on acquisition and processing. This is an important topic for future research.

Learning

Finally, one other component of the model should be mentioned as a potential basis for dyslexia. Ours is a learning model. Although other aspects of language are probably innate (e.g., the capacity to understand that things have names; Seidenberg & Petitto, 1987), the ability to read and pronounce words is not. The model learns by means of the back propagation learning algorithm, one member of the large class of connectionist learning procedures. It probably needs to be said that we are not committed to the idea that humans use this particular algorithm in learning. Using this algorithm does seem to result in knowledge about orthography and phonology becoming encoded in a way that permits us to simulate detailed aspects of human performance. However, it is likely that other algorithms will produce similar results, which is a good thing, given the biological implausibility of back propagation. It also may turn out that human learning is not limited to a single procedure. In any case, learning is obviously important to reading; dyslexia is sometimes thought to be secondary to a learning impairment. According to this view, learning to read draws on procedures that are also involved in acquiring other skills and knowledge. Hence, this hypothesis predicts that there should be children whose deficits are not reading specific but rather reflect a broader learning disability. Of course, there is evidence that such children exist. More interestingly, people such as Morrison (1984) have tried to identify the specific types of learning capacities involved in reading and their roles in the acquisition of other types of knowledge.

Although we have not done so as yet, it is possible to simulate learning impairments by modifying the learning algorithm in various ways. I think that one of the significant contributions of the connectionist movement is that it has invigorated the study of human learning, introducing a raft of new learning principles (and reintroducing a few old ones as well). It seems likely to me that there are general learning principles that are not task specific (or perhaps even species specific). As with the other hypotheses concerning dyslexia, the idea that some forms are due to impairments in learning, and that these impairments also have an impact on the acquisition of other types of knowledge is wholly consistent with our model. In the future we can expect to see more detailed proposals concerning the exact forms of human learning and their implications for the acquisition of various skills.

In summary, I have tried to suggest that the model we have developed provides a framework for exploring various proposals about the causes of dyslexia in a rigorous way. I hope it is clear that in this brief discussion I have not inventoried all of the possible ways in which the reading system could break down. Aside from investigating the effects of different types of damage, future research will have to address two additional issues. First, what are the effects of different degrees of damage; second, how do different types of damage interact? Of course, further progress also depends on developing a model of normal process-ing that addresses many of the limitations of our first-generation attempt.

BREAKDOWN: ACQUIRED DYSLEXIA

It is well known that brain injury (e.g., stroke) often results in selective impair-ments of word recognition. Patients' performance is typically assessed with respect to their capacity to name words and nonwords aloud, which is a task our model is intended to explain. Hence, our goal is to derive the impaired patterns of performance observed in patients by damaging the normal simulation model. Our preliminary experiments have focused on the pattern termed *surface dyslexia* (Patterson, Marshall, & Coltheart, 1985), a principal feature of which is rela-tively poor performance on irregular words (such as *pint* or *have*), with relatively spared performance on regular words (e.g., *tint, gave*) and on nonwords (e.g., *bint, mave*). We damaged the model by removing different proportions of hidden units or connections between units. The damaged model produces impaired output that closely resembles that of some surface dyslexic patients, ones we have termed *dysfluent*. These patients include JC, the original surface dyslexic described in Marshall and Newcombe's (1973) seminal study. There are other patients categorized as surface dyslexics, however, who do not fit this pattern (e.g., MP, studied by Bub, Cancelliere, & Kertesz, 1985).

This research, though preliminary, already suggests that the approach of deriv-ing impaired performance by "lesioning" a working simulation model may prove to be a powerful technique for understanding brain and behavior. First, we have shown that we can derive one of the patterns associated with surface dyslexia even though the model lacks the pronunciation rules implicated in all previous accounts of this disorder. Second, the model provides a basis for differ-entiating between two forms of surface dyslexia, the fluent and dysfluent forms. Our studies suggest that only the dysfluent type of surface dyslexia derives from ablating units or connections in the normal system. There are several other possible bases for the fluent form of the disorder that are consistent with the model, but they are outside the scope of the present implementation. Third, the method of damaging different proportions of units or connections may account for the different degrees of impairment exhibited by patients categorized as surface dyslexic.

Finally, the simulations illustrate the need to understand reading disorders in terms of explicit computational models of normal performance. Many surface dyslexics exhibit so-called "visual" errors, in which a word such as *spy* is read as *shy*. Our simulations of surface dyslexia produce these types of errors, but, importantly, they do not derive from a "visual" impairment. Rather, they derive from the same type of damage as "regularization" errors, such as *have/hevl*.

This case illustrates the difficulty of inferring the locus of an impairment solely from the pattern of impaired behavior. By attempting to derive impaired performance from the computational model of skilled performance, we found that errors often thought to arise from a visual processing impairment may in fact have a very different basis (see also Hinton & Shallice, 1991).

In sum, the preliminary attempts to model surface dyslexia suggest that our approach to reading impairments holds great promise. Our long-term goal is to extend our model to account for a broad range of acquired dyslexic disorders in terms of different types of damage to different components.

CONCLUSIONS

My principal goal in this chapter has been to convey some of the interest of an approach to understanding reading that emphasizes the role of computational modeling. The successes of the model, in simulating detailed aspects of normal and impaired performance, give us some reason to think we are on the right track. At the same time, I have tried, throughout the chapter, to be clear about limitations of the current implementation. I think that it comes as a shock to many people who are not intimately involved with this kind of research to realize that every computational model is, in a very real sense, false. By design, every model is limited in scope; these limitations ensure that at some level of detail the model will fail to behave correctly. Computational models are thus both easier and harder to evaluate than other types of theories in psychology; easier in the sense that because the model generates a broad range of specific behaviors it is easier to generate testable predictions about human performance; harder in the sense that it is necessary to distinguish real flaws in the model from cases in which its performance degrades for theoretically uninteresting reasons related to limitations in scope (see Seidenberg, 1989; Seidenberg & McClelland, 1990, for discussion). Despite these additional complications, I believe that this approach has begun to contribute to a deeper understanding of reading and reading disorders.

ACKNOWLEDGMENTS

I thank my colleagues James L. McClelland and Karalyn E. Patterson for input on this chapter.

REFERENCES

Adams, M. J. (1990). *Beginning to read: Thinking and learning about print.* Cambridge, MA: MIT Press.

Allport, D. A. (1985). Distributed memory, modular subsystems and dysphasia. In S. K. Newman & R. Epstein (Eds.), *Current perspectives in dysphasia.* (pp. 32–60) Edinburgh: Churchill Livingstone.

Balota, D., & Chumbley, J. (1984). Are lexical decisions a good measure of lexical access? The role of frequency in the neglected decision stage. *Journal of Experimental Psychology: Human Perception and Performance, 10,* 340–357.

Balota, D. A., & Chumbley, J. I. (1985). The locus of the word frequency effect in the pronunciation task: Lexical access and/or production? *Journal of Memory and Language, 24,* 89–106.

Baluch, B., & Besner, D. (in press). Visual word recognition: Evidence for strategic control of lexical and nonlexical routines in oral reading. *Journal of Experimental Psychology: Learning, Memory and Cognition.*

Besner, D., Twilley, L., McCann, R., & Seergobin, K. (1990). On the connection between connectionism and data: Are a few words necessary? *Psychological Review, 97,* 432–446.

Breitmeyer, B. G. (1978). Disinhibition in metacontrast masking of vernier acuity targets: Sustained channels inhibit transient channels. *Vision Research, 18,* 1401–1405.

Brown, G. D. A. (1987). Resolving inconsistency: A computational model of word naming. *Journal of Memory and Language, 26,* 1–23.

Bub, D., Cancelliere, A., & Kertesz, A. (1985). Whole-word and analytic translation of spelling to sound in a non-semantic reading. In K. E. Patterson, J. C. Marshall, & M. Coltheart (Eds.), *Surface dyslexia: Neuropsychological and cognitive studies of phonological reading* (pp. 15–34). Hillsdale, NJ: Lawrence Erlbaum Associates.

Caramazza, A. (1984). The logic of neuropsychological research and the problem of patient classification. *Brain and Language, 21,* 9–20.

Carr, T. H., & Pollatsek, A. (1985). Recognizing printed words: A look at current models. In D. Besner, T. G. Waller, & G. E. MacKinnon (Eds.), *Reading research: Advances in theory and practice* (Vol. 5, pp. 1–82). Orlando, FL: Academic Press.

Cohen, J. D., Dunbar, K., & McClelland, J. L. (1990). On the control of automatic processes: A parallel distributed processing account of the Stroop effect. *Psychological Review, 97,* 332–361.

Coltheart, M. (1987). Functional architecture of the language-processing system. In M. Coltheart, G. Sartori, & R. Job (Eds.), *Cognitive neuropsychology of language.* (pp. 1–25). Hillsdale, NJ: Lawrence Erlbaum Associates.

Derouesné, J., & Beauvois, M. F. (1979). Phonological processing in reading: Data from alexia. *Journal of Neurology, Neurosurgery and Psychiatry, 42,* 1125–1132.

Frost, R., Katz, L., & Bentin, S. (1987). Strategies for visual word recognition and orthographical depth. *Journal of Experimental Psychology: Human Perception and Performance, 13,* 104–115.

Galaburda, A. M., Sherman, G. F., Rosen, G. D., Aboitiz, F., & Geshwind, N. (1985). Developmental dyslexia: Four consecutive patients with cortical anomalies. *Annals of Neurology, 18,* 222–223.

Glushko, R. J. (1979). The organization and activation of orthographic knowledge in reading aloud. *Journal of Experimental Psychology: Human Perception and Performance, 5,* 674–691.

Hinton, G., & Shallice, T. (1991). Lesioning a connectionist network: Investigations of acquired dyslexia. *Psychological Review, 98,* 74–95.

Hynd, G., & Semrud-Clikeman, M. (1989). Dyslexia and brain morphology. *Psychological Bulletin, 106,* 447–482.

Jared, D., McRae, K., & Seidenberg, M. S. (1990). The basis of consistency effects in word naming. *Journal of Memory and Language, 29,* 687–715.

Jared, D., & Seidenberg, M. S. (1990). Naming multisyllabic words. *Journal of Experimental Psychology: Human Perception and Performance, 16,* 92–105.

Jared, D., & Seidenberg, M. S. (in press). Does visual word recognition proceed from spelling to sound to meaning? *Journal of Experimental Psychology: General.*

Jorm, A. F., & Share, D. L. (1983). Phonological recoding and reading acquisition. *Applied Psycholinguistics, 4,* 103–147.

Liberman, I. Y., & Shankweiler, D. (1979). Speech, the alphabet, and teaching to read. In L. B. Resnick and P. A. Weaver (Eds.), *Theory and practice of early reading, Vol. 2* (pp. 109–132). Hillsdale, NJ: Lawrence Erlbaum Associates.

Liberman, I., Shankweiler, D., Fischer, F. W., & Carter, B. (1974). Reading and the awareness of linguistic segments. *Journal of Experimental Child Psychology, 18,* 201–212.

Lovegrove, W., Martin, F., & Slaghuis, W. (1986). A theoretical and experimental case for a visual deficit in specific reading disability. *Cognitive Neuropsychology, 2,* 225–267.

Marshall, J. C., & Newcombe, F. (1973). Patterns of paralexia: A psycholinguistic approach. *Journal of Psycholinguistic Research, 2,* 175–179.

McCann, R., & Besner, D. (1987) Reading pseudohomophones: Implications for models of pronunciation assembly and the locus of word-frequency effects in naming. *Journal of Experimental Psychology: Human Perception and Performance, 13,* 14–24.

McCann, R., Besner, D., & Davelaar, E. (1988). Word recognition and identification: Do word-frequency effects reflect lexical access? *Journal of Experimental Psychology: Human Perception and Performance, 13,* 693–706.

McClelland, J. L. (1979). On the time relations of mental processes: An examination of systems of processing in cascade. *Psychological Review, 86,* 287–330.

McClelland, J. L., & Rumelhart, D. E. (1981). An interactive activation model of context effects in letter perception: Part 1. An account of basic findings. *Psychological Review, 88,* 375–407.

McRae, K., Jared, D., & Seidenberg, M. S. (1990). On the roles of frequency and lexical access in word naming. *Journal of Memory and Language, 29,* 43–65.

Meyer, D. E., Schvaneveldt, R. W., & Ruddy, M. G. (1974). Functions of graphemic and phonemic codes in visual word recognition. *Memory and Cognition, 2,* 309–321.

Monsell, S. (1987). On the relation between lexical input and output pathways for speech. In D. A. Allport, D. G. MacKay, W. Prinz, & E. Scheerer (Eds.), *Language perception and production: Relationships among listening, speaking, reading, and writing* (p. 273–311). San Diego, CA: Academic Press.

Monsell, S., Doyle, M. C., & Haggard, P. N. (1989). Effects of frequency on visual word recognition tasks: Where are they? *Journal of Experimental Psychology: General, 118,* 43–71.

Morrison, F. (1984). Reading disability: A problem in rule learning and word decoding. *Developmental Review, 4,* 36–47.

Morton, J. (1969). Interaction of information in word recognition. *Psychological Review, 76,* 165–178.

Paap, K. R., McDonald, J. E., Schvaneveldt, R. W., & Noel, R. W. (1987). Frequency and pronounceability in visually presented naming and lexical decision tasks. In M. Coltheart (Ed.), *Attention and performance XII: The psychology of reading* (pp. 221–243). Hillsdale, NJ: Lawrence Erlbaum Associates.

Paap, K., & Noel, R. (in press). Dual-route models of print to sound: Still a good horse race. *Psychological Research.*

Patterson, K. E., & Coltheart, V. (1987). Phonological processes in reading: A tutorial review. In M. Coltheart (Ed.), *Attention and performance XII: The psychology of reading* (pp. 421–447). London: Lawrence Erlbaum Associates.

Patterson, K. E., Marshall, J. C., & Coltheart, M. (1985). *Surface dyslexia: Neuropsychological and cognitive studies of phonological reading.* Hillsdale, NJ: Lawrence Erlbaum Associates.

Patterson, K. E., Seidenberg, M. S., & McClelland, J. L. (1989). Connections and disconnections: Dyslexia in a computational model of reading. In P. Morris (Ed.), *Parallel distributed processing: Implications for psychology and neuroscience* (pp. 131–181). London, England: Oxford University Press.

Peterson, S. E., Fox, P. T., Snyder, A. Z., & Raichle, M. E. (1990). Activation of extrastriate and frontal cortical areas by visual words and word-like stimuli. *Science, 249,* 1041–1043.

Rumelhart, D. E., Hinton, G. E., & Williams, R. J. (1986). Learning internal representations by error propogation. In D. Rumelhart & J. McLelland (Eds.), *parallel distributed processing: Explorations in the microstructure of cognition* (Vol. 1, pp. 318–362). Cambridge, MA: MIT Press.

Rumelhart, D. E., & McClelland, J. L., Eds. (1986). *Parallel distributed processing: Explorations in the microstructure of cognition* (Vol. 1). Cambridge, MA: MIT Press.

Seidenberg, M. S. (1985). The time course of information activation and utilization in visual word recognition. In D. Besner, T. G. Waller, & G. E. MacKinnon (Eds.), *Reading research: Advances in theory and practice* (Vol. 5, pp. 200–252). Orlando, FL: Academic Press.

Seidenberg, M. S. (1988). Cognitive neuropsychology and language: The state of the art. *Cognitive Neuropsychology, 5,* 403–426.

Seidenberg, M. S. (1989). Word recognition and naming: A computational model and its implications. In W. D. Marlsen-Wilson (Ed.), *Lexical representation and process* (pp. 25–73). Cambridge, MA: MIT Press.

Seidenberg, M. S., Bruck, M., Fornarolo, G., & Backman, J. (1986). Word recognition skills of poor and disabled readers: Do they necessarily differ? *Applied Psycholinguistics, 6,* 161–180.

Seidenberg, M. S., & McClelland, J. L. (1989). A distributed, developmental model of word recognition and naming. *Psychological Review, 96,* 523–568.

Seidenberg, M. S., & McClelland, J. L. (1990). More words but still no lexicon: Reply to Besner et al. *Psychological Review, 97,* 447–452.

Seidenberg, M. S., & Petitto, L. A. (1987). Communication, symbolic communication, and language. *Journal of Experimental Psychology: General, 116,* 279–287.

Seidenberg, M. S., & Tanenhaus, M. K. (1979). Orthographic effects on rhyme monitoring. *Journal of Experimental Psychology: Human Learning and Memory, 5,* 546–554.

Seidenberg, M. S., Waters, G. S., Barnes, M. A., & Tanenhaus, M. K. (1984). When does irregular spelling or pronunciation influence word recognition? *Journal of Verbal Learning and Verbal Behavior, 23,* 383–404.

Shallice, T., & Warrington, E. K. (1980). Single and multiple component central dyslexic syndromes. In M. Coltheart, K. E. Patterson, & J. C. Marshall (Eds.), *Deep dyslexia* (pp. 119–145). London: Routledge & Kegan Paul.

Shulman, H. G., Hornak, R., & Sanders, E. (1978). The effects of graphemic, phonetic, and semantic relationships on access to lexical structures. *Memory and Cognition, 6,* 115–123.

Smith, F. (1971). *Understanding reading.* New York: Holt, Rinehart & Winston.

Tanenhaus, M. K., Flanigan, H., & Seidenberg, M. S. (1980). Orthographic and phonological activation in auditory and visual word recognition. *Memory and Cognition, 8,* 513–520.

Taraban, R., & McClelland, J. L. (1987). Conspiracy effects in word pronunciation. *Journal of Memory and Language, 26,* 608–631.

Turvey, M. T., Feldman, L. B., & Lukatela, G. (1984). The Serbo-Croatian orthography constrains the reader to a phonologically analytic strategy. In L. Henderson (Ed.), *Orthographies and reading* (pp. 81–89). London: Erlbaum.

Van Orden, G. C. (1987). A ROWS is a ROSE: Spelling, sound, and reading. *Memory and Cognition, 15,* 181–198.

Van Orden, G. C., Johnston, J. C., & Hale, B. L. (1988). Word identification in reading proceeds from spelling to sound to meaning. *Journal of Experimental Psychology: Learning, Memory, and Cognition, 14,* 371–386.

Van Orden, G. C., Pennington, B. F., & Stone, G. O. (1990). Word identification in reading and the promise of a subsymbolic psycholinguistics. *Psychological Review, 97,* 488–522.

Vellutino, F. R. (1979). *Dyslexia.* Cambridge, MA: MIT Press.

Venezky, R. L. (1970). *The structure of English orthography.* The Hague: Mouton.

10 Identifying the Causes of Reading Disability

Donald Shankweiler
Stephen Crain
Susan Brady
Haskins Laboratories, New Haven, CT

Paul Macaruso
Massachusetts General Hospital

Everyone is aware of the hazards of determining cause and effect from observations that are essentially correlational. This thorny problem has surfaced recently in discussions of the interpretation of research on reading disability. It has been argued that the issue of whether causation can be inferred from obtained differences between good and poor readers turns on the selection of an appropriate control group. A much discussed proposal advocates the abandonment of designs that compare groups of children who differ in reading ability but who are matched in chronological age (the CA match control group). Instead, the critics would substitute comparison groups of children who are at the same reading level (RL) but who differ in age (Backman, Mamen, & Ferguson, 1984; Bryant & Bradley, 1985; Bryant & Goswami, 1986). Although we grant that the RL match control group allows one to determine the direction of causation in some cases, we do not agree that it is always the best approach to understanding reading disability. Comparisons of groups matched on chronological age can also yield knowledge of causation if certain conditions are met.

In our opinion, the debate in the reading research literature over the conditions that must be satisfied in order to permit inferences about causation has focused too narrowly on research method. Previous discussion has overlooked two critical ingredients that jointly constrain the direction of causation and thereby enable correlational data obtained from CA match designs to address questions about the causes of reading disorder. One ingredient is an articulated set of hypotheses that ties reading to an explicit model of language processing. The other prerequisite is a convergent pattern of results. The findings of individual studies, viewed piecemeal, are often ambiguous. Because the criticisms of research using age matched groups have generally been directed to studies in isolation, they have sometimes failed to take into account the full weight of the evidence. Our response to the criticisms is based on discussion of an interlocking set of research findings that support a specific model of language processing and a set of assumptions about the special demands of reading.

Here is the way we proceed. In the next section we summarize the arguments advanced by Bryant and his colleagues against matching on chronological age. Then, we present the case for the general usefulness of the CA match control group in testing hypotheses about the causes of reading disorder. We outline some assumptions about the reading process and we show how CA match comparisons can be used to narrow the range of causal factors. This section also considers the possibility, raised by Bryant and his colleagues, that differences between good and poor readers may be caused by differences in reading experience. The remainder of the paper is a general discussion of the problems of subject selection in research on reading. Included is a discussion of the role of the control group in assessing the significance of individual variation among poor readers. Lastly, we consider the uses of intelligence tests and educational achievement tests in selection of appropriately matched groups.

THE CASE AGAINST MATCHING ON CHRONOLOGICAL AGE

At issue is whether the CA match control group can, in principle, allow positive inferences to be drawn about the causes of reading disability. In considering this issue, our first task is to summarize the case that has been made against the CA match control group and to examine the alternative that has been recommended.

In a CA match design, good and poor readers (selected by standard reading tests) are matched in chronological age and, in addition, on measures such as IQ, oral vocabulary, etc. In an RL match design, poor readers are compared with younger normal readers who are performing at the same reading level. Bryant and Goswami (1986) concluded that positive and negative results have different values depending on which control group is used. Their argument went as follows: Consider first the interpretation of positive results obtained with a CA match design, where poor readers are inferior to good readers on some cognitive ability. Here it is impossible to distinguish cause from effect: the differences on the criterion measure(s) may have been a consequence, not a cause, of the differences in reading ability. That is to say, differences in reading experience might be the cause of obtained differences on a variety of abilities that could conceivably benefit from such experience. Thus, a positive result with a CA match comparison group is, in principle, uninformative. On the other hand, if the two groups were matched on reading level at the outset, differences in level of reading skill could not be the cause of any obtained differences between the groups on other measures. Therefore, obtaining a positive result with the RL match design can identify causes of poor reading.

It remains to consider the interpretation of negative results, when no between-group differences are obtained. Here, too, according to Bryant and Goswami, interpretation of the findings hinges on the choice of control group. In this case, negative results with CA match controls can be interpreted in causal terms, but only in a limited way, by ruling out the causal significance of any factor that failed to distinguish subjects who differ sharply in reading level. With an RL match control, negative results are inherently ambiguous. The failure to find differences could mean that the tested ability is irrelevant. Alternatively, the factor could be relevant to reading acquisition, but the older poor reader group might compensate for its absence by adopting a substitute strategy.

The principal implication that Bryant and Goswami drew from their analysis is that the CA match can be used only to rule out a factor's causal role in poor reading; it cannot affirmatively establish that a factor plays a causal role. In order to make such an inference, positive results with an RL match must be obtained. If this argument is valid, it would undermine many established hypotheses in the field—in effect, all hypotheses that are based on positive results with the CA match design.

An example chosen by Bryant and Goswami to illustrate the argument against the CA match design is the hypothesis that special limitations in working memory can cause reading problems. They rejected the inference, from use of the CA match design, that poor working memory is one of the causes of reading disability. They claimed that causation could just as well go in the opposite direction: ". . . the successful readers could have better STMs because of their greater experience of reading" (1986, p. 102). We will refer to this as the *reading experience hypothesis*. On this hypothesis, the problem with CA match designs is that they allow two things to vary: Reading experience and working memory. Although we agree that there is nothing in the empirical data per se that argues for the direction of causation, we contend that the direction of causation becomes readily traceable when the experimental findings are viewed from the perspective of a set of assumptions about reading and its relation to language acquisition. We illustrate how this theoretical framework constrains inference making by ruling out the reading experience hypothesis in some cases in which it might be invoked.

THE USE OF AGE MATCHED CONTROLS IN TESTING HYPOTHESES ABOUT READING

We begin by stating the assumptions that have guided our search for causative factors. Several considerations led us to believe that the origins of reading disorder should be sought in the language domain, rather than in some other cognitive system or in a general disruption of cognitive function. First is the observation that reading is largely parasitic upon primary language acquisition. The child who is learning to read does not have to acquire a new communication system, but can rely on preexisting language structures that have long been exploited in spoken communication by the time instruction in reading begins. To be sure, reading experience may modify the language of the reader. However, we contend that such modifications are acquired only by skilled readers and are limited to such secondary aspects of language as the enrichment of lexical knowledge and the enhancement of metalinguistic skills. Later, we indicate why we reject the possibility that the primary grammatical structure of language, including phonology, syntax, and semantics, could be acquired through reading. (For discussion of primary and secondary language abilities, see Liberman, 1983; Mattingly, 1984).

Many empirical findings support the contention that the source of the difficulties of reading is in the language domain. Reading difficulties do not reflect a general deficit in perceiving visual or auditory patterns, or in forming analytic strategies. For example, poor readers are impaired relative to good readers in the identification of acoustic stimuli masked by noise, but only when the stimuli are speech. Other kinds of sounds presented in noise are as accurately perceived by poor readers as by good readers (Brady, Shankweiler, & Mann, 1983). Moreover, poor readers have deficiencies in language-specific tasks. For instance, poor readers are reliably worse than good readers in memory for pictures of familiar objects, letters, nonsense syllables, and strings of unrelated words, but they are equivalent to good readers in memory for unfamiliar faces and nonsense designs (Katz, Shankweiler, & Liberman, 1981; Liberman, Mann, Shankweiler, & Werfelman, 1982; Liberman, Shankweiler, Liberman, Fowler, & Fischer, 1977).

From the earliest of these studies the same basic design was used: A group of poor readers was compared to a CA matched control group on parallel verbal and nonverbal tasks. These studies revealed positive differences between reader groups that could be attributed to poor readers' limitations in processing verbal materials, but negative findings when they were tested on materials that do not lend themselves to linguistic coding. Thus, we see a consistent pattern of positive and negative results indicating that the deficits of poor readers are language-related.

From further consideration of the internal organization of the language faculty, and the nature of alphabetic writing, we and our colleagues at Haskins Laboratories were led to expect that some limitation in the management of phonological structures might be the specific source of reading difficulty. It seemed obvious that mastery of reading requires the learner to discover how the segments of the orthography represent the phonological segments of the language. It also seemed obvious that until the learner has explicit awareness of phonological structure, it would prove impossible to grasp the orthographic code, let alone become skilled in its use.

In view of this, we asked whether explicit awareness of phonological structure is a natural consequence of knowing a language. Research beginning in the early 1970s showed that the answer is no. Preschool children, and even adult illiterates, find it difficult to abstract and manipulate phonological segments of spoken words (Liberman, 1973; Liberman, Shankweiler, Fischer, & Carter, 1974; Morais, Cary, Alegria, & Bertelson, 1979; Rozin & Gleitman, 1977). These facts have been confirmed repeatedly in research based on readers of several languages. Moreover, children who are poor readers typically have greater difficulty in analyzing spoken words into their constituent phonemes than those who are good readers. Indeed, measures of phonological awareness have emerged time and again as the best predictors of reading success (see Bryant & Bradley, 1985; Liberman & Shankweiler, 1985; Stanovich, 1986, for reviews). Evidence that the source of the difficulty is linguistic and does not stem from the general cognitive demands of these phonological tasks comes from several studies that fail to find reader group differences on nonlinguistic counterparts to these tasks (Morais, Cluytens, & Alegria, 1984; Pratt & Brady, 1988).

In addition to phonological awareness, we hypothesized that another prerequisite is needed to forge a link between the orthography and phonological structure: An efficient verbal working memory. If the fault in reading disorder is in phonological processes, one natural consequence would be that the affected individual would have special limitations in working memory. It has been known for many years that this form of memory relies heavily on coding based on phonological structure. We refer here to the classic findings of Conrad and others (Conrad, 1964; 1972; Baddeley, 1966) that confusions even of visual stimulus items in short-term memory typically have a phonological basis and are not based on visual or semantic similarity. Evidence from several laboratories finds that poor readers are inferior to their age-matched peers on memory tests that require them to retain the order of occurrence of a series of words or objects that can be named (Shankweiler, Liberman, Mark, Fowler, & Fischer, 1979; Wagner & Torgesen, 1987). As we saw, differences in recall have been obtained with a variety of verbal materials, including spoken sentences, but not with materials that cannot readily be coded phonologically.[1] These findings were interpreted, at

---

[1]Subsequent research investigated implications of the view that the problems of the largest group of poor readers are phonologic in origin. Examination of the nature of errors on verbal memory tasks revealed that both good and poor readers use phonetic coding in preference to some other strategy, but poor readers do so less accurately (Brady, Mann, & Schmidt, 1987). Further studies have supported the phonologic deficit hypothesis. For example, poor readers were found to be less accurate than good readers in articulation of dictated words. Performance on the articulation task correlated with measures of verbal memory, but not with measures of nonverbal spatial memory (Brady, 1986). In addition, studies of object naming uncovered deficits that, again, reflect deficient phonological processing (Denckla & Rudel, 1976; Katz, 1985; Wolf, 1981). For instance, even when the subjects were matched in vocabulary knowledge, differences between the reader groups in access to the phonological properties of particular words in the mental lexicon were evident (Katz, 1985). In these investigations we find, again, that a combination of positive and negative results has succeeded in further pinpointing the source of poor readers' deficits.

the time, as reflecting deficiencies of poor readers in verbal short-term memory buffer capacity (our more recent view is discussed below). Given deficient performance on various measures of verbal memory, a beginning reader with a severe limitation in storage capacity would have a double handicap. An abnormal limitation of capacity would impede learning the orthographic code, and would also hobble other on-line reading processes that make heavy demands on phonological storage (see also Baddeley, 1986; Perfetti, 1985).

So far we have reviewed the guiding assumptions and some of the major findings of our research. We have indicated how designs that employ CA match controls were used to narrow down the possible explanations of reading disability. The most basic application of the CA match was to show that the problems of the poor reader are in the language domain and not in visual processing or in some other cognitive domain. A second application was to show that the source of the problem lies at the phonological level of language. Children who fail to make expected progress in reading typically have difficulties in two phonologically-related areas: They have difficulty in becoming aware of the internal structure of words and they have special limitations in verbal working memory. Other findings, however, have led some researchers to question whether all the problems of disabled readers can be explained in these terms. In addition to several differences between good and poor readers that clearly implicate the phonological component of language, the reader group differences extend to spoken sentences as well. These findings have been confirmed repeatedly in experiments in which subjects are asked to act out sentence meanings with toy figures (e.g., Byrne, 1981; Mann, Shankweiler, & Smith, 1984).

Reading and Sentence Comprehension: A Problem of Interpretation

Because good and poor readers have been found to differ in comprehension of some spoken sentences, it became an important priority of our research to find out whether the observed differences were related to their differences in phonological processing. The conclusion we have reached is that both problems are tied together—the comprehension failures of poor readers are derived from their limitations in phonological processing. In reaching this conclusion, we directly confront the claim of Bryant and his colleagues that positive differences between age matched good and poor readers do not permit us to draw inferences about the direction of causation. Our research shows that this claim is unwarranted in light of the evidence we have gathered. In our view, the differences between reader groups in spoken language comprehension are best explained as a response by the language processing system to a deficit at the phonological level. If this explanation is correct, the direction of causation has been assigned: The poor readers in our studies were handicapped in several aspects of the reading process from the very beginning, because the phonological processing capabilities that they brought to the reading task were inadequate. We call this proposal the *processing limitation hypothesis* (PLH).

There is another point of view, however. Poor readers may lag behind good readers of the same age in the acquisition of certain linguistic structures, and they may fail to comprehend those structures in tests of spoken language understanding. We refer to this as the *structural lag hypothesis* (SLH). This hypothesis supposes that children who are poor readers are delayed relative to good readers in the acquisition of critical language structures. The structural lag hypothesis is tied to an implicit assumption about the course of language acquisition, as well as to an assumption about linguistic complexity. It supposes that some linguistic structures develop before others, with the course of development determined by the relative complexity of the structures. Our comments are directed to a version of the structural lag hypothesis that holds that some poor readers suffer from a developmental lag in syntactic knowledge. This version of the SLH appears to draw support from some classical studies in language acquisition that find the late emergence of certain constructions, for example, relative clauses, temporal terms, and adjectives with exceptional control properties (see C. Chomsky, 1969; Clark, 1970; Sheldon, 1974).

On the SLH, the differences between good and poor readers in spoken language comprehension are completely separate from their differences on phonological processing. If this position were upheld, the direction of causation would remain an open question. It would then be appropriate to ask, further, whether the poor readers had failed to acquire some of the structures needed for comprehension, or whether the good readers had advanced beyond their age-matched classmates because their greater experience in reading has enhanced their knowledge of critical grammatical structures. Either eventuality poses a challenge to our efforts to tie together the observed differences between good and poor readers at the sentence level and at the level of the phonology.

We will now sketch how we have countered these challenges to the processing limitation hypothesis (PLH). First we explain how the architecture of the language apparatus relates failures of spoken language comprehension to limitations in processing arising at the phonological level. Then we show how our research has succeeded in ruling out the alternative account (the SLH), which proposes that the differences between good and poor readers in spoken language are unrelated to their differences in phonological processing. The last step in the argument takes up the broader issue of the possible role of reading experience in explaining reader group differences.

To begin, let us explain how the failure of poor readers to interpret spoken sentences correctly is expected, given the conception of the language apparatus that underlies the PLH. We have long held the position that the language apparatus forms a biologically coherent system that is isolated from other parts of the cognitive and perceptual apparatus. In contemporary terms, language forms a "module" (Fodor, 1983). Our present view extends the notion of modularity, by differentiating subcomponents of the language faculty. As we conceive of it, the language module is composed of a hierarchy of structures and processors, each of which functions according to its own properties. The structures include the phonology, lexicon, syntax, and semantics. Each level of structure is served by a special-purpose parsing mechanism. A parser consists of algorithms for accessing rules used in assigning structural representations, as well as mechanisms for resolving ambiguities. Although the operations of the various components are interleaved in time, permitting the system as a whole to function "on-line," the flow of information between levels is tightly regulated. This control process is one of the chief functions of the working memory system, in our view. The strongest position, and the one that we adhere to in the absence of counterevidence, is that information transfer within the language apparatus is unidirectional, beginning at the lowest level with phonological processing and proceeding upward to the syntactic and semantic parsers (for discussion, see Crain & Steedman, 1985; Fodor, 1983; Forster, 1979; Shankweiler & Crain, 1986).

Because information flows bottom-up through the system, the first task of the "executive component" of working memory is to relay the partial results of the phonological analysis of the linguistic input upward through the system, thereby freeing this component for analysis of subsequent material. A low-level deficit in processing phonological information would create a bottleneck that would impede the transfer of information to higher levels in the system (for related discussion, see Crain, Shankweiler, Macaruso, & Bar-Shalom, 1990; Perfetti, 1985; Shankweiler & Crain, 1986). Our current view, then, gives less weight to limitations of buffer capacity, as such, than to limitations in the efficient transfer of phonological information to the higher components of the verbal working memory system in on-line language processing.

Poor readers, in this processing limitation view, should have difficulty comprehending spoken sentences that place heavy demands on working memory, but should be the equals of good readers on all other sentences, regardless of inherent complexity. Appealing to modularity principles, the PLH supposes that the acquisition of primary language structures is essentially complete by the time instruction in reading and writing begins. Early mastery of complex syntax is seen to be a consequence of the innate specification of many syntactic principles that either come "prewired" or are subject to rigid system-internal innate constraints on grammar construction (see, e.g., Chomsky, 1965, 1981). Because syntactic structures are largely built into the blueprint for language acquisition, it follows that inherent complexity of grammatical structures, as such, should not be a source of reader group differences (Crain & Shankweiler, 1988). Poor readers will be at a disadvantage, however, in contexts that stress verbal working memory. Whether the materials are presented by eye or by ear, their performance will reflect their working memory liabilities (Liberman & Shankweiler, 1985; Mann et al., 1984; Shankweiler & Crain, 1986).

Testing between the SLH and the PLH

As we saw, if the PLH is correct, the direction of causation between phonological limitations and reading difficulties can be assigned, but the issue is open if the SLH is correct. It is essential to show, then, how we have used CA matched controls to test between the PLH and its rival, the SLH.

The SLH and the PLH are broad hypotheses about the factors that make reading difficult to learn and about the characteristics that distinguish children who are making normal progress from those who are experiencing reading failures in the early grades. Both hypotheses view reading as building on earlier language acquisition, and both predict that children who are disabled in reading will also manifest specific deficits in the comprehension of spoken language. Despite these commonalities, the hypotheses ultimately diverge. First, on the SLH, the putative syntactic deficits are independent of further deficits the poor readers may have with phonological structures. By allowing at least two basic deficits in poor readers, this hypothesis abandons a unitary explanation of reading disability. The PLH, on the other hand, attempts to tie together the entire symptom complex of poor readers as a consequence of deficient phonological processing.

A second difference between the hypotheses concerns the possible role of reading experience. The PLH does not envision a role for reading experience in the acquisition of syntactic knowledge. In contrast, the SLH can readily accommodate the supposition that reading and writing contribute the experience needed for complete mastery of late-emerging syntactic structures. As we saw, there is evidence that several of these late emerging structures are more difficult in spoken language tasks for poor readers than for good readers (e.g., Byrne, 1981; Stein, Cairns, & Zurif, 1984). This evidence has been interpreted as indicating late maturation in poor readers of spoken-language competence, as befits the proposal that poor readers have not yet encountered the requisite data for complete acquisition of the finer points of syntax. The PLH explains these phenomena in other terms.

In the foregoing sections, we demonstrated how a combination of positive and negative results in studies using a CA match design allowed us to isolate the source of several symptoms of reading disability, most generally to the language domain, and subsequently, to the phonological component of language. We discussed how the sentence comprehension failures of poor readers could also occur as a by-product of deficiencies in phonological processing. We saw, though, that the SLH places in jeopardy the suggestion that all of the symptoms of reading disability arise from a deficit in phonological processing.

It is important to appreciate the role that CA match comparisons have played in recent research to test between the alternative explanations of the sentence comprehension problems of poor readers. The studies we have conducted called for pairs of tasks that vary memory load, while keeping syntactic structure constant. If reading disability stems from a structural lag, then children who have reading problems should perform poorly on both tasks. But according to the PLH, poor readers should have greater difficulty than their age-matched controls only in tasks that place heavy demands on working memory, whatever the inherent complexity of the linguistic structure being investigated. When the same test materials are presented in tasks that minimize processing load, poor readers should do as well as good readers. In short, confirmation of the PLH depends on obtaining both positive and negative results.[2] As discussed earlier, the same research strategy of establishing a pattern of positive and negative results was used previously to localize the short-term memory deficit of poor readers to the language domain.

In several studies, this pattern has been identified. We find that on tasks that are demanding of memory resources poor readers tend to make more errors than good readers. Positive differences have been obtained with sentences containing relative clauses (Mann et al., 1984), sentences containing adjectives with special control properties (Byrne, 1981), and sentences with the temporal terms *before* or *after* (Macaruso, Bar-Shalom, Crain & Shankweiler, 1989).[3] However, poor readers have proven to be the equals of good readers on each of these constructions when the same materials are presented in ways that lessen memory load (Crain, 1987; Crain et al., 1990; Smith, Macaruso, Shankweiler & Crain, 1989). Contrary to the expectations of the SLH, in these contexts both reader groups achieve such a high level of accuracy that competence with the constructions under investigation seems guaranteed. In short, the pattern of positive and negative findings clearly favors the PLH. In light of this research, it is apparent that CA match designs can successfully distinguish between these competing hypotheses about the source of spoken language comprehension problems in poor readers.[4]

---

[2]To address the question of a processing limitation versus a structural deficit, it is also useful to examine the pattern of errors across reader groups. Elsewhere we propose that a processing limitation, and not a structural deficit, can be inferred if (i) there is a decrement in performance by poor readers, as compared to good readers, but (ii) both reader groups reveal a similar pattern of errors across sentence-types, and (iii) poor readers manifest a sufficiently high rate of correct response on a subset of the sentences.

[3]It is worth noting that the differences between good and poor readers are greatest on temporal term sentences in which there is a conflict between the order in which the events are mentioned and the order in which they should be executed (e.g., "Move the biggest car after you move the red truck."). This is as expected, since this condition requires the subject to maintain information in memory while awaiting subsequent material.

[4]The research we have discussed has been followed in other studies of good and poor readers. As a further example, we mention an experiment by Fowler (1988), which tested several predictions of the PLH using a CA match design. The pattern of children's responses once again revealed clear-cut intercorrelations between measures of reading and various language-related measures: metaphonological awareness, working memory, and spoken sentence understanding. Children were com-

A Critique of the Reading Experience Hypothesis

We return to the criticisms that have been made against the CA match comparison. The argument against CA match designs turns, as we saw, on the premise that only negative results with this control group can lead to definite conclusions about the sources of reading disability. Positive results, on this argument, cannot justify definitive statements about causation, because limited reading experience may have been the cause of breakdowns in processing, instead of being caused by them (as Bryant and his colleagues suggest). Because the possible contribution of reading experience is at the heart of the criticism against CA match designs, it deserves closer scrutiny. Since we have chosen to allow reading experience to vary, we must show that this factor could not account for differences between reader groups on the dependent measures.

In the preceding section, a pattern of results was presented that defies explanation on the SLH, a hypothesis that was shown to accommodate the view that reading experience contributes to the acquisition of syntax. It remains to generalize the argument by showing how the theoretical framework we have adopted can overcome the challenge posed by other versions of the reading experience hypothesis. No one, to our knowledge, has explicitly worked through the various possible implications of the idea that reading experience creates the between-group differences identified by research. Therefore we limit discussion to possibilities that, in our view, are the most plausible ways in which reading experience could add to the primary language structures and processors involved in spoken language comprehension (keeping in mind, as we acknowledged earlier, that secondary language abilities can surely be expected to profit from reading experience).

First we consider the possibility that reading experience could enhance language understanding in the way Bryant and Goswami (1986) suggested, by improving the efficiency of verbal working memory. We contend, to the contrary, that it is *ad hoc* to invoke reading experience as an explanation of the working memory differences between good and poor readers, once these differences are viewed in conjunction with impairments in language processing found in other populations with working memory deficiencies.

We think it noteworthy that the experimental results we have summarized were predicted by a theoretical framework that is itself supported by a substantial

---

pared on two additional tasks. In the first, subjects performed grammaticality judgments, a task that is presumed to place minimal demands on working memory. A second task asked subjects to change some of the ungrammatical sentences from the judgment task, to make them grammatical. Clearly, correcting grammatical anomalies requires the ability to hold sentences in memory for some time. According to the PLH, both good and poor readers should do equally well on the grammaticality judgment task, but differences should occur on the correction task. This is exactly what was found. Reading ability was not significantly correlated with grammaticality judgments (a negative result) but it was correlated with the ability to make appropriate corrections (a positive result).

literature in other areas of psycholinguistic investigation, including language acquisition, language breakdown in aphasia, and normal sentence processing. We were guided by this theoretical and empirical base in selecting materials and tasks for our studies of reading disability. Thus, in order to provide support for the supposition that the cause of performance failures in poor readers lies within the working memory system, we chose structures that were known to be problematic for other groups with working memory limitations: for example, very young children (Tavakolian, 1981), mentally retarded adults (W. Crain, 1986), aphasics (Caramazza & Berndt, 1985) and, in some cases, even normal adults, when spoken sentences are presented in a way that stresses memory (Crain & Fodor, 1985). As we noted, the findings of studies using a CA match design revealed, in each case, that good and poor readers did not differ in their linguistic knowledge but did differ in their ability to use that knowledge when the task situation stresses working memory. This brings the data from poor readers into line with other populations with notable limitations in verbal working memory.

Impoverished reading experience cannot explain the difficulties that all these groups encounter with the problem structures. In light of the proposal that working memory underlies comprehension failures in each population, it would be arbitrary to invoke reading experience as a causal factor for the poor reader group alone. On the contrary, because these diverse groups share in common severe limitations in verbal working memory, it is reasonable to infer that this is the common cause of their problems in comprehension. In short, the reading experience hypothesis offers an explanation for the observed pattern of positive and negative results in poor readers that is logically possible, but implausible; it can be invoked only at the expense of a unitary account of the processing deficits that afflict diverse populations.[5]

Now we are prepared to deal with a version of the reading experience hypothesis that we sketched earlier—the proposal that differences exist between good and poor readers in grammatical competence, and that these arise from differences in reading experience. Though this idea might have seemed supportable, we have already given empirical grounds to reject it. To these we now present additional grounds to bolster the argument, by considering this hypothesis in the

---

[5]We readily concede that a case can be made, in principle, for the notion that reading experience could improve the efficiency of working memory for language, including spoken material. One possibility (suggested to us by Brian Byrne) is that orthographic imagery, which may be evoked in skilled readers during perception of spoken language, may reinforce the phonological representations evoked by the sound pattern. To the best of our knowledge, however, the critics of the CA match design, who contend that this design cannot establish a causal role for memory deficit in reading disorder, have not sought to argue their case along these lines, or, indeed, to offer any argument for the reading experience hypothesis as applied to working memory. In any case, we have seen that reading experience cannot explain the entire complex of language-related problems of the poor reader.

light of theoretical and empirical findings from language learnability. These findings make it highly implausible to suppose that reading experience can implant new syntactic knowledge. It follows that differences in sentence understanding between good and poor readers are not likely to be the product of reading experience.

To see this, suppose (counterfactually) that we had obtained the pattern of results predicted by the SLH, with the poor readers performing less well both on the task that stresses working memory and on the task that minimizes memory demands. This result would imply that the poor readers were missing critical syntactic structures. It could not reasonably be interpreted, on analogy with Bryant and Goswami's argument regarding working memory, as evidence that reading experience could have been the cause of good readers' superior performance. To draw that conclusion would undermine one of the basic tenets of the modularity perspective, namely the hypothesis that syntactic principles are in large part specified by an innate "Universal Grammar."[6]

The proposal that reading experience can implant primary syntactic knowledge hinges on the assumption that reading experience is better suited than spoken language to promote advancement through the later stages of language acquisition. In contrast, the theory of Universal Grammar requires that readily available data suffice for children's acquisition of syntactic knowledge (Lasnik & Crain, 1985). The necessary linguistic data must be abundant to ensure that each child encounters all experience needed in grammar construction. This means that input from speech sources alone is sufficient for completion of grammar acquisition. If we take the theory of Universal Grammar seriously, it makes little sense to suppose that the acquisition of primary syntactic structures could be enhanced by reading experience, especially at the early stages of reading. And this, in turn, means that it makes little sense to invoke reading experience to explain any disparity between good and poor readers in the acquisition of syntax.

Of course, children's convergence on the adult grammatical system sometimes requires extensive input from the environment. For example, specific experience is required to learn the properties associated with particular lexical items. So it is conceivable that reading experience could instill useful knowledge in these cases. However, for syntax, there is yet another reason to question the hypothesis that reading experience plays a fundamental role. Proponents of Universal Grammar hold that mastery of syntax requires exposure to a particular kind of input from the environment, in the form of sentence-meaning pairs (e.g.,

---

[6]Without postulating innate constraints it would be impossible, in our view, to account for the uniformity of natural languages, or to explain the efficiency of language acquisition in the absence of relevant linguistic experience. Further, there is direct empirical support for several specific properties of Universal Grammar, viz. evidence of young children's adherence to explicit structural constraints despite the "poverty of the stimulus" (e.g., Crain & McKee, 1985; Crain & Nakayama, 1987).

Pinker, 1984; Wexler & Culicover, 1980), or sentence-intonation pairs (Morgan, 1986). This is buttressed by a formal demonstration that "surface" data alone are insufficient to support grammar formation (Hamburger & Wexler, 1973). But acts of reading occur outside of normal social-communicative contexts. Lacking the nonlinguistic supports ordinarily present in spoken discourse, a reader must derive the meaning entirely from information supplied by the printed page. Although a reader may well infer the meaning of an unfamiliar *word* on the basis of what came before, it is highly unlikely that a reader could grasp an unfamiliar *structure* solely on that basis. The information provided by text is altogether too circumscribed to allow a reader to infer the meaning of a sentence with an unfamiliar syntactic structure. If this argument is correct, reading experience cannot supply the requisite data for the acquisition of syntactic principles.

It is time to take stock. We have illustrated the profitable use of CA match designs in testing between specific proposals about the causes of reading disorder. It proved meaningful to infer the direction of causation on the basis of a pattern of converging results that conforms to the predictions of the PLH. The greatest virtue of the PLH, in our view, is its power to explain a host of apparently diverse language deficits that are characteristic of poor readers. Although all of these problems are arguably phonologic in their origin, they manifest themselves as disturbances of both lower-level (phonologic) processes and higher-level (syntactic and semantic) processes. The SLH, in contrast, raises the possibility that poor readers suffer from more than one kind of deficit within the language domain. We noted evidence that at first seemed to support this position, but, ultimately, the PLH gave a better account of the data than the SLH. Finally, we turned to the narrower question of the possible role of reading experience in explaining the observed differences between reader groups. We rejected two versions of the reading experience hypothesis, the notion (suggested by Bryant and Goswami) that reading enhances working memory, and the notion that reading experience is needed to gain full mastery of syntactic structures.

The existence of individual variation among poor readers poses, for many workers in the field, another challenge to the PLH. As we noted, the findings we have reviewed led us tentatively to reject the hypothesis that there are poor readers who meet our selection criteria (see final section) and who suffer from a syntactic deficit in addition to their deficiencies in phonological processing. However, different selection criteria could be adopted, and the groups that are subsequently formed could present different patterns of deficit. To acknowledge the possibility of multiple basic deficits in poor readers and complex dissociations among them is to question, from another point of departure, the adequacy of a unitary explanation for reading disability and to open the issue of subtypes. In the following section, we discuss the role that RL and CA match control groups have played in assessing the significance of individual variations in the symptom picture associated with poor reading.

ROLE OF THE CONTROL GROUP IN ANSWERING
QUESTIONS ABOUT SUBTYPES

In any investigation of poor readers, it is readily apparent that they do not all look alike, even after steps have been taken to exclude from the experiment children with sensory deficits, behavior disorder, and low IQ. What one makes of variations in the symptom picture depends on one's basic assumptions about reading and where the problems ultimately lie. The data we have reviewed so far are in keeping with the phonologic hypothesis we have advanced. It could be argued, however, that the methods of investigation employed in this research have buried the variation by treating as "noise" differences that are potentially causally relevant (see Boder, 1973; Mattis, French, & Rapin, 1975). To maintain a unitary explanation in the face of individual differences, it must be shown that the differences reflect variations along a continuum, not qualitative differences.

In this section we confront the problem of individual variation within the population of disabled readers who meet our selection criteria. In doing this, we take a new tack. Whereas in the studies we considered previously, the spoken language problems of poor readers were the subject of investigation, in this section we focus on the reading process itself and examine how the pattern of errors bears on the question of whether some poor readers employ mechanisms that are not used by normal readers at any level of proficiency.

It is well known that damage to the dominant cerebral hemisphere can result in specific disturbances of reading and writing as well as disturbances of spoken language. When problems in reading and writing predominate in the symptom picture, the term "dyslexia" has standardly been used to designate the condition. Ever since the pioneering investigations of Hinshelwood (1917), resemblances have been reported in the clinical literature between the reading behavior of certain individual children who are experiencing inordinate difficulty in reading and that of brain-damaged adult dyslexics. It is easy to see why such parallels arouse keen interest. Their existence would support the idea that at least some children who fail to learn to read are not only retarded in the rate at which they learn, but they actually are deviant in the approach they adopt. The belief that there are qualitative signs that set the dyslexic child apart from other poor readers has been a recurring theme in the clinical neurological literature on reading problems. It is claimed that the adult syndromes of "deep dyslexia," "phonological dyslexia," and "surface dyslexia" find their counterparts in children (see Coltheart, Patterson & Marshall, 1980). If this claim is valid, it would imply that childhood reading problems, like the adult dyslexias, are causally diverse. An urgent priority for research, therefore, would be to characterize the major syndromes of developmental dyslexia in much the way they have been characterized in adult dyslexia.

The suggestion that syndromes of post-traumatic dyslexia in adults are mirrored in a closely corresponding set of developmental disorders is challenged by Bryant and Impey (1986). These authors employed the RL match design to investigate the question of whether there are special patterns of reading errors associated with some cases of developmental reading problems that set them apart from the normal course of development of reading and align them with particular varieties of acquired dyslexia (as claimed, for example, by Temple & Marshall, 1983, and Coltheart, Masterson, Byng, Prior, & Riddoch, 1983). Bryant and Impey maintain that the errors in question could only be used as a diagnostic for subtyping poor readers if they were found to be truly distinctive; that is, if they are absent in normal, younger children who are reading at the same overall level of proficiency. A similar comparison was made by Treiman and Hirsh-Pasek (1985). Except in these instances, previous comparisons between the reading error pattern of brain damaged adults and those of certain children and adolescents with severe reading difficulties failed to include an additional comparison with normal, but immature and only partially competent readers.

Bryant and Impey supplied the appropriate comparison. They studied a group of normal 10-year-old readers, matched in reading level with a 16-year-old reading-disabled adolescent whom Coltheart et al. (1983) had presented as a paradigm case of surface dyslexia. The normal children, like the reading-disabled adolescent, made many errors in reading orthographically irregular words. Moreover, when Bryant and Impey compared the adolescent's errors in reading and performance on a same-different test of word recognition with those of the normal ten-year-olds reading at grade level, they found much the same pattern of performance. A similar conclusion applied to a case described by Temple and Marshall (1983) as meeting the criteria for phonological dyslexia. Because reading errors have the same distribution in normal younger children, the pattern of errors evinced by each of the "dyslexic" cases cannot be regarded as qualitatively deviant. Bryant and Impey concluded (rightly, in our view) that reports in the literature of resemblances in error pattern between individual children with reading difficulty and reputedly distinct types of acquired dyslexia in adults have not yet brought us closer toward identification of separate causes for different reading problems among children. This is not to deny, of course, the existence of individual differences in reading strategies, which, as Bryant and Impey stress, are evident in both normal and reading-disabled children.

The lesson to be drawn from this application of the RL match bears emphasizing: That variation among cases of reading disability can only be evaluated against a background of variation in normal readers. It is worth noting that research strategies that use a CA match control group can lead to the same conclusion. One type of error to which diagnostic significance has been attached is the tendency to read letter sequences in reverse order and to reverse the orientation of individual letters. The purpose of the studies we are about to review was to evaluate an influential hypothesis concerning directional reversals.

It was claimed by Orton as early as 1925, and then reaffirmed in the literature,

that reversals are pathognomic of a syndrome of developmental reading distur-
bance that has a visual perceptual basis. But the question of the diagnostic
significance of reversals could not be meaningfully evaluated until data were
obtained on the kinds of errors normal children make at different stages of
learning to read. To this end, an early study by researchers at Haskins Laboratories explored the occurrence of reversal errors in an entire class of second-year
pupils in a suburban elementary school (Liberman, Shankweiler, Orlando, Harris, & Berti, 1971) and in a special group of children who had been selected by
members of the staff of a learning disability clinic as the result of screening the
school population in a large metropolitan area (Fischer, Liberman, & Shankweiler, 1978). The latter children met psychoeducational and medical-genetic
criteria for "developmental dyslexia." Although the "dyslexic" children were
somewhat poorer in word recognition than the worst of the poor readers recruited
in the earlier second grade sample, the groups did not differ in the incidence of
reversal errors.[7] Moreover, in both groups, reversals represented only a small
proportion of the total number of reading errors. Vowel errors and errors on
nonreversible consonants constituted the bulk of the misreadings.

The findings on the "dyslexic" children might have led to a different conclusion had the investigators failed to take the further step of assessing reversals in
an unselected school sample. Together, the findings of the two studies support
many other indications that the common error pattern is determined primarily by
the structure of the language and the orthography and not by visual form. Reversal errors among readers of some alphabetic orthographies are essentially a
transient normal phenomenon in the beginning stages of reading acquisition
(Mann, Tobin, & Wilson, 1987; Simner, 1982). Reversals cannot justifiably be
regarded as a symptom of a distinctive type of visual dyslexia. These findings,
together with those of Bryant and Impey, support the contention that there may
not be qualitative differences among children with reading disorder that pertain
specifically to reading. In other words, reading disorder may be on a continuum.
We therefore share with Bryant and his colleagues (Bryant & Bradley, 1985;
Bryant & Impey, 1986) a skeptical attitude regarding the existence of subtypes of
reading disorders.

The findings discussed in this section illustrate that the nature of the research
question may influence the choice of control group. As Backman et al. (1984)
remark, when questions are raised about the nature of the reading process itself,
as opposed to its cognitive underpinnings, the RL design has been successfully
employed. Although the RL design may be especially useful for this purpose, the
CA match design can also be used, as the foregoing research studies illustrate.

---

[7]When each error type was tabulated as a proportion of the total opportunities for an error of that
type to occur, reversals of letter sequence occurred with an incidence of 8 percent among the dyslexic
group and 7 percent among the school group. Similarly, reversals of letter orientation occurred with
an incidence of 12 percent and 13 percent, respectively (Fischer et al., 1978).

Both sets of studies discussed above are alike in their insistence that error patterns in reading disabled individuals must be interpreted with reference to the distribution of errors among normal learners. Research studies employing both RA and CA match designs find the empirical basis for subtypes to be unconvincing. For us, the significance of these negative findings is that they permit us to maintain a unitary hypothesis about the causes of reading disability—that the various manifestations arise from a single source. In the absence of counterevidence, either from studies of spoken language comprehension or from analysis of the error pattern in reading, we are compelled to continue to pursue the empirical consequences of this hypothesis.

In the following paragraphs, we take up several practical concerns that arise in selecting an appropriate control group and consequent problems of interpretation.

ACHIEVING MATCHED GROUPS: IN SEARCH OF PRINCIPLES

Because control groups are essential in testing hypotheses about the nature of reading disorder, it remains to ask whether any guidelines can be proposed for the selection of controls and for matching subjects in research on reading disorders. Obviously, not every objective can be met in a single study. It follows that there will be trade-offs in the use of one or another control measure, and that no absolute prescription can be given. Therefore it is appropriate to examine the consequences of adopting different criteria for matching subjects in research comparing good and poor readers, with some examples from the recent literature.

Controlling for Intelligence

The need for selection criteria in addition to age and reading ability is widely acknowledged, but which measures should we use? The choice of control measures in the research we have conducted has been guided by the aim of distinguishing cases of specific reading disability from reading problems that arise as only one of the manifestations of low intellectual function or insufficient motivation. Since a host of problems in addition to reading are associated with low IQ, any analytic goal would be defeated at the outset if uncontrolled variation in relevant intellectual abilities were allowed (see Jorm, Share, Maclean, & Matthews, 1986; Rutter & Yule, 1975). By equating groups on intelligence as well as on age we minimize the possibility that poor readers are failing to achieve normal progress because of generally poor learning ability. Although reading ability is certainly not independent of general intelligence, it has long been recognized that a significant segment of the population within the normal IQ range has special reading difficulties (see Stanovich, Cunningham, & Feeman, 1984, for a contemporary review).

Having decided to use IQ as a control measure, we are confronted with a range of choices. Should we use a Verbal or Performance IQ measure, or more specialized tests of verbal or nonverbal abilities, such as a vocabulary test or figure drawing? Of course there is no single answer, but the choices we make do influence the results we obtain (see Satz & Fletcher, 1980). On the one hand it could be argued that performance tests are the most appropriate control measures because children with reading disability commonly have additional problems in the language domain that could depress verbal IQ, and thus could introduce bias into the selection procedure. On the other hand, the overlap in IQ measures between disabled and normally achieving readers is so great that it has proved relatively easy to match good and poor readers, at least poor beginning readers, on IQ measures, even verbal IQ measures.

The choice of IQ measure depends on the research question at hand. For example, if we wish to assess abilities that may be affected by vocabulary knowledge, then use of an IQ measure that tests vocabulary knowledge is essential in order to ensure that the poor reading group does not simply comprise children who have impoverished vocabularies, which could lead to spuriously low performance on the comparison measure. Thus, if we wish to use speech perception measures in our comparisons of the phonological abilities of good and poor readers, where it is well known that word knowledge affects performance, the inclusion of a vocabulary test like the Peabody Picture Vocabulary Test is a critical control (Brady et al., 1983). It is equally critical in studies comparing people of different reading ability on lexical retrieval tasks, such as object naming (Katz, 1985; Wolf, 1981). Further benefits of controls for vocabulary are apparent: they guard against the possibility that the poor readers suffer from a general depression in linguistic processing. In addition, a vocabulary measure addresses, in part, the need to distinguish cases of specific reading disability from those that arise as one manifestation of low intelligence. Clearly, any factor that sets a floor or ceiling on spoken language comprehension will have the same effect on what can be interpreted in print. Lastly, measures like the Peabody correlate highly with other linguistic and nonlinguistic indicators of intellectual function, for example, the Wechsler Verbal and Performance tests (as in the WISC-R). Controlling for vocabulary, then, holds these other factors in check, to some degree.

Ideally, one would elect to match pairs of subjects or to equate groups on some measure or measures of intelligence. In our own research, we have usually not attempted to match individual subjects or to select groups in such a way as to equate mean scores for good and poor readers. Instead, exclusionary criteria have been used in the formation of groups by setting minimum standards for inclusion in the study, thereby excluding subjects whose IQs fell above or below the average range. In many of the studies we have done, in which good and poor

readers were selected from ordinary classrooms in suburban schools, the resulting groups did not differ significantly in mean score. However, in most of these
studies the direction of the IQ difference, though nonsignificant, favored the
better readers. Wolford and Fowler (1984), having surveyed the literature, find
this to be a quite general phenomenon. This being so, Crowder (1984) has urged
that any effects of IQ on the criterion measures be removed by statistical means,
such as partial correlation, covariance analyses, or repartitioning subjects into
groups based on IQ and comparing differences on the criterion measures for high
and low IQ with differences based on reader groups.[8]

The use of any test from which an IQ can be derived has been criticized by
those who point out that IQ tests are omnibus devices, and should not be employed when we have the option of using analytic tests that are more homogeneous in content. The point of these criticisms is well taken. That is why we have
typically used a specific verbal IQ measure (e.g., PPVT) that controls for level of
achievement in a relevant facet of spoken language comprehension (see above).
Whether we use general IQ measures or special purpose devices, standardized
tests have a powerful advantage that should not be overlooked: They alone give
us benchmarks that make it possible to compare research findings from different
laboratories, and, to a degree, across languages and writing systems (see Liberman, Liberman, Mattingly, & Shankweiler, 1980).

The problems of controlling for intelligence, not inconsiderable when comparing children of the same age, assume added dimensions of complexity when
persons of different ages are being compared, as in the RL match design. If the
subjects are children at different maturational and educational levels, equating for
IQ means equating on some normalized standard score, which is of course not to
equate on absolute level of performance. To return to an earlier example, suppose
we wish to compare children of different ages on a test of perception of spoken
words. We would very likely be forced to use different test words for the two
groups, even though both were matched on PPVT score, because their actual
vocabulary knowledge would differ. This difficulty is insuperable with the RL
match control group and would surely exclude its use for investigations that seek
to identify underlying cognitive problems. An important virtue of the CA match
design, overlooked in the recent enthusiasm for the RL match, is that it allows us
to employ more stringent criteria in selecting subjects.

---

[8]It has been our experience that when statistical controls were used to remove the effects of IQ
variation, differences between good and poor readers persisted (e.g., Brady et al., 1983; Fowler,
1988). Similarly, when we recombined groups according to IQ, the differences obtained for groups
based on reading ability disappeared (see Mark, Shankweiler, Liberman, & Fowler, 1977; Pratt &
Brady, 1988). The absence of major between-group differences on criterion measures attributable to
IQ is surely a reflection of the subject selection criteria used, and, in our view, is a further vindication
of the CA match control group.

Controlling on Tests of Achievement

Some of the critics of IQ measures would substitute measures of classroom achievement in their place. Given that the intent is to identify cases of specific reading disorder, these critics maintain that if we do not use achievement test criteria, we run the risk of including children who are generally low achievers ("under-achievers" perhaps, if IQ is high). Tests of mathematical achievement have been suggested for this purpose.

We agree that the objective has some merit, but again there are tradeoffs. Indeed, use of an achievement test may backfire by introducing a selection bias of its own. A study by Hall, Wilson, Humphreys, Tinzmann, and Bowyer (1983) is a case in point. The intent of this study was to investigate the hypothesis that poor readers are deficient in verbal working memory and in use of the phonological codes that are believed to support this memory system. These investigators elected to compare good and poor readers who were matched in math achievement on two subtests of the Woodcock-Johnson battery (Woodcock, 1977), one of which was a test of performance on orally presented word problems. This is surely a bad choice in any study whose objective is to test whether poor readers have abnormal limitations in verbal working memory, since word problems inevitably introduce heavy memory demands, particularly when presented orally. Thus, the effect of this selection procedure is to exclude children with special working memory limitations. In view of this it is hardly surprising that Hall et al. failed, in the main, to obtain differences between groups of good and poor readers in letter string and word string recall, and failed to confirm the results of many other investigations that implicate failures of working memory as a causal factor in reading disability.

Assessment of Reading

The success of any study of reading, whatever its design, depends on valid assessment of reading abilities. Here again, as in the case of language and cognitive measures, we are confronted with choices. Given the complexity of reading, we cannot expect to tap all the relevant skills with a single measure. Indeed, as Backman et al. (1984) rightly stressed, to equate groups on one measure of reading may result in great inequalities on other measures. For example, individuals matched on a test of reading isolated words may differ markedly on a test of comprehension. Less obviously, matching on a test of reading words does not guarantee that the subjects will be matched on decoding skills. In standardized word reading tests in common use, the items are drawn from graded reading texts. This results in the inclusion of words chiefly from the "sight word" vocabulary. Given this manner of construction, such tests do not require decoding skills for successful performance. Two children with the same score may have achieved it by use of very different strategies. Thus we cannot know, without further exploration, what skills contributed to performance.

Because extended testing is often impractical, it is important to consider which measures give the most information. Should we use comprehension measures or decoding measures, or some combination of the two? Comprehension measures are often chosen because they are presumed to have greater ecological validity. Although we can agree that the goal of reading is comprehension, we maintain that comprehension measures are unsatisfactory for many purposes. For one thing, measures of reading comprehension are uninterpretable until we have also assessed comprehension of comparable materials presented in spoken form. Because competence in spoken language sets a ceiling on reading, we cannot infer, without further investigation, whether failure to comprehend some portion of printed text can be viewed as a reading problem and not a general language problem.

Decoding measures, on the other hand, are strictly measures of reading. Properly constructed, they assess the ability to read new words never encountered in print before, a skill that is surely necessary for mastery of reading. Moreover, decoding measures show a moderately high correlation with more global reading measures, including comprehension measures (Perfetti & Hogaboam, 1975; Shankweiler & Liberman, 1972; Tunmer & Nesdale, 1985). Research on reading disorder has been handicapped by the absence of an analytic test of decoding. The Decoding Skills Test (Richardson & DiBenedetto, 1986) may prove to fill a long-standing need. It includes both words and pseudowords that sample all the spelling patterns of English.

One of the purported advantages of the RL match design is that it permits one to exclude the possibility that differences in reading experience could account for criterion performance differences between good and poor readers. But, obviously, to equate individuals on some measure or measures of reading is not to equate them in reading experience. Experience in reading might be expected to differ for normal and poor readers (Nagy & Anderson, 1984). At the very least we might expect that disabled readers engage in more (remedial) text reading and less reading for pleasure. But, even for young children from homogeneous family backgrounds, measures of experience with printed material have become available only recently (Cunningham & Stanovich, 1990). The potential for individual differences in reading experience increases as the age spread between subjects and their RL matched controls widens. In view of this, it seems wisest to avoid the assumption of equivalent experience, and instead to follow the more conservative course of restricting claims to comparisons based on measures of decoding performance.

ASSIGNING CAUSES: SOME CONCLUSIONS

Contemporary discussions of research on reading problems have correctly emphasized the importance of the decision an experimenter makes in choosing a control group. When inquiry focuses on reading behavior itself, the RL match comparison has been used to good effect in testing claims about isolable syndromes of reading disorder. The CA match, on the other hand, is often preferable in research aimed at isolating underlying processes. On the practical side, we offered some criteria for ruling out extraneous factors that may be spuriously associated with differences in reading ability, and we pointed to some of the difficulties in achieving suitably matched groups in either design.

Our defense of the CA match comparison has dealt chiefly with the claims of Bryant and his colleagues. Although we agree with many of their conclusions about the nature of reading problems and are cognizant of their important contributions to the research literature, we disagree with the implication that the matter of inferring cause and effect is chiefly a matter of selection of control group. We argued that, on the contrary, what enables us to infer causation is chiefly an articulated set of hypotheses about the reading process.

We began our defense of CA match comparisons by stating our basic theoretical assumptions that relate reading to the design features of the language apparatus. The manner in which reading is erected on preexisting language acquisitions led us to predict that the causes of reading disability would lie within the language domain. As predicted, seemingly normal school children who fail to make the expected progress in learning to read were found to have language-related difficulties, including problems in metaphonological awareness and unusual limitations in verbal working memory. Since both of these problems are arguably grounded in phonology, one of our central concerns has been to determine if all the language-related difficulties evinced by poor readers might stem from a single deficit in processing phonological information.

The observation that poor readers have difficulties in correctly interpreting some spoken sentences seemed, at first, to threaten the phonological deficit account. However, in the context of our assumptions about the architecture of the language apparatus, and in view of the phonological nature of the working memory code, we argued that a processing deficit might explain this problem too. If so, it would obviate the need to attribute the comprehension difficulties of reading disabled children to a developmental lag in structural competence, over and above their well-attested deficiencies in phonological processing. In order to tease apart the alternatives, tasks were constructed that stress processing in varying degrees, with syntactic structure held constant. It was found using CA match designs that good and poor readers could be distinguished only under task conditions that were most consuming of working memory resources. Poor readers attained the same high level of performance as good readers in contexts that reduced processing demands. This pattern of positive and negative results defies explanation on the hypothesis that poor readers have less syntactic knowledge than good readers. Moreover, any attempt to invoke the reading experience hypothesis to explain the pattern of positive and negative results obtained in tests of sentence interpretation seems *ad hoc,* since the same pattern of breakdown in spoken language understanding has been observed in other populations with severe memory limitations.

The view that reading experience inculcates syntactic competence also proved untenable in the light of language learnability considerations. These considerations provided us with a clear-cut example of how theory constrains the direction of causation. It was argued that spoken language experience plays a special role in syntactic development. In contrast, the input supplied by reading is too limited in kind and comes too late to promote basic grammar formation.

The conclusion that the problems of poor readers do not arise at the syntactic component of the language apparatus confirmed our expectation that the source of impairment is at a level of processing "below" the syntactic level; that is, at the level of phonological processing. Because this component feeds information either directly or indirectly to the syntactic component, and since poor readers are known to suffer from abnormal limitations in phonological processing, it is reasonable to infer that this is the source of their difficulties in interpreting both printed text and spoken sentences. The PLH alone seems capable of handling the whole network of empirical findings. Thus a unitary account of reading disability can still be entertained. The unitary account has been assailed also from the standpoint of variation in the symptom picture. We gave our reasons for considering that the arguments for subtypes are weak and inconclusive, a skepticism that is shared by others (Bryant & Bradley, 1985; Perfetti, 1985; Stanovich, 1986).

In sum, the available evidence does not sit well with the SLH or with any version of the idea that reading experience could supply the abilities that poor readers may critically lack, either in working memory or in syntactic competence. On the other hand, there is considerable empirical support for imputing a causal role to the phonological processing limitations of poor readers. The determination of causation rests on two critical ingredients: (i) a research strategy that makes use of both positive and negative results, and (ii) a set of guiding hypotheses about the reading process and its relation to an articulated model of spoken language processing. Since it is impossible to infer causation from correlation alone, both ingredients are necessary. And crucially, both are sufficient to counter the claim that causation can be inferred only when positive results are found with an RL match design. We argued that, taken together, positive and negative results based on CA match comparisons can be interpreted in terms of causation. In our view, the search for causation comes down to the search for the correct set of hypotheses. But, as with any adequate theory, it is not enough to explain the available facts: Other consequences of the theory must be pursued, which, if confirmed, lend additional weight to inferences about cause and effect, even when these inferences are based on correlational data.[9]

---

[9]The development in recent years of causal modeling techniques has potentially expanded the hypothesis-testing capacities of correlational studies (see Lomax, 1982). We have not attempted to evaluate these approaches here, but promising applications to reading research have been made by Lundberg, Olofsson, and Wall (1980) and Tunmer and Nesdale (1985) in addressing the question of how phonological awareness may promote reading acquisition. Other approaches that combine longitudinal study and training have also been used to good purpose, but these, too, are beyond the scope of this paper.

POSTSCRIPT

A draft of this chapter was circulated in 1987 and, after subsequent revision, the paper appeared in its present form in Haskins Laboratories Status Reports (SR-93/94, 1988). In the two years that have elapsed since then, the literature on the uses and misuses of the reading-level match design in investigations of reading disability has expanded. In reviewing our paper against this background we continue to believe that it brings added perspective to the problem of accurately assigning cause and effect to factors associated with reading disability. Accordingly, we decided to preserve the body of the paper without further revision. At the same time, we recognize the need to acknowledge discussion that appears in the current literature. This postscript supplies the needed update.

It is heartening to discover that many of the conclusions presented in the forgoing pages have also been reached in other critical discussion of the reading-level match design. We list these points of agreement first, and then we make note of arguments in our chapter that are not presented by others. Here, then, are the points of agreement:

1. In the absence of a theoretical framework, no research design by itself can distinguish cause and effect. In this regard, Vellutino and Scanlon (1989) stress the ambiguities in interpreting results obtained with either RL match or CA match designs. Like us, these authors emphasize the necessity of using theory to guide research.

2. We and others have suggested specific steps that may be taken to infer the direction of causation. Goswami and Bryant (1989) and Vellutino and Scanlon emphasize the value of a pattern of positive and negative results and the importance of coordinating their interpretation. If this principle is followed, we maintain that the much-criticized CA match design may be sufficient by itself for inferring the direction of causation. Like us, Vellutino and Scanlon and Jackson and Butterfield (1989) suggest the use of a variety of measures aimed at assessing the same ability. Our paper offers a further reason for testing the same ability with tasks that vary in their processing demands. Specifically, we show how alternative hypotheses about the underlying basis of reading disability predict different patterns of results across tasks.

3. Practical difficulties in equating groups on control factors, which is the focus of the second half of our paper, are also stressed by Morrison and Coltheart (1988) and Jackson and Butterfield, as well as by Vellutino and Scanlon. The latter also discussed the use of critical cut-off scores and exclusionary criteria in forming groups. In addition, the consequences of equating groups on some factors and not on others are discussed by Goswami and Bryant (1989) and Stanovich, Nathan and Zolman (1988). One result of the difficulties in equating groups is the ambiguity of interpreting differences in performance patterns, as we note. These

problems are further discussed in the subsequent literature by Goswami and Bryant and Morrison and Coltheart. In this regard, the latter authors question the validity of the distinction between a deficit (based on a putative "qualitative" difference) and a developmental delay (based on a putative "quantitative" difference).

4. At the heart of most criticisms of CA match designs is the possibility that reading experience may contribute to obtained differences between groups on the criterion measures. Vellutino and Scanlon counter this line of argument with illustrations from research findings, as we did. In this connection, our paper noted that no pure measures of reading experience had been devised. Although we remain convinced that this factor is extremely difficult to assess objectively, we should point out that a measure of "print exposure" has been proposed by Stanovich and his colleagues that accounts for some independent variance in reading performance. Incidentally, using this measure, Stanovich, West and Cunningham (in press) have confirmed one of our predictions: That reading experience would facilitate the development of lexical representations.

In sum, our survey of the contemporary literature yields several points of agreement regarding the use of control groups in studies of reading disability. The emphasis differs somewhat from paper to paper, but all reach the conclusion that the problem of drawing inferences about the direction of causation cannot be reduced to a formula.

In contrast to these points of convergence on matters of method, there is missing from the discussions we reviewed a wider perspective that we regard as indispensable to surmount the problems of inferring direction of causation. First, it is essential in our view to consider the problems of reading within the context of the development of spoken language. This forces us to confront the many differences between acquiring the spoken language and becoming a reader: For example, it forces us to consider a) why reading is learned later than speech, b) why learning to read is comparatively difficult whereas speech is acquired by nearly everyone, c) why children with reading disability so regularly have difficulties in understanding certain spoken sentences. Second, we continue to stress the value of viewing the difficulties of disabled readers in the context of findings obtained with other populations with known deficits in spoken language. These comparisons give us additional grounds for ruling out lack of reading experience as the source of several of the problems of the poor reader and they provide a basis for inferring the direction of causation from correlational data. Finally, it remains essential in our opinion to discuss theories and findings pertaining to reading against the background of theoretical and empirical research on language acquisition. In our own research we invoke principles of the theory of Universal Grammar in generating hypotheses about the origin of the basic difficulties that underlie reading disability. These principles have proven instrumental in our search for constraints on hypotheses about cause and effect in language processing.

ACKNOWLEDGMENT

The authors' research was supported in part by a Program Project Grant (HD-01994) to Haskins Laboratories from the National Institute of Child Health and Human Development. We are grateful to several colleagues and students who provided helpful comments on earlier drafts of this paper. We thank them all, but in particular we should mention Brian Byrne, Usha Goswami, Leonard Katz, Isabelle Y. Liberman, and Diane Lillo-Martin.

REFERENCES

Backman, J. E., Mamen, M., & Ferguson, H. B. (1984). Reading level design: Conceptual and methodological issues in reading research. *Psychological Bulletin, 96,* 560–568.

Baddeley, A. D. (1966). Short-term memory for word sequences as a function of acoustic, semantic and formal similarity. *Quarterly Journal of Experimental Psychology, 18,* 362–365.

Baddeley, A. D. (1986). *Working memory.* Oxford: Oxford University Press.

Boder, E. (1973). Developmental dyslexia: A diagnostic approach based on three atypical reading-spelling patterns. *Developmental Medicine and Child Neurology, 15,* 663–687.

Brady, S. (1986). Short-term memory, phonological processing and reading ability. *Annals of Dyslexia, 36,* 138–153.

Brady, S., Mann, V., & Schmidt, R. (1987). Errors in short-term memory for good readers and poor readers. *Memory & Cognition, 15,* 444–453.

Brady, S., Shankweiler, D., & Mann, V. A. (1983). Speech perception and memory code in relation to reading ability. *Journal of Experimental Child Psychology, 35,* 345–367.

Bryant, P., & Bradley, L. (1985). *Children's reading problems.* Oxford: Blackwell.

Bryant, P., & Goswami, U. (1986). Strengths and weaknesses of the reading level design: A comment on Backman, Mamen, and Ferguson. *Psychological Bulletin, 100,* 101–103.

Bryant, P., & Impey, L. (1986). The similarities between normal readers and developmental and acquired dyslexics. *Cognition, 24,* 121–137.

Byrne, B. (1981). Deficient syntactic control in poor readers: Is a weak phonetic memory code responsible? *Applied Psycholinguistics, 2,* 201–212.

Caramazza, A., & Berndt, R. S. (1985). A multicomponential deficit view of agrammatic Broca's aphasia. In M. L. Kean (Ed.), *Agrammatism.* (pp. 27–63). New York: Academic Press.

Chomsky, C. (1969). *The acquisition of syntax in children from 5 to 10.* Cambridge, MA: MIT Press.

Chomsky, N. (1965). *Aspects of the theory of syntax.* Cambridge, MA: MIT Press.

Chomsky, N. (1981). *Lectures on government and binding: The Pisa Lectures.* Dordrecht, Holland: Foris Publications.

Clark, E. V. (1970). How young children describe events in time. In G. B. Flores d'Arcais & W. J. M. Levelt (Eds.), *Advancements in psycholinguistics* (pp. 275–284). Amsterdam; North Holland.

Coltheart, M., Masterson, J., Byng, S., Prior, M., & Riddoch, J. (1983). Surface dyslexia. *Quarterly Journal of Experimental Psychology, 35,* 469–495.

Coltheart, M., Patterson, K., & Marshall, J. C. (1980). *Deep dyslexia.* London: Routledge & Kegan Paul.

Conrad, R. (1964). Acoustic confusions in immediate memory. *British Journal of Psychology, 3,* 75–84.

Conrad, R. (1972). Speech and reading. In J. F. Kavanagh & I. G. Mattingly (Eds.), *Language by ear and by eye: The relationships between speech and reading.* (pp. 205–240). Cambridge, MA: MIT Press.

Crain, S. (1987). On performability: Structure and process in language understanding. *Clinical Linguistics and Phonetics, 1,* 127–145.

Crain, S., & Fodor, J. D. (1985). On the innateness of Subjacency. *Proceedings of the Eastern States Conference on Linguistics (Vol. 1,* pp. 191–204). Columbus, OH: Ohio State University.

Crain, S., & McKee, C. (1985). Acquisition of structural restrictions on anaphora. *Proceedings of the Northeastern Linguistic Society, 16.* (pp. 94–110). Amherst, MA: University of Massachusetts.

Crain, S., & Nakayama, M. (1987). Structure dependence in grammar formation. *Language, 63,* 522–543.

Crain, S., & Shankweiler, D. (1988). Syntactic complexity and reading acquisition. In A. Davison & G. Green (Eds.), *Linguistic complexity and text comprehension: Readability issues reconsidered* (pp. 167–192). Hillsdale, NJ: Lawrence Erlbaum.

Crain, S., Shankweiler, D., Macaruso, P., & Bar-Shalom, E. (1990). Working memory and comprehension of spoken sentences: Investigations of children with reading disorders. In G. Vallar & T. Shallice (Eds.) *Neuropsychological impairments of short-term memory* (pp. 477–508). Cambridge: Cambridge University Press.

Crain, S., & Steedman, M. (1985). On not being led up the garden path: The use of context by the syntactic processor. In D. R. Dowty, L. Karttunen, & A. Zwicky (Eds.), *Natural language parsing: Psychological, computational, and theoretical perspectives.* (pp. 320–358). Cambridge: Cambridge University Press.

Crain, W. (1986). *Restrictions on the comprehension of syntax by mentally retarded adults.* Unpublished doctoral dissertation, Claremont Graduate School, Claremont, CA.

Crowder, R. G. (1984). Is it just reading? *Developmental Review, 4,* 48–61.

Cunningham, A. E., & Stanovich, K. E. (1990). Assessing print exposure and orthongraphic processing skill in children: A quick measure of reading experience. *Journal of Educational Psychology, 82,* 733–740.

Denckla, M. B., & Rudel, R. G. (1976). Naming of object-drawings by dyslexic and other learning disabled children. *Brain and Language, 3,* 1–15.

Fischer, F. W., Liberman, I. Y., & Shankweiler, D. (1978). Reading reversals and developmental dyslexia: A further study. *Cortex, 14,* 496–510.

Fodor, J. A. (1983). *The modularity of mind.* Cambridge, MA: MIT Press.

Forster, K. (1979). Levels of processing and the structure of the language processor. In W. E. Cooper & E. Walker (Eds.), *Sentence processing: Psycholinguistic studies presented to Merrill Garrett* (pp. 27–85). Hillsdale, NJ: Lawrence Erlbaum.

Fowler, A. E. (1988). Grammaticality judgments and reading skill in grade 2. *Annals of Dyslexia, 38,* 73–94.

Goswami, U. & Bryant, P. (1989). The interpretation of studies using the reading level design. *Journal of Reading Behavior, 21,* 413–424.

Hall, J. W., Wilson, K. P., Humphreys, M. S., Tinzmann, M. B., & Bowyer, P. M. (1983). Phonemic similarity effects in good vs. poor readers. *Memory & Cognition, 11,* 520–527.

Hamburger, H., & Wexler, K. (1973). Identifiability of a class of transformational grammars. In K. J. J. Hintakka, J. M. E. Moravcsik, & P. Suppes (Eds.), *Approaches to natural language* (pp. 153–166). Dordrecht, Holland: D. Reidel.

Hinshelwood, J. (1917). *Congenital word blindness.* London: H. K. Lewis.

Jackson, N. E. & Butterfield, E. C. (1989). Reading-level match designs: Myths and realities. *Journal of Reading Behavior, 21,* 387–411.

Jorm, A. F., Share, D. L., Maclean, R., & Matthews, R. (1986). Cognitive factors at school entry predictive of specific reading retardation and general reading backwardness: A research note. *Journal of Child Psychology and Psychiatry, 27,* 45–54.

Katz, R. B. (1985). Phonological deficiencies in children with reading disability: Evidence from an object-naming task. *Cognition, 22,* 250–257.

Katz, R. B., Shankweiler, D., & Liberman, I. Y. (1981). Memory for item order and phonetic recoding in the beginning reader. *Journal of Experimental Psychology, 32,* 474–484.

Lasnik, H., & Crain, S. (1985). On the acquisition of pronominal reference. *Lingua, 65,* 135–154.

Liberman, I. Y. (1973). Segmentation of the spoken word and reading acquisition. *Bulletin of the Orton Society, 23,* 65–77.

Liberman, I. Y. (1983). A language-oriented view of reading and its disabilities. In H. J. Myklebust (Ed.), *Progress in learning disabilities (Vol 5,* pp. 81–101). New York: Grune and Stratton.

Liberman, I. Y., Liberman, A. M., Mattingly, I. G., & Shankweiler, D. (1980). Orthography and the beginning reader. In J. F. Kavanagh & R. L. Venezky (Eds.), *Orthography, reading, and dyslexia* (pp. 137–153). Baltimore: University Park Press.

Liberman, I. Y., Mann, V. A., Shankweiler, D., & Werfelman, M. (1982). Children's memory for recurring linguistic and nonlinguistic material in relation to reading ability. *Cortex, 18,* 367–375.

Liberman, I. Y., & Shankweiler, D. (1985). Phonology and the problems of learning to read and write. *Remedial and Special Education, 6,* 8–17.

Liberman, I. Y., Shankweiler, D., Fischer, F. W., & Carter, B. (1974). Explicit syllable and phoneme segmentation in the young child. *Journal of Experimental Child Psychology, 18,* 201–212.

Liberman, I. Y., Shankweiler, D., Liberman, A. M., Fowler, C., & Fischer, F. W. (1977). Phonetic segmentation and recoding in the beginning reader. In A. S. Reber, & D. L. Scarborough (Eds.), *Toward a psychology of reading: The proceedings of the CUNY conferences* (pp. 207–225). Hillsdale, NJ: Lawrence Erlbaum.

Liberman, I. Y., Shankweiler, D., Orlando, C., Harris, K. S., & Berti, F. B. (1971). Letter confusions and reversals of sequence in the beginning reader: Implications for Orton's theory of developmental dyslexia. *Cortex, 7,* 127–142.

Lomax, R. G. (1982). Causal modeling of reading acquisition. *Journal of Reading Behavior, 14,* 341–345.

Lundberg, I., Olofsson, A., & Wall, S. (1980). Reading and spelling skills in the first school years predicted from phonemic awareness skills in kindergarten. *Scandinavian Journal of Psychology, 21,* 159–173.

Macaruso, P., Bar-Shalom, E. Crain, S. & Shankweiler, D. (1989). Comprehension of temporal terms by good and poor readers. *Language and Speech, 32,* 45–67.

Mann, V. A., Shankweiler, D., & Smith, S. T. (1984). The association between comprehension of spoken sentences and early reading ability: The role of phonetic representation. *Journal of Child Language, 11,* 627–643.

Mann, V., Tobin, P., & Wilson, R. (1987). Measuring phonological awareness through the invented spellings of kindergarten children. *Merrill-Palmer Quarterly, 33,* 365–391.

Mark, L. S., Shankweiler, D., Liberman, I. Y., & Fowler, C. A. (1977). Phonetic recoding and reading difficulty in beginning readers. *Memory & Cognition, 5,* 623–629.

Mattingly, I. G. (1984). Reading, linguistic awareness, and language acquisition. In J. Downing & R. Valtin (Eds.), *Language awareness and learning to read* (pp. 9–25). New York: Springer-Verlag.

Mattis, S., French, J. H., & Rapin, I. (1975). Dyslexia in children and young adults: Three independent neuropsychological syndromes. *Developmental Medicine and Child Neurology, 17,* 150–163.

Morais, J., Cary, L., Alegria, J., & Bertelson, P. (1979). Does awareness of speech as a sequence of phonemes arise spontaneously? *Cognition, 7,* 323–331.

Morais, J., Cluytens, M., & Alegria, J. (1984). Segmentation abilities of dyslexics and normal readers. *Perceptual and Motor Skills, 58,* 221–222.

Morgan, J. (1986). *From simple input to complex grammar.* Cambridge, MA: MIT Press.

Morrison, F. , & Coltheart, M. (1988). *Understanding reading disability: Conceptual and meth-odological strategies.* Paper presented at the Annual Meeting of the American Educational Research Association, New Orleans, April.

Nagy, W. E., & Anderson, R. C. (1984). How many words are there in printed school English? *Reading Research Quarterly, 19,* 304–330.

Orton, S. T. (1925). "Word-blindness" in school children. *Archives of Neurology, 14,* 581–615.

Perfetti, C. A. (1985). *Reading ability.* New York: Oxford University Press.

Perfetti, C. A., & Hogaboam, T. (1975). The relationship between single word decoding and reading comprehension skill. *Journal of Educational Psychology, 67,* 461–469.

Pinker, S. (1984). *Language learnability and language development.* Cambridge, MA: Harvard University Press.

Pratt, A., & Brady, S. (1988). Relation of phonological awareness to reading disability in children and adults. *Journal of Educational Psychology, 80,* 319–323.

Richardson, E., & DiBenedetto, B. (1986). *Decoding Skills Test.* Parkton, MD: York Press.

Rozin, P., & Gleitman, L. R. (1977). The structure and acquisition of reading II: The reading process and the acquisition of the alphabetic principle. In A. S. Reber & D. L. Scarborough (Eds.), *Toward a psychology of reading: The proceedings of the CUNY conferences* (pp. 55–141). Hillsdale, NJ: Lawrence Erlbaum.

Rutter, M., & Yule, W. (1975). The concept of specific reading retardation. *Journal of Child Psychology and Psychiatry, 16,* 181–197.

Satz, P., & Fletcher, J. M. (1980). Minimal brain dysfunctions: An appraisal of research concepts and methods. In H. Rie & E. Rie (Eds.), *Handbook of minimal brain dysfunctions.* New York: Wiley-Interscience.

Shankweiler, D., & Crain, S. (1986). Language mechanisms and reading disorders: A modular approach. *Cognition, 24,* 139–168.

Shankweiler, D., & Liberman, I. Y. (1972). Misreading: A search for causes. In J. F. Kavanaugh & I. G. Mattingly (Eds.), *Language by ear and by eye: The relationships between speech and reading* (pp. 293–317). Cambridge, MA: MIT Press.

Shankweiler, D., Liberman, I. Y., Mark, L. S., Fowler, C. A., & Fischer, F. W. (1979). The speech code and learning to read. *Journal of Experimental Psychology: Human Learning and Memory, 5,* 531–545.

Sheldon, A. (1974). The role of parallel function in the acquisition of relative clauses in English. *Journal of Verbal Learning and Verbal Behavior, 13,* 272–281.

Simner, M. (1982). Printing errors in kindergarten and the prediction of academic performance. *Journal of Learning Disabilities, 15,* 155–159.

Smith, S., Macaruso, P. Shankweiler, D., & Crain, S. (1989). Syntactic comprehension in young poor readers. *Applied Psycholinguistics, 10,* 429–454.

Stanovich, K. E. (1986). Matthew effects in reading: Some consequences of individual differences in the acquisition of literacy. *Reading Research Quarterly, 21,* 360–407.

Stanovich, K. E., Cunningham, A. E., & Feeman, D. J. (1984). Intelligence, cognitive skills and early reading progress. *Reading Research Quarterly, 19,* 278–303.

Stanovich, K. E., Nathan, R. G. & Zolman, J. E. (1988). The developmental lag hypothesis in reading: Longitudinal and matched reading-level comparisons. *Child Development, 59,* 71–86.

Stanovich, K. E., West, R. F. & Cunningham, A. E. (1991). Beyond phonological processes: Print exposure and orthographic processing. In S. A. Brady & D. P. Shankweiler (Eds.). *Phonological processes in literacy: A tribute to Isabelle Y. Liberman* (pp. 219–235). Hillsdale, NJ: Lawrence Erlbaum Associates.

Stein, C. L., Cairns, H. S., & Zurif, E. B. (1984). Sentence comprehension limitations related to syntactic deficits in reading-disabled children. *Applied Psycholinguistics, 5,* 305–322.

Tavakolian, S. L. (Ed.) (1981). *Language acquisition and linguistic theory.* Cambridge, MA: MIT Press.

Temple, C., & Marshall, J. (1983). A case study of developmental phonological dyslexia. *British Journal of Psychology, 74,* 517–533.

Treiman, R. & Hirsh-Pasek, K. (1985). Are there qualitative differences in reading behavior between dyslexics and normal readers? *Memory and Cognition, 13,* 357–364.

Tunmer, W. E., & Nesdale, A. R. (1985). Phonemic segmentation skill and beginning reading. *Journal of Educational Psychology, 77,* 417–427.

Vellutino, F. R. & Scanlon, D. M. (1989). Some prerequisites for interpreting results from reading level matched designs. *Journal of Reading Behavior, 21,* 361–385.

Wagner, R. K., & Torgesen, J. K. (1987). The nature of phonological processing and its causal role in the acquisition of reading skills. *Psychological Bulletin, 101,* 192–212.

Wexler, K., & Culicover, P. (1980). *Formal principles in language acquisition.* Cambridge, MA: MIT Press.

Wolf, M. (1981). The word-retrieval process and reading in children and aphasics. In K. Nelson (Ed.), *Children's language* (Vol. 3, pp. 437–493). New York: Gardner Press.

Wolford, G., & Fowler, C. (1984). Differential use of partial information by good and poor readers. *Developmental Review, 6,* 16–35.

Woodcock, R. W. (1977). *Woodcock-Johnson psycho-educational battery.* Boston: Teaching Resources.

11

Speculations on the Causes and Consequences of Individual Differences in Early Reading Acquisition

Keith E. Stanovich
Ontario Institute for Studies in Education

In this chapter I present some conclusions and speculations about the cognitive mechanisms that underlie individual differences in reading acquisition. I consider some of the processes and skills that have been widely discussed in the past decade in the literature on individual differences in reading. In addition to drawing some general conclusions about causal mechanisms in early reading, I devote equal attention to some of the implications that failing at early reading acquisition—and failing for particular reasons—has for later academic achievement and for cognitive development in general.

My readers are warned in advance that I paint with somewhat of a broad brush. Other chapters in this volume will undoubtedly give a more fine-grained partitioning of individual differences in the processes underlying early reading. However, I think that there are times when something can be gained from adopting a broad-brushed approach. In every science—not only biology—there are the "splitters" and the "lumpers." The splitters tend to see idiosyncrasies, lack of fit, and discrepancies in new empirical findings—discrepancies that for them, call for new concepts, theoretical change, or both. The lumpers view the same discrepancies as random variations from an established pattern—variations that for them, need no additional explanation. For lumpers, the splitters' data pattern is a mere temporary perturbation, not a real anomaly. Lumpers hope that further experimentation will demonstrate that the discrepancy is simply random fluctuation. The splitters hope that with further experimentation the perturbations will stand out as true anomalies and force theoretical adjustment.

The reason for my at least temporary stance in the lumper camp is that after spending my career as a splitter, writing sentences like "reading is a complex process determined by a multiplicity of factors," I have come to wonder whether our understanding of individual differences in reading has suffered a little from too much splitting. I certainly now think that educational practice has suffered (Stanovich, 1990a, 1991). Perhaps an overdose of arguments over fine distinctions has made us underestimate how much progress we are making at a grosser level of analysis. I have begun to think that it might be interesting to try a little lumping for a change and just see how far we can get. Such is the road by which I come to address you now as a lumper. No doubt, in my presentation I will make the "lumper's error": Classifying together phenomena, tasks, and patterns that really call for theoretical differentiation. Other chapters in this volume will surely balance out this bias. With this caveat in mind, I proceed to survey some of the major hypotheses that have been put forward as explanations of individual differences in the ability to acquire literacy.

CONTEXT USE BY EARLY READERS

Research has demonstrated that difficulty at using context to facilitate the recognition of words is not a major cause of reading failure or a major determinant of variability in reading achievement. The evidence for this conclusion is quite substantial for children in the late elementary and middle grades. It consists of numerous demonstrations that even less-skilled readers make substantial use of contextual information to facilitate the recognition of words (Briggs, Austin, & Underwood, 1984; Nicholson & Hill, 1985; Nicholson, Lillas, & Rzoska, 1988; Perfetti, Goldman, & Hogaboam, 1979; Perfetti & Roth, 1981; Pring & Snowling, 1986; Schwantes, 1985; Simons & Leu, 1987; Simpson & Foster, 1986; Stanovich, Nathan, West, & Vala-Rossi, 1985; Stanovich, West, & Feeman, 1981; West & Stanovich, 1978).

These demonstrations have generally ensured that the contextual information was available to the less-skilled readers in the study by using materials well within their capabilities. This important feature of the experimental design precludes the spurious observation of context-use deficiencies that naturally result when poor readers are given materials well beyond their abilities. In such cases, the efficiency of text processing can be so low that the reader may effectively have no context available. One may thus differentiate two explanations for the frequently reported description of problem readers as plodding through text, not using context, and understanding little. One—the "strategy" explanation—is often associated with top-down theories of the reading process. The idea is that these poor readers have adopted inefficient word recognition strategies. Often it is claimed that the inefficient strategy is one of overuse of phonics and that this strategy is mistakenly used in place of a more efficient strategy of "guessing from context." Alternatively, "plodder's" lack of contextual facilitation may be an epiphenomenon of extremely poor decoding skills (Stanovich, 1984, 1986b). The many experimental demonstrations indicating that, when they understand the context, poor readers display contextual priming effects on word recognition at least as large (and in many cases larger) than those shown by skilled readers favors this interpretation over the strategy explanation (for reviews, see Perfetti, 1985; Stanovich, 1986b).

What about the early stages of reading acquisition? It is possible that the linkages between processing operations at the initial stages of reading acquisition are quite different from what they are at more advanced stages. Nevertheless, there has been some research on the role of contextual facilitation in early reading acquisition. I argue here that the tentative conclusions from this research show continuity with the evidence on the role of context at more advanced stages of reading.

Because the reaction-time paradigms that can more specifically isolate the prelexical from the postlexical level of processing (Seidenberg, Waters, Sanders, & Langer, 1984; West & Stanovich, 1982, 1986) have generally not been applied to children at the earliest stages of reading acquisition, researchers have relied largely on analyses of oral reading errors to make inferences about the use of context by these children. This is problematic because, as has often been pointed out (e.g., Kibby, 1979; Leu, 1982; Wixson, 1979), an oral reading error can occur for a variety of reasons. Many oral reading errors reflect comprehension processes as well as word recognition processes. For example, this is certainly the case for self-corrections, which clearly implicate comprehension processes occurring well after lexical access. Creating indices of contextual processing that are based on measures such as self-corrections seriously confounds levels of processing and precludes testing predictions from models where differential predictions are made depending on the level of processing involved. For example, both verbal efficiency theory (Perfetti, 1985) and the interactive-compensatory model (Stanovich, 1980, 1984) posit that under some circumstances skilled readers will rely less on context to identify words than less skilled readers. However, neither theory denies that the better reader may have superior comprehension skill in addition to their superior decoding skills.

If the above caveats are acknowledged, results of oral reading error analyses provide some suggestive evidence. Many investigators have reported analyses of the syntactic and semantic appropriateness of the initial reading errors. Initial reading errors, although still not a pure index of processing at the word level, probably do implicate prelexical processes. The classic studies of Biemiller (1970) and Weber (1970) indicated considerable use of contextual information by their first-grade subjects. The vast majority of the errors made by the children were syntactically and semantically appropriate. Biemiller (1970) also reported that the children who were to become the better readers were those who rapidly moved out of what he characterized as an early stage of heavy context use to later stages that made greater use of graphic information. Although some of Biemiller's (1970) data patterns may have been caused by the instructional history of the children (Barr, 1974–1975), independent evidence supports one of the important general conclusions from his study: Better readers move more quickly from an early stage of context use and global processing to one that is more analytic at the word level (Bertelson, 1986; Byrne, this volume; Byrne & Field-ing-Barnsley, 1989; Ehri & Wilce, 1985; Goldsmith, 1981; Gough & Hillinger, 1980; Gough, Juel, & Griffith, this volume; Gough, Juel, & Roper/Schneider, 1983; Juel, 1980, 1988; Mason, 1980, Masonheimer, Drum, & Ehri, 1984; Nicholson, 1986; Whaley & Kibby, 1981).

Although the Biemiller (1970) and Weber (1970) results demonstrated ample use of context by beginning readers, Biemiller (1979) presented further results from first-grade children showing how important it is to take into account the relative difficulty of the materials when making inferences about context use from oral reading error studies. He found that as the difficulty of the reading material increased, the children made fewer contextually appropriate errors. When skilled and less-skilled readers were in materials of comparable difficulty they had similar proportions of contextually appropriate errors. From Biemiller's (1979) results one can see how easy it would be to create a pattern of less context use by the poorer readers: Simply put all of the children in the same materials. This will ensure less efficient decoding of the passage by the less-skilled readers and concomitantly less adequate contextual information for them to use.

Our research group (Stanovich, Cunningham, & Feeman, 1984b) has used a longitudinal design to produce data convergent with that of Biemiller (1979; see also Kibby, 1979). In the fall and spring the speed and accuracy with which skilled and less-skilled first-grade children read coherent story paragraphs and random word lists was assessed. A recognition efficiency score was constructed that reflected the mean number of words read correctly per second. Of course, the skilled readers were better in both types of materials. In the fall, the skilled readers also displayed more contextual facilitation; but, again, they were decod-ing the passages much better. The important question is whether the less-skilled readers display as much contextual facilitation as the skilled readers, *when at a comparable level of context-free decoding ability*. Our data speak to this question because the decoding efficiency of the less-skilled readers on the random lists measured in the spring was similar to that displayed by the skilled readers measured in the fall. Thus, by comparing the efficiency scores in the coherent paragraphs, one can ask whether these two groups were getting a similar con-textual "boost" when at comparable levels of context-free decoding ability. The data clearly indicated that the recognition efficiency scores of the less-skilled readers were facilitated at least as much by context as those of the skilled readers. These results support a decoding epiphenomenon explanation rather than a "strategy use" explanation of the contextual failures that some poor readers experience in some difficult reading materials.

THEN WHY DID WE BELIEVE
OTHERWISE FOR SO LONG?

Studies of early reading converge with the research with older children and adults in indicating that reading acquisition in less-skilled children seems not to be impeded by an inability to use context to facilitate word recognition. Why, if this evidence is so consistent, has the idea that poor readers fail at a "psycholinguistic guessing game" remained so popular among some reading researchers and practitioners? There are basically three reasons. One has been outlined already: The failure to take into account the interaction between the difficulty of materials and reader skill leads to a misinterpretation of the frequent reports from teachers of children who "just plod through and don't use context." These reports usually turn out to be spurious, not because they are untrue, but because the common interpretation—that the children are plodding (recognizing words slowly) *because* they are not using context—is false. The research reviewed previously leads to just the opposite conclusion: The children are not using context because they are plodding and decoding inefficiently.

The popularity of the context-use hypothesis as an explanation of reading failure also results from another conceptual misinterpretation. Advocates of top-down models of reading have repeatedly argued that skilled readers rely less on graphic cues than less-skilled readers (Smith, 1971, 1973, 1975). Smith's (1971) well-known hypothesis is that, being sensitive to the redundancy afforded by sentences, good readers develop hypotheses about upcoming words and are then able to confirm the identity of a word by sampling only a few features in the visual array. Good readers should process words faster because their use of redundancy lightens the load on their stimulus-analysis mechanisms. Despite its surface plausibility, this notion is contradicted by much recent data.

Recent advances in eye-movement technology have made available a host of powerful techniques for collecting data relevant to Smith's hypothesis. The results of studies employing these new methodologies have consistently indicated that fluent readers sample the visual array rather completely, even when reading fairly predictable words (Balota, Pollatsek, & Rayner, 1985; Just & Carpenter, 1980, 1987; Pollatsek, Rayner, & Balota, 1986; Rayner & Bertera, 1979; Rayner & Pollatsek, 1989; Zola, 1984). Fluent readers do not skip words wholesale, nor do they markedly reduce their sampling of visual features when context is present.

The top-down theorists seem to have confused the use of the features in the visual array with the cognitive resources necessary to process the features. It is not that the good reader relies less on visual information, but that the stimulus-analysis mechanisms of the good reader use less *capacity*. That is, good readers process print more efficiently in every sense; they completely sample the visual array and use fewer resources to do so. The good reader is not less reliant on the visual information, but the good reader does allocate less capacity to process this information.

In short, the insight from the top-down models—that skilled readers do not expend cognitive capacity at the word level—was correct, but not for the reasons that the top-down theorists suspected. The usefulness and importance of their insight about capacity usage led to a mistaken acceptance of the mechanism proposed to explain the insight: less capacity needed for graphic information because context use decreased the number of features to be processed. Actually, good readers expend less capacity not because they rely on contextual information, but because their stimulus-analysis mechanisms are so powerful and automatic. Once the mechanism responsible for the capacity insight is correctly specified, one can see more congruence between some of the insights that were the source of the popularity of the top-down models and the concepts in bottom-up models like Perfetti's (1985) verbal efficiency theory. For example, both classes of model agree that readers should expend processing capacity on higher-level comprehension processes rather than on word recognition.

Perhaps a third reason for the popularity of the context-use hypothesis as an explanation of individual differences in reading ability is that there is considerable confusion about the distinction between the importance of a mechanism as a determinant of a general developmental sequence and as a determinant of individual differences in the developmental sequence (McCall, 1981). Again, the top-down theorists seem to have taken an idea that was valid in one sphere and extended it into a domain where it was not applicable. Their error was not in emphasizing that context use occurs in reading, but in generalizing it as a mechanism that explained individual differences. In contrast, I argue here that the tendency to use context is so nearly universal among children that it cannot serve as a potent source of individual differences. The research reviewed previously indicates considerable use of context by early readers. This is clear from the fact that 70% to 95% of the oral reading errors of first-grade children are contextually appropriate (Biemiller, 1970, 1979; Weber, 1970). If the variability in ability to use context is low relative to the variability in other factors that determine reading ability (phonological processes, for example,), then context use will not be strongly related to individual differences in reading ability, despite its importance in every child's reading performance.

This point is similar to cautions that have been raised about interpreting genetic and environmental effects on intelligence test performance. It is often pointed out that if the variability in one factor is restricted then the other will necessarily relate more strongly to individual differences. For example, differences in the intelligence scores of identical twins must be entirely due to environmental differences because twins share the same genetic background. This of course does not mean that the general developmental sequence of identical twins is not partially under genetic control. Although heredity is contributing to the development of the organism, it cannot be linked to individual differences in this case.

An analogous phenomenon seems to be occurring in the case of contextual facilitation. All the empirical evidence indicates considerable context use by first-grade children, and models of first-grade reading acquisition often include at least one stage defined in part by context use. For example, Biemiller's (1970) proposed early reading stages include an initial stage of contextual dependency, a stage of increasing attention to graphic processing, and a stage where the integration of both graphic and contextual cues occurs. Bissex's (1980) case study also seems to confirm this sequence, and she particularly emphasized the importance of the third stage in which both context and graphophonemic information are used in a integrated manner. But even if one accepts the importance of a stage of graphic and contextual cue integration, is passage into this stage blocked by the inadequate development of context use skills or by the failure to develop skills of graphophonemic processing? All children may indeed go through a cue integration stage, but is the speed of its attainment actually determined by variation in context use skills? I suggest that the answer is no. Stages defined in part by ways of using context may indeed be real, but these stages misleadingly serve to suggest that context use is a source of individual differences. Compared to other prerequisite skills—such as phonological sensitivity, for example—the variability in the ability to use context to facilitate word recognition is so low that it is not a major determinant of individual differences in reading acquisition. The very ubiquity of contextual facilitation—the thing that has led some theorists to single it out as a mechanism for generating ability differences—is precisely the thing that prevents its association with individual differences.

VISUAL DEFICITS: A CLOSED CASE?

The context-use hypothesis is not the only hypothesis about individual differences in reading ability that has been in flux in recent years. Another popular hypothesis—that problems in reading acquisition are linked to deficient visual perception—has undergone a drastic reevaluation in the past two decades. Unlike the context-use hypothesis, which grew out of the general reading literature, the visual deficit hypothesis developed out of the study of dyslexia and reading disability. The visual deficit hypothesis was once very popular and still dominates presentations of dyslexia in the general media.

However, during the last two decades, the results of a series of controlled studies have served to undermine the visual deficit hypothesis to such an extent that several major reviews of the evidence have all concluded that visual deficits are not a major cause of reading disability or a major determinant of variability in reading ability (Mitchell, 1982; Rutter, 1978; Stanovich, 1982, 1986a; Vellutino, 1979). Some would state the conclusion even stronger and say that the case is closed, period. However, there are at least three reasons why the issue may not be completely closed, and the last of these reasons implicates early reading acquisition specifically.

First, some recent evidence may serve to reopen the issue of visual deficits (Willows, in press). There have been several recent reports of differences between disabled and nondisabled children in visual recognition experiments using nonverbal stimuli, brief presentations, and psychophysical procedures (Badcock & Lovegrove, 1981; DiLollo, Hanson, & McIntyre, 1983; Lovegrove & Slaghuis, 1989; Martin & Lovegrove, 1984, 1988; Slaghuis & Lovegrove, 1985, 1987; Solman & May, 1990; Willows, in press). Some of these investigators have argued that visual perception tasks where the stimulus is continuously exposed are not good indicators of the subtle visual problems of some disabled children (Willows, in press). Although some of the work leading to the general rejection of the visual deficit hypothesis did in fact use the sophisticated psychophysical procedures recommended by Badcock and Lovegrove (1981; see, for example, Morrison, Giordani, & Nagy, 1977), much of the evidence contradicting the idea of visual deficits comes from studies employing arrays exposed for several seconds or more. Clearly, then, these new reports will necessitate some further work with more sophisticated psychophysical techniques before the visual deficit hypothesis can be dismissed entirely (however, see Hulme, 1988).

A second point often raised in the context of discussions of visual deficits is that these processing problems may not be general but may characterize a small group of severely affected children. It is often argued that the data from this subgroup of children get swamped in samples containing mostly children with a variety of other deficits. This alternative explanation will remain a viable hypothesis until a large-scale epidemiological study is conducted that allows the precise demarcation of a subpopulation with visual deficits.

I fully agree that we should continue the search for reliably obtainable subgroups of reading disabled children. However, there is an important asymmetry in the research literature that serves to explain some of the seeming disagreement among reading disabilities researchers on the issue of visual deficits. Most investigators familiar with the literature would agree that the following generalization holds fairly well: Those researchers who champion the role of verbal or phonological factors in reading tend not to concern themselves with the subtype issue, whereas investigators supporting the visual deficit hypothesis tend to emphasize subtypes. There may be many reasons for this association, but at least part of the reason resides in the fact that the subtypes argument is quite often put forth as an alternative hypothesis to explain null findings in the area of visual processing. The argument—with which, it should be noted, I do not disagree—is that in heterogeneous groupings of reading disabled children, the visual processing problems of a small group of children with visual deficits will get swamped when the subgroup is combined with other groups of children with language and phonological deficits. This argument is correct and logical. But note that when investigating the hypothesis that there is a phonological problem, researchers do not have a similar worry. They are not concerned that the speech segmentation performance of the children with phonological problems will be statistically diluted by their being grouped together within a heterogeneous sample including children with visual problems. In short, phonological problems are so prevalent that they can be detected even under the most disadvantageous sampling conditions. This, of course, is not an argument against the idea of a visual subtype, but it does argue that researchers advocating the existence of the visual subtype will undermine their case by suggesting that it is as numerous as the phonological subtype.

The role of numbers in these disputes is not irrelevant, because therein lies part of the reason for the controversy in the literature and for why investigators in the various "camps" have had trouble reaching a rapprochement. The verbal deficit theorists often seem at first to admit that there is a small group of children with visual problems, but then slip in their writings into the assumption that they are entirely nonexistent. This understandably raises the ire of the visual deficit theorists. However, the latter are guilty of the same escalation by stealth. Their talk of a small subgroup of children with visual problems often graduates into an argument that large numbers of children are characterized by such a problem or that such children are "typical," language which teachers quite naturally translate to mean "most common." Thus, an underlying agreement grows into a full fledged controversy because both sides slip into defending their inflated claims.

There is, additionally, a third reason for keeping an open mind on the visual deficit hypothesis. Fletcher and Satz (1979; Fletcher, 1981; see also, Willows, in press) have proposed that there is a developmental trend in the nature of the cognitive deficits underlying reading failure, and that visual deficits characterize reading failure only in the earliest stages. They point out that many of the studies demonstrating null findings have been conducted with children beyond the age where their theory would predict a difference. Although some results inconsistent with the visual deficit hypothesis have been obtained with beginning readers (Calfee, 1977; Vellutino, 1979), the arguments of Satz and Fletcher are of import to researchers interested in early reading acquisition and should spur further research with younger children.

Thus, there are still questions surrounding the visual deficit issue that are worthy of further investigation. I remain skeptical, however, that there will be a large payoff in this area. Enough is already known to conclude that even if a real phenomenon is uncovered, it will not be the dominant cognitive locus of reading disability. Indeed, many of the researchers who argue for the possibility of visual deficits do not rule out the possibility of visual deficits coexisting with phonological deficits. But it will be easier to demarcate visual processing problems if they do not always co-occur with phonological or verbal problems. It would be convincing, for example, to demonstrate that a group of pre-kindergarten children with better than average phonological awareness, but visual processing problems, developed into children with reading disabilities. This convincing evidence will not be obtainable if the processing problems always co-occur. And in the absence of such evidence, researchers will quite rightly focus on the role of phonological processes in reading acquisition, about which much more is known.

PHONOLOGICAL PROCESSES: SPECULATIONS AND QUESTIONS

It will not surprise most readers of this chapter to hear me argue that variation in phonological processing ability is the primary specific mechanism that determines early reading success. Although general indicators of cognitive functioning such as intelligence, vocabulary, and listening comprehension all predict the ease of initial reading acquisition, phonological abilities stand out as the most potent predictors (Adams, 1990; Bradley & Bryant, 1983, 1985; Gough & Hillinger, 1980; Juel, 1988; Kamhi & Catts, 1989; Liberman, 1983; Mann, Tobin, & Wilson, 1987; Share, Jorm, Maclean, & Matthews, 1984; Stanovich, Cunningham, & Cramer, 1984; Stanovich, Cunningham, & Feeman, 1984a; Tunmer & Nesdale, 1985; Vellutino & Scanlon, 1987; Wagner, 1988; Wagner & Torgesen, 1987; Williams, 1984; Yopp, 1988). Although the strength of the observed correlations serves to draw attention to phonological abilities, it is not proof that these abilities are causally implicated in initial reading acquisition. Proof, of course, requires much stronger evidence than purely correlational data. However, a growing body of data supports the existence of a causal link. This evidence is of several different types.

First, there are several studies showing that measures of phonological sensitivity predict reading ability even when the former are assessed very early in development (Bradley & Bryant, 1983; Bryant, Bradley, Maclean, & Crossland, 1989; Fox & Routh, 1975; Lundberg & Hoien, 1989; Lundberg, Olofsson, & Wall, 1980; Maclean, Bryant, & Bradley, 1987; Share et al., 1984). Second, the results of longitudinal studies employing cross-lagged correlational methods, structural equation modeling, or both, suggest that the early development of phonological sensitivity leads to superior reading achievement (Perfetti, Beck, Bell, & Hughes, 1987; Tornéus, 1984). Evidence supporting this conclusion also comes from reading-level match designs, where older reading-disabled children have performed worse on phonological tasks than younger nondyslexic children matched on word recognition level (Baddeley, Ellis, Miles, & Lewis, 1982; Bradley & Bryant, 1978; Bruck, 1990; Bruck & Treiman, 1990; Holligan & Johnston, 1988; Olson, Wise, Conners, Rack, & Fulker, 1989; Siegel & Faux, 1989; Snowling, 1980, 1981; Snowling, Stackhouse, & Rack, 1986).

Finally, and of course most convincing, are the results of several studies where phonological skills were manipulated by means of training. The training resulted in significant experimental group advantages in reading, word recognition, and spelling (Ball & Blachman, 1988; Bradley, 1987; Bradley & Bryant, 1983, 1985; Cunningham, 1990; Fox & Routh, 1984; Lundberg, Frost, & Peterson, 1988; Olofsson & Lundberg, 1985; Tornéus, 1984; Treiman & Baron, 1983; Vellutino & Scanlon, 1987).

Several of the studies just cited have also supported Ehri's (1979, 1984, 1985; Ehri, Wilce, & Taylor, 1987) position that reading acquisition itself facilitates phonological awareness (see also Morais, Alegria, & Content, 1987; Perfetti et al., 1987). Thus, the situation appears to be one of reciprocal causation. Such situations of reciprocal causation can have important bootstrapping effects on reading achievement (see Stanovich, 1986b).

Ehri's (1979) early work also presaged the current controversy over precisely what level of phonological skill is a prerequisite to acquiring alphabetic literacy and what level is actually a product of that literacy (Bertelson, 1986; Bertelson,

Morais, Alegria, & Content, 1985; Bryant & Bradley, 1985; Morais et al., 1987; Perfetti et al., 1987). To untangle these questions, investigators have resorted to imaginative research designs that include comparisons of literates to illiterates and comparisons of different orthographies (Mann, 1986a; Morais, Bertelson, Cary, & Alegria, 1986; Read, Zhang, Nie, & Ding, 1986). There is as yet no firm consensus on the issue of just what level of phonological skill is a prerequisite to acquiring alphabetic literacy. In fact, researchers are still in disagreement over the proper terminology to use when referring to various aspects of phonological ability. For example, some investigators reserve the use of the term *phonological awareness* to refer to the ability to make explicit verbal reports of the phonemic level of language and the ability to manipulate representations at this level. Others use it as an umbrella term to refer to any task that involves sensitivity to speech sounds. References to phonological "knowledge" are similarly confusing.

In the interests of theoretical clarification, I suggest the following usages. First, the term *phonological awareness* should be divorced from the idea of "conscious" awareness, because there is no agreement among psychologists or philosophers on what "consciousness" means (Allport, 1980; Lycan, 1990; Lyons, 1986; Marcel & Bisiach, 1988; Stanovich, 1990b; Wilkes, 1984, 1988). In fact, "consciousness" may be a folk term of dubious usefulness for a science of psychology, because folk usage fails to coherently demarcate brain processes (P. M. Churchland, 1989; P. S. Churchland, 1986; Dennett, 1987; Rorty, 1979; Stich, 1983). It seems best not to link constructs in reading theory with inadequately operationalized, and thus slippery, folk language. Constructs in this particular domain of reading theory should be operationalized in terms of the type of reports that children can make in various types of tasks.

Some agreement on terminology would also foster better communication within this research area. I suggest that the generic term *phonological sensitivity* be used to cover the set of processing constructs being tapped by the various tasks used in research. Phonological sensitivity should be viewed as a continuum ranging from "deep" sensitivity to "shallow" sensitivity. Tasks indicating deeper levels of sensitivity require more explicit reports of smaller sized units (e.g., phonemes versus onset/rimes or syllables). The phoneme segmentation and sound isolation tasks studied by Yopp (1988) would fall on the deep end of the continuum. In contrast, examples of tasks tapping the most shallow forms of phonological sensitivity might be oddity tasks of rhyming stimuli. Tasks intermediate in phonological depth might be those like phoneme deletion (see Yopp, 1988), where the response is not a phoneme-sized unit, but segmentation has clearly been demonstrated.

If these rough distinctions are made, then a consensus in the research literature becomes apparent. Deep phonological sensitivity, in the sense just defined, appears not to be an absolute prerequisite to reading progress, but is itself fostered by the analytic attitude developed during initial learning of an alphabetic orthography (Morais et al., 1987). It should be emphasized that even if this conclusion is true, early development of deep phonological sensitivity is a powerful bootstrapping mechanism to further reading progress in stages that are still very early in the child's acquisition history. Just because the deeper forms of phonological sensitivity are not absolute prerequisites to any reading progress at all does not mean that they are not powerful facilitators in critically early stages of reading acquisition (during first grade, for example). In addition, it seems that a more shallow type of phonological sensitivity does serve as a prerequisite in acquiring alphabetic literacy (Bryant, Maclean, Bradley, & Crossland, 1990). This shallow phonological sensitivity may also be in a reciprocal relationship with reading, but the time course of its developmental effects may be different. These tentative conclusions do no grave injustices to the longitudinal studies, experiments comparing literates to illiterates, and the cross-cultural research.

INDIVIDUAL DIFFERENCES
IN ORTHOGRAPHIC ANALYSIS
AND ORTHOGRAPHIC MEMORY

Is phonological processing the end of the story? Do children with high levels of phonological skill acquire reading rapidly, and do children with low levels lag behind? Although the answer to the latter question appears to be "yes," the answer to the former is "not necessarily." That is, very few children with low levels of phonological sensitivity acquire reading rapidly, but not every child with high phonological skill becomes a good reader. Tunmer and Nesdale (1985) and Juel, Griffith, and Gough (1986) have demonstrated this by showing that phonemic segmentation is a necessary, but not sufficient, condition for rapid reading acquisition.

If phonological sensitivity is a necessary but not sufficient condition for efficient reading acquisition, there must exist at least one other cognitive "sticking point" where reading acquisition can run aground. What is this second problem area? For some, the prime candidate has been the code-breaking stage. The idea is that some children have particular problems with the irregularities in the orthography and therefore have difficulty cracking the code. Morrison (1984; Morrison & Manis, 1982) has argued for a very general deficit in learning irregular rule systems, a deficit that extends even to nonlinguistic materials. Other theorists see a more limited code-breaking problem.

There is another possible locus for the problem, however. Ehri (1979, 1980, 1984, 1985, 1987; see also Barron, 1981, 1986) has emphasized that lexical access depends on the establishment of accurate orthographic representations in memory—stored representations of the coded visual features of the letters in words. Certainly, the formation of orthographic representations would be facilitated by extensive spelling-to-sound knowledge (see Jorm & Share, 1983). Might there be individual differences in the ability to establish orthographic representations that are independent of phonological abilities and spelling-to-sound decoding skill? If so, then another potential sticking point for some problem readers might reside in a severe inability to form accurate orthographic representations, to access orthographic representations, or both.

Reitsma (1983) reported a key piece of evidence. He gave first-grade children practice at recognizing a set of words. Three days later, he tested their recognition of the practiced words and a matched set of homophonic spellings of the words. Only four trials of practice led to superior performance on the standard spellings three days later. This was true for both the skilled and less-skilled first-grade readers. Reitsma (1983) also tested a learning-disabled group two years older but approximately matched with the skilled first-graders on reading level. Interestingly, the learning-disabled children did not perform better on the standard spelling even after six trials of practice. This result suggests that some disabled readers have specific problems in forming visual–orthographic representations.

Case studies of adults with acquired surface dyslexia (Patterson, Marshall, & Coltheart, 1985) have suggested that there exist reading problems specifically associated with difficulties in accessing or forming representations, or both, in the orthographic lexicon. Additionally, some studies of individual differences across the normal continuum of ability have suggested that children show marked differences in their tendency to use print-specific information when recognizing words (Baron & Treiman, 1980; Bryant & Impey, 1986; Freebody & Byrne, 1988; Treiman, 1984). Our research group (Cunningham & Stanovich, 1990; Stanovich & West, 1989) has demonstrated that, in both children and adults, tasks assessing the efficiency of orthographic processing account for variance in word recognition ability even after the variance associated with phonological processing skills has been partialed out.

Perhaps evidence for individual differences in forming memory representations for words was also revealed in a study by Seymour and Elder (1986). They examined the word learning of a small group of children who were taught by a look–say method that included no phonics instruction. Although the children acquired virtually no phonological decoding skills, there were large individual differences in their acquisition of the sight vocabulary. More relevant evidence may come from studies that have explored the tendency of some children to use an analogy mechanism to aid in word decoding (Baron, 1977, 1979; Goswami, 1986, 1988, 1990; Manis, Szeszulski, Howell, & Horn, 1986; Marsh, Friedman, Welch, & Desberg, 1981). Analogy mechanisms share features with direct visual/orthographic recognition procedures and with grapheme-to-phoneme decoding procedures. The latter require complete phonological analysis but do not require that a precise orthographic representation be stored in memory; the former do require such a representation but do not require phonological analysis. Analogy mechanisms are similar to grapheme-to-phoneme decoding in that they require some (although not complete) phonological analysis. They are similar to direct visual access procedures in that they require rather precise orthographic representations to operate efficiently. Thus, experiments demonstrating differential use of analogy mechanisms may in fact be indirectly tapping individual differences in the quality of orthographic representations.

What is the precise mechanism that may be responsible for the hypothesized inability of some readers to form precise orthographic representations? For example, it is a common observation that poor readers tend not to fully analyze the interior components of words. If this tendency can be separated from phonological skill, then it could be a mechanism underlying a problem in developing orthographic representations. For example, Venezky (1976) examined the responses of second and fourth-grade children to invariant consonant spellings (b, d, l, m). Skilled and less-skilled readers differed very little in their responses to the consonants when they were in the initial position, but there were large differences when the consonants occupied medial and final positions in the word. Because the consonants all had virtually invariant spelling-to-sound mappings and because the poor readers responded correctly to them 90% of the time when they were in the initial position, Venezky (1976) argued that the problem was not lack of knowledge of letter–sound correspondences; he concluded that, "What appears to be lacking is a concern for word details beyond the beginning of the word" (p. 40).

Venezky's suggestion was echoed by Vellutino and Scanlon (1984) in their critique of Morrison's (1984) hypothesis of a rule-learning deficit as the cause of reading disability. They put forth an alternative interpretation of Morrison's experiments with nonverbal stimuli: "We suggest that these differences may be due to a cognitive style rather than to rule learning per se, a style characterized by a tendency to process letters, words, or information of any kind at a global and superficial level, with little inclination to discriminate in a fine grained or flexible matter" (Vellutino & Scanlon, 1984, p. 41). Frith (1985) echoed this conjecture: "Precise orthographic representations are acquired as the result of a reading strategy that gives equal attention to all letters in a word . . . Such a strategy would therefore involve more work than was necessary and sufficient for word recognition. It is conceivable that individual differences exist in terms of willingness/capacity to adopt such a wastefully inelegant strategy, and this would provide an explanation for arrest at this point in the sequence" (pp. 320–321). Another possibility is that the difference resides in the ability to use larger orthographic units, such as those that are based on correspondences with onset and rime (see Treiman, this volume).

Consistent with these ideas, several investigators (e.g., Adams, 1990; Barron, 1981, 1986; Henderson, 1982; Venezky & Massaro, 1979) have suggested that one reason for the effectiveness of phonics instruction is that it forces attention to the interior details of words, thus facilitating the development of accurate orthographic representations. It is intriguing to speculate that phonics training may indeed work, but for reasons other than those assumed by some of its most vociferous advocates.

It would be extremely interesting to know what the level of phonological sensitivity was for the children in the Venezky (1976) study. If these are the type of children for whom phonological sensitivity is not sufficient for the attainment of reading skill, one might be a step closer to identifying a specific problem in the formation of orthographic representations. However, to isolate a specific problem in forming orthographic images one must first ascertain that the child has no phonological problems and then make sure that the requisite letter–sound knowledge is present for completing the task.

A further reason for exploring the idea of a deficit in the ability to form orthographic representations caused by overly global processing is that the conjectures taken from Vellutino and Scanlon (1984) and from Frith (1985) seem to endorse a strategic interpretation of the underlying processing problem. This is also true of Venezky's (1976) original characterization: "Whatever the source of the problem—lack of appreciation of detail, low criterion level for identification, impulsivity, etc.—training procedures for overcoming it are needed before certain letter–sound relationships can be used" (p. 40). However, it is also possible that a more "hard-wired" process of orthographic pattern learning is responsible. This is why it is important to try to investigate the relative separability of phonological awareness, spelling–sound knowledge, orthographic pattern learning, and global processing strategies—a formidable task indeed.

The idea of a deficit in the process of forming orthographic representations leads to some interesting predictions about the effectiveness of certain remediation techniques. For example, Olson, Foltz, and Wise (1986; Wise et al., 1989; Wise, Olson, & Treiman, 1990) have developed computer-aided reading systems designed to partially eliminate the word processing problems of the poorer reader. The subject reads text on a monitor attached to a computer. When the subject encounters a word that cannot be decoded, he or she touches the word on the screen with a light pen. In less than a second, the word is "spoken" by an audio unit interfaced with the computer. For readers with primarily phonological, or spelling–sound decoding problems, or both, but no problem in orthographic pattern learning, the system could allow them to "break through" and develop the orthographic representations that they would not otherwise have amalgamated in memory (Ehri, 1980). However, the system should not be as effective for those children who have problems in forming accurate visual/orthographic representations.

HOW TO EXPLAIN
SPECIFIC READING DISABILITY:
PHONOLOGICAL PROCESSING
AND MODULARITY

For the moment, I wish to leave this other cognitive "sticking point" and return to phonological sensitivity. I want to explore some ways in which its cognitive status and psychometric properties could serve to clarify some puzzles in the literature on specific reading disability. Specifically, I refer to the research literature that has been generated in the hopes of clarifying the cognitive correlates of so-called "unexpected" reading failure—reading difficulties not predicted from knowledge of the child's other intellectual capabilities. This notion of unexpected reading failure has spawned new diagnostic categories and new educational classification systems. However, the literature on the information processing characteristics of this condition has been notable for its confusion (Stanovich, 1986a, 1988). Research in the domain of phonological processing can clarify this situation.

Several authors (e.g., Hall & Humphreys, 1982) in addition to myself (Stanovich, 1986a) have explored the implications of the fact that the concepts of dyslexia and specific reading disability (these terms will be used interchangeably in the discussion that follows) rest upon what has been termed the *assumption of specificity*. This assumption is implicit in all discussions of these concepts, even if it is not stated explicitly. Simply put, the idea is that a dyslexic child has a brain/cognitive deficit that is reasonably specific to the reading task. The concept of a specific learning disability—the very idea of unexpected reading failure—requires that the deficits displayed by the disabled reader not extend too far into other domains of cognitive functioning. If they did, there would already exist research and educational designations for such children (e.g., low intelligence), and the concept of reading disability would be superfluous.

A major problem in the area of reading disabilities research is that the literature on individual differences in the cognitive processes related to reading has undermined the assumption of specificity. When researchers went looking for cognitive differences between reading-disabled and nondisabled children, they found them virtually everywhere. Also troublesome was the fact that many of the differences were global in nature. The plethora of cognitive differences that have been uncovered threaten to undermine the concept of dyslexia, because they call into question the assumption of specificity. The results instead suggest that reading-disabled children exhibit rather generalized cognitive deficits.

For example, it has been claimed that language processing differences between disabled and nondisabled children exist at levels higher than phonology. Syntactic knowledge and awareness have been found to be deficient in the disabled reader (Byrne, 1981; Hallahan & Bryan, 1981; Menyuk & Flood, 1981; Newcomer & Magee, 1977; Semel & Wiig, 1975; Siegel & Ryan, 1984, 1988, 1989; Stein, Cairns, & Zurif, 1984; Vogel, 1974). Dyslexic children perform relatively poorly on tests of listening comprehension and linguistic awareness (Berger, 1978; Downing, 1980; Just & Carpenter, 1987; Kotsonis & Patterson, 1980; Menyuk & Flood, 1981; Newcomer & Magee, 1977; Siegel & Ryan, 1984, 1988, 1989; Smiley, Oakley, Worthen, Campione, & Brown, 1977). Comprehension strategies that are very general seem to be deficient.

Cognitive and developmental psychologists have linked a plethora of processing strategies to memory performance, and research has shown reading-disabled children to be deficient in their use and willingness to employ virtually every one of these strategies (Bauer, 1982; Foster & Gavelek, 1983; Newman & Hagen, 1981; Tarver, Hallahan, Kauffman, & Ball, 1976; Torgesen, 1977a, 1977b, 1978–1979; Torgesen & Goldman, 1977). These findings have led to characterizations of the underlying cognitive deficit of learning-disabled children that are notable for their generality. For example, Torgesen's (1977a, 1977b) early work on memory functioning led him to characterize the learning-disabled children as inactive learners who fail to apply even cognitive strategies that are within their capabilities.

Torgesen's notion is of course similar to the currently popular ideas regarding the importance of metacognitive or executive functioning. Indeed, recent work on the performance of learning-disabled children has reinforced Torgesen's earlier position and explicitly related his ideas to recent views on metacognitive functioning (Baker, 1982; Foster & Gavelek, 1983; Hagen, Barclay, & Newman, 1982; Hallahan & Bryan, 1981; Wong, 1984). However, the tendency to link deficiencies in metacognitive functioning with reading disability will serve to undermine the assumption of specificity. Recent conceptualizations (e.g., Baron, 1978; Campione & Brown, 1978; Sternberg, 1980, 1982, 1985) have stressed that metacognitive awareness of available strategies is a critical aspect of *intelligence!* We have encountered a paradox here. It is fundamental that hypotheses about the cognitive underpinnings of dyslexia must not undermine the assumption of specificity, but this is just what some lines of research in the learning disabilities field have done. The field, in a sense, threatens to devour itself. I want to save it from this fate.

The alternative hypothesis that I wish to advance is that all characterizations of the reading-disabled child like those outlined previously are on the wrong track—global processes like general linguistic awareness, comprehension, strategic functioning, active/inactive learning, and metacognitive functioning are the wrong places to look for the key to reading disability. The problem with all of these is that they are central processes, too critically intertwined with other aspects of intellectual functioning. My hypothesis (see Stanovich, 1986b) is that these global deficits are observed for two reasons. One is the widespread use of insufficiently selective procedures for defining reading disability. These procedures end up classifying a large number of children with generalized deficits as reading disabled. A second reason is that, although some of these findings of generalized deficits are indeed reliable, the observed performance deficits are the result of reading disability rather than its cause. This is probably particularly true of studies that have examined older disabled children.

The best candidates for key processing mechanisms underlying reading disability are those that are somewhat modular, in roughly Fodor's (1983) sense. Fodor conceptualized modular systems as those that are fast, automatic, and informationally encapsulated. The latter is the most important aspect of modularity. Encapsulation means that a module operates autonomously, that it is not under the direction of higher-level cognitive structures and is not supplemented by real-world knowledge. For our purposes, the important point is that modular processes do not strongly interact with central processes. They may provide data for central processing procedures, but they do not direct those central procedures, nor are they directed by them. Thus, a modular system may fail without disrupting the operations of central processes that do not depend on its output. This seems to me the only type of mechanism that could allow for the existence of reading disabilities in any appreciable numbers. The mechanisms listed previously—those that I argue are bad candidates—are in most cases central processes; they will interact strongly with a host of other cognitive mechanisms. Inefficiency in such a mechanism would surely affect the assessment of the child's intelligence. Modular processes, on the other hand, might fail without necessarily degrading certain central processes of the type needed for adequate performance on intelligence tests.

It is interesting to look at some of the psychometric properties of phonological tasks in light of this modularity framework. One extremely interesting trend running through the correlational work on phonological processing and early reading acquisition is the tendency for the phonological measures to predict reading ability better than comprehensive, standardized intelligence tests. A nonexhaustive sampling of these correlations is provided in Table 11.1, where it is apparent that the trend is highly consistent.

The mean correlation between the phonological measures and reading ability is .54 (median = .535), whereas the mean correlation between intelligence test performance and reading ability is .35 (median = .34). The relative strength of the phonological measures as predictors is even more impressive when one considers that most of them can be administered in under 10 minutes.

Sometimes I think we have been too cautious in our presentations of what has been discovered in this area. We typically present correlations like those in Table 11.1 with the warning that, when squared, we are still only accounting for a small portion of the variance in reading ability. But these phonological tasks are often quite brief, typically only 10–20 trials, and their reliabilities may be quite low. Perhaps the relationships that many investigators are observing are more impressive than is readily apparent. Certainly, the trend in Table 11.1 is magnified when one takes reliability into account, because the reliabilities of the phonological tasks are surely lower than those of the standardized intelligence measures.

Unfortunately, few investigators have reported the reliabilities of their tasks. Our own data (Stanovich et al., 1984) are mixed on this point. Several of the tasks we investigated (e.g., deletion of initial phoneme, supply initial phoneme) actually did have reliabilities greater than .90. However, most of the oddity tasks we investigated had reliabilities in the .60–.75 range. Yopp's (1988) reliabilities were higher, however, averaging .83. Bryant et al. (1989) reported reliabilities of .78, .94, .76, and .83 for several different tasks.

Consider what might happen if investigators in this area were to engage in a practice popular with our colleagues in differential psychology who champion the cause of psychometric concepts such as g: correction for attenuation due to the imperfect reliability of the variables. Suppose we chose .55 as a not atypical correlation between phonological sensitivity and reading. Because most of the correlations in Table 11.1 involve reading tests administered to first-grade children, and in some cases to kindergarten children, a reliability of .85 for the reading test is not unreasonable. If the reliability of the phonological task is only .65, then the corrected "true" correlation is in the .75 range. Of course, there are cautions to be observed in applying the disattenuation procedure (Winne & Belfry, 1982), but this never dissuaded Spearman from reporting disattentuated correlations greater than 1.0! In any case, I raise the reliability issue more as food for thought than as something I wish to push strongly.

Another interesting aspect of phonological sensitivity measures as predictors is their relative uniqueness. Several investigators (Bradley & Bryant, 1983, 1985; Goldstein, 1976; Juel et al., 1986; Lundberg et al., 1980; Mann, 1984; Tunmer & Nesdale, 1985; Vellutino & Scanlon, 1987; Wagner & Torgesen, 1987) have demonstrated that phonological tasks account for a statistically significant proportion of variance in reading ability after the variance associated with standardized intelligence measures has been partialed out. For example, Bradley and Bryant (1985) found that their sound categorization task accounted for a significant increase in variance explained even after chronological age, a picture vocabulary test, the WISC, and a memory test had been entered into the regression equation. Similarly, in our first-grade data (Stanovich et al., 1984a), two phonological awareness measures accounted for significant variance in reading ability after the variance associated with Raven's Progressive Matrices, the Peabody Picture Vocabulary Test, and two measures of listening comprehension had been partialed out.

This relative uniqueness of the phonological measures is quite striking to anyone who has explored multivariate data sets containing several cognitive tasks and thus knows how quickly the uniqueness values of most tasks drop when just a few variables have gone into the equation. The phonological tasks seem to be tapping something very different from the cognitive processes measured by our standard intelligence, cognitive, and reading readiness tasks. This impression is bolstered by a consideration of the third column of Table 11.1, where one sees the correlations between the phonological and the intelligence measures. These correlations are quite low. The mean correlation between performance on the phonological and intelligence measures was .37 (median = .36). Of course, these low correlations are the reason for the regression patterns described previously, so these are not independent findings. Nevertheless, looking at the zero-order correlations helps one to get a feel for the relative separability of phonological skill and intelligence.

In short, phonological sensitivity is not closely related to other higher-level

TABLE 11.1
Examples of Correlations Between Phonological Sensitivity (PS), Intelligence Test Performance
(IQ), and Early Reading Ability (R)

Study	PS and R	IQ and R	PS and IQ
Bradley and Bryant (1985)	.52	.52	
		.45	
	.57	.51	
Bryant, Bradley, Maclean, and Crossland (1989)	.67	.66	.58
	.64	.42	.58
	.66		.61
			.28
			.46
			.34
Helfgott (1976)	.72	.41	
	.49		
Juel, Griffith, and Gough (1986)	.56	.34	.40
	.69		.36
	.67		.43
Lundberg, Olofsson, and Wall (1980)	.37	.19	.29
	.34	.15	.29
Share, Jorm, Maclean, and Mathews (1984)	.66	.47	
	.62	.50	
Stanovich, Cunningham, and Cramer (1984)	.47	.25	.55
Stanovich, Cunningham, and Freeman (1984a)	.43	.33	.29
	.44	.34	.07
Torneus (1984)	.33	.24	.30
	.41		.31
	.41		.42
	.52		.50
Tunmer and Nesdale (1985)	.48	.28	.11
Tunmer, Herriman, and Nesdale (1988)	.41	.10	.13
	.44	.34	.42
	.27	.11	
	.32	.43	
	.54		
Vellutino and Scanlon (1987)	.46	.34	
	.48	.39	
	.55	.39	
	.53	.32	
Yopp (1988)	.63		
	.66		
	.67		
	.55		
	.47		
	.71		
	.67		
	.72		
	.53		
Zifcak (1981)	.64	.27	
	.66	.33	

Note. Some AS correlations are averages of correlations from several different tasks employed in the study;
in some cases multiple values are reported when different intelligence and reading tests were used in the
same study, or children of different ages, or different subgroups; the time of PS assessment in these studies
varied from prekindergarten, to kindergarten, to first grade.

cognitive skills. Thus, it is a good candidate for the mechanism that leads to specific reading disability. To be far off the regression line when reading ability is plotted against intelligence (that is, to be specifically reading disabled), the assumption of specificity must be met: The child must have a cognitive problem that depresses reading but not other global intellectual skills. The dissociation between phonological skills and global cognitive measures makes phonological skills one of the few mechanisms we know of that fits this bill. However, it is possible that there are other word-level mechanisms that might also be candidates. Perhaps the processes underlying the formation of visual–orthographic representations or the processes underlying the induction and use of spelling–sound knowledge are similarly dissociated from central cognitive functions. However, because we have much less evidence on the relative dissociation of these processes, the subsequent discussion will focus on phonological sensitivity.

THE CONSEQUENCES
OF EARLY READING FAILURE

Is it possible that there is one cause of reading failure, but there are many consequences? How far can we get by defending this strongly stated hypothesis? Does it clarify any of the puzzles in the literature on reading disability? These are the questions of the present section, where I intend to weave together the following hypothesis: (a) Early development of phonological sensitivity is crucial to the successful completion of the initial stages of reading acquisition; (b) initial success or lack of success in early reading becomes magnified because reading is embedded in a particular social, instructional, and cognitive context; (c) as reading skill develops, it becomes more tightly intertwined with other cognitive skills and knowledge bases; and (d) because of (a) and (b), the cognitive consequences of reading failure are profound.

Many chapters in this volume demonstrate that to set the stage for future success a beginning reader must at some point discover the alphabetic principle: that units of print map on to units of sound (see also Gough & Hillinger, 1980; Juel, 1988; Liberman, 1983; Perfetti, 1984). This principle may be induced; it may be acquired through direct instruction; it may be acquired along with or after the build-up of a visually based sight vocabulary; but it must be acquired if a child is to progress successfully in reading. Children must be able to decode independently the many unknown words that they will encounter in the early stages of reading. Only some knowledge of grapheme-to-phoneme mappings will enable the child to gain the reading independence that eventually leads to the levels of practice that are a prerequisite to fluent reading. The research cited previously appears to indicate that some minimal level of phonemic sensitivity is required for the acquisition of the spelling-to-sound knowledge that supports independent decoding.

In Allington's (1984) first-grade sample, the total number of words read during a week of school reading-group sessions ranged from a low of 16 for one of the children in the less-skilled group to a high of 1933 for one of the children in the skilled reading group. Allington observed that some of the skilled reading groups were reading three times as many words per week as some of the less-skilled groups. Of course, these results say nothing about the relative differences in home reading, which are at least as large (Anderson, Wilson, & Fielding, 1988). The important point is that very early in the initial acquisition process poor readers, who experience greater difficulty in breaking the spelling-to-sound code, are exposed to much less text than their more skilled peers.

These exposure differences contribute to the enormous spread of decoding ability that is already present by the end of Grade 1. In a previous study (Stanovich, 1981), I measured the speed and accuracy with which first-grade children named a set of 20 words at the end of the school year. Not surprisingly, the less-skilled group made three times as many errors as the skilled group (9.7 vs. 3.3). Reaction times were computed on only those words that the subject named correctly. This ensures a confounding of stimuli with subject group: The times of the skilled readers came from words that were considerably more difficult than the words named by the less-skilled group. Nevertheless, the naming times of the skilled readers were still 340 msec faster than those of the less-skilled readers. The skilled children were decoding more difficult material and decoding it more efficiently than the less-skilled children.

Further exacerbating the problem of differential exposure is the fact that less-skilled readers often find themselves in materials that are too difficult for them (Allington, 1977, 1983, 1984; Bristow, 1985; Forell, 1985; Gambrell, Wilson, & Gantt, 1981). The combination of deficient decoding skills, lack of practice, and difficult materials results in unrewarding early reading experiences that lead to less involvement in reading-related activities. Lack of exposure and practice on the part of the less-skilled reader delays the development of automaticity and speed at the word recognition level. Thus, reading for meaning is hindered, unrewarding reading experiences multiply, and practice is avoided or merely tolerated without real cognitive involvement.

With maturation and further practice in an alphabetic orthography the phonological sensitivity of the less-skilled reader does develop. But at the point when the poorer readers finally acquire the necessary level of phonological sensitivity they of course do not suddenly become facile readers (Fox & Routh, 1983). Children with slowly developing phonological sensitivity are unfortunately subject to other disadvantages. Those who have difficulty using spelling–sound cues to decode will tend to rely on other mechanisms. They may rely heavily on context and the development of a sight vocabulary to deal with the reading demands of school. These mechanisms will eventually prove insufficient to sustain fluent reading, but if they are all the child has they will certainly be used. A problem may arise if the child cannot be weaned from these inefficient strategies at the time when the requisite phonological sensitivity has been achieved. This will be less of a problem for the reader who has relatively advanced phonological skills, because such a child will have a much shorter history of reliance on other strategies.

The more frequent and richer reading experiences of the skilled reader have other consequences that in turn facilitate subsequent reading experiences. The better reader is more rapidly approaching a stage where decoding efficiency is no longer the primary determinant of reading level. As word recognition demands fewer resources, more general language skills become the limiting factor on reading ability (Chall, 1983; Gough & Tunmer, 1986; Sticht, 1979; Sticht & James, 1984). But the reading experience of the better reader has provided an enormous advantage even here. Reading itself contributes importantly to the development of many language and cognitive skills. For example, much vocabulary growth probably takes place through the learning of word meanings from context during reading (Hayes, 1988; Nagy & Anderson, 1984; Nagy, Herman, & Anderson, 1985; Stanovich, 1986b; Sternberg, 1985). Similarly, much general information and knowledge about more complex syntactic structures probably also takes place through reading itself (Mann, 1986b; Perfetti, 1985, p. 172–173). In short, many things that facilitate further growth in reading comprehension ability—general knowledge, vocabulary, syntactic knowledge—are developed by reading itself. These in turn serve to fuel further increases in reading comprehension ability. The increased reading experiences of children who crack the spelling-to-sound code early have important positive feedback effects that are denied the slowly progressing reader. Such feedback appears to be a potent source of individual differences in reading-related cognitive skills (Anderson et al., 1988; Cunningham & Stanovich, 1990, 1991; Hayes, 1988; Hayes & Ahrens, 1988; Share, McGee, & Silva, 1989; Share & Silva, 1987; Stanovich, 1986b; Stanovich & West, 1989; van den Bos, 1989).

Just as important as the cognitive spinoffs of reading failure are the motivational side effects. These are starting to receive the increasing attention of researchers (Johnston & Winograd, 1985; Oka & Paris, 1986). Butkowsky and Willows (1980) manipulated success and failure in a reading and a nonreading task. The poor readers in their experiment were less likely to attribute success to ability and were more likely to attribute it to luck or to the easiness of the task than were the better readers. Following failure, however, they were more likely to attribute their performance to ability and less likely to attribute it to luck or to task difficulty. The poorer readers also displayed less task persistence. Their behavior displayed characteristics of academic learned helplessness (Diener & Dweck, 1978; Fowler & Peterson, 1981; Licht & Dweck, 1984; Torgesen & Licht, 1983). Interestingly, the children displayed the same behavioral and attributional patterns on the nonreading task as on the reading task. Thus, the learned helplessness that may have resulted from reading failure was beginning to influence performance on other cognitive tasks, perhaps eventually leading to an general inability to deal with all types of academic and cognitive tasks. In addition to the negative cognitive effects of reading failure, motivational spinoffs can also lead to increasingly global performance deficits.

To summarize, it is hypothesized that there are developmental changes in the degree to which the deficits of reading-disabled children display cognitive specificity. The performance of reading-disabled children is characterized by a relatively high degree of specificity upon entering school; it is localized in the phonological domain. But the specificity eventually breaks down, in part because of the consequences of reading failure. Of course, the exact time course of this developmental sequence and its feedback effects remains to be worked out. The aspect of the argument that is critical for the present discussion is the hypothesis that at some point slower progress at reading acquisition begins to have more generalized effects—effects on processes of import to a broader range of tasks and skills than just reading. That is, the initial specificity of the problem may turn into a wider deficit due to the behavioral, cognitive, and motivational spinoffs from failure at such a crucial educational task as reading.

A developmental trend in the applicability of the specificity hypothesis may in part explain why the literature has not uncovered strong evidence for specificity and instead has indicated a plethora of cognitive deficits: The subjects in many of the studies may have been so developmentally advanced that generalized cognitive deficiencies had begun to appear. This is certainly true of studies of cognitive differences among adult readers of varying skill. Studies examining the differing reading subskill profiles of older disabled children may be looking not at differing causes of reading failure but at different methods of coping with a disability that has a common cause.

The hypothesis that initial advantages in reading acquisition have strong feedback effects on other reading-related cognitive skills (the "Matthew effects" hypothesis; see Stanovich, 1986b) argues for emphasizing early remediation. It also affects how we interpret the absolute magnitude of the outcomes of preventative efforts. For example, a critic of the Bradley and Bryant (1983, 1985) phonological training study might argue that the achievement difference between the sound categorization experimental group and the control group was fairly small in magnitude (e.g., Yaden, 1984). However, one inference that follows from the developmental hypothesis outlined previously is that small achievement differences that appear early can cause large differences later on (see Bradley, 1987).

When viewed in light of possible reciprocal and feedback relationships, the achievement differences observed by Bradley and Bryant (1983, 1985) can hardly be deemed unimportant. A longitudinal study by Jorm, Share, Maclean, and Matthews (1984; see also Juel, 1988) illustrates how variation in phonological skills may generate individual differences in reading acquisition that increase with development. Jorm and his colleagues formed two groups of kindergarten children who differed on phonological recoding skill but were matched on verbal intelligence and sight word reading. By the first grade, the group superior in phonological recoding skill was four months advanced in reading achievement. However, the two groups tended to diverge with time, the performance difference increasing to nine months by the second grade.

CONCLUSION

In advancing their "simple view of reading," Gough and Tunmer (1986; Hoover & Gough, 1990) suggested that as a useful simplifying assumption we treat decoding as the proximal cause of reading disability. This chapter is in the spirit of their analysis. I have suggested a simplifying assumption for those investigations that probe one step distal from decoding, that there are only a very small number of cognitive mechanisms that are responsible for decoding problems. A further useful simplifying assumption was used to clarify the literature on reading disability. I argued that the best candidates for cognitive mechanisms mediating the reading problem are those that are not too global in nature, in short, mechanisms that display some modular properties. For this reason, the phonological domain was viewed as a good candidate for the cognitive mechanism that could cause specific reading disability, whereas generalized rule-learning mechanisms, strategic processing, and metacogitive functioning were viewed as doubtful candidates.

The developmental hypothesis that I have advanced fits well within the modularity framework. It explains how failure in a specific subsystem can selectively damage performance in one cognitive task while leaving others relatively unscathed. The hypothesis accounts for how central processes can operate efficiently in a variety of tasks even while a deficient module is depressing performance in a selective domain, which is a prerequisite pattern for the idea of specific reading disability.

A focus on gradually developing cognitive skill deficits could enrich some of our ideas about the logic of an intelligence made up of both modular and central systems (Fodor, 1983). For example, to say that a modular system may fail without disrupting the *current* operations of some central systems not dependent on its current output is not to say that the consistent failure of a module will have no long-term *indirect* effects on central systems. This is precisely what I think is happening in reading. If the continued development of a central process depends on a deficient module for information that cannot be derived from other input systems, then a modular failure could lead to the deterioration of a central system. The persistent failure of the word recognition module to present central processes with the real-world knowledge, complex syntactic structures, decontextualized arguments, and vocabulary that are present in written language may have severe and snowballing effects on the development of higher-level processing operations. This idea is increasingly emphasized by reading theorists (e.g.,

Anderson et al., 1988; Chall, 1983; Chall, Jacobs, & Baldwin, 1990; Mann, 1986b; Morrison & Manis, 1982; Perfetti, 1985; Stanovich, 1986b; Torgesen, 1985).

REFERENCES

Adams, M. J. (1990). *Beginning to read: Thinking and learning about print*. Cambridge, MA: MIT Press.

Allington, R. L. (1977). If they don't read much, how they ever gonna get good? *Journal of Reading, 21*, 57–61.

Allington, R. L. (1980). Poor readers don't get to read much in reading groups. *Language Arts, 57*, 872–876.

Allington, R. L. (1983). The reading instruction provided readers of differing reading abilities. *The Elementary School Journal, 83*, 548–559.

Allington, R. L. (1984). Content coverage and contextual reading in reading groups. *Journal of Reading Behavior, 16*, 85–96.

Allport, D. A. (1980). Attention and performance. In G. Claxton (Ed.), *Cognitive psychology: New directions* (pp. 112–153). London: Routledge & Kegan Paul.

Anderson, R. C., Wilson, P. T., & Fielding, L. G. (1988). Growth in reading and how children spend their time outside of school. *Reading Research Quarterly, 23*, 285–303.

Badcock, D., & Lovegrove, W. (1981). The effects of contrast, stimulus duration, and spatial frequency on visible persistence in normal and specifically disabled readers. *Journal of Experimental Psychology: Human Perception and Performance, 7*, 495–505.

Baddeley, A. D., Ellis, N. C., Miles, T. R., & Lewis, V. J. (1982). Developmental and acquired dyslexia: A comparison. *Cognition, 11*, 185–199.

Baker, L. (1982). An evaluation of the role of metacognitive deficits in learning disabilities. *Topics in Learning and Learning Disabilities, 2*, 27–35.

Ball, E. W., & Blachman, B. A. (1988). Phoneme segmentation training: Effect on reading readiness. *Annals of Dyslexia, 38*, 208–225.

Balota, D., Pollatsek, A., & Rayner, K. (1985). The interaction of contextual constraints and parafoveal visual information in reading. *Cognitive Psychology, 17*, 364–390.

Baron, J. (1977). Mechanisms for pronouncing printed words: Use and acquisition. In D. LaBerge & S. J. Samuels (Eds.), *Basic processes in reading: Perception and comprehension* (pp. 175–216). Hillsdale, NJ: Lawrence Erlbaum Associates.

Baron, J. (1978). Intelligence and general strategies. In G. Underwood (Ed.), *Strategies in information processing* (pp. 403–450). San Diego, CA: Academic Press.

Baron, J. (1979). Orthographic and word-specific mechanisms in children's reading of words. *Child Development, 50*, 60–72.

Baron, J., & Treiman, R. (1980). Use of orthography in reading and learning to read. In J. F. Kavanagh & R. L. Venezky (Eds.), *Orthography, reading, and dyslexia* (pp. 171–189). Baltimore, MD: Park Press.

Barr, R. C. (1974–1975). The effect of instruction on pupil reading strategies. *Reading Research Quarterly, 10*, 555–582.

Barron, R. (1981). Reading skill and spelling strategies. In A. Lesgold & C. A. Perfetti (Eds.), *Interactive processes in reading* (pp. 299–327). Hillsdale, NJ: Lawrence Erlbaum Associates.

Barron, R. (1986). Word recognition in early reading: A review of the direct and indirect access hypothesis. *Cognition, 24*, 93–119.

Bauer, R. (1982). Information processing as a way of understanding and diagnosing learning disabilities. *Topics in Learning and Learning Disabilities, 2*, 33–45.

Berger, N. (1978). Why can't John read? Perhaps he's not a good listener. *Journal of Learning Disabilities, 11,* 633–638.

Bertelson, P. (1986). The onset of literacy: Liminal remarks. *Cognition, 24,* 1–30.

Bertelson, P., Morais, J., Alegria, J., & Content, A. (1985). Phonetic analysis capacity and learning to read. *Nature, 313,* 73–74.

Biemiller, A. (1970). The development of the use of graphic and contextual information as children learn to read. *Reading Research Quarterly, 6,* 75–96.

Biemiller, A. (1979). Changes in the use of graphic and contextual information as functions of passage difficulty and reading achievement level. *Journal of Reading Behavior, 11,* 307–319.

Bissex, G. L. (1980). *Gnys at wrk.* Cambridge, MA: Harvard University Press.

Bradley, L. (1987, December). *Categorising sounds, early intervention and learning to read: A follow-up study.* Paper presented at the meeting of the British Psychological Society, London.

Bradley, L., & Bryant, P. E. (1978). Difficulties in auditory organisation as a possible cause of reading backwardness. *Nature, 271,* 746–747.

Bradley, L., & Bryant, P. E. (1983). Categorizing sounds and learning to read—a causal connection. *Nature, 301,* 419–421.

Bradley, L., & Bryant, P. E. (1985). *Rhyme and reason in reading and spelling.* Ann Arbor: University of Michigan Press.

Briggs, P., Austin, S., & Underwood, G. (1984). The effects of sentence context in good and poor readers: A test of Stanovich's interactive-compensatory model. *Reading Research Quarterly, 20,* 54–61.

Bristow, P. S. (1985). Are poor readers passive readers?: Some evidence, possible explanations, and potential solutions. *The Reading Teacher, 39,* 318–325.

Bruck, M. (1990). Word-recognition skills of adults with childhood diagnoses of dyslexia. *Developmental Psychology, 26,* 439–454.

Bruck, M., & Treiman, R. (1990). Phonological awareness and spelling in normal children and dyslexics: The case of initial consonant clusters. *Journal of Experimental Child Psychology, 50,* 156–178.

Bryant, P. E., & Bradley, L. (1985). Reply to Bertelson et al. *Nature, 313,* 74.

Bryant, P. E., Bradley, L., Maclean, M., & Crossland, J. (1989). Nursery rhymes, phonological skills and reading. *Journal of Child Language, 16,* 407–428.

Bryant, P. E., & Impey, L. (1986). The similarities between normal readers and developmental and acquired dyslexics. *Cognition, 24,* 121–137.

Bryant, P. E., Maclean, M., Bradley, L., & Crossland, J. (1990). Rhyme and alliteration, phoneme detection, and learning to read. *Developmental Psychology, 26,* 429–438.

Butkowsky, S., & Willows, D. (1980). Cognitive-motivational characteristics of children varying in reading ability: Evidence for learned helplessness in poor readers. *Journal of Educational Psychology, 72,* 408–422.

Byrne, B. (1981). Deficient syntactic control in poor readers: Is a weak phonetic memory code responsible? *Applied Psycholinguistics, 2,* 201–212.

Byrne, B., & Fielding-Barnsley, R. (1989). Phonemic awareness and letter knowledge in the child's acquisition of the alphabetic principle. *Journal of Educational Psychology, 81,* 313–321.

Calfee, R. C. (1977). Assessment of independent reading skills: Basic research and practical applications. In A. S. Reber & D. L. Scarborough (Eds.), *Toward a psychology of reading: The proceedings of the CUNY conferences.* (pp. 289–323). Hillsdale, NJ: Lawrence Erlbaum Associates.

Campione, J., & Brown, A. (1978). Toward a theory of intelligence: Contributions from research with retarded children. *Intelligence, 2,* 279–304.

Chall, J. S. (1983). *Stages of reading development.* New York: McGraw-Hill.

Chall, J. S., Jacobs, V. A., & Baldwin, L. E. (1990). *The reading crisis: Why poor children fall behind.* Cambridge, MA: Harvard University Press.

Churchland, P. M. (1989). *A neurocomputational perspective: The nature of mind and the structure of science.* Cambridge, MA: MIT Press.

Churchland, P. S. (1986). *Neurophilosophy: Toward a unified science of the mind/brain.* Cambridge, MA: MIT Press.

Cunningham, A. E. (1990). Explicit versus implicit instruction in phonological awareness. *Journal of Experimental Child Psychology, 50,* 429–444.

Cunningham, A. E., & Stanovich, K. E. (1990). Assessing print exposure and orthographic processing skill in children: A quick measure of reading experience. *Journal of Educational Psychology, 82,* 733–740.

Cunningham, A. E., & Stanovich, K. E. (1991). Tracking the unique effects of print exposure in children: Associations with vocabulary, general knowledge, and spelling. *Journal of Educational Psychology, 83,* 264–274.

Dennett, D. (1987). *The intentional stance.* Cambridge, MA: MIT Press.

Diener, C., & Dweck, C. (1978). An analysis of learned helplessness: Continuous changes in performance, strategy, and achievement cognitions following failure. *Journal of Personality and Social Psychology, 36,* 451–462.

DiLollo, V., Hanson, D., & McIntyre, J. S. (1983). Initial stages of visual information processing in dyslexia. *Journal of Experimental Psychology: Human Perception and Performance, 9,* 923–935.

Downing, J. (1980). Learning to read with understanding. In C. M. McCullough (Ed.), *Persistent problems in reading education* (pp. 163–178). Newark, DE: International Reading Association.

Ehri, L. C. (1979). Linguistic insight: Threshold of reading acquisition. In T. G. Waller & G. E. MacKinnon (Eds.), *Reading research: Advances in research and theory* (Vol. 1, pp. 63–114). San Diego, CA: Academic Press.

Ehri, L. C. (1980). The development of orthographic images. In U. Frith (Ed.), *Cognitive processes in spelling* (pp. 311–338). San Diego, CA: Academic Press.

Ehri, L. C. (1984). How orthography alters spoken language competencies in children learning to read and spell. In J. Downing & R. Valtin (Eds.), *Language awareness and learning to read* (pp. 119–147). New York: Springer-Verlag.

Ehri, L. C. (1985). Effects of printed language acquisition on speech. In D. Olson, N. Torrance, & A. Hildyard (Eds.), *Literacy, language, and learning* (pp. 333–367). Cambridge, England: Cambridge University Press.

Ehri, L. C. (1987). Learning to read and spell words. *Journal of Reading Behavior, 19,* 5–31.

Ehri, L. C., & Wilce, L. (1985). Movement into reading: Is the first stage of printed word learning visual or phonetic? *Reading Research Quarterly, 20,* 163–179.

Ehri, L. C., Wilce, L., & Taylor, B. B. (1987). Children's categorization of short vowels in words and the influence of spellings. *Merrill-Palmer Quarterly, 33,* 393–421.

Fletcher, J. M. (1981). Linguistic factors in reading acquisition. In F. Pirozzolo & M. Wittrock (Eds.), *Neuropsychology and cognitive processes in reading* (pp. 261–294). San Diego, CA: Academic Press.

Fletcher, J. M., & Satz, P. (1979). Unitary deficit hypotheses of reading disabilities. *Journal of Learning Disabilities, 12,* 22–26.

Fodor, J. (1983). *Modularity of mind.* Cambridge, MA: MIT Press.

Forell, E. R. (1985). The case for conservative reader placement. *The Reading Teacher, 35,* 857–862.

Foster, R., & Gavelek, J. (1983). Development of intentional forgetting in normal and reading-delayed children. *Journal of Educational Psychology, 75,* 431–440.

Fowler, J., & Peterson, P. (1981). Increasing reading persistence and altering attributional style of learned helpless children. *Journal of Educational Psychology, 73,* 251–260.

Fox, B., & Routh, D. K. (1975). Analyzing spoken language into words, syllables, and phonemes: A developmental study. *Journal of Psycholinguistic Research, 4,* 331–342.

Fox, B., & Routh, D. K. (1983). Reading disability, phonemic analysis, and dysphonic spelling: A follow-up study. *Journal of Clinical Child Psychology, 12,* 28–32.

Fox, B., & Routh, D. K. (1984). Phonemic analysis and synthesis as word attack skills: Revisited. *Journal of Educational Psychology, 76,* 1059–1064.

Freebody, P., & Byrne, B. (1988). Word-reading strategies in elementary school children: Relations to comprehension, reading time, and phonemic awareness. *Reading Research Quarterly, 23,* 441–453.

Frith, U. (1985). Beneath the surface of developmental dyslexia. In K. E. Patterson, J. C. Marshall, & M. Coltheart (Eds.), *Surface dyslexia: Neuropsychologic and cognitive studies of phonologic reading.* (pp. 301–330). Hillsdale, NJ: Lawrence Erlbaum Associates.

Gambrell, L. B., Wilson, R. M., & Gantt, W. N. (1981). Classroom observations of task-attending behaviors of good and poor readers. *Journal of Educational Research, 74,* 400–404.

Goldsmith, J. S. (1981). Decoding reexamined. *Elementary School Journal, 82,* 152–159.

Goldstein, D. (1976). Cognitive-linguistic functioning and learning to read in preschoolers. *Journal of Educational Psychology, 68,* 680–688.

Goswami, U. (1986). Children's use of analogy in learning to read: A developmental study. *Journal of Experimental Child Psychology, 42,* 73–83.

Goswami, U. (1988). Orthographic analogies and reading development. *Quarterly Journal of Experimental Psychology, 40A,* 239–268.

Goswami, U. (1990). A special link between rhyming skills and the use of orthographic analogies by beginning readers. *Journal of Child Psychology and Psychiatry, 31,* 301–311.

Gough, P. B., & Hillinger, M. L. (1980). Learning to read: An unnatural act. *Bulletin of the Orton Society, 30,* 171–176.

Gough, P. B., Juel, C., & Roper/Schneider, D. (1983). Code and cipher: A two-stage conception of initial reading acquisition. In J. Niles & L. Harris (Eds.), *Thirty-second yearbook of the National Reading Conference* (pp. 207–211). National Reading Conference, Rochester, New York.

Gough, P. B., & Tunmer, W. E. (1986). Decoding reading, and reading disability. *Remedial and Special Education, 7,* 6–10.

Hagen, J., Barclay, C., & Newman, R. (1982). Metacognition, self-knowledge, and learning disabilities: Some thoughts on knowing and doing. *Topics in Learning and Learning Disabilities, 2,* 19–26.

Hall, J., & Humphreys, M. (1982). Research on specific learning disabilities: Deficits and remediation. *Topics in Learning and Learning Disabilities, 2,* 68–78.

Hallahan, D., & Bryan, T. (1981). Learning disabilities. In J. Kauffman & D. Hallahan (Eds.), *Handbook of special education* (pp. 141–164). Englewood Cliffs, NJ: Prentice-Hall.

Hayes, D. P. (1988). Speaking and writing: Distinct patterns of word choice. *Journal of Memory and Language, 27,* 572–585.

Hayes, D. P., & Ahrens, M. (1988). Vocabulary simplification for children: A special case of 'motherese'? *Journal of Child Language, 15,* 395–410.

Henderson, L. (1982). *Orthography and word recognition in reading.* San Diego, CA: Academic Press.

Holligan, C., & Johnston, R. S. (1988). The use of phonological information by good and poor readers in memory and reading tasks. *Memory and Cognition, 16,* 522–532.

Hoover, W. A., & Gough, P. B. (1990). The simple view of reading. *Reading and Writing: An Interdisciplinary Journal, 2,* 127–160.

Hulme, C. (1988). The implausibility of low-level visual deficits as a cause of children's reading difficulties. *Cognitive Neuropsychology, 5,* 369–374.

Johnston, P. H., & Winograd, P. N. (1985). Passive failure in reading. *Journal of Reading Behavior, 17,* 279–301.

Jorm, A. F., & Share, D. L. (1983). Phonological recoding and reading acquisition. *Applied Psycholinguistics, 4,* 103–147.

Jorm, A. F., Share, D. L., Maclean, R., & Matthews, R. (1984). Phonological recoding skills and learning to read: A longitudinal study. *Applied Psycholinguistics, 5,* 201–207.

Juel, C. (1980). Comparison of word identification strategies with varying context, word type, and reader skill. *Reading Research Quarterly, 15,* 358–376.

Juel, C. (1988). Learning to read and write: A longitudinal study of 54 children from first through fourth grades. *Journal of Educational Psychology, 80,* 437–447.

Juel, C., Griffith, P. L., & Gough, P. B. (1986). Acquisition of literacy: A longitudinal study of children in first and second grade. *Journal of Educational Psychology, 78,* 243–255.

Just, M. A., & Carpenter, P. A. (1980). A theory of reading: From eye fixations to comprehension. *Psychological Review, 4,* 329–354.

Just, M. A., & Carpenter, P. A. (1987). *The psychology of reading and language comprehension.* Boston: Allyn & Bacon.

Kamhi, A., & Catts, H. (1989). *Reading disabilities: A developmental language perspective.* Boston: College-Hill Press.

Kibby, M. W. (1979). Passage readability affects the oral reading strategies of disabled readers. *The Reading Teacher, 32,* 390–396.

Kotsonis, M., & Patterson, C. (1980). Comprehension-monitoring skills in learning-disabled children. *Developmental Psychology, 16,* 541–542.

Leu, D. (1982). Oral reading error analysis: A critical review of research and application. *Reading Research Quarterly, 17,* 420–437.

Liberman, I. Y. (1983). A language-orientated view of reading and its disabilities. In H. Myklebust (Ed.), *Progress in learning disabilities* (Vol. 5, pp. 81–101). New York: Grune & Stratton.

Licht, B., & Dweck, C. (1984). Determinants of academic achievement: The interaction of children's achievement orientations with skill area. *Developmental Psychology, 20,* 628–636.

Lovegrove, W., & Slaghuis, W. (1989). How reliable are visual differences found in dyslexics? *Irish Journal of Psychology, 10,* 542–550.

Lundberg, I., Frost, J., & Petersen, O.-P. (1988). Effects of an extensive program for stimulating phonological awareness in preschool children. *Reading Research Quarterly, 23,* 263–284.

Lundberg, I., & Hoien, T. (1989). Phonemic deficits: A core symptom of developmental dyslexia? *Irish Journal of Psychology, 10,* 579–592.

Lundberg, I., Olofsson, A., & Wall, S. (1980). Reading and spelling skills in the first school years predicted from phonemic awareness skills in kindergarten. *Scandinavian Journal of Psychology, 21,* 159–173.

Lycan, W. G. (1990). *Mind and cognition: A reader.* Cambridge, MA: Basil Blackwell.

Lyons, W. (1986). *The disappearance of introspection.* Cambridge, MA: MIT Press.

Maclean, M., Bryant, P., & Bradley, L. (1987). Rhymes, nursery rhymes, and reading in early childhood. *Merrill-Palmer Quarterly, 33,* 255–281.

Manis, F. R., Szeszulski, P., Howell, M., & Horn, C. (1986). A comparison of analogy- and rule-based decoding strategies in normal and dyslexic children. *Journal of Reading Behavior, 18,* 203–218.

Mann, V. (1984). Reading skill and language skill. *Developmental Review, 4,* 1–15.

Mann, V. (1986a). Phonological awareness: The role of reading experience. *Cognition, 24,* 65–92.

Mann, V. (1986b). Why some children encounter reading problems. In J. Torgesen & B. Wong (Eds.), *Psychological and educational perspectives on learning disabilities* (pp. 133–159). San Diego, CA: Academic Press.

Mann, V., Tobin, P., & Wilson, R. (1987). Measuring phonological awareness through the invented spelling of kindergarten children. *Merrill-Palmer Quarterly, 33,* 365–391.

Marcel, A. J., & Bisiach, E. (1988). *Consciousness in contemporary science.* London: Oxford University Press.

Marsh, G., Friedman, M., Welch, V., & Desberg, P. (1981). A cognitive-developmental theory of reading acquisition. In G. MacKinnon & T. Waller (Eds.), *Reading research: Advances in theory and practice* (Vol. 3, pp. 199–221). San Diego, CA: Academic Press.

Martin, F., & Lovegrove, W. (1984). The effects of field size and luminance on contrast sensitivity differences between specifically reading disabled and normal children. *Neuropsychologia, 22,* 73–77.

Martin, F., & Lovegrove, W. (1988). Uniform and field flicker in control and specifically disabled readers. *Perception, 17,* 203–214.

Mason, J. M. (1980). When do children begin to read: An exploration of four year old children's letter and word reading competencies. *Reading Research Quarterly, 15,* 203–227.

Masonheimer, P. E., Drum, P. A., & Ehri, L. C. (1984). Does environmental print identification lead children into word reading? *Journal of Reading Behavior, 16,* 257–271.

McCall, R. B. (1981). Nature-nurture and the two realms of development: A proposed integration with respect to mental development. *Child Development, 52,* 1–12.

Menyuk, P., & Flood, J. (1981). Linguistic competence, reading, writing problems, and remediation. *Bulletin of the Orton Society, 31,* 13–28.

Mitchell, D. (1982). *The process of reading: A cognitive analysis of fluent reading and learning to read.* New York: Wiley.

Morais, J., Alegria, J., & Content, A. (1987). The relationships between segmental analysis and alphabetic literacy: An interactive view. *Cahiers de Psychologie Cognitive, 7,* 415–438.

Morais, J., Bertelson, P., Cary, L., & Alegria, J. (1986). Literacy training and speech segmentation. *Cognition, 24,* 45–64.

Morrison, F. (1984). Word decoding and rule-learning in normal and disabled readers. *Remedial and Special Education, 5,* 20–27.

Morrison, F., & Giordani, B., & Nagy, J. (1977). Reading disability: An information processing analysis. *Science, 196,* 77–79.

Morrison, F., & Manis, F. (1982). Cognitive processes and reading disability: A critique and proposal. In C. Brainerd & M. Pressley (Eds.), *Program in cognitive development research* (Vol. 2, pp. 59–94). New York: Springer-Verlag.

Nagy, W. E., & Anderson, R. C. (1984). How many words are there in printed school English? *Reading Research Quarterly, 19,* 304–330.

Nagy, W. E., Herman, P. A., & Anderson, R. C. (1985). Learning words from context. *Reading Research Quarterly, 20,* 233–253.

Newcomer, P., & Magee, P. (1977). The performance of learning (reading) disabled children on a test of spoken language. *The Reading Teacher, 30,* 896–900.

Newman, R. S., & Hagen, J. W. (1981). Memory strategies in children with learning disabilities. *Journal of Applied Developmental Psychology, 1,* 297–312.

Nicholson, T. (1986). Reading is not a guessing game—The great debate revisited. *Reading Psychology, 7,* 197–210.

Nicholson, T., & Hill, D. (1985). Good readers don't guess—Taking another look at the issue of whether children read words better in context or in isolation. *Reading Psychology, 6,* 181–198.

Nicholson, T., Lillas, C., & Rzoska, M. (1988). Have we been misled by miscues? *The Reading Teacher, 42,* 6–10.

Oka, E., & Paris, S. (1986). Patterns of motivation and reading skills in underachieving children. In S. Ceci (Ed.), *Handbook of cognitive, social, and neuropsychological aspects of learning disabilities* (Vol. 2, pp. 115–145). Hillsdale, NJ: Lawrence Erlbaum Associates.

Olofsson, A., & Lundberg, I. (1985). Evaluation of long term effects of phonemic awareness training in kindergarten. *Scandanavian Journal of Psychology, 26,* 21–34.

Olson, R. K., Foltz, G., & Wise, B. W. (1986). Reading instruction and remediation with the aid of computer speech. *Behavior Research Methods, Instruments, and Computers, 18,* 93–99.

Olson, R. K., Wise, B., Conners, F., Rack, J., & Fulker, D. (1989). Specific deficits in component reading and language skills: Genetic and environmental influences. *Journal of Learning Disabilities, 22,* 339–348.

Patterson, K. E., Marshall, J. C., & Coltheart, M. (1985). *Surface dyslexia: Neurological and cognitive studies of phonological reading.* Hillsdale, NJ: Lawrence Erlbaum Associates.

Perfetti, C. A. (1984). Reading acquisition and beyond: Decoding includes cognition. *American Journal of Education, 92,* 40–60.

Perfetti, C. A. (1985). *Reading ability.* New York: Oxford University Press.

Perfetti, C. A., Beck, I., Bell, L., & Hughes, C. (1987). Phonemic knowledge and learning to read are reciprocal: A longitudinal study of first grade children. *Merrill-Palmer Quarterly, 33,* 283–319.

Perfetti, C. A., Goldman, S., & Hogaboam, T. (1979). Reading skill and the identification of words in discourse context. *Memory and Cognition, 7,* 273–282.

Perfetti, C. A., & Roth, S. (1981). Some of the interactive processes in reading and their role in reading skill. In A. Lesgold & C. Perfetti (Eds.), *Interactive processes in reading* (pp. 269–297). Hillsdale, NJ: Lawrence Erlbaum Associates.

Pollatsek, A., Rayner, K., & Balota, D. A. (1986). Inferences about eye movement control from the perceptual span in reading. *Perception and Psychophysics, 40,* 123–130.

Pring, L., & Snowling, M. (1986). Developmental changes in word recognition: An information-processing account. *Quarterly Journal of Experimental Psychology, 38A,* 395–418.

Rayner, K., & Bertera, J. H. (1979). Reading without a fovea. *Science, 206,* 468–469.

Rayner, K., & Pollatsek, A. (1989). *The psychology of reading.* Englewood Cliffs, NJ: Prentice-Hall.

Read, C., Zhang, Y., Nie, H., & Ding, B. (1986). The ability to manipulate speech sounds depends on knowing alphabetic reading. *Cognition, 24,* 31–44.

Reitsma, P. (1983). Printed word learning in beginning readers. *Journal of Experimental Child Psychology, 36,* 321–339.

Rorty, R. (1979). *Philosophy and the mirror of nature.* Princeton, NJ: Princeton University Press.

Rutter, M. (1978). Prevalence and types of dyslexia. In A. Benton & D. Pearl (Eds.), *Dyslexia: An appraisal of current knowledge* (pp. 5–28). New York: Oxford University Press.

Schwantes, F. M. (1985). Expectancy, integration, and interactional processes: Age differences in the nature of words affected by sentence context. *Journal of Experimental Child Psychology, 39,* 212–229.

Seidenberg, M. S., Waters, G. S., Sanders, M., & Langer, P. (1984). Pre- and post-lexical loci of contextual effects on word recognition. *Memory and Cognition, 12,* 315–328.

Semel, E., & Wiig, E. (1975). Comprehension of syntactic structures and critical verbal elements by children with learning disabilities. *Journal of Learning Disabilities, 8,* 53–58.

Seymour, P. H. K., & Elder, L. (1986). Beginning reading without phonology. *Cognitive Neuropsychology, 3,* 1–36.

Share, D. L., Jorm, A. F., Maclean, R., & Matthews, R. (1984). Sources of individual differences in reading acquisition. *Journal of Educational Psychology, 76,* 1309–1324.

Share, D. L., McGee, R., & Silva, P. A. (1989). IQ and reading progress: A test of the capacity notion of IQ. *Journal of the American Academy of Child and Adolescent Psychiatry, 28,* 97–100.

Share, D. L., & Silva, P. A. (1987). Language deficits and specific reading retardation: Cause or effect? *British Journal of Disorders of Communication, 22,* 219–226.

Siegel, L. S., & Faux, D. (1989). Acquisition of certain grapheme–phoneme correspondences in normally achieving and disabled readers. *Reading and Writing: An Interdisciplinary Journal, 1,* 37–52.

Siegel, L. S., & Ryan, E. B. (1984). Reading disability as a language disorder. *Remedial and Special Education, 5,* 28–33.

Siegel, L. S., & Ryan, E. B. (1988). Development of grammatical-sensitivity, phonological, and short-term memory skills in normally achieving and learning disabled children. *Developmental Psychology, 24,* 28–37.

Siegel, L. S., & Ryan, E. B. (1989). Subtypes of developmental dyslexia: The influence of definitional variables. *Reading and Writing: An Interdisciplinary Journal, 1,* 257–287.

Simons, H. D., & Leu, D. J. (1987). The use of contextual and graphic information in word recognition by second-, fourth-, and sixth-grade readers. *Journal of Reading Behavior, 19,* 33–47.

Simpson, G. B., & Foster, M. R. (1986). Lexical ambiguity and children's word recognition. *Developmental Psychology, 22,* 147–154.

Slaghuis, W. L., & Lovegrove, W. S. (1985). Spatial-frequency dependent visible persistence and specific reading disability. *Brain and Language, 4,* 219–240.

Slaghuis, W. L., & Lovegrove, W. S. (1987). The effect of field size and luminance on spatial-frequency dependent visible persistence and specific reading disability. *Bulletin of the Psychonomic Society, 25,* 38–40.

Smiley, S., Oakley, D., Worthen, D., Campione, J., & Brown, A. (1977). Recall of thematically relevant material by adolescent good and poor readers as a function of written versus oral presentation. *Journal of Educational Psychology, 69,* 381–387.

Smith, F. (1971). *Understanding reading.* New York: Holt, Rinehart & Winston.

Smith, F. (1973). *Psycholinguistics and reading.* New York: Holt, Rinehart & Winston.

Smith, F. (1975). The role of prediction in reading. *Elementary English, 52,* 305–311.

Snowling, M. (1980). The development of grapheme–phoneme correspondence in normal and dyslexic readers. *Journal of Experimental Child Psychology, 29,* 294–305.

Snowling, M. (1981). Phonemic deficits in developmental dyslexia. *Psychological Research, 43,* 219–234.

Snowling, M., Stackhouse, J., & Rack, J. (1986). Phonological dyslexia and dysgraphia—a developmental analysis. *Cognitive Neuropsychology, 3,* 309–339.

Solman, R. T., & May, J. G. (1990). Spatial locatization discrepancies: A visual deficiency in poor readers. *American Journal of Psychology, 103,* 243–263.

Stanovich, K. E. (1980). Toward an interactive-compensatory model of individual differences in the development of reading fluency. *Reading Research Quarterly, 16,* 32–71.

Stanovich, K. E. (1981). Relationships between word decoding speed, general name-retrieval ability, and reading progress in first-grade children. *Journal of Educational Psychology, 73,* 809–815.

Stanovich, K. E. (1982). Individual differences in the cognitive processes of reading: I. Word decoding. *Journal of Learning Disabilities, 15,* 485–493.

Stanovich, K. E. (1984). The interactive-compensatory model of reading: A confluence of developmental, experimental, and educational psychology. *Remedial and Special Education, 5,* 11–19.

Stanovich, K. E. (1986a). Cognitive processes and the reading problems of learning disabled children: Evaluating the assumption of specificity. In J. Torgesen & B. Wong (Eds.), *Psychological and educational perspectives on learning disabilities* (pp. 87–131). San Diego, CA: Academic Press.

Stanovich, K. E. (1986b). Matthew effects in reading: Some consequences of individual differences in the acquisition of literacy. *Reading Research Quarterly, 21,* 360–407.

Stanovich, K. E. (1988). The right and wrong places to look for the cognitive locus of reading disability. *Annals of Dyslexia, 38,* 154–177.

Stanovich, K. E. (1990a). A call for an end to the paradigm wars in reading research. *Journal of Reading Behavior, 22,* 221–231.

Stanovich, K. E. (1990b). Concepts in developmental theories of reading skill: Cognitive resources, automaticity, and modularity. *Developmental Review, 10,* 72–100.

Stanovich, K. E. (1991). Discrepancy definitions of reading disability: Has intelligence led us astray? *Reading Research Quarterly, 26,* 7–29.

Stanovich, K. E., Cunningham, A. E., & Cramer, B. (1984). Assessing phonological awareness in kindergarten children: Issues of task comparability. *Journal of Experimental Child Psychology, 38,* 175–190.

Stanovich, K. E., Cunningham, A. E., & Feeman, D. J. (1984a). Intelligence, cognitive skills, and early reading progress. *Reading Research Quarterly, 19,* 278–303.

Stanovich, K. E., Cunningham, A. E., & Feeman, D. J. (1984b). Relation between early reading acquisition and word decoding with and without context: A longitudinal study of first-grade children. *Journal of Educational Psychology, 76,* 668–677.

Stanovich, K. E., Nathan, R. G., West, R. F., & Vala-Rossi, M. (1985). Children's word recognition in context: Spreading activation, expectancy, and modularity. *Child Development, 56,* 1418–1429.

Stanovich, K. E., & West, R. F. (1989). Exposure to print and orthographic processing. *Reading Research Quarterly, 24,* 402–433.

Stanovich, K. E., West, R. F., & Feeman, D. J. (1981). A longitudinal study of sentence context effects in second-grade children: Tests of an interactive-compensatory model. *Journal of Experimental Child Psychology, 32,* 185–199.

Stein, C. L., Cairns, H. S., & Zurif, E. B. (1984). Sentence comprehension limitations related to syntactic deficits in reading-disabled children. *Applied Psycholinguistics, 5,* 305–322.

Sternberg, R. (1980). Sketch of a componential subtheory of human intelligence. *Behavioral and Brain Sciences, 3,* 573–584.

Sternberg, R. (1982). Introduction: Some common themes in contemporary approaches to the training of intelligent performances. In D. Detterman & R. Sternberg (Eds.), *How and how much can intelligence be increased?* (pp. 141–146). Norwood, NJ: Ablex.

Sternberg, R. (1985). *Beyond IQ: A triarchic theory of human intelligence.* Cambridge, England: Cambridge University Press.

Stich, S. (1983). *From folk psychology to cognitive science.* Cambridge, MA: MIT Press.

Sticht, T. G. (1979). Applications of the audread model to reading evaluation and instruction. In L. B. Resnick & P. A. Weaver (Eds.), *Theory and practice of early reading* (Vol. 1, pp. 209–226). Hillsdale, NJ: Lawrence Erlbaum Associates.

Sticht, T. G., & James, J. H. (1984). Listening and reading. In P. D. Pearson (Ed.), *Handbook of reading research* (pp. 293–317). New York: Longman.

Tarver, S. G., Hallahan, D. P., Kauffman, J. M., & Ball, D. W. (1976). Verbal rehearsal and selective attention in children with learning disabilities: A developmental lag. *Journal of Experimental Child Psychology, 22,* 275–285.

Torgesen, J. (1977a). Memorization processes in reading-disabled children. *Journal of Educational Psychology, 69,* 571–578.

Torgesen, J. (1977b). The role of nonspecific factors in the task performance of learning disabled children: A theoretical assessment. *Journal of Learning Disabilities, 10,* 27–34.

Torgesen, J. (1978–79). Performance of reading disabled children on serial memory tasks. *Reading Research Quarterly, 14,* 57–87.

Torgesen, J. (1985). Memory processes in reading disabled children. *Journal of Learning Disabilities, 18,* 350–357.

Torgesen, J., & Goldman, T. (1977). Verbal rehearsal and short-term memory in reading-disabled children. *Child Development, 48,* 56–60.

Torgesen, J., & Licht, B. (1983). The learning disabled child as an inactive learner: Retrospect and prospects. In J. McKinney & L. Feagans (Eds.), *Topics in learning disabilities* (Vol. 1, pp. 100–130). Norwood, NJ: Ablex.

Tornéus, M. (1984). Phonological awareness and reading: A chicken and egg problem? *Journal of Educational Psychology, 70,* 1346–1358.

Treiman, R. (1984). Individual differences among children in reading and spelling styles. *Journal of Experimental Child Psychology, 37,* 463–477.

Treiman, R., & Baron, J. (1983). Phonemic-analysis training helps children benefit from spelling-sound rules. *Memory and Cognition, 11,* 382–389.

Tunmer, W. E., & Nesdale, A. R. (1985). Phonemic segmentation skill and beginning reading. *Journal of Educational Psychology, 77,* 417–427.

van den Bos, K. P. (1989). Relationship between cognitive development, decoding skill, and reading comprehension in learning disabled Dutch children. In P. Aaron & M. Joshi (Eds.), *Reading and writing disorders in different orthographic systems* (pp. 75–86). Norwell, MA: Kluwer Academic.

Vellutino, F. R. (1979). *Dyslexia: Theory and research.* Cambridge, MA: MIT Press.

Vellutino, F. R., & Scanlon, D. M. (1984). Converging perspectives in the study of the reading process: Reactions to the papers presented by Morrison, Siegel and Ryan, and Stanovich. *Remedial and Special Education, 5,* 39–44.

Vellutino, F. R., & Scanlon, D. M. (1987). Phonological coding, phonological awareness, and reading ability: Evidence from a longitudinal and experimental study. *Merrill-Palmer Quarterly, 33,* 321–363.

Venezky, R. L. (1976). *Theoretical and experimental base for teaching reading.* The Hague: Mouton.

Venezky, R. L., & Massaro, D. W. (1979). The role of orthographic regularity in word recognition. In L. B. Resnick & P. A. Weaver (Eds.), *Theory and practice of early reading* (Vol. 1, pp. 85–107). Hillsdale, NJ: Lawrence Erlbaum Associates.

Vogel, S. (1974). Syntactic abilities in normal and dyslexic children. *Journal of Learning Disabilities, 7,* 103–109.

Wagner, R. K. (1988). Causal relations between the development of phonological processing abilities and the acquisition of reading skills: A meta-analysis. *Merrill-Palmer Quarterly, 34,* 261–279.

Wagner, R. K., & Torgesen, J. K. (1987). The nature of phonological processing and its causal role in the acquisition of reading skills. *Psychological Bulletin, 101,* 192–212.

Weber, R. M. (1970). A linguistic analysis of first-grade reading errors. *Reading Research Quarterly, 5,* 427–451.

West, R. F., & Stanovich, K. E. (1978). Automatic contextual facilitation in readers of three ages. *Child Development, 49,* 717–727.

West, R. F., & Stanovich, K. E. (1982). Sources of inhibition in experiments on the effect of sentence context on word recognition. *Journal of Experimental Psychology: Learning, Memory, and Cognition, 8,* 385–399.

West, R. F., & Stanovich, K. E. (1986). Robust effects of syntactic structure on visual word processing. *Memory and Cognition, 14,* 104–112.

Whaley, J., & Kibby, M. (1981). The relative importance of reliance on intraword characteristics and interword constraints for beginning reading achievement. *Journal of Educational Research, 74,* 315–320.

Wilkes, K. V. (1984). Is consciousness important? *British Journal of Philosophy of Science, 35,* 223–243.

Wilkes, K. V. (1988). *Real people: Personal identity without thought experiments.* London: Oxford University Press.

Williams, J. P. (1984). Phonemic analysis and how it relates to reading. *Journal of Learning Disabilities, 17,* 240–245.

Willows, D. M. (in press). Visual processes in learning disabilities. In B. Wong (Ed.), *Learning about learning disabilities.* San Diego, CA: Academic Press.

Winne, P. H., & Belfry, M. J. (1982). Interpretive problems when correcting for attenuation. *Journal of Educational Measurement, 19,* 125–133.

Wise, B. W., Olson, R. K., Anstett, M., Andrews, L., Terjak, M., Schneider, V., Kostuch, J., & Kriho, L. (1989). Implementing a long-term computerized remedial reading program with synthetic speech feedback. *Behavior Research Methods, Instruments, and Computers, 21,* 173–180.

Wise, B. W., Olson, R. K., & Treiman, R. (1990). Subsyllabic units in computerized reading instruction: Onset-rime vs. postvowel segmentation. *Journal of Experimental Child Psychology, 49,* 1–19.

Wixson, K. L. (1979). Miscue analysis: A critical review. *Journal of Reading Behavior, 11,* 163–175.

Wong, B. (1984). Metacognition and learning disabilities. In T. Waller, D. Forrest, & E. MacKinnon (Eds.), *Metacognition, cognition, and human performance* (pp. 137–180). San Diego, CA: Academic Press.

Yaden, D. (1984). Reading research in metalinguistic awareness: Findings, problems, and classroom applications. *Visible Language, 18,* 5–47.

Yopp, H. K. (1988). The validity and reliability of phonemic awareness tests. *Reading Research Quarterly, 23,* 159–177.

Zola, D. (1984). Redundancy and word perception during reading. *Perception and Psychophysics, 36,* 277–284.

12

Whole Language Versus Code Emphasis: Underlying Assumptions and Their Implications for Reading Instruction*

I. Y. Liberman
A. M. Liberman
Haskins Laboratories, New Haven, Connecticut

Various studies have estimated the number of children who fail at reading to be 20%–25% of the school population (Stedman & Kaestle, 1987). Although it is generally agreed that this presents a serious problem, opinion is deeply divided about its underlying causes and inevitably, therefore, about the proper route to its solution. In this chapter we will explore two current views. One of these is commonly referred to by its partisans as *Whole Language;* the other, which we embrace, we call *Code Emphasis,* borrowing the name given it by Jeanne Chall (1967).

At the level of their most fundamental assumptions, Whole Language and Code Emphasis stand in stark contrast. Whole Language proceeds from the premise that learning to speak and learning to read are entirely comparable instances of language development. From this it follows that learning to read can and should be as effortless as learning to speak. Code Emphasis, on the other hand, recognizes that speech and reading must follow very different developmental paths. Speech is wholly natural, an integral part of the child's specialization for language. Because this specialization provides an automatic, tacit command of the complex relation between the sounds of speech and the abstract phonological structures they communicate, the acquisition of speech, whether in production or perception, is relatively effortless. A writing system, on the other hand, is an artifact, a biologically secondary code that maps to its natural language base in ways that must be consciously understood if it is to be used properly. Accordingly, learning to read is, in the Code Emphasis view, a cog-

---

*Chapter reprinted by permission from *Annals of Dyslexia*, 1990, *40*, 51–76.

nitive, intellectual achievement in a way that learning to speak is not. It is simply wrong to suppose, as Whole Language does, that they can be learned in the same epigenetic way.

WHAT'S RIGHT WITH WHOLE LANGUAGE

Some of what Whole Language espouses is undeniably right and inherently appealing, which may account for the wide currency it now enjoys. But this is so, in our view, only to the extent that it offers suggestions about instruction that sensible people like your grandmothers and ours would have regarded as truisms. Other, more fundamental, aspects of the Whole Language position are demonstrably false in ways that we will develop later.

But first let us consider some of the truisms. In a parent–teacher guide to the Whole Language movement that we take as our primary source (Goodman, 1986), Kenneth Goodman (past president of the International Reading Association as well as a founding father and leading writer in the Whole Language movement) made numerous suggestions that no good teacher we know would quarrel with. For example, he said that we need committed teachers who will serve eagerly as "guides, facilitators, kid watchers" (p. 44), that in the preschool years children would profit from "literate environments with functional print everywhere" (that is, homes and schools with freely available books and magazines), as they would from "environments in which teachers and parents themselves enjoy reading, read to their children, take them to libraries, and generally expand the children's awareness of the functions of print" (p. 44).

The parent–teacher guide offers some equally unobjectionable ideas for the beginning literacy program. For example, it says that the best books for first graders are those with predictable stories that use frequent word repetitions, together with cyclical sequencing that provides lots of productive, self-motivating practice (p. 47). We cannot take exception to these notions either, except to remark that they are hardly original with Whole Language or with us, having been preempted by writers of children's stories from Mother Goose to Dr. Seuss.

The guide also recommends that reading and writing be integrated so that children can understand their reciprocal relationship (p. 47). It urges that schools should build on the language development children have attained before they reach school and expand it (p. 10). And it urges further that schools "respect learners: who they are, where they come from, how they talk, what experiences they had before coming to school" (p. 10).

There is a good deal more of this kind of advice in the parent–teacher guide. Though obvious, much of it nevertheless deserves more emphasis than it usually gets, and the Whole Language people are right to provide it. Surely, it is good to

identify and promote practices that have been part of every good teacher's repertoire since the teaching of reading began.

WHAT'S WRONG WITH WHOLE LANGUAGE

To find the important differences between Whole Language and Code Emphasis,
one must put aside the easy truisms and look more deeply into the assumptions
the two views make about the nature of language itself, and about the similarities
or differences between the processes that underlie its spoken and written forms.
What we see there, and what we mean now to say, is that the basic assumptions
of Whole Language are wrong, and that they lead to recommendations about
reading instruction that we consider grievously misguided. To avoid a common
misunderstanding, we should recognize at this point that lots of children—
perhaps as many as 75%—will discover the alphabetic principle, which is what
they must understand if they are to read, no matter how unhelpful the instruction.
But we find it ironic that, in order to succeed, these children might have to
prevail over the misunderstandings of their teachers. Would even they not be
better served by instruction that is designed to teach them what they need to
know? In any case, we are left with the 20%–25% who will *not* discover the
point of the alphabet except as it is made apparent to them by appropriate
instruction.

So let us examine a basic assumption of Whole Language, as exemplified by
Goodman's description of a paradox he sees in the contrast between the ease of
learning to speak and the relative difficulty of learning to read. He reminds us
that infants learn to speak a language in a very short time and without formal
training, but, when they reach school age, many of them begin to have difficulty
with the kind of language development that Goodman associates with learning to
read. In his view, infants are "good at learning language when they need it to
express themselves, as long as they are surrounded by people who are using
language meaningfully and purposefully" (1986, p. 7). As he sees it, children
would be just as good at learning to read if only the task were made similarly
meaningful and purposeful. Unfortunately, according to Goodman, teachers
make learning to read difficult, "by breaking whole (natural) language into bite-
size, abstract little pieces." School traditions, he says, "took apart the language
into words, syllables, and isolated sounds," and this "postponed its natural purpose—the communication of meaning—and turned it into a set of abstractions
unrelated to the needs and experiences of the child we sought to help" (p. 7).

That may sound plausible, but in our view it could hardly be more wrong. We
agree, of course, that most children quickly master speech well enough to communicate usefully and that, typically, they do this without explicit instruction,

whereas in contrast many fail to learn to read and write. But before we accept Goodman's explanation that the schools are at fault by making a naturally easy task difficult (p. 8), we should ask two questions: First, is reading, like speaking, really all that natural; and, second, if not, what more is required if the child is to read and write?

To understand that the answer to the first question is an unqualified "no," one has only to consider such obvious facts about language as the following:

1. All communities of humans have a fully developed spoken language, but only a minority of these exists in a written form. Where there is a written form, many competent speakers do not, and indeed, cannot use it effectively, no matter how strong the pressure to do so.

2. In the history of the race, as in the development of the child, speech comes first, reading second. Apparently, speech is as old as the human species, having evolved with it as perhaps the most important of its species-typical characteristics; alphabets, on the other hand, are developments of the last three or four thousand years, and they are cultural achievements, not the primary products of biological evolution.

3. Reflecting biological roots that run deep, speech employs a single, universal strategy for constructing utterances. All languages form all words (hence all utterances) by combining and permuting a few dozen consonants and vowels, meaningless segments that we sill sometimes refer to, loosely, as phonemes. On the other hand, scripts, being artifacts, choose variably from a menu of strategies. Some, like the one we use, represent the phonemes. Others represent the more numerous syllables or, as in the case of Japanese, moras. Still others, like the Chinese, take the considerably more numerous morphemes as their irreducible units.

4. To develop speech, the normal child need only be in an environment where language is spoken; reading, on the other hand, almost always requires explicit tuition.

Given these telling facts about the differences between speech and script, it has to be both wrong and misleading to suppose, as Whole Language seems to, that they are psychologically and biologically equivalent vehicles for language. It must be equally wrong, though perhaps even more misleading, to conclude then as the parent–teacher guide does (p. 24) that learning to read is, or can be, as natural a part of language development as learning to speak. Surely, it is plain that speech is biologically primary in a way that reading and writing are not. Accordingly, we suppose that learning to speak is, by the very nature of the underlying process, much like learning to walk or to perceive visual depth and distance, whereas learning to read and write is more like learning to do arithmetic or to play checkers. Just because learning to speak and learning to read can both be viewed as forms of language development—in the vacuous sense that both reflect the effect of experience on language behavior—it simply does not follow, as Whole Language would have it, that they are therefore equivalent forms of development, or that they can be instructed by experience in the same natural, unconscious way.

And so we are brought to the second question: Given children who have learned to speak, typically without conscious awareness of the underlying linguistic structures and processes they naturally deploy, what more must they learn if they would exploit their already impressive command of the language for the purpose of reading and writing it by means of an alphabet?

To see what more the would-be reader must learn about language, we need first to appreciate the critical differences between language and other natural means of communicating meanings, because that is where the most important aspects of the disagreement between Whole Language and Code Emphasis have their roots, and where we find the basis for the very different ways they and we understand the reading problem. We begin by reminding ourselves that consonants and vowels are the essential structural elements of the phonological component of the child's natural capacity for language. The obvious and critically important function of the phonology is to form meaningful words by combining and permuting its small inventory of meaningless and abstract units in the elegantly principled ways that linguists have been concerned to characterize. For our purposes, however, it is important to know about the phonological strategy only that it is crucial for language because it makes possible vocabularies tens or even hundred of thousands of times larger than could ever be managed if, as in all nonhuman systems, the signal for each "word" were holistically different from every other one (see A. M. Liberman & Studdert-Kennedy, 1978, for further discussion). Thus, the phonology is not merely an inventory of sounds, but a marvelous system that comprehends all the words of the language, including even those that have yet to be uttered. It relates sound to meaning in a way that makes it one of the two properties (syntax is the other) that permits languages to be open and generative—that is, to convey an indefinitely large number of meaningful messages, including novel ones.

Communication among nonhuman animals is different in a critically important way, because, so far as anyone has been able to determine, the natural animal systems have no phonology (nor do they have syntax, for that matter), and, as a consequence, their message-carrying potential is severely limited. Lacking the phonological structures that make lexical generativity possible, nonhuman animals can convey in their natural communication only as many word-meanings as there are distinctively different signals they can make and perceive, and that is, at most, a few dozen. Moreover, short of calling a convention and getting all the animals to agree on a hitherto unused signal-to-meaning link, there is no way the animals can communicate a novel message. Thus, in contrast to language, which is lexically open because word meanings are conveyed by arranging and rearranging meaningless signal elements, the nonhuman systems attach meaning directly to each element and are, as a consequence, tightly and irremediably closed.

We see, then, that language would pay a terrible price if it were not phonologically based. Perhaps it would be of some comfort to the Whole Language people that in such a nonphonological world there would be no "bite-size, abstract little pieces" for teachers to break a word into, and so postpone its natural purpose—the communication of meaning. Each word would be conveyed by an unanalyzable signal, so meaning would be conveyed directly, just as Whole Language seems to think it should be. Unfortunately, there would not be many words.

In telling its very different story about the human and nonhuman capacities for communication, Whole Language scants the phonological faculty, emphasizing instead that our communication system is as it is because, by comparison with other species, we have more to say, a greater capacity for using symbols, a need for social interaction, and intelligence. The clear implication is that it is primarily these factors that make it possible for the child, but not the monkey, to learn language either in its spoken or its written form.

But, surely, animals do have something to say, and the most superficial study of the science of ethology reveals that many of them say it unerringly, often, and insistently. Whether what they say is "symbolic" depends on just exactly what one means by a symbol. Is a bird behaving symbolically when it produces a so-called "mobbing" call? Does this call "symbolize" the presence of a predator, as well as the bird's desire to enlist the cooperation of its fellows in protecting their common interests? As for social interaction, many animal species are dependent on it for their very survival, and the biologically necessary interaction is always maintained, as it is in us, by communication. This leaves intelligence, about which we would only offer the notion that, whatever intelligence is taken to be, there is no strong reason to suppose that language is its inevitable product. Indeed, the matter might better be put the other way around: We may be intelligent, or, at least, appear so, because, being endowed with the species-typical and biologically distinct devices of phonology (and syntax)—the devices that critically distinguish language from all other forms of natural communication—we can manage cognitive processes in ways that creatures not so endowed must find impossible. Seen this way, language is not so much a result of intelligence as it is a critically important tool that an intelligence can use. Of course, a person with low intelligence will find that much less to do with the tool, and his or her use of it will surely reveal the poverty of his or her cognitive resources. But intelligence does not *cause* language, and it is not a truly sufficient condition for learning to read. Surely, there are intelligent people in societies that boast no readers.

So, in its most fundamental assumptions about language and its expression in speech or script, we find the parent–teacher guide doubly mistaken; first, in its assertion that learning to read can be like learning to speak, and second, in its assumptions about the conditions that cause either kinds of learning to occur. We take it as undeniable that learning to read is *not* like learning to speak. As for the conditions that underlie learning to speak, they are but two: being neurologically normal in the several aspects of the language faculty, and having a normal exposure to the mother tongue. Learning to read imposes further requirements, of which more later.

Being neurologically normal for language means, *inter alia,* that the child has a natural capacity—indeed, a positive affinity—for phonological structures. This is why children are, in George Miller's apt phrase, "spontaneous apprentices" in the business of language (Miller, 1977), acquiring new words at such a phenomenal rate that by the time they are 6 years of age they command a vocabulary of 13,000 words, of which 7800 are root forms. One year later their vocabulary comprises 21,600 words (12,400 roots), and just one year after that it has grown to 28,300 words and 17,600 roots (Templin, 1957). Such prodigies of language development would not be possible if there were no phonological system, and if children did not have, by virtue of their biology, a tacit command of its underlying structures and mechanisms (see Studdert-Kennedy, 1987, and M. Y. Liberman, 1983, for pertinent discussions).

We take it as given, therefore, that in teaching children to read and write, our aim must be to transfer the wonders of phonology from speech to script. In our view, this can be done only if the child comes to understand the alphabetic principle, the insight that words are distinguished from each other by the phonological structure that the alphabet represents. Surely, this is the principle that links the less natural mode of written communication to its natural, spoken base, and so makes available to the reader–writer the ready-made phonological system that gives to speech the incalculable advantages it enjoys.

But why might it be hard for children to grasp the alphabetic principle and so gain access to a phonology they have already pretty well mastered? To answer that question, which takes us to the very heart of the reading problem, we must first bother to understand how the phonemes are produced and perceived in speech, for only then can we see precisely how far these processes must be different in writing and reading.

Consider, then, that if as in every language all utterances must be formed by variously stringing together two or three dozen consonants and vowels, the strings inevitably must run to considerable lengths. As a practical matter, then, there must be a way of producing these strings at some reasonable rate. Speech (and language, for that matter) would be impossible if, instead of saying "bag," we could only say "buh, a, guh" ; for to say "buh a guh" is not to speak but to spell. In that case, language production would be impossibly tedious. To get a feel for what speech perception would be like, have someone spell a Victorian novel to you, letter by painful letter. Not only would communication be slow, but it would likely overreach the limits of working memory, and so make sentence comprehension all but impossible.

Of course, if speech were a matter of saying "buh a guh" in place of "bag," then, as in the nonphonological case just described, the fundamental assumption of Whole Language would be more nearly right: Reading and writing would be no more difficult and no less natural than speaking and listening, for any child who could say a word would, *ipso facto,* know how to spell and read it. But there would be no language worth writing and reading. Speech and language became possible only because there evolved in speech a specialization for the rapid and effortless production and perception of phonological structures. We and some of our colleagues believe that the strategy underlying this specialization was to define the phonemes not as sounds but as motor control structures we choose to call gestures. Thus, the phoneme we write as *b* is a closing and opening at the lips; the phoneme we write as *m* is that same closing and opening at the lips, combined with an opening of the velum, and so forth. In fact, the gestures are far more complex and abstract than this (see, for example, Browman & Goldstein, 1985; A. M. Liberman & Mattingly, 1985; A. M. Liberman & Mattingly, 1989), but for our purposes the important consideration is only that the gestural strategy permits coarticulation. That is, it permits the speaker to overlap gestures that are realized by different organs of articulation (as in the case of lips and tongue in /ba/) and to merge gestures that are produced by different parts of the same organ (as in the case of the tip and blade of the tongue in /da/). The consequence is that people can and do regularly speak at rates of 10 to 20 phonemes per second, which is nearly an order of magnitude faster than they could otherwise manage. That phonological elements are best defined as gestures is a hypothesis. Coarticulation, on the other hand, is a fact, an essential characteristic of every language in the world.

But coarticulation was not there for the taking. It required the evolution of special articulatory gestures that lend themselves to being coarticulated and that have come to serve a linguistic purpose and no other. (Thus, they are not engaged in eating, swallowing, breathing, or worrying a blackberry seed with the tongue.) It also required the evolution of a special method of controlling and coordinating these gestures, for speech mechanisms must produce enough overlap and merging to make high rates possible, while yet preserving the small set of invariant phonological structures that form all words (A. M. Liberman & Mattingly, 1989).

The relevance of all this to our concerns becomes apparent when one considers that, like other biologically specialized processes, those that exploit coarticulation to produce phonological structures go on automatically, below the level of awareness. The obvious consequence is that, to speak a word, a person need not know how to spell it or even that it can be spelled. Nor does he or she need to know what articulatory gestures to make or how to make them. The speaker need only think of the word; the speech specialization does all the hard work, automatically selecting and coordinating the linguistically significant gestures that form the appropriate phonological structure.

Coarticulation has important consequences for speech perception as well (and hence for the would-be reader), for it folds into a single segment of sound information about several successive phonemes, and so relaxes the constraint on rate of perception imposed by the temporal resolving power of the ear (A. M. Liberman, Cooper, Shankweiler, & Studdert-Kennedy, 1967). This produces a very complex relation between the sound and the phonological structure it conveys, but this considerable complication causes the listener no trouble; he or she has only to listen, for phonological specialization parses the signal automatically, recovering the several coarticulated gestures that produced it. Once recovered in this automatic, precognitive way, the phonological structure that uniquely specifies the word is available for whatever further use is to be made of it. We see, then, that production and perception of speech are easy, not because its processes are simple—for they are, in fact, marvelously intricate—but because the underlying specialization is so wonderfully adapted to its complex task.

But why make such a fuss about how we produce and perceive phonological structures if our concern is with reading and writing and the difficulties that attend them? The point is obvious, or so it seems to us. Given the biological specialization we have described, there is ordinarily nothing in children's experience with speech that will acquaint them with the alphabetic principle—that is, nothing to make them aware that all words are specified by an internal phonological structure, the shortest elements of which are the phonemes that the letters of the alphabet represent. Thus, the speech specialization causes a word like *bag* to be coarticulated into a single, seamless piece of sound, even though it comprises three discrete phonemes. Given the automaticity of that specialization, the constituent phonemes do not ordinarily rise to the level of awareness. Therefore, the beginning reader does not understand why a word like *bag* should be represented by three letters, or why its spelling should differ from that of *sag* in the first letter, from *big* in the second, and from *bat* in the third. Moreover, the problem may resist the most obvious solution, because there is simply no way the teacher can divide the sound of *bag* so as to recover its three phonemes. Saying "buh a guh" to the child does not necessarily help all that much, because "buh a guh" is the wrong word. At all events, we can now see that the normal processes of speech not only fail to reveal the internal structures of words, but may, indeed, obscure them. Of course, the requisite awareness can be developed, as it obviously has been in all literate people. Indeed, developing that awareness should be the first aim of the reading teacher. But that takes some doing.

All that we have said about the beginning reader applies to the condition of our ancestors at the time they developed the alphabet. After all, human beings had been producing and perceiving speech for tens or hundreds of thousands of years before that moment, just three or four thousand years ago, when it occurred to someone that words did not differ holistically, one from another, but only in the particulars of their internal structure. Given that momentous, if seemingly simple, linguistic discovery, it only remained for someone to get the idea that if each phonological element were represented by an identifiable, but wholly arbitrary, optical shape, then all could read and write, provided only that they knew the language and were consciously aware of the internal structure of its words.

Once again the wrong assumptions by Whole Language theory about the nature of spoken and written language leads it to advice about instruction that is, in our view, likely to be unhelpful. Thus, they assert in the guide (p. 9) that one trouble with reading instruction as it is sometimes practiced is that it is designed to make the child into a linguist. This, they say, is entirely unnecessary—after all, the child need not be a linguist in order to speak—and even harmful, because it makes learning to read an intellectual, and therefore disagreeable, task. For exactly the reasons we have just given, Code Emphasis agrees that a child need not be a linguist in order to speak. But it holds that to use an alphabetic writing system properly, the child must be led to the same linguistic insight—and it was a linguistic insight—that underlay the development of the alphabet. Becoming enough of a linguist to appreciate that all words have an internal structure need not be a disagreeable task, as we will argue later, but, agreeable or not, it is a necessary achievement for anyone who would take advantage of the alphabetic mode for the purpose of reading and writing.

So much, then, for the differences between Whole Language and Code Emphasis in the assumptions they make about spoken and written language. We turn now, though only briefly, to an equally important difference between the two views in what they have to say about the nature of the reading process itself. Put with admirable succinctness by Goodman himself, the Whole Language assumption is that reading is a "psycholinguistic guessing game" (Goodman, 1976). By this, Goodman means that (presumably skilled) readers merely sample the print, apprehending some words and skipping others. Then, using their normal and natural language processes, they guess at the message by taking advantage of context, their knowledge of the world, or, indeed, anything else that will spare them the inconvenience of actually reading what the writer had, in fact, written. As we will see later, this leads the Whole Language people to advocate actually *teaching* the child to guess. But, for now, the point is simply that their fundamental assumption about skilled reading is contrary to fact. The elegant studies of eye movements during reading by Rayner and his associates have shown conclusively that good readers read every word (Rayner & Pollatsek, 1987). It is only the poor readers who sample the print, picking out words here and there, and then guessing at the rest. Other studies by Perfetti's group in Pittsburgh show that truly literate people are much less likely to use a guessing strategy (Perfetti & Lesgold, 1979). And, finally, there is the demonstration by Gough and associates (Gough, Alford, & Holley-Wilcox, 1981) that, more often than not, guessing from context leads to errors of a most egregious sort. Thus, their well-educated skilled reader, given appropriate context and unlimited time, correctly guessed only 1 word in 4.

RELEVANT RESEARCH

We have pointed to differences between Whole Language and Code Emphasis in their general hypotheses about the nature and causes of reading disability, and we have said how well or how poorly those hypotheses accord with some of the most basic facts about the nature of spoken and written language. It is time, now, to make these hypotheses more specific and explicit, and to inquire, at least briefly, into the research by which they are to be evaluated. We would, of course, like to be even handed in this matter, offering data on both sides of the argument. Unfortunately for that purpose, Whole Language seems to have led to little, if any, relevant research. Based, as it is, on the assumption that children should learn to read just as they learned to speak, Whole Language cannot have thought it relevant to discover what is necessary for reading beyond the conditions that were sufficient for the development of speech. Yet obvious and undeniable facts about language tell us that something more *is* necessary, and common sense suggests that identifying this something provides the basis for knowing what a proper program of instruction must be designed to do. At all events, Whole Language has made no research contribution to this important issue. Nor have its partisans mounted studies aimed at finding out what distinguishes those children who become good readers from those who do not, or how to predict at an early stage which children are at risk of failure. In the case of the research that is relevant to one tenet of Whole Language—that is, the data we cited in connection with the claim that reading is psycholinguistic guessing—the outcome was, as we said, directly contrary to what Whole Language had, in the absence of any data, supposed to be the case. We therefore turn to the specific, testable questions about reading that Code Emphasis has led to, and to the research studies by which those questions have been and are being answered.

As we have said, our guiding premise is that proper use of an alphabetic script requires, most importantly, an awareness of the fact that words are specified by their internal phonemic structure and, further, that such awareness does not come for free. This has seemed to us quite obvious, given what we know about language and the way an alphabet conveys it. But it seems not to appear so to everyone—certainly not to the proponents of Whole Language—so we seek further support for it, not in anything more we might learn about language and alphabets—for the evidence there seems full and convincing—but rather more directly in the results of research on learning to read and on the difference between those who succeed and those who do not.

Is knowing a language sufficient to provide beginning readers with the phonological awareness that they need if they are to apply the alphabetic principle?

Phonological awareness means simply the more or less explicit understanding that words are made of discrete units—that a word like *bag* has 3 such units, that *brag* has 4, and that *brags* has 5. It does not entail knowing how to spell a word, only that it *can* be spelled. On the basis of all the considerations about speech and the development of the alphabet that we summarized in the earlier parts of this chapter, we many years ago (I. Y. Liberman, 1973) assumed, as we have already said, that beginning readers would usually lack phonological awareness. Then, seeking direct support for our assumption, we tested it on preschoolers (I. Y. Liberman, Shankweiler, Fischer, & Carter, 1974). Using a task that was presented (and accepted) as a tapping game, we found that only 17% of the kindergarteners "passed" according to any reasonable criterion of passing. (Many more—about 48%—performed well with syllables, which was to have been expected, because syllables, unlike phonemes, are always marked acoustically by a discrete, vocalic center.) Thus, we found that relatively few kindergarteners are aware that words can be taken apart into units like those the alphabet represents. Following that study, many others, using different kinds of measures, have arrived at the same conclusion (for reviews, see Blachman, 1988; Routh & Fox, 1984). Indeed, research on illiterate adults has shown that they, too, are lacking in phonological awareness (Byrne & Ledez, 1983; I. Y. Liberman, Rubin, Duques, & Carlisle, 1985; Lukatela, I. Y. Liberman, & Shankweiler, in preparation; Marcel, 1980; Morais, Cary, Alegria, & Bertelson, 1979; Pratt & Brady, 1988; Read & Ruyter, 1985).

So it is now quite firmly established that neither experience with speech nor cognitive maturation is sufficient to acquaint a person with the principle that underlies all alphabets. As for the relatively few kindergarteners who have the awareness that the use of an alphabet presupposes, we might guess that they have acquired it as a result of the kinds of more or less analytic linguistic activities they may have engaged in at home (rhyming and various linguistic games, for example) or even by observing the print of stories read aloud to them. In any case, the teacher should never assume that the beginning reader has achieved the cognitive insight about language that reading requires.

Are there individual differences in degree of phonological awareness that correlate with (are predictive of) reading achievement? The answer to that question is presented very pointedly by Bryant and Goswami (1987), who say that "the discovery of a strong relationship between children's phonological awareness and their progress in learning to read is one of the great successes of modern psychology" (p. 439). The relevant evidence is most impressive, coming as it does from studies that covered a wide range of cultural and economic backgrounds, as well as a number of different languages: in English (Blachman, 1984; Bradley & Bryant, 1983; Fox & Routh, 1980; Goldstein, 1976; Helfgott, 1976; I. Y. Liberman, 1973; Mann & I. Y. Liberman, 1984; Olson, Wise, Conners, & Rack, 1989; Treiman & Baron, 1981); in Swedish (Lundberg, 1989; Lundberg, Olofsson, & Wall, 1980; Magnusson & Naucler, 1987); in French (Bertelson, 1987; Morais, Cluytens, & Alegria, 1984); in Spanish (de Manrique

& Gramigna, 1984); in Italian (Cossu, Shankweiler, I. Y. Liberman, Tola, & Katz, 1988); and in Serbo-Croatian (Lukatela et al., in preparation). Indeed, several investigators have arrived at the conclusion that, of all possible tests, the kind that measures some aspect of phonological awareness is the best single predictor of reading achievement (Blachman, 1988; Golinkoff, 1978; Lundberg et al., 1980; Mann, 1984; Routh & Fox, 1984; Stanovich, 1985; Vellutino & Scanlon, 1987).

Can phonological awareness, as such, be taught to prereaders, and, if so, does teaching it have consequences for later achievement in reading? Appropriate methods of reading instruction are, by their very nature, likely to make learners sufficiently aware of phonological structure to allow them to appreciate, and hence to apply, the alphabetic principle. Whether or not the teacher is aware of the importance of phonological awareness, he or she is likely, given common sense and a reasonable approach to instruction, to call the children's attention to the internal structure of words and to how this structure is reflected in the alphabetic spelling. Indeed, it is presumably by this route that most of us learned what we needed to know. Moreover, as we pointed out earlier in this chapter, some children will infer the principle, no matter how ill-advised the method of instruction. Still, it is important to know whether phonological awareness can be taught as a prelude to reading instruction, and whether such teaching has happy consequences, especially for children who are at risk. As for children at risk, Bradley and Bryant (1983) at Oxford University first identified them by appropriate measures of phonological ability at ages 4 and 5, and then showed that specific training in phonological classification caused them to progress better in learning to read, as measured even 4 years later (Bradley, 1987), than control groups that had equivalent training in semantic (as opposed to phonological) classification, or that received no linguistic training at all. Subsequently, Bertelson's group in Belgium (Content, Kolinsky, Morais, & Bertelson, 1986), Blachman in Syracuse (Ball & Blachman, 1988), Lundberg's laboratory in Sweden (Lundberg, Frost, & Peterson, 1988; Olofsson & Lundberg, 1983) and Vellutino and Scanlon (1987) in Albany have all achieved salutary effects with training of normal randomly selected groups of kindergarteners.

There is, then, considerable research support for the conclusion that phonological awareness can be trained in the prereader and that such training causes children to make better and faster progress when they later undertake to learn how to read and to spell. This conclusion applies to normal children and also to children who, because of deficiencies in measurable aspects of phonological awareness, are presumably at risk.

Given the differences among children in the ease with which they can be made aware of phonological structure, differences that correlate so highly with achievement in reading, where do we look to find the source of these differences? Together with our colleagues, we are currently pursuing the hypothesis that the source is the phonological component of the child's specialization for language. If that hypothesis is correct, then relative difficulty in achieving phonological awareness should be only one of several symptoms. Among other symptoms of a weak phonology, we should expect problems with verbal short-term memory, because, as is well known (Baddeley, 1968; Conrad, 1964; A. M. Liberman, Mattingly, & Turvey, 1972), such memory requires the use of phonological structures. If those structures are weak, short-term memory should suffer. We are not surprised, therefore, to find that poor readers do, in fact, perform more poorly than age-matched good readers on tasks requiring immediate memory of verbal items, though with nonverbal tasks, such as those that require memory for nonsense shapes or photographs of unfamiliar faces, the poor readers are not at a disadvantage (Gathercole & Baddeley, 1989; Katz, Shankweiler, & I. Y. Liberman, 1981; I. Y. Liberman, Mann, Shankweiler, & Werfelman, 1982; Mann & I. Y. Liberman, 1984; Rapala & Brady, 1990; but see Pennington, 1989).

Also consistent with the assumption that poor readers suffer from a relatively weak phonology is the finding by Brady and associates (Brady, Shankweiler, & Mann, 1983) that poor readers need a higher quality of signal than good readers for error-free performance in the perception of speech, but not for the identification of nonspeech environmental sounds. The other side of this coin is the finding by Catts (1986) that reading-disabled junior-high students made significantly more errors than matched normal pupils on demanding tasks of speech production (tongue twisters, polysyllabic words, and the like).

Even the well-documented naming problems of reading-disabled second-graders—problems that, on their face, invite an interpretation that places the problem in the semantic component–turn out on investigation to lie in the phonology. Thus, in a series of carefully controlled studies with the Boston Naming Test, Katz (1986) found that poor readers who misnamed objects could nevertheless describe their functions accurately, recognize the correct names when given a series of choices, or even generate the correct name when given a phonological prompt. Apparently, their problem was that they could not access the right phonological structure, presumably because it was weakly established.

Though this issue is far from settled, we are encouraged to believe that individual differences in the ease with which children grasp the alphabetic principle originate in the phonological component of their language faculty, not in some cognitive (for example, analytic) capacity that cuts across linguistic and nonlinguistic domains (for a review of the evidence, see Wagner & Torgesen, 1987). Until we see compelling evidence to the contrary, we will suppose that this is the right way to understand the child whose difficulties with reading do not extend to all intellectual tasks.

INSTRUCTION BY WHOLE LANGUAGE

Given the profound differences in the underlying assumptions of Whole Language and Code Emphasis, we should expect equally profound differences in the instructional methods they rationalize. In fact, these differences exist, though they are sometimes papered over by a throw-away line or two in the parent–teacher guide. Thus, the parent–teacher guide does say (p. 46) "Cultivate the alphabetic principle." But it does not tell parent or teacher just exactly how it is to be cultivated or why. Instead, it devotes considerable space to promoting procedures that seem designed, not to reveal the principle, but to obscure it. Thus, it says (p. 43) that "literacy development is a matter of learning to use just enough print, language structure, and meaning, and to keep it all in the proper personal and cultural perspective." We are not told exactly how the beginner arrives at the decision that he or she has used "just enough print" or how he or she uses "the proper personal and cultural perspective" to learn to read. In any case, the guide repeatedly leaves the teacher with the notion that the alphabetically represented word is somehow an encumbrance rather than a medium for conveying meaning. Thus, the guide says "Readers are seeking meaning, not sounds or words," (p. 38), but does not explain how one reaches the meaning without grasping the words.

The guide does permit a little leeway—it allows readers to "use their developing phonic generalizations to help when the going gets tough," but goes on to warn that "If they are lucky enough not to have been taught phonics in isolation, with each letter equally important, then they will not be diverted from developing the strategies necessary to select just enough graphic information to get to the sense they are seeking" (p. 38). The guide suggests that instead of bothering with all the graphic information, "learners need to know which available cues are most useful in a particular written context." Figure 12.1 displays an exercise seen on a poster board in a reading-methods classroom in a school of education where the Whole Language approach was in operation. The exercise was presumably meant to develop just such guessing skills. We find the message it appeared to convey shocking—that learning to guess meaning from that most minimal of graphic cues, the initial consonant or two, is a desirable route to reading acquisition.

In much the same vein, the guide explains that in its natural, easy-going classrooms, "trial and error risk-taking on the part of the learner is an absolute requirement" (p. 43). In the risk-taking, guessing approach, the learner necessarily makes errors. Not to worry. The parent–teacher guide assures us that learners' errors are accepted, indeed "celebrated," if they contribute to making sense: "No one is perfect," says the guide, "and sense, rather than error-free performance, is the main point of reading" (p. 47). Therefore, we are not surprised to learn from graduate students taking a course in reading at a university where Whole Language was favored that they are told to reward children who, for example, read "Crest" instead of "toothpaste" in a story about brushing teeth. Crest is a toothpaste, after all, their professor reminded them. Similarly, we see a feature story in the *New York Times* (March 31, 1990) about an adult in a community literacy class who reads "kids" for "children." Presumably, Whole Language would find this quite acceptable, even praiseworthy. Children are kids, aren't they? Surely, this is wholly consistent with what we learn from

Hey la la, Ho la la

My d ___ and I

Tr ___ to m ___

With ch ___ and p ___

Hey ___ ___, ___ ___ ___

Oh d ___ t ___ c ___

If y ___ ___ st ___

We'll n ___ g ___ th ___

FIG. 12.1. Poster found in a reading clinic classroom in a school of education, apparently used to train children in guessing from context.

the parent–teacher guide, where we are told that such errors may be viewed as "charming indications of growth toward control of language processes" (p. 19). We fear that they may serve, instead, as indicators that the children are wholly ignorant of what the game is about. They will probably not figure it out on their own, and their errors will become less and less charming as time goes on. We can only hope that when these readers graduate into the real world they will not skip the words they cannot read or substitute their own words in the instruction manuals they use to operate the machinery of the workplace.

Lest you suppose that the parent–teacher guide we have been quoting is not representative of the thinking of the Whole Language movement (even though it is written by their leading author), let us quote from a recent issue of the *Whole Language Teachers Newsletter* (1988) about what to do if the reader encounters an unfamiliar word (we are grateful to Professor Charles Read for calling our attention to this). The newsletter says:

Foremost on the list of Don'ts are sound-it-out and look-for-familiar-word-parts-within-the-word because these activities divert the reader's attention from meaning . . . Good Things to Do include skip it, use prior information . . . read ahead, re-read, or put in another word that makes sense.

But all of this has got to be bad advice. For, surely, what the reader wants to get from the printed page is what the writer *actually* said, not what the reader thinks *might* have been said, given the reader's guess from context and "cultural and personal perspective." Is it not just the most accomplished writers who, in an effort at precision and style, tend to avoid the inexact, soggy, and cliché-ridden prose that results when words are made to appear only in those contexts so very usual that guessing is, in fact, as good as reading? And is it not just that text that is designed to inform the readers, instead of repeating what they already know, that will necessarily lie outside their "personal and cultural perspective?" If the readers are relying on what they already know, as Whole Language would have them do, how on earth are they ever going to use reading to learn something new? And how, if they follow the prescriptions of Whole Language, could they ever appreciate the beauty of poetry or the majesty of the Gettysburg Address? Are the readers to substitute their guesses for the words of Shakespeare and Lincoln? Are not the "cultural and personal perspective" of the writer more important than those of the reader if the reader is to understand what the writer wrote?

We are reminded here of a pertinent example of how a dyslexic boy in the third grade, a child who had not mastered the alphabetic principle, attempted to follow a "psycholinguistic-guessing-game" approach and the principles recommended in the Whole Language newsletter. (Though this episode occurred in the clinical practice of one of us some thirty years ago, she has never forgotten it.)

The child was given a passage to read, the first sentence of which was: "A boy said, 'Run little girl.' " The child knew how to read the word *A* correctly, probably because it is the name of the letter. When he came to the word *boy* he engaged in guessing and risk-taking as recommended in the guide and produced "baby," presumably on the basis of a cue available to him—the *b*. Now he had *A baby*. He did not know *said* so he looked ahead and found *run*, which he did know. But what to do with the word between *baby* and *run?* Well, he used his "intact language skills" and figured that because there was an *s* in the word, and because he needed something to fill in there, he would say "is running" because that would make sense syntactically (though it may be somewhat dubious semantically). But then he ran into a big snag. Unfortunately, *little* was a word he knew by sight, so he was forced to read it correctly. Now his sentence said, "A baby is running little," and he was confronted with the word *girl,* which he did not know. At this point he gave up trying to make sense and simply threw in "go," which he knew begins with the right letter. And his sentence now read "A baby is running little go." So much for the guide's assumption that "kids are universally able to sort out language as they use it to meet their functional needs." So much for children's ability to use their "developing phonics generalizations to help when the going gets tough" (p. 38) and so much for using "their prior learning and experience to make sense of the texts, guessing what will occur next." And so much for their ability "to select just enough graphic information to get to the sense [they are] seeking."

A three-step Whole Language procedure for introducing children to the reading process that appeared recently in an academic journal seems to rise above the print altogether, disregarding the information that letters, as opposed to pictures, are supposed to convey (Norris, 1989). In the first step, after reading the children the story of Goldilocks and the Three Bears, the teacher asks them to draw pictures of the story. We are told that the teacher then "reads the pictures" the child has drawn, saying "Once upon a time there were three bears—a papa bear, a mama bear, and a baby bear." In the second step, the teacher asks the children to add letters to the picture. The children, who apparently have not been taught much about letters, scrawl some marks on the paper. The teacher points to the marks while saying: "This says, 'Papa bear's porridge was too hot.' This word says, 'Mama bear's porridge is too hot.' " (In our day Mama bear's porridge was too cold and Baby bear's was just right—but this is apparently a different story.) Finally, the teacher asks the children to use the bears' names in their story and shows them how the names are represented in the book. The children copy some of the letters, apparently at random—in the figure accompanying the article the letters include a string of *L*s and *T*s and another of capital- and lower-case *B*s and some figures that look like *8*s. The teacher points to the child's letters while saying: "You wrote about Baby Bear. Baby Bear's porridge was too hot." This sort of thing might be acceptable as a game for two- and three-year-olds, but it is so misleading as to be questionable even for them. Those pictures the children drew do not say "Once upon a time there were three bears." The scrawls they made tell nothing about the heat of the porridge. Nor do the letters the children selected to copy from the printed story relate to the words in the story. Encouraging a child in this way to believe that they do may plant the false notion that print is like a picture.

CODE EMPHASIS
AND THE ALPHABETIC PRINCIPLE

We have offered ample reason to believe that, by the very nature of the difference in underlying process, learning to read will not be so easy and effortless as learning to speak, whether the approach is Whole Language or Code Emphasis. But just because Code Emphasis makes intellectual demands of the child, it does not follow that its procedures must entail the mindless, sounding-out drills that the parent–teacher guide fears. In fact, Code Emphasis can be carried out in a pleasant, game-like atmosphere, with children participating happily, and with rapidly growing understanding of the alphabetic principle. Appropriate procedures have been described in detail elsewhere (e.g., Blachman, 1987; Elkonin, 1973; Engelmann, 1969; Gallistel, Fischer, & Blackburn, 1977; Gillingham & Stillman, 1956; I. Y. Liberman, 1989; I. Y. Liberman, Shankweiler, Blachman, Camp, & Werfelman, 1980; Lindamood & Lindamood, 1975; Rosner, 1975;

Slingerland, 1971), and cannot, for want of space, be given here. Suffice it to say that not only can all these procedures be presented in ways that are enjoyable for the child, but they can also be effective, even in inner-city schools, as is strongly suggested by the dramatic increases in reading scores that were obtained after the procedures were introduced (Blachman, 1987; Calfee, Lindamood, & Lindamood, 1973; Enfield, 1987; Wallach & Wallach, 1976; Williams, 1985).

The gains in reading in some of these studies were measured by determining how well a child could read isolated words (e.g., Calfee et al., 1973), but in others (Blachman, 1987; Enfield, 1987), standard tests of reading comprehension were used. Moreover, research evidence supports the intuitively obvious view that skill in comprehension is highly correlated with skill in decoding of single words (Curtis, 1980; Jastak & Jastak, 1978; Perfetti & Hogaboam, 1975; for a general discussion of this matter, see Gough & Tunmer, 1986). We remark on this only because the Whole Language people so often suggest that Code Emphasis produces children who decode but do not comprehend. It is of course true, as we have noted earlier, that children who are not adept at decoding will invest so much time and attention in just getting the word that they will overreach the capacity of the working memory that is essential to processing the sentence (Perfetti & Lesgold, 1979). However, this is not a reason for encouraging them to skip or to fill the words in by guessing; rather it is a sign that they need, by practice, to make the decoding process automatic and relatively effortless. Even when children appear to have mastered the words, they may still have trouble with the sentence, not because they have bothered to read words, but because they have a deficiency in the syntactic component of their language faculty, independently of whether the constituent words are spoken or read. Indeed, there is evidence that poor readers do have relatively greater syntactic difficulties than good readers, even when the sentences are spoken to them (Smith, Macaruso, Shankweiler, & Crain, 1989), and it is interesting from our point of view that there are some reasons for supposing that such difficulties may, in fact, be traceable to the same phonological deficiencies that underlie the problems with decoding (Shankweiler, 1989). Finally, we offer the common-sense observation that comprehension will sometimes be impossible for reasons that have nothing to do with either reading or language ability. Thus, no matter how skillful or linguistically gifted, readers will, for example, not comprehend a paper on a scientific subject in a field utterly foreign to them. But whatever the reasons for failing to understand a text, none of them in any way suggests that the remedy is to teach the reader to guess at the words or to skip them. Given the nature of language, it is simply inconceivable that texts can be understood except by taking account of the words they comprise. Teaching the children what they need to know in order to read those words fluently must be the primary aim of reading instruction. What they need to know, and what their experience with language has not taught them, is no more and no less than the alphabetic principle.

ACKNOWLEDGMENTS

The preparation of this chapter was aided by grants to Haskins Laboratories (NIH-NICHD-HD-01994) and to Yale University/Haskins Laboratories (NIH-21888-01A1). We are grateful to Anne Fowler and Donald Shankweiler for valuable criticisms. A special debt is owed to Alice Dadourian for her skill and infinite patience in helping us with the manuscript.

REFERENCES

Baddeley, A. D. (1968). How does acoustic similarity influence short-term memory? *Quarterly Journal of Experimental Psychology, 20*, 242–264.

Ball, E. W., & Blachman, B. A. (1988). Phoneme segmentation training: Effect on reading readiness. *Annals of Dyslexia, 38*, 208–225.

Bertelson, P. (1987). *The onset of literacy: Cognitive processes in reading acquisition.* Cambridge: MA: MIT Press.

Blachman, B. A. (1988). Phonological awareness and word recognition: Assessment and intervention. In A. G. Kamhi & H. W. Catts (Eds.), *Reading disorders: A developmental language perspective* (pp. 133–158). San Diego, CA: College-Hill Press.

Blachman, B. A. (1984). Relationship of rapid naming ability and language analysis skills to kindergarten and first-grade achievement. *Journal of Educational Psychology, 76*, 610–622.

Blachman, B. (1987). An alternative classroom reading program for learning disabled and other low-achieving children. In R. F. Bowler (Ed.), *Intimacy with language: A forgotten basic in teacher education* (pp. 49–55). Baltimore: Orton Dyslexia Society.

Bradley, L., & Bryant, P. E. (1983). Categorizing sounds and learning to read—A causal connection. *Nature, 30*, 419–421.

Brady, S. A., Shankweiler, D., & Mann, V. A. (1983). Speech perception and memory coding in relation to reading ability. *Journal of Experimental Child Psychology, 35*, 345–367.

Browman, C. P., & Goldstein, L. M. (1985). Dynamic modeling of phonetic structure. In V. Fromkin (Ed.), *Phonetic linguistics* (pp. 35–53). San Diego, CA: Academic Press.

Bryant, P. E., & Goswami, U. (1987). Beyond grapheme-phoneme correspondence. *Cahiers de Psychologie Cognitive, 7*, 439–443.

Byrne, B., & Ledez, J. (1983). Phonological awareness in reading disabled adults. *Australian Journal of Psychology, 35*, 345-367.

Calfee, R. C., Lindamood, P., & Lindamood, C. (1973). Acoustic-phonetic skills and reading: Kindergarten through twelfth grade. *Journal of Educational Psychology, 64*, 293–298.

Catts, H. W. (1986). Speech production/phonological deficits in reading disordered children. *Journal of Learning Disabilities, 19*, 504–508.

Chall, J. (1967). *Learning to read: The great debate.* New York: McGraw-Hill.

Conrad, R. (1964). Acoustic confusions in immediate memory. *British Journal of Psychology, 55*, 75–84.

Content, A., Kolinsky, R., Morais, J., & Bertelson, P. (1986). Phonetic segmentation in prereaders: Effect of corrective information. *Journal of Experimental Child Psychology, 42*, 49–72.

Cossu, G., Shankweiler, D., Liberman, I. Y., Tola, G., & Katz, L. (1988). Awareness of phonological segments and reading ability in Italian children. *Applied Psychology, 9*, 1–16.

Curtis, M. E. (1980). Development of components of reading skill. *Journal of Educational Psychology, 72*, 656–669.

de Manrique, A. M. B., & Gramigna, S. (1984). La segmentacion fonologica y silabica en ninos de preescolar y primer grado. *Lectura y Vida, 5,* 4–13.

Elkonin, D. B. (1973). U. S. S. R. In J. Downing (Ed.), *Comparative reading* (pp. 551–579). New York: Macmillan.

Enfield, M. L. (1987). A cost-effective classroom alternative to "pull-out programs". In R. F. Bowler (Ed.), *Intimacy with language: A forgotten basic in teacher education* (pp. 45–55). Baltimore: Orton Dyslexia Society.

Engelmann, S. (1969). *Preventing failure in the primary grades.* Chicago: Science Research Associates.

Fox, B., & Routh, D. K. (1980). Phonetic analysis and severe reading disability in children. *Journal of Psycholinguistic Research, 9,* 115–119.

Gallistel, E., Fischer, P., & Blackburn, M. (1977). *Manual: GFB sequence of objectives for teaching and testing reading in the concept transfer sequence.* Hamden, CT: Montage Press.

Gathercole, S. E., & Baddeley, A. D. (1989). The role of phonological memory in normal and disordered language development. In C. von Euler, I. Lundberg, & G. Lennerstrand (Eds.), *Wenner-Gren Symposium Series 54, Brain and Reading* (pp. 245–255). New York: MacMillan.

Gillingham, A., & Stillman, B. (1956). *Remedial training for children with specific disability in reading, spelling, and penmanship* (Rev. Ed.). Cambridge, MA: Educators Publishing Service.

Goldstein, D. M. (1976). Cognitive-linguistic functioning and learning to read in preschoolers. *Journal of Experimental Psychology, 68,* 680–688.

Golinkoff, R. M. (1978). Phonemic awareness skills and reading achievement. In F. B. Murray & J. H. Pikulski (Eds.), *The acquisition of reading: Cognitive, linguistic, and perceptual prerequisites* (pp. 23–41). Baltimore: University Park Press.

Goodman, K. S. (1976). Reading: A psycholinguistic guessing game. In H. Singer & R. B. Ruddell (Eds.), *Theoretical models and processes of reading* (pp. 497–508). Newark, DE: International Reading Association.

Goodman, K. S. (1986). *What's whole in whole language: A parent-teacher guide.* Portsmouth, NH: Heinemann.

Gough, P. B., Alford, J. A., Jr., & Holley-Wilcox, P. (1981). Words and contexts. In O. J. L. Tzeng & H. Singer (Eds.), *Perception of print: Reading research in experimental psychology* (pp. 85–102). Hillsdale, NJ: Lawrence Erlbaum Associates.

Gough, P. B., & Tunmer, W. E. (1986). Decoding, reading, and reading disability. *Remedial and Special Education, 7,* 6–10.

Helfgott, J. (1976). Phoneme segmentation and blending skills of kindergarten children: Implications for beginning reading acquisition. *Contemporary Educational Psychology, 1,* 157–169.

Jastak, J. F., & Jastak, S. (1978). *The Wide Range Achievement Test.* Wilmington, DE: Jastak Associates.

Katz, R. B. (1986). Phonological deficiencies in children with reading disability: Evidence from an object-naming rask. *Cognition, 22,* 225–257.

Katz, R. B., Shankweiler, D., & Liberman, I. Y. (1981). Memory for item order and phonetic reading in the beginning reader. *Journal of Experimental Child Psychology, 32,* 474–484.

Liberman, A. M., Cooper, F. S., Shankweiler, D. P., & Studdert-Kennedy, M. (1967). Perception of the speech code. *Psychological Review, 74,* 431–461.

Liberman, A. M., & Mattingly, I. G. (1985). The motor theory of speech perception revised. *Cognition, 21,* 1–36.

Liberman, A. M., & Mattingly, I. G. (1989). A specialization for speech perception. *Science, 243,* 489–494.

Liberman, A. M., Mattingly, I. G., & Turvey, M. (1972). Language codes and memory codes. In

A. W. Melton & E. Martin (Eds.), *Coding processes and human memory* (pp. 307–334). Washington: V. H. Winston.

Liberman, A. M., & Studdert-Kennedy, M. (1978). Phonetic perception. In R. Held, H. W. Leibowitz, H. -L. Teuber (Eds.), *Handbook of sensory physiology: Vol. VIII, Perception* (pp. 143–178). Berlin: Springer-Verlag.

Liberman, I. Y. (1973). Segmentation of the spoken word and reading acquisition. *Bulletin of the Orton Society, 23,* 65–77.

Liberman, I. Y. (1989). Phonology and beginning reading revisited. In C. von Euler, I. Lundberg, & G. Lennerstrand (Eds.), *Wenner-Gren Symposium Series 54: Brain and reading* (pp. 207–220). New York: Macmillan.

Liberman, I. Y., Mann, V., Shankweiler, D., & Werfelman, M. (1982). Children's memory for recurring linguistic and nonlinguistic material in relation to reading ability. *Cortex, 18,* 367–375.

Liberman, I. Y., Rubin, H., Duques, S., & Carlisle, J. (1985). Linguistic skills and spelling proficiency in kindergartners and adult poor spellers. In D. B. Gray & J. F. Kavanagh (Eds.), *Biobehavioral measures of dyslexia* (pp. 163–176). Parkton, MD: York Press.

Liberman, I. Y., Shankweiler, D., Blachman, B., Camp, L., & Werfelman, M. (1980). Steps toward literacy: A linguistic approach. In P. Levinson & C. Sloan (Eds.), *Auditory processing and language: Clinical and research perspectives* (pp. 189–215). New York: Grune and Stratton.

Liberman, I. Y., Shankweiler, D., Fischer, F. W., & Carter, B. (1974). Explicit syllable and phoneme segmentation in the young child. *Journal of Experimental Child Psychology, 18,* 201–212.

Liberman, M. Y. (1983). A linguistic approach. In M. Studdert-Kennedy (Ed.), *Psychobiology of language.* Cambridge, MA: MIT Press.

Lindamood, C. H., & Lindamood, P. C. (1975). *The A.D.D. Program, Auditory discrimination in depth.* Hingham, MA: Teaching Resources.

Lukatela, K., Liberman, I. Y., & Shankweiler, D. (in preparation). Phonological awareness in illiterates: Observations from Serbo-Croatian. . New York: Macmillan.

Lundberg, I. (1989). Lack of phonological awareness—a critical factor in developmental dyslexia. In C. von Euler, I. Lundberg, & G. Lennerstrand (Eds.), *Wenner-Gren Symposium Series 54, Brain and Reading.* New York: Macmillan.

Lundberg, I., Frost, J., & Petersen, O. -P. (1988). Effects of an extensive program for stimulating phonological awareness in preschool children. *Reading Research Quarterly, 23,* 263–284.

Lundberg, I., Olofsson, A., & Wall, S. (1980). Reading and spelling skills in the first school years predicted from phonemic awareness skills in kindergarten. *Scandinavian Journal of Psychology, 21,* 159–173.

Magnusson, E. & Naucler, K. (1987). *Language disordered and normally speaking children's development of spoken and written language: Preliminary results from a longitudinal study.* Report, Uppsala University Linguistics Department, 16, 35–63.

Mann, V. & Liberman, I. Y. (1984). Phonological awareness and verbal short-term memory. *Journal of Learning Disabilities, 17,* 592–598.

Mann, V. (1984). Longitudinal prediction and prevention of reading difficulty. *Annals of Dyslexia, 34,* 117–137.

Marcel, T. (1980). Phonological awareness and phonological representation: Investigation of a specific spelling problem. In U. Frith (Ed.), *Cognitive processes in spelling* (pp. 373–403). San Diego, CA: Academic Press.

Martin, D. (1990, March 31). When every day brings a lesson in being a hero. *The New York Times,* p. 27.

Miller, G. (1977). *Spontaneous apprentices.* New York: Seabury Press.

Morais, J., Cluytens, M., & Alegria, J. (1984). Segmentation abilities of dyslexics and normal readers. *Perceptual and Motor Skills, 58,* 221–222.

Morais, J., Cary, L., Alegria, J., & Bertelson, P. (1979). Does awareness of speech as a sequence of phones arise spontaneously? *Cognition, 7,* 323–331.

Norris, J. A. (1989). Facilitating developmental changes in spelling. *Academic Therapy, 251,* 97–108.

Olofsson, A., & Lundberg, I. (1983). Can phonemic awareness be trained in kindergarten? *Scandinavian Journal of Psychology, 24,* 35–44.

Olson, R., Wise, B., Conners, F., & Rack, J. (1989). Deficits in disabled readers' phonological and orthographic coding: Etiology and remediation. In C. von Euler, I. Lundberg, & G. Lennerstrand (Eds.), *Wenner-Gren Symposium Series 54, Brain and Reading* (pp. 233–242). New York: Macmillan.

Pennington, B. F. (1989). Using genetics to understand dyslexia. *Annals of Dyslexia, 39,* 81–93.

Perfetti, C. A., & Hogaboam, T. (1975). The relationship between single word decoding and reading comprehension skill. *Journal of Educational Psychology, 67,* 461–469.

Perfetti, C. A., & Lesgold, A. M. (1979). Coding and comprehension in skilled reading and implications for reading instruction. In L. B. Resnick & P. A. Weaver (Eds.), *Theory and practice of early reading* (Vol. 1, pp. 57–84). Hillsdale, NJ: Lawrence Erlbaum Associates.

Pratt, A. C., & Brady, S. (1988). Relation of phonological awareness to reading disability in children and adults. *Journal of Educational Psychology, 80,* 3, 319–323.

Rapala, M. M., & Brady, S. (1990). Reading ability and short-term memory: The role of phonological processing. *Reading and Writing: An Interdisciplinary Journal, 2,* 1–25.

Rayner, K., & Pollatsek, A. (1987). Eye movements in reading: A tutorial review. In M. Coltheart (Ed.), *Attention & performance XIII: The psychology of reading* (pp. 327–362). Hillsdale, NJ: Lawrence Erlbaum Associates.

Read, C., & Ruyter, L. (1985). Reading and spelling skills in adults of low literacy. *Remedial and Special Education, 6,* 43–52.

Rosner, J. (1975). *Helping children overcome learning disabilities.* New York: Walker and Co.

Routh, D. K., & Fox, B. (1984). "Mm . . . is a little bit of may: Phonemes, reading, and spelling. In K. D. Gadow & P. Bialen (Eds.), *Advances in learning and behavioral disabilities* (Vol. 3, pp. 95–125). Greenwich, CT: JAI Press.

Shankweiler, D. (1989). How problems of comprehension are related to difficulties in decoding. In D. Shankweiler & I. Y. Liberman (Eds.), *Phonology and reading disability: Solving the reading puzzle.* Ann Arbor: The University of Michigan Press.

Slingerland, B. H. (1971). *A multisensory approach to language arts for specific language disability children: A guide for primary teachers.* Cambridge, MA: Educators Publishing Service.

Smith, S. T., Macaruso, P., Shankweiler, D., & Crain, S. (1989). Syntactic comprehension in young poor readers. *Applied Psycholinguistics, 10,* 429–454.

Stanovich, K. E. (1985). Explaining the variance in reading ability in terms of psychological processes: What have we learned? *Annals of Dyslexia, 35,* 67–96.

Stedman, L. C., & Kaestle, C. E. (1987). Literacy and reading performance in the United States from 1880 to the present. *Reading Research Quarterly, 22,* 8–46.

Studdert-Kennedy, M. (1987). The phoneme as a perceptuomotor structure. In A. Allport, D. MacKay, W. Prinz, & E. Scheerer (Eds.), *Language, perception and production* (pp. 67–84). London: Academic Press.

Templin, M. (1957). *Certain language skills in children.* Chicago: University of Chicago Press.

The Whole Language Teachers Association Newsletter (Spring, 1988). Sudbury, MA.

Treiman, R. A., & Baron, J. (1981). Segmental analysis ability: Development and relation to reading ability. In G. E. MacKinnon & T. G. Waller (Eds.), *Reading research: Advances in theory and practice, Vol. 3.* New York: Academic Press.

Vellutino, F. R., & Scanlon, D. (1987). Phonological coding and phonological awareness and reading ability: Evidence from a longitudinal and experimental study. *Merrill-Palmer Quarterly, 33,* 321–363.

Wagner, R. K., & Torgesen, J. K. (1987). The nature of phonological processing and its causal role in the acquisition of reading skills. *Psychological Bulletin, 101,* 192–212.

Wallach, M. A., & Wallach, L. (1976). *Teaching all children to read.* Chicago: The University of Chicago Press.

Williams, J. P. (1985). The case for explicit decoding instruction. In J. Osborn, P. Wilson, & R. Anderson (Eds.), *Reading education: Foundations for a literate America* (pp. 205–213). Lexington, MA: D. C. Heath.

Author Index

A

Aboitiz, F., 264, *271*
Adams, M. J., 125, *139*, 199, *209*, 215, *238*, 243, 263, 266, 267, *270*, 316, 320, *322*
Ahrens, M., 329, *335*
Alegria, J., 4, *33*, 59, *62*, 76, *104*, 167, *171*, 190, 192, 194, *211*, 279, *303*, 316, 317, 318, *333*, *337*, 354, *364*, *365*
Alford, J. A., Jr., 38, *47*, *48*, 352, *363*
Allen, J., 220, *238*, *239*
Allington, R. L., 328, 332
Allport, D. A., 245, *271*, 317, *332*
Altwerger, B., 125, *141*
Amsterdam, L., 220, *238*
Anderson, R. C., 216, *238*, *239*, 328, 329, 332, *332*, *337*
Anderson-Inman, L., 137, *140*
Andrews, L., 321, *341*
Anstett, M., 321, *341*
Austin, S., 308, *333*

B

Backman, J. E., 80, 81, 85, *102*, *105*, 183, 199, *209*, 264, *273*, 275, 291, 295, *301*
Badcock, D., 313, 314, *332*
Baddeley, A. D., 279, 280, *301*, 316, 332, 356, *362*, *363*

Baker, L., 198, 205, *209*, 323, *332*
Bakker, D. J., 2, *32*
Baldwin, L. E., 332, *333*
Ball, D. W., 323, *340*
Ball, E. W., 98, *102*, 355, *362*
Balota, D. A., 248, 251, 256, *271*, 311, *332*, *338*
Baluch, B., 252, *271*
Bar-Shalom, E., 282, 284, *302*, *303*
Barclay, C., 323, *335*
Barnes, M. A., 248, *273*
Barnhart, C. L., 6, *32*
Baron, J., 40, 43, *47*, 56, 57, *62*, 70, 80, 81, 85, 98, *102*, *105*, *106*, 110, 111, 112, 113, *139*, *140*, *142*, 155, 165, 167, *171*, *174*, 182, *213*, 316, 319, 323, *332*, *340*, 354, *365*
Barr, R. C., 27, *32*, 109, *139*, 309, *332*
Barron, R. W., 110, 111, 112, 113, 116, *139*, *140*, 184, *209*, 318, 320, *323*
Barton, D., 73, 91, *102*
Bauer, R., 323, *332*
Beauvois, M. F., 252, *271*
Beck, I. L., 109, *140*, 166, *173*, 193, *212*, 309, 316, 317, *338*
Becker, W. C., 137, *140*
Belfry, M. J., 325, *341*
Bell, L., 151, 166, 168, *171*, *173*, 193, *212*, 309, 316, 317, *338*
Belmont, L., 2, 3, *32*
Bentin, S., 251, *271*
Benton, A. L., 2, *32*
Berger, N., 322, *333*
Berndt, R. S., 286, *301*

Bertelson, P., 59, *62*, 77, *102*, 194, *211*, 279, *303*, 310, 316, 317, *333*, 337, 354, 355, *362*, *365*

Bertera, J. H., 311, *388*

Berti, F. B., 158, *172*, 291, *303*

Besner, D., 110, *140*, 252, 256, 258, 258, 259, 260, *271*, *272*

Bhavnagri, N., 218, *240*

Bickley, A., 197, *209*

Bickley, R., 197, *209*

Biemiller, A., 112, *140*, 199, 200, *210*, 309, 310, 312, *333*

Bienkowski, M., 148, 151, *173*

Birch, H., 2, 3, *32*

Bisiach, E., 317, *336*

Bissex, G. L., 312, *333*

Blachman, B. A., 98, *102*, 316, *332*, 354, 355, 360, 361, *362*, *364*

Blackburn, M., 360, *363*

Bloomfield, L., 6, *32*

Blum, I., 190, *210*

Blumberg, E. L., 157, *174*

Bock, J. K., 220, *238*

Boder, E., 31, *32*, 168, *171*, 289, *301*

Bohannon, J., 210, *210*

Boies, S. J., 164, *173*

Bowey, J. A., 70, 72, 76, 81, *102*, *106*, 190, 196, 197, *210*, *212*, *213*

Bowyer, P. M., 295, *302*

Bradley, L., 10, 27, 29, *32*, 45, *47*, 49, 50, 52, 53, 54, 59, *62*, *63*, 71, 72, 76, 91, *102*, *104*, 110, *140*, 153, 165, 167, 168, 169, *171*, *172*, 191, 192, 207, *210*, 275, 279, 291, 298, *301*, 316, 317, 318, 324, 325, 330, *333*, *336*, 354, 355, *362*

Brady, S. A., 165, *171*, 356, *362*

Breaux, A. M., 23, *34*

Breitmeyer, B. G., 263, *271*

Brewer, W., 220, *238*

Briggs, P., 308, *333*

Bristow, P. S., 328, *333*

Britton, D., 27, *32*

Brooks, L. R., 9, *32*, 117, 118, 120, 122, *140*

Browman, C. P., 350, *362*

Brown, A. L., 16, *32*, 198, 205, *209*, 323, *333*, *339*

Brown, G. D. A., 248, *271*

Bruce, D. J., 50, *62*

Bruck, M., 74, 76, 80, 81, 84, 85, 89, 91, 92, *102*, *103*, *105*, *106*, 168, *174*, 183, 199, *209*, 264, *273*, 316, *333*

Bryan, T., 322, 323, *335*

Bryant, P. E., 10, 27, 29, *32*, 45, *47*, *48*, 49, 50, 52, 53, 54, 59, 62, *62*, *63*, 71, 72, 76, 91, *102*, *104*, 110, *140*, 153, 165, 167, 168, 169, *171*, *172*, 191, 192, 207, *210*, 275, 276, 277, 279, 285, 290, 291, 298, 299, *301*, *302*, 316, 317, 318, 319, 324, 325, 330, *333*, *336*, 354, 355, *362*

Bub, D., 269, *271*

Burke, C. L., 125, *141*

Butkowsky, S., 329, *333*

Butterfield, E. C., 299, *302*

Byng, S., 290, *301*

Byrne, B., 4, 7, 8, 9, 10, 15, 19, 27, *32*, *34*, 153, *171*, 195, *210*, 280, 283, 284, *301*, 310, 319, 322, *333*, *335*, 354, *362*

C

Cairns, H. S., 283, *304*, 322, *340*

Calfee, R. C., 31, *33*, 71, 72, *103*, 315, *333*, 361, *362*

Camp, L., 360, *364*

Campbell, R., 88, 97, *103*

Campione, J., 322, 323, *333*, *339*

Cancelliere, A., 269, *271*

Cantor, J. H., 23, *33*, 72, *104*

Caramazza, A., 260, *271*, 286, *301*

Carlisle, J., 196, *211*, 354, *364*

Carnine, D. W., 15, *33*

Caroll, J., 219, *238*

Carpenter, P. A., 311, 322, *336*

Carr, T. H., 200, *210*, 243, 245, *271*

Carroll, M., 7, 9, *32*

Carter, B., 50, *63*, 70, *104*, 265, *272*, 279, *303*, 354, *364*

Carter, D. B., 204, *212*

Cary, L., 194, *211*, 279, *303*, 317, *337*, 354, *365*

Cattell, J. M., 146, *171*

Catts, H. W., 316, *336*, 356, *362*

Chafe, W., 216, 217, *238*

Chafetz, J., 81, *106*

Chall, J. S., 112, *140*, 153, *171*, 323, 329, 332, *333*, 343, *362*

Chapman, R. S., 71, 72, *103*

Chomsky, C., 216, *238*, 281, *301*

Chomsky, N., 282, *301*

Chumbley, J. I., 248, 251, 256, *271*

Churchland, P. M., 317, *334*

Churchland, P. S., 317, *334*

Clark, E. V., 281, *301*

Clay, M., 216, *238*

Clements, G. N., 66, *103*

Clover, J., 204, *211*

Cluytens, M., 4, *33*, 76, *104*, 279, *303*, 354, *364*

Cohen, J. D., 257, *271*

Coltheart, M., 5, 30, *34*, 79, *103*, 110, *140*, 243, 245, 269, *271*, *272*, 289, 290, 299, *301*, *303*, 319, *338*

Coltheart, V., 248, *272*

Conners, F., 316, *337*, 354, *365*

Conrad, R., 279, *301*, 356, *362*

Content, A., 4, *33*, 59, 62, 190, 192, *211*, 316, 317, 318, *333*, *337*, 355, *362*

Cooper, F. S., 191, *211*, 351, *363*

Cooper, J., 56, *63*, 153, *173*

Cossu, G., 355, *362*

Crain, S., 15, *33*, 207, *212*, 282, 284, 286, 287, *302*, *303*, *304*, 361, *365*

Crain, W., 286, *302*

Cramer, B., 49, 54, 55, *63*, 71, 72, 76, 98, *105*, 165, *174*, 316, 324, *339*

Crossland, J., 27, *32*, 207, *210*, 316, 318, 324, *333*

Crowder, R. G., 294, *303*

Culicover, P., 288, *305*

Cunningham, A. E., 40, *48*, 49, 54, 55, *63*, 71, 72, 76, 98, *105*, 164, 165, *174*, 178, 183, 191, 201, 202, 205, *213*, *214*, 215, *238*, 293, 300, *304*, 310, 316, 319, 324, 325, 329, *334*, *339*, 340

Curtis, M. E., 40, *47*, 179, *210*, 361, *362*

D

Danis, C., 74, 93, *106*

DaPolito, F., 15, *33*

Davelaar, E., 110, *140*, 259, *272*

Davey, T. C., 216, *239*

Davies, P., 219, *238*

Davis, S., 66, 69, *103*

de Gelder, B., 77, *102*

de Manrique, A. M. B., 355, *363*

de Paola, T., 226, *238*

Deffner, N. D., 138, *140*

DeGroot, A. M. B., 149, *171*

Delaney, S., 151, *173*

Denckla, M. B., 279, *302*

Dennett, D., 317, *334*

Derouesné, J., 252, *271*

Desberg, P., 5, *33*, 56, 57, *63*, 109, *142*, 153, *173*, 319, *337*

Dewitz, P., 125, *140*

DiBenedetto, B., 296, *304*

Diener, C., 329, *334*

DiLollo, V., 313, *334*

Dimino, J., 215, *239*

Ding, B., 194, *212*, 317, *338*

Dixon, R., 137, *140*

Dolch, E. W., 109, *140*

Dow, M. L., 72, *103*

Downing, J., 322, *334*

Doyle, M. C., 248, *272*

Drum, P. A., 125, *142*, 310, *337*

Dunbar, K., 257, *271*

Dunn, L. M., 61, *62*

Dunn, L. M., 61, *62*

Dunning, D., 231, *239*

Duques, S., 196, *211*, 354, *364*

Durrell, D. D., 86, 101, *106*
Dweck, C., 329, *334, 336*

E

Ehri, L. C., 5, 15, *33*, 36, *47*, 93, *103*, 109, 110, 113, 118, 120, 121, 122, 123, 124, 125, 127, 129, 130, 133, 134, 136, 137, 138, 139, *140, 141, 142*, 153, 159, 161, 165, *171, 172*
Ehrlich, S. F., 149, *172*, 185, 190, 192, 194, *210*, 215, 219, *238, 239*, 310, 316, 318, 321, *334, 337*
Elder, L., 10, 27, *34*, 319, *338*
Elkonin, D. B., 360, *363*
Elley, W., 216, 219, *239*
Ellington, B., 197, *209*
Ellis, A. W., 88, *103*
Ellis, N. C., 53, *62*, 316, *332*
Enfield, M. L., 361, *363*
Engelmann, S., 360, *363*
Evans, M., 190, 200, *210*
Evett, L. J., 87, *104*, 111, *141*
Ewing, A., 4, *33*

F

Faux, D., 316, *338*
Feeman, D. J., 40, *48*, 178, 183, 191, 201, 205, *213, 214*, 293, *304*, 308, 310, 316, 325, *340*
Feitelson, D., 236, *239*
Feldman, L. B., 251, *273*
Ferguson, H. B., 275, 291, 295, *301*
Ferreiro, E., 217, *239*
Fielding, L. G., 328, 329, 332, *332*
Fielding-Barnsley, R., 10, 27, 29, *32*, 195, *210*, 310, *333*
Firth, I., 113, *141*
Fischer, F. W., 4, *34*, 50, *63*, 70, *104*, 112, 139, *142*, 153, *173*, 265, *272*, 278, 279, 291, *302, 303, 304*, 354, *364*
Fischer, P., 360, *363*
Flanigan, H., 253, *273*

Flavell, J. H., 189, 203, *210*
Fletcher, J. M., 293, *304*, 315, *334*
Flood, J., 322, *337*
Fodor, J. A., 281, 282, *302*, 323, 331, *334*
Fodor, J. D., 162, *172*, 286, *302*
Foltz, G., 321, *337*
Forell, E. R., 328, *334*
Fornarolo, G., 85, *105*, 264, *273*
Forster, K. I., 147, 149, 164, *172*, 282, *302*
Foster, M. R., 308, *339*
Foster, R., 323, *334*
Fowler, A. E., 284, 294, *302*
Fowler, C. A., 2, 3, *34*, 85, *103*, 112, 139, *142*, 153, *173*, 278, 279, 294, *303, 304, 305*
Fowler, J., 329, *334*
Fox, B., 19, *33*, 49, *63*, 70, 98, *103*, 316, 328, *334, 335*, 354, 355, *363, 365*
Fox, P. T., 243, *272*
Francis, J., 72, 76, *102*
Freebody, P., 319, *335*
French, J. H., 289, *303*
Friedman, M., 5, *33*, 56, 57, *63*, 109, *142*, 319, *337*
Frith, U., 5, *30, 33*, 110, 124, *141*, 168, *172*, 320, 321, *335*
Frost, J., 98, *104*, 165, *172*, 192, *211*, 316, *336*, 355, *364*
Frost, R., 251, *271*
Frostig, M., 2, *33*
Fudge, E. C., 66, 69, *103*
Fulker, D., 316, *337*

G

Galaburda, A. M., 264, *271*
Gallistel, E., 360, *363*
Gambrell, L. B., 328, *335*
Gantt, W. N., 328, *335*
Garner, R., 205, *210*
Gathercole, S. E., 356, *363*
Gattuso, B., 77, *103*

Gavelek, J., 323, *334*
Gentry, J. R., 93, 96, *103*
Gerstein, R., 215, *239*
Geshwind, N., 264, *271*
Gibson, E. J., 146, *172*
Gillingham, A., 360, *363*
Giordani, B., 314, *337*
Gleitman, L. R., 4, 25, *33, 34,* 70, 77,
    98, 99, 101, *105,* 112, *141, 142,*
    279, *304*
Glucksberg, S., 148, *172,* 204, *210*
Glushko, R. J., 56, *63,* 81, 87, 88, *103,*
    111, *141,* 247, 248, *271*
Goldman, S. R., 197, *212,* 308, *338*
Goldman, T., 323, *340*
Goldsmith, J. S., 310, *335*
Goldstein, D. M., 49, *63,* 325, *335*
Goldstein, L. M., 350, *362*
Goldstein, Z., 236, *239*
Golinkoff, R. M., 75, 77, *103,* 355,
    363
Goodacre, E., 58, *63*
Goodman, K. S., 176, 181, 182, *210,*
    344, 345, 352, *363*
Goodman, Y. M., 125, *141*
Goswami, U., 39, *47,* 52, 54, 58, 62,
    62, 63, 81, 82, 83, 84, 86, 88, *103,*
    106, 115, *141,* 275, 276, 277, 285,
    299, *301, 302,* 319, *335,* 354, *362*
Gough, P. B., 5, 10, 28, *33,* 35, 36,
    38, 39, 40, 41, 42, 43, 44, *47, 48,*
    65, 70, 97, *103,* 109, 111, 112,
    113, 123, 124, 126, 138, *141,* 147,
    153, 165, *172,* 178, 179, 180, 182,
    183, 184, 185, 186, 191, 192, 199,
    210, 211, 310, 316, 318, 325, 327,
    329, 331, *335, 336,* 352, 361, *363*
Gramigna, S., 355, *363*
Green, D. W., 149, *173*
Greeno, J. G., 15, *33*
Grieve, R., 190, *193*
Griffith, P. L., 42, 43, 45, *48,* 179, 183,
    191, 192, *211,* 318, 325, *336*
Guttentag, R. E., 164, *172*

H

Haddock, M., 15, *33*
Hagen, J. W., 323, *335, 337*
Haggard, P. N., 248, *272*
Haines, C. F., 70, *104*
Haith, M., 164, *172*
Hale, B. L., 254, 255, *273*
Hall, J. W., 4, *33,* 295, *302,* 322, *335*
Hall, W., 219, *239*
Hallahan, D. P., 322, 323, *335, 340*
Halle, M., 66, 69, *106*
Halliday, M. A. K., 218, *239*
Hamburger, H., 15, *33,* 288, *302*
Hammil, D., 197, *212*
Hammond, K., 181, *211,* 231, 236, *239*
Hanson, D., 313, *334*
Hardy, M., 70, *103*
Harris, K. S., 158, *172,* 291, *303*
Harste, J. C., 125, *141*
Hasan, R., 218, *239*
Hayes, D. P., 329, *335*
Heath, S. B., 215, *239*
Hébert, M., 80, 81, *102,* 183, 199, *209*
Helfgott, J., 354,, *363*
Henderson, E. H., 93, 96, *104*
Henderson, L., 111, *141,* 320, *335*
Hepler, N., 201, *210*
Herman, P. A., 329, *337*
Herriman, M. L., 28, *34,* 126, *143,*
    183, 188, 189, 190, 191, 195, 203,
    205, 207, *213*
Hewison, J., 236, *239*
Hiebert, E. H., 125, *141,* 216, *238*
Hill, D., 308, *337*
Hillinger, M. L., 5, 10, *33,* 39, 40, *48,*
    65, 70, 97, *103,* 109, 112, 124, *141,*
    153, 165, *172,* 182, 199, *210,* 310,
    316, 327, *335*
Hinshelwood, J., 289, *302*
Hinton, G. E., 246, 261, 270, *271, 273*
Hirsh-Pasek, K., 290, *304*
Hockett, C. F., 66, *104*
Hoff, S., 221, *239*

Hogaboam, T. W., 110, *142,* 183, 197, *212,* 296, *304,* 308, *338,* 361, *365*
Hoien, T., 316, *336*
Holdaway, D., 216, *239*
Holley-Wilcox, P., 38, *48,* 352, *363*
Holligan, C., 316, *335*
Hood, J., 108, *141*
Hooper, J. B., 65, *104*
Hoover, W. A., 35, *48,* 179, 182, 183, 185, 186, *211,* 311, *335*
Horn, C. C., 164, *172,* 319, *336*
Hornak, R., 254, *273*
Howell, M., 319, *336*
Huggins, A., 199, *209*
Hughes, C., 166, *173,* 193, *212,* 309, 316, 317, *338*
Hulme, C., 314, *335*
Humphreys, G. W., 87, *104,* 111, *141*
Humphreys, L. G., 216, *239*
Humphreys, M. S., 295, *302,* 322, *335*
Hynd, G., 264, *271*

I, J

Imai, M., 216, *239*
Impey, L., 290, 291, *301,* 319, *333*
Iverson, B., 230, *239*
Jackson, N. E., 299, *302*
Jacobs, V. A., 332, *333*
James, C. T., 15, *33*
James, J. H., 329, *340*
Jared, D., 248, 251, 255, 260, *271, 272*
Jastak, J. F., 361, *363*
Jastak, S., 361, *363*
Johnson, D. D., 81, *104*
Johnston, J. C., 254, 255, *273*
Johnston, P. H., 31, 33, 329, *335*
Johnston, R. S., 316, *335*
Jonasson, J. T., 110, *140*
Jorm, A. F., 112, 113, 132, *142,* 168, *172,* 182, 183, 184, 192, 194, 199, 200, *211, 212,* 230, *240,* 266, *272,* 292, *302,* 316, 318, 330, *336, 338*

Juel, C., 28, *33,* 40, 42, *48,* 109, 116, 126, *141, 142,* 153, *172,* 179, 183, 184, 191, 192, 205, 206, *211,* 310, 316, 318, 325, 327, 330, *335, 336*
Just, M. A., 311, 322, *336*

K

Kaestle, C. E., 215, *240,* 343, *365*
Kahn, D., 38, *48*
Kamhi, A., 316, *336*
Kane, M. J., 16, *32*
Katz, L., 251, *271,* 355, *363*
Katz, R. B., 278, 279, *302, 303,* 356, *363*
Kauffman, J. M., 323, *340*
Kay, J., 56, *63,* 81, *104*
Kennedy, D., 197, *211*
Kerr, B., 221, 223, 226, 237, *239, 240*
Kertesz, A., 269, *271*
Keyser, S. J., 66, *103*
Kibby, M. W., 309, 310, *336, 341*
Kimura, Y., 47, *48*
Kintsch, W., 148, *172*
Kirtley, C., 50, *63,* 72, 76, *104*
Kister, M. C., 204, *212*
Kita, B., 236, *239*
Knafle, J. D., 71, *104*
Kneuz, R. J., 148, *172*
Kolinsky, R., 355, *362*
Kostuch, J., 321, *341*
Kotsonis, M. E., 204, *212,* 322, *336*
Krauss, R., 204, *210*
Kriho, L., 321, *341*

L

Lally, M. R., 195, *213*
Langer, P., 309, *338*
Large, B., 53, *62*
Lartz, M., 221, *239*
Lasnik, H., 287, *303*
Ledez, J., 4, *32,* 354, *362*
Ledger, G., 200, *212*

Lenel, J. C., 23, *33*, 72, *104*

Leong, C. K., 70, *104*

Lesgold, A. M., 3, *34*, 181, 211, 231, 236, *239*, 352, 361, 365

Leu, D. J., 220, *239*, 308, 309, *336, 339*

Levin, H., 146, 157, *172*

Lewis, V. J., 316, *332*

Liberman, A. M., 112, 139, *142*, 191, 207, *211*, 278, 294, *303*, 347, 350, 351, 356, *363, 364*

Liberman, M. Y., 349, *364*

Liberman, I. Y., 2, 3, 4, 19, *33, 34*, 50, *63*, 65, 70, 85, 86, 97, *103, 104, 105, 106*, 112, 139, *142*, 153, 158, 165, *172, 173*, 191, 196, 207, 209, *211*, 265, *272*, 278, 279, 291, 294, 296, *302, 303, 304*, 316, 327, *336*, 354, 355, 356, 360, *362, 363, 364*

Licht, B., 329, *336, 340*

Lieman, J. M., 148, 151, *173, 174*

Lillas, C., 308, *337*

Limber, J., 76, 91, *104*

Lindamood, C. H., 360, 361, *362, 364*

Lindamood, P. C., 360, 361, *362, 364*

Linn, R., 219, *239*

Lipscomb, L., 36, *48*

Lomax, R. G., 298, *303*

Long, C., 16, *32*

Lovegrove, W. S., 2, *33*, 263, *272*, 313, 314, *332, 336, 337, 339*

Lovett, M. W., 112, *142*

Lukatela, G., 251, *273*

Lukatela, K., 354, 355, *364*

Lundberg, I., 49, 52, *63*, 98, *104*, 165, *172*, 192, *211, 212*, 298, *303*, 316, 325, *336, 337*, 354, 355, *364, 365*

Lycan, W. G., 317, *336*

Lyons, W., 317, *336*

M

Macaruso, P., 282, 284, *302, 303*, 304, 361, *365*

MacKay, D. G., 68, *104*

Macken, M. A., 73, 91, *102*

Maclean, M., 27, *32*, 50, *63*, 71, 72, 76, *104*, 167, *172*, 194, 207, *210*, 316, 318, 324, *333, 336*

Maclean, R., 113, 132, *142*, 183, 184, 192, *211, 212*, 230, *240*, 292, *302*, 316, 330, *336, 338*

Magee, P., 322, *327*

Magnusson, E., 354, *364*

Makita, K., 4, *33*

Mamen, M., 275, 291, 295, *301*

Manis, F. R., 164, *172*, 183, 198, 199, *211*, 318, 319, 332, *336, 337*

Mann, V. A., 165, *172*, 180, *211*, 278, 279, 280, 282, 284, 291, 293, 294, *301, 303*, 316, 317, 325, 329, 332, *336*, 354, 355, 356, *362, 364*

Marcel, A. J., 56, *63*, 91, *104*, 316, *336*, 354, *364*

Marchbanks, G., 157, *172*

Mark, L. S., 4, *34*, 153, *173*, 279, 294, *303, 304*

Markman, E., 204, *211*

March, G., 5, *33*, 56, 57, *63*, 109, *142*, 153, *173*, 319, *337*

Marshall, J. C., 243, 245, 269, *272*, 289, 290, *301*, 304, 319, *338*

Martin, D., 357, *364*

Martin, F., 2, *33*, 263, *272*, 313, *337*

Maslow, P., 2, *33*

Mason, J. M., 126, *142*, 215, 216, 218, 219, 220, 221, 223, 226, 231, 236, 237, *239, 240*, 310, *337*

Masonheimer, P. E., 125, *142*, 310, *337*

Massaro, D. W., 147, *173*, 320, *337*

Masterson, J., 290, *301*

Matluck, J. H., 180, *211*

Matthews, R., 113, 132, *142*, 183, 184, 192, 194, *211, 212*, 230, *240*, 292, *302*, 316, 330, *336, 338*

Mattingly, I. G., 278, 294, *303*, 350, 356, *363, 364*

Mattis, S., 289, *303*

May, J. G., 313, *339*
McCall, R. B., 312, *337*
McCann, R., 252, 256, 258, 259, 260, *271, 272*
McClelland, J. L., 39, *48,* 81, 87, 88, *105,* 147, 148, 149, 150, *173,* 243, 244, 245, 246, 247, 248, 252, 254, 256, 257, 258, 259, 260, 263, 270, *271, 272, 273*
McCormick, C., 218, 223, 231, 237, *239, 240*
McCutchen, D., 151, *173*
McDonald, J. E., 253, *272*
McGee, R., 329, *338*
McIntyre, J. S., 313, *334*
McKee, C., 287, *302*
McNinch, G. H., 190, *211*
McRae, K., 248, 251, 260, *271, 272*
Menyuk, P., 322, *337*
Meyer, D. E., 253, 254, *272*
Miles, T. R., 316, *332*
Miller, G., 349, *364*
Miller, P., 76, 91, *104*
Miller, R., 73, 91, *102*
Milz, V., 219, *240*
Mitchell, D. C., 149, *173,* 313, *337*
Monsell, S., 248, 267, *272*
Moon, C., 230, *240*
Morais, J., 4, *33,* 59, *62,* 76, *104,* 167, *171,* 190, 192, *211,* 279, *303,* 316, 317, 318, *333, 337,* 354, 355, *362, 364, 365*
Morgan, J., 288, *303*
Morrison, F. J., 2, *33,* 183, 198, 199, *211,* 268, *272,* 299, *303,* 314, 318, 320, 332, *337*
Morton, J. C., 87, 88, *104,* 147, *173,* 245, *272*
Mross, F., 148, *172*

N

Nagy, J., 314, *337*
Nagy, W. E., 219, *239,* 329, *337*
Nakayama, M., 287, *302*

Nathan, R. G., 299, *304,* 308, *340*
Naucler, K., 354, *364*
Nesdale, A. R., 28, *34,* 126, *143,* 183, 189, 191, 194, 195, 200, 201, 202, 203, 204, 205, 207, *211, 212, 213,* 296, 298, *305,* 316, 318, 325, *341*
Newcombe, F., 269, *272*
Newcomer, P., 197, *212,* 322, *337*
Newman, R. S., 323, *335, 337*
Nicholson, T., 308, 310, *337*
Nie, H., 194, *212,* 317, *338*
Noel, R. W., 252, 253, *272*
Norris, J. A., 360, *365*
Norris, S., 237, *240*

O

O'Brien, C., 204, *212*
Oakley, D., 322, *339*
Oka, E., 205, *212,* 329, *337*
Olofsson, A., 49, 52, *63,* 98, *104,* 165, *172,* 192, *212,* 298, *303,* 316, 325, *336, 337,* 354, 355, *364, 365*
Olson, D., 216, *240*
Olson, R., 354, *365*
Olson, R. K., 83, *106,* 316, 321, *337, 341,* 354, *365*
Omura, A., 216, *239*
Orlando, C., 158, *172,* 291, *303*
Orton, S. T., 2, *33,* 290, *304*
Otto, W., 10, *33*

P

Paap, K. R., 252, 253, *272*
Pappas, C., 216, *240*
Paris, S., 205, *212,* 329, *337*
Patterson, C. J., 204, *212,* 322, *336*
Patterson, K. E., 87, 88, *104,* 243, 244, 245, 248, 252, 260, 269, *272,* 289, *301,* 319, *338*
Pennington, B. F., 251, 254, *273,* 356, *365*
Perera, K., 217, 220, *240*

Perfetti, C. A., 2, 3, *33, 34,* 110, 112, 138, *142,* 151, 162, 165, 166, 168, *171, 173,* 181, 182, 183, 193, 197, *212,* 280, 282, 296, 298, *304,* 308, 309, 312, 316, 317, 327, 329, 332, *338,* 352, 361, *365*
Perin, D., 194, *212*
Peterman, C., 216, 221, 226, *240*
Petersen, O. -P., 98, *104,* 165, *172,* 192, *211,* 316, *336,* 355, *364*
Peterson, P., 329, *334*
Peterson, S. E., 243, *272*
Petitto, L. A., 268, *273*
Phillips, L., 237, *240*
Pinker, S., 288, *304*
Pizzilo, C., 2, *33*
Pollatsek, A., 243, 245, *271,* 311, *332, 338,* 352, *365*
Polson, P. G., 15, *33*
Poritsky, S., 4, *34*
Posnansky, C., 164, *173*
Posner, M. I., 164, *173*
Powell, B., 221, 226, *240*
Pratt, A. C., 279, 294, *304,* 354, *365*
Pratt, C., 189, 190, 196, 203, 204, *210, 211, 213*
Pring, L., 308, *338*
Prior, M., 290, *301*
Purcell-Gates, V., 216, *240*

R

Rack, J., 316, *337,* 354, *365*
Raichle, M. E., 243, *272*
Rapala, M. M., 356, *365*
Rapin, I., 289, *303*
Rayner, K., 149, 164, *172, 173,* 311, *332, 338,* 352, *365*
Read, C., 42, *48,* 91, *105,* 194, 196, *212,* 317, *338,* 354, *365*
Reber, A. S., 9, *34*
Reeds, J. A., 133, *142*
Reitsma, P., 121, 122, 136, *142,* 319, *338*
Resnick, L. B., 145, *173,* 181, *211,*

231, 236, *239*
Rho, S., 148, *172*
Richards, M. M., 22, *34*
Richardson, E., 296, *304*
Richek, M. A., 109, *142*
Richman, B., 219, *238*
Riddoch, J., 290, *301*
Rieben, L., 165, *173*
Rohl, M., 192, 193, 196, *212, 213*
Roper/Schneider, D., 40, *48,* 109, 126, *141, 142,* 310, *335*
Rorty, R., 317, *338*
Rosen, G. D., 264, *271*
Rosner, J., 50, *63,* 77, 78, *105,* 360, *365*
Roth, S. F., 162, *173,* 308, *338*
Routh, D. K., 19, *33,* 49, *63,* 70, 98, *103,* 316, 328, *334, 335,* 354, 355, *363, 365*
Rozin, P., 4, 25, *33, 34,* 70, 77, 98, 99, 101, *105,* 112, *141, 142,* 279, *304*
Rubin, H., 196, *211,* 354, *364*
Ruddy, M. G., 253, 254, *272*
Rudel, R. G., 279, *302*
Rumelhart, D. E., 147, 149, 150, *173,* 243, 246, 254, *272, 273*
Rutter, M., 292, *304,* 313, *338*
Ruyter, L., 354, *365*
Ryan, E. B., 200, 212, *214,* 322, *338, 339*
Rzoska, M., 308, *337*

S

Sanders, E., 254, *273*
Sanders, M., 309, *338*
Santa, C. M., 81, 82, *105*
Santa, J. L., 81, *105*
Saterdahl, K., 56, *63*
Satz, P., 293, *304,* 315, *334*
Scanlon, D. M., 191, 192, *214,* 299, *305,* 316, 320, 321, 325, *341,* 355, *364*
Schadler, M., 164, *173*
Schmidt, R., 279, 293, *301*

Schneider, V., 321, *341*

Schonell, F., 58, *63*

Schvaneveldt, R. W., 253, 254, *272*

Schwantes, F. M., 308, *338*

Scott, J. A., 216, *238*

Scragg, D. G., 39, *48*

Seidenberg, M. S., 39, *48*, 80, 81, 85, 87, 88, 89, *102, 105, 106*, 148, 150, 151, 168, *173, 174*, 183, 199, *209*, 244, 245, 246, 247, 248, 249, 250, 251, 252, 253, 255, 256, 258, 259, 260, 262, 263, 264, 268, 270, *271, 272, 273*, 309, *338*

Selkirk, E. O., 66, 67, 69, *105*

Semel, E., 322, *338*

Semrud-Clikeman, M., 264, *271*

Seymour, P. H. K., 10, 27, *34*, 319, *338*

Shallice, T., 261, 266, 270, *271, 273*

Shankweiler, D. P., 2, 3, 4, 19, *33, 34*, 50, *63*, 70, 85, 86, *103, 104, 105, 106*, 112, 139, *142*, 153, 158, 165, *171, 172, 173*, 182, 183, 184, 192, 194, 199, 200, 209, *211, 212*, 278, 279, 280, 282, 284, 291, 294, 296, *301, 302, 303, 304*, 351, 354, 355, 356, 360, 361, *362, 363, 364, 365*

Share, D. L., 112, 113, 132, *142*, 168, *172*, 182, 183, 184, 192, 194, 199, 200, *211, 212*, 230, *240*, 265, 266, *272*, 292, 294, *302, 303*

Shattuck-Hufnagel, S., 68, *105*

Shea, P., 4, *32*

Sheldon, A., 281, *304*

Sherman, G. F., 264, *271*

Shulman, H. G., 254, *273*

Siegel, L. S., 316, 322, *338, 339*

Silva, P. A., 329, *338*

Simner, M., 291, *304*

Simon, D. P., 50, 63

Simons, H. D., 308, *339*

Simpson, G. B., 308, *339*

Simpson, L., 4, *34*

Sinha, S., 237, *239*

Slaghuis, W. L., 2, *33*, 263, *272*, 313, *336, 339*

Slingerland, B. H., 361, *365*

Smiley, S., 322, *339*

Smith, E. E., 81, *105*

Smith, F., 176, 181, 182, *212, 250, 273*, 311, *339*

Smith, L. B., 77, *103*

Smith, S. T., 280, 282, 284, *303, 304*, 361, *365*

Smythe, P. C., 70, *103*

Snowling, M., 183, *212*, 308, 316, *338, 339*

Snyder, A. Z., 243, *272*

Solman, R. T., 313, *339*

Sotsky, R., 4, *34*

Souther, A., 40, *48*

Spring, C., 117, 120, *142*

Stackhouse, J., 316, *339*

Stammer, J., 125, *140*

Stanovich, K. E., 2, *34*, 40, 41, *48*, 49, 54, 55, *63*, 71, 72, 76, 98, *105*, 112, 127, *142*, 153, 155, 162, 164, 165, *174*, 177, 178, 181, 183, 191, 192, 201, 202, 205, 207, 209, *212, 213, 214*, 279, 293, 298, 299, 300, *304*, 308, 309, 310, 313, 316, 317, 319, 322, 323, 324, 325, 328, 329, 330, 332, *334, 339, 340, 341*, 355, *365*

Stedman, L. C., 215, *240*, 343, *365*

Steedman, M., 282, *302*

Stein, C. L., 283, *304*, 322, *340*

Stemberger, J. P., 68, 93, *105*

Stennett, R. G., 70, *103*

Sternberg, R., 198, *213*, 323, 329, *340*

Stich, S., 317, *340*

Sticht, T. G., 329, *340*

Stillman, B., 360, *363*

Stone, G. O., 251, 254, *273*

Stuart, M., 5, 30, *34*

Studdert-Kennedy, M., 191, *211*, 351, *363*, 347, 349, *364, 365*

Sulzby, E., 35, *48*, 216, *240*

Swinney, D. A., 148, *174*

Szeszulski, P., 319, *336*

T

Tanenhaus, M. K., 148, 151, *173, 174,*
248, 253, 262, *273*
Tannen, D., 216, *241*
Taraban, R., 81, *105,* 248, *273*
Tarver, S. G., 323, *340*
Tavakolian, S. L., 286, *304*
Taylor, B. B., 133, 136, *141,* 316, *334*
Taylor, N., 190, *210*
Teale, W., 35, *48*
Teberosky, A., 217, *239*
Temple, C., 290, *304*
Templin, M., 349, *365*
Terjak, M., 321, *341*
Thissen, D. M., 164, *173*
Thompson, G. B., 27, *34,* 183, *213*
Thorndike, R., 230, *241*
Tinzmann, M. B., 4, *33,* 295, *302*
Tizard, J., 236, *239, 241*
Tobin, P., 291, *303,* 316, *336*
Tola, G., 355, *362*
Torgesen, J. K., 165, *174,* 279, *305,*
316, 323, 325, 329, 332, *340, 341,*
356, *366*
Tornéus, M., 316, *340*
Treiman, R., 23, *34,* 43, 48, 67, 68, 69,
70, 72, 73, 74, 76, 77, 81, 83, 84, 85,
88, 89, 90, 91, 92, 93, 98, *103, 105,*
106, 110, 112, 127, 133, *142,* 165,
167, *174*
Tunmer, W. E., 28, *34,* 35, *48,* 70, *106,*
112, 113, 126, 138, *141, 143,* 165,
174, 178, 179, 180, 183, 186, 188,
189, 190, 191, 193, 194, 195, 196,
200, 201, 202, 203, 204, 205, 207,
208, *210, 211, 212, 213,* 215, *241,*
296, 298, *305,* 316, 318, 325, 329,
331, *335, 341,* 361, *363*
Turvey, M. T., 251, *273,* 356, *365*
Twilley, L., 252, 256, 258, 259, 260,
271

U

Uchida, N., 216, *239*

Uhrey, J., 109, *143*
Underwood, B. J., 11, 14, *34*
Underwood, G., 308, *333*

V

Vala-Rossi, M., 308, *340*
van den Bos, K. P., 329, *341*
Van Orden, G. C., 151, *174,* 251, 254,
255, *273*
Vellutino, F. R., 2, *34,* 113, *143,* 191,
192, *214,* 263, *273,* 299, *305,* 313,
315, 316, 320, 321, 325, *341,* 355,
365
Venezky, R. L., 71, 72, 81, 85, 86, *103,*
104, 106, 133, 137, *143,* 179, *214,*
250, *273,* 320, 321, *341*
Vergnaud, J. -R., 66, 69, *106*
Vogel, S. A., 197, *214,* 322, *341*

W

Wagner, R. K., 165, *174,* 279, *305,*
316, 325, *341,* 356, *366*
Wagoner, S. A., 197, 205, *214*
Walberg, H., 230, *239*
Wall, S., 49, 52, *63,* 98, *104,* 165, *172,*
298, *303,* 316, 325, *336,* 354, 355,
364
Wallach, L., 361, *366*
Wallach, M. A., 361, *366*
Walsh, M., 44, *48,* 184, *211*
Wang, W. S. -Y., 13, *142*
Warren-Leubecker, A., 201, *210, 214*
Warrington, E. K., 266, *273*
Waterman, B., 230, *240*
Waters, G. S., 89, *106,* 168, *174,* 248,
273, 309, *338*
Weaver, P. A., 145, *173*
Weber, R. M., 198, *214,* 309, 310, 312,
341
Weener, P., 197, *211*
Welch, V., 5, *33,* 56, 57, *63,* 109, *142,*
319, *337*
Wells, G., 215, 216, 230, 231, *240, 241*

Werfelman, M., 278, *303,* 356, 360, *364*

West, R. F., 155, 164, *174,* 205, *214,* 300, *304,* 308, 309, 319, 329, *340, 341*

Wexler, K., 288, *302, 305*

Whaley, J., 310, *341*

Whetton, C., 61, *62*

White, K., 230, *241*

Wiig, E., 322, *338*

Wilce, L., 153, *172*

Wilce, L. S., 36, *47,* 109, 110, 118, 121, 124, 127, 129, 130, 133, 134, 136, 138, *140, 141,* 153, 159, 165, *172,* 194, *210,* 219, *239,* 310, 316, *334*

Wilkes, K. V., 317, *341*

Wilkinson, I. A. G., 216, *238*

Williams, D. V., 157, *174*

Williams, J. P., 10, 28, *34,* 49, *63,* 77, 98, 99, 101, *106,* 146, 157, *174,* 316, *341,* 361, *366*

Williams, R. J., 246, *273*

Willows, D. M., 200, *214,* 313, 314, 315, 329, *333, 341*

Wilson, K. P., 4, *33,* 295, *302*

Wilson, P. T., 328, 329, 332, *332*

Wilson, R., 291, *303,* 316, *336*

Wilson, R. M., 328, *335*

Winbury, N. E., 4, *34*

Winne, P. H., 325, *341*

Winograd, P. N., 329, *335*

Wise, B. W., 83, *106,* 316, 321, *337, 341,* 354, *365*

Wixson, K. L., 309, *342*

Wolf, M., 279, 293, *305*

Wolford, G., 2, *34,* 294, *305*

Wong, B., 323, *342*

Woodcock, R. W., 295, *305*

Woodward, V. A., 125, *141*

Worthen, D., 322, *339*

Wright, A. D., 200, *213*

Wylie, R. E., 86, 101, *106*

Y

Yaden, D., 330, *342*

Yopp, H. K., 71, 72, *106,* 193, 194, *214,* 317, 324, *342*

Yule, W., 292, *304*

Z

Zhang, Y., 194, *212,* 317, *338*

Zinna, D. R., 86, *106*

Zola, D., 311, *342*

Zolman, J. E., 299, *304*

Zukowski, A., 72, 81, 88, 89, 90, *106*

Zurif, E. B., 283, *304,* 322, *340*

Subject Index

A

Acquired reading disability, 269-270, 289, 290, 319

Alliteration, 50, 51, 53, 71 (*see also* Phonological awareness, Phonological awareness tasks)

Alphabetic principle, 15-30, 327, 353-354, 357, 360-361

Alphabetic stage of reading, 5-6, 126-137

Analogies
relation to rhyming ability, 59-62
use in reading, 55-62, 83, 87-88, 319-320

Artificial orthography, acquisition of by adults, 6-10, 117-118, 122-123

Automaticity, 163, 164, 178

C

"Chinese" readers, 44, 182

Chronological age match design, 275-280, 285-288, 292-298

Cipher (*see* Orthographic cipher)

Cipher stage of reading, 132-137

Cloze task, 197, 202

Coarticulation, 191, 350-351

Coda of syllable, 67 (*see also* Syllables)

Code Emphasis, 343-361

Cognitive neuropsychology, 249

Comprehension monitoring, 197, 203-205

Connectionist models of word recognition, 147-148, 150, 243-270

Consistent vs. inconsistent words, 80, 89, 247-249

Consonant clusters (*see* Syllables)

Context use in reading, 38, 41, 148-149, 157, 162, 176-178, 181, 182, 197, 199-200, 308-313, 352, 353, 357-359

Cue reading, 36-42, 124-137 (*see also* Logographic stage of reading, Paired-associate reading)
visual, 124-126
phonetic 126-132

D

Decentration, 207-209

Decoding (*see* Phonological recoding)

Default acquisition procedure for reading, 1, 5-31

Disabled readers, 243-270, 275-305, 307-332
acquired reading disability, 269-270, 289-290, 319
adults, 31, 168-169
brain correlates, 264
chronological age match design, 275-280, 285-288, 292-298
computational model, 260-270
impaired phonological representation, 265-267
learning deficits, 268
limited computational resources,

263-265
orthographic deficits, 261-263
conditional rules, 183-184
context use, 181, 199, 308-313
different kinds of, 3, 180, 186-187,
    260-270, 289-291, 314-315
homographic spelling patterns, 198-
    199
intelligence, 292-294, 323
motivation, 329-330
oral language comprehension, 180-
    181, 205-206, 280-288, 297-298,
    322, 361
orthographic representations, 318-
    321
phonological awareness, 2-3, 279,
    315-318
reading level match design, 275-
    277, 289-292, 296-297
reversal errors, 290-291
specificity, 321-327, 330
speech perception and production,
    356
spelling, 168-169
syntactic awareness, 197-201, 322
visual processing, 2, 263, 265, 313-
    315
working memory, 3-4, 277, 279-
    280, 295, 356
Dual route models of word recognition,
    50, 79, 87-88, 107-120, 155, 184,
    252-254
flaws, 87, 111-120, 248-251
modified, 87-88
standard, 79, 87
Dyslexia (*see* Disabled readers)

E

Emergent literacy, 35, 124-132, 215-
    238
Environmental print, 124-126, 233
Exception words (*see* Regular vs.
    irregular words)
Eye movements in reading, 311, 352

G

Grapheme-phoneme relations, 56-57,
    79, 98-99, 114-139, 182-187, 191,
    219, 247-251, 327
computational vs. reflective
    knowledge, 165, 167
conditional rules, 183-184, 198
as weighted connections between
    units, 250

H

Holistic word perception, 108, 146-147
Homographic spelling patterns, 198-
    199
Hyperlexia, 187

I

Illiterate adults, 77, 354
Inconsistent words (*see* Consistent vs.
    inconsistent words)
Instruction in reading (*see* Teaching of
    reading)
Intelligence, 53-54, 113, 201-203, 208,
    292-294, 312, 324-327, 348
Irregular words (see Regular vs.
    irregular words)

L

Letter-name knowledge
    use in reading, 126, 194-195
    use in spelling, 93-96, 196
Lexical decision task, 255-258
Letter-sound relations (*see* Grapheme-
    phoneme relations)
Lexical representations, 107-139, 145-
    170, 243-270
acquisition, 145-170
    autonomous system, 153, 161-170
    complete vs. partial, 126-137,
        157-159

functional system, 153, 154-161, 163
    grapheme-phoneme connections, 159-161
    number of entries, 154-165
    precision, 157-159
    redundancy, 159-161
computational model of, 243-270
    distributed representations, 245
    lack of lexical nodes, 258-260
impenetrable vs. interactive, 162
vs. lexical access, 146
and spelling, 163
vowels vs. consonants, 157-158
Listening comprehension (*see* Oral language comprehension)
Logographic stage of reading, 5- 6, 124-132 (*see also* Cue reading, Paired-associate reading)

M

Matthew effects, 205, 330
Metacognition, 206, 289, 323
Metalinguistic awareness, 188-209
    (see also Phonological awareness, Syntactic awareness, Pragmatic awareness, Word awareness)
Models of word recognition
    analogy, 56, 87, 88
    computational, 243-270
        lack of lexical nodes, 258-260
        use of error scores, 256-258
    connectionist, 147-148, 150, 243-270
    connections during acquisition, 114-138, 160
    decoding, 155
    dual route, 50, 79, 87-88, 107-120, 155, 184, 252-254
        flaws, 87, 111-120, 248-251
        modified, 87-88
        standard, 79, 87
    interactive, 147, 148
    modularity, 162

restricted-interactive, 147-152
specific word learning, 107-139, 155
    positive learning trials, 113
    rote memory, 111
stage model of development of word recognition, 5-6, 56-59, 123-137
Models of reading
    cognitive-developmental model, 206-209
    simple view, 179-187, 331
    verbal efficiency theory, 181-182
Modularity, 161-164, 281-282, 323-324, 331-332
Morphophonemic rules, 182
Multiletter units, 79-88, 115, 150, 182

N

Nonwords
    reading of, 40-41, 44, 58-59, 80, 83-85, 112, 121-122, 134-135, 183-184, 192, 259-260, 263-264, 267, 269
    spelling of, 89-90, 95-96, 196

O

Onset of syllable, 8, 23, 66-76, 90-93
    (*see also* Syllables, Alliteration)
Oral language comprehension
    and reading achievement, 35, 179-181, 185-186, 208, 215-238
    disabled readers, 180-181, 205-206, 280-288, 297-298
    intuitive vs. metalinguistic, 188-191
Oral vs. written language
    acquisition differences, 343-344, 345-353
    context dependence, 204-205, 216
    form differences, 219
    functional differences, 218-219
    physical differences, 217-218
    redundancy, 220
    situational differences, 218

story reading to link, 220-229
structural differences, 220
Orthographic cipher
and reading, 38-42
and spelling, 42-43
Orthographic depth, 251
Orthographic representations, 137, 145-170, 262, 318-321
Orthographic stage of reading, 5

P

Paired-associate reading, 5, 10-15, 117
(*see also* Cue reading, Logographic stage of reading)
Parallel distributed processes, 243-270
Peak of syllable, 66-67
(*see also* Syllables)
Phonemic awareness
(*see* Phonological awareness)
Phonetic features 7-8, 10, 133
Phonics, 6, 27, 39, 109, 138, 250, 320
(*see also* Code Emphasis)
Phonological awareness
development of, 70-77, 192
in illiterate adults, 77, 354
influence of spelling knowledge on, 136-137, 193-194
intrasyllabic units and, 70-78
and metalinguistic awareness, 188
relation to letter-name knowledge, 194-195
relation to spelling, 132, 195-196
relation to word reading, 5-6, 27-28, 49-52, 113, 127, 166-167, 190-196, 215, 265-267, 279, 315-318, 324-327, 353-356
syllabic awareness versus phonemic awareness, 70
training in, 27-31, 49, 54-55, 77-78, 98, 192, 316, 355
Phonological awareness tasks

alliteration, 50-51, 53, 71
blending, 50, 166
comparison, 72
counting, 50, 70, 194, 354
deletion, 50-51, 59, 72, 76, 166, 193-194, 317
oddity, 59, 72, 76
phoneme identity, 28-30
phoneme recognition, 73-74
reversal, 193-194
rhyming, 50-55, 59-62, 71-72, 167, 317
segmentation, 28-30, 50, 73, 317
substitution, 74-77
Phonological recoding, 107-139, 243-270
grapheme-phoneme rules and, 79-88, 98-99, 182-183, 327
intrasyllabic units and, 79-88
relation to reading comprehension, 35, 179-187, 361
role of syntactic awareness in developing, 198, 201
as self-teaching mechanism, 182
Pragmatic awareness, 188, 203-206
Predictors of reading skill, 52-54, 113, 132, 194, 205, 230-236, 316, 324-325
Pretend reading, 216, 221-223, 237
Pseudowords (*see* Nonwords)
Psycholinguistic guessing game, 176, 311, 352, 359

R

Reading comprehension
factors predicting, 205, 231-237
relation to oral language comprehension, 179-181, 185-186, 215-238, 296
relation to phonological recoding, 35, 179-187, 361
Reading level match design, 275-277, 289-292, 296-297
Redundancy, 159-161

Regular vs. irregular words, 43-44,
50, 56, 86, 111-112, 151-152, 154,
157, 183, 199, 248-251, 254-255,
263, 264, 269, 290
Repeated readings, 216
Restricted-interactive model of word
recognition, 147-152
Reversal errors, 290-291
Rhyming, 50-55, 59-62, 71, 72, 167,
317 (*see also* Phonological awareness, Phonological awareness tasks)
Rime of syllable, 8, 23, 66-73, 76-77,
93-96 (*see also* Syllables, Rhyming)

S

Selective association in early reading
acquisition, 15, 36-38, 124-132, 182
Sight word learning, 107-139
letter-sounds, role of 111-139, 191
meaningfulness, 131
orthographic regularity and, 116
positive learning trials, 113, 185
practice effects, 121
selective association and, 36-38
stages, 123-137
Similar vs. dissimilar words 10-14, 36-
37
Skilled vs. beginning reading, 145-146,
175-179
Speech errors, 68
Speech recoding
(*see* Phonological recoding)
Spelling
cipher and, 42-43
in dyslexics, 168-169
errors, 42-43, 90-97, 168-169, 196
intrasyllabic units and, 88-97
invented, 42, 90, 196
and letter-name knowledge, 93-96,
196
and phonological awareness, 88-97,
132, 195-196

visual vs. phonemic routes, 168-169
and word reading, 44-47, 119-
120, 122, 129-132, 135, 167-170,
233
and word representation, 152, 163
word-specific knowledge and, 43,
44
Stage models of reading acquisition, 5-
6, 56-59, 123-137
Story reading to children, 215-238
adult-child interaction, 221-229
cultural differences, 215
in kindergarten, 226-229
pictures, importance of, 218, 223-
224
primerese vs. natural language, 220
relation to reading achievement,
215-216, 230-238
retellings by child, 221-223
vocabulary development, 216
Syllables
internal structure of, 65-70
relation to phonological awareness,
70-78
relation to reading, 70-88
relation to spelling, 88-97
role in teaching of reading, 97-101
Syntactic awareness, 188, 196-203
Syntax acquisition, 282-283, 287-288,
329

T

Teaching of reading, 343-361
decoding oriented, 200
language experience method, 90,
200
linguistic method, 6
meaning emphasis, 109
phonological awareness training
and, 27-31, 49, 54-55, 77-78, 97-
101, 192, 316
phonics method, 6, 27, 39, 109, 138,
250, 320
syllable structure and, 97-101

whole word method, 10, 27, 109,
138-139, 192
Whole Language vs. Code Emphasis, 343-361

T

Teaching of spelling, 97-101

U

Universal Grammar, 287-288

V

Vocabulary, 202-203, 216, 219, 293,
329, 349

W

Whole Language, 343-361
Word awareness, 190-196
Word families, 15-27, 101
Word frequency, 41, 151-152, 247-
251, 267
Word recognition
automaticity, 163-164, 178
autonomous vs. interactive, 147-149
context effects, 38, 41, 148-149,
157, 162, 176-178, 181, 182, 197,
199-200, 308-313, 352-353, 357-
359
frequency effects, 41, 151-152, 247-
251, 267
instantaneous, 116-117
phonemic activation, 150-151
phonological recoding vs. direct
access, 107-139, 150, 253-255
by sight, 107-139
Word-specific associations, 43-44, 79,
107-139, 184, 319
Word superiority effect, 147
Working memory
bottleneck, 181-182, 282, 361
deficiencies in disabled readers, 3-
4, 277, 279-280, 295, 356